T0214551

Lecture Notes in Computer Science   11259

Commenced Publication in 1973
Founding and Former Series Editors:
Gerhard Goos, Juris Hartmanis, and Jan van Leeuwen

More information about this series at http://www.springer.com/series/7412

Jian-Huang Lai · Cheng-Lin Liu
Xilin Chen · Jie Zhou · Tieniu Tan
Nanning Zheng · Hongbin Zha (Eds.)

Pattern Recognition and Computer Vision

First Chinese Conference, PRCV 2018
Guangzhou, China, November 23–26, 2018
Proceedings, Part IV

 Springer

Editors
Jian-Huang Lai
Sun Yat-sen University
Guangzhou, China

Cheng-Lin Liu
Institute of Automation
Chinese Academy of Sciences
Beijing, China

Xilin Chen
Institute of Computing Technology
Chinese Academy of Sciences
Beijing, China

Jie Zhou
Tsinghua University
Beijing, China

Tieniu Tan
Institute of Automation
Chinese Academy of Sciences
Beijing, China

Nanning Zheng
Xi'an Jiaotong University
Xi'an, China

Hongbin Zha
Peking University
Beijing, China

ISSN 0302-9743   ISSN 1611-3349 (electronic)
Lecture Notes in Computer Science
ISBN 978-3-030-03340-8   ISBN 978-3-030-03341-5 (eBook)
https://doi.org/10.1007/978-3-030-03341-5

Library of Congress Control Number: 2018959435

LNCS Sublibrary: SL6 – Image Processing, Computer Vision, Pattern Recognition, and Graphics

This Springer imprint is published by the registered company Springer Nature Switzerland AG
The registered company address is: Gewerbestrasse 11, 6330 Cham, Switzerland

Preface

Welcome to the proceedings of the First Chinese Conference on Pattern Recognition and Computer Vision (PRCV 2018) held in Guangzhou, China!

PRCV emerged from CCPR (Chinese Conference on Pattern Recognition) and CCCV (Chinese Conference on Computer Vision), which are both the most influential Chinese conferences on pattern recognition and computer vision, respectively. Pattern recognition and computer vision are closely inter-related and the two communities are largely overlapping. The goal of merging CCPR and CCCV into PRCV is to further boost the impact of the Chinese community in these two core areas of artificial intelligence and further improve the quality of academic communication. Accordingly, PRCV is co-sponsored by four major academic societies of China: the Chinese Association for Artificial Intelligence (CAAI), the China Computer Federation (CCF), the Chinese Association of Automation (CAA), and the China Society of Image and Graphics (CSIG).

PRCV aims at providing an interactive communication platform for researchers from academia and from industry. It promotes not only academic exchange, but also communication between academia and industry. In order to keep track of the frontier of academic trends and share the latest research achievements, innovative ideas, and scientific methods in the fields of pattern recognition and computer vision, international and local leading experts and professors are invited to deliver keynote speeches, introducing the latest advances in theories and methods in the fields of pattern recognition and computer vision.

PRCV 2018 was hosted by Sun Yat-sen University. We received 397 full submissions. Each submission was reviewed by at least two reviewers selected from the Program Committee and other qualified researchers. Based on the reviewers' reports, 178 papers were finally accepted for presentation at the conference, including 24 oral and 154 posters. The acceptance rate is 45%. The proceedings of the PRCV 2018 are published by Springer.

We are grateful to the keynote speakers, Prof. David Forsyth from University of Illinois at Urbana-Champaign, Dr. Zhengyou Zhang from Tencent, Prof. Tamara Berg from University of North Carolina Chapel Hill, and Prof. Michael S. Brown from York University.

We give sincere thanks to the authors of all submitted papers, the Program Committee members and the reviewers, and the Organizing Committee. Without their contributions, this conference would not be a success. Special thanks also go to all of the sponsors and the organizers of the special forums; their support made the conference a success. We are also grateful to Springer for publishing the proceedings and especially to Ms. Celine (Lanlan) Chang of Springer Asia for her efforts in coordinating the publication.

We hope you find the proceedings enjoyable and fruitful reading.

September 2018

Tieniu Tan
Nanning Zheng
Hongbin Zha
Jian-Huang Lai
Cheng-Lin Liu
Xilin Chen
Jie Zhou

Organization

Steering Chairs

Tieniu Tan	Institute of Automation, Chinese Academy of Sciences, China
Hongbin Zha	Peking University, China
Jie Zhou	Tsinghua University, China
Xilin Chen	Institute of Computing Technology, Chinese Academy of Sciences, China
Cheng-Lin Liu	Institute of Automation, Chinese Academy of Sciences, China
Long Quan	Hong Kong University of Science and Technology, SAR China
Yong Rui	Lenovo Group

General Chairs

Tieniu Tan	Institute of Automation, Chinese Academy of Sciences, China
Nanning Zheng	Xi'an Jiaotong University, China
Hongbin Zha	Peking University, China

Program Chairs

Jian-Huang Lai	Sun Yat-sen University, China
Cheng-Lin Liu	Institute of Automation, Chinese Academy of Sciences, China
Xilin Chen	Institute of Computing Technology, Chinese Academy of Sciences, China
Jie Zhou	Tsinghua University, China

Organizing Chairs

Liang Wang	Institute of Automation, Chinese Academy of Sciences, China
Wei-Shi Zheng	Sun Yat-sen University, China

Publicity Chairs

Huimin Ma	Tsinghua University, China
Jian Yu	Beijing Jiaotong University, China
Xin Geng	Southeast University, China

International Liaison Chairs

Jingyi Yu	ShanghaiTech University, China
Pong C. Yuen	Hong Kong Baptist University, SAR China

Publication Chairs

Zhouchen Lin	Peking University, China
Zhenhua Guo	Tsinghua University, China

Tutorial Chairs

Huchuan Lu	Dalian University of Technology, China
Zhaoxiang Zhang	Institute of Automation, Chinese Academy of Sciences, China

Workshop Chairs

Yao Zhao	Beijing Jiaotong University, China
Yanning Zhang	Northwestern Polytechnical University, China

Sponsorship Chairs

Tao Wang	iQIYI Company, China
Jinfeng Yang	Civil Aviation University of China, China
Liang Lin	Sun Yat-sen University, China

Demo Chairs

Yunhong Wang	Beihang University, China
Junyong Zhu	Sun Yat-sen University, China

Competition Chairs

Xiaohua Xie	Sun Yat-sen University, China
Jiwen Lu	Tsinghua University, China

Website Chairs

Ming-Ming Cheng	Nankai University, China
Changdong Wang	Sun Yat-sen University, China

Finance Chairs

Huicheng Zheng	Sun Yat-sen University, China
Ruiping Wang	Institute of Computing Technology, Chinese Academy of Sciences, China

Program Committee

Haizhou Ai	Tsinghua University, China
Xiang Bai	Huazhong University of Science and Technology, China

Xiaochun Cao	Institute of Information Engineering, Chinese Academy of Sciences, China
Hong Chang	Institute of Computing Technology, China
Songcan Chen	Chinese Academy of Sciences, China
Xilin Chen	Institute of Computing Technology, China
Hong Cheng	University of Electronic Science and Technology of China, China
Jian Cheng	Chinese Academy of Sciences, China
Ming-Ming Cheng	Nankai University, China
Yang Cong	Chinese Academy of Science, China
Dao-Qing Dai	Sun Yat-sen University, China
Junyu Dong	Ocean University of China, China
Yuchun Fang	Shanghai University, China
Jianjiang Feng	Tsinghua University, China
Shenghua Gao	ShanghaiTech University, China
Xinbo Gao	Xidian University, China
Xin Geng	Southeast University, China
Ping Guo	Beijing Normal University, China
Zhenhua Guo	Tsinghua University, China
Huiguang He	Institute of Automation, Chinese Academy of Sciences, China
Ran He	National Laboratory of Pattern Recognition, China
Richang Hong	Hefei University of Technology, China
Baogang Hu	Institute of Automation, Chinese Academy of Sciences, China
Hua Huang	Beijing Institute of Technology, China
Kaizhu Huang	Xi'an Jiaotong-Liverpool University, China
Rongrong Ji	Xiamen University, China
Wei Jia	Hefei University of Technology, China
Yunde Jia	Beijing Institute of Technology, China
Feng Jiang	Harbin Institute of Technology, China
Zhiguo Jiang	Beihang University, China
Lianwen Jin	South China University of Technology, China
Xiao-Yuan Jing	Wuhan University, China
Xiangwei Kong	Dalian University of Technology, China
Jian-Huang Lai	Sun Yat-sen University, China
Hua Li	Institute of Computing Technology, Chinese Academy of Sciences, China
Peihua Li	Dalian University of Technology, China
Shutao Li	Hunan University, China
Wu-Jun Li	Nanjing University, China
Xiu Li	Tsinghua University, China
Xuelong Li	Xi'an Institute of Optics and Precision Mechanics, Chinese Academy of Sciences, China
Yongjie Li	University of Electronic Science and Technology of China, China
Ronghua Liang	Zhejiang University of Technology, China
Zhouchen Lin	Peking University, China

Contents – Part IV

Object Detection and Tracking

Asymmetric Two-Stream Networks for RGB-Disparity Based
Object Detection 3
   Ruizhi Lu, Jianhuang Lai, and Xiaohua Xie

Crack Detection for Concrete Architecture Images Using Feature
Enhancement Filtering and Shape Guided Active Contour Model 16
   Xiaomin Xie, Tingting Wang, Bo Liu, Kui Li, and Lin Zhang

Domain Attention Model for Domain Generalization in Object Detection 27
   Weixiong He, Huicheng Zheng, and Jianhuang Lai

Exploring Multi-scale Deep Feature Fusion for Object Detection 40
   Quan Zhang, Jianhuang Lai, Xiaohua Xie, and Junyong Zhu

Infrared Small Target Detection Using Multiscale Gray and Variance
Difference 53
   Jinyan Gao, Yulan Guo, Zaiping Lin, and Wei An

A Local Top-Down Module for Object Detection with
Multi-scale Features 65
   Shihua Huang, Lu Wang, Peiyu Yang, and Qingxu Deng

Parallel Connecting Deep and Shallow CNNs for Simultaneous Detection
of Big and Small Objects 78
   Canlong Zhang, Dongcheng He, Zhixin Li, and Zhiwen Wang

Penalty Non-maximum Suppression in Object Detection 90
   Wenqing Zhao and Hai Yan

Self-Paced Densely Connected Convolutional Neural Network
for Visual Tracking 103
   *Daohui Ge, Jianfeng Song, Yutao Qi, Chongxiao Wang,
and Qiguang Miao*

A Saliency-Based Object Tracking Method for UAV Application 115
   Jinyu Yang, Wenrui Ding, Chunlei Liu, and Zechen Ha

Research on Real-Time Vehicle Detection Algorithm Based
on Deep Learning 126
   Wei Yang, Ji Zhang, Zhongbao Zhang, and Hongyuan Wang

Vehicle Detection Based on Separable Reverse Connected Network   138
Enze Yang, Linlin Huang, and Jian Hu

Online Multiple Person Tracking Using Fully-Convolutional Neural
Networks and Motion Invariance Constraints   150
Nan Wang, Qi Zou, Yaping Huang, and Qiulin Ma

Conductive Particles Detection in the TFT-LCD Manufacturing
Process with U-ResNet   162
Kangping Chen and Eryun Liu

A New Monocular 3D Object Detection with Neural Network   174
Weijie Hong, Yiguang Liu, Yunan Zheng, Ying Wang, and Xuelei Shi

SalNet: Edge Constraint Based End-to-End Model for Salient
Object Detection   186
Le Han, Xuelong Li, and Yongsheng Dong

Gated Feature Pyramid Network for Object Detection   199
Xuemei Xie, Quan Liao, Lihua Ma, and Xing Jin

Learning Non-local Representation for Visual Tracking   209
Peng Zhang and Zengfu Wang

Discriminative Visual Tracking Using Multi-feature and Adaptive
Dictionary Learning.   221
Penggen Zheng, Jin Zhan, Huimin Zhao, and Jujian Lv

Oscillation Detection and Parameter-Adaptive Hedge Algorithm
for Real-Time Visual Tracking   233
Bolin Lv, Xiaolong Zhou, and Shengyong Chen

Asymmetrical Reverse Connection and Smooth-NMS
for Object Detection   245
Juan Peng, Zhicheng Wang, Xuan Lv, Gang Wei, Jingjing Fei,
and Hongwei Zhang

External Damage Risk Detection of Transmission Lines Using E-OHEM
Enhanced Faster R-CNN   260
Lei Qu, Kuixiang Liu, Qi He, Jun Tang, and Dong Liang

Parallel Search by Reinforcement Learning for Object Detection   272
Ye Huang, Chaochen Gu, Kaijie Wu, and Xinping Guan

A Novel Visual Tracking Method Based on Moth-Flame
Optimization Algorithm   284
Huanlong Zhang, Xiujiao Zhang, Xiaoliang Qian, Yibin Chen,
and Fang Wang

Learning Soft-Consistent Correlation Filters for RGB-T Object Tracking   295
  Yulong Wang, Chenglong Li, and Jin Tang

Performance Evaluation and Database

A Touching Character Database from Tibetan Historical Documents
to Evaluate the Segmentation Algorithm   309
  Quanchao Zhao, Long-long Ma, and Lijuan Duan

Nighttime FIR Pedestrian Detection Benchmark Dataset for ADAS   322
  Zhewei Xu, Jiajun Zhuang, Qiong Liu, Jingkai Zhou, and Shaowu Peng

How Many Labeled License Plates Are Needed?   334
  Changhao Wu, Shugong Xu, Guocong Song, and Shunqing Zhang

Evaluation of Lightweight Local Descriptors for Level Ground Navigation
with Monocular SLAM   347
  Weiya Chen, Yulin Wan, Shiqi Ou, and Zhidong Xue

Establishing a Large Scale Dataset for Image Emotion Analysis Using
Chinese Emotion Ontology.   359
  *Lifang Wu, Mingchao Qi, Heng Zhang, Meng Jian, Bowen Yang,
  and Dai Zhang*

Remote Sensing

Attention-Based Convolutional Networks for Ship Detection
in High-Resolution Remote Sensing Images   373
  Xiaofeng Ma, Wenyuan Li, and Zhenwei Shi

An Improved Camouflage Target Detection Using Hyperspectral Image
Based on Block-Diagonal and Low-Rank Representation   384
  *Fei Li, Xiuwei Zhang, Lei Zhang, Yanning Zhang, Dongmei Jiang,
  and Genping Zhao*

Hyperspectral Band Selection with Convolutional Neural Network   396
  Rui Cai, Yuan Yuan, and Xiaoqiang Lu

Integrating Convolutional Neural Network and Gated Recurrent Unit
for Hyperspectral Image Spectral-Spatial Classification   409
  Feng Zhou, Renlong Hang, Qingshan Liu, and Xiaotong Yuan

Disparity-Based Robust Unstructured Terrain Segmentation   421
  *Pengbo Zhang, Xinzhu Ma, Zhihui Wang, Haojie Li,
  and Zhongxuan Luo*

Author Index   433

Object Detection and Tracking

Asymmetric Two-Stream Networks for RGB-Disparity Based Object Detection

Ruizhi Lu[1,2,3], Jianhuang Lai[1,2,3(✉)], and Xiaohua Xie[1,2,3]

[1] School of Data and Computer Science, Sun Yat-sen University, Guangzhou, China
lurzh3@mail2.sysu.edu.cn, {stsljh,xiexiaoh6}@mail.sysu.edu.cn
[2] Guangdong Key Laboratory of Information Security Technology,
Guangzhou, China
[3] Key Laboratory of Machine Intelligence and Advanced Computing,
Ministry of Education, Beijing, China

Abstract. Currently, most methods of object detection are monocular-based. However, due to the sensitivity to color, these methods can not handle many hard samples. With the depth information, disparity maps are helpful to get over this problem. In this paper, we propose the asymmetric two-stream networks for RGB-Disparity based object detection. Our method consists of two networks, Disparity Representations Mining Network (DRMN) and Muti-Modal Detection Network (MMDN), to combine RGB and disparity data for more accurate detection. Unlike normal two-stream networks, our model is asymmetric because of the different capacity of RGB and disparity data. We are the first to propose a deep learning based framework utilizing only binocular information for object detection. The experiment results on KITTI and our proposed BPD dataset demonstrate that our method can achieve a significant increase in performance efficiently and get the state-of-the-art.

Keywords: Object detection · Two-stream networks · RGBD data

1 Introduction

With the help of deep neural networks, object detection has achieved great progress in recent years. However, in many real-world applications, it is still challenging for object detection to deal with a dramatic variety of illumination, occlusions, viewpoints, and busy backgrounds, etc.

Currently most approaches of object detection are monocular-based [7,8, 11,13,15,16,18,19], in other words, they take as input RGB images from single camera. Rich information of color and textures can be extracted from monocular RGB images, and the data only depend on one RGB camera with low cost. Therefore, monocular RGB images are popular in researches on object detection. Nevertheless, monocular-based methods utilizing only RGB data are likely to be mistaken on some hard-negative and hard-positive samples. As illustrated in

© Springer Nature Switzerland AG 2018
J.-H. Lai et al. (Eds.): PRCV 2018, LNCS 11259, pp. 3–15, 2018.
https://doi.org/10.1007/978-3-030-03341-5_1

Fig. 1(a), in RGB image, a lamp has the similar appearance with people's head, so it tends to be mistaken for a pedestrian. In addition, a white hat of the person brings an unusual color of the head, so monocular-based methods recognize him with low confidence due to the sensibility to color. However, if the depth features of objects are known, we can find that lamp's shape is flat, and pedestrian's shape is a paraboloid (Fig. 1(b)), then hard-negative and hard-positive samples can be distinguished, also the confidence of true pedestrian improves, such as Fig. 1(c).

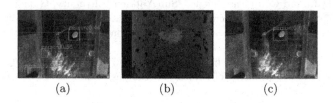

(a)   (b)   (c)

Fig. 1. An example of pedestrian detection. (a) A lamp is likely to be mistaken for a pedestrian because it looks like a head for the monocular-based methods. In addition, a white hat of the person brings an unusual color of head, so monocular-based methods recognize him with low confidence. But (b) from disparity map we can find that lamp's actual shape is flat, and pedestrian's shape is a paraboloid. According to these, (c) hard-negative and hard-positive samples can be distinguished, also the confidence of true pedestrian improves. Best viewed in color. (Color figure online)

Learning depth features of objects contributes to locating objects accurately. There are two ways to achieve this. On one hand, RGB cameras and extra equipment, such as LIDAR and Microsoft Kinect, can be utilized to get depth information of objects. Some methods took as input LIDAR bird views (3D) [1–3] or depth images (2.5D) [5] with RGB images to locate objects more accurately. However, these approaches need extra expensive equipment, which is unavailable in normal public places. As a result, currently they are too costly to be applied in most public cases, except for some special ones such as autonomous driving, which desperately needs accurate object detection and can afford it.

Besides, from disparity maps we can also get depth information of objects, and these will help learn more discriminative features, such as Fig. 1(b). Furthermore, disparity maps can be got only depending on a pair of normal RGB cameras, so RGB-Disparity based approaches are more feasible and they have much lower cost than the above polymorphic-based approaches. Object detection utilizing only binocular information has not drawn much attention so far. Some approaches regarded binocular information as the correction of monocular detection. For example, Zhang et al. [22] adjusted the detection results of left images with that of right images, but it needed to detect respectively on binocular images so brought much higher computational cost.

In this paper, we propose the asymmetric two-stream networks for RGB-Disparity based object detection. Different from normal two-stream networks [3–5, 21, 23, 24], where both streams were similarly designed as complete network structures, in our networks one of the streams is based on only part of the whole backbone network with lower computational cost. Our method can significantly improve the performance of basic network. The main contributions of this paper are as follows.

- We propose the asymmetric two-stream networks for RGB-Disparity based object detection. To our knowledge, we are the first to raise a deep learning based framework utilizing only binocular information for object detection.
- Asymmetric two-stream networks are designed to combine RGB and disparity data, so the proposed method can learn discriminative features more easily. Besides, our approach only depends on a pair of normal RGB cameras, so it's low-cost and more feasible in public places.
- The experiment results on KITTI and our proposed BPD dataset have shown that, with less complexity, our method can improve the performance and have comparable effect with some complicated monocular-based methods.

2   Related Work

Object detection has made great progress during these years. For more accurate localization, researchers worldwide have made a lot of efforts, which are twofold: designing stronger networks and utilizing other more reliable equipment.

On the aspect of designing stronger networks, proposal-based methods [7, 8, 11, 18], generating proposals first and then applying high-quality classifiers, have developed for their performances but with higher computational cost. Ren et al. [18] proposed faster R-CNN, which employed RPN and following classification into an end-to-end network. Lin et al. [11] exploited the inherent pyramidal hierarchy of deep convolutional network to construct feature pyramid. On the other hand, [12,13,15,16,19] established regression-based frameworks to locate objects, which removed the step of generating proposals and trained end-to-end detectors directly with higher computational efficiency. Liu et al. [13] proposed SSD, predicting object locations on multi-scale layers thus obtaining desirable performance for objects with different scales. In this paper, for the excellent trade-off between performance and computational cost, our proposed method is based on the SSD network [13].

More complex networks can learn more discriminative features, yet with higher computational cost. On the other hand, some methods utilized other more reliable equipment to locate objects, such as LIDAR and Kinect. [1–3] took as input both LIDAR point clouds and RGB images to predict oriented 3D bounding boxes. Deng et al. [5] stuck to the 2.5D representation framework, taking as input RGB images and Kinect depth maps, to find 3D locations of objects. With the help of other reliable equipment, depth features of objects can be caught, thus localization would be more accurate. However, such expensive devices are not available in most public places. Furthermore, in most public cases 2D localization is enough instead of 3D. As a result, these methods are not feasible in normal public places. In our work, we propose the asymmetric two-stream networks utilizing RGB and disparity data for 2D object detection, which only require a pair of normal RGB cameras and can achieve a significant increase in performance.

Object detection utilizing only binocular information has not drawn much attention so far. Actually, with the binocular images by a pair of normal RGB cameras, disparity maps can be got and represent the distances between objects and cameras. Utilizing it we can learn more discriminative features of objects. Zhang et al. [22] detected pedestrians, aided by the fusion of binocular information. However, detections were based on traditional sliding-window methods and needed to be processed on binocular images respectively, where disparity maps were used for preprocessing only. To our knowledge, we are the first to propose a deep learning based framework utilizing binocular information for object detection, and it needs to be processed only once per image.

The structure of two-stream networks is popular in dealing with cross-modal data. [21,23,24] designed two-stream networks to fuse RGB and flow features in action recognition. [4] proposed two-stream networks to utilize ensembles of RGB and hypothetical thermal data in pedestrian detection. However, to maintain the symmetry of networks, in existed methods both streams were similarly tended to be designed as complete network structures, so they were multi-parameter and computationally costly. In this paper, we establish a framework of asymmetric two-stream networks, where one of the streams is based on only part of the whole backbone network with lower computational cost. RGB and disparity data go through different networks respectively, and then discriminative features can be learned and fused for better object detection.

3   Two-Stream Networks for Learning and Fusing RGB-Disparity Representations

In this section, the proposed asymmetric two-stream networks for RGB-Disparity based object detection will be described in details. We first present the overview of our approach in Sect. 3.1. Then in Sect. 3.2, the design of asymmetric two-stream networks will be discussed in particular. Finally, specific to the construction of two-stream networks, we will talk about our training strategy in Sect. 3.2.

3.1   Overview

The overview of our asymmetric two-stream networks is illustrated in Fig. 2. Given a pair of binocular RGB images, a disparity map can be got by stereo matching methods, and then two-stream networks get processed. Our proposed two-stream networks consist of two different networks, Disparity Representations Mining Network (DRMN) and Muti-Modal Detection Network (MMDN). DRMN takes as input disparity maps in order to learn discriminative features from them, which will be aided to MMDN later. On the other hand, MMDN learns representations from RGB images and fuses them with the output of DRMN. According to representations from both sides, MMDN processes the

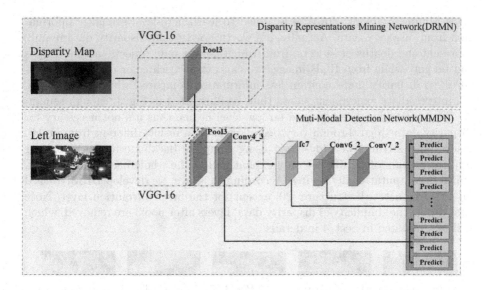

Fig. 2. The overview of our asymmetric two-stream networks.

final detection. With the two-stream networks, representations from RGB and disparity data can be learned and fused to generate more discriminative information, helpful to detection.

3.2   Two-Stream Networks

Given RGB images x_{rgb} and disparity maps x_d, the easy ways to fuse them are addition of them, maximum of them, and concatenation of them. However, features from RGB images and disparity maps, representing information of color and depth respectively, are cross-modal, and it's hard for models to directly learn from them. As a result, We need to learn transform functions $F_1(\cdot)$, $F_2(\cdot)$, projecting them into a common space S, where the fusion of them will be much easier.

$$\tilde{X}_1 = F_1(x_{rgb}), \quad \tilde{X}_2 = F_2(x_d), \quad \tilde{X}_1, \tilde{X}_2 \in S \tag{1}$$

To deal with cross-modal features, referring to [4,24], we establish a framework of asymmetric two-stream networks to model $F_1(\cdot)$ and $F_2(\cdot)$ separately. RGB and disparity data go through different convolution networks respectively, after that semantic information learned can be fused more easily. According to above, our proposed asymmetric two-stream networks consist of two different networks, Disparity Representations Mining Network (DRMN) and Muti-Modal Detection Network (MMDN).

Disparity Representations Mining Network (DRMN). In order to narrow the apparent gap between RGB and disparity data, Disparity Representations Mining Network (DRMN) is aimed to learn high-level semantic information from disparity data. Actually, it's worth noting that disparity data mainly represent the depths of objects, from which almost only objects' actual shapes can be got, while from RGB images we can extract rich color and texture features, so disparity maps contain less information compared with RGB images. An intermediate experiment shows that, as illustrated in Fig. 3, enough semantic information has been learned on low-level layers, thus it's not necessary for disparity data to go through very deep layers. As a result, different from [4,24], where both streams were designed using complete backbone networks, in our implementation of DRMN we only exploit half of the whole backbone network, which is computationally saving. According to above, we develop DRMN based on VGG-16 network structure [20] except for the first convolution layer. Note that due to the simplicity of disparity data, layers after pool3 are removed, which will be evaluated in Sect. 4 in details.

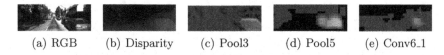

(a) RGB   (b) Disparity   (c) Pool3   (d) Pool5   (e) Conv6_1

Fig. 3. Feature maps output from different layers for disparity data. Note that the saliency of a car has already been learned on the layer of pool3 (c), getting approximately the same effects with that from pool5 (d) and conv6_1 (e). Best viewed in color. (Color figure online)

Muti-Modal Detection Network (MMDN). The aim of Muti-Modal Detection Network (MMDN) is to fuse multi-modal data and then process the final detection. There are 3 main steps in MMDN, learning representations from RGB data, fusing heterogeneous features from RGB and disparity, and determining the final detection. With the help of multi-modal data, localization will be more accurate.

For excellent performance on objects with different scales, we develop our MMDN on SSD backbone network [13] to finish the above 3 steps. There are 2 main differences between our method and [13]. Firstly, features learned from RGB data and DRMN will be concatenated on the layer of pool3. At this moment semantic information of them can be fused more easily. Secondly, in [13], feature maps in a layer were responsible for the regression of bounding boxes with a range of size. But if the range was too large, the accuracy of regression will be affected. Referring to [17], we discretize the range of bounding boxes' size and assign 4 regressions for features maps in a layer. However, different from [17], we do not exploit Recurrent Rolling Convolution architecture because of the large computational cost, and evaluations in Sect. 4 will show that our asymmetric two-stream networks have comparable performance with [17], but with less time consumption.

Training Strategy. As discussed above, our proposed two-stream networks consist of 2 different networks. To avoid the problem of slow convergence, the training process includes 3 main phases. Firstly, DRMN is trained on the SSD network [13], initialized using the parameters of VGG-16 [20] pre-trained on ImageNet dataset. After training the layers after pool3 are removed. Secondly, MMDN is trained with the output of DRMN deactivated. The layers of MMDN are initialized similar to DRMM. Finally, the layer of pool3 in MMDN is concatenated with the output of DRMN. The combined two-stream networks are finetuned together, where the coefficients of learning rates of the layers before pool3 drop to 0.1 and others remain 1.

4   Experiment

In this section, details of evaluation will be described. Experiments are performed on KITTI Object Detection Benchmark [6], a publicly available dataset, and our proposed Binocular Pedestrian Detection (BPD) dataset, captured by binocular devices. To evaluate the effectiveness of our method, we conduct 3 experiments in this section. Firstly, we process our method under different stereo matching methods to demonstrate the insensitivity of our algorithm to different stereo matching approaches. Secondly, because DRMN is based on part of the whole backbone network, exploration of different DRMN's depths is performed. Finally, the analysis of performances on both datasets is provided.

4.1   Datasets

The KITTI dataset [6] consists of 7481 images for training and validation, and 7518 images for testing, captured by driving cars with stereo cameras. The groundtruth of the test set is not available, and everyone has only one chance to submit results to a dedicated server for evaluation on the test set. Following [17], We employ an image similarity metric for the training set and validation set separation, which makes our resulting validation set contain 2741 images. In the meanwhile, for a fair comparison, as described in [17], the experiments on KITTI are carried out with only car dataset because the pedestrian data are scarce.

The Binocular Pedestrian Detection (BPD) dataset is captured by ourselves using top-view binocular devices, which covers plenty of indoor and outdoor real-world scenes, such as offices, corridors, laboratory, teaching building, and scenic spots, etc. Besides the BPD dataset is very challenging with many hard samples, and a low image resolution of 320×240, as illustrated in Fig. 4. The BPD dataset consists of 65093 images for training and 12330 images for testing. Specially, all images are captured in the top-view. All left and right images are provided so that we can get a disparity map for each pair of images using stereo matching methods.

Fig. 4. The BPD dataset. Plenty of indoor and outdoor real-world scenes are covered, such as offices (a), corridors (b, c), laboratory (d), teaching building (e), and scenic spots (f), etc. The dataset is challenging with a low image resolution of 320×240, and a lot of hard samples, for instance, the pedestrians in the dark.

4.2   Experiment Setting

The following settings are used throughout the experiments. In training, we adopt the data augmentation methods described in SSD [13]. Stochastic gradient descent (SGD) is chosen for optimization. Besides, the initial learning rate is set to 0.0005, which will be divided by 10 at iterations of 20000 and 100000. Training is processed for 120000 iterations in total. In the whole evaluation, mAP with IoU of 0.5 is adopted as the criteria, and all experiments on speed are measured with batch size 1 using TITAN X with Intel Xeon E5-2620@2.10 GHz.

4.3   Exploration Under Different Stereo Matching Methods

Our proposed DRMN takes as input disparity map, which can be got using various of stereo matching methods. To demonstrate that our method is insensitive to different stereo matching approaches, we process our method under two typical stereo matching methods, CRL [14] and SGBM [9]. CRL [14] is CNN-based so it's time-consuming but performs very well. SGBM [9] is a time-saving method with the help of classical semi-global matching, but the disparity maps got are coarser, such as Fig. 5. Table 1 shows the performances of the proposed method under these two stereo matching approaches on the KITTI validation set, where all images are resized to 640×192. We can find that although there is a large gap between both of disparity maps, our asymmetric two-stream networks get almost the same accuracy under them (84.1% vs 83.8%). We argue that it's because, on one hand, the semantic information learned by our DRMN can help to reduce the discrepancy on appearances of them. On the other hand, features learned by MMDN can correct the results of DRMN. As a result, it can be confirmed that our method is insensitive to stereo matching approaches, which means we can adopt fast stereo matching (e.g. SGBM (40 ms/frame)) for practical feasibility instead of CNN based ones (e.g. CRL (190 ms/frame)).

4.4   Evaluation of Performances Under Different Depths of DRMN

As mentioned in Sect. 3, DRMN is based on part of the whole backbone network. To explore the depth of DRMN, Table 2 shows the performances under different depths of DRMN on the KITTI validation set, where disparity maps are generated using SGBM [9]. Noting that *Asymmetric Two-Stream Networks (data)*

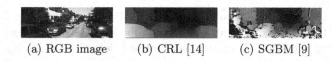

      (a) RGB image   (b) CRL [14]   (c) SGBM [9]

Fig. 5. Disparity maps from CRL [14] and SGBM [9]. Best viewed in color. (Color figure online)

Table 1. Performances of our method under two different stereo matching methods on KITTI validation set.

	Our mAP (%)	Time (per image)
CRL [14]	84.1	190 ms
SGBM [9]	83.8	40 ms

means the depth of DRMN is zero and raw disparity data are concatenated with RGB data directly. Other *Asymmetric Two-Stream Networks (X)* mean DRMN forwards until the layer of X and then the output are concatenated on the corresponding layer in MMDN. In addition, *One-Stream Network (only RGB)* is also chosen for comparison, where DRMN is removed and MMDN utilizing only RGB data works without the output of DRMN. We can see that because RGB and disparity are cross-modal data, concatenating them directly without two-stream networks even results in a worse accuracy than one-stream network utilizing only RGB data (73.7% vs 80.8%), which strongly confirms the necessity of DRMN. Besides, we demonstrate that performance is not better as DRMN goes deeper, and concatenating features on a low-level layer of pool3 can achieve better performance boost than other high-level layers (i.e. pool5 and conv6_1). As discussed in Sect. 3, the reason is that disparity maps are simpler than RGB images, and enough semantic information has been learned on low-level layers, thus it's not necessary to forward very deep layers. According to above, in our implementation of DRMN, layers after pool3 are removed.

4.5   Results on the KITTI Dataset

To demonstrate the effectiveness of our asymmetric two-stream networks, our method is evaluated on the KITTI validation set. Because our method is regression-based, for fairness, we compare our method only with regression-based methods. Thereinto, our method is compared with the recently published state-of-the-art method, Recurrent Rolling Convolution Detector (RRC) [17], which ranked the first for the hardest category of the car on KITTI testing set by the time this paper was written. Note that our method is not compared with other two-stream or binocular-based methods because of the different applications. Firstly, existed two-stream networks for detection [1–3,5] were mostly designed for 3D localization instead of 2D, and they required data from LIDAR or Kinect, which is not consistent with our case. [4] was for 2D localization but it needed thermal data for training. Secondly, binocular-based approach [22] was based on traditional sliding-window methods inefficiently and designed for front-view pedestrian detection only. We are the first to propose an end-to-end deep learning based framework for RGB-Disparity based object detection, which only utilizes binocular information.

Table 2. Detection results on KITTI validation set.

Methods	mAP (%)	FPS
One-stream network (only RGB)	80.8	25
Asymmetric two-stream networks (data)	73.7	20
Asymmetric two-stream networks (pool3)	**83.8**	17
Asymmetric two-stream networks (pool5)	82.3	15
Asymmetric two-stream networks (conv6_1)	82.2	14
RRC [17][a]	84.0	11
Asymmetric two-stream RRC	**85.6**	9

[a]The accuracy is lower than that reported in [17], mainly because in [17] an image size of 2560×768 was adopted but here all images are resized to 640×192. Actually, the increase in input size significantly boosts detection accuracy, as pointed out in [10], but it will cause overloaded occupation of GPU memory and be impractical.

Table 2 shows the results on the KITTI validation set. It needs to be pointed out that, in [17], to achieve the best performance, an image size of 2560×768 was adopted, which would cause overloaded occupation of GPU memory and be divorced from reality. In order to develop feasible methods available in most public places, all images are resized to 640×192 and we retrain RRC carefully for evaluation. From the results we can observe that, on one side, our proposed asymmetric two-stream networks exploiting RGB and disparity get the accuracy of 83.8%, outperforming one-stream network exploiting RGB by 3%. On the other side, our method can get comparable accuracy with RRC (83.8% vs 84.0%), while our method runs faster than RRC (17 FPS vs 11 FPS). It can be confirmed that our method exploits disparity data well so that it can learn discriminative features more easily without the large increase in network complexity. Finally, since RRC is based on SSD network too, we employ our asymmetric two-stream networks in it, which achieves the state-of-the-art with an accuracy of 85.6%. All of the above have shown the effectiveness of our asymmetric two-stream networks.

4.6   Results on the BPD Dataset

In this section, we evaluate methods on our proposed BPD dataset, which is captured by ourselves using top-view binocular devices, including lots of hard samples. Following the settings in Sect. 4.5 except that image size of 320×240

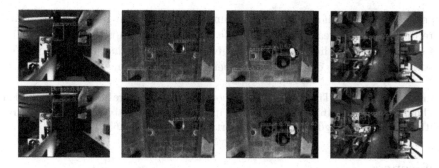

Fig. 6. Examples of detection results on the BPD dataset. The top and bottom rows refer to results of one-stream network and our asymmetric two-stream networks respectively. Compared with the other, Our method can handle more hard samples (e.g. objects on the sofa, lamps, and pedestrians with hats on). Best viewed in color. (Color figure online)

Table 3. Detection results on BPD dataset.

Methods	mAP (%)	FPS
One-stream network (only RGB)	77.8	28
Asymmetric two-stream networks	**83.0**	22
RRC [17]	83.3	14
Asymmetric two-stream RRC	**84.7**	11

is adopted here, results on the BPD dataset are illustrated as Table 3. Similar to results in Sect. 4.5, we can see that our asymmetric two-stream networks bring a significant increase in performance over the one-stream network (83.0% vs 77.8%). Figure 6 shows the qualitative results of one-stream network exploiting only RGB data and our asymmetric two-stream networks respectively, we can see that our method can handle more hard samples. Besides, our method achieves comparable accuracy with RRC (83.0% vs 83.3%), while RRC runs at 14 FPS, slower than our methods (22 FPS). Obviously, our asymmetric two-stream networks utilizing both RGB and disparity information can get comparable performance with lower network complexity. Finally, we employ our asymmetric two-stream networks in RRC, with an accuracy of 84.7%, getting the state-of-the-art. The results shown in this section demonstrate the effectiveness of our asymmetric two-stream networks again.

5 Conclusion

In this paper, we propose the asymmetric two-stream networks for RGB-Disparity based object detection, which exploit both RGB and disparity data to get a higher accuracy of localization. Unlike normal two-stream networks, our model is asymmetric due to the different capacity of RGB and disparity data.

Experiment results show that our asymmetric two-stream networks can learn more discriminative features without the large increase in network complexity, and get the state-of-the-art. In the future, we plan to refine disparity data by detection, to generate disparity better benefitting detection.

Acknowledgement. This project is supported by the Natural Science Foundation of China (61573387, 61672544), and the Tip-top Scientific and Technical Innovative Youth Talents of Guangdong special support program (No. 2016TQ03X263).

References

1. Chen, X., et al.: 3D object proposals for accurate object class detection. In: NIPS, pp. 424–432. MIT Press (2015)
2. Chen, X., Kundu, K., Zhu, Y., Ma, H., Fidler, S., Urtasun, R.: 3D object proposals using stereo imagery for accurate object class detection. PAMI **40**(5), 1259–1272 (2018)
3. Chen, X., Ma, H., Wan, J., Li, B., Xia, T.: Multi-view 3D object detection network for autonomous driving. In: CVPR, pp. 6526–6534. IEEE (2017)
4. Dan, X., Ouyang, W., Ricci, E., Wang, X., Sebe, N., et al.: Learning cross-modal deep representations for robust pedestrian detection. In: CVPR, pp. 4236–4244. IEEE (2017)
5. Deng, Z., Latecki, L.J.: Amodal detection of 3D objects: Inferring 3D bounding boxes from 2D ones in RGB-depth images. In: CVPR, pp. 398–406. IEEE (2017)
6. Geiger, A., Lenz, P., Urtasun, R.: Are we ready for autonomous driving? The KITTI vision benchmark suite. In: CVPR, pp. 3354–3361. IEEE (2012)
7. Girshick, R.: Fast R-CNN. In: ICCV, pp. 1440–1448. IEEE (2015)
8. He, K., Gkioxari, G., Dollár, P., Girshick, R.: Mask R-CNN. In: ICCV, pp. 2980–2988. IEEE (2017)
9. Hirschmuller, H.: Stereo processing by semiglobal matching and mutual information. PAMI **30**(2), 328–341 (2008)
10. Huang, J., et al.: Speed/accuracy trade-offs for modern convolutional object detectors. In: CVPR, pp. 7310–7311. IEEE (2017)
11. Lin, T.Y., Dollar, P., Girshick, R., He, K., Hariharan, B., Belongie, S.: Feature pyramid networks for object detection. In: CVPR, pp. 2117–2125. IEEE (2017)
12. Lin, T.Y., Goyal, P., Girshick, R., He, K., Dollar, P.: Focal loss for dense object detection. In: CVPR, pp. 2980–2988. IEEE (2017)
13. Liu, W., et al.: SSD: single shot multibox detector. In: Leibe, B., Matas, J., Sebe, N., Welling, M. (eds.) ECCV 2016. LNCS, vol. 9905, pp. 21–37. Springer, Cham (2016). https://doi.org/10.1007/978-3-319-46448-0_2
14. Pang, J., Sun, W., Ren, J.S., Yang, C., Yan, Q.: Cascade residual learning: a two-stage convolutional neural network for stereo matching. In: ICCV, pp. 887–895. IEEE (2017)
15. Redmon, J., Divvala, S., Girshick, R., Farhadi, A.: You only look once: Unified, real-time object detection. In: CVPR, pp. 779–788. IEEE (2016)
16. Redmon, J., Farhadi, A.: Yolo9000: better, faster, stronger. In: CVPR, pp. 6517–6525. IEEE (2017)
17. Ren, J., et al.: Accurate single stage detector using recurrent rolling convolution. In: CVPR, pp. 752–760. IEEE (2017)

18. Ren, S., He, K., Girshick, R., Sun, J.: Faster R-CNN: towards real-time object detection with region proposal networks. PAMI **39**(6), 1137–1149 (2017)
19. Shen, Z., Liu, Z., Li, J., Jiang, Y.G., Chen, Y., Xue, X.: DSOD: learning deeply supervised object detectors from scratch. In: CVPR, pp. 1919–1927. IEEE (2017)
20. Simonyan, K., Zisserman, A.: Very deep convolutional networks for large-scale image recognition. arXiv preprint arXiv:1409.1556 (2014)
21. Sun, S., Kuang, Z., Ouyang, W., Sheng, L., Zhang, W.: Optical flow guided feature: a fast and robust motion representation for video action recognition. arXiv preprint arXiv:1711.11152 (2017)
22. Zhang, Z., Tao, W., Sun, K., Hu, W., Yao, L.: Pedestrian detection aided by fusion of binocular information. Pattern Recognit. **60**, 227–238 (2016)
23. Zhu, J., Zou, W., Zhu, Z.: End-to-end video-level representation learning for action recognition. arXiv preprint arXiv:1711.04161 (2017)
24. Zhu, Y., Lan, Z., Newsam, S., Hauptmann, A.G.: Hidden two-stream convolutional networks for action recognition. arXiv preprint arXiv:1704.00389 (2017)

Crack Detection for Concrete Architecture Images Using Feature Enhancement Filtering and Shape Guided Active Contour Model

Xiaomin Xie[✉], Tingting Wang, Bo Liu, Kui Li, and Lin Zhang

College of Mechanical and Electrical Engineering, Hohai University,
Changzhou 213022, Jiangsu, China
yu_jian_wo@126.com

Abstract. Accurate and automatic crack detection for concrete architecture images is quite important and challenging. A joint crack detection model is presented in this paper, integrating the nonlocal means model for the noise removing, the multi-scale Hessian filtering for line-like feature enhancement, the morphological operations for the coarse segmentation, and the localized active contour model for the fine results. Firstly, the nonlocal mean filtering is adopted to reduce the noise which appears during the acquisition of the concrete architecture image, preserving the details of the edges information simultaneously. Secondly, an improved multi-scale linear feature enhancement filtering is used to strengthen the crack target; Then, a set of morphological operations and the thresholding model are employed to ameliorate the results and output a binary image which is used to initialize the level set function and guide the evolution of the active contours. Finally, the localized active contour model integrating the intensity and the shape information is utilized to refine the coarse results. Experiments and comparisons on the crack images show the effectiveness of the proposed model.

Keywords: Crack segmentation · Non-local mean image denoising
Multi-scale Hessian filtering · Active contour model

1 Introduction

Concrete architectures are the most common infrastructure in the city. After years of service, the occurrence of cracks in different degrees will harm the safety of concrete buildings. Therefore, the accurate detection of cracks is of great significance to the evaluation and restoration of structures. So far, there have been a variety of crack detection methods, such as the artificial detection, the ultrasonic detection and the machine vision detection [1, 2]. The artificial detection is dependent on the experienced workers, which is time consuming and gradually replaced by the visual based methods. The visual based detection methods have aroused the interest of the researchers [1–4].

Over the past few decades, a large number of crack detection algorithms based on image processing have been proposed in the literature. According to the difference of the information used by the approaches, these models are roughly divided into the following categories: intensities based methods [5, 6], edge based methods [7, 8], shape

© Springer Nature Switzerland AG 2018
J.-H. Lai et al. (Eds.): PRCV 2018, LNCS 11259, pp. 16–26, 2018.
https://doi.org/10.1007/978-3-030-03341-5_2

based methods [9, 10] and the integrated methods [10, 11]. Normally, the cracks in the structure images are mainly characterized as follows: (1) The pixels intensities belonging to the crack are darker than the ones of the background; (2) The local crack patches are approximated as linear, which distribution contains longitudinal, transverse, diagonal and the like [9]; (3) The pixel number of the crack is much less than the one of the background.

Initially, the researchers take the gray level information into consideration to find the thresholding value between the crack target and the background. However, these methods are affected by the noise and lack the global constraints, which result in poor detection results. Since the differences in cracks and background grayscale are distinct, the gradient based edges are the important features for crack detection. Hence, the edge detection algorithms such as the Canny and Sobel are used to deal with different types of surface cracks [8, 12]. Similarly, the edge detection models are easily effected by the noise and the complex background. To address these problems, more feature information is utilized to guide the crack segmentation, such as the geometric features and the textures [13, 14]. Given the linear structures of the crack, the Hessian filter, which is developed for the vessel enhancement [16], is employed to emphasize the characteristics of the crack [15]. The drawback of the model is that serious inhomogeneity would easily lead to error detection since the step edges would be taken as crack.

Meanwhile, machine learning based methods have been another important approaches for crack detection. For this kind of methods, the 2-D geometric characteristics such as the longitudinal, transverse, diagonal, are as the input features of the classifiers [9, 17, 18]. The supervised classifiers, for example the SVM [17], the neural network [18] are used to classify the crack and non-crack. However, the techniques work on every pixel or local sub-image, and therefore lack global constraints. Further, some model-based crack segmentation methods are proposed [10, 19, 20] in the field. The active contour model (ACM) [11, 20], which objective function is constructed by the features of the crack (intensity, edges, shape, etc.), is considered as a general framework. In general, The existing problems of aforementioned models could be solved to certain extent by the ACM. For example, the Region-Scalable Fitting (RSF) model and the like, which are put forward in [21, 22], work in spatially varying local region, and hence segment images with intensity inhomogeneity effectively. The model is subjected to the global constraints of the length and area, so it is robust to noise.

In this paper, a joint crack detection model is proposed. Firstly, the nonlocal mean filtering is employed to reduce the noise which appears during the acquisition of the concrete architecture image, preserving the details of the edges information simultaneously. Secondly, an improved multi-scale linear feature enhancement filtering is used to strengthen the crack target; Then, a set of morphological operations and the thresholding model are employed to ameliorate the results and output a binary image which is used to initialize the level sets and guide the evolution of the active contours. Finally, the localized active contour model integrating the intensity and the shape information is utilized to refine the coarse results.

The rest of the paper is arranged as follows: Sect. 2 provides the detailed description of the whole algorithm; experiments and analysis are carried out in Sect. 3; finally, the conclusion is drawn in Sect. 4.

2   The Proposed Model

In the section, the proposed automatic crack detection is described in detail. The whole flowchart of the proposed model is shown in Fig. 1. The whole framework can be divided into four parts: In the first part, the nonlocal mean denoising filter is employed to smooth the crack image while preserve the object edge information. In the second part, the improved multi-scale Hessian-based filter is used to enhance the dark line-like object. Meanwhile, two morphology operators: the dilation reconstruction and the erosion reconstruction, are introduced to remove the noise and the pseudo small targets in the image, which are followed by the Otsu thresholding to output a binary image. The binary image has two major roles: on the one hand, it works as the initial active contour; on the other hand, it works as the shape constraint term of the energy functional. The results of each step are shown in Fig. 2.

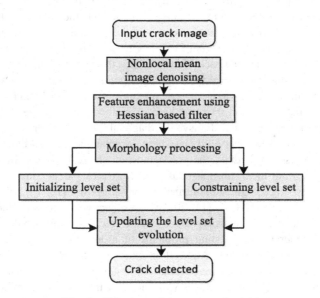

Fig. 1. Flowchart of the proposed model

2.1   Nonlocal Mean Image Denoising

The nonlocal mean image filter (NLM) [23] makes full use of the redundant information in the image, and maintains the details of the image while de-noising. The basic idea of the NLM filter lies in: the pixels in the image are weighted averagely by the pixels with similar structures in the neighborhood of the image. However, the NLM filter takes a lot of time to calculate the weight value, which limits its application. Later, some fast NLM models are proposed to accelerate the denoising process [24]. In this paper, the fast NLM filter in [24] is introduced to smooth the images (refer to [24] for details). The filtering results could be observed in Fig. 2(b), which demonstrates that the noise is effectively suppressed and the crack edges are well maintained simultaneously.

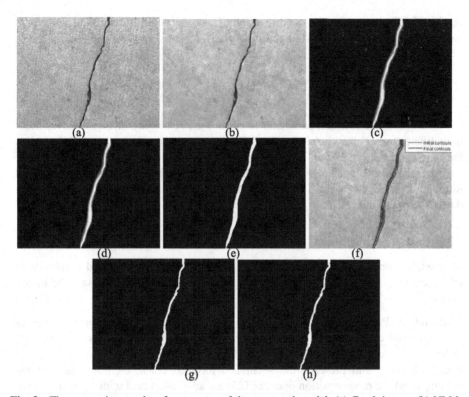

Fig. 2. The processing results of every step of the proposed model. (a) Crack image. (b) NLM filtered result. (c) Hessian based filtered result. (d) The result of the application of morphology opening reconstruction and closing reconstruction. (e) Thresholding result. (d) Final contours of the ACM. (g) The corresponding binary result determined by the final contours. (h) Postprocessing results (if necessary).

2.2   Hessian Based Multi-scale Filtering

The Hessian matrix calculates the second order information of the pixels (x, y) in the image $I\colon \Omega \to \Re$.

$$H(x, y) = \begin{bmatrix} \frac{\partial^2 L}{\partial^2 x} & \frac{\partial^2 L}{\partial x \partial y} \\ \frac{\partial^2 L}{\partial y \partial x} & \frac{\partial^2 L}{\partial^2 y} \end{bmatrix} \qquad (1)$$

Where, $L = G(x, y, s) * I(x, y)$ denotes the convolution of the original image and the Gaussian function, where, s is the scale parameter. The eigenvalues $(\lambda_1, \lambda_2, \quad |\lambda_1| \le |\lambda_2|)$ and the corresponding eigenvectors are important shape indices, and the larger eigenvalues represent the direction of the larger curvature. With these eigenvalues, the likelihood function is developed in [16] according to the two measures: $R_a = |\lambda_1|/|\lambda_2|$, $R_b = \sqrt{|\lambda_1|^2 + \left||\lambda_2|^2\right|}$. However, the response in [16] between cracks of different transverse radii is usually inhomogeneous. Given that, the cracks have complex textures, the likelihood function is designed in this paper as:

$$V(x, y, s) = \begin{cases} 0, & \text{if } \lambda_2 \leq 0 \\ e^{\left(-(\lambda_1 + \lambda_2)/R_b^2\right)} \left(1 - e^{\left(-R_b^2/2c\right)}\right) & \text{otherwise} \end{cases} \quad (2)$$

Where, c is the constant parameter to control the sensitivity of measures R_b. Note that, different scales parameters lead to different response results, and the final result is the maximum response of all the responses.

After the NLM denoising, the enhancement result of the multi-scale Hessian based filtering is displayed in Fig. 2(c), which demonstrates the ability of the approach to detect the linear targets.

2.3   Coarse Segmentation

Meanwhile, some noise and other small linear noncracks are detected as shown in Fig. 2(c). Thus some subsequent processing approaches are used to obtain the binary image.

Morphology Processing. The morphology opening operators with linear structures element could detect the crack in a certain shape. Thus the structures element with different angular rotations and sizes could detect all the linear shape. To eliminate the effects of noise, and preserve the small and tortuous crack, the supremum of the openings and the reconstruction operator [25] are adopted to deal with the result of the Hessian based enhancement. Then, the dual filter, which replaces the opening operator by the closing one, is used to fill in the hole of the result as in [25]. The result of the morphology operators could be seen in Fig. 2(d).

Otsu Thresholding. Further, the Otsu thresholding is introduced to generate the binary image. It is assumed that the image pixels can be divided into two parts: the background and the objects according to the threshold. And the threshold is determined based on the maximum variance of the inter classes. The binary output mask is shown in Fig. 2(e), which could be considered as a coarse segmentation of the crack.

2.4   Localized Region Based ACM

The proposed localized region based ACM integrates the advantages of the LCV [22] and the multi-scale Hessian based enhancement. The LCV model uses the local image information to segment the images with intensity inhomogeneity effectively. The energy function consists of six terms: the first two terms are the fitting energy terms which measure the similarity between the image pixel and the local intensity mean; The third and fourth terms are the length term and the area term which smooth the zero level contours. The fifth term is the penalty term which penalizes the deviation of the level set function from the signed distance function. The last one is the shape constraint term, where the $\varphi(x)$ is the signed distance function obtained mainly by the Hessian based denoising. The energy function is expressed as:

$$E(\phi(\mathbf{x}), f_1, f_2) = \int (I - f_1(\mathbf{x}))^2 H(\phi(\mathbf{x})) d\mathbf{x} + \int (I - f_2(\mathbf{x}))^2 (1 - H(\phi(\mathbf{x}))) d\mathbf{x}$$
$$+ \alpha \int |\nabla H(\phi(\mathbf{x}))| d\mathbf{x} + \beta \int H(\phi(\mathbf{x})) d\mathbf{x}$$
$$+ \mu \int \frac{1}{2} |\nabla \phi(H) - 1|^2 d\mathbf{x} + v \int (H(\phi(\mathbf{x})) - H(\varphi(\mathbf{x})))^2 d\mathbf{x}$$

$$(3)$$

Where, α, β, μ, v are the weight parameters of the energy terms. $f_1(\mathbf{x})$, $f_2(\mathbf{x})$ locally approximate the intensities on both sides of the zero level set curve, which are calculated as:

$$f_1(\mathbf{x}) = \frac{\int K(\mathbf{x}) I(\mathbf{x}) H(\phi(\mathbf{x})) d\mathbf{x}}{\int H(\phi(\mathbf{x})) d\mathbf{x}}, \quad f_2(\mathbf{x}) = \frac{\int K(\mathbf{x}) I(\mathbf{x}) (1 - H(\phi(\mathbf{x}))) d\mathbf{x}}{\int K(\mathbf{x}) (1 - H(\phi(\mathbf{x}))) d\mathbf{x}} \quad (4)$$

Where, $H(\mathbf{x})$ is the Heaviside function which denotes the internal region of the active curve while $(1 - H(\mathbf{x}))$ represents the external region. K is the Gaussian kernel function. Minimize the functional of (3), we obtain the corresponding Euler-Lagrange equation:

$$\frac{\partial \phi}{\partial t} = -\delta(\phi) \left[(I - f_2(\mathbf{x}))^2 - (I - f_1(\mathbf{x}))^2 \right] + \alpha \delta(\phi) div \left(\frac{\nabla \phi}{|\nabla \phi|} \right) + \beta \delta(\phi)$$
$$+ \mu \left(\Delta \phi - div \left(\frac{\nabla \phi}{|\nabla \phi|} \right) \right) + v \delta(\phi) (H(\phi(\mathbf{x})) - H(\varphi(\mathbf{x})))$$

$$(5)$$

Where, $\delta(\phi)$ is the Dirac function. In this paper, the initialized level set function is obtained by:

$$\phi_0(\mathbf{x}) = \varphi(\mathbf{x}) = 4 \times (0.5 - B(\mathbf{x})) \quad (6)$$

Where, the mask $B(\mathbf{x})$ is the binary result of the thresholding segmentation. Thus the difference between the constant 0.5 and the mask could obtain the different signs on both sides of the contour. Thus the initialization is performed automatically.

3 Experiments

In this section, several experiments are carried out to show the effectiveness of the proposed approach. All the experiments are conducted in MATLAB R2015a, on a personal computer.

First, we compare several filters that can protect the edges while denoising. A lot of fine particles in the concrete building images interfere with the cracks, which would further have a negative impact on crack detection. The bilateral filter, the guided filter and the NLM filter used in this paper are carried out on the original crack images, which can be seen in Fig. 3(b)–(d).

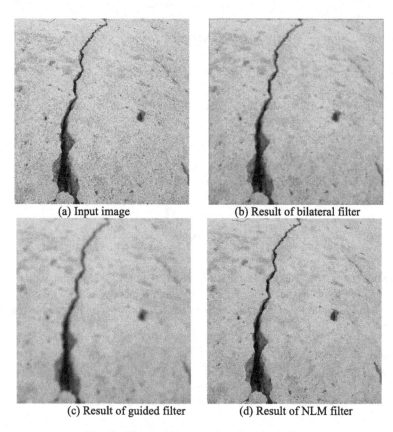

(a) Input image   (b) Result of bilateral filter

(c) Result of guided filter   (d) Result of NLM filter

Fig. 3. The denoising results using three filters

Using the guided filter, the noise is suppressed and hence it provides the most smoothest background. Meanwhile, the cracks are largely blurred as shown in Fig. 3(c). On the contrary, the bilateral filter shows better performance than the guide filter, which reduces some noise in the background and keeps the target edge to some extent, as shown in Fig. 3(b). Among all the evaluated models, the NLM filter obtain the best performance, providing the clear edges and the similar background to the guided filter as shown in Fig. 3(d).

Then, we demonstrate the ability of the improved Hessian based enhancement model in this paper. The classical Frangi's model [16] is proved to be an effective method of linear object enhancement, which is shown in Fig. 4(b). However, the response of the Frangi's model is lower at the transition and bifurcations, which are marked with yellow circles in Fig. 4(b). Consequently, small cracks could not be extracted by the detection. On the contrary, the improved model is able to enhance all the cracks, which is clearly seen in Fig. 4(c).

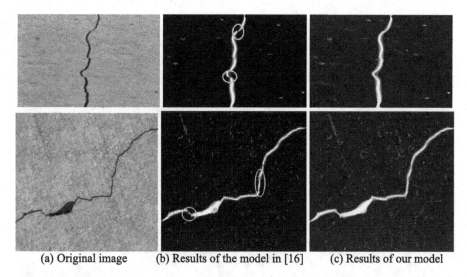

(a) Original image   (b) Results of the model in [16]   (c) Results of our model

Fig. 4. The enhancement results using two kinds of Hessian based models

The experiments on several crack images in Fig. 5 are conducted to compare the proposed model to the state-of-art ACM models, i.e. the GC model [20], and the LCV model [22]. The GC model (Geodesic active contours model) is based on the gradient and curvature to detect the crack boundary. The precision and speed of the ACM models depend greatly on the initial contour curve. And one need to set the initial contours carefully to get better performance. Thus, we set the same initialization obtained by the Hessian based enhancement and the thresholding for the GC model and the LCV model, which could be seen in Fig. 5(a).

Figure 5(a) reveals that, when the crack is simple, all the methods can detect the crack successfully, benefiting from the initialization technique. As the crack becomes complex, the segmentation results of the GC model get worse. However, the LCV model provides satisfactory results, despite some unsmooth and abrupt edges. The proposed method achieves the best performance for all images, confirming that it is an effective approach for crack detection.

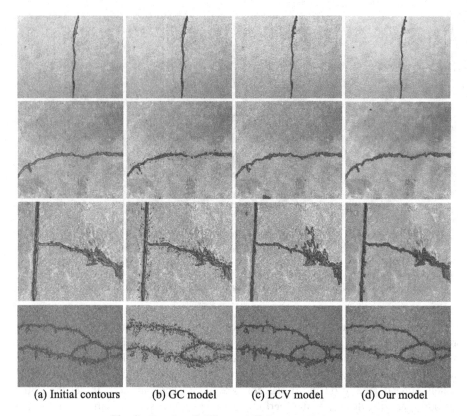

(a) Initial contours   (b) GC model   (c) LCV model   (d) Our model

Fig. 5. Results of different ACMs on crack images.

4 Conclusion

Our main contribution is to present a hybrid framework for crack detection, which integrates the advantages of the NLM filter, the Hessian based enhancement and the localized ACM. Both the intensity and the shape information of the crack is utilized to construct the level set functional. Also, the automatic initialization of the active contour is realized through the results based on the Hessian-based enhancement. Some experiments have demonstrated the functions of each part of the hybrid framework. The proposed approach has the potential to be an effective way for crack detection.

Acknowledgments. This work was supported by 'the Fundamental Research Funds for the Central Universities' (2016B02914), Science and Technology Development Funds of Jiangsu Province (grant 2015030-03).

References

1. Lins, R.G., Givigi, S.N.: Automatic crack detection and measurement based on image analysis. IEEE Trans. Instrum. Meas. **65**(3), 583–590 (2016)
2. Rabih, A., Sylvie, C., Jérôme, I., Vincent, B.: Automatic crack detection on two-dimensional pavement images: an algorithm based on minimal path selection. IEEE Trans. Intell. Transp. Syst. **17**(10), 2718–2729 (2016)
3. Sylvie, C., Jean-Marc, M.: Automatic road pavement assessment with image processing: review and comparison. Int. J. Geophys. **2011**, 1–20 (2011)
4. Mohan, A., Poobal, S.: Crack detection using image processing: a critical review and analysis. Alex. Eng. J. (2017). http://dx.doi.org/10.1016/j.aej.2017.01.020
5. Li, Q., Liu, X.: Novel approach to pavement image segmentation based on neighboring difference histogram method. In: IEEE Congress on Image and Signal Processing (CISP 2008), Sanya, China, pp. 792–796 (2008)
6. Wei, W., Liu, B.: Automatic road crack image preprocessing for detection and identification. In: Proceedings IEEE 2nd ICINIS, Tianjin, China, pp. 319–322 (2009)
7. Hutchinson, T.C., M.ASCE, Chen, Z.Q.: Improved image analysis for evaluating concrete damage. J. Comput. Civ. Eng. **20**(3), 210–216 (2006)
8. Zhao, H., Qin, G., Wang, X.: Improvement of canny algorithm based on pavement edge detection. In: Proceedings on 3rd International Congress on Image and Signal Processing, vol. 2, pp. 964–967. IEEE, Yantai (2010)
9. Shi, Y., Cui, L., Qi, Z.Q., Meng, F., Chen, Z.S.: Automatic road crack detection using random structured forests. IEEE Trans. Intell. Transp. Syst. **17**(12), 3434–3445 (2016)
10. Nguyen, H.N., Kam, T.Y., Cheng, P.Y.: Automatic crack detection from 2D images using a crack measure-based B-spline level set model. Multidimens. Syst. Signal Process. https://doi.org/10.1007/s11045-016-0461-9
11. Li, G., Zhao, X.X., Du, K., Ru, F., Zhang, Y.B.: Recognition and evaluation of bridge cracks with modified active contour model and greedy search-based support vector machine. Autom. Constr. **78**, 51–61 (2017)
12. Ayenu-Prah, A., Attoh-Okine, N.: Evaluating pavement cracks with bidimensional empirical mode decomposition. EURASIP J. Adv. Signal Process. **2008**(1), 861701 (2008)
13. Hu, Y., Zhao, C.X.: A local binary pattern based methods for pavement crack detection. J. Pattern Recognit. Res. **1**(20103), 140–147 (2010)
14. Nguyen, H.N., Kam, T.Y., Cheng, P.Y.: An automatic approach for accurate edge detection of concrete crack utilizing 2D geometric features of crack. J. Signal Process. Syst. **77**(3), 221–240 (2014)
15. Yusuke, F., Yoshihiko, H.: A robust automatic crack detection method from noisy concrete surfaces. Mach. Vis. Appl. **22**(2), 245–254 (2011)
16. Frangi, A.F., Niessen, W.J., Vincken, K.L., Viergever, M.A.: Multiscale vessel enhancement filtering. Med. Image Comput. Comput. Assist. Interv. **1496**, 130–137 (1998)
17. Tsai, Y.C., Kaul, V., Mersereau, R.M.: Critical assessment of pavement distress segmentation methods. J. Transp. Eng. **136**(1), 11–19 (2010)
18. Cheng, H.: Novel approach to pavement cracking detection based on neural network. Transp. Res. Rec. J. Transp. Res. Board **1764**, 119–127 (2001)
19. Tang, J., Gu, Y.: Automatic crack detection and segmentation using a hybrid algorithm for road distress analysis. In: Proceedings of the 2013 IEEE International Conference on Systems, Man, and Cybernetics, pp. 3026–3030. IEEE, Manchester (2013)

20. Chambon, S.: Detection of points of interest for geodesic contours: application on road images for crack detection. In: Proceedings on International Conference on Computer VISAPP, pp. 210–213. SciTePress (2011)
21. Li, C.M., Kao, C., Gore, J., Ding, Z.: Implicit active contours driven by local binary fitting energy. In: IEEE Conference on Computer Vision and Pattern Recognition (CVPR), pp. 1–7. IEEE Computer Society, Washington, DC (2007)
22. Liu, S.G., Peng, Y.L.: A local region-based Chan-Vese model for image segmentation. Pattern Recognit. **45**, 2769–2779 (2012)
23. Li, C.M., Kao, C., Gore, J., Ding, Z.: Minimization of region-scalable fitting energy for image segmentation. IEEE Trans. Image Process. **17**(10), 1940–1949 (2008)
24. Buades, A., Coll, B., Morel, J.M.: A review of image denoising algorithms, with a new one. Multiscale Model. Simul. **4**(2), 490–530 (2005)
25. Darbon, J., Cunha, A., Chan, T.F., Osher, S., Jensen, G.J.: Fast nonlocal filtering applied to electron cryomicroscopy. In: 5th IEEE International Symposium on Biomedical Imaging: From Nano to Macro, ISBI 2008, 14–17 May 2008, pp. 1331–1334. IEEE, Paris (2008)

Domain Attention Model for Domain Generalization in Object Detection

Weixiong He[1,2,3], Huicheng Zheng[1,2,3](✉), and Jianhuang Lai[1,2,3]

[1] School of Data and Computer Science, Sun Yat-sen University, Guangzhou, China
[2] Key Laboratory of Machine Intelligence and Advanced Computing,
Ministry of Education, Guangzhou, China
[3] Guangdong Key Laboratory of Information Security Technology,
Guangzhou, China
hewx5@mail2.sysu.edu.cn,{zhenghch,stsljh}@mail.sysu.edu.cn

Abstract. Domain generalization methods in object detection aim to learn a domain-invariant detector for different domains. However, it is difficult to obtain a domain-invariant detector when there is large discrepancy between different domains. Based on the idea of biasing the allocation of available processing resources towards the most informative components of an input, attention models have shown promising performance on different tasks. In this paper, we provide a framework for addressing the issue of visual domain generalization with domain attention. Specifically, we build a domain attention block utilizing the source domain discrepancy to learn different weights for different source domains on the input features, so that the input features similar to the source domains will be enhanced and the features different from all the source domains will be suppressed. Thus we can obtain a domain-general representation effective for localization and classification in the proposed model. In order to demonstrate the merits of the proposed approach, we put forward a HD-16 dataset for object detection in different scenes. Extensive experiments on HD-16 dataset verify the effectiveness of the proposed approach.

Keywords: Domain generalization · Object detection
Attention model

1 Introduction

Object detection, the task that locates specific objects in images, is a fundamental problem in computer vision. In recent years, driven by the development of deep convolutional neural networks (CNNs) [14], many CNN-based object detection approaches [15,17,23,25] have been proposed and the performance of object detection was improved drastically. However, detectors trained on benchmark datasets would not always obtain satisfactory detection results when being applied to a new scene in the wild, due to the domain shift between the training source domains and the unknown testing target domains. In order to overcome the impact of domain shift, domain adaption (DA) methods [3,18,27] and domain generalization (DG) methods [1,3,6,7,20–22] are proposed to improve the performance in target domains. DA methods require target data to train a new model when facing a new target scene, and thus their performances depend largely on the distributions of target domains. Moreover, DA methods are based on the assumption that the target samples can be commodiously obtained, which is impractical in some cases. On the other hand, DG methods learn domain-invariant models without target samples, and can be more conveniently implemented in practice. The basic idea of DG methods is to combine source data in a way to produce models invariant for the specific target data, so that the model has satisfactory performance on different target scenes. However, existing DG methods seem to become degraded when the discrepancy between source domains and target domains is large, since the models trained on the source domains may not represent samples from the target scene well.

Based on the idea of biasing the allocation of available processing resources of an input, attention model [11,12,19,29] can dynamically weight the information of a signal. Therefore attention model can increase the ability to represent samples and has shown promising performances on different tasks. Nonetheless, little development is obtained in using the existing attention methods for domain generalization, because the labeled target samples are unobtainable and no supervised information is provided for biasing the suitable allocation of target domains.

In this work, we introduce a domain generalization approach for objection detection. Different from the previous work that tried to learn a domain-invariant model, we propose to utilize the discrepancy between different source domains to build an attention model and let the model put attention on the features that are similar to the source domains.

Our motivation comes from the observation that though source domains have different forms of distribution (Fig. 1(a)–(c)) with target domain (Fig. 1(d)), in which some of them have high similarity with the distribution of target domain while the others do not. If we treat these source domains all in the same way, the final distribution (Fig. 1(e)) may have a large gap with the target representation. However, a satisfactory result (Fig. 1(f)) can be obtained by combining these domains with different weights. Equivalently, target domain can also be resolved into sources domains after applying different weights on its domain specific features, and the output will be represented by the model easier. In order to achieve this goal, we propose the domain attention block to extract the domain specific weights of input and then differently weight each channel of the input, finally output an adaptive representation which is generalized for the model trained on the source domains. A large-scale human detection dataset with more than 90k images in 16 scenes is proposed to demonstrate the merits of proposed approach. The main contributions of this paper can be summarized as follows:

1. To address the domain generalization problem in object detection, we propose a novel domain attention model by introducing the domain attention blocks

to the baseline one-step detection model, which differently weight channels of the input according to the domain specific weights.

2. Given the images without domain labels in practice, we further present our method using the effective clustering method to generate pseudo domain labels.

3. We extensively perform comparative evaluations to show the superiority of our approach on the proposed dataset.

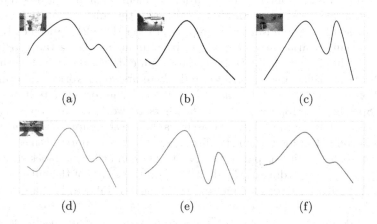

Fig. 1. Illustration of the distributions of different domains, (a)–(c) denotes the distributions of three source domains, (d) denotes the distribution of the target domain. The results of combining source representations in equal/unequal weights are shown in (e)/(f) respectively. Images in left corner of (a)–(d) come from different domains.

2 Related Work

2.1 Object Detection

Object detection has been a classical problem in computer vision, resulting in a plentitude of approaches. Classical work [4,5] usually formulated object detection as a sliding-window-based classification problem. Following the rise of deep convolutional neural networks (CNNs) [14] in computer vision, the performance of object detection was improved drastically. Among the large number of CNN-based approaches [8,15–17,23,24], two-step detectors [8,15,24] have received significant attention due to their performances. This line of work starts from R-CNN [8], which extracts region proposals from the image and classifies each region of interest (ROI) independently. Besides, one-step detectors [16,17,23] were proposed and popularly used in recent years due to their superiority in terms of speed. One-step detectors begin with YOLO [23], which treats object detection as a regression problem that jointly predicts the locations and confidence based on the output features from convolutional network backbone. Developed from YOLO, SSD [17] exploits features from multiple convolutional layers to achieve a multi-scale prediction for object localization and obtain a satisfactory detection performance. Thus, we use SSD as the baseline detection model, and further improve its generalization ability for object detection in new target domains.

2.2 Domain Generalization

In the previous works, domain generalization problem is mainly addressed in two ways. On the one hand, some methods aggregate the information from source domains to learn a domain-invariant representation [1,20,21]. Specifically, [21] learns a domain-invariant transformation by minimizing the distance between domains. [1] simply put all the training data from different domains together to learn a SVM classifier. On the other hand, there are some works exploiting all information from the source domains to train a classifier or regulate its weights [13,30]. Specifically, [13] weights the classifiers to work well on an unknown dataset, and [30] fuses the scores of classifiers for a test sample. However, those methods become degraded when the discrepancy between source scenes and the target scene is large. In this paper, we use the domain attention block to weight the input features according to the domain specific weights of the current input features. Actually, the proposed method is similar but inherently different from the first kind of methods. In our work, we try to resolve the target domain into source domains by applying different weights on domain specific features and finally output an adaptive representation which is generalized for the model trained on the source domains.

2.3 Attention Mechanism

Attention is a tool to bias the allocation of available processing resources towards the most informative components of an input signal [11,12,19,29]. In recent years, attention mechanisms have achieved great success in a range of tasks such as object localization, image classification and sequence-based models [2]. Specifically, [29] introduces a powerful trunk-and-mask attention mechanism using a hourglass model. [11] proposes SE block, which is a lightweight gating mechanism specialised to model channel-wise relationships in a computationally efficient manner and enhance the representational power of basic modules throughout the network. In this work, we propose domain attention block which is developed from SE block [11] to solve the domain generalization problem in object detection. However, the proposed domain attention block has a goal entirely different from SE block. While SE block try to model channel-wise relationships using the spatial information, domain attention block models the domain specific weights of the input features and differently weights the features using these weights. As a whole, the proposed domain attention block has better performance and adaptation in domain generalization problem.

3 Proposed Method

In this section, we firstly introduce the structure of domain attention block in Sect. 3.1. After that, a framework for the proposed domain attention model will be described in Sect. 3.2. We further propose a general method in Sect. 3.3 to deal with the situation that no domain label is available.

3.1 Domain Attention Block

Figure 2 shows the structure of the domain attention block, which consists of two branches, i.e., the domain specific branch and the domain aggregation branch. Taking as input the feature maps X, the domain specific branch can extract the domain specific scores of X, which are the confidence of X belonging to various source domains. Once the domain scores are obtained, domain aggregation branch will aggregate these scores to generate domain specific weights and finally output the weighted feature maps. In the following, we present more details about the domain attention block.

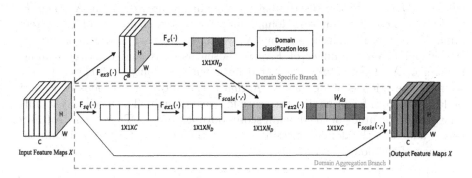

Fig. 2. Illustration of the structure of domain attention block.

Let $D = \{D_i\}_{i=1,2,...,N_D}$ denote the dataset consisting of N_D source domains, $i = 1, 2, ..., N_D$ is the domain labels of samples in D_i. Given the feature maps $X \in R^{H \times W \times C}$, we aim to learn a transformation $F(\cdot) : X \to \tilde{X}, \tilde{X} \in R^{H \times W \times C}$ which outputs the feature maps $\tilde{X}$ that are differently weighted for each channel according to the domain specific weights. We formulate $F(X)$ as

$$F(X) = F_{scale}(W_{ds}, X) \tag{1}$$

where W_{ds} represents the domain specific weights, and F_{scale} uses W_{ds} to differently weight each channel of X. Intuitively, a direct idea is using the domain scores as W_{ds} since we hope W_{ds} is specific for each domain. However, the number of domain scores is usually much less than the number of feature channels, thus it is unreliable to only take the domain scores as W_{ds} due to the imbalance between the scores and number of feature channels. What's more, the scores can not directly be used as the domain specific weights because of the different dimensionality. Therefore we design function F_w which takes both the domain scores and X into account to obtain reasonable weights. Specifically we formulate the composite function F_w as

$$F_w = F_{scale}(F_{sq} \circ F_{ex1}, F_s) \circ F_{ex2} \tag{2}$$

where $\circ$ denotes an operation that composites two functions and F_{sq} generates channel-wise statistics using global average pooling. After the channel-wise statistics are generated, F_{ex1} processes them using a 1×1 convolution with N_D output channels, then F_{scale} weights these channels by the domain scores which are provided by a composite function F_s. Finally, F_{ex2} transforms these weighted features using 1×1 convolution with the same channel number as X, and applies a softmax operation to obtain the domain specific weights of X. When it comes to the generation of domain scores, we firstly extract the discriminative domain features of X, and hope that the domain score is easily generated based on these discriminative features. Therefore, we define F_s as

$$F_s = F_{ex3} \circ F_c \tag{3}$$

where F_{ex3} extracts the discriminative domain features of input X, then F_c transforms these discriminative domain into scores for each domain of the current input X. Specifically, given the input X, we firstly use 1×1 convolution as F_{ex3}, the output channel number of F_{ex3} is chosen as $C/16$ and C is the channel number of X. Then a fully connected layer with N_D outputs followed by the softmax operation is chosen as F_c. Actually, the above descriptions of F_s just build a structure for providing the score for each domain. The feasibility mainly relies on the accuracy of the domain scores output from F_c. Therefore, a softmax loss is added as the domain classifier loss on the output of F_c to maintain the accuracy of the domain scores.

3.2 The Overall Framework

We apply the domain attention block on the one-step detection model, resulting in the proposed domain attention model. An one-step detection model generally consists of two parts, the backbone convolution network and the unified classification/localization component. As shown in Fig. 3, we apply the domain attention block to the last several convolution layers in the backbone. There are two main reasons why we apply the attention block in such format. Firstly, discrepancy between different domains is more capturable in the high-level semantic information from top convolution layers [28]. Secondly, though difference between domains is existed, they still share some common information which are reflected in bottom layers [18]. As for the number of layers for applying domain attention block, we regard it as a hyper-parameter in the proposed method.

3.3 General Situation Without Domain Labels

We discuss our method above based on the assumption that the total dataset D consists of a certain number of source datasets, and there is a priori domain

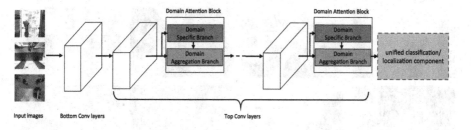

Fig. 3. Illustration of domain attention model.

label for each image, which means we know corresponding source dataset for each image coming from D. Actually, this assumption is not always satisfied because it is time consuming to identify the relationships between each image and its corresponding source dataset. In the general condition, the number of source datasets and the relationships between the images and the source datasets are unknown.

In this situation, D is represented as $\{D_i\}_{i=1,2,...,N}$ where $N \geq 1$ and N is unknown. We adjust the proposed method by a simple preprocessing for the total dataset D. Specifically, we firstly assume the certain number n of source datasets, then we use unsupervised clustering methods to generate the source dataset and label each image with a pseudo domain label. After the preprocessing above, the dataset D will conform to the assumption of Sect. 3.1, and the following process is the same as Sect. 3.1. The experimental results prove that this preprocessing is effective when there is not much difference between the assumption n and the ground truth N.

4   Experiments

In this section, we evaluate the proposed domain attention model for domain generalization in object detection. We construct a human detection dataset with images from 16 scenes (HD-16) for evaluation. Extensive experiments are conducted in order to demonstrate the merits of the proposed method.

4.1   HD-16 Dataset

HD-16 is a large human detection dataset which has $93,371$ images in total captured by the top-view cameras in 16 different scenes. The number of images of each scene various from $1,362$ to $17,510$. Each image in the dataset is in the top-view and at the scale of 320×240 in pixel. HD-16 is challenging due to the large discrepancy in uncontrolled illumination and background between the images from different scenes. Figure 4 shows some examples of HD-16.

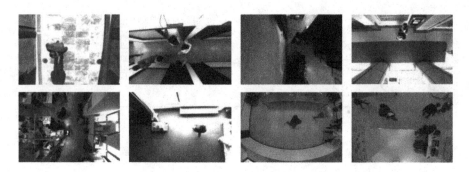

Fig. 4. Example images from different scenes in HD-16.

4.2 Experiment Setting

Baseline Detector. In experiment, we choose the SSD [17] as the baseline detector due to its outstanding performance in multi-scale object detection. In order to demonstrate the generalization of the proposed method, we respectively choose VGG-16 network [26] and MobileNet [10] as the backbone of SSD, and then apply the domain attention model on them for comparison.

Training Strategy. In the training process, we adopt the same data augmentation methods in SSD [17]. Moreover, we set the initial learning rate to 5×10^{-3} and the max-iteration of the training process is $300,000$.

Dataset Partition and Evaluation Protocol. Following the ordinary experimental protocol [18,28] for domain generalization datasets, we partition the HD-16 based on scenes. Specially, we randomly choose 12 scenes for training and the other 4 scenes for testing, resulting in a training set consisting of $65,534$ images and a testing set with $27,837$ images. For simplicity, we simply denote these 4 testing scenes as $T1 - T4$ and the combined testing set as C. Following the general criteria, we adopt mean average precision (mAP) with IoU of 0.5 for evaluation on HD-16.

4.3 Experiments on VGG-16 Based SSD

We firstly compare the proposed methods with SSD [17] based on VGG-16 network [26]. Because the image in the dataset is 320×240 in pixel and a person covers limited pixels in the image, we remove the conv7-9 layers as these layers have bigger receptive field than the actual area of a person. Then, we apply domain attention blocks after fc7, conv6_1, and conv6_2 in VGG-16. Since the proposed method develops from SENet [11], for fair comparison we further experiment on SSD with backbone of SENet (VGG-16 based), the results are shown in Table 1. It is evident from Table 1 that our method outperforms both competitors, for example, surpassing all compared methods by 3.7%(62.2%-56.0%),

Table 1. mAP(%) on VGG-16 based SSD.

	$T1$	$T2$	$T3$	$T4$	C
SSD [17]	56.0	57.0	71.5	72.8	56.4
SSD-SENet [11]	58.5	56.4	73.2	73.2	56.9
Ours	**62.2**	**59.3**	**75.9**	**74.7**	**59.8**

2.3%(59.3%-57.0%), 2.7%(75.9%-73.2%), 1.5%(74.7%-73.2%) and 2.9%(59.8%-56.9%) on $T1, T2, T3, T4$, and C, respectively. This indicates the advantages of the proposed method in handling domain generalization. The performance superiority is mainly because the proposed method effectively weights the input features and outputs adaptive representations which are generalized for the model trained on the source domains.

4.4 Experiments on MobileNet Based SSD

We evaluate the benefits of the proposed methods when integrate with other CNN architectures in addition to VGG-16. Specially, we select MobileNet architecture [10] for particularly testing the potentials in mobile vision application. For the same reason stated in Sect. 4.3, we remove conv14-17 and apply domain attention blocks after conv12 and conv13 in MobileNet. Table 2 shows the generic capability of the proposed method in weighting the input features and outputting adaptive representations for domain generalization when combined with a smaller MobileNet CNN architecture.

Table 2. mAP(%) on MobileNet based SSD.

	$T1$	$T2$	$T3$	$T4$	C
SSD [17]	55.1	53.3	65.7	72.0	55.9
SSD-SENet [11]	52.2	58.8	**67.2**	71.0	56.3
Ours	**56.2**	**59.6**	66.6	**72.3**	**58.9**

4.5 Experiments on General Situation Without Domain Labels

We further evaluate the proposed method in general situation without domain labels, which was discussed in Sect. 3.3. VGG-16 based SSD [17] is used for the baseline. Moreover, the result of the proposed method with ground-truth domain labels is used for comparison. For the training images without domain labels, we firstly choose n as the domain number. Specially, we choose the k-means algorithm [9] as the unlabeled cluster method by setting the hyper-parameter $k = n$. As for the representation of each image used in k-means algorithm, we simply resize each image to 40×30 and flatten to a feature vector. For simplicity, we use gt to denote the ground-truth domain number. We adjust n from 8 to 16,

Fig. 5(a) shows the clustering results and Fig. 5(b) shows the results on $T2$. We can infer from Fig. 5(a) that when $n < gt$, several domains tend to be merged into a cluster, and a domain is splited into several clusters when we set $n > gt$. It's the same as we expected that the proposed method has the best result when $n = gt = 12$, and the mAP is 0.6% lower (58.7% vs 59.3%) than the situation without domain labels. Moreover, the proposed method still outperforms the baseline (57.0%) in most situations, even when we set $n = 16$ that produces great deviation between the pre-set domain number and gt. In the situation that $n = 8$, the experiment result of the proposed method is worse than the baseline, we hold the opinion that when n is far less than gt, the model tends to treat all the samples in the same way and domain specific features are insufficient. Therefore, the domain attention block will degrade the performance to a small degree as the domain attention block may provide inaccurate weights.

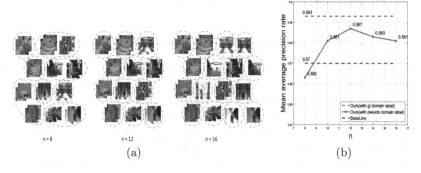

(a)   (b)

Fig. 5. (a) Clustering results when $n = 8, 12, 16$. (b) Evaluation of $T2$ on the general situation.

4.6   Model Complexity

Evaluation is also carried out on the proposed model from the aspect of model complexity. The model complexity of SSD based on VGG-16 and MobileNet will be used as the baseline for comparison. To further demonstrate the superiority of the proposed method in terms of model complexity, we also compare with the SENet-based SSD model, which has an attractive advantage in model complexity. We select the combined testing set C for evaluation. Table 3 shows the experiment result, the number in bracket denotes the percent of added capacity compared to the baseline. We can infer from Table 3 that SENet costs larger model capacity and obtains lower improvement (0.4%–0.5%) compared to the proposed method. Furthermore, the proposed method greatly improves the mAP (3%–3.4%) with less than 10% (1.9% in VGG-16) additional model capacity.

Table 3. Comprehensive evaluation on model complexity and detection performance

	Model capacity (MB)	mAP (%)
SSD-VGG16	88.0	56.4
SSD-VGG16 + SENet	90.0 (2.3%)	56.9
Ours-VGG16	89.7 (1.9%)	59.8
SSD-MobileNet	12.8	55.9
SSD-MobileNet + SENet	14.6 (12.8%)	56.3
Ours-MobileNet	14.0 (8.5%)	58.9

5 Conclusion

In this paper, we propose a domain attention model to solve the domain generalization problem for object detection in novel target domains. Based on the idea that target domain can be resolved into the sources domains, we propose to build a domain attention block by utilizing the discrepancy between different source domains, to weight the input data which contains domain specific features. The proposed approach is built on the state-of-the-art one-step object detector SSD and can be trained end-to-end using the standard SGD optimization. Moreover, we construct a HD-16 dataset for object detection in different scenes to demonstrate the merits of the proposed approach. Extensive experiments on HD-16 dataset have demonstrated the merits of the proposed approach.

Acknowledgement. This work was supported by National Natural Science Foundation of China (U1611461), Special Program for Applied Research on Super Computation of the NSFC-Guangdong Joint Fund (the second phase, No. U1501501), and Science and Technology Program of Guangzhou (No. 201803030029).

References

1. Blanchard, G., Lee, G., Scott, C.: Generalizing from several related classification tasks to a new unlabeled sample. In: NIPS, pp. 2178–2186 (2011)
2. Bluche, T.: Joint line segmentation and transcription for end-to-end handwritten paragraph recognition. In: NIPS, pp. 838–846 (2016)
3. Chen, Y., Li, W., Sakaridis, C., Dai, D., Van Gool, L.: Domain adaptive faster R-CNN for object detection in the wild. arXiv preprint arXiv:1803.03243 (2018)
4. Dalal, N., Triggs, B.: Histograms of oriented gradients for human detection. In: CVPR, vol. 1, pp. 886–893. IEEE (2005)
5. Everingham, M., Van Gool, L., Williams, C.K., Winn, J., Zisserman, A.: The PASCAL Visual Object Classes (VOC) challenge. Int. J. Comput. Vis. **88**(2), 303–338 (2010)
6. Ghifary, M., Balduzzi, D., Kleijn, W.B., Zhang, M.: Scatter component analysis: a unified framework for domain adaptation and domain generalization. T-PAMI **39**(7), 1414–1430 (2017)

7. Ghifary, M., Bastiaan Kleijn, W., Zhang, M., Balduzzi, D.: Domain generalization for object recognition with multi-task autoencoders. In: ICCV, pp. 2551–2559 (2015)
8. Girshick, R., Donahue, J., Darrell, T., Malik, J.: Rich feature hierarchies for accurate object detection and semantic segmentation. In: CVPR, pp. 580–587 (2014)
9. Hartigan, J.A., Wong, M.A.: Algorithm as 136: a K-means clustering algorithm. J. Royal Stat. Soc. **28**(1), 100–108 (1979)
10. Howard, A.G., et al.: Mobilenets: efficient convolutional neural networks for mobile vision applications. arXiv preprint arXiv:1704.04861 (2017)
11. Hu, J., Shen, L., Sun, G.: Squeeze-and-excitation networks. arXiv preprint arXiv:1709.01507 (2017)
12. Itti, L., Koch, C., Niebur, E.: A model of saliency-based visual attention for rapid scene analysis. T-PAMI **20**(11), 1254–1259 (1998)
13. Khosla, A., Zhou, T., Malisiewicz, T., Efros, A.A., Torralba, A.: Undoing the damage of dataset bias. In: Fitzgibbon, A., Lazebnik, S., Perona, P., Sato, Y., Schmid, C. (eds.) ECCV 2012. LNCS, vol. 7572, pp. 158–171. Springer, Heidelberg (2012). https://doi.org/10.1007/978-3-642-33718-5_12
14. Krizhevsky, A., Sutskever, I., Hinton, G.E.: ImageNet classification with deep convolutional neural networks. In: NIPS, pp. 1097–1105 (2012)
15. Lin, T.Y., Dollar, P., Girshick, R., He, K., Hariharan, B., Belongie, S.: Feature pyramid networks for object detection. In: CVPR, pp. 2117–2125. IEEE (2017)
16. Lin, T.Y., Goyal, P., Girshick, R., He, K., Dollar, P.: Focal loss for dense object detection. In: CVPR, pp. 2980–2988. IEEE (2017)
17. Liu, W., et al.: SSD: single shot multibox detector. In: Leibe, B., Matas, J., Sebe, N., Welling, M. (eds.) ECCV 2016. LNCS, vol. 9905, pp. 21–37. Springer, Cham (2016). https://doi.org/10.1007/978-3-319-46448-0_2
18. Long, M., Cao, Y., Wang, J., Jordan, M.I.: Learning transferable features with deep adaptation networks. arXiv preprint arXiv:1502.02791 (2015)
19. Mnih, V., Heess, N., Graves, A., et al.: Recurrent models of visual attention. In: NIPS, pp. 2204–2212 (2014)
20. Motiian, S., Piccirilli, M., Adjeroh, D.A., Doretto, G.: Unified deep supervised domain adaptation and generalization. In: ICCV, pp. 5716–5726 (2017)
21. Muandet, K., Balduzzi, D., Schölkopf, B.: Domain generalization via invariant feature representation. In: ICML, pp. 10–18 (2013)
22. Niu, L., Li, W., Xu, D., Cai, J.: An exemplar-based multi-view domain generalization framework for visual recognition. T-PAMI **29**(2), 259–272 (2016)
23. Redmon, J., Divvala, S., Girshick, R., Farhadi, A.: You only look once: unified, real-time object detection. In: CVPR, pp. 779–788. IEEE (2016)
24. Ren, S., He, K., Girshick, R., Sun, J.: Faster R-CNN: towards real-time object detection with region proposal networks. T-PAMI **39**(6), 1137–1149 (2017)
25. Shen, Z., Liu, Z., Li, J., Jiang, Y.G., Chen, Y., Xue, X.: DSOD: learning deeply supervised object detectors from scratch. In: CVPR, pp. 1919–1927. IEEE (2017)
26. Simonyan, K., Zisserman, A.: Very deep convolutional networks for large-scale image recognition. arXiv preprint arXiv:1409.1556 (2014)
27. Tzeng, E., Hoffman, J., Darrell, T., Saenko, K.: Simultaneous deep transfer across domains and tasks. In: ICCV, pp. 4068–4076. IEEE (2015)

28. Tzeng, E., Hoffman, J., Zhang, N., Saenko, K., Darrell, T.: Deep domain confusion: Maximizing for domain invariance. arXiv preprint arXiv:1412.3474 (2014)
29. Wang, F., et al.: Residual attention network for image classification. arXiv:1704.06904 (2017)
30. Xu, Z., Li, W., Niu, L., Xu, D.: Exploiting low-rank structure from latent domains for domain generalization. In: Fleet, D., Pajdla, T., Schiele, B., Tuytelaars, T. (eds.) ECCV 2014. LNCS, vol. 8691, pp. 628–643. Springer, Cham (2014). https://doi.org/10.1007/978-3-319-10578-9_41

Exploring Multi-scale Deep Feature Fusion for Object Detection

Quan Zhang[1], Jianhuang Lai[1,2,3(✉)], Xiaohua Xie[1,2,3], and Junyong Zhu[1,2,3]

[1] School of Data and Computer Science, Sun Yat-sen University, Guangzhou, China
zhangq48@mail2.sysu.edu.cn, {stsljh,xiexiaoh6,zhujuny5}@mail.sysu.edu.cn
[2] Guangdong Key Laboratory of Information Security Technology,
Guangzhou, China
[3] Key Laboratory of Machine Intelligence and Advanced Computing,
Ministry of Education, Beijing, China

Abstract. The ability to extract the discriminative features remains a fundamental task of object detection, especially for small objects. Many mainstream object detection models, use the feature pyramids structure, a kind of fusion approaches, to predict objects of different scales. This traditional fusion strategy aims to merge different feature maps by linear operation, which does not allow the model to learn the complementary relationship between spatial information and semantic information. To address this problem, we develop a non-linear embedded network (NlENet) to achieve multi-scale fusion, which can learn the potential complementary relationship through end-to-end autonomous learning and get a more accurate performance. There are three main blocks in this proposed network, residual convolution unit (RCU), multi-resolution fusion and chained residual pooling. Due to the flexibility of the NlENet, we can embed it into many mainstream detection frameworks with few modification. We confirm that our fusion network can extract richer and more accurate features and achieve a better object detection performance on the COCO2017 dataset.

Keywords: Object detection · Non-linear fusion
Multi-resolution strategy

1 Introduction

Object detection is a fundamental task of computer vision. Object detection is defined as locating and classifying all objects in an input image. One of the most effective ways to improve results is learning robust and comprehensive feature representation. So some early works, such as Fast R-CNN [2], try to compute a single feature map through a CNN and use it to complete detection. However, as the network gets deeper, the feature map we computed will lose a lot of spatial detail information, which is disadvantageous for detection because the detection requires precise spatial position. So many current works focus on how to get more

© Springer Nature Switzerland AG 2018
J.-H. Lai et al. (Eds.): PRCV 2018, LNCS 11259, pp. 40–52, 2018.
https://doi.org/10.1007/978-3-030-03341-5_4

accurate spatial information and more discriminative semantic information. In many current mainstream methods, such as RetinaNet [14], Mask-RCNN [5], feature fusion is an essential tool to improve the accuracy of object detection, especially for small objects. As shown in Fig. 1, The core fusion idea of these work is the feature pyramid network(FPN) [13], which fuses feature maps at different sacles which are extracted from the original image in the backbone network instead of using single feature map. It is known that the high-level feature maps in the network are rich in semantic information but lacking spatial information, while the low-level feature maps, in contrast, contain rich spatial information but lack semantic information. FPN makes use of both high level feature maps and low level feature maps via adding a upside down path to transfer the semantic information to the lower part of the network, leading to a feature representation containing both rich semantic information and rich spatial information, which can probably improve the detection result. Howerver, there is no nonlinear structure in FPN, and the complementary relationship between spatial information and semantic information can not be captured, which limits the performance of the model. Therefore, the core contribution of this paper is to propose a new fusion rule based on network learning, which can obtain the potential complementary relationship between spatial information and semantic information through end-to-end autonomous learning.

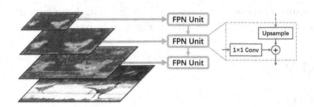

Fig. 1. FPN framework. These feature maps are extracted from different locations in the backbone network. The yellow boxes represent the fusion operator of FPN. For each input feature map, FPN will give a corresponding fused feature map. The specific fusion strategy is shown in the yellow dotted box. It consists of an upsampled layer, a convolutional layer and a linear summation. In particular, the upsampled layer is not necessary if there is only one input. (Color figure online)

In this paper, we adopt a elaborated feature fusion strategy for object detection. The main idea is to develop a non-linear embedded network to achieve multi-scale fusion. Non-linear operators have advantages over linear operators about extracting features. The idea of non-linearity is widely used in machine learning, manifold learning and neural networks, which is shown good performance. The embedded network structure makes our method more flexible and can be integrated into multiple network structures. Specifically, we design a refined network to capture both semantic and spatial information at the same time, allowing it automatically extract discriminant information from different layers and learn the optimal combination. There are three main blocks in our fusion network, residual convolution unit (RCU), multi-resolution fusion and chained residual pooling. Compared to the FPN, the non-linear fusion will exploit more semantic information and spatial information, leading a more accurate object detector. We propose a convolutional network named NlENet, that is, non-linear embedded network, by incorporating this new feature fusion strategy. Experimental evaluation was conducted on the COCO dataset [7] and the results validated that our fusion framework do have better performance.

In our paper, the contributions can be summarized as the followings.

1. We introduce a non-linear embedded network (NlENet) which can obtain the potential complementary relationship between spatial information and semantic information through end-to-end autonomous learning and combine them to get a more accurate performance.
2. We give a concise and persuasive theoretical analysis to prove that our method is theoretically valid.
3. According to experimental results, our method can improve the performance of object detection tasks, and due to the flexibility of the NlENet, we can embed it into the backbone network of many mainstream detection tasks with minor modifications.

The rest of this paper is organized as follows. Section 2 briefly reviews the related works on object detection and fusion strategy. Details of the proposed method and some analysis are presented in Sect. 3. Experimental results are reported in Sect. 4, and Sect. 5 concludes the whole paper.

2 Related Work

2.1 Object Detectors

The sliding-window method, in which a classifier is applied on a dense image grid, has a long history [14]. For example, Viola *et al.* [16] used boosted object detectors for face detection. At this stage, many feature extraction methods are based on hand-engineered features due to computational constraints. The HOG and SIFT feature [18] have been widely used at this stage. The DPMs [17] extends the original dense approach to make the entire framework more flexible, and this approach ranks top-one result for many years on the PASCAL dataset [19]. Although the sliding-window method has been very successful in the traditional computer vision, with the arrival of deep learning [6], more frameworks based on convolutional neural networks [14] appear and become the mainstream method of object detection rapidly.

2.2 Two-Stage Detectors

In the modern object detection, the most famous method is based on a two-stage approch [14]. This kind of method divides object detection into two steps. The first step is to generate a series of candidate proposals that contain all the objects in the image and remove a large number of backgrounds. The second step is to classify these proposals into foreground classes or background. R-CNN [3] is a classical two-stage framework based on deep learning, which upgraded the second-stage classifier to a convolutional network and improved a lot in accuracy. There are many works to extend R-CNN. For example, Fast R-CNN [2] speeded up by employing an end-to-end training procedure. Faster R-CNN [20] introduces a new module, namely Region Proposal Networks(RPN), which integrated proposal generation with the second-stage classifier into a single convolution network. Until now, the Faster R-CNN method was still the classic way of two-step detection, and a lot of work was done in order to improve its performance [4].

2.3   One-Stage Detectors

Although the two-step approach has been very successful, there are still some limitations. The main disadvantage is that it takes too much time to generate the candidate proposals in the first step. The one-step approaches are to improve speed, but their accuracy trails that of two-stage methods. It is a trade-off problem. OverFeat [11] was one of the first modern one-stage object detectors based on deep network. The SSD [8] and YOLO [10] are recent models in one-stage methods. The core idea is to divide the original image into several grids, and to execute classification and regression on each grid. SSD has a nearly 10% higher AP than YOLO while the speed of YOLO is almost three times faster than that of SSD [14].

Based on the strengths and weaknesses of one-step and two-step approaches, there are also some works [14] to design a good and fast framework. There are two common ways to consider this problem, which are making two-step models faster or make one-step models more accurate. RetinaNet [14] is a simple one-step network designed to achieve the accuracy of two-step models and the speed of one-step models. This model uses a new loss function that adjusts the weight of the positive and negative samples in the one-step method to improve the accuracy of the model.

2.4   Multi-scale Fusion

When an input image is forwardly calculated in the network, the feature maps will contain less spatial information, and the semantic information will gradually increase. This phenomenon will result in inaccurate location about object detection, especially for some small objects. Feature fusion is an effective way to improve the ability of feature representation. A number of recent methods [24] improve detection and segmentation by using different layers in a convolution network, beacuse the low-level feature contains more spatial information and the high-level feature contains more semantic information. For example, SSD [8] and MS-CNN [1] predict objects at multiple layers but do not fuse the hierarchical features. U-Net [21] and Stacked Hourglass networks [22] exploits sample fusion, lateral or skip connections, that associate low-level feature maps through spatial and semantic levels. FPN and RetinaNet combine traditional feature pyramid methods with neural networks to produce more discriminative features by using multi-scale methods while guaranteeing detection speed. However, this linear fusion operator does not make full use of these two kind information, which is just a linear combination.

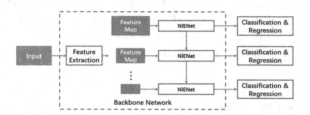

Fig. 2. Our framework. Our framework mainly consists of three processes. The first one is feature extraction, which uses the forward calculation of the network to extract feature maps with different sizes. The second one is the NlENet, which use the non-linear operator and embedded way to fuse the feature maps and enhance the information in each feature map. The last one is detection, sending each feature map to the corresponding detection sub-network to perform the corresponding task.

3   Proposed Method

3.1   Framework

Our model consists of a backbone network and a series of sub-networks, and each of sub-networks contains two tasks, classification and regression. The number of sub-networks depends on the number of NlENet. For the input image, the backbone network is used to extract the feature maps of different network layers and create new corresponding fused feature maps by our fusion strategy, which is similar to FPN but the core idea is completely different. The classification network and the regression network accept the output of the backbone network, and the final result is calculated through a corresponding network structure. In order to ensure the speed of the one-step method, both sub-networks only contain few regular units, which is shown in Fig. 2. Following the work [13], we design a pyramid based on the ResNet architecture [23]. We extract feature maps in the backbone network from the bottom to up, where the feature map scale changes, and donate as { C_3, C_4, C_5, C_6, C_7 } where the subscript means pyramid level. From C_3 to C_7, the scale of feature maps in the pyramid is reduced by 2 times. All of these feature maps have 256 channels.

In order to handle the unbalanced samples problem, we use focal loss [14] as our optimization goal, which is defined as Eq. 1. The variable p_t is a simple variant of the binary classification probability that can be derived from the model. Focal loss is essentially an extension of the cross-entropy loss. The parameters

α_t and γ are control factors based on experience. In practice, we usually set $\alpha_t = 0.25$ and $\gamma = 2$.

$$F(p_t) = -\alpha_t(1 - p_t)^\gamma log(p_t) \tag{1}$$

3.2 Fusion Strategy

The structure of the NlENet is shown in Fig. 3. The whole process of fusion can be divided into three main steps, residual convolution unit, multi-resolution fusion and chained residual pooling, which is inspired by the general structure of RefineNet [15] used in semantic segmentation.

The residual convolution unit (RCU), is a simplified version of the convolutional block in the ResNet, and the original batch-normalization layer is removed. The number of filters is equal to that of the feature map channels in backbone network. This is a transitional module, which finetunes the weights of original backbone network layer to adapt our object detection task. Considering the time consume and numbers of parameters, we usually use two RCUs in one blocks for tuning in our network.

The multi-resolution fusion block aims to integrate all inputs into a fused high-resolution feature map. This block first apply convolutions for multi-inputs in odrer to adaption. This convolution does not change the shape of each feature map. After that, we upsample all the small feature maps to the largest scale and add up all of them to get the fused feature maps. If there is only one input, the addition is not needed, but the rest operations of the block can not be ignored.

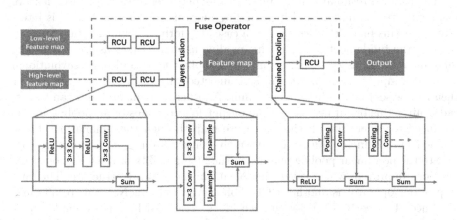

Fig. 3. Fusion network. There are three main blocks in NlENet, including residual convolution unit (RCU), multi-resolution fusion and chained residual pooling. The dashed line of the input feature maps indicates that the module can accept up to two inputs, and if there is only one input, the middle layer's operation, multi-resolution fusion is not needed. Due to multi-layer pooling, this structure as a whole is a non-linear operator.

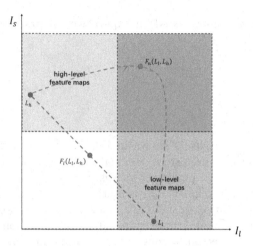

Fig. 4. The distribution of the information amount. The x-axis represents the amount of spatial information and the y-axis represents the amount of semantic information. The yellow area is mainly the range of high-level feature maps, and the blue area represents the range of low-level feature maps. The red dotted line is the output of $F_l(L_l, L_h)$ which represents the location of the output after the linear fusion, and the green dotted line, the output of $F_n(L_l, L_h)$, represents the distribution of the output after executing the non-linear fusion. Solid dots of different colors represent an instance of different distributions. It can be very intuitive to find that non-linear strategy is able to capture more information. (Color figure online)

The chained residual pooling block is a higher-level process for fused feature maps and we can understand it as finding more useful information. It is interested that this module is designed as a cascaded form. This means that you can connect the fundamental unit in this module as many times as you want. The fundamental unit is consisted of only one pooling layer and one convolutional layer. The inputs of this block will be connected with an ReLU activation layer then will be sent to this fundamental unit. Another fundamental unit can be cascaded after this one if necessary. The output feature maps of all pooling blocks are fused together with the input feature map through the summation. These chained units aim to capture more widely context from a large image region. Due to the non-linear pooling operation, the fitting ability of the whole operator has been improved, which is very important in the network structure. The final step of our operator is another RCU. Following the RefineNet, this results in a sequence of three RCUs between each block. The goal here is to employ non-linearity operations for further processing or for final prediction [15]. In addition, this layer does not change the feature shape.

3.3   Analysis

In this part we will give a simple and intuitive proof to explain why our non-linear operator works, compared with other fusion strategies. We define I as the information contained in the feature maps. Next, we define I_s as semantic information and I_l as spatial information in the feature map. We can naturally get the equation $I = I_s \oplus I_l$ when ignoring the noise and other random factors.

Table 1. Bounding box proposal results(%) using RetinaNet and our fusion operator.

Method	AP	AP_s	AP_m	AP_l	AR
YOLOv2	**21.6**	**5.0**	**22.4**	**35.5**	–
SSD513	**29.6**	**9.8**	**31.2**	**47.7**	**36.8**
ION [25]	**30.7**	**11.8**	**32.8**	**44.8**	**27.7**
RetinaNet-FPN	**30.7**	**12.9**	**32.2**	**46.9**	**37.9**
RetinaNet-NlENet (Ours)	**34.3**	**17.2**	**34.0**	**51.8**	**39.6**

We define a parameter space D consisting of I_s and I_l. As mentioned, the high-level feature map contains rich semantic information and little spatial information, but the low-level feature map is on the opposite. We divide the parameter space into four regions to roughly describe the distribution of the information amount for the different feature maps. As shown in Fig. 4, high-level feature maps will be concentrated in the yellow block, the low-level features will gather in the blue block. The green dot represents an instance of a specific feature map in our network.

Let's consider the fusion operation. We define a binary operator $F(\cdot, \cdot)$ accepting that two different layers of feature maps as input. We use L_l and L_h to represent the features from the lower level and the features from the upper level respectively. If we use a linear version of the F, noted as F_l, the output is only a weighted summation of the original input information. This strategy indeed gather the two information together, but at the same time, there is a loss of both kinds of information, which is more like the "average" of the two kinds of information. In the parameter space D, the output is only distributed on the red dotted line between the two green dots because the output is only linear weighted sum of the input. If we use the our fusion operator in this paper, noted as F_n, the operator's non-linear fusion ability is increased, which allows the operator to capture more information and make the fused feature map more discriminative.

In short, because of the introduction of nonlinear operations in NLEnet, such as chained residual pooling, the two kinds of information are more complementary in the fusion process, rather than a simple linear combination, which embodies the advantages of each feature. There is a significant improvement in the detection results.

4 Experiments

4.1 Dataset

We conducted our experiment on the COCO dataset [7] with 80 categories. For training, we use the COCO trainval35k split. We report our result by evaluating on the minival split [14]. We evaluate the COCO-style Average Recall(AR) and Average Precision(AP) on small, medium and large objects, whose definition is in the work [7]. In order to obtain a good model, the backbone network is pre-trained on the ImageNet classification set [23] and then fintuned on our COCO detection dataset. We use the pre-trained ResNet-50 models that are publicly available. Our code is implemented using Keras.

4.2 Implementation Detail

Our structure is trained end-to-end. We adopt Adam training on 4 GPUs. The size of the image entered on the network is fixed to 224×224. A mini-batch contains 4 images and 256 anchors per images. During training, network converges after 1500 epochs. The learning rate is first set to 10^{-4}, which is then divided by 10 at 600 iterations. Training the whole framework on 4 GPUs takes about 2 days on COCO. We use a random horizontal flip and vertical flip, the probability is 0.5. In addition, we also introduce a random translation (up to one-tenth of its side length) and scaling (between 1 and 1.2 times), which make our model more robust. During testing, execution time on NVIDIA GeForce 1080Ti is roughly 84msec for an image of shape $1000 \times 800 \times 3$.

At the same time, we have designed a contrast network, RetinaNet-FPN, to prove the validity of our framework. The structure of this network is basically the same as that of Fig. 2. The only difference is that we have replaced the NLE unit with the FPN element as shown in Fig. 1. In the process of experiment, the same experimental parameters and training process are adopted.

4.3 Parameter Analysis

Due to the flexibility of NlENet, we can insert it into the backbone network through a variety of ways. In this section, we will analyze the relationship between the number of NLENet and the detection results and the whole network performance. We denote K as the number of NlENet, and different K correspond to different pyramid structures. For example, when $K = 2$, that means that we want to fuse C_3 and C_4, these two feature maps. The first NlENet receives C_3 and outputs N_3, and the second NlENet receives N_3 and C_4 and outputs N_4. Specifically, when K equals 0, there is no feature fusion in the network at this time, and this will be used as the baseline in our experiment.

We use two evaluation methods to evaluate the network performance, that is, AP curve and performance curve. AP has already been introduced in the Sect. 4.1. The performance curve describes the average contribution of each embedded network to the whole network performance improvement, which can be described by the formula as:

$$\eta(K) = \frac{AP(K) - AP(K = 0)}{K}. \tag{2}$$

As shown in Fig. 5, with the increase of K, the accuracy of network is also improved. This phenomenon confirms that our NlENet in this paper can learn the potential complementary relationship between spatial information and semantic information. However, the performance curve tells us that NlENet can not be stacked indefinitely. With the increase of K, the performance of each embedded network first rises and then gradually decreasing when reaching the maximum. When $K = 4$, each NlENet can reach the best performance. If we continue to fuse more features, the network will pay too much attention to detail information, such as background noise, which is detrimental to performance.

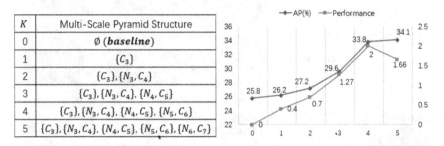

K	Multi-Scale Pyramid Structure
0	Ø (*baseline*)
1	$\{C_3\}$
2	$\{C_3\}, \{N_3, C_4\}$
3	$\{C_3\}, \{N_3, C_4\}, \{N_4, C_5\}$
4	$\{C_3\}, \{N_3, C_4\}, \{N_4, C_5\}, \{N_5, C_6\}$
5	$\{C_3\}, \{N_3, C_4\}, \{N_4, C_5\}, \{N_5, C_6\}, \{N_6, C_7\}$

Fig. 5. Parameter Analysis. The left diagram shows the different stacking structures of NlENet under different K value. K represents the number of NlENet, and N_i represents the output of the network when N_{i-1} and C_i are input. Specifically, N_3 has only one input C_3. The right picture shows the accuracy of detection (blue curve) and the average performance (yellow curve) of each NlENet under different K value. The horizontal axis represents the value of K. (Color figure online)

4.4 Result

Our experiment is designed to prove the effectiveness of our fusion operator. In this experiment, we compare our method with another widely used fusion structure, FPN. The experimental results are shown in Table 1. The experimental results show that our embeded network improves the result of object detection, which has a 4% performance improvement over the RetinaNet. Specifically, the detection of small objects is the largest increase on AP evaluation, which shows that our method can indeed capture more spatial information in the feature map, and also have a good performance for small objects.

We also made a visualization to clearly show the improvement of NlENet in Fig. 6. This visualization result shows the different fusion of the feature maps extracted from the backbone network. We can also treat each line in this diagram as a process of information integration during the network forward computation. It can be clearly seen that (a) NlENet alleviates the dissipation of spatial information, which promotes high-level feature maps can also capture spatial information transmitted from lower layers, especially for small objects; (b) high-level semantics gradually penetrate into lower layers, which leads to higher response values of semantic-related content in low-level feature maps; (c) NlENet guides the overall detection framework to focus on areas closely related to high-level semantics, greatly suppressing background and noise, especially for edge noise. Compared with the fusion strategy in the RetinaNet, our method is more powerful and accurate.

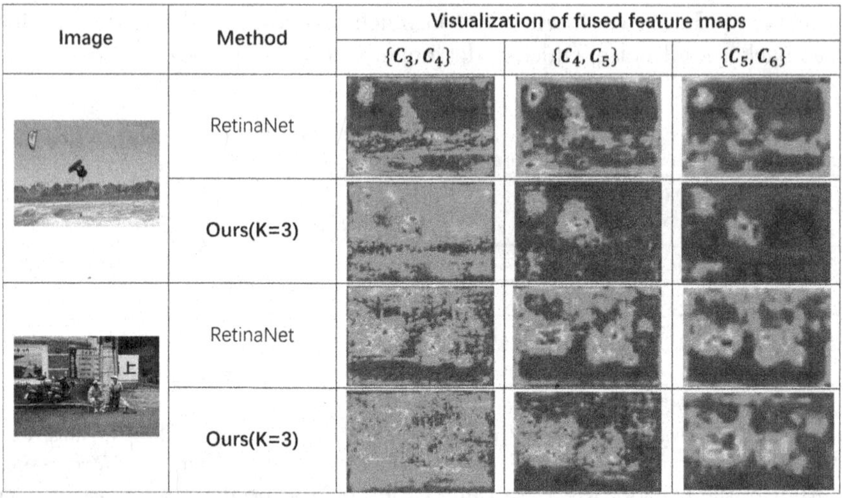

Image	Method	Visualization of fused feature maps		
		$\{C_3, C_4\}$	$\{C_4, C_5\}$	$\{C_5, C_6\}$
	RetinaNet			
	Ours(K=3)			
	RetinaNet			
	Ours(K=3)			

Fig. 6. Visualization of feature maps. This picture respectively visualizes the results of the fusion under the RetinaNet and our framework. Each column in the figure is a fusion of feature maps extracted from different locations in the backbone network.

5   Conclusion

In this work, we develop a elaborated embeded feature fusion network for object detection, which can obtain the potential complementary relationship between spatial information and semantic information through end-to-end autonomous learning and combine them to get a more accurate performance. Then we give a brief analysis about the advantages of our fusion strategy. Finally, NIENet is pretty flexible and can be integrated into other networks with minor modifications.

Acknowledgment. This project is supported by the Natural Science Foundation of China (61702566, 61573387).

References

1. Cai, Z., Fan, Q., Feris, R.S., Vasconcelos, N.: A unified multi-scale deep convolutional neural network for fast object detection. In: Leibe, B., Matas, J., Sebe, N., Welling, M. (eds.) ECCV 2016. LNCS, vol. 9908, pp. 354–370. Springer, Cham (2016). https://doi.org/10.1007/978-3-319-46493-0_22
2. Girshick, R.: Fast R-CNN. In: ICCV (2015)
3. Girshick, R., Donahue, J., Darrell, T., Malik, J.: Rich feature hierarchies for accurate object detection and semantic segmentation. In: CVPR (2014)
4. Hariharan, B., Arbeláez, P., Girshick, R., Malik, J.: Hypercolumns for object segmentation and fine-grained localization. In: CVPR (2015)
5. He, K., Gkioxari, G., Dollár, P., Girshick, R.: Mask R-CNN. In: arXiv:1703.06870 (2017)
6. Krizhevsky, A., Sutskever, I., Hinton, G.: ImageNet classification with deep convolutional neural networks. In: NIPS (2012)
7. Lin, T.-Y., Maire, M., Belongie, S., Hays, J., Perona, P., Ramanan, D., Dollár, P., Zitnick, C.L.: Microsoft COCO: common objects in context. In: Fleet, D., Pajdla, T., Schiele, B., Tuytelaars, T. (eds.) ECCV 2014. LNCS, vol. 8693, pp. 740–755. Springer, Cham (2014). https://doi.org/10.1007/978-3-319-10602-1_48
8. Fu, C.-Y., Liu, W., Ranga, A., Tyagi, A., Berg, A.C.: DSSD: Deconvolutional single shot detector. In: arXiv:1701.06659 (2016)
9. Liu, W., Anguelov, D., Erhan, D., Szegedy, C., Reed, S., Fu, C.-Y., Berg, A.C.: SSD: single shot multibox detector. In: Leibe, B., Matas, J., Sebe, N., Welling, M. (eds.) ECCV 2016. LNCS, vol. 9905, pp. 21–37. Springer, Cham (2016). https://doi.org/10.1007/978-3-319-46448-0_2
10. Redmon, J., Divvala, S., Girshick, R., Farhadi, A.: You only look once: unified, real-time object detection. In: CVPR (2016)
11. Sermanet, P., Eigen, D., Zhang, X., Mathieu, M., Fergus, R., LeCun, Y.: Overfeat: Integrated recognition, localization and detection using convolutional networks. In: ICLR (2014)
12. Shrivastava, A., Gupta, A., Girshick, R.: Training region-based object detectors with online hard example mining. In: CVPR (2016)
13. Lin, T.-Y., Dollár, P., Girshick, R., He, K., Hariharan, B., Belongie, S.: Feature pyramid networks for object detection. In: CVPR (2017)
14. Lin, T.-Y., Goyal, P., Girshick, R., He, K., Dollár, P.: Focal loss for dense object detection. In: ICCV (2017)
15. Lin, G., Milan, A., Shen, C., Reid, I.: RefineNet: multi-path refinement networks for high-resolution semantic segmentation. In: CVPR (2017)
16. Viola, P., Jones, M.: Rapid object detection using a boosted cascade of simple features. In: CVPR (2001)
17. Felzenszwalb, P.F., Girshick, R.B., McAllester, D.: Cascade object detection with deformable part models. In: CVPR (2010)
18. Lowe, D.G.: Distinctive image features from scale-invariant keypoints. IJCV 60(2), 91–110 (2004)
19. Everingham, M., Van Gool, L., Williams, C.K., Winn, J., Zisserman, A.: The PASCAL Visual Object Classes (VOC) challenge. IJCV 88(2), 303–338 (2010)

20. Ren, S., He, K., Girshick, R., Sun, J.: Faster R-CNN: towards real-time object detection with region proposal networks. In: NIPS (2015)
21. Ronneberger, O., Fischer, P., Brox, T.: U-Net: convolutional networks for biomedical image segmentation. In: Navab, N., Hornegger, J., Wells, W.M., Frangi, A.F. (eds.) MICCAI 2015. LNCS, vol. 9351, pp. 234–241. Springer, Cham (2015). https://doi.org/10.1007/978-3-319-24574-4_28
22. Newell, A., Yang, K., Deng, J.: Stacked hourglass networks for human pose estimation. In: Leibe, B., Matas, J., Sebe, N., Welling, M. (eds.) ECCV 2016. LNCS, vol. 9912, pp. 483–499. Springer, Cham (2016). https://doi.org/10.1007/978-3-319-46484-8_29
23. Russakovsky, O.: ImageNet large scale visual recognition challenge. IJCV **115**(3), 211–252 (2015)
24. Fu, H., Cheng, J., Xu, Y., Wong, D.W.K., Liu, J., Cao, X.: Joint optic disc and cup segmentation based on multi-label deep network and polar transformation. IEEE Trans. Med. Imaging **37**(7), 1597–1605 (2018)
25. Bell, S., Zitnick, C.L., Bala, K.: Inside-outside net: detecting objects in context with skip pooling and recurrent neural networks. In: CVPR (2016)

Infrared Small Target Detection Using Multiscale Gray and Variance Difference

Jinyan Gao[1], Yulan Guo[1,2](✉), Zaiping Lin[1], and Wei An[1]

[1] College of Electronic Science,
National University of Defense Technology, Changsha 410073, China
{gaojinyan15,yulan.guo,anwei}@nudt.edu.cn, linzaiping@sina.com
[2] Institute of Computing Technology, Chinese Academy of Sciences,
Beijing 100080, China

Abstract. Infrared small target detection plays an important role in infrared monitoring and early warning systems. This paper proposes a local adaptive contrast measure for robust infrared small target detection using gray and variance difference. First, a size-adaptive gray-level target enhancement process is performed. Then, an improved multiscale variance difference method is proposed for target enhancement and cloud clutter removal. To demonstrate the effectiveness of the proposed approach, a test dataset consisting of two infrared image sequences with different backgrounds was collected. Experiments on the test dataset demonstrate that the proposed infrared small target detection method can achieve better detection performance than the state-of-the-art approaches.

Keywords: Infrared image · Small target detection
Local difference measures

1 Introduction

It is challenging to detect infrared (IR) small targets due to several reasons. First, an infrared small target only occupies a few pixels in an image since the detection distance is long [3,13]. Second, the target has a point spread characteristic due to reflection, refraction, and sensor aperture diffraction [23,24]. Besides, the intensity and shape of a small IR target can be changed under different seasons, weathers, and time [8,12]. In addition, sunlight reflections can also be caused by ocean and cirrus clouds. Moreover, broken cloud and cloud edges are always the main causes for false alarms in infrared small target detection [9,21].

Recently, the progress in Human Visual Systems (HVS) has been widely used to improve the performance of small IR target detection. According to

---

Supported by the National Natural Science Foundation of China (Nos. 61602499 and 61471371), and the National Postdoctoral Program for Innovative Talents (No. BX201600172).

© Springer Nature Switzerland AG 2018
J.-H. Lai et al. (Eds.): PRCV 2018, LNCS 11259, pp. 53–64, 2018.
https://doi.org/10.1007/978-3-030-03341-5_5

the HVS attention mechanism, the local contrasts between targets and their surrounding backgrounds are more important than the absolute intensities of visual signals in an attention system [19]. In the literature, several local contrast measures have been proposed to imitate the HVS selective attention mechanism [2,4,6,7,11,16–18,22]. These measures have shown great potential in infrared small target detection. For example, Chen et al. [2] proposed a Local Contrast Map (LCM) for local target enhancement and background clutter suppression. Han et al. [11] proposed an improved LCM (ILCM) to enhance the detection rate. Wei et al. [22] produced a Multiscale Patch-based Contrast Measure (MPCM) for small target enhancement and background clutter suppression, although it is able to simultaneously detect bright and dark targets in IR images, some discrete points still remain in heavy clutters. Deng et al. [4] introduced a Novel Weighted Image Entropy (NWIE) measure using multiscale gray-level difference and local information entropy. It focuses on the suppression of cloud edges. Nasiri et al. [16] recently proposed a performance-leading Variance Difference (VARD) based method. However, the detection performance is still limited by its fixed-size sliding window.

Inspired by the multiscale gray difference used in [4,20], we propose a joint filter using multiscale gray and variance difference to improve VARD. Two major contributions of this work can be summarized as follows.

(1) A maximum contrast measure is used to extract the maximum cross-scale gray difference. Meanwhile, the optimal size map of the internal window is obtained for subsequent use.
(2) A revised multiscale variance difference measure is designed to alleviate the impact of the background fluctuation and optimize the calculation of variance in each internal window.

The rest of this paper is organized as follows. In Sect. 2, we review the VARD method. In Sect. 3, we describe our proposed MGVD joint filter. In Sect. 4, several experiments are conducted to test our method. The paper is concluded in Sect. 5.

2   The VARD Method

Local contrast has been widely used in HVS inspired IR small target detection [2,16,18]. Nasiri et al. [16] recently proposed the VARD method for small target detection. In VARD, a fixed-size sliding window with three windows is first extracted from an IR image, as shown in the right part of Fig. 1. The sizes of the internal, middle and external windows are set to 7×7, 11×11, 15×15, respectively.

Given a target with Gaussian shape in an IR image, the target is usually brighter than its surroundings. Therefore, when a target exists in an internal window, the intensity in the internal window is higher than that in the middle window.

$$P_{rem}(x_0, y_0) = M_{in} - M_{mid} \tag{1}$$

where M_{in}, M_{mid}, P_{rem} represent the mean values of the internal window, the mean values of the middle window and their difference, respectively. (x_0, y_0) represents the central pixel under investigation.

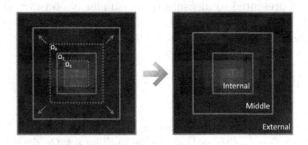

Fig. 1. Target with its surrounding regions.

Note that, some areas in an IR image with strong evolving clouds are similar to target regions, therefore, the variance difference between the internal and external window around the investigated image patch is calculated as follows.

$$VARD = V_{in} - V_e \qquad (2)$$

$$M_{VARD} = \frac{1}{D_{in}^2 - 1} \sum_{j=1}^{D_{in}^2 - 1} VARD_j \qquad (3)$$

where V_{in} and V_e represent the variance of the internal and external windows, respectively. D_{in} is the size of the internal window, $D_{in}^2 - 1$ is the number of neighbors of an image patch.

In fact, the size of a small target can range from 2×2 to about 9×9 pixels. In the ideal case, the size of the internal window should be the same as the target size. To deal with this problem, LCM [11], MPCM [22], NWIE [4] define several multiscale sliding windows to match the size of a real target. The VARD method achieves a state-of-the-art detection performance and efficiency. However, the intensity and variance estimation of the internal window defined in Eqs. 1 and 2 is inaccurate as its internal window has a fixed size. Besides, the number of neighboring image patches for the calculation of variance difference (Eq. 3) is insufficient. That is because it only considers the situations when a sliding window enters a target region, but do not consider the situations when a sliding window leaves a target region, as shown in Fig. 2. These factors decrease the accuracy of local gray and variance difference, and finally affects the detection rate and false alarm rate of the algorithm. Therefore, MGVD is proposed to improve VARD.

3 MGVD-based Small Target Detection

In this section, we introduce a new multiscale IR small target detection method to improve VARD.

3.1 Multiscale Gray Difference

As demonstrated in literature [4,14,15], an IR small target has a signature discontinuous with its neighborhood (as shown in Fig. 1). In this paper, multiscale gray difference is presented to measure the dissimilarity of a target region from its surrounding areas. For an image I, the kth gray difference at point (x, y) can be formulated as:

$$D(x,y) = \left| \frac{1}{N_{\Omega_k}} \sum_{(x,y)\in\Omega_k} I(x,y) - \frac{1}{N_{\Omega_{max}}} \sum_{(p,q)\in\Omega_{max}} I(p,q) \right|^2 \tag{4}$$

where $k = 1, 2, \ldots, K$, which corresponds to the variable sizes of the internal window 3×3, 5×5, $\ldots$, $(2K + 1) \times (2K + 1)$. The set Ω_k denotes the pixels contained in the internal window, the set Ω_{max} denotes the pixels contained in the maximal neighboring area (corresponding to the middle window). $I(x, y)$ and $I(p, q)$ represent the gray value at point in Ω_k and Ω_{max}, N_{Ω_k} and $N_{\Omega_{max}}$ are the number of pixels in sets Ω_k and Ω_{max}. K is the number of variable internal windows.

Using different sizes of the internal windows, we can obtain a set of corresponding gray difference $D_k(x, y)$. Then, the maximum difference measure $D_{max}(x, y)$ at point (x, y) is

$$D_{max}(x,y) = \max\{D_1(x,y),\ D_2(x,y),\ \ldots,\ D_K(x,y)\} \tag{5}$$

Consequently, we can obtain the maximum contrast map (i.e., D_{max}) between the internal window and the middle window.

3.2 Multiscale Variance Difference

Some areas in an IR image with strong evolving clouds are similar to target regions, therefore, using gray difference only is insufficient to extract a target. In addition, the grayscale value in the middle window may be affected by the target, we further consider the variance difference between different internal and external windows of its neighboring image patches.

Different from VARD, we increase the number of neighboring image patches for the calculation of variance difference, as illustrated in Fig. 2. In our method, the size of the internal window is set to $D_{in}^*(x, y)$, which corresponds to the maximum difference measure in Eq. 5. The number of neighboring image patches is $D_2 = 2D_{in}^* - 1$. Finally, the multiscale variance difference can be calculated as:

$$VARD' = V_{in}' - V_{e_j} \tag{6}$$

$$M_{VARD'} = \frac{1}{D_2^2 - 1} \sum_{j=1}^{D_2^2 - 1} VARD_j' \tag{7}$$

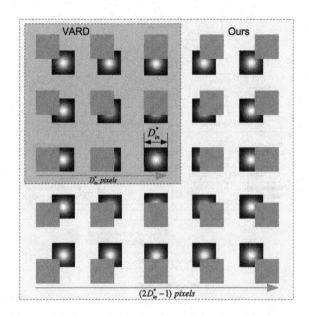

Fig. 2. A sliding neighboring internal window (blue square). (Color figure online)

where V'_{in} represents the variance of the internal window, V_{e_j} represents the variance of the external window in neighboring image patches, $VARD'$ represents our revised variance difference for a single image patch. Consequently, the multiscale variance difference is calculated as:

$$MGVD = D_{max} \odot M^2_{VARD'} \qquad (8)$$

where $\odot$ means the Hadamard product.

3.3 MGVD-based Small Target Detection

The proposed algorithm has five major steps, a flow chart is shown in Fig. 3. First, image patches with three windows are first extracted from an IR image. Second, the maximum contrast measure between the internal window and the middle window is calculated on each image patch. Third, the variance difference is calculated between the internal window and its surrounding background in the external windows. Fourth, the multiscale gray difference map is multiplied with the multiscale variance difference map. Finally, we used the same adaptive-threshold segmentation method as [1,2,10] to extract candidate targets. The threshold is computed according to

$$T = \mu + k \times \sigma \qquad (9)$$

where μ and σ are the mean and standard deviation of the final enhanced map, respectively. In our experience, k ranges from 2 to 15.

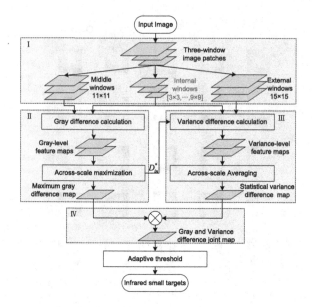

Fig. 3. Overview of our proposed MGVD small target detection method.

4 Experimental Results and Analysis

To test the performance of our proposed method, qualitative and quantitative experiments are presented in this section.

4.1 Experimental Setup

To demonstrate the effectiveness of our proposed method, two real IR image sequences with heavy clutters are tested. Example images are shown in Fig. 4 and the details of these two real sequences are summarized in Table 1.

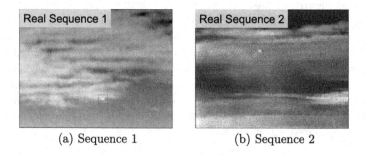

(a) Sequence 1   (b) Sequence 2

Fig. 4. Original images.

Table 1. Details of 2 real IR image sequences.

	Frame	Image resolution	Target description	Background description
Dataset 1 [21]	40	128 × 128	an airplane with small size.	sky scene with changing banded cloud.
Dataset 2 [2]	30	200 × 256	an airplane with changing size.	gloomy sky with heavy cloudy clutters.

Five recent HVS-based single frame target detection methods have been used as baseline methods, including Average Gray Absolute Difference Maximum Map (AGADM) [20], LCM [2], NLCM [18], NWIE [4], and VARD [16]. LCM is a traditional HVS-based local contrast method, AGADM and NWIE are two multiscale gray difference based methods, NLCM and VARD are two joint target detection methods using both grayscale and variance.

Three evaluation criteria have been used to measure the target enhancement and background suppression performance, including Signal to Clutter Ratio Gain (SCRG) and Background Suppression Factor (BSF) and Receiver Operating Characteristic (ROC) curves [4, 18, 25]. They are defined as:

$$SCRG = \frac{S_{out}/C_{out}}{S_{in}/C_{in}} \tag{10}$$

$$BSF = \frac{C_{in}}{C_{out}} \tag{11}$$

where S_{in} and S_{out}, C_{in} and C_{out} are the amplitude of target signal and the standard deviations of clutter in the input and output images, respectively.

A ROC curve represents the relationship between the probability of detection and false alarm rate. Specifically, for a given threshold T in Eq. 9, the probability of detection P_d and false alarm rate P_f [3, 5, 16] can be calculated as:

$$P_d = \frac{n_t}{n_c} \tag{12}$$

$$P_f = \frac{n_f}{n} \tag{13}$$

where n_t, n_c, n_f and n represent the number of detected true pixels, ground-truth target pixels, false alarm pixels and the total number of image pixels, respectively.

4.2   Qualitative Results

The target enhancement and detection results achieved by different methods on the two sequences are shown in Figs. 5 and 6. It can be seen that the image processed by our method has less clutter and residual noise under different clutter backgrounds as compared to the baseline methods. That is attributed to

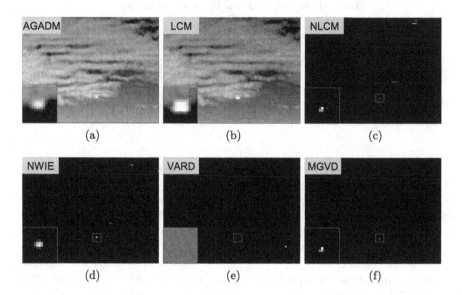

Fig. 5. Target enhancement results obtained by different methods on Sequence 1. Real targets are shown in red rectangles, with a close-up version shown in the left bottom part of each figure. (Color figure online)

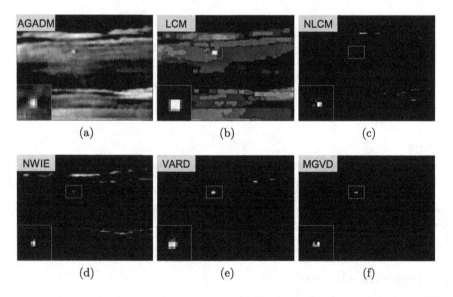

Fig. 6. Target enhancement results obtained by different methods on Sequence 2, Real targets are shown in red rectangles, with a close-up version shown in the left bottom part of each figure. (Color figure online)

the adaptive calculation of grayscale maximum contrast measure and variance difference in each image patch. The AGADM and LCM methods are inferior to the other four methods in background suppression. Although the NLCM and NWIE methods can preserve the target to a certain extent, several strong cloud edges remain in the filtered results of the two image sequences. Since the size of the sliding window in VARD is fixed, the targets with various sizes cannot be optimally enhanced. Therefore, they are missed in some frames in Sequence 1. Besides, cloud edges are also enhanced and still remain in strong evolving background in Sequence 2 after filtered by VARD.

In summary, the above qualitative results demonstrate that the proposed method obtains the best target enhancement and background suppression performance. However, there are still few deficiencies of our MGVD method. For example, when a target is so far away from the imaging system that it only occupies 2–3 pixels in an image, the temporal cues in multiple frames should be used to extract targets.

4.3 Quantitative Results

The average SCRG and BSF results obtained by our method and the baseline methods are shown in Fig. 7 and Table 2. We can find that the SCRGs and BSFs achieved by AGADM and LCM method are relatively low. The VARD method is the second best method in BSF. In contrast, our proposed method removes isolated clutter residuals and preserves the target missed by VARD in strong cloud edges (as shown in Sequence 1). Consequently, our MGVD method obtains the highest scores in both SCRG and BSF, with remarkable background suppression performance being achieved. It is clear that the performance of the NLCM and NWIE methods are poor for the removal of strong evolving cloud edges, especially in Sequence 2.

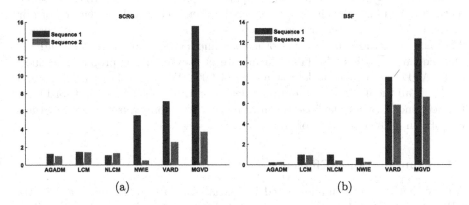

Fig. 7. The average SCRG and BSF results achieved by different methods on two sequences. (a) The average SCRG results. (b) The average BSF results.

Table 2. The average SCRG and BSF results.

Method	Sequence 1		Sequence 2	
	SCRG	BSF	SCRG	BSF
AGADM [20]	1.2109	0.2012	0.9732	0.2250
LCM [2]	1.4365	0.9389	1.4027	0.8625
NLCM [18]	1.0492	0.9509	1.2972	0.3734
NWIE [4]	5.5243	0.6268	0.4361	0.2329
VARD [16]	7.0765	8.5662	2.5477	5.8326
MGVD	**15.5178**	**12.3488**	**3.6658**	**6.6185**

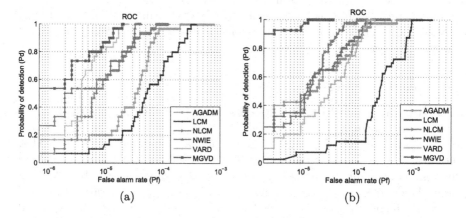

Fig. 8. ROC curves. (a) ROC curves of Sequence 1. (b) ROC curves of Sequence 2.

ROC curves are used to further compare our proposed method to the baseline methods. As illustrated in Fig. 8, it can be seen that the ROC curves of our method on the two real image sequences are close to the upper left corner. That is, our method outperforms other baseline methods in terms of P_d and P_f. On Sequence 1, when the false alarm rate is 2×10^{-5}, our proposed method and VARD can achieve a detection rate of 90%. When the false alarm rate is 1×10^{-4}, all the methods can obtain a detection rate over 90%, except for LCM. On Sequence 2, when the false alarm rate is 1×10^{-5}, only our proposed method can obtain a detection rate of 90%.

4.4   Computational Efficiency

All the methods were implemented in Matlab 2014a on a PC with a 2.7 GHz CPU and 4.0 GB RAM. We ran our method on 2 real IR image sequences. The run time on each dataset is 5.73 s and 17.20 s. Since our method uses a sliding window to check all possible locations in an image, it is not very efficient. Its efficiency should be further improved in future.

5 Conclusion

This paper presented a joint filter for small target detection using multiscale gray and variance difference. Maximum gray difference is first extracted by an absolute gray difference method. The optimal size of the internal window is then used to calculate the variance of the internal window. Finally, the neighboring image patches are expanded for the estimation of variance difference. Experiments shows that the proposed method achieves promising target enhancement and background suppression performance on complicated real IR images.

References

1. Bai, X., Bi, Y.: Derivative entropy-based contrast measure for infrared small-target detection. IEEE Trans. Geosci. Remote Sens. **56**(99), 2452–2466 (2018)
2. Chen, C.P., Li, H., Wei, Y., Xia, T., Tang, Y.Y.: A local contrast method for small infrared target detection. IEEE Trans. Geosci. Remote Sens. **52**(1), 574–581 (2014)
3. Dai, Y., Wu, Y.: Reweighted infrared patch-tensor model with both nonlocal and local priors for single-frame small target detection. IEEE J. Sel. Top. Appl. Earth Obs. Remote Sens. **10**(8), 3752–3767 (2017)
4. Deng, H., Sun, X., Liu, M., Ye, C., Zhou, X.: Infrared small-target detection using multiscale gray difference weighted image entropy. IEEE Trans. Aerosp. Electron. Syst. **52**(1), 60–72 (2016)
5. Deng, H., Sun, X., Liu, M., Ye, C., Zhou, X.: Small infrared target detection based on weighted local difference measure. IEEE Trans. Geosci. Remote Sens. **54**(7), 4204–4214 (2016)
6. Deng, H., Sun, X., Liu, M., Ye, C., Zhou, X.: Entropy-based window selection for detecting dim and small infrared targets. Pattern Recogn. **61**, 66–77 (2017)
7. Dong, L., Wang, B., Zhao, M., Xu, W.: Robust infrared maritime target detection based on visual attention and spatiotemporal filtering. IEEE Trans. Geosci. Remote Sens. **55**(5), 3037–3050 (2017)
8. Fan, Z., Bi, D., Xiong, L., Ma, S., He, L., Ding, W.: Dim infrared image enhancement based on convolutional neural network. Neurocomputing **272**, 396–404 (2018)
9. Gao, C., Wang, L., Xiao, Y., Zhao, Q., Meng, D.: Infrared small-dim target detection based on Markov random field guided noise modeling. Pattern Recogn. **76**, 463–475 (2018)
10. Gao, J., Lin, Z., Guo, Y., An, W.: TVPCF: a spatial and temporal filter for small target detection in IR images. In: Digital Image Computing: Techniques and Applications (DICTA), pp. 1–7 (2017)
11. Han, J., Ma, Y., Zhou, B., Fan, F., Liang, K., Fang, Y.: A robust infrared small target detection algorithm based on human visual system. IEEE Geosci. Remote Sens. Lett. **11**(12), 2168–2172 (2014)
12. Kim, S.: Infrared variation reduction by simultaneous background suppression and target contrast enhancement for deep convolutional neural network-based automatic target recognition. Opt. Eng. **56**(6), 063108 (2017)
13. Li, Y., Zhang, Y.: Robust infrared small target detection using local steering kernel reconstruction. Pattern Recogn. **77**, 113–125 (2018)
14. Liu, D., Li, Z., Liu, B., Chen, W., Liu, T., Cao, L.: Infrared small target detection in heavy sky scene clutter based on sparse representation. Infrared Phys. Technol. **85**, 13–31 (2017)

15. Liu, R., Wang, J., Yang, H., Gong, C., Zhou, Y., Liu, L., Zhang, Z., Shen, S.: Tensor Fukunaga-Koontz transform for small target detection in infrared images. Infrared Phys. Technol. **78**, 147–155 (2016)
16. Nasiri, M., Chehresa, S.: Infrared small target enhancement based on variance difference. Infrared Phys. Technol. **82**, 107–119 (2017)
17. Nie, J., Qu, S., Wei, Y., Zhang, L., Deng, L.: An infrared small target detection method based on multiscale local homogeneity measure. Infrared Phys. Technol. **90**, 186–194 (2018)
18. Qin, Y., Li, B.: Effective infrared small target detection utilizing a novel local contrast method. IEEE Geosci. Remote Sens. Lett. **13**(12), 1890–1894 (2016)
19. Shi, Y., Wei, Y., Yao, H., Pan, D., Xiao, G.: High-boost-based multiscale local contrast measure for infrared small target detection. IEEE Geosci. Remote Sens. Lett. **15**(99), 1–5 (2018)
20. Wang, G., Zhang, T., Wei, L., Sang, N.: Efficient method for multiscale small target detection from a natural scene. Opt. Eng. **35**(3), 761–769 (1996)
21. Wang, X., Peng, Z., Kong, D., He, Y.: Infrared dim and small target detection based on stable multisubspace learning in heterogeneous scene. IEEE Trans. Geosci. Remote Sens. **55**(10), 5481–5493 (2017)
22. Wei, Y., You, X., Li, H.: Multiscale patch-based contrast measure for small infrared target detection. Pattern Recogn. **58**, 216–226 (2016)
23. Xin, Y.H., Zhou, J., Chen, Y.S.: Dual multi-scale filter with SSS and GW for infrared small target detection. Infrared Phys. Technol. **81**, 97–108 (2017)
24. Zhang, H., Bai, J., Li, Z., Liu, Y., Liu, K.: Scale invariant SURF detector and automatic clustering segmentation for infrared small targets detection. Infrared Phys. Technol. **83**, 7–16 (2017)
25. Zhang, X., Ding, Q., Luo, H., Hui, B., Chang, Z., Zhang, J.: Infrared small target detection based on directional zero-crossing measure. Infrared Phys. Technol. **87**, 113–123 (2017)

A Local Top-Down Module for Object Detection with Multi-scale Features

Shihua Huang, Lu Wang[✉], Peiyu Yang, and Qingxu Deng

School of Computer Science and Engineering,
Northeastern University, Shenyang, Liaoning, China
wanglu@cse.neu.edu.cn

Abstract. Object detection methods based on deep models and multi-scale features have achieved the state-of-the-art performance. However, since each feature layer operates independently, several issues such as box-in-box detections and less effective performance on small objects need to be addressed. In this paper, we tackle these issues by integrating contextual and semantic information from higher layer features into the prediction layer. Existing methods adopting similar ideas mostly apply full top-down modules, which may increase computational loads significantly. Instead, we present an efficient while general local top-down module, in which each prediction layer is integrated only with the upsampled features from its two succeeding layers. Experimental results show that the proposed algorithm performs favorably against the state-of-the-art methods on the VOC, COCO and HollywoodHeads datasets, while introducing little computational overhead. Compared with methods using full top-down modules, the proposed algorithm achieves comparable or higher accuracy while operates at a higher frame rate. The code is available at https://github.com/Hshihua/Local-Top-Down-Detection-Network.

Keywords: Object detection · SSD · Deconvolution
Local top-down module

1 Introduction

Object detection plays a pivotal role in image understanding that can be applied to numerous applications, e.g., image indexing and retrieval, image and video understanding, among others. Recent progress in object detection has been mainly based on deep Convolutional Neural Networks (CNNs). Existing CNN based object detection approaches can be categorized into two groups, based on image regions [1,14] or bounding boxes [10,11].

Among the state-of-the-art detection methods, the single shot multibox detector (SSD) approach [10] is fast and robust to scale variations because it makes use of multiple convolution layers for object detection. Although the SSD method performs well in terms of speed and accuracy, there are several issues

© Springer Nature Switzerland AG 2018
J.-H. Lai et al. (Eds.): PRCV 2018, LNCS 11259, pp. 65–77, 2018.
https://doi.org/10.1007/978-3-030-03341-5_6

that need to addressed. First, each layer in the feature pyramid of the SSD method is used independently as an input to the classifier network. Thus, the same object can be detected at multiple scales, which is known as box-in-box detections. Second, the first prediction layer has a smaller receptive field than others and thus has less context and weak semantic information. This is the main reason that the SSD method is less effective in detecting small objects.

In contrast to the existing bottom-up CNN models, top-down modules that forward information from top layers to lower layers have been shown to be critical for achieving the state-of-the-art performance. The top-down modules introduce abstract semantic information and context into lower level layers for better box classification [3,9,15] by continually upsampling features from the uppermost layer of the bottom-up pyramid to the lowest prediction layer. This operation does not stop until the finest resolution level of the feature pyramid has been reached. As such, approaches with such top-down modules may entail heavy computational loads.

In this paper, we show that it is possible to solve the problems of detectors using multi-scale feature maps by adding a simple and efficient Local Top-Down Module (LTD) that integrates the information from two succeeding convolutional layers instead of all the upper convolutional layers while introducing much less computational cost. For concreteness, we use the SSD detector as the baseline method with the proposed LTD module.

The contributions of this paper are summarized as follows:

- To solve the typical problems of detecting objects using multi-scale features, we propose a local top-down module to integrate high level semantic information and context into the lower prediction layers, which differs from the widely used full top-down module.
- Our method obtains significant improvement over the SSD method on different benchmark datasets. Compared with detectors using full top-down modules, our approach gets comparable or even higher accuracy.
- Our method runs at 37 FPS on a single 1080 GPU for images of 300×300 pixels, which is significantly faster than most existing detectors using full top-down modules.

2   Related Work

ConvNet Based Object Detectors. With significant progress of deep learning on large scale object recognition [4,5], numerous detection methods based on ConvNet have been proposed. Two-stage or region-based methods such as Faster R-CNN [14] and R-FCN [1] achieve high accuracy but with high computational loads. On the other hand, one-stage or region-free detectors such as YOLO [11, 12] and SSD [10] perform efficiently and accurately. The SSD [10] and YOLO9000 [12] methods do not entail the computationally expensive processes to generate region proposals while performing favorably against the state-of-the-art two-stage detectors. The recently proposed one-stage detector RefineDet [18] retains the merits of both one-stage and two-stage approaches by introducing an anchor refinement module that is able to filter out negative anchors as well as adjust the locations and sizes of anchors.

SSD Based Object Detectors. Numerous methods based on the SSD method have been developed. To generate high quality bounding boxes, Ren et al. propose the RRC scheme [13] by introducing a recurrent rolling convolution architecture over multi-scale feature maps to construct object classifiers and bounding box regressors. This method achieves the state-of-the-art performance on the KITTI dataset based on the IoU threshold of 0.7. Based on the observation that detecting small objects without enlarging the image requires more context information, the DSSD method [3] augments the ResNet [4] based SSD approach with deconvolution layers to introduce additional large-scale context. Recently, the R-SSD method [6] presents a feature concatenation structure that fully exploits the relationship among layers in the feature pyramid through pooling and deconvolution. By using the deconvolution module, both DSSD and R-SSD methods obtain about 1% performance gain over the SSD approach on the PASCAL VOC dataset.

Top-Down Module for Object Detection. Recent detection methods adopt top-down modules to add context and decode abstract but semantic information into low level feature maps for better box classification based on Faster R-CNN [14]. Lin et al. [9] propose a top-down model with lateral connections to construct semantic feature pyramid and achieve significant performance gain with a single model. In [8], Kong et al. use reverse connection with objectness of a prior network to combine fine-grained details with highly abstract information, which obtains performance gain in accuracy and speed. The TDM [15] method uses a top-down network that handles the selection and integration of contextual information and low level features. On the other hand, some recent methods are developed based on the SSD detector. The DSSD scheme [3] uses a deconvolution module with feature integration based on element-wise products. In the BlitzeNet [2] method, the ResSkip block is used to integrate feature maps from bottom-up and top-down streams with skip and residual connection. We note the above-mentioned methods all adopt full top-down module to construct top-down or backward feature pyramids.

3 Proposed Algorithm

Our goal is to improve the accuracy of object detectors using multi-scale features via a local top-down module. We implement our work based on the SSD method. Figure 1 illustrates the overall architecture of the proposed approach.

In the following, we first justify the necessity of using a local top-down module, and then describe the proposed local top-down module in details.

3.1 Main Ideas

The SSD method [10] is constructed based on a truncated base network that ends with several convolutional layers by adding a serial of progressively smaller

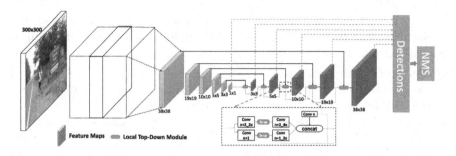

Fig. 1. Architecture of the proposed network.

convolutional layers. Each added layer together with some of the earlier base network layers are used to predict scores and corrections for the predefined default bounding boxes. However, the SSD method (or other detectors that utilize bottom-up multi-scale features) does not exploit the information between the lower layers and upper layers, e.g., the pathway that introduces more semantic information and context from high level features into low level ones. In particular, we show that not all the information propagated backward from the higher layers is useful for lower layers.

Considering the case that the input to a detector is an image of 300×300 pixels and an object to be detected is of 30×30 pixels, it is likely that the object can be detected on the 38×38 feature maps as there are much stronger activations in this layer than the others that can help locate this object effectively. However, in general the semantic information of such an object begins to vanish after the 10×10 feature maps ($300 : 30 = 10 : 1$), and the pixels within this object may then become the context of the other larger objects. Therefore, feature maps with resolution smaller than 10×10 are of little help in detecting this object. In other words, the most useful semantic information only exists in the next two higher layers (10×10 and 19×19 in this case) of the prediction layer (38×38 in this case). Furthermore, as the next two higher layers already have much larger receptive fields, they can provide sufficient context to the prediction layer.

Regarding the box-in-box detection issue, we observe that the scale of the outside box is usually at most 2 to 3 times the scale of the inside box, meaning that the visual information within three consecutive layers (4 times scale difference) is sufficient to solve this problem effectively.

As such, the effective top-down semantic and context information should be within local ranges (e.g., involving three feature layers), rather than the whole feature pyramid. Thus, we propose to use a local top-down module to propagate the upper layer information to the lower layers (e.g., within two to three layers).

3.2   Local Top-Down Module

Figure 2(a) shows our building block that constructs the local top-down feature maps for the n-th prediction layer, which are the concatenation of the bottom-up Conv n, upsampled Conv $n + 1$ and Conv $n + 2$ features. Specifically, the

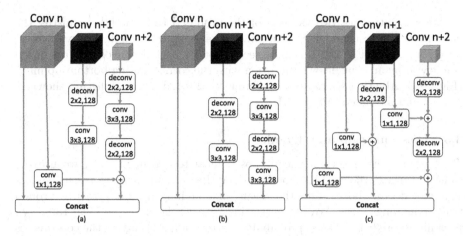

Fig. 2. Variants of the local top-down module. The difference lies in the block after deconvolution. (a) The convolutional block is integrated with the element-wise sum block (used in the proposed network); (b) all are convolutional blocks; (c) all are element-wise sum blocks.

Conv $n+1$ feature maps are first upsampled to the same spatial resolution as their pervious layer (Conv n) maps while being reduced to d channels via a learned deconvolution layer ($d = 128$ in our implementation). In case of information divergence and the aliasing effect of upsampling, the upsampled features are convolved with 3×3 kernels before being concatenated to the Conv n maps.

The Conv $n + 2$ maps need to be upsampled twice before the concatenation. For the first deconvolution operation, they are processed in the same way as Conv $n+1$ maps (i.e., deconv + conv). The resulting features are used to construct the top-down maps of the Conv $n + 1$ layer and then upsampled for the second time. Because the semantic information contained in the Conv $n + 2$ layer is diluted significantly after two continuous upsampling operations, the results are summed element-wisely with the Conv n maps (which undergo a 1×1 convolutional layer to reduce the channel dimension) to enhance the upampled features. The resulting features are finally concatenated to the bottom-up Conv n maps to form the local top-down feature maps for the n-th prediction layer.

In the proposed LTD module, for each prediction layer, the number of feature channels is increased for just two times that of the upsampled features, i.e., $2d$ (256 in our implementation). This is much smaller than that in the top-down module used by the R-SSD [6] method, which increases the feature dimension for up to 2304 channels. In addition, in our LTD module, the dimension of upper layer feature maps is reduced before they are merged with the prediction layer, whereas for the full top-down module, such as the DSSD scheme, feature channels need to be increased for certain layers before integration so as to make the element-wise product operation feasible through the whole feature pyramid. Hence, our LTD module is more efficient than these full top-down modules.

We also introduce two variants of the proposed LTD module to justify the design. For the first model, each deconvolution operation is followed by a convolution operation (Fig. 2(b)). For the second model, each deconvolution operation is followed by an element-wise addition with the corresponding bottom-up maps (Fig. 2(c)). Ablation studies with different local top-down modules are shown in Table 3 and discussed in Sect. 4.1.

3.3 Loss Function and Training

To illustrate the merits of the proposed local top-down module, we use the same settings as the SSD method including the data augmentation scheme, loss function, default boxes, and the means of matching default boxes to ground truth bounding boxes. We use activations of each layer in the local top-down pyramid to predict the class probability distribution and regress the coordinates of the default boxes.

4 Experimental Results

We evaluate the proposed algorithm against the state-of-the-art object detection methods on the PASCAL VOC 2007, PASCAL VOC 2012, MS COCO and HollywoodHeads datasets [17]. We also carry out ablation studies on the VOC 2007 dataset to better demonstrate the effectiveness of each component. All the hyperparameters are set according to the SSD method unless otherwise specified.

4.1 Results on the VOC 2007 Dataset

For the VOC 2007 dataset, all models are trained on the VOC 2007 trainval + 2012 trainval and evaluated on the VOC 2007 test set. The training process takes 120k iterations with initial learning rate being 10^{-3}, which is then decreased to 10^{-4} at 80k steps and to 10^{-5} at 100k steps. The detection performance of all evaluated methods is presented in Table 1. Overall, the proposed algorithm gains more than 2% improvement over the SSD method, and outperforms the others when the input image size is either 300×300 or 512×512 pixels.

We also carry out ablation studies to analyze the proposed method using the VOC 2007 datasets. The results are shown in Tables 2, 3 and 4 and discussed in the following. Unless specified explicitly, all the results are based on input images of 300×300 pixels.

Batch Normalization. Although batch normalization is a useful method in training deep models, it is not used in the SSD method. In this work, we add the batch normalization layer to convolutional layers from the last convolutional layer of the backbone until the last convolutional layer of the detection network. The experimental results show that this can increase the mAP for 0.8% on the VOC 2007 test set.

Backbone Network. We replace the VGGNet in SSD and our method with the MobileNet and ResNet-101 models as the backbone convolutional network to

Table 1. Detection results on the PASCAL VOC dataset. To exclude the effect of the different testing environments on the inference speed, the R-FPS metric is used to measure the relative processing speed of each SSD-based detector compared with that of the SSD detector running in the same environment. The letters M and P denote the Titan X Maxwell and Pascal architectures respectively. Bold fonts indicate the best

Method	Backbone	mAP(%)		FPS	R-FPS	GPU
		VOC 2007	VOC 2012			
two-stage:						
Faster R-CNN [14]	VGGNet	73.2	70.4	7		TITAN X(M)
R-FCN [1]	ResNet101	80.5	77.6	9		TITAN X(M)
DeNet-101 [16]	ResNet-101	77.0	73.9	33		Tesla P100
CoupleNet [19]	ResNet101	81.7	**80.4**	9.8		TITAN X(P)
one-stage:						
YOLOv2-352 [12]	Darknet	73.7	-	81	-	TITAN X(M)
SSD300 [10]	VGGNet	77.2	75.8	46	-	TITAN X(M)
R-SSD300 [6]	VGGNet	78.5	76.4	35	57%	TITAN X(P)
Blitznet300 [2]	ResNet-50	78.5	75.4	24	52%	TITAN X(M)
DSSD321 [3]	ResNet-101	78.6	76.3	15.3	33%	TITAN X(M)
YOLOv2-544 [12]	Darknet	78.6	73.4	40	-	TITAN X(M)
SSD512 [10]	VGGNet	79.8	78.5	19	-	TITAN X(M)
Blitznet512 [2]	ResNet-50	80.7	79.0	19.5	**103%**	TITAN X(M)
R-SSD512 [6]	VGGNet	80.8	-	16.6	66%	TITAN X(P)
DSSD513 [3]	ResNet-101	81.5	80.0	6.3	33%	TITAN X(M)
Ours300	VGGNet	79.4	76.7	37	85%	GTX1080
Ours512	VGGNet	**81.8**	79.7	16.7	87%	GTX1080

analyze the generalibility of the proposed algorithm. Table 2 shows the evaluation results with different backbone networks. Note that our method obtains at least 2% performance gain over the SSD method for different backbone networks. For the MobileNet, our method achieves about 4% gain. These results demonstrate the proposed method can be integrated with different backbone networks.

Variants of the LTD Module. To better understand the design options of the proposed local top-down module, we implement three variants as shown in Fig. 2. Table 3 shows the detection results of these variants. Note that the module with all element-wise sum blocks performs the worst while the proposed model based on convolution and element-wise performs best. These results show that the adopted model with convolution and summation operation performs better than the model with pure convolution or summation operations.

Number of Upsampled Convolutional Layers. Table 4 shows the detection results when different number of succeeding upsampled convolutional layers are integrated with the prediction layer. When incorporating three upsampled

Table 2. Detection performance with different pre-trained backbones.

Backbone	Method	mAP(%)
MobileNet [5]	SSD	68.3
	ours	**72.3**
VGGNet [7]	SSD	77.2
	ours	**79.4**
ResNet-101 [4]	SSD	73.3
	ours	**75.5**

Table 3. Comparison of detection performance with different local top-down modules.

Input size	LTD Module	mAP(%)
300 × 300	all-elementwise-sum	78.9
	all-conv	79.3
	conv-and-sum (Proposed)	**79.4**
512 × 512	all-elementwise-sum	81.4
	all-conv	81.5
	conv-and-sum (Proposed)	**81.8**

layers, the Conv $n + 3$ feature maps additionally undergo a 3×3 convolution, a deconvolution and an element-wise sum operation after those processing steps for the Conv $n + 2$ features. The results in Table 4 show that incorporating the upsampled feature maps from the two succeeding convolutional layers performs best, which justifies our design and proves that layers that are far away from the prediction layer does not help in achieving better detection performance.

To evaluate the inference time, we test the SSD method and ours on the VOC 2007 dataset with a single 1080 GPU. For input images of 300×300 pixels, the proposed method runs at 37 FPS while the SSD scheme runs at 43.6 FPS. For input images of 512×512 pixels, the proposed method runs at 16.7 FPS while the SSD scheme runs at 19.2 FPS. By introducing the local top-down module, the speed difference is no more than 15%. More run-time evaluation results with other methods are shown in Table 1, which demonstrates that our method introduces much less overhead than the other SSD based detectors, except for the BlitzNet512 detector. Note that the BlitzNet512 uses the ResNet50 as the backbone, which is 2 times faster than the VGG backbone used by us, and the mAP of BlitzNet is 1.1% lower than our method.

Table 4. Results for integration with different number of succeeding upsampled convolutional layers.

# upsampled layers	0	1	2	3
mAP(%)		77.2	79.1	**79.4**	78.7

4.2 Results on the VOC 2012 Dataset

We also test our method on the PASCAL VOC 2012 dataset. For VOC 2012 test set, we train our network on data consisting of PASCAL VOC 2007 trainval, 2007 test and 2012 trainval. The training process takes 240k iterations with initial learning rate being 10^{-3}, which is decreased to 10^{-4} at 160k steps and to 10^{-5} at 200k steps.

The detection results are shown in Table 1. We see that our method gains 0.9% and 1.2% improvement over the SSD method and compares favorably against the other state-of-the-art object detectors. Note that the performance gap between our method and the DSSD method becomes smaller than that on the PASCAL VOC 2007 test set. Specifically, when the input is about 300×300 pixels, the mAP gap between our method and the DSSD scheme is 0.4%, while the gap is 0.8% on the VOC 2007 dataset; When the input is around 512×512 pixels, the DSSD method outperforms our method by 0.3%. We think the main reason behind this is that DSSD is based on the deeper ResNet101 [4] backbone and the complicated classifiers, which can benefit more from the larger amount of training data than the VGGNet [7] used in our method. This assert can be justified by the fact that the SSD detector with the ResNet101 backbone performs worse on PASCAL VOC 2007 test set than the SSD with the VGGNet backbone, but better on PASCAL VOC 2012 test set and MS COCO test-dev2015 data.

4.3 Results on the MS COCO Dataset

We conduct experiments on the MS COCO 2015 dataset where the models are trained on the trainval35k set and evaluated on the test-dev. The training process takes 400k iterations with the initial learning rate being 10^{-3}, which is decreased at 280k and 360k steps to 10^{-4} and 10^{-5} respectively. We report the standard COCO metrics including AP (averaged over IoU thresholds), AP_{50} and AP_{75} (measured under IoU threshold of 0.5 and 0.75 respectively). In addition, we present the COCO AP on objects of small, medium, and large size (namely, AP_S, AP_M, and AP_L).

Table 5 shows the detection performance of different detectors on the MS COCO dataset. Note that both SSD321 and DSSD methods achieves better mAP than our algorithm. However, most the performance gain is from the deeper ResNet-101 backbone network and strong classifiers. When comparing the SSD321 with the DSSD321, although the deconvolution module of DSSD achieves 1.2% improvement for small object detection, it does not improve the overall accuracy of SSD, i.e., the performance of DSSD is inferior to SSD in detecting medium- and large- size objects. On the other hand, our method consistently outperforms the SSD scheme significantly under all the evaluation conditions.

4.4 Results on the HollywoodHeads Dataset

As heads usually correspond to small objects in images and head detection is useful for various applications, we evaluate our method on the HollywoodHeads

Table 5. Detection performance on the MS COCO test-dev2015.

Method	Training data	Backbone	Input Size	AP	AP$_{50}$	AP$_{75}$	AP$_S$	AP$_M$	AP$_L$
two-stage:									
Faster-RCNN [14]	trainval	VGGNet	$\sim 1000 \times 600$	21.9	42.7	-	-	-	-
R-FCN [1]	trainval	ResNet101	$\sim 1000 \times 600$	29.9	51.9	-	10.8	32.8	45.0
DeNet-101 [16]	trainval35k	ResNet101	512×512	31.9	50.5	34.2	9.7	34.9	50.6
CoupleNet [19]	trainval	ResNet101	$\sim 1000 \times 600$	33.1	53.5	35.4	11.6	36.3	50.1
one-stage:									
YOLOv2 [12]	trainval35k	DarkNet	544×544	21.6	44.0	19.2	5.0	22.4	35.5
SSD300 [10]	trainval35k	VGGNet	300×300	25.1	43.1	25.8	6.6	25.9	41.4
SSD321 [3]	trainval35k	ResNet101	321×321	28.0	45.4	29.3	6.2	28.3	49.3
DSSD321 [3]	trainval35k	ResNet101	321×321	28.0	46.1	29.2	7.4	28.1	47.6
SSD512 [10]	trainval35k	VGGNet	512×512	28.8	48.5	30.3	10.9	31.8	43.5
SSD513 [3]	trainval35k	ResNet101	513×513	31.2	50.4	33.3	10.2	34.5	49.8
DSSD513 [3]	trainval35k	ResNet101	513×513	**33.2**	53.3	35.2	13.0	35.4	51.1
Ours300	trainval35k	VGGNet	300×300	27.5	47.7	28.1	**9.2**	28.7	43.0
Ours512	trainval35k	VGGNet	512×512	31.3	53.1	32.5	**14.3**	33.5	45.4

Table 6. Experimental results on the HollywoodHead test set.

Method	Training data	mAP(%)
Baseline [17]	training set	72.7
SSD300 [10]	validation set	70.0
Ours 300	validation set	**75.6**

dataset [17]. This dataset contains $369,846$ human heads annotated in $224,740$ frames from 21 Hollywood movies. The movies vary in genres and contain different time epochs. The training set contains $216,719$ frames, the validation set consists of $6,719$ frames and the test set is composed of 1,302 frames.

In this experiment, we use the validation set as the training set to train SSD and our method, as the original training set is large that either determining the proper train parameters or the training process itself is computationally prohibitive. We set the learning rate to be 0.01 for the first 16 k iterations, 10^{-4} for the next 4k iterations and 10^{-5} for the last 4k iterations. Table 6 shows that our method outperforms both the detectors in [17] and the SSD method, even when the detector in [17] is trained on a much larger training set.

4.5   Visual Illustration of the Detection Results

Figure 3 shows some examples of the detection results of SSD and our algorithm, when the threshold of the detection confidence score is 0.6 for both methods. The first two rows show the detection results on the VOC and MS COCO datasets

Fig. 3. Illustration of the detection results. The first and second rows show some improved results of our method (right) over SSD (left) on the VOC, COCO and HollywoodHeads datasets. The last row shows some failure cases of our method.

and next two rows display the results on the HollywoodHeads datasets. Overall, the proposed LTD method can deal with some difficult detection cases such as box-in-box, small objects and occlusion better than the SSD scheme. The last row of Fig. 3 illustrates some failure cases of our method. There are occasional missing detections, inaccurate box localizations and false positives caused by various reasons. The missing and inaccurate detections in the first two images are mainly due to the ambiguous appearance of the objects. In the third failure case, the false positive detection occurs due to the fact that the shape formed by the belt happens to look like a surfboard while the person on top of it and the sea form a reasonable context to support its existence. In the fourth image, the laptop is also detected as a TV due to the similarity between the two classes.

5 Conclusion

In this paper, we present a local top-down module to solve the problems of object detectors with multi-scale features. Although the proposed approach is simple, i.e., only concatenating the features upsampled from the two succeeding convolutional layers with the current prediction layer, it is effective and efficient in achieving performance gain on large datasets based on the SSD method. The proposed LTD module can be applied to other detection frameworks that utilize multi-scale features. Our future work is to incorporate the proposed LTD module into other state-of-the-art object detectors such as RON [8].

Acknowledgements. This work is supported by Natural Science Foundation of Liaoning Province, China, #20170540312.

References

1. Dai, J., Li, Y., He, K., Sun, J.: R-FCN: object detection via region-based fully convolutional networks. In: NIPS, pp. 379–387 (2016)
2. Dvornik, N., Shmelkov, K., Marial, J., Schmid, C.: BlitzNet: a real-time deep network for scene understanding. In: ICCV, pp. 4174–4182 (2017)
3. Fu, C.Y., Liu, W., Ranga, A., Tyagi, A., Berg, A.C.: DSSD: deconvolutional single shot detector. arXiv preprint arXiv: 1701.06659 (2017)
4. He, K., Zhang, X., Ren, S., Sun, J.: Deep residual learning for image recognition. In: CVPR, pp. 770–778 (2016)
5. Howard, A.G., et al.: MobileNets: efficient convolutional neural networks for mobile vision applications. arXiv preprint arXiv: 1704.04861 (2017)
6. Jeong, J., Park, H., Kwak, N.: Enhancement of SSD by concatenating feature maps for object detection. In: BMVC (2017)
7. Simonyan, K., Zisserman, A.: Very deep convolutional networks for large-scale image recognition. In: ICLR (2015)
8. Kong, T., Sun, F., Yao, A., Liu, H., Lu, M., Chen, Y.: RON: reverse connection with objectness prior networks for object detection. In: CVPR, pp. 5244–5252 (2017)
9. Lin, T.Y., Dollár, P., Girshick, R., He, K., Hariharan, B., Belongie, S.: Feature pyramid networks for object detection. In: ICCV, pp. 936–944 (2017)
10. Liu, W., et al.: SSD: Single shot multibox detector. In: Leibe, B., Matas, J., Sebe, N., Welling, M. (eds.) ECCV 2016. LNCS, vol. 9905, pp. 21–37. Springer, Cham (2016). https://doi.org/10.1007/978-3-319-46448-0_2
11. Redmon, J., Divvala, S., Girshick, R., Farhadi, A.: You only look once: unified, real-time object detection. In: CVPR, pp. 779–788 (2016)
12. Redmon, J., Farhadi, X.: YOLO9000: better, faster, stronger. In: CVPR, pp. 6517–6525 (2017)
13. Ren, J., et al.: Accurate single stage detector using recurrent rolling convolution. In: CVPR, pp. 752–760 (2017)
14. Ren, S., He, K., Girshick, R., Sun, J.: Faster R-CNN: towards real-time object detection with region proposal network. In: NIPS, pp. 91–99 (2015)
15. Shrivastava, A., Sukthankar, R., Malik, J., Gupta, A.: Beyond skip connections: top-down modulation for object detection. arXiv preprint arXiv: 1612.06851 (2016)

16. Tychsen-Smith, L., Petersson, L.: Denet: scalable real-time object detection with directed sparse sampling. In: ICCV, pp. 428–436 (2017)
17. Vu, T.H., Osokin, A., Laptev, I.: Contex-aware CNNs for person head detection. In: ICCV, pp. 2893–2901 (2015)
18. Zhang, S., Wen, L., Bian, X., Lei, Z., Li, S.Z.: Single-shot refinement neural network for object detection. In: CVPR (2018)
19. Zhu, Y., Zhao, C., Wang, J., Zhao, X., Wu, Y., Lu, H.: Couplenet: coupling global structure with local parts for object detection. In: ICCV, pp. 4146–4154 (2017)

Parallel Connecting Deep and Shallow CNNs for Simultaneous Detection of Big and Small Objects

Canlong Zhang[1]([✉]), Dongcheng He[1], Zhixin Li[1], and Zhiwen Wang[2]

[1] Guangxi Key Lab of Multi-source Information Mining and Security,
Guangxi Normal University, Guilin, China
zcltyp@163.com
[2] College of Computer Science and Communication Engineering,
Guangxi University of Science and Technology, Liuzhou, China

Abstract. In order to improve the real-time and accuracy of Faster R-CNN (Region based Convolutional Neural Networks) for detecting small object, a novel object detection model is proposed in this paper. Our model not only keeps the detection accuracy for big object, but also improves significantly the accuracy for small object, and with very little reduction in term of detection speed. Firstly, a shallow CNN is designed and connected with an improved deep CNN by using skip-layers connection method, which makes full use of the convolution characteristics with different layers to improve the detection ability for small object; Secondly, the detection accuracy of our model is improved further by incorporating the region proposal mechanism in Faster R-CNN, and using 12 kinds of anchors to generate object candidates; Finally, a dimensional reducer is designed by connecting ROI-Pool layer and 1×1 convolutional layer, which accelerates the detection of overall network. The test results on image datasets PASCAL VOC and MS COCO show that the detection accuracy of our model is higher than some current advanced models, and small objects is significantly improved.

Keywords: Object detection · Convolutional neural networks
Region proposal · Skip-layers connection

1 Introduction

Object detection technology has been widely used in intelligent transportation, road detection and military target detection. With the advent of deep learning and large-scale visual identification datasets, object detection has developed rapidly, among which the two-step object detection framework based on R-CNN [1–4] and one-step object detection framework based on regression [5–7] are the most representative.

Object detection framework based on R-CNN mainly consists of image convolution, region proposal, classification and regression of the region. In 2014,

© Springer Nature Switzerland AG 2018
J.-H. Lai et al. (Eds.): PRCV 2018, LNCS 11259, pp. 78–89, 2018.
https://doi.org/10.1007/978-3-030-03341-5_7

Girshick et al. [1] proposed the object detection framework based R-CNN by combining region proposal with CNN, which opened a new era for object detection with deep learning. After that, around the detection accuracy and speed, many improved versions of the R-CNN model have been proposed, such as, the Fast R-CNN [2] incorporating the ROI-Pool layer and multi-task loss function, the Faster R-CNN [3] incorporating Region Proposal Network (RPN), and the Mask R-CNN [4] cooperating instance segmentation for multitask collaboration. Compared with the traditional method of target detection, the R-CNN methods avoid the subjectivity of the manual feature extraction, and realize the end-to-end object feature extraction and classification.

In view of the two-step object detection be very slow, the one-step object detection method avoids the process of region proposal, and performs the object detection by using regression method directly to output category and bounding box of each regions in the image. The YOLO [5] divides the image into grids, and performs regression computation on those grids to gain category and bounding box of the objects, which boosts the detection speed to 45 fps. The SSD [6] introduces the anchor representation of Faster R-CNN into YOLO to general multi-scale regions at each location in the image, which not only improves greatly the accuracy of detector but also makes the detection speed be up to 58 fps. DSSD [7] fuses the deep convolution layers and the shallow convolution layers by using encode-decode network, which can leverage high-level semantic and low-level image feature, so boosts the detection performance on small object and dense object. Above methods do not require region proposal, so compared to the methods based on R-CNN, their detection speed are faster but the accuracy be lower.

The shortage of above two methods is that the detection accuracy of small objects is poor. Therefore, in this paper, an object detection model based on parallel connection of Deep and Shallow CNN (DS-CNN) is designed via innovative use of skip-layers connection, region proposal and anchors. This model not only keeps the detection accuracy for big object, but also improves significantly the accuracy for small object, and with very little reduction in term of detection speed.

2   DS-CNN

The framework of our detection model is shown in Fig. 1, and it consists of four parts: the first part is the feature extraction network, including deep CNN and shallow CNN; the second part is the region proposal network, which is used to generate object candidates; the third part is dimensional reducer, which is used to reduce the dimension of feature of object candidate; the fourth part is fully-connected (FC) layer, classification and regression network.

2.1   The Design of Deep and Shallow CNN

In general, the deeper the level of convolution is, the more obvious the semantic characteristic is, and the easier it is to classify the object, but the more

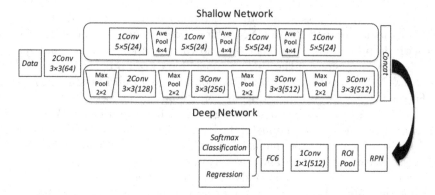

Fig. 1. The framework of DS-CNN. Given an input image, after dealing with two layers of convolutional layers, we use shallow network and deep network to process the feature map into the same size and combine them in the concat layer. The RPN generates 500 region proposals, and then the feature map is processed by the dimensional reducer and fully-connected layer. Finally, we use softmax for classification and multi-task loss function for regression.

information lost. For large-scale objects, this loss is not enough to affect their classification and identification, but it is not the same for small objects. Taking Fast R-CNN [2] as an example, the feature map of last convolutional layer conv5-3 has been reduced by 16 times. For a 500×300 image, the size of the small object is about 32×32, and it becomes 2×2 after conv5-3. Although the upsampling can expand the image to 7×7, the loss of information is irreversible. This is the reason why the series method of R-CNN model has a relatively poor detection accuracy on small objects.

For this purpose, we designed deep CNN and shallow CNN based on the VGG16 network. The deep network is used to capture the high-level semantics of large objects, while the shallow network is used to hold the low-level image features of small objects. In the deep network, the parameters of conv1-1 to pool4 are the same as those of VGG16, but the conv5-1 to conv5-3 layers are all modified using dilated convolution with a pad of 2, a kernel size of 3×3, a stride of 1, and a dilation of 2. Dilated convolution [8] is a common method in the image segmentation, it can expand the receptive field without changing the size of the feature map, and thus contains more global information. The principle is shown in Fig. 2, where (a) is the normal feature map, and (b) is a dilated convolutional map with a dilatation factor of 2. For the 7×7 feature area, the actual convolution kernel size is 3×3 and the hole is 1, that is, the weights of other points except 9 black points are 0. Although there is no change in kernel size compared to (a), the receptive field of this convolution has increased to 7×7, which allows each convolution output to contain more global information.

In the shallow network, it is no longer necessary to capture high-level semantic features of the image, but rather to obtain the low-level image features, so we don't need a very deep network, that is, we don't need to use a large number of

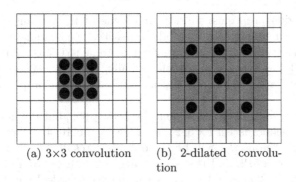

(a) 3×3 convolution   (b) 2-dilated convolution

Fig. 2. Principle of dilated convolution.

convolutional layers. In order to achieve better results for the parallel structure, we use the skip-layers connection method to share the parameters of conv1-1 and conv1-2. Starting from conv2-1, only 4 convolutional layers are used, each of these layers has 24 filters with a kernel size of 5 × 5. In order to make the final deep network and shallow network have the same spatial resolution, we design an average pooling layer with a kernel size of 4 × 4 and a stride of 2 after each convolutional layer in the shallow network. Using average pooling instead of maximum pooling in this model ensures that no excessive image information is lost.

After extracting image features, we need to combine the feature maps of the deep network and the shallow network, and to integrate them into a unified space. In this paper, we employ the concat layer to do it, and the dimension of joint features is 536-d.

2.2 Object Candidate Generation

The number and quality of object candidate region proposals affects directly the speed and accuracy of the object detection. RPN [3] directly generates candidate regions on the convolutional map by using the "anchor". Although RPN is still in the way of window sliding in essence, the detection speed of the whole network is greatly improved because of its regional recommendation, classification and regression sharing the feature of convolution map, so we refer the RPN in the proposed DS-CNN.

RPN scans and convolves the feature maps by using a 3 × 3 sliding window. At the center of 3 × 3 sliding window, we give 4 scales(64, 128, 256, 512) and 3 aspect ratios(1:1, 1:2, 2:1), which can generate 12 different region proposal boxes, i.e., 12 kind of anchor. Thus, for the 14 × 14 feature map, there are about 2300 (14 × 14 × 12) region proposal boxes. After that, all region proposal boxes are sent to the fully connection classification layer and regression layer to classify and refine the region. The classification layer contains two elements for calculating the probability of the target or non-target. The regression layer contains four coordinate elements (x, y, w, h) for determining the target position. In order to obtain valid region proposals, we adjusted some of the parameters and using the non-maximum suppression method to preserve the candidate region whose overlap rate with truth region is greater than or equal to 0.5 as a positive sample, and less than 0.3 as a negative sample. Finally, the first 500 positive samples with highest overlap rate are selected as the final region proposals for object detection.

In RPN, the input image can scale up to 1000×600, but the maximum scale in 12 kinds of anchors is 1024×512, resulting to the 1024 be beyond 1000, so the parts beyond the border will be cut out. As a result, the maximum size of the anchor is 1000×512, and this size is large enough to cover the big object in image. Similarly, 256 and 128 scales can be used to deal with medium-size objects. Because each anchor is single-label detection, large object with obvious feature will cover small object with obscure feature. However, by using the minimum scale 64, we can avoid the small objects to be covered by large objects when detecting small objects, so improve the detection accuracy of small objects.

2.3   Dimensional Reducer

The FC layer can integrate the extracted image features, and plays the role of classification in CNN. Because the FC layer is easy to cause parameter redundancy, many classical methods choose to use other types of layers instead of the FC layer. For example, fully convolutional network uses a convolutional layer instead of FC layer, and ResNet [9] and GoogLeNet [10] all use the global average pooling instead of FC layer. Because our model draws on the classification and regression layer of Fast R-CNN, it cannot completely remove the FC layer. Therefore, in our model, a dimensional reducer is designed to replace one FC layer of VGG16 to reduce parameter redundancy. The dimensional reducer consists of a ROI-Pool layer and a 1×1 convolutional layer. The ROI-Pool layer is able to output a fixed size feature map after the RPN, which is used to compress feature maps in this paper. The convolutional layer with a kernel size of 1×1 and a step size of 1 is behind the ROI-Pool layer, which can not only make the structure more compact, but also reduce the dimension of the feature map. We use dimensional reducer to fix the size of feature maps to 7×7, and to reduce dimension of features from 536 to 512. The compressed features are then input the FC layer. The experimental results show that our structure of dimensional reducer+FC6+Loss is faster than the one of FC6+FC7+Loss in VGG16, and the detection accuracy is also slightly improved.

Similar to the series method of R-CNN, in FC layer, we uses SoftmaxWith-Loss for classification and SmoothL1Loss for regression when training, and uses Softmax for classification when testing.

2.4   Joint Training

Like some advanced models, the DS-CNN can also accept end-to-end training and testing. However, by comparison, we find that the alternate training method can obtain better mAP than end-to-end training method on our model. The main steps of the alternate optimization training are as follows: Firstly, we initialize the feature extraction network with the pre-trained model of ImageNet [11], and gain candidate regions by training the RPN alone on PASCAL VOC. Secondly, we reinitialize the feature extraction network with the pre-trained model of ImageNet, and add the candidate regions generated in the first step. Meanwhile, a separate detection network is trained on the PASCAL VOC dataset using DS-CNN so as to obtain the parameters of convolutional layer through the loss values of the fully-connected layer and the candidate regions of the RPN. Thirdly, we retrain DS-CNN, and use the model obtainded in the second step to initialize and fix the parameters of the convolutional layer so that the convolutional layer does not participate the back propagation, and using the RPN model trained in the first step to initialize and fix the parameters of the RPN in the DS-CNN so that the RPN isn't involved in the back propagation. The total purpose of this step is to connect the feature extraction network with the RPN. Finally, we use the parameters of both convolutional layer and RPN obtained in the third step to reinitialize and fix the DS-CNN model so that both the convolutional layer and the RPN isn't involved in the back propagation. The purpose of training in this step is to fine-tune the fully-connected layer and get the most optimized results.

3   Experimental Evaluation

PASCAL VOC [12] and MS COCO [17] are two used widely datasets in the object detection field, and are used to evaluate our DS-CNN. The mAP is used as the main evaluation criterion, and the convergence and detect speed of model are used as two auxiliary evaluation criteria. We also compare our model with state-of-the-art models, and they all use VGG16. All experimental results are obtained by running these models on a PC with Intel Core i7-7700K 4.20 GHz CPU, GeForce GTX 1080Ti GPU, and 16 GB RAM.

3.1   Experiments on PASCAL VOC

The PASCAL VOC 2007 dataset includes 20 object categories, about 5k training images and 5k testing images, and the PASCAL VOC 2012 dataset is similar to PASCAL VOC 2007, but the volume of data has doubled. Small objects of PASCAL VOC dataset are mostly indoor, including bottle, chair, dining table, potted plant, sofa, and tv.

In the first experiment, we use alternate training method to train our DS-CNN on the training dataset of PASCAL VOC 2007, and test the model on the testing dataset of PASCAL VOC 2007. Experimental results are shown in Table 1, where the bold fonts, such as **bottle, chair**, are small objects. From the table, we can observe that the mAP of DS-CNN is 72.1%, which is higher than other models. For small objects, the detection accuracy of our model is significantly improved, where the bottle and plant is the most obvious. Although the accuracy of tv is lower than OHEM+FRCN [14], it is also 3.2% better than Faster R-CNN. However, the detection results on larger objects seem to be unstable, but we notice that most of them can maintain a high accuracy. In order to express object detection results more intuitively, Fig. 3 shows some examples of results on the PASCAL VOC 2007 dataset.

Table 1. The average detection precision (%) of all models on PASCAL VOC 2007, where the training dataset is from PASCAL VOC 2007, and the best score is highlighted in red color.

	mAP	areo	bike	bird	boat	bottle	bus	car	cat	chair	cow
FRCN [2]	66.9	74.5	78.3	69.2	53.2	36.6	77.3	78.2	82.0	40.7	72.7
Faster R-CNN	69.9	70.0	80.6	70.1	57.3	49.9	78.2	80.4	82.0	52.2	75.3
locNET [13]	65.4	70.7	74.2	62.2	48.1	45.2	84.0	74.7	78.6	42.9	73.0
OHEM+FRCN	69.9	71.2	78.3	69.2	57.9	46.5	81.8	79.1	83.2	47.9	76.2
DS-CNN	72.1	71.8	82.3	71.1	58.4	51.3	80.1	82.8	82.5	53.1	78.8
	table	dog	horse	motor	person	**plant**	sheep	**sofa**	train	**tv**	
FRCN [2]	67.9	79.6	79.2	73.0	69.0	30.1	65.4	70.2	75.8	65.8	
Faster R-CNN	67.2	80.3	79.8	75.0	76.3	39.1	68.3	67.3	81.1	67.6	
locNET [13]	67.0	75.4	77.9	66.9	58.1	30.9	65.5	69.3	73.6	69.0	
OHEM+FRCN	68.9	83.2	80.8	75.8	72.7	39.9	67.5	66.2	75.6	75.9	
DS-CNN	69.1	80.5	82.2	79.9	81.5	45.1	71.2	70.2	79.9	70.8	

In order to eliminate the interference caused by the insufficiency of the dataset, we designed the second experiment. Similarly to the first experiment, we still used the testing dataset of PASCAL VOC 2007 for testing, but the training dataset were from PASCAL VOC 2007+2012, by which the volume of training dataset was expanded to three times of the first experiment. The experimental results are shown in Table 2. It is easy to see that the mAP of DS-CNN is 75.8%. Similar to our method, SSD500 also parallel connects the convolution features from different layers. However, its features all are from high-level instead of low-level layers, so the features of small objects cannot be effectively extracted and trained. On the contrary, in our model, the shallow network and the average pooling layer are used to preserve the information of small objects, and the scale 64 is used to enhance the detection of small objects in the RPN, so the DS-CNN performs better than SSD on the detection of small objects. However, SSD enhances the combination of different convolutional layers, uses data augments, and abandons the fully-connected layers and candidate region generating, so the overall performance of object detection is better than DS-CNN. In structure, DS-CNN is similar to Faster R-CNN, and also draws on RPN of Faster R-CNN, so there is a high comparability between them. The accuracy of DS-CNN is higher than that of Faster R-CNN on all objects except boat, where the detection accuracy on small objects is increased significantly, which demonstrates the effectiveness of DS-CNN.

In order to illustrate that our model can also achieve good results in different datasets, we design the third experiment. In this experiment, the training dataset

Fig. 3. Some elected examples of object detection results on the PASCAL VOC 2007

Table 2. The average detection precision (%) of all models on testing dataset of PASCAL VOC 2007, where the training dataset is from PASCAL VOC 2007+2012, and the best score is highlighted in red color.

	mAP	areo	bike	bird	boat	bottle	bus	car	cat	chair	cow
FRCN	70.0	77.0	78.1	69.3	59.4	38.3	81.6	78.6	86.7	42.8	78.8
Faster R-CNN	73.2	76.5	79.0	70.9	65.5	52.1	83.1	84.7	86.4	52.0	81.9
Noc [15]	73.3	76.3	81.4	74.4	61.7	60.8	84.7	78.2	82.9	53.0	79.2
SSD500	75.1	79.8	79.5	74.5	63.4	51.9	84.9	85.6	87.2	56.6	80.1
DS-CNN	75.8	76.9	80.4	75.3	65.3	60.8	85.4	85.7	88.2	60.4	82.7
	table	dog	horse	motor	person	plant	sheep	sofa	train	tv	
FRCN	68.9	84.7	82.0	76.6	69.9	31.8	70.1	74.8	80.4	70.4	
Faster R-CNN	65.7	84.8	84.6	77.5	76.7	38.8	73.6	73.9	83.0	72.6	
Noc [15]	69.2	83.2	83.2	78.5	68.0	45.0	71.6	76.7	82.2	75.7	
SSD500	70.0	85.4	84.9	80.9	78.2	49.0	78.4	72.4	84.6	75.5	
DS-CNN	70.3	85.1	85.8	78.8	79.2	45.6	76.1	76.8	84.2	74.3	

consists of training dataset of PASCAL VOC 2007+2012 and testing dataset of PASCAL VOC 2007, and testing dataset is from testing dataset of PASCAL VOC 2012. We also compare DS-CNN with FRCN+YOLO [5] and HyperNet [16], and the experimental results are illustrated in Table 3. It is easy to see that our model not only keeps the high detection accuracy for big object, but also improves significantly the detection accuracy for small object, and with very little reduction in detection speed.

Table 3. The average detection precision (%) of all models on testing dataset of PASCAL VOC 2012, where the training dataset is from PASCAL VOC 2007+2012, and the best score is highlighted in red color.

	mAP	areo	bike	bird	boat	**bottle**	bus	car	cat	**chair**	cow
Faster R-CNN	70.4	84.9	79.8	74.3	53.9	49.8	77.5	75.9	88.5	45.6	77.1
FRCN+YOLO	70.4	83.0	78.5	73.7	55.8	43.1	78.3	73.0	89.2	49.1	74.3
HyperNet	71.4	84.2	78.5	73.6	55.6	53.7	78.7	79.8	87.7	49.6	74.9
OHEM+FRCN	71.9	83.0	81.3	72.5	55.6	49.0	78.9	74.7	89.5	52.3	75.0
DS-CNN	73.1	82.7	81.1	73.9	55.9	53.7	80.0	76.1	89.8	54.9	76.6
		table	dog	horse	motor	person	**plant**	sheep	**sofa**	train	**tv**
Faster R-CNN		55.3	86.9	81.7	80.9	79.6	40.1	72.6	60.9	81.2	61.5
FRCN+YOLO		56.6	87.2	80.5	80.5	74.7	42.1	70.8	68.3	81.5	67.0
HyperNet		52.1	86.0	81.7	83.3	81.8	48.6	73.5	59.4	79.9	65.7
OHEM+FRCN		61.0	87.9	80.9	82.4	76.3	47.1	72.5	67.3	80.6	71.2
DS-CNN		62.2	89.5	81.8	83.9	79.8	48.6	73.6	68.5	81.5	69.4

3.2 Experiments on MS COCO

The MS COCO dataset is more complex than PASCAL VOC, and contains 80 object categories, about 80k images on the training set and 40k images on the validation set. Especially, the dataset has many small objects, so is very suitable for evaluating DS-CNN. We use the end-to-end training method, and set the basic learning rate be 0.001 and the learning strategy be 'step'. The total iteration step is 490k, and the learning rate is reduced to 0.0001 after 350k iterations. We calculate the mAP@IoU$\in$[0.5:0.05:0.95] (COCO's standard metric) and mAP@0.50 (PASCAL VOC's metric). Experimental results are shown in Table 4. It can be seen that our model has 23.1% mAP on the COCO metric and 43.6% mAP on the VOC metric. It is also interesting to notice that our model performs well on the detection of small and medium objects, and its mAP reaches 6.3% and 25.4% respectively. However, its performance on the large objects seem to be mediocre.

Table 4. MS COCO 2015 test-dev detection average precision (%). All methods use VGG16, and area infers to the size of object.

	Area	FRCN	OHEM	DS-CNN
mAP@[0.50:0.95]	All	19.7	22.6	23.1
mAP@0.50	All	35.9	42.5	43.6
mAP@[0.50:0.95]	Small	3.5	5.0	6.3
mAP@[0.50:0.95]	Medium	18.8	23.7	25.4
mAP@[0.50:0.95]	Large	34.9	37.9	36.3

3.3   Combine from Which Layers?

When using the skip-layers connection method, we need to consider which layers be combined can get the best detection result. For example, the combination of conv3+conv4 +conv5 is the best in ION [18], while the combination of conv1+conv3+conv5 is the best in HyperNet [16]. We give different combinations of cov1, cov2, cov3 and cov5, and use the end-to-end method to train and test each combination on the PASCAL VOC 2007 dataset. The experimental results are shown in Table 5. We found it is no true that the more the number of layers is, the higher the accuracy is, and the best combination is conv1+conv5.

Table 5. The detection accuracy of different combinations of multiple layers.

layers	data+5	1 + 5	2+5	3+5	1+2+5	1+3+5
mAP	69.7%	71.4%	70.8%	69.4%	70.2%	68.6%

3.4   The Evaluation of Speed

Detection speed and convergence speed are two important indexes for evaluating the performance of an object detection model. We compare the DS-CNN with Faster R-CNN on PASCAL VOC 2007. For fair comparison, we also set the number of final candidate regions in Faster R-CNN to 500, and run two models on our PC. We collected each detection time of the model, and averaged all detection times. The detection speed of DS-CNN was about 12 fps, while Faster R-CNN was about 14 fps. In fact, this is an expected result, because DS-CNN consumes more time than Faster R-CNN in feature extraction. However, the difference between 12 and 14 is very little, so the speed has also met our standard: the detection speed has little reduction.

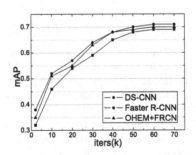

Fig. 4. The mAP at different iterations.

We also used the end-to-end training and testing method to evaluate the convergence speeds of two models on PASCAL VOC 2007 dataset, and recorded the mAPs of intermediate models with different iterations before generating the final models. The comparison result is shown in Fig. 4. It is easy to see that the two models all had converged when iterating 70k times, and the mAP of DS-CNN is 71.4% while Faster R-CNN is 69.5%. DS-CNN has a faster convergence speed than Faster R-CNN, because it is about 6% higher than Faster R-CNN when iterating 2k times, and it starts to converge after 50k iterations.

4   Conclusions

We designed a new object detection model based on R-CNN. Firstly, we used dilated convolution to design deep neural networks and shallow neural networks, and used skip-layers connection method to connect the two networks. Secondly, we used the RPN to generate object candidates. Thirdly, we designed a dimensional reducer to reduce the dimension of feature maps. Finally, the model output the results of classification and regression. The experimental results illustrated that our model not only keeps the detection accuracy for big object, but also improves significantly the detection accuracy for small object, and with very little reduction in detection speed. However, many more advanced structures cannot be applied to our model due to the limitations of the VGG16 and Fast R-CNN frameworks. In the future, we will research more advanced image feature extraction methods to further improve the accuracy and speed of object detection.

Acknowledgments. The authors would like to thank the anonymous reviewers for their constructive comments. This work was supported by the National Natural Science Foundation of China (Grant nos. 61866004, 61663004, 61462008, 61751213), the Natural Science Foundation of Guangxi Province (Grant nos. 2017GXNSFAA198365, 2016GXNSFAA380146), the Scientific Research and Technology Development Project of Liuzhou (Grant no. 2016C050205), and Guangxi Collaborative Innovation Center of Multisource Information Integration and Intelligent Processing.

References

1. Girshick, R., Donahue, J., Darrell, T, Malik, J.: Rich feature hierarchies for accurate object detection and semantic segmentation. In: IEEE Conference on Computer Vision and Pattern Recognition, pp. 580–587 (2014)
2. Girshick, R.: Fast R-CNN. In: IEEE International Conference on Computer Vision, pp. 1440–1448 (2015)
3. Ren, S., He, K., Girshick, R., Sun, J.: Faster R-CNN: towards real-time object detection with region proposal networks. In: International Conference on Neural Information Processing Systems, pp. 91–99 (2015)
4. He, K., Gkioxari, G., Dollár, P., Girshick, R.: Mask R-CNN. In: IEEE International Conference on Computer Vision, pp. 2980–2988 (2017)
5. Redmon, J., Divvala, S., Girshick, R., Farhadi, A.: You only look once: unified, real-time object detection. In: IEEE Conference on Computer Vision and Pattern Recognition, pp. 779–788 (2016)

6. Liu, W., Anguelov, D., Erhan, D., Szegedy, C., Reed, S., Fu, C.-Y., Berg, A.C.: SSD: single shot multibox detector. In: Leibe, B., Matas, J., Sebe, N., Welling, M. (eds.) ECCV 2016. LNCS, vol. 9905, pp. 21–37. Springer, Cham (2016). https://doi.org/10.1007/978-3-319-46448-0_2

7. Fu, C.Y., Liu, W., Ranga, A., Tyagi, A., Berg, A.C.: DSSD : Deconvolutional single shot detector (2017)

8. Yu, F., Koltun, V.: Multi-scale context aggregation by dilated convolutions (2015)

9. He, K., Zhang, X., Ren, S., Sun, J.: Deep residual learning for image recognition, pp. 770–778 (2015)

10. Szegedy, C., et al.: Going deeper with convolutions, pp. 1–9 (2014)

11. Russakovsky, O., et al.: Imagenet large scale visual recognition challenge. Int. J. Comput. Vis. **115**(3), 211–252 (2014)

12. Everingham, M., Eslami, S.A., Van Gool, L., Williams, C.K., Winn, J., Zisserman, A.: The pascal visual object classes challenge: a retrospective. Int. J. Comput. Vis. **111**(1), 98–136 (2015)

13. Gidaris, S., Komodakis, N.: LocNet: improving localization accuracy for object detection, vol. 766–767, no. 121, pp. 789–798 (2015)

14. Shrivastava, A., Gupta, A., Girshick, R.: Training region-based object detectors with online hard example mining, pp. 761–769 (2016)

15. Ren, S., He, K., Girshick, R., Zhang, X., Sun, J.: Object detection networks on convolutional feature maps. IEEE Trans. Pattern Anal. Mach. Intell. **39**(7), 1476–1481 (2016)

16. Kong, T., Yao, A., Chen, Y., Sun, F.: Hypernet: towards accurate region proposal generation and joint object detection. In: Computer Vision and Pattern Recognition, pp. 845–853 (2016)

17. Lin, T.-Y., Maire, M., Belongie, S., Hays, J., Perona, P., Ramanan, D., Dollár, P., Zitnick, C.L.: Microsoft COCO: common objects in context. In: Fleet, D., Pajdla, T., Schiele, B., Tuytelaars, T. (eds.) ECCV 2014. LNCS, vol. 8693, pp. 740–755. Springer, Cham (2014). https://doi.org/10.1007/978-3-319-10602-1_48

18. Bell, S., Lawrence Zitnick, C., Bala, K., Girshick, R.: Inside-outside net: detecting objects in con-text with skip pooling and recurrent neural networks, pp. 2874–2883 (2015)

Penalty Non-maximum Suppression
in Object Detection

Wenqing Zhao$^{(\boxtimes)}$ and Hai Yan

North China Electric Power University, Baoding 071003, China
jbzwq@126.com

Abstract. As a post-processing step, Non-Maximum Suppression (NMS) is always used to obtain final detection boxes. It suppresses all detection boxes which have a higher intersection-over-union (IoU) overlap than threshold T with pre-selected detection box p with the maximum score in each iteration. However, it removes the positive object, if the positive object is adjacent to p with a higher IoU. To overcome these shortages, we propose Penalty-NMS method which according to the different overlap to assign penalty coefficient to decay detections scores. In this process, we will not eliminate any detection boxes. And we keep all detection boxes temporarily until the detections with lower score will be eliminated after many rounds of iteration. Our method obtains significant improvements on standard datasets like PASCAL VOC (1.9% for Faster RCNN) and MS COCO (1.6% for R-FCN and 1.8% for Faster RCNN) without any additional computational and parameters.

Keywords: Non-Maximum suppression · Detection boxes · Penalty coefficient
Intersection-over-union

1 Introduction

Object detection has always been a popular research topic in the field of computer vision. In the past decade, traditional methods [26–28] have reached the bottleneck and the accuracy is also not satisfying. However, owing to the image recognition which is based on Convolutional Neural Network, has fulfilled remarkable achievements, thus in the basis of the development of network, [3] has successfully made remarkable progress by introducing Convolutional Neural Network into object detection. Subsequently, many methods [1–3, 7, 32–34] based on the idea of [3] have significantly improved in the part of accuracy and speed. At the meantime, many current object detection pipelines due to the deep learning can be divided into three stages as follows: (1) extracts region proposals, (2) classifies and refines each region proposal, and (3) removes extra detection boxes that might belong to the same object. NMS is frequently used in Stage (3) as an essential part of object detection and obtains impressive effect in [1–3, 7, 8]. However, traditional NMS algorithm suppresses any detection box which exceeds the threshold T. That is, it removes detection boxes which have a IoU of pre-selected detection p exceed the given threshold T. Average precision would drop as a result of the missing positives, thus, traditional NMS could also be named as GreedyNMS. The current state-of-the-art object detection Faster RCNN

J.-H. Lai et al. (Eds.): PRCV 2018, LNCS 11259, pp. 90–102, 2018.
https://doi.org/10.1007/978-3-030-03341-5_8

based on ImageNet model [10–12] extracts feature maps and generates many region proposals by Region Proposal Network(RPN) [2]. Then it uses GreedyNMS to get final detections.

For any IoU threshold, GreedyNMS always tradeoffs between recall and precision. This paper is devoted to solving the problem which leads to a miss due to the setting of the threshold T. As a post-processing step, GreedyNMS aims to remove redundant detections. When we solve its defects, we should not add any additional computation or parameters. [9] proposed Tyrolean network (Tnet) to rescore all detections, then the network can choose the best detection. Although this method improves detection performance, it also adds extra training.

Static images which are addressed by stage (1) and (2) will generate multiple detection boxes (denoted as set P), each detection box attaches a corresponding detection score (denoted as set C). GreedyNMS selects the detection box p with the highest score in the set P, removes p from set P and appends it to set K (final detection boxes set). Then it calculates the IoU of p with the rest detection boxes, suppressing all detections in which the IoU is higher than threshold T. At last, repetitively executing the remaining detection boxes with the same procedures, then T plays an essential role in object detection. When we selected a lower threshold T, the object which has a IoU higher than T would be missed. Instead, when we select a larger threshold T, it would generate more false positives which will lead to a drop in average precision. Hence, GreedyNMS always compromises between recall and precision. For this purpose, we propose Penalty Non-maximum suppression (Penalty-NMS) which penalizes all detection boxes except detection box which has the highest score in each iteration. Owing to the different overlap values, assigning penalty coefficient to reduce the detection boxes score without using threshold T. In comparison with the box in which the GreedyNMS suppression is greater than the threshold T, we'd like to use the quadratic function to calculate the penalty coefficient to reduce detection score which has different overlap values. Penalty-NMS obtains significant improvements in average precision for Faster RCNN and R-FCN on standard datasets like PASCAL VOC and MS COCO.

2 Related Work

Although the NMS algorithm is a core part of object detection, Numerous studies have focused on feature design, classifier design, and object proposals in the past. Surprisingly, Few studies on the NMS algorithms exist.

NMS was first employed in edge detection which is performed edge thinning to remove spurious responses [35]. Subsequently, it has been applied to face detection [29] and object detection [16]. [16] demonstrated that a greedy NMS algorithm, where a detection box with the maximum score is selected and its neighboring boxes are suppressed using a threshold improves performance over the approach used for face detection [29]. Since then, greedy NMS has been the de-facto algorithm used in object detection [1–3, 7, 24, 32].

For clustering detections, principled clustering formulation has been proposed in [15, 16] which obtain good performance for object class detection. Several other clustering algorithms have been explored for the task of NMS: mean-shift clustering [16], agglomerative clustering [17] and affinity propagation clustering [18]. However, they have yet to surpass the performance of GreedyNMS. To link convnets and NMS [26], directly generates a sparse set of detections by training an LSTM that NMS is unnecessary. [21] designs a convnet that combines decisions of GreedyNMS with different overlap thresholds, allowing the network to choose the GreedyNMS operating point locally. [20] proposed a proposal subset optimization algorithm for detecting salient objects as an alternative to NMS. [22] has proposed a true end-to-end learning algorithm which makes the classifier aware of the NMS procedure at test time by including GreedyNMS at training time. [23] operates on graphs, but requires a preprocessing that defines a node ordering. [4, 30] tend to produce fewer spread-out double detections and improve overall detection quality. [19, 24] propose to detect pairs of objects instead of each individual objects in order to handle strong occlusion. But there is a problem that single and double detections need to be handled.

In summary, most of the proposed algorithms can replace GreedyNMS. However, we find that GreedyNMS still obtain the greatest performance for generic object detection. [21] has obtain better results which is capable of performing NMS without being given a set of suppression alternatives to choose from and without having another final suppression step. But an additional deep network with vast parameters and Computation is required. [25] proposed Soft-NMS that Our algorithm is similar to it but does not add any parameters.

Although the traditional NMS algorithm can obtain better performance in several generations of detector [1–3, 13, 14], it is still a greedy algorithm with obvious defects. This paper aims to improve the NMS algorithm without any additional parameters or computation.

3   Penalty-NMS

This section is divided into two parts. First of all, we review the details of the traditional NMS (i.e. GreedyNMS) and analyze the shortcomings of GreedyNMS as a postprocessing in object detection. Then we introduce Penalty-NMS which is proposed in this paper in detail.

3.1   GreedyNMS

When a test image passes the detection system without post-processing, multiple detections are generated around each object. However, each object only needs one detection box. Therefore, GreedyNMS is used as a post-processing to eliminate redundant detection boxes. GreedyNMS process is as follows:

1. Detection boxes set $p\{p_1, p_2 \cdots p_n\}$ and the corresponding scores set $C\{c_1, c_2 \ldots c_n\}$.
2. Choose the detection box p_{max} which has a maximum score and merge it into set K (the final detection boxes set). Then remove p_{max} from set P and calculate the IOU overlap of the remaining detections with p_{max}.

3. Set the threshold T. Remove all detections which have a IoU overlap that is greater than T from set P.
4. Repeat steps 2 and 3 until set P is empty.

Threshold T in step 3 has a decisive influence on the final result of the entire detection system. However, it's hard for us to find a suitable value.

3.2   Penalty-NMS

The neighbor detection boxes have a higher likelihood of detecting the same object. However, GreedyNMS always falls into local optimal, since it removes all the detection boxes which have a IoU overlap that is greater than threshold T. Unlike GreedyNMS, we penalize all detection boxes that should be suppressed in GreedyNMS in **Piecewise Penalty-NMS** or penalize all detection boxes regardless of whether they have an overlap with detection box p in **Continuous Penalty-NMS**. The detection boxes with lower scores are removed after multiple penalties.

(Piecewise Penalty-NMS). As it is shown in Eq. (1), Piecewise Penalty-NMS penalizes any detection which has a higher IoU than T and the detection boxes with a IoU less than T keep its original score. The penalty coefficient is $\beta(1 - overlap^2)$.

$$\mu_i = \begin{cases} 1, & overlap < T \\ \beta(1 - overlap^2), & overlap \geq T \end{cases} \tag{1}$$

Here μ_i is the penalty coefficient for detection box i, overlap ($0 \leq overlap \leq 1$) is the IoU overlap of the detection box p_i with the pre-selected detection box, β ($\beta > 0$) is the regulatory factor.

In Eq. (1) we change the score of the detection boxes which have a IoU overlap is greater than threshold T in GreedyNMS from 0 to $\beta(1 - overlap^2)$ · confidence(detection boxes' score). Therefore, we can regard GreedyNMS as a special form of Piecewise Penalty-NMS. As we have analyzed in Sect. 3.1, there are always some positive objects which are missed in GreedyNMS. So penalizing detections to decay the scores seems to be a better approach. Eq. (1) decreases the scores of the detection boxes whose IoU overlap is greater than threshold T. However, the Piecewise Penalty-NMS still needs to set threshold T manually. The performance of the algorithm is still limited by the threshold T.

(Continuous Penalty-NMS). Continuous Penalty-NMS algorithm is shown in Fig. 3. The penalty coefficient is shown in Eqs. (2) and (3). In Continuous Penalty-NMS, we no longer use threshold T, but directly penalize all detection boxes. In Eqs. (2) and (3), the growth of penalty has the opposite change. In the following sections, Continuous Penalty-NMS$_1$ and Continuous Penalty-NMS$_2$ correspond to Eqs. (2) and (3) respectively.

$$\mu_i = \beta\left(1 - overlap^2\right) \tag{2}$$

$$\mu_i = \beta(overlap - 1)^2 \tag{3}$$

In Sect. 3.1, we have analyzed the performance of the traditional NMS which is strictly limited by the threshold T. Piecewise Penalty-NMS is a better way to improve the performance of GreedyNMS algorithm, but it's still unable to get rid of the threshold T. Therefore, we further propose Continuous Penalty-NMS which is different from [25] that does not penalize detection boxes with no overlap. Instead, Continuous Penalty-NMS penalizes all detections except detection box with maximum score in each iteration.

Quadratic functions are used as the penalty coefficients in this paper. The first derivative of Eqs. (1) and (2) is $-2\beta \cdot overlap$ and the first derivative of Eq. (3) is $2\beta(overlap - 1)$. All of them are less than 0. Therefore, the penalty coefficient becomes smaller as the value of IoU becomes higher to decay the score of detection box. The second derivative of Eqs. (1) and (2) are both less than 0 that are convex function. Equation (3) is opposite to it but is the same as Gaussian function which is presented in [25]. The growth proportion of Penalty in Eq. (2) increases as the IoU overlap increases. However, the growth proportion of Penalty in Eq. (3) decreases as the IoU overlap increases.

Penalty-NMS algorithm is used in each iteration and removes detections whose scores are less than σ. Compared with the influence of the threshold T in GreedyNMS, the parameter β and σ in Penalty-NMS is less sensitive to the performance of the algorithm. We can also set β to 1.0 which means that our algorithm does not add any parameters. Besides, the computational complexity for Penalty-NMS is $O(n^2)$ which is the same as GreedyNMS, the n is the number of detection boxes. Although Penalty-NMS algorithm does not get the global optimal solution, compared with GreedyNMS algorithm, a better sub-optimal global solution is obtained without any additional computation and can be easily embedded in any detection system (Fig. 1).

4   Experiment

4.1   Experiment on PASCAL VOC

Our experiment is based on Faster RCNN on PASCAL VOC [4] that has 20 object categories and the basic network is VGG16 [11]. We train the models on the union set of VOC 2007 *trainval* and evaluate on VOC 2007 *test* set. Object detection accuracy is measured by mean Average Precision (mAP). In this section, we analyze and compare the performance of Piecewise Penalty-NMS, Continuous Penalty-NMS$_1$, Continuous Penalty-NMS$_2$ and traditional NMS algorithm. We also analyze the sensitivity of parameters β and σ.

(Penalty-NMS Performance Analysis). In Table 1, we analyze the changes of mAP values at different threshold T by GreedyNMS and Piecewise Penalty-NMS. We also compare the performance of Piecewise Penalty-NMS at different values of β.

Penalty-NMS: $\mathcal{P}$ is the set of detections

        K is the set of the final detections

        S is the set of the scores

        μ_i is the penalty coefficient of detection box i

        c_i is the score of detection box i, σ is the lowest score.

while $\mathcal{P} \neq \emptyset$:

    $p_m = maximum(\mathcal{P})$

    $K = K \cup p_m$

    $\mathcal{P} = \mathcal{P} - p_m$

    for p_i in $\mathcal{P}$:

        $c_i = \mu_i c_i$ ---------   Continuous Penalty-NMS

        if overlap > T:

            $c_i = \mu_i c_i$ ---------   Piecewise Penalty-NMS

        else:

            $c_i = c_i$

    if $c_i < \sigma$

        $\mathcal{P} = \mathcal{P} - p_i$

return K, S

Fig. 1. The pseudo code for Penalty-NMS algorithm

Table 1 shows that when the threshold T is 0.3 or 0.4, compared with GreedyNMS, Piecewise Penalty-NMS has a significant improvement up to 1.9%(higher than [25]) in mAP. Although Piecewise Penalty-NMS adds a parameter β, analyzing the red box in Table 1, we can see that the different values of β has no significant distinction in mAP. The fluctuation range is only 0–0.7%. The blue box in Table 1 shows that Piecewise Penalty-NMS does not obtain any performance improvement when the threshold T $\geq$ 0.5. We analyze the main reason for this situation is that the positive detections which should be suppressed is directly kept. The effect is similar to our algorithm when we set higher threshold. However, this growth of positive is much less than the growth of false positive, which leads a drop in average precision.

Table 1. Results on PASCAL VOC 2007 test set, PPenalty-NMS denotes Piecewise Penalty-NMS. 0.5, 0.6, 0.7, 0.8 denotes the value of β

NMS	T				
	0.3	0.4	0.5	0.6	0.7
GreedyNMS	69.6	**70.0**	69.2	64.6	56.4
PPenalty-NMS$_{0.5}$	71.5	71.1	69.0	64.7	56.5
PPenalty-NMS$_{0.6}$	**71.9**	71.2	68.8	64.1	56.6
PPenalty-NMS$_{0.7}$	71.5	71.4	68.6	64.8	56.3
PPenalty-NMS$_{0.8}$	71.2	71.4	68.9	64.7	56.5

Table 2 shows that Continuous Penalty-NMS$_1$ and Continuous Penalty-NMS$_2$ algorithm still obtain significant improvement without using threshold T. The highest growth reached 1.9% and 1.8% respectively which are Equal to Piecewise Penalty-NMS. Empirically, the detection boxes with higher overlap should be penalized more. The growth proportion of Penalty in Eq. (2) increases as the IoU increases. However, the growth proportion of Penalty in Eq. (3) decreases as the IoU increases. As parameter β changes, although Penalty-NMS$_1$ and Continuous Penalty-NMS$_2$ are two different modes of penal growth, both of them obtain similar improvement. Therefore, the growth mode of penalty is not the key factor which can affect the performance of the algorithm. In Table 2, row 4 and 5 show that the value of mAP decreases continuously as the threshold T increases. Compared with Continuous Penalty-NMS1 and Continuous Penalty-NMS2 whose ranges of variation are from 0.3% to 0.8%, the performance of the traditional NMS is totally depended on the setting of threshold T.

Table 2. Results on PASCAL VOC 2007 test set, CPenalty-NMS$_1$ denotes Continuous Penalty-NMS$_1$, CPenalty-NMS$_2$ denotes Continuous Penalty-NMS$_2$.

NMS	β							
	0.3	0.4	0.5	0.6	0.7	0.8	0.9	1.0
CPenalty-NMS$_1$	71.6	71.5	71.3	**71.9**	71.4	71.2	71.4	71.1
CPenalty-NMS$_2$	71.4	71.1	71.1	71.5	71.5	71.4	71.1	**71.8**
T		0.3	0.4	0.5	0.6	0.7	0.8	0.9	1.0
GreedyNMS		69.6	**70.0**	69.2	64.6	56.4	42.9	–	–

(Sensitivity Analysis). The function of the parameter σ is the same as the threshold T in GreedyNMS. But its effect on the performance of the algorithm is far less than T. As shown in Fig. 4, Piecewise Penalty-NMS$_1$ and Continuous Penalty-NMS$_2$ obtain better performance from a range between 0.001 to 0.004. The mAP for Piecewise Penalty-NMS (β = 0.6, T = 0.3) are maintained at 71.4%–71.9%. Likewise, Continuous Penalty-NMS$_1$ (β = 0.6) also stays at 71.6%–71.9%. The fluctuation range is kept within 0.5% and less than the GreedyNMS (Fig. 2).

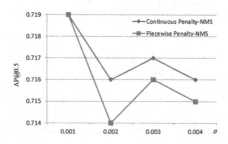

Fig. 2. Sensitivity Analysis to parameter σ

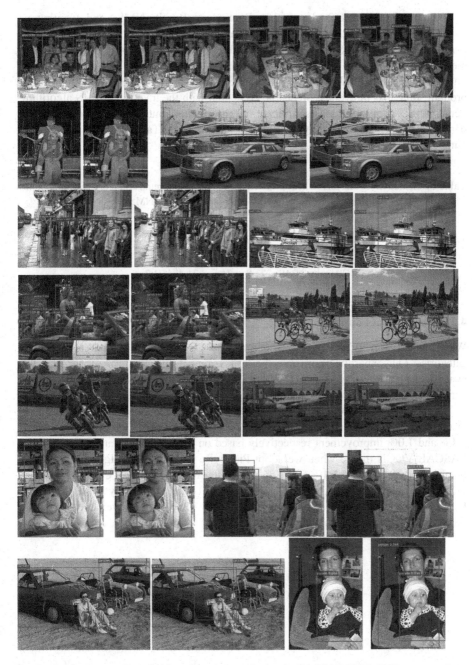

Fig. 3. Selected examples of object detection results on the PASCAL VOC 2007 test set using the Faster R-CNN system. The model is VGG-16 and the training data is 07 trainval. Left for NMS algorithm and right for Continuous Penalty-NMS1 algorithm.

Column 9 of Table 2 shows that Continuous Penalty-NMS$_1$ and Continuous Penalty-NMS$_2$ reach 71.1% and 71.8% respectively which also obtain better performance than GreedyNMS. So we have a further experiment that sets β to 1.0, which means that we also no longer use parameter β. In Table 3, we still obtain a better improvement by 1.0%–1.8%, when the range is from 0.001 to 0.004. Although it has brought some loss in average precision, compared with the traditional NMS algorithm, Penalty-NMS not only has significant improvements, but also is freer to select parameter σ, which has a slight influence on accuracy. Table 4 show the detailed numbers.

Table 3. Sensitivity Analysis when β is equal to 1.0. Continuous Penalty-NMS$_1$ denotes CPenalty-NMS$_1$ and Continuous Penalty-NMS$_2$ denotes CPenalty-NMS$_2$.

NMS	σ			
	0.001	0.002	0.003	0.004
CPenalty-NMS$_1$	71.1	71.2	**71.0**	71.1
CPenalty-NMS$_2$	**71.8**	71.6	71.4	71.3

4.2 Experiments on MS COCO

We evaluate Faster RCNN and R-FCN on the MS COCO dataset [5] that has 80 object categories. Our experiments involve the 80 k *train* set and 40 k *val* set for test. We evaluate the mAP average for IoU ∈ [0.5:0.05:0.95] (COCO's standard metric, simply denoted as mAP@[0.5, 0.95]) and mAP@0.5 (PASCAL VOC's metric).

The results are in Table 5. R-FCN [24] with single-scale trained baseline has a *val* result of 48.9%/27.6% and Faster RCNN has a baseline 48.4%/27.2%. R-FCN obtained 1.1% and 1.0% improvement respectively based on MS COCO's standard metric and PASCAL VOC's metric when we adopt Piecewise Penalty-NMS algorithm. We also obtain improvements of 1.4% and 1.3% for Faster RCNN. For MS COCO's standard metric we obtain an improvement of 1.6% and 1.8% respectively for R-FCN and Faster RCNN which are higher than Soft-NMS [25]'s improvements 1.1% for Faster RCNN and 1.3% for R-FCN.

Table 4. Results on PASCAL VOC 2007 test set with Faster R-CNN detectors and VGG-16

method	mAP	areo	bike	bird	boat	bottle	bus	car	cat	chair	cow	table	dog	horse	mbike	person	plant	sheep	sofa	train	tv
GreedyNMS	70.0	68.8	78.7	69.3	51.5	54.2	81.3	80.1	83.9	50.0	77.1	64.7	83.7	83.4	76.1	77.0	38.4	68.7	64.9	75.1	73.4
Soft-NMS [25] -L	71.2	71.4	81.4	70.5	54.6	52.9	77.6	82.1	83.4	51.8	78.9	66.7	81.2	82.1	78.9	79.7	39.5	71.7	64.4	79.2	75.2
Soft-NMS [25] -G	71.2	71.3	80.7	70.9	54.9	53.0	78.2	81.9	83.8	51.9	78.6	67.1	80.1	81.9	79.4	80.0	39.7	71.8	64.6	78.8	75.6
PPenalty-NMS	71.9	71.8	80.9	73.3	60.0	53.9	79.0	82.5	83.8	51.7	79.9	68.5	79.7	83.7	75.8	79.9	42.5	72.3	66.3	77.9	74.8
CPenalty-NMS$_1$	71.9	72.3	83.0	72.4	58.6	54.5	78.7	82.8	82.9	51.1	80.0	69.1	81.0	81.7	76.8	79.5	43.6	68.4	68.5	80.1	72.0
CPenalty-NMS$_2$	71.8	71.4	81.7	70.5	58.5	54.8	79.9	82.1	85.5	51.9	80.3	66.1	81.7	82.6	75.7	79.6	42.7	72.2	67.4	79.4	72.1

Table 5. Results on MS COCO dataset with ResNet-101. G denotes GreedyNMS, P denotes Piecewise Penalty-NMS and C denotes Continuous Penalty-NMS$_1$.

	Training data	Test data	AP@0.5	mAP@[0.5,0.95]
Faster RCNN-G	Train	Val	48.4	27.2
Faster RCNN-P	Train	Val	49.7	28.6
Faster RCNN-C	Train	Val	49.9	29.0
R-FCN-G	Train	Val	48.9	27.6
R-FCN-P	Train	Val	49.9	28.7
R-FCN-C	Train	Val	50.1	29.2

5　Conclusion

As the greedy algorithm, NMS usually serves as post-processing. In this paper, we analyze in detail the limitations of GreedyNMS, which bring about a miss due to the setting of threshold T. We propose Penalty-NMS algorithm which penalizes detection boxes rather than the direct suppress one. What's more, our method solves the limitations without using any additional computations or parameters. The experimental results indicate that compared to the traditional NMS algorithm, Penalty-NMS achieves salient progress. Notes should be observed that we do not obtain the overall optimal result and Penalty-NMS is still a greedy algorithm. But the penalty idea gets a good effect on applying NMS algorithm. Moreover, other functions are proper to be penalty coefficient. The future work will focus on the way of learning to get penalty coefficient instead of adopting the fixed function.

References

1. Girshick, R.: Fast R-CNN. In: ICCV (2015)
2. Ren, S., He, K., Girshick, R., Sun, J.: Faster R-CNN: towards real-time object detection with region proposal networks. In: NIPS (2015)
3. Girshick, R., Donahue, J., Darrell, T., Malik, J.: Rich feature hierarchies for accurate object detection and semantic segmentation. In CVPR (2014)
4. Everingham, M., Van Gool, L., Williams, C.K.I., Winn, J., Zisserman, A.: The PASCAL Visual Object Classes Challenge 2007 (VOC2007) Results (2007)
5. Lin, T.-Y., et al.: Microsoft COCO: common objects in context. In: Fleet, D., Pajdla, T., Schiele, B., Tuytelaars, T. (eds.) ECCV 2014. LNCS, vol. 8693, pp. 740–755. Springer, Cham (2014). https://doi.org/10.1007/978-3-319-10602-1_48
6. Uijlings, J., van de Sande, K., Gevers, T., Smeulders, A.: Selective search for object recognition. IJCV **104**, 154–171 (2013)
7. Redmon, J., Divvala, S., Girshick, R., Farhadi, A.: You only look once: unified, real-time object detection. ArXiv preprint arXiv:1506.02640 (2015)
8. He, K., Zhang, X., Ren, S., Sun, J.: Spatial pyramid pooling in deep convolutional networks for visual recognition. In: Fleet, D., Pajdla, T., Schiele, B., Tuytelaars, T. (eds.) ECCV 2014. LNCS, vol. 8691, pp. 346–361. Springer, Cham (2014). https://doi.org/10.1007/978-3-319-10578-9_23

9. Hosang, J., Benenson, R., Schiele, B.: A convent for non-maximum suppression. In: GCPR (2016)
10. Zeiler, M.D., Fergus, R.: Visualizing and understanding convolutional networks. In: Fleet, D., Pajdla, T., Schiele, B., Tuytelaars, T. (eds.) ECCV 2014. LNCS, vol. 8689, pp. 818–833. Springer, Cham (2014). https://doi.org/10.1007/978-3-319-10590-1_53
11. Simonyan, K., Zisserman, A.: Very deep convolutional networks for large-scale image recognition. In: International Conference on Learning Representations (ICLR) (2015)
12. He, K., Zhang, X., Ren, S., Sun, J.: Deep residual learning for image recognition. arXiv: 1512.03385 (2015)
13. Viola, P., Jones, M.: Robust real-time face detection. IJCV **57**, 137–154 (2004)
14. Felzenszwalb, P., Girshick, R., McAllester, D., Ramanan, D.: Object detection with discriminatively trained part-based models. In: PAMI (2010)
15. Rothe, R., Guillaumin, M., Van Gool, L.: Non-maximum suppression for object detection by passing messages between windows. In: Cremers, D., Reid, I., Saito, H., Yang, M.-H. (eds.) ACCV 2014. LNCS, vol. 9003, pp. 290–306. Springer, Cham (2015). https://doi.org/10. 1007/978-3-319-16865-4_19
16. Dalal, N., Triggs, B.: Histograms of oriented gradients for human detection. In: CVPR (2005)
17. Bourdev, L., Maji, S., Brox, T., Malik, J.: Detecting people using mutually consistent poselet activations. In: Daniilidis, K., Maragos, P., Paragios, N. (eds.) ECCV 2010. LNCS, vol. 6316, pp. 168–181. Springer, Heidelberg (2010). https://doi.org/10.1007/978-3-642-15567-3_13
18. Mrowca, D., Rohrbach, M., Hoffman, J., Hu, R., Saenko, K., Darrell, T.: Spatial semantic regularisation for large scale object detection. In: ICCV (2015)
19. Stewart. R., Andriluka, M.: End-to-end people detection in crowded scenes. In: CVPR (2016)
20. Zhang, J., Sclaroff, S., Lin, Z., Shen, X., Price, B., Mech, R.: Unconstrained salient object detection via proposal subset optimization. In: Proceedings of the IEEE Conference on Computer Vision and Pattern Recognition, pp. 5733–5742 (2016)
21. Hosang, J., Benenson, R., Schiele, B.: Learning non-maximum suppression (2017)
22. Henderson, P., Ferrari, V.: End-to-end training of object class detectors for mean average precision. In: Lai, S.-H., Lepetit, V., Nishino, K., Sato, Y. (eds.) ACCV 2016. LNCS, vol. 10115, pp. 198–213. Springer, Cham (2017). https://doi.org/10.1007/978-3-319-54193-8_13
23. Blaschko, M.B.: Branch and bound strategies for non-maximal suppression in object detection. In: Boykov, Y., Kahl, F., Lempitsky, V., Schmidt, Frank R. (eds.) EMMCVPR 2011. LNCS, vol. 6819, pp. 385–398. Springer, Heidelberg (2011). https://doi.org/10.1007/ 978-3-642-23094-3_28
24. Dai, J., Li, Y., He, K., et al.: R-FCN: object detection via region-based fully convolutional networks (2016)
25. Bodla, N., Singh, B., Chellappa, R., et al.: Improving object detection with one line of code (2017)
26. Felzenszwalb, P., Girshick, R., McAllester, D., Ramanan, D.: Object detection with discriminatively trained part based models. In: TPAMI (2010)
27. Viola, P., Jones, M.: Rapid object detection using a boosted cascade of simple features. In: Proceedings of the 2001 IEEE Computer Society Conference on Computer Vision and Pattern Recognition, CVPR 2001, vol. 1, pp. I. IEEE (2001)
28. Felzenszwalb, P., Mcallester, D., Ramanan, D.: A discriminatively trained, multiscale, deformable part model. In: IEEE Conference on Computer Vision and Pattern Recognition, CVPR 2008. IEEE (2008)

29. Krizhevsky, A., Sutskever, I., Hinton, G.E.: ImageNet classification with deep convolutional neural networks. In: International Conference on Neural Information Processing Systems, pp. 1097–1105. Curran Associates Inc (2012)
30. Simonyan, K., Zisserman, A.: Very deep convolutional networks for large-scale image recognition. Comput. Sci. (2014)
31. Szegedy, C., Liu, W., Jia, Y., et al.: Going deeper with convolutions. In: Computer Vision and Pattern Recognition. IEEE (2015)
32. Redmonand, J., Farhadi, A.: Yolo9000: better, faster, stronger. In: CVPR (2017)
33. Liu, W., et al.: SSD: Single Shot MultiBox Detector. In: Leibe, B., Matas, J., Sebe, N., Welling, M. (eds.) ECCV 2016. LNCS, vol. 9905, pp. 21–37. Springer, Cham (2016). https://doi.org/10.1007/978-3-319-46448-0_2
34. Shen, Z., Liu, Z., Li, J., et al.: DSOD: Learning deeply supervised object detectors from scratch (2017)
35. Rosenfeld, A., Thurston, M.: Edge and curve detection for visual scene analysis. IEEE Trans. Comput. **100**(5), 562–569 (1971)

Self-Paced Densely Connected Convolutional Neural Network for Visual Tracking

Daohui Ge[1,2], Jianfeng Song[1,2(✉)], Yutao Qi[1,2], Chongxiao Wang[1,2], and Qiguang Miao[1,2]

[1] School of Computer Science and Technology, Xidian University,
Xi'an 710071, Shaanxi, China
jfsong@mail.xidian.edu.cn
[2] Xian Key Laboratory of Big Data and Intelligent Vision,
Xi'an 710071, Shaanxi, China

Abstract. Convolutional neural networks (CNNs) have achieved surprising results in visual tracking. To address the model drift problem, we propose a novel self-paced densely connected convolutional neural netwrok (SPDCT) to distinguish the reliable data from noisy and confusing data. In the proposed model, each sample is given a weight, which is estimated by SPDCT to indicate the reliability of the sample. The self-paced learning framework is then integrated into the online update phase to improve the robustness of CNNs. In order to determine the pace parameter of self-paced learning effectively, we propose an adaptive method based on the number of training samples. Meanwhile, with the aim of facilitating the representation power of the features, we enhance the feature reuse and the information flow by applying the densely connected learning. Extensive experimental results demonstrate competing performance of the proposed tracker over a number of state-of-the-art algorithms.

Keywords: Model drift problem · Self-paced learning
Densely connected learning · Convolutional neural networks

1 Introduction

Visual Tracking is a fundamental problem in computer vision, which has been widely applied into video surveillance, robotic, medical imaging, and so on. Given the initial bounding box of the target, the process of the visual tracking is to estimate the location and scale of the target in the subsequent frames. Although visual tracking has been researched for several years, it remains an extremely challenging problem due to appearance changes, partial occlusion, motion blur, and background clutters. CNN-based trackers have been drawing increasing attention and have achieved excellent results in visual tracking.

© Springer Nature Switzerland AG 2018
J.-H. Lai et al. (Eds.): PRCV 2018, LNCS 11259, pp. 103–114, 2018.
https://doi.org/10.1007/978-3-030-03341-5_9

Most existing trackers adopt an online update strategy to capture the appearance changes. FCNT [19] only updates the specific network using the most confident tracking result to avoid introducing background noise. CREST [15] collects all estimated locations to update the model every fixed frame. The process of updating brings the model drift problem due to factors such as tracking failure, occlusions, and inaccurate scale estimation.

The way to improve the robustness of online update is to reduce the introduction of the noisy and confusing data. Self-paced learning (SPL), which is recently proposed, is such a representative approach for robust learning. The origin of SPL is curriculum learning (CL) [1] proposed by Bengio et al. Furthermore, a set of training samples organized in ascending order of learning difficulty are defined in a curriculum from the CL. However, the curriculum is always fixed during the iterations and not affected by the subsequent learning. Then, inspired by the learning process of humans/animals, Kumar et al. propose the SPL to generate the dynamic curriculum according to what the model has already learned. SPL has the benefit of avoiding the bad local minima and achieving a more reasonable solution. Based on the above analysis, we propose a novel self-paced sample space model by distinguishing the reliable data from the noisy and confusing data to avert the model drifts.

The current trackers employ existing deep learning networks which have been offline pre-trained for a large amount of data to extract features. In the traditional CNNs structure, only the nearest previous layers output is used as the input of the current layer, resulting in the discarding of other existing features. [5] proposed a densely connected network by adding shortcut connections to enhance the information flow between layers and the feature reusing of the network. Inspired by the DenseNet, we apply the densely connected learning to reduce the dependency of the adjacent layers in the CNNs and improve the ability of feature representations.

The contributions of this paper are mainly summarized as three folds: (i) We propose a novel self-paced sample space model that integrate the SPL framework into the visual tracking. It avoids the drifts of online update by choosing the reliable data from noisy and confusing data. (ii) We apply the densely connected learning to enhance the information flow and feature reuse of the network. It effectively facilitates the representation power of the features. (iii) We conduct extensive experiments on the benchmark datasets. The results show that our tracker achieves the state-of-the-art performance.

The rest of this paper is organized as follows. We first introduce the existing visual tracking algorithm and self-paced learning framework in Sect. 2. Then, our SPDCT model and visual tracking algorithm are discussed in Sect. 3 and Sect. 4. Experiments are detailed in Sect. 5 and concluding remarks are given in Sect. 6.

2   Related Work

CNN-Based Tracking. The capability of feature representations is very important for visual tracking. Deep neural network, especially CNNs, is developing rapidly and has been successfully applied into visual tracking [11,19,20]. FCNT [19] employs a fully convolutional neural and proposes a feature map selection method to improve tracking accuracy. HCFT [11] adopts the hierarchical features to train correlation filters. STCT [20] casts online training CNN as learning ensembles to reduce over-fitting. Other CNN-based trackers consider that transfer pre-trained deep features may not be appropriate for online tracking. These methods mentioned above directly employ the traditional CNNs structure to capture the appearance change of target. Different from existing tracking methods that based on convolutional neural network, we propose a densely connected learning method to improve the robustness of visual representation through feature reuse.

Self-Paced Learning. Self-paced learning [10,12] is to learn the model iteratively from easy to complex samples inspired by the learning process of humans/animals. Compared with other machine learning methods, SPL jointly learns the curriculum and model parameters by incorporating a self-paced function and a pace parameter into the objective function. When pace is small, only 'easy' samples with small costs will be chosen into training data. As the value of pace grows, more samples with larger losses will be gradually appended to train a more 'mature' model. [12] has proven that the learning process of traditional SPL regime can be guaranteed to converge to rational critical points of the corresponding implicit NCRP objective. SPL has been successfully applied to various applications, such as action and event detection [7], reranking [6], segmentation [8], and co-saliency detection [22]. [16] employs self-paced learning to solve long-term tracking problems. Compared with [16], we use self-paced learning method to select reliable frames. However, this paper adopts feature pyramid method to fuse multi-layer CNN features and densely connected learning to improve the robustness of feature representation.

3   Proposed Visual Tracking Method

The main idea of the self-paced densely connected convolutional neural network is integrating the SPL framework into visual tracking algorithm. Specifically, SPDCT tends to distinguish the reliable data from the noisy data, and then uses them to update tracker to ensure the robust of the model. Figure 1 shows our SPDCT model pipeline. The details are discussed as follows.

3.1   Self-paced Sample Space Model

We propose a self-paced sample space model (SPSS) to avoid introducing background noise through online update. Formally, we denote the training dataset as $D = \{(x_1, y_1), (x_2, y_2), ..., (x_n, y_n)\}$, where x_i and y_i denote the observed samples and correspond labels, respectively. Such an idea can be formulated as an optimization problem as follows,

$$\min_{w,v} E(w, v) = \sum_{i=1}^{n} v_i L(y_i, g(x_i; w, b)) + f(\lambda, v) \tag{1}$$

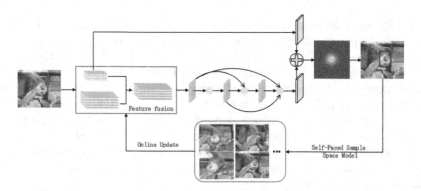

Fig. 1. The pipeline of SPDCT tracking algorithm. We first extract the hierarchy convolutional features of the target and fuse multi-layer features. Then, feed the fused features to densely connected learning to get the response map. When updating the model, we adopt the self-paced sample space model to choose reliable samples.

where $L(x)$ denotes the quadratic loss function under the estimated response value $g(x_i, w)$ with the weight vector w and bias parameter b. $v = [v_1, v_2, ..., v_n]$, $v \in [0,1]^n$ denotes the important weights for all training samples, $v = 1$ indicates a reliable sample and λ is the pace parameter for controlling the selecting pace. The capability of the self-paced sample space model is determined by the self-paced function that avoids the negative influence brought by large-noise-outliers. The formula of the self-paced function as the following form:

$$f(\lambda, v) = -\|v_1\| = -\lambda \sum_{i=1}^{n} v_i \qquad (2)$$

Similar to SPL, the optimization problem of Eq. 1 can be solved by alternately optimizing the important weight v and the weight vector w of a sample of variables. Under fixed v, weight vector w can be optimized by existing off-the-shelf supervised learning methods, such as back propagation algorithm. Under fixed $\{w, b\}$, $v = [v_1, v_2, ..., v_n]$ can be easily calculated by

$$v_i^* = \begin{cases} 1, L(y_i, g(x_i, w)) < \lambda \\ 0, otherwise \end{cases} \qquad (3)$$

In traditional SPL methods, the parameter of pace adds a fixed value for each iteration to choose more hard samples, and it is difficult to effectively determine the fixed value. In this paper, we propose an adaptive strategy based on the number of samples. In the tth iteration, N_t denotes the total number of training samples and N_p means the proportion of samples selected. We first get the L_{sort} by sorting the samples in ascending order according to their weights, and the $(N_t * N_p)^{th}$ loss value of L_{sort} is used as the parameter value of pace in the SPL. As shown in Eq. 4.

$$\lambda = L_{sort}[(N_t * N_p)] \qquad (4)$$

Fig. 2. Visualization of the training set during the online update phase. Our approach selects some training samples with target in the center of the image to better suppress the background noise in each iteration update.

Fig. 2 shows the comparison between the SPDCT algorithm(bottom row) and the CREST(top row) method. In CREST, the training data is composed of continuous video frames, which is easy to overfit the current video frames. For example, when occlusion occurs, CREST learns more background information, which causes tracking drift. In contrast, our model chooses reliable training samples through SPSS model to avoid introducing background noise.

3.2 Densely Connected Learning

The quality of the features determines the performance of the tracker based on convolutional neural networks. Most of CNN-based trackers employ the traditional CNNs structure directly to capture the appearance change of target. In the traditional CNN network structure, only the output of the previous layer is used as the input of the current layer, which leads to discarding existing features and hindering in convolutional neural networks. To enhance the reuse of the features and reduce the dependence of adjacent layers, we apply the densely connected convolutional network instead of the traditional CNNs, which connects each layer to every other layer in a feed-forward fashion. Figure 3 shows structure of the densely connected learning. The lth layer receives the feature maps generated by all of previous layers as input. This form of densely connected learning can be formulated as follows:

$$x_l = H_l \left([x_0, x_1, ..., x_{l-1}] \right) \tag{5}$$

where $H_l(x)$ denotes the non-linear transformation function composed of convolution (Conv) and rectified linear units (ReLU). Similar to [5], we concatenate the multiple inputs of $H_l(x)$. x_l is the output of the lth layer. We adopt four layers in the densely connected learning with a small growth rate.

Densely connected layer enhances feature reuse and maximize the information flow through the neural network. According to the results in Sect. 5, the learned features are more robust for appearance change.

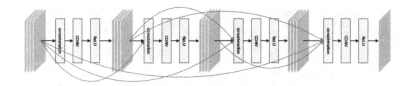

Fig. 3. The structure of the densely connected learning.

3.3 Multi-layer Features Fusion

According to FCNT [19], convolutional layers at different levels focus on different perspectives of target. A top layer encodes more semantic features with low-resolution map, while a lower layer carries more spatial information with high-resolution map. In order to maintain the spatial and semantic information of features, we adopt feature pyramid method as described in Feature pyramid networks (FPN) [9] to achieve multi-layer fusion, as shown in Fig. 4.

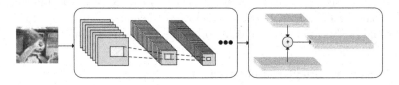

Fig. 4. Multi-layer features fusion.

4   Tracking with SPDCT

We illustrate the detailed procedure of SPDCT from model initialization, detection, scale estimation, and online update, as listed in algorithm 1.

Model Initialization. Similar to CREST [15], given the first frame with the target location, we extract a training patch centered on the target location and send the patch to an existing deep neural network to extract the features. Soft labels are used as the input to the densely connected learning to train weight and bias parameters of the network. All the parameters in the densely connected layers are randomly initialized following zero mean Gaussian distribution.

Detection. After a new frame's arrival, we crop a search patch centered on the tracking results of the previous frame. The patch and the training data have the same size. We obtain the response map through the densely connected layers, which locates the target position based on the maximum response value. The online tracking strategy is extremely simple and straightforward.

Scale Estimation. When we obtain the center location of the target, we crop the frame at different scales to get some patches. We send these patches to SPDCT to get the response values of target. We evaluate the scale of target by searching for the maximum response value.

Algorithm 1. Algorithm of SPDCT tracking.

Require: A video sequence, Initial state of target.
Ensure: the location of target in the following frames.
 1: For the initial frame, crop the image five times as large as the target and generate
    the corresponding two-dimensional Gaussian soft label. Train the SPDCT model.
 2: **for** $nFrames = 2, 3, ...$ **do**
 3:     Extract the candidate patch based on the target position of the previous frame.
 4:     Feed the candidate patch to the SPDCT model to generate the response map.
 5:     Locate the target by finding the maximum of the response map.
 6:     Extract the different scale patches and send them to the SPDCT model. Search
        for the maximum response value to determine the target scale.
 7:     **if** $mod(nFrames - 1, 5) == 0$ **then**
 8:         calculate the v by Equation 3
 9:         choose the samples where $v = 1$.
10:        update SPDCT model.
11:        calculate the λ by Equation 4
12:     **end if**
13: **end for**
14: **return** the tracking results.

Online Update. We adopt self-paced sample space model to obtain the reliable training data for model update. We first collect tracking results as training samples. For each frame, the corresponding soft label can be generated according to the predicted location. When obtaining the response map of target, we calculate the sample weight by Eq. 3 and choose samples with $v = 1$ for online update. In order to reduce the over-fitting of recent samples and to satisfy the memory constraint, we select a maximum of N samples at a time and online update the model every fixed frames.

5 Experiments

In this section, we first explain the implementation details and then analyze the effects of self-paced sample space model and densely connected learning. We validate the performance of our SPDCT tracker against state-of-the-art trackers on three benchmark dataset: OTB-50,OTB-100 [21] and UAV123 [13].

5.1 Experiments Setups

Implementation Details. Consistenting with the existing trackers, we set up the VGG model as feature extractor. We obtain the features from the output of conv3-3 and con4-3 layers of the VGG model. In the first frame, we obtain the training sample with five times the size of the target bounding box. The soft label and the learning rate are set to a two-dimensional Gaussian function with peak value of 1 and $5e-7$, respectively. In the online update, we calculate the λ by Eq. 4 and choose the reliable data with the adaptive percentage N_p of 0.5.

N is set to 11. The SPDCT model is fine-tuned for 2 iterations with the learning rate of 1e−8 for every 5 frames. The SPDCT is implemented in MATLAB based on the wrapper of MatConvNet [18].

Benchmark Datasets. We conduct our experiments on three benchmark datasets: OTB-50,OTB-100 [21] and UAV123 [13]. The OTB-50 and OTB-100 datasets have 50, 100 real-world targets for tracking, respectively. There are 11 attributes, such as occlusion, scale variation, motion blur, and background clutters. The UAV123 dataset consists of 123 aerial videos with more than 110 K frames.

Evaluation Methodology. We use the one-pass evaluation (OPE) with precision and success plots to evaluate the current state-of-the-art trackers. Precision plot shows the percentage of frames where the distance between the estimated location and the ground truth within 20 pixels. Success plot demonstrates the percentage of frames where the estimated box and the ground truth box overlap. All the trackers are ranked according to the area under curve (AUC) of each success plot.

5.2   Ablation Studies

The SPDCT algorithm consists of self-paced sample space model and densely connected learning. Based on the experimental results on the OTB-50 dataset, we apply the ablation studies method to analyze the effect of each part. We set up four contrast experiments including a standard SPDCT tracker, SPDCT tracker without the self-paced sample space model (SPDCT-spss free), SPDCT tracker without the densely connected model (SPDCT-densely learning free), and SPDCT with neither self-paced sample space model nor densely connected learning (SPDCT-neither).

Figure 5 shows the precision and success plots of the above ablative experiments. The experimental results show that both models of self-paced sample space model and densely connected learning are helpful to improve the performance. Self-paced sample space model enhances the ability of the tracker to

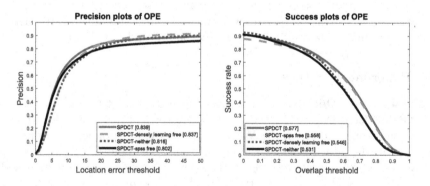

Fig. 5. Ablative experiments on the OTB-50 benchmark.

discern the target because of the selection of a reliable sample for updating the model to avoid introducing noise. Densely connected learning model enriches the input of convolutional layers by reusing the convolutional features, alleviates over-fitting and enhances the representation power of features. In precision plots, SPDCT-spss free performs worse than SPDCT-neither. Because densely connected learning is more capable of learning. When there is noise in a training sample, the model learns features unrelated to the target and loses its representation power. The standard SPDCT has the best results.

5.3   Comparisons to State-of-the-art Trackers

In this section, we compare the SPDCT model with the recent state-of-the-art trackers, including HDT [14], CREST [15], SRDCFdecon [4], DeepSRDCF [2], HCFT [11], SINT [17], FCNT [19], MEEM [23], SRDCF [3], and other 29 trackers from OTB-2015 benchmark [21] and UAV123 [13]. We initialize the model randomly, and then use the first frame of video as the training sample. The ten best results are shown in Figs. 6, 7 and 8. On the OTB-50, OTB-100 and UVA123, the experimental results show that our SPDCT tracking algorithm performs a best among these trackers. On the OTB-50, the performance of precision plot is 3.5% and 3.6% higher than the performance of HDT and HCFT separately. The performance of success plot is 0.7% and 0.9% higher than the performance of CREST and BACF separately. On the OTB-100, the performance of precision plot is 1.7% and 2.0% higher than DeepSRDCF and HDT separately, and reaches the fourth best on success plots. On the UAV123, the performance of precision plot is 2.1% higher than the performance of SRDCF, and reaches the second best on success plots. Our SPDCT model does not use any auxiliary training data. We consider the reliability of the samples by self-paced sample space model and feature reuse by densely connected learning, improving the robustness of the model. The results reached the state-of-the-art performance and shows that our SPDCT model has good generalization ability. Figure 9 visualizes quantitative evaluation results. We compare three top performing trackers: DeepSRDCF,

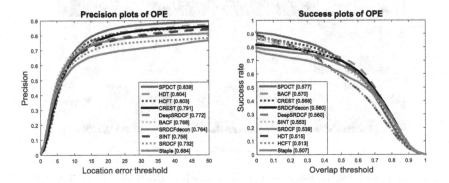

Fig. 6. Precision and success plots on the OTB-50 dateset.

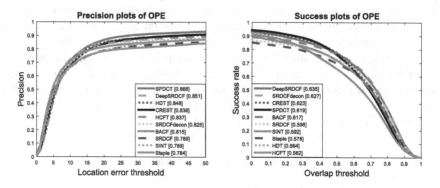

Fig. 7. Precision and success plots on the OTB-100 dateset.

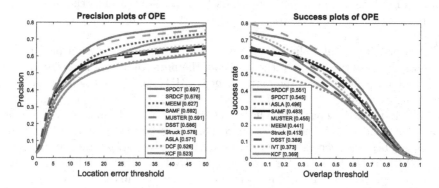

Fig. 8. Precision and success plots on the UAV123 dateset.

Fig. 9. Qualitative evaluation of our SPDCT tracker, DeepSRDCF, HCFT, CREST on three challenging sequences, from top to down, ClifBar, Human3, Ironman.

HCFT, CREST with our SPDCT tracker on three challenging sequences. The results show that our SPDCT model achieves the state-of-the-art trackers.

6 Conclusion

In this paper, we have proposed a novel self-paced sample space model that integrate the SPL framework into the visual tracking for distinguishing the reliable date from noisy and confusing data to avoid the model drifts problem. We also apply the densely connected learning to improve the information flow and feature reuse of the network, while enhancing the representation power of the features effectively. Experiments on three benchmark datasets demonstrate that our SPDCT model achieves state-off-the-art performance. In the future, we will consider how to effectively construct the diversity samples of visual tracking in self-paced learning framework.

Acknowledgements. The work was jointly supported by the National Key R&D Program of China under Grant No. 2018YFC0807500, the National Natural Science Foundations of China under grant No. 61772396, 61472302, 61772392, the Fundamental Research Funds for the Central Universities under grant No. JB170306, JB170304, No. JBF180301 and Xi'an Key Laboratory of Big Data and Intelligent Vision under grant No. 201805053ZD4CG37.

References

1. Bengio, Y., Louradour, J., Collobert, R., Weston, J.: Curriculum learning. In: Proceedings of the 26th Annual International Conference on Machine Learning, pp. 41–48. ACM (2009)
2. Danelljan, M., Hager, G., Shahbaz Khan, F., Felsberg, M.: Convolutional features for correlation filter based visual tracking. In: Proceedings of the IEEE International Conference on Computer Vision Workshops, pp. 58–66 (2015)
3. Danelljan, M., Hager, G., Shahbaz Khan, F., Felsberg, M.: Learning spatially regularized correlation filters for visual tracking. In: Proceedings of the IEEE International Conference on Computer Vision, pp. 4310–4318 (2015)
4. Danelljan, M., Hager, G., Shahbaz Khan, F., Felsberg, M.: Adaptive decontamination of the training set: a unified formulation for discriminative visual tracking. In: Proceedings of the IEEE Conference on Computer Vision and Pattern Recognition, pp. 1430–1438 (2016)
5. Huang, G., Liu, Z., Weinberger, K.Q., van der Maaten, L.: Densely connected convolutional networks. In: Proceedings of the IEEE Conference on Computer Vision and Pattern Recognition, vol. 1, p. 3 (2017)
6. Jiang, L., Meng, D., Mitamura, T., Hauptmann, A.G.: Easy samples first: self-paced reranking for zero-example multimedia search. In: Proceedings of the 22nd ACM International Conference on Multimedia, pp. 547–556. ACM (2014)
7. Jiang, L., Meng, D., Yu, S.I., Lan, Z., Shan, S., Hauptmann, A.: Self-paced learning with diversity. In: Advances in Neural Information Processing Systems, pp. 2078–2086 (2014)

8. Kumar, M.P., Turki, H., Preston, D., Koller, D.: Learning specific-class segmentation from diverse data. In: 2011 IEEE International Conference on Computer Vision (ICCV), pp. 1800–1807. IEEE (2011)
9. Lin, T.Y., Dollár, P., Girshick, R., He, K., Hariharan, B., Belongie, S.: Feature pyramid networks for object detection. In: CVPR, vol. 1, p. 4 (2017)
10. Liu, S., Ma, Z., Meng, D.: Understanding self-paced learning under concave conjugacy theory. Commun. Inf. Syst. **18**, 1–35 (2018)
11. Ma, C., Huang, J.B., Yang, X., Yang, M.H.: Hierarchical convolutional features for visual tracking. In: Proceedings of the IEEE International Conference on Computer Vision (2015)
12. Ma, Z., Liu, S., Meng, D.: On convergence property of implicit self-paced objective. Inf. Sci. **462**, 132–140 (2018)
13. Mueller, M., Smith, N., Ghanem, B.: A benchmark and simulator for UAV tracking. In: Leibe, B., Matas, J., Sebe, N., Welling, M. (eds.) ECCV 2016. LNCS, vol. 9905, pp. 445–461. Springer, Cham (2016). https://doi.org/10.1007/978-3-319-46448-0_27
14. Qi, Y., et al.: Hedging deep features for visual tracking. IEEE Trans. Pattern Anal. Mach. Intell. **PP**(99), 1 (2018)
15. Song, Y., Ma, C., Gong, L., Zhang, J., Lau, R., Yang, M.H.: Crest: convolutional residual learning for visual tracking. In: IEEE International Conference on Computer Vision, pp. 2555–2564 (2017)
16. Supancic III, J.S., Ramanan, D.: Self-paced learning for long-term tracking. In: 2013 IEEE Conference on Computer Vision and Pattern Recognition (CVPR), pp. 2379–2386. IEEE (2013)
17. Tao, R., Gavves, E., Smeulders, A.W.: Siamese instance search for tracking. In: 2016 IEEE Conference on Computer Vision and Pattern Recognition (CVPR), pp. 1420–1429. IEEE (2016)
18. Vedaldi, A., Lenc, K.: MatConvNet: convolutional neural networks for MATLAB. In: Proceedings of the 23rd ACM International Conference on Multimedia, pp. 689–692. ACM (2015)
19. Wang, L., Ouyang, W., Wang, X., Lu, H.: Visual tracking with fully convolutional networks. In: IEEE International Conference on Computer Vision (ICCV) (2015)
20. Wang, L., Ouyang, W., Wang, X., Lu, H.: STCT: Sequentially training convolutional networks for visual tracking. In: Proceedings of the IEEE Conference on Computer Vision and Pattern Recognition, pp. 1373–1381 (2016)
21. Wu, Y., Lim, J., Yang, M.H.: Object tracking benchmark. IEEE Trans. Pattern Anal. Mach. Intell. **37**(9), 1834–1848 (2015)
22. Zhang, D., Meng, D., Li, C., Jiang, L., Zhao, Q., Han, J.: A self-paced multiple-instance learning framework for co-saliency detection. In: Proceedings of the IEEE International Conference on Computer Vision, pp. 594–602 (2015)
23. Zhang, J., Ma, S., Sclaroff, S.: MEEM: robust tracking via multiple experts using entropy minimization. In: Fleet, D., Pajdla, T., Schiele, B., Tuytelaars, T. (eds.) ECCV 2014. LNCS, vol. 8694, pp. 188–203. Springer, Cham (2014). https://doi.org/10.1007/978-3-319-10599-4_13

A Saliency-Based Object Tracking Method for UAV Application

Jinyu Yang[1] , Wenrui Ding[2], Chunlei Liu[2(✉)], and Zechen Ha[2]

[1] The Hong Kong University of Science and Technology,
Clear Water Bay, Hong Kong
yangjinyu@buaa.edu.cn
[2] Beihang University, Beijing, China
{ding,liuchunlei,hazechen36}@buaa.edu.cn

Abstract. Visual tracking has been an active and complicated research area in computer vision for recent decades. In the area of unmanned aerial vehicle (UAV) application, establishing a robust tracking model is still a challenge. The kernelized correlation filter (KCF) is one of the state-of-the-art object trackers. However, it could not reasonably handle the severe special situations in UAV application during tracking process, especially when targets undergo significant appearance changes due to camera shaking or deformation. In this paper, we proposed a new compounded feature to track the object by combining saliency feature and color features for the conspicuousness of the objects in the videos captured by UAVs. Considering the speed of real-time application, we use a spectrum-based saliency detection method - quaternion type-II DCT image signatures. In addition, severe drifting can be detected and adjusted by the relocation mechanism. Extensive experiments on the UAV tracking sequences show that the proposed method significantly improves KCF, and achieves better performance than other state-of-the-art trackers.

Keywords: Saliency feature · UAV · Object tracking · KCF

1 Introduction

Unmanned aerial vehicle (UAV) is one of the most important tools for obtaining information, which is implemented by multiple tasks both in civilian and military areas such as normal observation, disaster monitoring, and battlefield detection, etc. Among these applications, UAV object tracking is rather challenging due to various factors like illumination change, occlusion, motion blur, and texture variation [3–6]. To this end, the conventional data association and temporal filters always fail due to the fast motion and changing object or background appearances.

In object tracking filed, generative tracking methods always search for best matched regions in successive frames as results. Most of recent generative methods such as [13–15] focus on building a good representation of the target. Because the generative method focuses on the representation of the target itself and ignores the background information, it is prone to drift when the object changes violently or under occlusion.

J.-H. Lai et al. (Eds.): PRCV 2018, LNCS 11259, pp. 115–125, 2018.
https://doi.org/10.1007/978-3-030-03341-5_10

On the other hand, a popular trend of visual tracking research in recent years is the use of discriminative learning methods, such as [7, 8]. Discriminative method can be more robust than generative method because it distinguishes the background and foreground information significantly. However, these methods face such problems as lack of samples and confusion of boundary demarcation. In addition, many existing methods are slow in operation and expensive in computation, which limits their practical applications [9].

Though many attempts have been made to mitigate these tracking problems for general videos, none of them can be perfectly applied to UAV videos due to the characteristic of small target caused by the long-distance imaging and movement of both target and background caused by the violent motion of the airframe. Inspired by the visual attention mechanism, our works establish a more robust feature representation by combining the saliency feature with the ordinary feature on the basis of the kernelized correlation filter (KCF).

The rest of the paper is organized as follows. Section 2 introduces our method including details about how saliency feature can be efficiently embedded in the KCF framework and the relocation mechanism used to detect and adjust the tracking failure. Section 3 shows the extensive experiments we designed to evaluate the results of our method in comparison of other state-in-the-art methods. Finally, conclusions are put forward in Sect. 4.

2   Methodology

2.1   Tracking by Correlation Framework

Discriminative trackers [9] are thought more robust than generative trackers because the former regard visual tracking as a problem of binary classification. Utilizing the trained classifier, trackers can distinguish foreground and background and estimate target position among vast candidates.

In 2010, correlation filter was introduced into tracking to raise efficiency when facing a large number of samples [1]. Using the circulant structure and ridge regression, Henriques et al. [7] simplify the training and testing process. The purpose of ridge regression training is to find a filter ω which can minimize the squared error over training samples x and their label y. The training problem is formulated as

$$\min_{\omega} ||\phi\omega - y|| + \lambda||\omega|| \tag{1}$$

where ϕ denotes the mapping of all the circular shifts of the template x. If the mapping ϕ is linear, Eq. 1 could be solved directly using the DFT matrix and the target's position could be located when we get its filter ω.

Then the appealing method being able to work solely with diagonal matrices by Fourier diagonalizing circulant matrices can be used simplify the linear regression in Eq. 2.

$$X = Fdiag(\hat{x}^*)F^H \tag{2}$$

From the Eq. 2, we have

$$\alpha = (K + \lambda I)^{-1}y \tag{3}$$

with the gaussian kernel k, the matrix $K_{i,j} = k(P^i x, P^j x)$ is circulant. Using the quick calculation of the Eq. 3, the FFT of α is calculated by:

$$\hat{\alpha} = \frac{\hat{y}}{\hat{k}^{xx} + \lambda} \tag{4}$$

where the notation "^" represents discrete Fourier operator, k^{xx} is the first row of the circulant matrix K, and test patch z are evaluated by:

$$\hat{y} = \hat{k}^{zx} \Theta \hat{\alpha} \tag{5}$$

where Θ is the element-wise product. $\hat{y}$ is the output response for all the testing patches in frequency domain. Then we have

$$response = \max(ifft(\hat{y})) \tag{6}$$

The target position is the one with the maximal value among response calculated by Eq. 6. Finally, a new model is trained at the new position, and the obtained values of α and x are linearly interpolated with the ones from the previous frame, to provide the tracker with some memory.

Despite of the huge success of correlation tracking, these trackers could not represent the small target of UAV application robustly since the ground targets always "weak" and "small", which showing low representation. Therefore, how to find a more robust feature and solve the critical drift problem in the UAV application should be a challenging problem.

2.2 Tracking by Compounded Features

Due to the weakly representation of the small target, we can use a saliency method, which is thought to be one of the guiding mechanisms of human visual tracking, to get close to the approximate target position. There have been some works using visual saliency for object tracking. For example, [24] used multiple trackers to modulate the attention distribution and [25] embedded three kinds of attention to help locate the object, while they are both time-consuming. In this paper, we propose a simple and efficient feature model based on the image saliency, combing the saliency feature and the ordinary feature, which can be represented as:

$$C_o(z) = \gamma C_f(z) + (1 - \gamma)C_s(z) \tag{7}$$

in which $C_o(z)$ represents the compounded feature, $C_f(z)$ represents the ordinary feature such as gray and HoG, $C_s(z)$ represents the saliency feature, γ represents the weight coefficient, z means the candidate target. This combination of two parts provides a more robust feature representation. And we will introduce the two parts in detail below respectively.

Ordinary Feature Representation. Low-level features, such as intensity, color, orientation, motion, etc., are widely used. It is because that fast guidance of image key content is usually believed to be driven by bottom-up features. For simplicity and speed, we omit other cues but intensity. Color cue does not exist in gray-scale image sequences. Besides, the computational cost of color or motion is rather expensive. It is not a good trade-off to trade significant amount of computing time for a little performance improvement, especially when our main task is tracking, in which speed is a key performance metric. Therefore, an intensity map $I(z)$ is used to model appearance distribution.

$$I(z) = (r(z) + g(z) + b(z))/3 \tag{8}$$

in which $r(z), g(z), b(z)$ represents the three color channels, respectively.

Saliency Feature Representation. By investigating different saliency models, we note that computational models, especially spectral models, fit the UAV tracking situation better to the real-time application for its speediness. Therefore, to get the saliency feature representation, we cite the image signature method [22], providing an approach to the figure-ground separation problem using a binary, holistic image descriptor.

$$Imagesignature(x) = \text{sign}[\text{DCT(x)}] \tag{9}$$

$$\tilde{x} = IDCT[sign(\bar{x})] \tag{10}$$

$$m = g \cdot [\tilde{x} \circ \tilde{x}] \tag{11}$$

where x represents the image, g is a Gaussian kernel, $\cdot$ denotes the convolution operation and $\circ$ denotes the Hadamard production. It has been verified experimentally that this method efficiently suppresses the background and highlight the foreground.

Then, through transferring the single-channel definition of the DCT signature to quaternion DCT(QDCT) signature, we derive a sparsity map using the QDCT method [23], describing the possible target candidates of image around the target in the last frame.

$$m_{QDCT}(I_Q) = g \cdot [\tilde{I}_Q \circ \tilde{I}_Q] \tag{12}$$

$$\tilde{I}_Q = IQDCT^L\{sign[QDCT^L(I_Q)]\} \tag{13}$$

where I_Q is the quaternion image, g is a 10×10 Gaussian kernel with $\sigma=2.5$. Using the QDCT method, color information can be totally covered in the saliency detection. The mixture of spectral method and low-level features (color in our method only) improves the performance of original image signature method.

$$QDCT^L(p,q) = \alpha_p^M \alpha_q^N \sum_{m=0}^{M-1} \sum_{n=0}^{N-1} u_Q I_Q(m,n) \beta_{p,m}^M \beta_{q,n}^N \tag{14}$$

$$QDCT^R(p,q) = \alpha_p^M \alpha_q^N \sum_{m=0}^{M-1} \sum_{n=0}^{N-1} I_Q(m,n) \beta_{p,m}^M \beta_{q,n}^N u_Q \tag{15}$$

$$IQDCT^L(m,n) = \sum_{p=0}^{M-1} \sum_{q=0}^{N-1} \alpha_p^M \alpha_q^N u_Q C_Q(p,q) \beta_{p,q}^M \beta_{m,n}^N \tag{16}$$

$$IQDCT^R(m,n) = \sum_{p=0}^{M-1} \sum_{q=0}^{N-1} \alpha_p^M \alpha_q^N C_Q(p,q) \beta_{p,q}^M \beta_{m,n}^N u_Q \tag{17}$$

Where u_Q is a unit (pure) quaternion, $u_Q^2 = -1$ that serves as DCT axis, I_Q is the $M \times N$ quaternion matrix. In accordance with the definition of the traditional type-II DCT, we define α, β and u_Q as follows:

$$\alpha_p^M = \begin{cases} \sqrt{1/M} & for \quad p = 0 \\ \sqrt{2/M} & for \quad p \neq 0 \end{cases} \tag{18}$$

$$\beta_{p,m}^M = \cos[\frac{\pi}{M}(m + \frac{1}{2})p] \tag{19}$$

$$u_Q = -\sqrt{1/3}i - \sqrt{1/3}j - \sqrt{1/3}k \tag{20}$$

Figure 1 shows the process of obtaining saliency feature. In this model, the red, blue and green channels are extracted respectively in the candidate patch, occupying three channels of the QDCT (the residual channel is set as void). Then we get the saliency map of each channel. Through QDCT and IQDCT transform, three channel maps are grouped to the final saliency map, which can be combined with the gray feature.

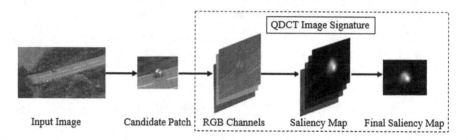

Fig. 1. Process of obtaining saliency feature.

2.3   Tracking by Relocation Mechanism

As shown in the failure detection case in the output constraint transfer theory, the output of the test image is reasonably considered to follow a Gaussian distribution, which is theoretically transferred to be a constraint condition in the Bayesian optimization problem, and successfully used to detect the tracking failure problem. Here, we argue that the Gaussian prior [12] can well help to detect failure by setting $|(y_{max}^t - \mu^t)/\sigma^t| < T_g$, where μ^t and σ^t are the average and variance of response calculated based on all previous frames in the tracking procedure, y_{max}^t represents the maximum response, and according to [12], T_g is set as 0.7.

After judging and entering the drift processing mechanism, we get N samples from the target position in the last frame to relocate the target position by a linear stochastic differential equation:

$$p_t^{(n)} = p_{t-1}^{(n)} + A\delta_t^{(n)} \tag{21}$$

where $\delta_t^{(n)}$ is a multivariate Gaussian random variable, t represent t^{th} frame, n represent n^{th} sample and p represents the position, A is the proportionality factor, which can be updated by:

$$A = \frac{P(\delta_t^{(n)}(x))P(\delta_t^{(n)}(y))P(F_t^{(n)})}{1 - P(\delta_t^{(n)}(x))P(\delta_t^{(n)}(y))P(F_t^{(n)})} \tag{22}$$

where x, y represents two directions in a two-dimensional image, $P(\delta_t^{(n)})$ is Gauss probability and $P(F_t^{(n)})$ is the likelihood calculated by Euclidean distance of the feature between the candidate targets and the target. Through Eq. 22, we can refine the candidate location so that obtain a more precise tracking result.

Algorithm 1 Saliency-based Object Tracking Method

1: Initial target bounding box $b_0 = [x_0, y_0, w, h]$

2: if the frame $n < 20$

3: repeat

4:    Crop out the search windows according to b_{n-1}, and extract the saliency-based feature representation.

5:    Obtain the target position according to KCF algorithm.

6:    Updating essential parameters of the KCF tracker.

7: until $n = 20$

8: end

9: Compute the mean μ and variance σ^2 using all previous frames.

10: if $n > Num$

11: repeat

12:    Crop out the search window and extract the compounded feature representation.

13:    Obtain the target position according to KCF algorithm.

14:    if satisfy $|(y_{max}^t - \mu^t)/\sigma^t| < T_g$

15:    Crop out N samples using Eq. 21.

16:    Assign different weight to each region using KCF algorithm to obtain the target position.

17:    Updating essential parameters of KCF tracker.

18:    Updating μ and σ^2

19: until End of the video sequence.

20: end

---

3 Experiments

Most visual tracking models have been tested on the commonly used benchmark [10] with many datasets like OTB50 [10], ALOV300++ [21] and so on, which have abundant natural scenes. However, in the field of UAV object tracking, few datasets have been proposed to test the tracking models. In 2016, a new dataset (UAV123) [11] with sequences from an aerial viewpoint was proposed, which contains a total of 123 video sequences and more than 110 K frames, making it the second largest object tracking dataset after ALOV300++. To evaluate the effectiveness and robustness of trackers, we selected 45 challenging sequences from UAV123 dataset, covering typical UAV tracking problems. According to the benchmark [10], each sequence is manually tagged with 11 attributes which represent challenging aspects including illumination variations (IV), scale variations (SV), occlusions (OCC), deformations (DEF), motion blur (MB), fast motion (FM), in-plane rotation (IPR), out-of-plane rotation (OPR), out-of-view (OV), background clutters (BC), and low resolution (LR). In addition, we compare our tracker with 10 state-of-the–art trackers covering correlation filter-based tracker CT [18], CSK [7], KCF [19], OCT [12], saliency-based tracker SPC [20] and other representative trackers, such as LOT [2], ORIA [17] and DFT [16]. The platform of our experiments is Intel I7 2.7 GZ (4 cores) CPU with 8G RAM.

3.1 Objective Evaluation

Figure 2 shows qualitative results comparing with the other state-of-the-art trackers on challenging sequences. In the first row, our tracker can precisely track the wakeboard, while the conventional KCF tracker fails. The famous OCT tracker could also relocate the target because of the Gaussian prior, although the tracking bounding boxes of the OCT is not as precise as those of ours. While in *uav*, the appearances of the target are weak and small, with severe changing and drifting. Most trackers drift easily due to poor robustness. While our tracker could locate the target accurately because of the robust compounded feature and utilization of relocation method. It is also observed that our proposed tracker works very well in other sequences, e.g., *road* and *truck*. In contrast, all other compared trackers get false or imprecise results in one sequence at least.

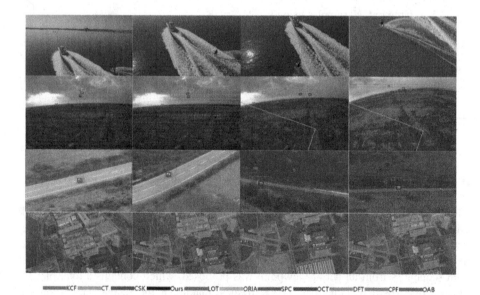

Fig. 2. Illustration of some key frames.

3.2 Subjective Evaluation

In Fig. 3, the overall success and precision plots generated by the benchmark toolbox are reported. These plots report 11 performing trackers in the benchmarks. Our tracker and OCT achieve 90.8% and 84.7% based on the average precision rate when the threshold is set to 20, while the famous KCF and CSK trackers, respectively, achieve 74.1% and 72.4%. In terms of success rate, Ours and OCT, respectively, achieve 56.9% and 55.8%. We also compare with SPC, which presents a saliency prior context model, showing that our tracker achieves a significant performance in terms of precision (18.4% higher) and success rate (10.3% higher). These results confirm that our method performs better than most state-of-the-art trackers.

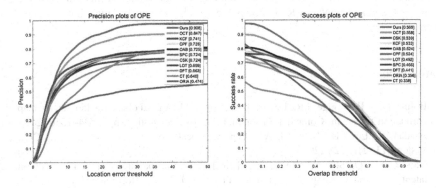

Fig. 3. Success and precision plots.

Results about average success rate for 8 typical attributes are summarized in Table 1. In this table we use bold fonts to indicate the best tracker of different attributes among KCF, OCT and our tracker. Statistic data shows that our method is effective and efficient in front of the challenges including in-plane rotation, out-of-plane rotation, scale variation and fast motion, which occurs frequently in UAV videos. We are pleasantly surprised that our method outperforms the KCF and OCT for low resolution videos, with a success rate of 0.55, meaning our method can perform well although the target is weak and small. Besides, our method hold a tracking speed of 92FPS, so it can realize real-time UAV object tracking.

Table 1. Results for success rate of different attributes

attribute	SV	MB	FM	IPR	OPR	OV	BC	LR
KCF	0.310	**0.689**	0.596	0.336	0.346	0.582	0.585	0.512
OCT	0.378	0.574	0.568	0.396	0.391	**0.587**	**0.621**	0.542
Ours	**0.479**	0.671	**0.614**	**0.468**	**0.482**	0.580	0.591	**0.550**

4 Conclusion

In this paper, we propose a compounded feature and a relocation method to enhance KCF for object tracking in UAV applications. We explore that the incorporation of low-level features and saliency feature could effectively solve the tough problems in UAV tracking, i.e. low resolution and fast motion. Also, we show that the failure judgement and relocation mechanism is appropriate for the weak and small targets in UAV tracking process. In the experimental section, we implement our tracking framework under the compounded feature – the combination of QDCT image signatures and gray feature. It's worth noting that the proposed method could be extended to other features and extensive tracking situations. Extensive experiments of the UAV videos and comparisons on the benchmark show that the proposed method significantly improves the performance of KCF, and achieves a better performance than state-of-the-art tracker.

References

1. Bolme, D.S., Beveridge, J.R., Draper, B.A., Lui, Y.M.: Visual object tracking using adaptive correlation filters. In: Computer Vision and Pattern Recognition, pp. 2544–2550 (2010)
2. Avidan, S., Levi, D., Barhillel, A., Oron, S.: Locally orderless tracking. Int. J. Comput. Vision **111**, 213–228 (2015)
3. Yao, R., Shi, Q., Shen, C., Zhang, Y., Hengel, A.V.: Part-based visual tracking with online latent structural learning. In: Computer Vision and Pattern Recognition, pp. 2363–2370, Portland, OR, USA (2013)
4. Adam, A., Rivlin, E., Shimshoni, I.: Robust fragments-based tracking using the integral histogram. In: Computer Vision and Pattern Recognition, pp. 798–805, New York, NY, USA (2006)
5. Ross, D.A., Lim, J., Lin, R.-S., Yang, M.-H.: Incremental learning for robust visual tracking. Int. J. Comput. Vis. **77**, 125–141 (2008)
6. Zhuang, B., Lu, H., Xiao, Z., Wang, D.: Visual tracking via discriminative sparse similarity map. IEEE Trans. Image Process. **23**, 1872–1881 (2014)
7. Henriques, J.F., Caseiro, R., Martins, P., Batista, J.: Exploiting the circulant structure of tracking-by-detection with kernels. In: Fitzgibbon, A., Lazebnik, S., Perona, P., Sato, Y., Schmid, C. (eds.) ECCV 2012. LNCS, vol. 7575, pp. 702–715. Springer, Heidelberg (2012). https://doi.org/10.1007/978-3-642-33765-9_50
8. Kalal, Z., Mikolajczyk, K., Matas, J.: Tracking-learning-detection. IEEE Trans. Pattern Anal. Mach. Intell. **34**, 1409–1422 (2012)
9. Hare, S., Saffari, A., Torr, P.H.: Struck: structured output tracking with kernels. In: International Conference on Computer Vision, pp. 263–270 (2011)
10. Wu, Y., Lim, J., Yang, M.H.: Online object tracking: a benchmark. In: Computer Vision and Pattern Recognition, pp. 2411–2418 (2013)
11. Mueller, M., Smith, N., Ghanem, B.: A benchmark and simulator for UAV tracking. In: Leibe, B., Matas, J., Sebe, N., Welling, M. (eds.) ECCV 2016. LNCS, vol. 9905, pp. 445–461. Springer, Cham (2016). https://doi.org/10.1007/978-3-319-46448-0_27
12. Zhang, B., Li, Z., Cao, X., Ye, Q., Chen, C., Shen, L., et al.: Output constraint transfer for kernelized correlation filter in tracking. IEEE Trans. Syst. Man Cybernet. Syst. **47**, 693–703 (2017)

13. Arulampalam, M.S., Maskell, S., Gordon, N., et al.: A tutorial on particle filters for online nonlinear/non-Gaussian Bayesian tracking. IEEE Trans. Signal Process. **50**, 174–188 (2002)
14. X.Q. Zhang, W.M. Hu, S. Maybank, X. Li and M.L. Zhu: Sequential particle swarm optimization for visual tracking. In: Computer Vision and Pattern Recognition, Anchorage, AK, USA, pp. 1–8 (2008)
15. Yang, C., Duraiswami, R., Davis, L.: Efficient mean-shift tracking via a new similarity measure. In: Computer Vision and Pattern Recognition, pp. 176–183 (2005)
16. Learnedmiller, E., Sevillalara, L.: Distribution fields for tracking. In: Computer Vision and Pattern Recognition, pp. 1910–1917 (2012)
17. Wu, Y., Shen, B., Ling, H.: Online robust image alignment via iterative convex optimization. In: Computer Vision and Pattern Recognition, pp. 1808–1814 (2012)
18. Zhang, K., Zhang, L., Yang, M.-H.: Real-time compressive tracking. In: Fitzgibbon, A., Lazebnik, S., Perona, P., Sato, Y., Schmid, C. (eds.) ECCV 2012. LNCS, vol. 7574, pp. 864–877. Springer, Heidelberg (2012). https://doi.org/10.1007/978-3-642-33712-3_62
19. Henriques, J.F., Caseiro, R., Martins, P., Batista, J.: High-speed tracking with kernelized correlation filters. IEEE Trans. Pattern Anal. Mach. Intell. **37**, 583–596 (2015)
20. Ma, C., Miao, Z., Zhang, X.P., Li, M.: A saliency prior context model for real-time object tracking. IEEE Trans. Multimedia **19**, 2415–2424 (2017)
21. Liang, P., Blasch, E., Ling, H.: Encoding color information for visual tracking: algorithms and benchmark. In: IEEE Trans. Image Process. 1–14 (2015)
22. Hou, X., Harel, J., Koch, C.: Image signature: highlighting sparse salient regions. IEEE Trans. Pattern Anal. Mach. Intell. **34**(1), 194–201 (2012)
23. Schauerte, B., Stiefelhagen, R.: Quaternion-based spectral saliency detection for eye fixation prediction. In: Fitzgibbon, A., Lazebnik, S., Perona, P., Sato, Y., Schmid, C. (eds.) ECCV 2012. LNCS, pp. 116–129. Springer, Heidelberg (2012). https://doi.org/10.1007/978-3-642-33709-3_9
24. Choi, J., Chang, H.J., Jeong, J., et al.: Visual tracking using attention-modulated disintegration and integration. In: Computer Vision and Pattern Recognition, pp. 4321–4330 (2016)
25. Wang, Q., Teng, Z., Xing, J., Gao, J., Hu, W., Maybank, S.: Learning attentions: residual attentional siamese network for high performance online visual tracking. In: Computer Vision and Pattern Recognition (2018)

Research on Real-Time Vehicle Detection Algorithm Based on Deep Learning

Wei Yang, Ji Zhang, Zhongbao Zhang, and Hongyuan Wang[✉]

Changzhou University, Changzhou, Jiangsu, China
hywang@cczu.edu.cn

Abstract. At present, the demand for transportation is continuously increasing, and the consequent traffic congestion problem has become more and more prominent. How to automatically and timely detect vehicles to analyze road traffic information is an important issue for intelligent traffic monitoring systems (ITS). In some existing methods for to detect vehicles, real-time performance and precision cannot be taken into account at the same time. Hereby, a method of automatic vehicle detection, which has the high performance on real-time and precision, is proposed in this paper. This method improves the YOLOv2 framework model in following aspects: introducing a new loss function, expanding the grid size, and optimizing the number and size of anchors in the model to automatically learn vehicle characteristics. Compared with YOLOv2, YOLOv3 and Faster RCNN, both the precision and the real-time performance of this method are improved competitively.

Keywords: Vehicle detection · Real-time detection · YOLOv2
Loss function

1 Introduction

At present, the level of urbanization in China has exceeded 50% and the number of car ownership has reached 310 million by the end of 2017. With traffic congestion and numerous potential safety issues emerged, it is on rise for the demand for intelligent traffic monitoring systems (ITS). Countries all over the world have invested a large amount of manpower and material resources into the research and development of various transportation technologies. Object detection is an indispensable part of ITS. It is also one of the most important research topics in computer vision, artificial intelligence, pattern recognition, image processing and machine learning. It can provide strong information to support for many traffic links such as road traffic control, highway management and emergency management. Its performance has a direct impact on follow-up objection tracking, objection classification, and objection recognition.

Detection of moving objects from video sequences is an important research issue in computer vision and other application fields. The traditional object detection is generally divided into three stages (Fig. 1): selecting candidate regions, extracting the corresponding features and classification. In the feature extraction process, it usually uses artificial methods, such as Histogram of Oriented Gradient (HOG) [1–3], Scale-invariant Feature Transform (SIFT) [4, 5]. The effect of the model recognition by

© Springer Nature Switzerland AG 2018
J.-H. Lai et al. (Eds.): PRCV 2018, LNCS 11259, pp. 126–137, 2018.
https://doi.org/10.1007/978-3-030-03341-5_11

this method is greatly influenced by the artificial. The extracted features are inputted into the classification, such as the Support Vector Machine (SVM) [6], the AdaBoost [7], DPM [8] and RF [9]. In 2010, Felzenszwalb et al. proposed DPM, in which the features extraction doesn't needed to be separated from the classifier training, and make full use of the advantages of HOG and SVM. This has greatly improved the detection effect. However, the disadvantage of the DPM model is its high complexity and low object detection speed and precision.

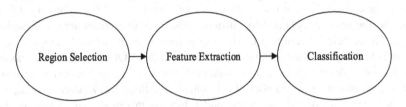

Fig. 1. Three stages of traditional object detection

However, as the traffic environment becomes more and more complex, the characteristics of the manual design are not very robust to the diversity of the objection. Therefore, the application of deep learning to object detection is a research trend. The RCNN [10] proposed by Ross et al. has made great breakthroughs in the field of object detection, followed by SPP-net [11], Fast-RCNN [12], Faster-RCNN [13], R-FCN [14], and YOLO [15], SSD [16] and other algorithms. CNN was first added to RCNN [10] for object detection. The method solves the problem that how to train high-quality models with a small amount of the labeled data and becomes the mainstream method in the field of object detection. However, RCNN [10] needs to perform a forward CNN to carry out feature extraction for each proposal extracted from Selective Search [17] (SS). Therefore, the calculation volume is too large to be updated in real time. Fast-RCNN [12] model is an improvement on RCNN [10], which avoids the redundant feature extraction operation in RCNN [10], and adopts adaptive scale pooling to optimize the entire network to improve the precision of deep network detection and recognition. However, Fast-RCNN [12] uses the Selective Search Algorithm (SS) [9] to extract candidate regions, which takes a long time. And the Faster-RCNN [13] algorithm introduces the RPN network on this foundation, which shortens the time of proposal extraction obviously, and achieves the highest object detection precision on the VOC2007 and VOC2012 datasets. Although the RCNN series have high detection precision, they still can't meet the real-time requirement on the detection speed. On the other hand, Ross et al. proposed the YOLO [11] algorithm, which can achieve 45FPS using GPU acceleration on PASCAL VOC, and YOLOv2 algorithm, which can achieve 67FPS in a specific environment. However, YOLO is not effective in detecting small and low-precision objects, its generalization ability is weak, and the error of location influences the detection effect seriously. In response to these problems of YOLO, SSD [12] combines with RPN structure to improve YOLO and achieves higher detection precision and speed. Subsequently, YOLOv2 makes a balance between precision and speed. At the same time, YOLO9000 [18] is trained in

COCO and ImageNet datasets to achieve real-time detection of over 9000 species. In 2018, Redman et al. proposes YOLOv3 [19] based on YOLO algorithm. YOLOv3 has improved a lot in speed while maintaining its original precision. At the same time, its ability to detect small objects has increased, but its performance on medium-sized and larger objects has been relatively poor.

In summary, YOLOv2 model is a better choice for real-time vehicle detection in the real scene. However, it is still insufficient for vehicle detection: (1) the precision is lower than Faster RCNN. (2) YOLOv2 is trained and tested on VOC2007 and COCO datasets, these datasets have many categories and some categories have very different shapes. So the anchors obtained by clustering the bounding boxes are not completely suitable for vehicle detection. (3) The recognition rate of difficult samples on the datasets is not high. In view of the above, based on the YOLOv2 model an improved algorithm for to detect vehicle is presented in this paper. The method introduces a new loss function, increases the number of cell units in the detection window and improves the number and sizes of anchors in the model. Finally, this model automatically learns the vehicle characteristics and realizes real-time and high-precision vehicle automatic detection and vehicle category recognition.

2   Real-Time Object Detection YOLOv2 Algorithm

Reference to the YOLO and SSD network structure, YOLOv2 designs a new classification network Darkne-19 as the basis of the network model, which is improved on the basis of YOLOv1 (YOLOv1 structure is shown in Fig. 2). Most object detection frameworks use VGG-16 as the feature extraction network before YOLOv2, but VGG-16 is more complex and requires more computation. The YOLO framework uses a network structure similar to GoogleNet, and the amount of calculation is less than VGG-16, but the precision is slightly lower than VGG-16.

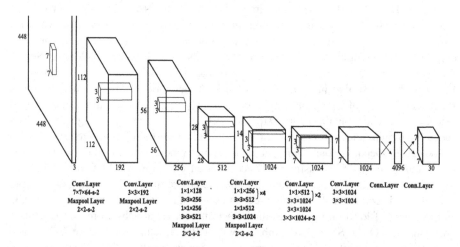

Fig. 2. YOLOv1 network structure

YOLOv2 detection network extracts features based on Darknet-19 and then modifies its network structure accordingly. The last convolution layer of the Darknet-19 is changed to three convolution layers, which the size of is 3 * 3 and the channel is 1024. In order to compress features and increase the depth of the network, the number of channels will be doubled after each pooling operation and places the 1 * 1 convolution kernel between the convolution kernels of 3 * 3. Compared with YOLOv2, the paper draws on the idea of anchor in Faster RCNN: using k-means [20] algorithm to cluster the bounding boxes in the dataset and determine the size and quantity of the anchor. In order to introduce anchor boxes to predict bounding boxes, the author removes the full connection layer from the network. The model contains only the convolutional layer and the pooling layer, so the input size can be changed at any time. During training, the model input size is changed every few rounds to make the model robust to different size images. Class prediction in YOLOv2 is no longer bound to each cell, but the anchor is used to predict categories and coordinates at the same time. Instead of direct prediction of the coordinates, the prediction of the relative offset is used to simplify the problem and facilitate the learning of network. Each time after 10 training, the model randomly chooses a new input image size to continue training. This training rule forces the model to adapt to different resolutions. The model is faster for small size, so YOLOv2 can adjust speed and precision according to the demand.

3 Improved Method Based on YOLOv2 Model

Although YOLOv2 has achieved good real-time detection results, the precision is still lower than that of the Faster RCNN and the algorithm does not fully apply to vehicle detection. For the specific problems in the application, this paper makes following improvements based on YOLOv2:

1. Constructing a new loss function to reduce the weight of easy-to-classify samples, so that the model was more focused on hard-to-classify samples during training.
2. K-means is used to cluster the bounding boxes of KITTI dataset to determine the number and size of the anchor. The anchor of YOLOv2 is determined by the VOC2007 and VOC2012 datasets clustering. These datasets are rich in categories and have different shapes. The anchor's parameters are universal, but not suitable for data in KITTI dataset. The clustering operation needed to be redone in KITTI dataset.
3. Improving the size of the network's feature map behind the multiple convolutional layers and pooling operations, which enabled more bounding boxes to be detected to reduce missed detection rates.

3.1 Construct New Loss Function

The design goal of the loss function is to achieve a good balance between the coordinates, the confidence of the bounding boxes and the category. The total loss function of YOLOv2 is shown in Formula 1:

$$\lambda_{noobj} \sum_{i=0}^{l.h*l.w} \sum_{j=0}^{l.n} l_{ij}^{noobj} \left(c_i - \hat{c}_i\right)^2 + \lambda_{obj} \sum_{i=0}^{l.h*l.w} \sum_{j=0}^{l.n} l_{ij}^{obj} \left(c_i - \hat{c}_i\right)^2$$

$$+ \lambda_{class} \sum_{i=0}^{l.w*l.h} \sum_{j=0}^{l.n} l_{ij}^{obj} \sum_{c \in classes} \left(p_i(c) - \hat{p}_i(c)\right)^2$$

$$+ \lambda_{coord} \sum_{i=0}^{l.w*l.h} \sum_{j=0}^{j.n} l_{ij}^{obj} (2 - w_i * h_i) \left[\left(x_i - \hat{x}_i\right)^2 + \left(y_i - \hat{y}_i\right)^2 + \left(w_i - \hat{w}_i\right)^2 + \left(h_i - \hat{h}_i\right)^2\right] \qquad (1)$$

$$+ 0.01 * \sum_{i=0}^{l.w*l.h} \sum_{j=0}^{j.n} l_{ij}^{noobj} \left[\left(p_{jx} - \hat{x}_i\right)^2 + \left(p_{jy} - \hat{y}_i\right)^2 + \left(p_{jw} - \hat{w}_i\right)^2 + \left(p_{jh} - \hat{h}_i\right)^2\right]$$

In the loss function, c_i is the real category, $\hat{c}$ is the prediction category; (x_i, y_i, w_i, h_i) is the boundary box information of the real object, $(\hat{x}_i, \hat{y}_i, \hat{w}_i, \hat{h}_i)$ is the boundary box information of the prediction object, and $\lambda_{noobj}, \lambda_{class}, \lambda_{coord}$ are the weight parameters. The first two items calculate the IOU loss of the anchors containing the object and the non-object, that is the prediction of the confidence of the bounding boxes with or without the object; the third item represents the category prediction; the forth item represents the coordinate prediction, that is, for each objection, calculate the nearest coordinate gradient of the anchor; The last item calculates the loss of those anchors that failed to provide a valid prediction of truth in the anchors. It is somewhat similar to the difference in loss for cells that contain object and no objects. The anchors that do not provide valid predictions use the weight of scale = 0.01 to calculate the loss. The main purpose is to be more stable in the early stages of model training.

However, the YOLO algorithm is unipolar and has low precision. The reason is that the background and foreground is unbalanced. This imbalance leads to a large number of easy sample classes (including easy positive and easy negative, but mainly easy negative) during training. Although the loss of each sample class is small, because of the large number, it dominates the final loss, and results in a degenerate model that is eventually trained. Therefore, this paper prepares to change term of the third item and adds a modulation factor $(1 - p_i(c))^\gamma$ to increase the precision. The specific loss function is as follows:

$$\lambda_{noobj} \sum_{i=0}^{l.h*l.w} \sum_{j=0}^{l.n} l_{ij}^{noobj} \left(c_i - \hat{c}_i\right)^2 + \lambda_{obj} \sum_{i=0}^{l.h*l.w} \sum_{j=0}^{l.n} l_{ij}^{obj} \left(c_i - \hat{c}_i\right)^2$$

$$+ \lambda_{class} (1 - p_i(c))^\gamma \sum_{i=0}^{l.w*l.h} \sum_{j=0}^{l.n} l_{ij}^{obj} \sum_{c \in classes} \left(p_i(c) - \hat{p}_i(c)\right)^2$$

$$+ \lambda_{coord} \sum_{i=0}^{l.w*l.h} \sum_{j=0}^{j.n} l_{ij}^{obj} (2 - w_i * h_i) \left[\left(x_i - \hat{x}_i\right)^2 + \left(y_i - \hat{y}_i\right)^2 + \left(w_i - \hat{w}_i\right)^2 + \left(h_i - \hat{h}_i\right)^2\right] \qquad (2)$$

$$+ 0.01 * \sum_{i=0}^{l.w*l.h} \sum_{j=0}^{j.n} l_{ij}^{noobj} \left[\left(p_{jx} - \hat{x}_i\right)^2 + \left(p_{jy} - \hat{y}_i\right)^2 + \left(p_{jw} - \hat{w}_i\right)^2 + \left(p_{jh} - \hat{h}_i\right)^2\right]$$

3.2   K-Means Dimension Clustering

Drawing on the idea of Faster RCNN, YOLOv2 introduces k-means to cluster the bounding boxes in dataset by dimension, which can determine the sizes and number of anchors. Anchors are a set of initial candidates of fixed size and aspect ratio. The quality of the anchors affects the speed of the object detection and the precision of the location of bounding box. However, because the number and width dimensions of the anchor in the Faster-RCNN are manually set, Redmon et al. proposes a method of dimensional clustering to cluster bounding boxes manually labeled in the dataset by k-means. The clustering result of VOC and COCO datasets is 5, so the number of anchors in YOLOv2 network is 5. However, this clustering result is not suitable for the KITTI datasets. In this paper, the method of dimensional clustering is used to find the proper K by adjusting the objective function $d(box, centroid) = 1 - IOU(box, centroid)$ to the minimum, variable box represents the information of the bounding box and $centroid$ represents the information of the cluster center. Then, the k-means algorithm is used to cluster the bounding boxes corresponding to the object area in the KITTI datasets, and the optimal number of anchors and the width-height dimension suitable for the detection data set are obtained.

3.3   Grid Size Expansion

In YOLOv2, all of the images must be divided into $S * S$ grids. In different environments, the number of grids affects the precision of detection. When multiple objects are included in the images, especially small objects, the expanded network size can increase the number of objects extracted and improve recognition precision of the system. However, for sparse objects, increasing the number of grids will not greatly improve the detection effect, and will increase the complexity and calculation of the model. Therefore, selecting the appropriate parameter S is also critical for the precision and speed of the object detection. Since the object density in the image varied with the traffic flow, several sets of contrast experiments are conducted when determining the size of S. In the experiment, $S = 7$, 9 and 14 are taken, and recall rate and precision have improved when $S = 14$, so takes $S = 14$ in this paper.

4   Result and Analysis

4.1   Experimental Data

Based on YOLOv2, the train phase of vehicle detection model needs a large amount of labeled vehicle data. The larger number of training data brings the improvement of the recognition rate and the generalization performance of the model. Therefore, the establishment of vehicle detection dataset is very important for to improve YOLOv2 algorithm.

This paper uses the KITTI dataset a public computer vision algorithm evaluation dataset under the world's largest autopilot scenario. KITTI dataset contains real image data collected from urban, rural, and highway scenes with a maximum of 15 cars and 30 pedestrians per image. There are various degrees of occlusion and truncation. In the experiment, 4000 images are selected as the training set A and 3481 images are used as the test set A* from the KITTI dataset. Considering the actual situation, the dataset was expanded by left and right flipping. In addition, in order to verify the validity of the model and the generalization ability, 7000 images are selected from the public dataset BIT-Vehicle Dataset as test set B, 7000 images under different conditions in the actual scene were collected as test set C. Table 1 shows the dataset information.

Table 1. Sample number information

Dataset	Quantity	Left and right flip	Resolution/pixel
training set A	4000	8000	1242 * 375
test set A*	3481	6962	1242 * 375
test set B	9850	–	1600 * 1200
test set C	8041	–	1920 * 1080

4.2 Experimental Configuration and Training

Our experiments are performed on a computer equipped with an Ubuntu 16.04 system. The model of the graphics card is a TITAN XP discrete graphics card produced by NVIDIA, and a GPU development package CUDA8.0 and a deep learning acceleration library cudnn5.1 are installed. Development environment is Python2.7, and the framework is Darknet-19.

The network parameters are as follows: learning-rate is 0.0001; policy is steps; batch is 128; steps respectively take 100, 20000, 35000; max-batch is 40000; scales are 10, 0.1, 0.1; momentum is 0.9 and decay is 0.0005. As shown in Fig. 3, the horizontal ordinate represents the number of iterations, ranging from 0 to 40,000 times. After the number of network iterations exceeds 15,000 times, the parameters have stabilized. During the training, the changes of average-loss, class, region- average IOU and average recall are important parameters to measure the quality of the model. In the training phase, average-loss needs to decline, and finally maintains a stable range. In addition, the value of region average IOU and average recall tend to be as good as 1, as can be seen from the figure, which basically meets the requirements.

4.3 Comparison of Different Threshold on the Dataset

The merger of sub-regions will cause redundancy in the detection window. The sub-region detection window itself is redundant, which can lead to the main objection may be repeatedly selected and affect the detection results. In order to be able to select a better object area, the non-maximum suppression algorithm (NMS) is a common method to solve this problem. The optimal threshold can be determined based on the detection effect obtained by different thresholds. As shown in Table 2, Rps/Img represents the number of bounding boxes in each sample. Seen from Fig. 4, the precision and recall rate are inversely proportional to the change of threshold value. By observing

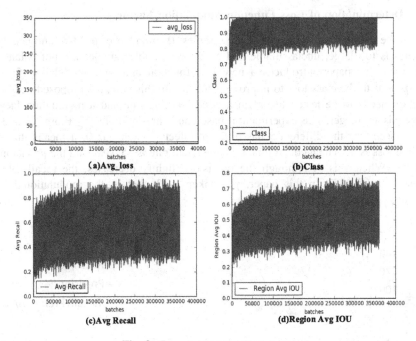

Fig. 3. Important parameters curves

the data changes of them, when the threshold is about 0.45, the recall rate is 35.08% and the precision is 93.47% and the detection effect of both recall rate and precision can be obtained. Therefore, after completing the network training by using the improved method, the threshold is set to 0.50, and the training effect is verified by using the sample of the validation set.

Table 2. The Comparison of verification results for different threshold

Threshold	Rps/Img	Recall/%	Precision/%	Recall + Precision/%
0.001	79.94	63.15	3.54	66.69
0.050	4.65	56.17	54.12	110.29
0.100	3.69	53.01	64.28	117.29
0.150	3.21	50.62	70.58	121.20
0.200	2.88	48.29	75.18	123.47
0.250	2.63	46.25	78.73	124.98
0.300	2.39	43.96	82.39	126.35
0.350	2.16	41.49	86.17	127.66
0.400	1.93	38.62	89.77	128.39
0.450	**1.68**	**35.08**	**93.47**	**128.55**
0.500	1.41	30.71	95.31	126.02
0.550	1.17	26.08	96.20	122.28
0.600	1.08	23.14	97.58	120.72

4.4   Determination of Loss Function Modulation Factor γ

Due to the unbalanced categories of the samples, the number of positive and negative samples is too large, unclassifiable and easily classifiable samples are not balanced. Therefore, this paper introduces a new loss function and adds modulation factors $(1 - p_i(c))^\gamma$ to the class loss to improve precision. In this case, the proposed new loss function needs to be tested to obtain a good learning rate and a modulation factor, where γ is an integer. This experiment is based on a threshold of 0.45. From Table 3, it can be seen that the different γ has different effects. When γ is 0, it means that the original loss is not changed. At this time, the recall rate is 35.08%, and the precision is 93.47%. When γ is 3, although the precision slightly decreases, the recall rate is increased by 5.23%. In this paper, γ is taken as 3, that is, the modulation factor $(1 - p_i(c))^3$ is increased.

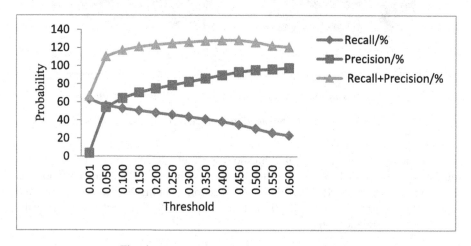

Fig. 4. The variation of precision and recall rate

4.5   The Results of the Dimension Clustering of Bounding Boxes

This paper adopts the method of dimensional clustering. The criteria evaluation is related to the IOU score. The objective function formula is $d(box, centroid) = 1 - IOU(box, centroid)$. The purpose of k-means is to adjust the objective function to the minimum, that is, the IOU is the largest. As can be seen from Fig. 5, when k is 5, the objective function reaches the minimum, so the number of anchors is 5, and k is 5 for exclusive clustering to obtain anchors. The final anchors are (0.39, 1.18), (0.69, 5.29), (0.94, 1.77), (1.78, 5.28), (3.10, 6.28). After getting the values of the anchors, the configuration file is changed to train the model, eventually increasing the precision to 95.04% and the recall rate to 41.37%.

Table 3. The model performance of different γ

γ	Recall/%	Precision/%	Recall + Precision/%
0	35.08	93.47	128.55
1	33.77	91.46	125.23
2	41.48	91.68	133.16
3	**40.31**	**93.27**	**133.58**
4	38.82	92.47	131.29

4.6 Comparison of Test Results of Different Test Sets

In order to evaluate the quality of this algorithm, we carry out a test model on three different test sets. The test results are shown in Table 4. A* is the test set in the KITTI data set, B is a test set selected in the BIT-Vehicle Dataset, and C is selected from the home-made dataset. As can be seen from the table, the algorithm has good generalization ability and the overall robustness is very good. As can be seen from Table 5, the precision and recall rate of Test Set B are particularly high. It is because BIT-Vehicle Dataset only has one vehicle per picture, and the vehicle is large and easy to identify. While Test Set C is homemade, vehicles in the dataset are relatively intensive and there are many small objects, so the recall rate is low.

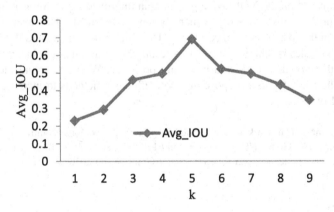

Fig. 5. The change curve of AVG-IOU

Table 4. Performance of models under different test sets

Test set	Quantity	Left and right flip	Precision/%	Recall/%
A*	6962	1242 * 375	94.45	36.33
B	9850	1600 * 1200	95.86	68.92
C	8041	1920 * 1080	92.21	62.25

Table 5. Performance of different object detection algorithms

Object detection algorithm	mAP/%	Detection speed(s/piece)
Ours	**78.35**	**0.023**
YOLOv2	75.18	0.025
YOLOv3	67.13	0.024
Faster RCNN	75.80	0.039

4.7   Comparison with Other Object Detection Algorithms

In this paper, the improved algorithm based on YOLOv2 is compared with YOLOv2, YOLOv3 and Faster RCNN. The comparison results are shown in Table 5. It can be seen from the table that the algorithm in this paper is improved in real time and precision. It can be seen from the table that detection effect in the actual application scenario is worse than that in the verification. This is because in the actual application scenario, the distant objects (such as, the small object) in the video has a poor detection effect, which needs to be improved.

5   Conclusion

In this paper, based on the YOLOv2 algorithm, an improved algorithm is proposed and its performance is validated with in many set of experiments. However, the KITTI dataset used in this paper has a maximum of 15 vehicles per image, and the number of small object samples is relatively less. As a result, the recall rate of vehicle detection is not high in the crowded roads and in distant positions. We will expand the scope of research in the next step and propose the more effective methods to increase the recall rate of small objects.

Acknowledgments. This work was supported in part by the National Natural Science Foundation of China under Grants NO. 61502058 and 61572085, and part by Jiangsu Joint Research Project of Industry, Education and Research under Grant No.BY2016029-15.

References

1. Wang, S., Yan, J., Wang, Z.: Improved moving object detection algorithm based on local united feature. Chin. J. Sci. Instrum. **36**(10), 2241–2248 (2015)
2. Viola, P., Jones, M.J.: Rapid object detection using a boosted cascade of simple features. In: IEEE CVPR, pp. 511–518 (2001)
3. Dalal, N., Triggs, B.: Histograms of oriented gradients for human detection. In: IEEE Computer Society Conference on Computer Vision and Pattern Recognition, vol. 1, pp. 886–893 (2005)
4. Lowe, D.G.: Object recognition from local scale-invariant features. In: International Conference on Computer Vision, Corfu, Greece, pp. 1150–1157 (1999)
5. Lowe, D.G.: Distinctive image features from scale-invariant keypoints. Int. J. Comput. Vis. **60**(2), 91–110 (2004)

6. Wang, L. (ed.): Support Vector Machines: Theory and Applications. Springer, Heidelberg (2005). https://doi.org/10.1007/b95439
7. Ferreira, A.J., Figueiredo, M.A.T.: Boosting algorithms: a review of methods, theory, and applications. In: Zhang, C., Ma, Y. (eds.) Ensemble Machine Learning, pp. 35–85. Springer, Boston (2012). https://doi.org/10.1007/978-1-4419-9326-7_2
8. Felzenszwalb, P., Ross, G., McAllester, D.: Object detection with discriminatively trained part based models. IEEE Trans. Pattern Anal. Mach. Intell. **32**(9), 1627–1645 (2010)
9. Breiman, L.: Machine Learning. Mach. Learn. **45**(1), 5–32 (2001)
10. Girshick, R., Donahue, J., Darrell, T., Malik, J.: Rich feature hierarchies for accurate object detection and semantic segmentation. In: 2014 IEEE Conference on Computer Vision and Pattern Recognition (CVPR), pp. 580–587. IEEE (2014)
11. He, K., Zhang, X., Ren, S., Sun, J.: Spatial pyramid pooling in deep convolutional networks for visual recognition. In: Fleet, D., Pajdla, T., Schiele, B., Tuytelaars, T. (eds.) ECCV 2014. LNCS, vol. 8691, pp. 346–361. Springer, Heidelberg (2014). https://doi.org/10.1007/978-3-319-10578-9_23
12. Girshick, R.: Fast R-CNN. In: International Conference on Computer Vision, pp. 1440–1448 (2015)
13. Ren, S., He, K., Girshick, R., Sun, J.: Faster R-CNN: towards real-time object detection with region proposal networks. In: Advances in Neural Information Processing Systems, pp. 91–99 (2015)
14. Dai, J., Li, Y., He, K.: R-FCN: object detection via region-based fully convolutional networks (2016)
15. Redmon, J., Divvala, S., Girshick, R., Farhadi, A.: You only look once: unified, real-time object detection. In: Computer Vision and Pattern Recognition, pp. 779–788 (2016)
16. Liu, W., et al.: SSD: single shot multibox detector. In: Leibe, B., Matas, J., Sebe, N., Welling, M. (eds.) ECCV 2016. LNCS, vol. 9905, pp. 21–37. Springer, Cham (2016). https://doi.org/10.1007/978-3-319-46448-0_2
17. Uijlings, J.R., Sande, K.E., Gevers, T., Smeulders, A.W.: Selective search for object recognition. Int. J. Comput. Vis. **104**, 154–171 (2013)
18. Redmon, J., Farhadi, A.: YOLO9000: better, faster, stronger, pp. 6517–6525 (2016)
19. Redmon J, Farhadi A.: YOLOv3: An Incremental Improvement (2018). arXiv: 1804.02767
20. Huang, Z.: Extensions to the k-means algorithm for clustering large data sets with categorical values. Data Min. Knowl. Discov. **2**(3), 283–304 (1998)

Vehicle Detection Based on Separable Reverse Connected Network

Enze Yang, Linlin Huang[(⊠)], and Jian Hu

Beijingjiaotong University, Beijing, China
{16120028,huangll,jhu}@bjtu.edu.cn

Abstract. Vehicle detection is a challenging problem which plays an important role in a wide range of traffic applications. In this paper, we propose a fast and accurate framework for detection vehicles on multi-scale using Separable Reverse Connected network. Reverse connected structure enriches the semantic information of former layers, while separable convolution is introduced for reducing computation costs. Further, optimization methods based on multi-scale training and model compressing are employed to make training process more efficient and reduce the parameters of the network with slightly loss of accuracy. Comprehensive evaluations on Pascal VOC 2007+2012 and MSCOCO 2014 show that proposed method outperforms that using Feature Pyramid Network (FPN) about 3% in mAP of vehicle categories. Model compressing accelerates the network of two-stage detector about 10 times without distinct drop of accuracy, which brings about high quality for real-time vehicle detection.

Keywords: Vehicle detection · Separable Reverse Connected network
Model compression · Convolutional neural networks

1 Introduction

Vehicle detection is one of the most fundamental and significant tasks in surveillance systems, driver-assistance systems and a wide range of intelligent traffic applications.

Traditional vehicle detectors were mainly designed by hand-engineered feature extractor such as HOG [12], SIFT [13], Haar-like [14], and sliding-window algorithms such as Selective Search [15] and Edge Box [16] which were used to generate a large number of redundant windows. The performance of the detectors is dominated by the method of feature extraction with heavy computational costs and limited ability of representation. With the rapid progress of deep convolutional neural networks in recent years, CNN based vehicle detectors have achieved remarkable performance and become a new trend in detection tasks.

However, detect vehicles in modern urban environment is challenging because that the detection network should be robust to different weather conditions and frequent occlusion. Besides, from the perspective of design and network optimization, several key issues are caused widespread concern recently: (i) Multiple vehicle attributes recognition. In order to analyze the traffic scene from a comprehensive point of view, a vehicle detector should not only locate appearing vehicles but also extract the attributes from specific vehicle categories. (ii) Multi-scale detection. Recognizing vehicles at

© Springer Nature Switzerland AG 2018
J.-H. Lai et al. (Eds.): PRCV 2018, LNCS 11259, pp. 138–149, 2018.
https://doi.org/10.1007/978-3-030-03341-5_12

vastly different scales has been a challenge in vehicle detection. In other words, detecting vehicles of small size usually shows lower accuracy. (iii) Real-time detection. The demand of real-time vehicle detection is increasing rapidly, reducing storage and compressing network models are mainly methods adopted to achieve acceleration.

Recent CNN based vehicle detectors are categorized into two-stage and single-stage detectors. The two-stage detectors consist of region proposal network and a pipeline for classification and bounding box regression. The most famous R-CNN series network [1–3] are proposed gradually for detection tasks. R-CNN [1] predict objects from region proposals generated by Selective Search through CNN layers. Fast R-CNN [2] propose entire-image convolution for network acceleration. As a milestone, Faster R-CNN [3] introduce Region Proposal Network (RPN) to generate proposals using convoluted features. R-FCN [4] intend to generate a fully convolutional network and position sensitive feature map for more precise region proposals. Dai et al. propose Deformable Convolutional Networks [5] for geometric transformations by learning additional offsets without supervision. Feature Pyramid Network [6] is constructed upon image pyramid for multi-scale detection, which enables a model to detect objects across multiple scales. A top-down architecture with skip connections are utilized to merge the feature maps. FPN brings an idea of multi-scale detection, however the method of up-sample brings partial void information from deep layers, which is not efficient for feature fusion.

The single-stage detectors directly predict object instance with modified backbone. YOLO [7] employ a light feature extractor and simplifies detection as a regression problem. Even though YOLO could hardly achieve the accuracy as region based networks, it provides surprisingly speed of detection in return. A series steps is made on previous work by YOLO v2 [8], which gains a great improvement of speed and accuracy in detection. Benefited from YOLO and Faster R-CNN, Single Shot Multi-box Detector [9] is proposed to detect objects in different aspect ratios and scales on hierarchical feature maps. However, from the perspective of multi-scale detection and network efficiency, there is a certain space for both single-stage and two-stage detectors to improve their performance.

In this paper, Separable Reverse Connected network was proposed to achieve higher accuracy in multi-scale vehicle detection. Compared with Feature Pyramid Network [6], reverse connected structure enriches the semantic information of former layers by merging de-convoluted feature from deeper layers. Furthermore, separable convolution is introduced for the purpose of fewer parameters and lower computation costs. Prediction layers are designed in 3 scales that represent the detected vehicles of large middle and small size respectively. For optimization, Multi-scale training and OHEM [10] are employed to make the training process more efficient. Deep compression [11] is applied to reduce the storage requirement of neural networks which achieve acceleration with slightly loss of accuracy. By integrating the works above, an advanced vehicle detection framework with high quality of multi-scale detection and fast speed of processing based on modern object detectors were proposed in this paper.

2 Our Approach

Convolutional neural networks have become the leading method of vehicle detection, in this section, we introduce a Separable Reverse Connected network based on an analysis of existing vehicle detectors, the key idea of our approach is taking full advantage of semantic information from deeper feature maps, and by introducing separable convolution can we reduce the parameters and computational costs. Moreover, methods for optimization are implied for a better performance of the network.

2.1 Network Selection

A series of comparative experiments are conducted for an analysis of the modern detectors. As a representative of high performance object detectors among all the existing detection frameworks, two-stage detectors like Faster R-CNN, R-FCN and FPN applied on Faster R-CNN, and single-stage detectors like YOLO, YOLO v2 and SSD are as representatives of efficient detectors come into our sight. Among two-stage approaches, R-FCN and FPN are the networks to strengthen Faster-RCNN in different aspects. ZF, VGG and ResNet are introduced as feature extractors. And for single-stage approaches, darknet and VGG are utilized by default.

2.2 Separable Reverse Connected Network

A network with high quality of multi-scale vehicle detection is proposed in this subsection. The purpose of our work is to enrich the semantic information of former feature maps, meanwhile, the increasing scale of parameters is a problem should be taken into consideration.

Reverse Connected Structure. The method of combining fine-grained features from former feature maps with high resolution feature maps from deeper layers is widely accepted in multi-scale detection tasks. Benefitted from Feature Pyramid Network [6] which introduce a top-down pathway and lateral connections, fine-grained features are extracted in a proper way. Top-down pathways enhance the low-level semantics feature maps by up-sampling spatially coarser, together with lateral connections from bottom-up pathway, merged feature maps are provided with comprehensive information.

Inspired from FPN, the significant improvement of multi-scale objects detection by combining multiple features should be noticed. From this point of view, we try to enhance the low-level feature maps in an intense method. Thus, rich features brought by deeper layers are further enhanced in our reverse connected structure.

Reverse connected structure compared with FPN is shown in Fig. 1, in our approach, de-convolution layer is connected with deeper feature map instead of up-sample layer of top-down pathway in FPN. Similarly, lateral pathways and de-convoluted feature maps are combined by element-wise addition. This process is applied on the prediction layers for feature enhancement which will be discussed in following sections. Clearly, the ability of multi-scale representation enables the network to detect vehicles in wider scales. However, as a price of more semantic features for former layers, de-convolution in fusing feature maps bring more parameters than up-sample method, which leads to efficiency decline of the network.

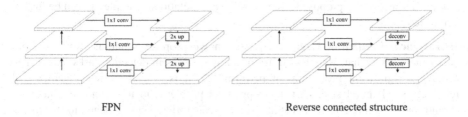

FPN   Reverse connected structure

Fig. 1. Feature Pyramid Network (FPN) merges the feature map by 2x up-sampling while Reverse connected structure utilizes de-convolution instead.

Separable Convolution. Following the discussion above, multi-scale detection is achieved in a reverse connected structure, but meanwhile the network brings more computational costs, which is exactly the problem will be considered in the process of framework design. An efficient structure in Inception V3 [18] for reducing parameters from deep feature maps is proposed as spatial factorization.

The crucial part of the method is asymmetric convolution which separate the original $k \times k$ convolutions into $k \times 1$ followed by $1 \times k$ convolutions, the scale of parameters is significant reduced from k^2 to $2k$. Additionally, the scale of the feature map can be controlled by C_{mid} and C_{out} according to Fig. 2, as mentioned in Inception V3, very good results could be achieved by employing spatial factorization on deeper layers, thus, a similar implementation is introduced as separable convolution after feature extractors in our framework.

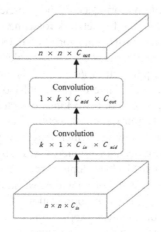

Separable Convolution

Fig. 2. Separable convolution implied on feature map

Separable convolution is presented for the purpose of parameters decrease, which offsets the efficiency loss caused by reverse connected structure. Besides, the capability of feature map could be adjusted by separable convolution through setting channels of output. By integrating proposed structures, the computational complexity can be further controlled.

Hierarchical Prediction Layers. The reason we propose Separable Reverse Connected network is that, vehicles are from multiple scales in detection tasks, in order to achieve a significant promotion of performance, it is crucial to detect vehicles of relatively small pixel size. Driven by practical problems in this work, our network should show its strength of detecting vehicle categories. Hence, benefitted from the image pyramid of SSD [9], which predict objects in hierarchical layers for more accurate results, vehicles in multi-scales are supposed to be sort out in fused feature maps generated from Separable Reverse Connected network. Notice that the vehicle categories are the main targets that we need to characterize, prediction layers are designed in 3 scales for network efficiency, each layers represents the corresponding scale of vehicles to be detected.

From the suggested structure, Fig. 3 shows the entire pipeline of vehicle detection proposed in our work. Firstly, original image is sent to the feature extractor, fused feature maps are created by Separable Reverse Connected network afterwards, vehicles will be predicted in multiple scale on the basis of rich semantic information. The top layer predicts vehicles of large size (most buses and trucks, partial cars), the layer in between predicts middle size vehicles (most cars, partial buses, trucks, motors and people), and the bottom layer is for small size vehicles (most motors and people, partial cars).

2.3 Optimization

As the network structure presented above, further studies will be conducted in this section to improve the overall performance of the vehicle detection task.

We employ multi-scale training for network robustness and a better adaptability for multi-scale detection. Among most frameworks of detection, resizing images for a certain input is widely accepted. However, diverse scales of input images bring about enhancement of datasets. In practical, a portion of dataset is extracted, and then we change the resolution in a certain range of {256, 608} by resizing images randomly. Multi-scale training is adopted by both two kinds of detectors.

Another strategy for training process of detectors aims at the imbalance between the positive and negative training examples which may cause inefficient training because the standard cross-entropy loss cannot provide useful supervision signals, instead of using negative examples, OHEM [10] adopts a re-weighting scheme to address this problem, which leads to a faster and more stable network. By implementing online hard example mining algorithm, the network optimization of training process is achieved.

From the perspective of practical application, the single-stage detectors are designed for real-time detection while the two-stage detectors are always lack of efficiency due to expensive computational costs and intensive memory. Therefore, we introduce model compression for optimizing two-stage detectors in this work.

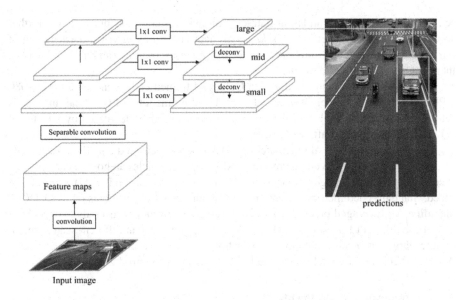

Separable Reverse Connected network

Fig. 3. The pipeline of proposed Separable Reverse Connected network. In a design of hierarchical prediction, vehicles are predicted in multiple feature maps.

According to [11], parameter pruning and sharing is the effective method in reducing the network complexity and addressing the over-fitting problem.

By means of an implementation of model compressing, significant reduction has been shown on the scale of two-stage models, which enable the two-stage detectors toward real-time vehicle detection.

3   Experiments

In this section, the constitution of datasets will be introduced at first, then we list the results of comparative experiments in two-stage and single-stage detectors, the performance of our approach in multi-scale vehicle detection and optimization will be evaluated in following subsections.

One of the purpose of our work is that proposed vehicle detectors have the ability to recognize variable categories as much as possible in real-world traffic environment. Additionally, there are much more connections between the location of other objects like pedestrians which should be taken into consideration in traffic environment. For this reason, we aiming two standard object detection datasets Pascal VOC 0712 and MS COCO for network training and evaluation. Pascal VOC has 20 object categories which including car, bus, motor and person in vehicle categories. We trained all the models on the union set of VOC 2007 *trainval* and VOC 2012 *trainval* ("07+12"), and evaluate on VOC 2007 *test* set. MS COCO has 80 objects categories which including car, bus, truck, motor and person in vehicle categories. There are 80k images in training set, and 40k images in validation dataset. Following a common practice, we further split the 40k validation set into 35k *large-val* datasets and 5k *mini-val* datasets. All of our experiments involve training set and the *large-val* for training (about 115k images), then test on 5k *mini-val* datasets.

The models are implemented within Caffe and trained end-to-end on a GTX 1080 GPU, with SGD and a weight decay of 0.0001 and momentum of 0.9. Learning rate is set to 0.001 at the beginning of the training process, and then decreased by a factor of 0.1 every 50k iterations after 90k iterations.

The evaluation results of the models listed below are measured equally. Pascal VOC results are evaluated by Average Precision (AP) for each vehicle category, mean Average Precision of vehicle categories (vehs mAP) and frame per second (FPS) as detection speed. Standard coco metrics are employed to evaluate our experiments on MS COCO, including AP (averaged precision over intersection-over-union thresholds), AP_{50}, AP_{75} (AP at use different IoU thresholds), and AP_S, AP_M, AP_L (AP at different scales: small, middle, large) as a representation of detection performance in different scales, mean Average Precision of vehicle categories (vehs mAP) is also introduced in evaluation.

3.1   Comparative Experiments

Corresponding comparative experiments are conducted for an analysis of modern vehicle detectors.

Experiments on Two-Stage Detectors. Faster R-CNN, R-FCN and FPN based on Faster R-CNN are mainly discussed in two-stage detectors.

For Faster R-CNN, the detector with a backbone of VGG shows a higher accuracy in detecting vehicles, while ZF holds a faster result because of fewer parameters. R-FCN has been improved on the basis of the Faster R-CNN networks. VGG, ResNet50 and ResNet101 are the feature extractors for R-FCN, and clearly ResNet101 possesses advantages against other backbones especially for detection tasks of buses and trucks. Also as an improved network, FPN aims at detecting vehicles of relatively small size which is obvious in AP_S and AP_M of COCO benchmark. And with a ResNet101 backbone, FPN based on Faster R-CNN get the best results of mean precision.

From the speed perspective, most two-stage detectors in Table 1 are provided with the test speed under 5 frames per second, which could hardly meet the requirement of real-time detection. Thus, FPN based on Faster R-CNN with ResNet101 gains the best trade off in two-stage detectors (Table 2).

Table 1. Comparative results evaluated on Pascal VOC0712 of two-stage detectors.

Network	Backbone	Person	Car	Motor	Bus	vehs mAP	FPS
Faster R-CNN	ZF	65.3	73.9	69.1	68.4	69.1	18
Faster R-CNN	VGG	69.9	84.7	77.5	83.1	78.8	7
R-FCN	VGG	75.5	84.9	75.4	80.3	79.0	4.7
R-FCN	ResNet50	77.9	85.2	75.9	81.2	80.1	4.9
R-FCN	ResNet101	78.5	86.3	82.3	**86.0**	83.3	3.3
FPN	VGG	76.1	85.7	81.7	83.3	81.7	4.4
FPN	ResNet101	**79.1**	**87.1**	**83.4**	85.5	**83.8**	4.0

Table 2. Comparative results evaluated on MS COCO of two-stage detectors

Network	Backbone	AP	AP_{50}	AP_{75}	AP_S	AP_M	AP_L
Faster R-CNN	ZF	20.1	38.5	19.9	5.7	24.9	34.2
Faster R-CNN	VGG	24.2	45.3	23.5	7.7	26.4	37.1
R-FCN	VGG	21.4	39.4	28.8	7.0	26.2	35.1
R-FCN	ResNet50	22.9	40.0	32.7	7.6	26.5	36.4
R-FCN	ResNet101	25.3	44.3	38.0	7.2	28.1	**39.0**
FPN	VGG	24.9	44.9	38.4	10.9	26.9	38.5
FPN	ResNet101	**26.2**	**45.3**	**39.1**	**11.1**	**29.5**	38.7

Experiments on Single-Stage Detectors. YOLO, YOLO v2 and SSD are typical single-stage detectors to be evaluated.

The results of single-stage detectors are evaluated in Tables 3 and 4. Apparently, SSD512 with a VGG feature extractor shows its advantage in detecting cars, however, a remarkable improvement of accuracy has been made by YOLO v2 which shows a high performance in detecting person and motors.

Table 3. Comparative results evaluated on Pascal VOC0712 of single-stage detectors.

Network	Backbone	Person	Car	Motor	Bus	vehs mAP	FPS
SSD 300	VGG	74.5	80.8	80.6	81.1	79.3	46
SSD 512	VGG	78.2	**85.6**	80.9	**84.9**	**82.4**	19
YOLO	GoogLeNet	63.5	55.9	71.3	68.3	64.6	45
YOLOv2	Darknet	**81.3**	76.5	**83.4**	79.8	80.3	**81**

Table 4. Comparative results evaluated on MS COCO of single-stage detectors.

Network	Backbone	vehs mAP	AP	AP_{50}	AP_{75}	AP_S	AP_M	AP_L
SSD 300	VGG	25.1	23.2	41.2	23.4	5.3	23.2	39.6
SSD 512	VGG	**29.8**	**23.7**	**46.2**	**23.8**	8.0	**28.9**	**40.6**
YOLO	GoogLeNet	23.3	19.8	40.4	17.9	4.3	19.3	31.2
YOLOv2	Darknet	28.2	23.4	44.0	23.2	**8.7**	22.4	35.5

In terms of speed, a significant progress is made by YOLO v2 from Pascal VOC evaluations. Compared with SSD512 which has high accuracy but lack of efficiency, YOLO v2 with a feature extractor of darknet show its strength in a comprehensive consideration.

3.2 Vehicle Detection with Separable Reverse Connected Network

Learn from the comparative experiments of the previous section, FPN based on Faster R-CNN with ResNet101 and YOLO v2 with darknet are as representative networks for two kinds of detectors. For a further promotion of accuracy, Separable Reverse Connected network (SRC) is applied on corresponding networks. The same strategy as mentioned at the beginning of Sect. 3 is adopted for training and testing.

SRC Applied on Two-Stage Detector. The performance of Separable Reverse Connected network and FPN based on Faster R-CNN are investigated. Tables 5 and 6 gives the detection results. We can see from the tables that SRC achieves better results in detecting vehicles of small size. Moreover, the detection speed of SRC is 2–3 faster than FPN due to effective design of separable convolution.

Table 5. Results on FPN and Separable Reverse Connected (SRC) network based on Faster R-CNN evaluated on Pascal VOC0712.

Network	Backbone	Person	Car	Motor	Bus	vehs mAP	FPS
Faster R-CNN FPN	ResNet101	79.1	**87.1**	83.4	**85.5**	83.8	4.0
Faster R-CNN SRC	ResNet101	**80.2**	86.7	**83.9**	85.2	**84.0**	**10.6**

Table 6. Results on FPN and Separable Reverse Connected (SRC) network based on Faster R-CNN evaluated on MS COCO.

Network	Backbone	vehs mAP	AP	AP_{50}	AP_{75}	AP_S	AP_M	AP_L
Faster R-CNN FPN	ResNet101	34.6	26.2	45.3	39.1	11.1	29.5	**38.7**
Faster R-CNN SRC	ResNet101	**34.9**	**26.4**	**45.6**	**40.2**	**13.2**	**29.6**	38.4

SRC Applied on Single-Stage Detector. Comparison with SSD, YOLO v2 and SRC structure applied on YOLO v2 are illustrated in Tables 7 and 8. The results show that application of SRC gives the best results on mAP and better results in most vehicle categories excepting slightly lower in "car" detection. Compared with YOLOv2, it is a little bit slower, which can be tolerated in real application.

Table 7. Results on SSD, YOLO v2 and Separable Reverse Connected (SRC) network evaluated on Pascal VOC0712.

Network	Backbone	Person	Car	Motor	Bus	vehs mAP	FPS
SSD 512	VGG	78.2	**85.6**	80.9	84.9	82.4	19
YOLOv2	Darknet	81.3	76.5	83.4	79.8	80.3	**81**
SRC	Darknet	**83.6**	84.3	**83.8**	**85.3**	**84.3**	34

Table 8. Results on SSD, YOLO v2 and Separable Reverse Connected (SRC) network evaluated on MS COCO.

Network	Backbone	vehs mAP	AP	AP_{50}	AP_{75}	AP_S	AP_M	AP_L
SSD 512	VGG	29.8	23.7	46.2	23.8	8.0	**28.9**	40.6
YOLOv2	Darknet	28.2	23.4	44.0	23.2	8.7	22.4	35.5
SRC	Darknet	**31.7**	**29.0**	**47.1**	**25.5**	**11.3**	28.6	**40.9**

3.3 Optimization Results

In the light of algorithms mentioned in Sect. 2.3, specific optimization employed on SRC networks for the process of training and model compressing. The experiments are mainly conducted on COCO dataset.

Training Optimization. For an experimental set, multi-scale training and OHEM are applied for an observation of their contributions in Table 9. Each method indicates a promotion on original SRC by about 2% mAP of vehicles. Meanwhile according to Table 10, more improvements for vehicles mAP are brought by multi-scale training on a single-stage SRC, which shows the achievement of training optimization.

Table 9. Optimization applied on SRC of two-stage. Results are evaluated on MS COCO.

Network	Backbone	vehs mAP	AP_S	AP_M	AP_L
SRC	ResNet101	34.9	13.2	29.6	38.4
+ms-train	ResNet101	36.8	13.5	30.1	39.6
+ms-train OHEM	ResNet101	**38.5**	**15.1**	**32.4**	**42.3**

Table 10. Optimization applied on SRC of single-stage. Results are evaluated on MS COCO.

Network	Backbone	vehs mAP	AP_S	AP_M	AP_L
SRC	Darknet	31.7	11.3	28.6	40.9
+ms-train	Darknet	**34.8**	**13.8**	**33.7**	**41.5**

Model Compressing. In practice, parameter pruning and sharing are introduced for compressing the two-stage SRC++ model. We apply different intensities of compressing for a measurement in Table 11, significant progress of speed shall be noticed which enables the network to detect vehicles at 28 frames per second in set A and 35 frames per second in set B.

Table 11. Model compressing applied on SRC++ of two-stage evaluated on MS COCO.

Network	Backbone	vehs mAP	AP_S	AP_M	AP_L	Params	FPS
SRC++	ResNet101	38.5	15.1	32.4	42.3	215.8M	9.7
Compressed SRC++: A	ResNet101	38.2	14.9	31.8	42.0	129.8M	28
Compressed SRC++: B	ResNet101	37.7	14.1	30.2	41.4	67.3M	35

Although, slightly drops of mean average precision in vehicle categories are caused by decreased parameters of the network, compared with FPN, there is still a promotion of accuracy in detecting vehicles about 3% in mAP. Moreover, an impressive acceleration about 10 times faster than FPN is achieved, which is capable for real-time vehicle detection.

4 Conclusion

To conclude our works, we firstly conduct a series of comparative experiments in modern vehicle detectors for base networks selection of further improvements. A Separable Reverse Connected (SRC) network is proposed in this paper to achieve multi-scale vehicle detection of high performance, aiming at the semantic information, feature maps are fused by a de-convolution method. Together with optimization of multi-scale training and OHEM, our proposed model outperforms FPN about 3% in mAP of vehicle categories. For YOLO v2 of single-stage detectors, an implementation of SRC beats the original structure by about 7% vehicles mAP. Model compression are applied to reduce the storage requirement of neural networks which achieve 10 times acceleration with slightly loss of accuracy.

References

1. Girshick, R., Donahue, J., Darrell, T., Malik, J.: Rich feature hierarchies for accurate object detection and semantic segmentation. In: IEEE Conference on Computer Vision and Pattern Recognition, pp. 580–587 (2014)
2. Girshick, R.: Fast R-CNN. Computer Science (2015)
3. Ren, S., He, K., Girshick, R., Sun, J.: Faster R-CNN: towards real-time object detection with region proposal networks. In: International Conference on Neural Information Processing Systems, pp. 91–99 (2015)
4. Dai, J., Li, Y., He, K., Sun, J.: R-FCN: object detection via region-based fully convolutional networks (2016)
5. Dai, J., Qi, H., Xiong, Y., Li, Y., Zhang, G., Hu, H., Wei, Y.: Deformable convolutional networks, pp. 764–773 (2017)
6. Lin, T.Y., Dollar, P., Girshick, R., He, K., Hariharan, B., Belongie, S.: Feature pyramid networks for object detection, pp. 936–944 (2016)
7. Redmon, J., Divvala, S., Girshick, R., Farhadi, A.: You only look once: unified, real-time object detection. In: Computer Vision and Pattern Recognition, pp. 779–788 (2016)
8. Redmon, J., Farhadi, A.: Yolo9000: better, faster, stronger, pp. 6517–6525 (2016)
9. Liu, W., et al.: SSD: single shot multibox detector. In: Leibe, B., Matas, J., Sebe, N., Welling, M. (eds.) ECCV 2016. LNCS, vol. 9905, pp. 21–37. Springer, Cham (2016). https://doi.org/10.1007/978-3-319-46448-0_2
10. Shrivastava, A., Gupta, A., Girshick, R.: Training region-based object detectors with online hard example mining, pp. 761–769 (2016)
11. Han, S., Mao, H., Dally, W.J.: Deep compression: Compressing deep neural networks with pruning, trained quantization and Huffman coding. Fiber 56(4), 3–7 (2015)
12. Dalal, N., Triggs, B.: Histograms of oriented gradients for human detection. In: IEEE Computer Society Conference on Computer Vision and Pattern Recognition, pp. 886–893 (2005)
13. Lowe, D.G.: Distinctive image features from scale-invariant keypoints. Int. J. Comput. Vis. 60(2), 91–110 (2004)
14. Lienhart, R., Maydt, J.: An extended set of haar-like features for rapid object detection. In: Proceedings of International Conference on Image Processing, vol. 1, pp. I-900–I-903 (2002)

15. Uijlings, J.R.R., Van De Sande, K.E.A., Gevers, T., Smeulders, A.W.M.: Selective search for object recognition. Int. J. Comput. Vis. **104**(2), 154–171 (2013)
16. Zitnick, C.L., Dollár, P.: Edge boxes: locating object proposals from edges. In: Fleet, D., Pajdla, T., Schiele, B., Tuytelaars, T. (eds.) ECCV 2014. LNCS, vol. 8693, pp. 391–405. Springer, Cham (2014). https://doi.org/10.1007/978-3-319-10602-1_26
17. Tsai, L.W., Hsieh, J.W., Fan, K.C.: Vehicle detection using normalized color and edge map. IEEE Trans. Image Process. **16**(3), 850–864 (2007)
18. Szegedy, C., Vanhoucke, V., Ioffe, S., Shlens, J., Wojna, Z.: Rethinking the inception architecture for computer vision. Computer Science, pp. 2818–2826 (2015)
19. Szegedy, C., Ioffe, S., Vanhoucke, V., Alemi, A.: Inception-v4, inception-ResNet and the impact of residual connections on learning (2016)
20. Li, Z., Peng, C., Yu, G., Zhang, X., Deng, Y., Sun, J.: Light-head R-CNN: in defense of two-stage object detector (2017)
21. Huang, J., et al.: Speed/accuracy trade-offs for modern convolutional object detectors, pp. 3296–3297 (2016)
22. Sandler, M., Howard, A., Zhu, M., Zhmoginov, A., Chen, L.C.: Inverted residuals and linear bottlenecks: mobile networks for classification, detection and segmentation (2018)
23. He, K., Gkioxari, G., Dollr, P., Girshick, R.: Mask r-cnn (2017)
24. Xie, S., Girshick, R., Dollar, P., Tu, Z., He, K.: Aggregated residual transformations for deep neural networks pp. 5987–5995 (2016)
25. Kong, T., Sun, F., Yao, A., Liu, H., Lu, M., Chen, Y.: RON: reverse connection with objectness prior networks for object detection, pp. 5244–5252 (2017)
26. Zhu, X., Wang, Y., Dai, J., Yuan, L., Wei, Y.: Flow-guided feature aggregation for video object detection, pp. 408–417 (2017)
27. Li, J., Liang, X., Wei, Y., Xu, T., Feng, J., Yan, S.: Perceptual generative adversarial networks for small object detection, pp. 1951–1959 (2017)
28. Chollet, F.: Xception: deep learning with depthwise separable convolutions, pp. 1800–1807 (2016)
29. Peng, C., et al.: MegDet: a large mini-batch object detector (2017)
30. Szegedy, C., et al.: Going deeper with convolutions, pp. 1–9 (2014)

Online Multiple Person Tracking Using Fully-Convolutional Neural Networks and Motion Invariance Constraints

Nan Wang[✉], Qi Zou, Yaping Huang, and Qiulin Ma

Beijing Key Laboratory of Traffic Data Analysis and Mining,
Beijing Jiaotong University, Beijing, China
{16112070,qzou,yphuang,17112075}@bjtu.edu.cn

Abstract. We propose a novel framework for multiple person tracking in crowded scenes with the tracking-by-detection paradigm. In such scenes, noisy detections and frequent occlusions are major challenges. A common way to handle the challenges is to use Convolutional Neural Networks (CNNs) based appearance features to discriminate objects. However, to get sufficiently discriminative features, CNNs demand a large amount of training data and sometimes compromise efficiency. We address the challenges in two ways. Firstly, an Appearance Net modified from a Siamese network is proposed to identify persons in crowed scenes. Compared to other CNNs with deep layers and careful fine-tuning, our Appearance Net is efficient and accurate enough without any fine-tuning. Secondly, a motion invariance model is designed to tackle noisy detections caused by cluttered background or inaccurate bounding box localization, and missing objects caused by occlusions. By utilizing spatial geometric constraints, our tracker can generate reliable trajectories under challenging scenes. Extensive experiments on the two largest multi-object tracking (MOT) benchmarks, namely MOT15 and MOT17, demonstrate competing performance of the proposed tracker over a number of state-of-the-art trackers.

Keywords: Fully-convolutional neural networks · Motion invariance
Multiple object tracking

1 Introduction

MOT, especially multiple person tracking, is a fundamental task in computer vision. It is important in many applications such as video surveillance, autonomous driving, and augmented reality. Thanks to the advancement of object detection methods, a framework called tracking-by-detection is widely used in MOT. The framework includes two phases: a detection phase which is

This work is supported by National Nature Science Foundation of China (61473031, 61472029) and Beijing Natural Science Foundation (4152042).

J.-H. Lai et al. (Eds.): PRCV 2018, LNCS 11259, pp. 150–161, 2018.
https://doi.org/10.1007/978-3-030-03341-5_13

employed in each frame to locate objects (actually presented as bounding boxes), and a matching phase where the candidate objects are associated to form trajectories across frames. Although it is a good decomposition, the tracking-by-detection is also challenged by some factors like occlusions, missing objects, and false alarms, especially in monocular videos and crowded scenes.

To address these problems, many algorithms are proposed, which can be divided into online and off-line models. The off-line methods [1,3,4,26] use global information from both the past and future frames to achieve good performance. However, in some real-time applications, future information is unavailable which limits the usage of offline methods. In contrast, online methods only use information from the past and current frames [6,15,17] and concern more about high efficiency.

As the noticeable progress of deep learning in object detection and other related fields [5,18,19], CNNs-based methods are also used in MOT. One popular way is to employ the appearance features generated by a generic CNNs model [29]. Other researchers also propose online learning methods for discriminative appearance models or data association tasks or both [2,22]. A closely related work designed a Fully-Convolutional Siamese Networks (FCSNs) [6] to compute the appearance similarity between detection pairs. Unlike us, they focus on single person tracking. Though some CNNs-based methods achieve good performance by designing sophisticated network architecture and elaborate fine-tuning, they require high-quality training samples for specific scenes and usually scarify the efficiency. It seems that most of the high-accurate algorithms suffer from high computational cost. To this end, we propose an online framework for compromising the accuracy and speed. The main contributions of our work are as follows:

1. We propose a fully-convolutional neural networks (FCNNs) for extracting appearance features which provides a good trade-off between the speed and accuracy. In addition, a recognition strategy is designed on our Appearance Net and the experiments show that it is very robust to long-term reappearance.
2. A motion model is designed to predict the state of an object and correspondingly a strategy to recover the short-term missing is proposed.
3. We demonstrate the effectiveness of our online MOT framework using challenging MOT15 [8] and MOT17 [9] benchmarks.

2 Related Work

With the tracking-by-detection paradigm becoming an standard framework, many works of MOT focus on designing more discriminative feature representations and robust data association methods.

Appearance Feature. Besides hand-crafted features such as HOG [37] and color histogram [36], many new feature representations are proposed by exploiting context information [26,33]. In [26], they use optical flow information to form an aggregated descriptor. As we mentioned above, many researchers also employ deep architectures as their feature extractors [2,3,14,16,22]. [14] train their descriptors encoding local spatio-temporal information and aggregate the pixel values and optical flow information into a comprehensive feature. Furthermore, some works attempt to combine all these features in a unified model. [2] employs spatial-temporal attention mechanism and ROI-pooling to fuse the appearance feature and context information together. [3] even use a quadruplet convolutional architectures to model the tracker in an end-to-end way.

Data Association. The other trend is to design more robust and efficient data association methods. A popular way is to formulate the tracking problem as a graph, where each node indicates a detection and the edge indicates a possible matching. Then the data association can be solved efficiently by linear programming methods [11–13,20]. Recently, deep neural network architectures have been used not only for modeling appearance feature but also for association [1,3]. These works employ a CNNs-based architecture to model the whole tracking-by-detection framework in an end-to-end way.

In general, the more sophisticated and carefully fine-tuning the model is, the better performance will be achieved. However, the added complexity can also exhibit a significantly higher computational cost and the performance may not be perfect for more general scene as they are usually trained for special tasks or situations. To address this, our Appearance Net is trained offline without online updating. Furthermore, there is no data association methods fusing in the architecture elaborately, as our network is designed to link with other off-the-shelf frameworks easily. Hence, we design an efficient motion model in case of missing detections and simply use the Hungarian [10] algorithm for online tracking.

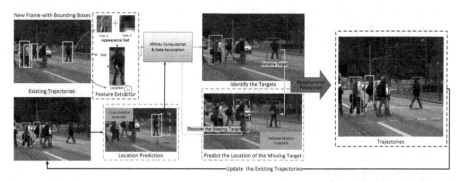

Fig. 1. Overview of the framework: the blue dotted box and green dotted boxes represent the feature extractor and motion models, respectively. (Color figure online)

3   Online MOT Framework

Overview of our online framework is shown in Fig. 1. As a routine, we use a public detector provided by MOT benchmark for object detection. When a new frame I_t arrives, the tracker computes the similarity scores between the existing targets and new detections according to their features (more details in Sect. 3.1). Then the data association between detections and targets is model by a bipartite graph where nodes are detections or targets, edges indicate the assignments, and the weights on edges are computed by their similarity scores. Next, there are some additional strategies (as shown with the yellow arrow in Fig. 1) in case of occlusions and missing detections. We employ the motion model illustrated in Sect. 3.2 and a recognition strategy for reappearing explained in Sect. 3.3 as supplements. Specifically, our online system works in a sequentially forward way: after reading in a new frame, current trajectories are prolonged and objects information is updated . Then the system proceeds to the next frame.

For a frame I_t, let $D_t = \{d_t^k | k = 1, 2, \cdots, M_t\}$ be all the detections in I_t, where $d_t^k = [x_t^k, y_t^k, w_t^k, h_t^k]$ with (x_t^k, y_t^k) denoting the center location and (w_t^k, h_t^k) denoting the scale of the corresponding detection respectively.

Similarly, the trajectories can be represented by $\mathbb{T}_t = \{\mathscr{T}_t^i | i = 1, 2, \cdots, N_t\}$ where $\mathscr{T}_t^i = [x_t^i, y_t^i, w_t^i, h_t^i, v_t^i, R_t^i]$. x_t^i, y_t^i, w_t^i, and h_t^i are obtained from the matched detection, indicating the location and size of the target respectively. v_t^i denotes the velocity vector of the target at t. Furthermore, R_t^i describes the set of pairwise motion features of $\mathscr{T}_t^i$ (more details in Sect. 3.2).

For the similarity scores mentioned above, we use three measures including the appearance feature F_a, size constraint F_s and location constraint F_L. The cost between an object and a detection is computed as:

$$C_t^{i,k} = F_a(\mathscr{T}_{t-1}^i, d_t^k) + F_s(\mathscr{T}_{t-1}^i, d_t^k) + F_L(\mathscr{T}_{t-1}^i, d_t^k). \tag{1}$$

The objective of the association is to minimize the total cost of frame I_t as:

$$A_t = \arg\min_A \sum_i \sum_k a_t^{i,k} C_t^{i,k}$$

$$s.t. \sum_i a_t^{i,k} \leq 1 \wedge \sum_k a_t^{i,k} \leq 1, \tag{2}$$

The assignment of I_t is $A_t = \{a_t^{i,k} | i = 1, 2, \cdots, N_{t-1}, k = 1, 2, \cdots, M_t\}$. If d_t^k is assigned to i-th target, $a_t^{i,k}$ is equal to 1, otherwise it is 0. The optimization problem in (2) is solved by the Hungarian algorithm [10].

3.1 Appearance Model

We propose a fully-convolutional Appearance Net to extract appearance features. Our networks only contain four successively convolutional layers with two pooling layers following the first two layer. The reason why we choose such a tiny model is that it is not only fast, but also very suitable to the MOT tracking.

Architecture. Before using the four-layer architecture, we designed a deep network based on the VGG-16 model and the computational cost of which is too high to accept for online applications. To address this problem and inspired by [6], we use their fully-convolutional siamese networks as our baseline. Since we desire an appearance extractor without affinity comparison, we only modify the branch used for exemplar images to design our Appearance Net. The original exemplar branch is a five-layer network and we utilize the first four layers according to our further experiment results about the model (more details about their work, please refer [6]).

For further researching, we visualized every feature map of each channel belong to different convolutional layers and found that the Conv_1 and Conv_2 contain more low-level features and Conv_3 to Conv_5 contain more middle-level or high-level features. In general, objects of MOT tasks tend to be small or fuzzy, i.e. the resolution may be not enough for multi-layer convolution. Furthermore, when we extract the image patch following the detected bounding box, the background information is inevitable included. These noisy data will propagate with the positive data along the network and make negative effect. With the architecture becoming deeper, the proportion of the noisy data may become larger. Additionally, we quantified the performance of using each layer and every two layers combined together. The results show that Conv_4 presents the best accuracy when only one layer is employed and the best performance comes from the combination feature of Conv_2 and Conv_4.

Training. The training parameters and datasets are same as the FCSNs of [6]. The main difference between ours and the FCSNs is that our network only has one input without a symmetrical architecture for comparing two image patches. Furthermore, the FCSNs is designed for VOT tasks, while ours is for extracting features with no need to extend range for searching the possible position of the object. Specifically, ours is trained on the ILSVRC [38] dataset without refining on any training sets of MOT tasks. The experimental results demonstrate the robustness on object representation.

Feature Measure. As we mentioned above, there are three costs for associating. The cost of the appearance between $\mathscr{T}_{t-1}^i$ and d_t^k is defined as:

$$F_a(\mathscr{T}_{t-1}^i, d_t^k) = -\log(m - \frac{\sum |\varphi(d_t^k) - \varphi(\mathscr{T}_{t-1}^i)|}{Z}) \qquad (3)$$

where $\varphi(.)$ is the operation of the Appearance Net. m controls the range of the distance and Z is the normalized factor. In our experiment, we set $m = 1$ for range $[0, 1]$. In addition, $\varphi(\mathscr{T}_{t-1}^i)$ is extracted from the last frame where the target appeared. In the following sections, all appearance costs between two objects are calculated according to (3) by using the corresponding appearance features. Furthermore, the costs of scale and location are defined as follows:

$$F_s(\mathscr{T}_{t-1}^i, d_t^k) = -\log(1 - \frac{|w_{t-1}^i - w_t^k|}{2\left(w_{t-1}^i + w_t^k\right)} - \frac{|h_{t-1}^i - h_t^k|}{2\left(h_{t-1}^i + h_t^k\right)}) \qquad (4)$$

$$F_L(\mathscr{T}_{t-1}^i, d_t^k) = -\log(1 - \frac{|x_t^i - x_t^k|}{2\left(w_{t-1}^i + w_t^k\right)} - \frac{|y_t^i - y_t^k|}{2\left(h_{t-1}^i + h_t^k\right)}) \qquad (5)$$

Note that, the location (x_t^i, y_t^i) used in (5) is predicted by the unary motion invariance, as shown in the green dotted box on the bottom-left of Fig. 1.

3.2 Motion Model

Our motion model includes two parts: unary motion and pairwise motion. As described in Fig. 1, each part can predict an object state.

Unary Motion. The unary motion invariance assumes that the speed of a target is invariant in a short period and can be represented by a linear model. Our tracker estimates the velocity of each target online and predicts the location by:

$$p_{t-\Delta t+\bar{t}}^i = l_{t-\Delta t}^i + v^i * \bar{t}$$
$$s.t. 1 \leq \Delta t < \tau \wedge 1 \leq \bar{t} \leq \Delta t \tag{6}$$

where Δt is the time span of missing or for prediction. $l_{t-\Delta t}^i = (x_{t-\Delta t}^i, y_{t-\Delta t}^i)$ is the center location of $\mathcal{T}_{t-\Delta t}^i$. For two adjacent frames, Δt is equal to 1 and the location used in (5) is predicted by (6). If a target disappears for a short term during tracking, the location in each missing frame could also be predicted by (6) subjecting to the two constraints. In (6) τ is the max gap that the unary motion can keep reliable and $\bar{t}$ indicates the frame for prediction.

Pairwise Motion. The pairwise motion invariance depicts structure relationships between the target and its neighbors. It assumes that the relative distance between two targets in a short term would keep invariant. According to this, one target could be estimated by its neighbors. Each relationship between a pair of targets of I_t is described by:

$$r_t^{i,j} = (\dot{x}_t^{i,j}, \dot{y}_t^{i,j}) = (x_t^i - x_t^j, y_t^i - y_t^j) \tag{7}$$

where the superscript i and j denote the indexes of two different targets. The relationship set of target i is represented as $R_t^i = \{r_t^{i,j} | j = 1, 2, \cdots, N_t, j \neq i\}$ and the set of all relative motion relationship at frame t is $R_t = \{R_t^i | i = 1, 2, \cdots, N_t\}$. Similar to appearance features, the pairwise motion feature updates online and is used according to the last existing frame I_{t-1}:

$$p_t^i = (x_t^j, y_t^j) + (\dot{x}_{t-1}^{i,j}, \dot{y}_{t-1}^{i,j}) \tag{8}$$

where (x_t^j, y_t^j) represents the center location of the target j in I_t and $(\dot{x}_{t-1}^{i,j}, \dot{y}_{t-1}^{i,j})$ is the pairwise motion extracted in the last frame. Notably, the near targets used for predicting are those who have been associated with corresponding detections. It means that only the neighbor who is reliable would be used in the pairwise prediction. Since the uncertainty of the motion, the pairwise motion is more reliable than the unary motion in a short period. Whereas, the same reason causes that the structure relationship cannot keep more than a few frames.

Recovery Strategy. The recovery includes two phases. First, if there is any missing target which has not been associated with any detection at the current frame, the data association will conduct again according to the predictions estimated by the pairwise motion invariance (yellow arrow of Fig. 1). The detection assignments for missing targets are given by:

$$\hat{A}_t = \arg\min_A C(\hat{\mathbb{T}}_t, R_{t-1}, \hat{D}_t)$$

$$s.t. \sum_{i \in \hat{N}_t} a_t^{i,k} \le 1 \wedge \sum_{k \in \hat{M}_t \bigcup\{0\}} a_t^{i,k} = 1, \tag{9}$$

$$C(\hat{\mathbb{T}}_t, R_{t-1}, \hat{D}_t) = \sum_{i=1}^{\hat{N}_t} \sum_{k=1}^{\hat{M}_t} a_t^{i,k} \hat{C}_t^{i,k} \tag{10}$$

$$\hat{C}_t^{i,k} = F_a(\mathscr{T}_{t-1}^i, d_t^k) + F_s(\mathscr{T}_{t-1}^i, d_t^k) + F_L(\mathbb{T}_t - \hat{\mathbb{T}}_t, R_{t-1}^i, d_t^k) \tag{11}$$

where $\hat{\mathbb{T}}_t$ is the set of missing targets at t and $\hat{D}_t$ is the set of detections which have not been matched to any target. In addition, $\hat{D}_t$ contains a dummy detection d_t^0 in case of missing again. The assignments for missing targets are denoted as $\hat{A}_t = \{a_t^{i,k} \big| i \in \hat{N}_t, k \in \hat{M}_t \bigcup\{0\}\}$. If the target i is matched with detection k, $a_t^{i,k}$ is equal to 1. Otherwise it is assigned with d_t^0. In formulation (11), the features of the missing target used for F_a and F_s are extracted from its latest appearing frame I_{t-1}. Besides, the location cost F_L is obtained by:

$$F_L(\mathbb{T}_t - \hat{\mathbb{T}}_t, R_{t-1}^i, d_t^k) = \min_{j \in N_t - \hat{N}_t} (-\log(1 - \frac{|x_t^j - x_t^k|}{2(w_{t-1}^i + w_t^k)} - \frac{|y_t^j - y_t^k|}{2(h_{t-1}^i + h_t^k)})) \tag{12}$$

where (x_t^j, y_t^j) presents the location predicted by the pairwise motion invariance and j is the index of the predictions estimated by the reliable neighbors.

Second, if a target is re-identified by one of the two motion models after a short-term disappearing, its locations in the missing frames will be predicted with using corresponding model. Specially, since the relationships between two targets change rapidly, our tracker will only recovery the target which has been missing within τ frames.

3.3   Reappearance Recognition Model

The other contribution of our framework is a recognition strategy conducted after tracking. The strategy merely relied on the features extracted by the Appearance Net. Specifically, if a new trajectory is generated in a frame, it will be compared with the terminated ones based on the affinity only considering appearance distance, i.e. following (3).

As it depicts in Fig. 3, our strategy for recognition is very promising compared with other similar works [1,22] in some aspects. Firstly, the time cost is very competitive since our appearance model is fast. Secondly, our strategy could handle a long-term disappearing, even if the object has been disappeared for

174 frames (the first row of Fig. 3). Thirdly, the experiment demonstrates our Appearance Net is robust to the rotation out of the plane (also shown in the first row). Moreover, our strategy is naturally suitable to parallelization for further speeding up.

4 Experiments

In this section, we present the details about the implementation and experimental results of the proposed tracking framework.

4.1 Implementation Details

The proposed framework is implemented on MATLAB with matconv [40]. The training details is in Sect. 3.1. In our implementation, we use an IoU (Intersection-over-Union) ratio 0.5 for removing the redundant detections which overlap with others in the same frame. The threshold τ in (6) is set to 7 which is also the termination threshold of tracking. Since our tracker will predict the missing object, τ couldn't be too small or too large, we choose 7 for a trade-off. For tracking managing, we start a new trajectory more than five frames.

Datasets. We evaluate our online MOT framework on the public available MOT15 [8] benchmarks containing 22 (11 training, 11 test) video sequences in unconstrained environments. It provides public object detections generated by the ACF detector [39] and the ground truth of the training sequences. So we use the training sequences for performance analysis of the proposed framework. In addition, as we mentioned above, our appearance model doesn't use any MOT training datasets to train or refine. Our results have been submitted to the benchmark for fair comparison.[1]

Evaluation MetricEvaluation Metric. We follow the standard CLEAR MOT metrics [7] for evaluating multiple people tracking performance. The metrics includes multiple object tracking accuracy (MOTA), which combines identity switches (IDs), false positives (FP), and false negatives (FN). Furthermore, we also report multiple object tracking precision (MOTP), mostly tracked (MT), mostly lost (ML) and frame per second (HZ).

4.2 Ablation Study

To further investigate different components of our framework, we perform ablation study on MOT15 training sets, because the groundtruth is only provided for training sets but not the test sets.

---

[1] https://motchallenge.net/results/2D_MOT_2015/.

Ablation Study on Appearance Features. We compare the appearance features extracted by the Appearance Net with several hand-crafted and CNNs-based appearance features in Table 1. The color histogram (CHIST), histogram of oriented gradient (HOG) and a six channel color histogram (6HIST) including RGB and HSV channels are used as representatives of hand-crafted features. For the CNNs-based appearance methods, we employ the exemplar branch of our baseline in [6] and the methods used in MHT [5,29]. As it depicts, the accuracy (MOTA) of ours is higher than other results.

Table 1. Ablation analysis of different features on MOT15 training set.

	MOTA	MOTP	FP	FN	IDs	FM
CHIST	12.18	71.08	10596	22126	2321	1726
HOG [37]	15.61	71.13	9846	21892	1940	1588
6HIST	22.42	71.41	8344	21662	952	1115
FCNNs [6]	23.64	71.32	7416	22148	905	1262
MHTCNN [5,29]	27.88	71.64	5556	22572	652	1046
OURS	29.54	71.88	4410	23212	495	960

Table 2. Ablation analysis of different motion models on MOT15 training set.

	MOTA	MOTP	FP	FN	IDs	FM
AppNet+KF [41]	27.37	72.09	3369	24943	670	797
OURS_w/o_P	27.61	72.14	3899	24410	578	942
OURS_w/o_U	28.11	72.11	4116	24046	529	987
AppNet+SCEA [33]	28.83	71.86	5437	22487	477	794
OURS	29.54	71.88	4410	23212	495	960

Ablation Study on Motion Model. We employ two typical motion-based models, namely Structural Constraint Event Aggregation (SCEA) [33] and Kalman filtering (KF) [40], for comparison. Furthermore, two variants of our motion model are tested: ours without pairwise motion (OURS_w/o_P) and ours without unary motion (OURS_w/o_U). As depicted in Table 2, although the SCEA method uses not only motion constraints but also an optimal strategy for association, our full model (OURS) presents the best performance among the five results. It is because that both the two components of our motion model are useful for improving the performance and they are supplemental for each other.

Comparisons with State-of-the-Art Methods. We evaluate our tracking performance on the test sequences of MOT15 benchmarks and compare it with state-of-the-art trackers. All these compared methods including ours use the same public detections provided by the benchmark for fair comparison. The quantitative comparison results are shown in Table 3. Furthermore, since we concern more on online tracking, we visualize the relation between speed (HZ) and accuracy (MOTA) of the methods whose MOTA are higher than 30.

As Fig. 2 depicts, our speed is the highest. For those whose accuracies are higher, their speeds are less than half of our speed. Specially, we can find the methods NOMT and SiameseCNN are very competitive. However, their environments are 16 cores and 24 cores respectively, as shown in Table 3.

Our results on MOT17 benchmark are public available[2] and are not listed here due to the page limit. All experimental results demonstrate our efficient Appearance Net and the effective motion model.

---

[2] https://motchallenge.net/results/MOT17/.

Table 3. Comparison on MOT15 testing set. Best in bold, second best in blue.

Tracker	Online	MOTA	MOTP	MT	ML	FP	FN	IDS	HZ (fps)	Cores
TO [35]	N	25.7	72.2	4.3%	57.4%	**4779**	40511	383	5	8
SiameseCNN [14]	N	29	71.2	8.5%	48.4%	5160	37798	639	52.8	24
CNNTCM [32]	N	29.6	71.8	11.2%	44.0%	7786	34733	712	1.7	4
MCF_PHD [31]	N	29.9	71.7	11.9%	44.0%	8892	33529	656	12.2	1
MHT_DAM [29]	N	32.4	71.8	16.0%	43.8%	9064	32060	435	0.7	4
NOMT [26]	N	33.7	71.9	12.2%	44.0%	7762	32547	442	11.5	16
QuadMOT [3]	N	33.8	**73.4**	12.9%	36.9%	7898	32061	703	3.7	1
TSMLCDEnew [25]	N	34.3	71.7	14.0%	39.4%	7869	31908	618	6.5	4
JointMC [23]	N	35.6	71.9	**23.2%**	39.3%	10580	**28508**	457	0.6	1
oICF [34]	Y	27.1	70	6.4%	48.7%	7594	36757	454	1.4	2
SCEA [33]	Y	29.1	71.1	8.9%	47.3%	6060	36912	604	6.8	1
MDP [30]	Y	30.3	71.3	13.0%	38.4%	9717	32422	680	1.1	8
CDA_DDALpb [28]	Y	32.8	70.7	9.7%	42.2%	4983	35690	614	2.3	1
TDAM [27]	Y	33	72.8	13.3%	39.1%	10064	30617	464	5.9	1
AM [2]	Y	34.3	70.5	11.4%	43.4%	5154	34848	**348**	0.5	1
HybridDAT [24]	Y	35	72.6	11.4%	42.2%	8455	31140	358	4.6	1
AMIR15 [22]	Y	**37.6**	71.7	15.8%	**26.8%**	7933	29397	1026	1.9	1
Ours	Y	31.3	70.2	12.6%	35.4%	8903	32393	926	**14.8**	1

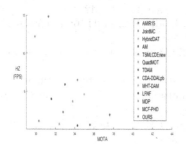

Fig. 2. MOTA & HZ

Fig. 3. Reappearance recognition

5   Conclusion

In this paper, we propose an online MOT framework that efficiently utilizes the fully-convolutional neural networks and motion invariance. For the FCNNs-based feature model, we employ a four-layers structure to extract the appearance features quickly and accurately. The motion invariance assumes that the motion of an object is invariant and independent with other objects in a short-term period. Equipped with our FCNNs-based feature, the experiments show that our framework makes a good balance between the speed and accuracy.

References

1. Tang, S., Andriluka, M., Andres, B., Schiele, B.: Multiple people tracking by lifted multicut and person re-identification. In: CVPR 2017, pp. 3539–3548 (2017)
2. Chu, Q., Ouyang, W., Li, H., Wang, X., Liu, B., Yu, N.: Online multi-object tracking using CNN-based single object tracker with spatial-temporal attention mechanism. In: ICCV 2017, pp. 4846–4855 (2017)
3. Son, J., Baek, M., Cho, M., Han, B.: Multi-object tracking with quadruplet convolutional neural networks. In: CVPR 2017, pp. 5620–5629 (2017)
4. Tang, S., Andres, B., Andriluka, M., Schiele, B.: Multi-person tracking by multicut and deep matching. In: Hua, G., Jégou, H. (eds.) ECCV 2016. LNCS, vol. 9914, pp. 100–111. Springer, Cham (2016). https://doi.org/10.1007/978-3-319-48881-3_8
5. Girshick, R., Donahue, J., Darrell, T., Malik, J.: Rich feature hierarchies for accurate object detection and semantic segmentation. In: CVPR 2014, pp. 580–587 (2014)
6. Bertinetto, L., Valmadre, J., Henriques, J.F., Vedaldi, A., Torr, P.H.S.: Fully-convolutional Siamese networks for object tracking. In: Hua, G., Jégou, H. (eds.) ECCV 2016. LNCS, vol. 9914, pp. 850–865. Springer, Cham (2016). https://doi.org/10.1007/978-3-319-48881-3_56
7. Bernardin, K., Stiefelhagen, R.: Evaluating multiple object tracking performance: the CLEAR MOT metrics. J. Image Video Process. **2008**(1), 1–10 (2008)
8. Leal-Taixé, L., Milan, A., Reid, I., Roth, S., Schindler, K.: Motchallenge 2015: towards a benchmark for multi-target tracking. arXiv:1504.01942 (2015)
9. Milan, A., Leal-Taixé, L., Reid, I., Roth, S., Schindler, K.: MOT16: a benchmark for multi-object tracking. arXiv:1603.00831 (2016)
10. Munkres, J.: Algorithms for the assignment and transportation problems. J. Soc. Ind. Appl. Math. **5**(1), 32–38 (1957)
11. Dehghan, A., Modiri Assari, S., Shah, M.: GMMCP-tracker: globally optimal generalized maximum multi clique problem for multiple object tracking. In: CVPR 2015, pp. 4091–4099 (2015)
12. Zhang, L., Li, Y., Nevatia, R.: Global data association for multi-object tracking using network flows. In: CVPR 2008, pp. 1–8 (2008)
13. Tang, S., Andres, B., Andriluka, M., Schiele, B.: Subgraph decomposition for multi-target tracking. In: CVPR 2015, pp. 5033–5041 (2015)
14. Leal-Taixé, L., Canton-Ferrer, C., Schindler, K.: Learning by tracking: Siamese CNN for robust target association. In: CVPR 2016 Workshops, pp. 33–40 (2016)
15. Murray, S.: Real-Time multiple object tracking - a study on the importance of speed. arXiv:1709.03572 (2017)
16. Milan, A., Rezatofighi, S.H., Dick, A.R., Reid, I.D., Schindler, K.: Online multi-target tracking using recurrent neural networks. In: AAAI 2017, pp. 4225–4232 (2017)
17. Bochinski, E., Eiselein, V., Sikora, T.: High-Speed tracking-by-detection without using image information. In: AVSS 2017, pp. 1–6 (2017)
18. Girshick, R.: Fast R-CNN. arXiv:1504.08083 (2015)
19. He, K., Zhang, X., Ren, S., Sun, J.: Deep residual learning for image recognition. In: CVPR 2016, pp. 770–778 (2016)
20. Jiang, H., Fels, S., Little, J.J.: A linear programming approach for multiple object tracking. In: CVPR 2007, pp. 1–8 (2007)
21. Leal-Taixé, L., Fenzi, M., Kuznetsova, A., Rosenhahn, B., Savarese, S.: Learning an image-based motion context for multiple people tracking. In: CVPR 2014, pp. 3542–3549 (2014)

22. Sadeghian, A., Alahi, A., Savarese, S.: Tracking the untrackable: Learning to track multiple cues with long-term dependencies. In: ICCV 2017, pp. 300–311 (2017)
23. Keuper, M., Tang, S., Zhongjie, Y., Andres, B., Brox, T., Schiele, B.: A multi-cut formulation for joint segmentation and tracking of multiple objects. arXiv:1607.06317 (2016)
24. Yang, M., Wu, Y., Jia, Y.: A hybrid data association framework for robust online multi-object tracking. J. Soc. Ind. Appl. Math. **26**(12), 5667–5679 (2017)
25. Wang, B., Wang, G., Chan, K.L., Wang, L.: Tracklet association by online target-specific metric learning and coherent dynamics estimation. PAMI **39**(3), 589–602 (2017)
26. Choi, W.: Near-online multi-target tracking with aggregated local flow descriptor. In: ICCV 2015, pp. 3029–3037 (2015)
27. Yang, M., Jia, Y.: Temporal dynamic appearance modeling for online multi-person tracking. Comput. Vis. Image Underst. **153**, 16–28 (2016)
28. Bae, S.H., Yoon, K.J.: Confidence-based data association and discriminative deep appearance learning for robust online multi-object tracking. PAMI **40**(3), 595–610 (2018)
29. Kim, C., Li, F., Ciptadi, A., Rehg, J.M.: Multiple hypothesis tracking revisited. In: ICCV 2015, pp. 4696–4704 (2015)
30. Xiang, Y., Alahi, A., Savarese, S.: Learning to track: online multi-object tracking by decision making. In: ICCV 2015, pp. 4705–4713 (2015)
31. Wojke, N., Paulus, D.: Global data association for the probability hypothesis density filter using network flows. In: ICRA 2016, pp. 567–572 (2016)
32. Wang, B., et al.: Joint learning of convolutional neural networks and temporally constrained metrics for tracklet association. In: CVPR 2016 Workshops, pp. 1–8 (2016)
33. Hong Yoon, J., Lee, C.R., Yang, M.H., Yoon, K.J.: Online multi-object tracking via structural constraint event aggregation. In: CVPR 2016, pp. 1392–1400 (2016)
34. Kieritz, H., Becker, S., Hübner, W., Arens, M.: Online multi-person tracking using integral channel features. In: AVSS 2016, pp. 122–130 (2016)
35. Manen, S., Timofte, R., Dai, D., Van Gool, L.: Leveraging single for multi-target tracking using a novel trajectory overlap affinity measure. In: WACV 2016, pp. 1–9 (2016)
36. Novak, C.L., Shafer, S.A.: Anatomy of a color histogram. In: CVPR 1992, pp. 599–605 (1992)
37. Dalal, N., Triggs, B.: Histograms of oriented gradients for human detection. In: CVPR 2005, pp. 886–893 (2005)
38. Russakovsky, O., Deng, J., Su, H., Krause, J., et al.: Imagenet large scale visual recognition challenge. Int. J. Comput. Vis. **115**(3), 211–252 (2015)
39. Dollár, P., Appel, R., Belongie, S., Perona, P.: Fast feature pyramids for object detection. PAMI **36**(8), 1532–1545 (2014)
40. Vedaldi, A., Lenc, K.: MatConvNet: convolutional neural networks for MATLAB. In: Proceedings of the 23rd ACM International Conference on Multimedia, pp. 689–692 (2015)
41. Kalman, R.E.: A new approach to linear filtering and prediction problems. J. Basic Eng. **82**(1), 35–45 (1960)

Conductive Particles Detection in the TFT-LCD Manufacturing Process with U-ResNet

Kangping Chen$^{(\boxtimes)}$ and Eryun Liu

Department of Information Science and Electronic Engineering,
Zhejiang University, Hangzhou, China
{chenkp,eryunliu}@zju.edu.cn

Abstract. The inspection of conductive particles after Anisotropic Conductive Film (ACF) bonding is a common and crucial step in the TFT-LCD manufacturing process since quality of conductive particles is an indicator of ACF bonding quality. Manual inspection under microscope is a time consuming and tedious work. There is a demand in industry for automatic conductive particle inspection system. The challenge of automatic conductive particle quality inspection is the complex background noise and diversified particle appearance, including shape, size, clustering and overlapping etc. As a result, there lacks effective automatic detection method to handle all the complex particle patterns. In this paper, we propose a U-shaped deep residual neural network (U-ResNet), which can learn features of particle from massive labeled data. The experimental results show that the proposed method achieves high accuracy and recall rate, which exceedingly outperforms the previous work.

Keywords: Conductive particles · TFT-LCD
Deep convolutional network · U-ResNet

1 Introduction

The Anisotropic Conductive Film (ACF) bonding technique has been widely used in the Thin Film Transistor Liquid Crystal Display (TFT-LCD) industry, such as Film on Glass (FOG) and Chip on Glass (COG) [5,12,14]. The ACF is an electrical conductive adhesive, containing small conductive particles distributed on the insulated pad. During the bonding process, the particles deform and make electrical interconnections between the conductive areas on LCD panel and the flexible circuit vertically [14]. In general, validly deformed particles have clear bright parts and dark parts to be seen when projecting tilted light (see Fig. 1). As the bonding conditions are critical, such as pressure, temperature, time and alignment of the parts, the particles may fail in deformation and be unable to make electrical conductions if any of them is not satisfied (see Fig. 2) [6]. Insufficient number of valid particles may result in poor conductivity and even electrical failure between the panel and flexible circuit [6,14], which leads

© Springer Nature Switzerland AG 2018
J.-H. Lai et al. (Eds.): PRCV 2018, LNCS 11259, pp. 162–173, 2018.
https://doi.org/10.1007/978-3-030-03341-5_14

to inferior products and waste of material. To guarantee the electrical quality at the bonding step and not affect the following manufacturing procedures, an after-bonding inspection of conductive particles is indispensable.

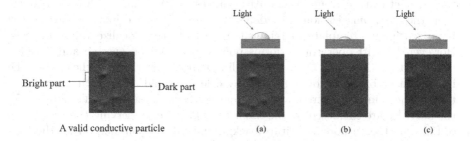

Fig. 1. An example of valid particle, which has a bright part and a dark part to be seen when projecting light.

Fig. 2. (a) Valid conductive particles; (b) invalid particles with too little deformation; (c) invalid particles with too much deformation.

The current practice of after-bonding inspection is to detect the number of valid conductive particles under the microscope manually. Fully automatic particle inspection is still an open problem due to numerous factors, such as clustering and overlapping of the conductive particles after the bonding process (see Fig. 3). We see that sometimes it is even hard to distinguish the particles on such small area, not to mention detecting the valids.

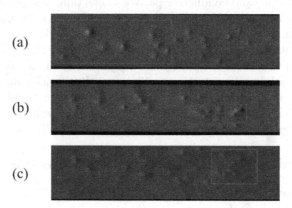

Fig. 3. Challenges in the particle detection. (a) *Variant size*: The particles in the box are valid but in different size; (b) *overlapping and mixture*: The particles in the box overlaps while the valids and invalids are in mixture; (c) *poor illumination and clustering*: The box region is much darker than it in (a) or (b). Meanwhile, the particles are in clusters.

With the development of Automatic Optic Inspection (AOI) technology, a series of researches [5,6,9,12,15] have been made to address the problem. These researches focus on how to design appropriate description to the valid particles. In Lin's (2011) [6], the particles are extracted with *Prewitt operator*, utilizing the gradient feature around them. After processing the image with Prewitt operator, the Otsu binarization is carried out on the processed image. Then on the binarized image, template matching is used to further localize valid particles. However, Prewitt operator performs poor when particles overlap and is sensitive to noise. Moreover, Otsu thresholding is based on the hypothesis that the image can be binarized by a global grayscale threshold [11], which is not practical in the complex environment of circuit surface. Later in Chen's (2017) [15], the particles are extracted by the *intensity difference*. Observing the drawbacks of Lin's [6], the authors substitute background subtraction method for the Prewitt operator process to divide the images into background and foreground, also suppress the noise. And then, instead of a simple binarization, k-means is used to classify the pixels, which is more suitable for the overlapping situation and $k = 4$ shows the best performance in the authors' experiment. Though the method shows higher precision than Lin's [6], it is more time-consuming and still hard to cope with complex situation. In addition to the pure 2D analyses, Guangming Ni [9] designed a special differential interference contrast (DIC) system to detect the particles in 3D space with predefined parameters. Though it gains more information in the additional dimension, the detection is still done by handcrafted features. The handcrafted features are created by the researchers from limited samples. Since the conductive particles vary in shape and size, these handcrafted-feature based method may fail to deal with complex situations.

In this paper, we incorporate the learning-based idea [2,7] and design a convolutional network for valid conductive particles detection. The proposed network architecture is inspired by U-NET [10], which has been widely used in medical analysis [1,10] and autonomous driving [13]. Based on the U-shaped network, we add skip connections to cascade convolutional layers to make residual blocks [4], which is helpful to recover the full spatial resolution at the network output [1]. Also, instead of solving the detection problem in a classification manner, our task is reduced to a more straight-forward regression problem. Besides, we make a series of improvements for better fitting our task. The experimental results show our method outperforms the previous methods both in precision and recall rate.

2   Proposed AOI System for Particle Detection

2.1   Overview

The AOI system is designed to work on the assembly line. As shown in Fig. 4, the full pipeline of our AOI system includes three major steps:

1. Image acquisition and ROI extraction. The raw image is obtained by a line scan camera. One image includes thousands of pads, each of them is a ROI containing particles. The ROIs are detected by aligning the marker points which located on the corner of LCD panel.

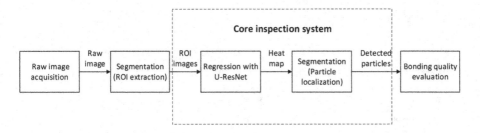

Fig. 4. The full pipeline of our proposed AOI system.

2. Particle detection. This step is the focus of our work in this paper. Given a list of ROI images, the proposed algorithm detects valid particles on the ROIs one by one.
3. Bonding quality evaluation. With the detected particles on each pad, a final decision about the effectiveness of ACF bonding is made based on the quality of particles, such as number of valid particles.

2.2 Pixelwise Regression

As shown in the flowchart (see Fig. 4), the particle detection is separated into two problems, namely particle heat map estimation and particle localization.

The particle heat map is a map with value range in $[0, 1]$ indicating strength of particle. A higher value indicates higher probability that there is a particle. The heat map estimation can be modeled as a pixelwise regression problem as follows:

$$\mathbf{Y}^* = F(\mathbf{X}), \tag{1}$$

where $\mathbf{X}$ is the input ROI image, $\mathbf{Y}^*$ is the output heat map of the same size as $\mathbf{X}$, and F is the pixelwise regression model, such as deep neural network, that mapping the ROI image to the heat map image.

2.3 U-ResNet: U-Shaped Architecture with Residual Blocks

In general, there are two types of technologies for particle strength heat map estimation, namely the knowledge driven and the data driven methods.

The knowledge driven based methods estimate the heat map by extracting handcrafted particle features, while the data driven methods learn the estimation model from markup data.

The existing methods are mainly based on the handcrafted features. However, there are rare methods based on learning from data in the literature. Learning based methods have the advantage to handle complex background.

In this section, we proposed a data driven method based on deep learning. The network structure is shown in Fig. 5.

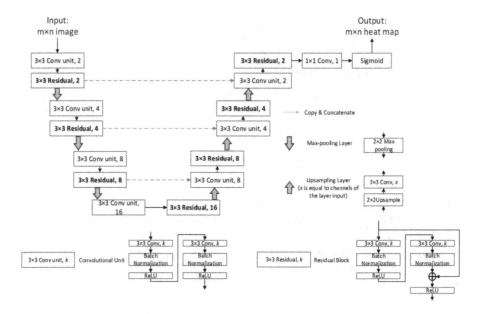

Fig. 5. The architecture of U-ResNet-7.

Architecture. The proposed U-ResNet is a U-shaped network with a down path and an up path, consisting of 14 basic blocks, a 1×1 convolutional layer and a sigmoid layer as output, as shown in Fig. 5. The basic block refers to the convolutional unit or the residual block, either composing of two 3×3 convolutional layers with stride 1 and zero-padding, each followed by a batch normalization layer and a rectified linear unit (ReLU). Differently, the residual block contains additional shortcut connection between the layer input and the latter ReLU. Every two blocks makes a step. After taking a step, a 2×2 max-pooling layer is followed in the down path while an upsampling layer is in the up path.

It should be noted that the proposed network architecture is inspired by the U-NET [10] and ResNet [4]. The feature channels are doubled every step on the down path and halved on the up path, which is brought from U-NET [10]. The structure of *copy & concatenate* is also adopted for combining the feature hierarchy and refining the spatial precision [8].

The network shown in Fig. 5 includes 7 residual blocks, which we call U-ResNet-7. This network structure can be further extended to have deeper layers. By substituting residual blocks for the remaining convolutional units, the U-ResNet-14 is built. By further replacing the three convolutions in the upsampling layers, we design the U-ResNet-17, which doesn't contain any seperate convolutional layer except for the last 1×1 convolution.

Heat Map Regression. The output layer in our networks is a sigmoid layer, which normalizes the output to range $[0, 1]$. Overall, the network takes an $m \times n$

image as input and generates a heat map of the same size. Each value on the heat map indicates the strength of being a valid conductive particle center at the corresponding position on the ROI image.

2.4 Loss Function

Given the predicted heat map and label image, the loss function defined for the regression task is

$$L(\mathbf{Y}^*, \mathbf{Y}) = \sqrt{\sum_{i=1}^{m}\sum_{j=1}^{n} \alpha_{ij}(y_{ij}^* - y_{ij})^2}, \qquad (2)$$

where m and n refer to the size of the input image, $\mathbf{Y}$ represents the label map of the conductive particles while $\mathbf{Y}^*$ refers to the predicted heat map, y_{ij} and y_{ij}^* stands for the strength value at (i, j) on the respective maps. As the number of pixels of particles and background in the label image is unbalanced, the weight coefficient α_{ij} is large for the particles and small for the background, which penalizes more on the labeled particles while keeps the robustness for the wrong labels, as shown in Eq. (3).

$$\alpha_{ij} = 0.05 \times (1 - y_{ij}) + 0.95 \times y_{ij} = \begin{cases} 0.05 & \text{if } y_{ij} = 0, \\ 0.95 & \text{if } y_{ij} = 1. \end{cases} \qquad (3)$$

2.5 Particle Localization

Given the predicted heat map, the particle can be localized in two steps:

1. Particle segmentation. The value in the heat map indicates the strength of being center of particle. A threshold k can be selected to segment the particle region.
2. Given the segmented particle area, the particle center is estimated as the centroid of segmented objects.

3 Experiments

3.1 The Dataset

As far as we know, there is no conductive particle dataset in the public domain that is available for research. A large amount of data is necessary for both training and validation. We created a dataset for algorithm evaluation. The training and validation datasets are both created in two steps.

1. ROI Extraction: The raw images are of 8-bit grayscale, captured by a 64 kHz, 4k TDI Line Scan camera of $0.72\,\mu m$/pixel in resolution. The size of raw image is 42036×1635. As the particles only appear on the pin area of LCD screen,

Table 1. Detailed information of the annotated datasets.

Dataset Name	Set-A	Set-B	Set-C
Image Size	1024×128	128×64	92×24
Training Set Count	3304	5665	5792
Validation Set Count	827	1417	1448
Total Count	4131	7082	7235

the detection algorithm focuses only on the ROI images. There are three different sizes of ROI images according to the pin size of LCD screen used tested in our experiments, namely 1024×128, 128×64, and 92×24, which we call Set-A, Set-B and Set-C, respectively. The particle characteristics on these three types of ROI images are slightly different.

2. Particle Location Annotation: Given a ROI image $\mathbf{X}$, the label image $\mathbf{Y}$ of the same size is obtained, where $y_{ij} = 1$ with (i, j) is the manually marked center of particles otherwise $y_{ij} = 0$. The ROI images along with corresponding label images in three categories compose the final datasets called Set-A, Set-B and Set-C (see Table 1).

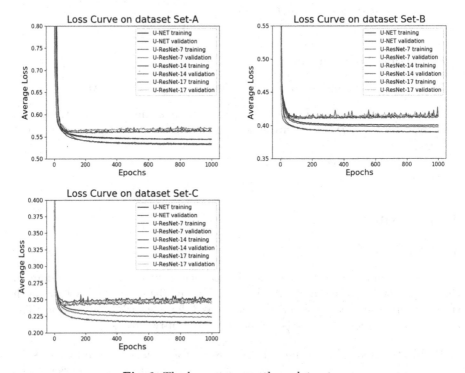

Fig. 6. The loss curves on three datasets.

3.2   Training the Model

To speed the training process, we divide the grayscaled value of pixels by 255 to normalize the values into range $[0, 1]$. We also added a batch normalization layer after each convolutional layer (see Fig. 5).

The weights of our network are first initialized by the way introduced by Kaiming He [3]. Then the model is trained via backpropagation algorithm with GPU accelaration. We use Adam optimizer with a batch size of 64 samples, learning rate of 0.001, the first momentum $\beta_1 = 0.9$, the second momentum $\beta_2 = 0.999$, and weight decay of 0.01. It takes about 20 h to train for 1000 epochs on a single NVIDIA TITAN X GPU. The training and validation loss curves are shown in Fig. 6. As we can see in the figure, both loss curves are converged.

From the loss curves, we see that all U-ResNet based networks have lower loss than the original U-NET [10]. The U-ResNet-14 and U-ResNet-17 have the lowerest training loss. But on the validation sets, U-ResNet-7 always has the lowerest loss, which indicates that U-ResNet-7 may have the best particle localization performance.

3.3   Precision and Recall Evaluation

Previous loss analysis indicates that U-ResNet-7 has the best convergence performance on dataset Set-A while U-ResNet-14 wins on Set-B and Set-C. But the output from the networks is actually a heat map rather than the detection results. As mentioned above, we need to determine the segmentation threshold k for further processing to localize particles. To evaluate the final results, we introduce precision and recall as quantitative criterions.

The precision and recall are defined as:

$$Precision = \frac{|U \cap U^*|}{|U|} \times 100\% \tag{4}$$

$$Recall = \frac{|U \cap U^*|}{|U^*|} \times 100\% \tag{5}$$

where U is the set of ground truth particles on the label map, U^* is the set of localized particles, the intersection $U \cap U^*$ refers to the set of correctly localized particles, and $|.|$ is the number of elements in the set. To determine the intersection, the location (i^*, j^*) of each particle in set U^* and the location (i, j) of its nearest neighbor in set U is measured with Euclidean distance D, as shown in Eq. 6.

$$D = \sqrt{(i^* - i)^2 + (j^* - j)^2}. \tag{6}$$

The tolerance of D is set to 5 in the experiment, which corresponds to the nearly maximum radius of valid particle in our dataset.

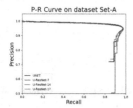 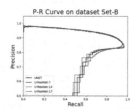 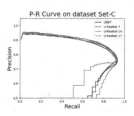

Fig. 7. Precision-Recall curves of the proposed model.

Table 2. Performance comparison on three datasets.

		Lin's [6]	Chen's [15]	U-NET [10]	U-ResNet-7	U-ResNet-14	U-ResNet-17
Set-A	Precision	74.8%	77.5%	96.0%	**96.1%**	95.9%	96.0%
	Recall	74.8%	77.5%	96.0%	**96.1%**	95.9%	96.0%
Set-B	Precision	83.8%	81.0%	89.6%	**89.9%**	89.8%	89.7%
	Recall	31.0%	33.1%	89.6%	**89.9%**	89.8%	89.7%
Set-C	Precision	75.4%	77.0%	83.5%	84.5%	**84.7%**	84.6%
	Recall	30.9%	30.7%	83.5%	84.5%	**84.7%**	84.6%

Tradeoff Between Precision and Recall. To evaluate the tradeoff between precision and recall, the P-R curves with respect to threshold k on heat map are shown in Fig. 7.

We see that all 4 networks have similar performance on dataset Set-A. But on Set-B and Set-C, whose image data contains denser particles with more variant size, we observe that the curves are discriminate. The curve of U-ResNet-17 decays the most saliently after reaching the turning point, especially on Set-C. Combined with loss curve of U-ResNet-17, we infer that it's caused by slightly overfitting, because U-ResNet-17 with the most layers among the models, has the best training error but performs poor on the validation set. The curve of U-NET [10] decays the second most saliently while the U-ResNet-7 and U-ResNet-14 perform excellent on three datasets.

The curves also manifest that we cannot make both precision and recall close to 1. To tradeoff between the two criterions, we seek for a threshold k that makes them close to each other. The equal value determines the best precision and recall on the dataset (see Table 2). In accord with the result from loss curve, U-ResNet-7 has the best precision and recall on dataset Set-A and Set-B while U-ResNet-14 performs the best on Set-C. U-ResNet-7 and U-ResNet-14 outperforms U-NET [10] on all datasets, which demonstrates that U-ResNet is more suitable for our particle detection task.

3.4 Comparison with Traditional Methods

The biggest difference between the traditional methods and the proposed method is how to extract features. Figure 8 shows several examples from three datasets. As we can see, the method based on U-ResNet or U-NET [10] performs better than the traditional methods. Lin's method [6] has poor performance in region with dense or overlapping particles, especially on Set-B and Set-C. Chen's [15] has better result than Lin's method but still loses a number of particles.

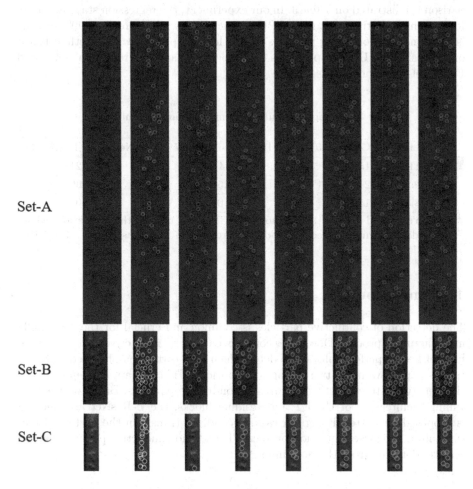

Fig. 8. Examples of particle detection results on three datasets. From left to right: ROI image, Ground truth, Lin's [6], Chen's [15], U-NET [10], U-ResNet-7, U-ResNet-14, U-ResNet-17

Table 2 illustrates the precision and recall values of the methods on three datasets. We see on the table that on Set-B and Set-C, the two traditional methods have very low recall rate while all deep learning based methods exceedingly outperform the two traditional methods. This fact implies that learning-from-data methods are more suitable for detecting valid conductive particles.

3.5   Computation Time

The system was implemented on a Ubuntu 14.04 LTS OS system with 3.5 GHz i7-5930 CPU, 32 G RAM and TITAN X GPU. The total computation time comparison is illustrated on Table 3. In our experiment, the regression stage accounts for less than 1% time cost with GPU acceleration, while more than 99% of time is consumed for localizing particles on the heat map. We see the method based on U-ResNet or U-NET performs much better than the traditional ones and U-ResNet-7 is more time-saving.

Table 3. Average computation time comparison (unit: ms).[1]

	Lin's [6]	Chen's [15]	U-NET [10]	U-ResNet-7	U-ResNet-14	U-ResNet-17
Set-A	11.08	151.11	**5.37**	5.44	6.60	7.21
Set-B	9.28	21.92	2.61	**2.58**	2.64	2.66
Set-C	8.45	14.10	1.98	**1.96**	2.05	2.06

[1] For Lin's [6] and Chen's [15] methods, no GPU was used in the evaluation, while for the deep learning based methods, the regression step was tested with GPU acceleration.

4   Conclusion

The detection of conductive particles is common and crucial for the TFT-LCD manufacturing process. Due to the complex pattern of conductive particles, there has not been a perfect solution to detect them with certain handcrafted features. In this paper, we make two major contributions. First, we apply deep convolutional network to extracting features of conductive particles. Based on the prevailing architecture of U-NET and residual blocks, the U-ResNet architecture is proposed for better fitting our task. Second, we transform the particle detection into a pixelwise regression problem. Then valid conductive particles can be directly detected from the heat map.

References

1. Drozdzal, M., Vorontsov, E., Chartrand, G., Kadoury, S., Pal, C.: The importance of skip connections in biomedical image segmentation. In: Carneiro, G., et al. (eds.) LABELS/DLMIA -2016. LNCS, vol. 10008, pp. 179–187. Springer, Cham (2016). https://doi.org/10.1007/978-3-319-46976-8_19
2. Ferguson, M., Ak, R., Lee, Y.T.T., Law, K.H.: Automatic localization of casting defects with convolutional neural networks. In: 2017 IEEE International Conference on Big Data (Big Data), pp. 1726–1735. IEEE (2017)
3. He, K., Zhang, X., Ren, S., Sun, J.: Delving deep into rectifiers: surpassing human-level performance on imagenet classification. In: Proceedings of the IEEE International Conference on Computer Vision, pp. 1026–1034 (2015)

4. He, K., Zhang, X., Ren, S., Sun, J.: Deep residual learning for image recognition. In: Proceedings of the IEEE Conference on Computer Vision and Pattern Recognition, pp. 770–778 (2016)
5. Jia, L., Sheng, X., Xiong, Z., Wang, Z., Ding, H.: Particle on bump (POB) technique for ultra-fine pitch chip on glass (COG) applications by conductive particles and adhesives. Microelectron. Reliab. **54**(4), 825–832 (2014)
6. Lin, C.S., Huang, K.H., Lin, T.C., Shei, H.J., Tien, C.L.: An automatic inspection method for the fracture conditions of anisotropic conductive film in the TFT-LCD assembly process. Int. J. Optomechatronics **5**(3), 286–298 (2011)
7. Lin, H., Li, B., Wang, X., Shu, Y., Niu, S.: Automated defect inspection of led chip using deep convolutional neural network. J. Intell. Manuf., 1–10 (2018)
8. Long, J., Shelhamer, E., Darrell, T.: Fully convolutional networks for semantic segmentation. In: Proceedings of the IEEE Conference on Computer Vision and Pattern Recognition, pp. 3431–3440 (2015)
9. Ni, G., Liu, L., Du, X., Zhang, J., Liu, J., Liu, Y.: Accurate AOI inspection of resistance in LCD anisotropic conductive film bonding using differential interference contrast. Opt. Int. J. Light. Electron Opt. **130**, 786–796 (2017)
10. Ronneberger, O., Fischer, P., Brox, T.: U-Net: convolutional networks for biomedical image segmentation. In: Navab, N., Hornegger, J., Wells, W.M., Frangi, A.F. (eds.) MICCAI 2015. LNCS, vol. 9351, pp. 234–241. Springer, Cham (2015). https://doi.org/10.1007/978-3-319-24574-4_28
11. Sezgin, M., Sankur, B.: Survey over image thresholding techniques and quantitative performance evaluation. J. Electron. Imaging **13**(1), 146–166 (2004)
12. Sheng, X., Jia, L., Xiong, Z., Wang, Z., Ding, H.: ACF-COG interconnection conductivity inspection system using conductive area. Microelectron. Reliab. **53**(4), 622–628 (2013)
13. Wirges, S., Hartenbach, F., Stiller, C.: Evidential occupancy grid map augmentation using deep learning. arXiv preprint arXiv:1801.05297 (2018)
14. Yen, Y.W., Lee, C.Y.: ACF particle distribution in COG process. Microelectron. Reliab. **51**(3), 676–684 (2011)
15. Yu-ye, C., Ke, X., Zhen-xiong, G., Jun-jie, H., Chang, L., Song-yan, C.: Detection of conducting particles bonding in the circuit of liquid crystal display. Chin. J. Liq. Cryst. Disp. **32**(7), 553–559 (2017)

A New Monocular 3D Object Detection with Neural Network

Weijie Hong, Yiguang Liu$^{(\boxtimes)}$, Yunan Zheng, Ying Wang, and Xuelei Shi

Vision and Image Processing Lab (VIPL), College of Computer Science,
Sichuan University, Chengdu 610065, People's Republic of China
liuyg@scu.edu.cn

Abstract. Coherently recognizing objects and localizing its 3D position is vital in a large number of practical applications such as robot, autonomous unmanned systems, etc. To tackle this problem, we present a new framework composed of two coupled deep networks. The framework involves three tight steps: first, by implanting a pyramid strategy into the end-to-end detection network, the goal of detecting and recognizing objects with large or small scales is attained in 2D pictures; second, by a novel lost function we proposed for the depth networks, the 3D points of the objects are accurately estimated; and finally, we propose a windowed point cloud segmentation: combing 3D norm direction, curvature and color information, outlier 3D points are removed from windows, thus the clean object is extracted with its 3D position. The obvious advantage of the framework lies on that most the steps are implemented by the fused networks, and this makes the frame-work efficient, accurate and robust provided with enough training data. The framework is evaluated on the KITTI benchmark, and the efficiency is superior to the state-of-the-art methods while the accuracy is comparable. Our method is several tens of times faster than most of previous methods and capable of applications with real time constraint. In addition, we only use weak supervision learning methods in our framework that need less manual annotations.

Keywords: 3D Object Detection · Deep network
Windowed point cloud segmentation

1 Introduction

The problem of object detection is particularly important in the real word, such as auto-driving and robot that need to make decisions or interact with objects in the real world. The recent two-dimensional detection algorithms can handle a lot of viewpoints including noise. Although 2D detection has a great progress, accurate three-dimensional objects detection is still an open question in some way. Predictably 3D position plays a critical role in the context of auto-driving or robotics. In many cases, it is necessary to enable recovery of 3D position and recognizing classes of surrounding object in real-time. In this paper, we are focused on both 2D and 3D object analysis from monocular images.

© Springer Nature Switzerland AG 2018
J.-H. Lai et al. (Eds.): PRCV 2018, LNCS 11259, pp. 174–185, 2018.
https://doi.org/10.1007/978-3-030-03341-5_15

Up to now there are two ways to achieve 2D object detection without considering the traditional standard sliding window scheme method. The first one is the proposal-based methods [5,14]. The goal of object proposal methods is to propose several regions with high confidence scores. Then these proposals are given to the classification-detector which has strong ability to classify objects. The main advantage of object proposal methods is to reduce the time when searching space in comparison with traditional methods. The second one is the 2D object end-to-end detection [13]. From the network structure, there is no middle region proposal to find the objects. The determination of position and category is completed by direct regression. And the main advantage of these methods is that they can quickly detect and identify multiple objects in some image with certain accuracy (Fig. 1).

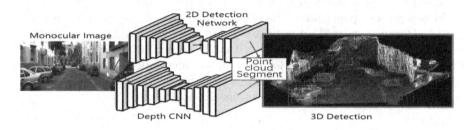

Fig. 1. Our new framework for 3D object detection

Several recent methods have explored 3D object detection. Chen et al. [1] addresses the problem by sampling 3D boxes in the real world assuming the flat ground plane constraint. The boxes are scored using high level contextual, shape and category specific features. Arsalan et al. [11] present a method that combines relatively stable 3D object properties with geometric constraints provided by a 2D object bounding box. It aims to produce a complete 3D bounding box for 3D object detection and pose estimation from a single image. Another related approach by Florian et al. [7] propose a supervised approach based on the Many-task CNN (Deep MANTA) which achieve accurate 3D vehicle bounding boxes using multiple refinement steps. All of the above approaches require complex preprocessing including high level features such as segmentation or 3D shape repositories. And they may not be suitable for robots or other applications with limited computational resources. Further more they only calculate the 3D box, without getting the sufficient 3D description of the object.

In this paper, we aim to build a framework to detect 3D information of surrounding object in real time. We propose a new framework from a single view, which is designed to achieve the detection of 3D point cloud information. And our approach is based on the improvement of the deep convolutional network combined with Stereo Geometry. Our monocular framework consists three steps: first, we get 2D bounding boxes and classification from a image, which depend on our improved 2D object detection network; second, we get a depth image using a depth network that is used to predict the depth from a single view; finally, combining information from both above network, we compute accurate point clouds of objects by using windowed point cloud segmentation that is implemented in narrow fields bounded by 2D boxes. Remarkably, we implant a feature pyramid network into our 2D detection network when it infers, which greatly increased the accuracy of tiny object. Predictably the detection of dim objects is crucial for the accuracy of flowing 3D detection. In the second step, we adopt an unsupervised network to predict depth. Specifically, we improve the depth network, and simplify the loss function, and we find that improvement boots the predict of depth. Predictably both improvements play a vital role in 3d detection. In the third step, we propose a windowed point cloud segmentation. Combining norm direction, curvature and color information, we remove outlier 3D points in order to recover point cloud information and locate objects accurately. In addition, these steps are quite fast that it only cost 0.32s per image.

In general, our paper makes these main contributions: firstly, we propose a new ideal for monocular 3D object detection that need little tagging information; secondly, through our improvement to the 2D detection, depth inference and windowed point cloud segmentation, we build a framework that can infer the 3D information of surrounding objects in real time; finally, through our method, we can get more accurate 3D detection results–3D point cloud.

2   Method

In this section we introduce our framework in detail. Our method will be separated three pipelines to explain: step 1, we set up an improved 2D-box detection network; step 2, we design an unsupervised depth prediction network from one picture; step 3, we generate the point cloud and remove outlier points of object by using point cloud segmentation.

2.1   Improved 2D-BOX Object Detector

Recently deep learning has achieved a great breakthrough in the two-dimension object detection, and the algorithm of object detection is divided into two major categories: the proposal-based approach and the end-to-end approach. Although the accuracy is reduced a little, the end-to-end object detection algorithm has a significant advantage in time-consuming. In many applications of different scenarios, it is necessary to achieve real-time detection. Therefore we adapt the end-to-end object detection method for our framework in this paper. Then we made some improvements, so that it can ensure the accuracy and real-time performance.

Multi-scale Pyramid. In the work of object detection, there are many problems. Especially in the case of tiny object detection, it is very difficult to detect. In the deeper network layer, the receptive field expands, which means that the stride can ignore some important information. Traditional solutions to this problem is feature stratification that forces different layers to learn the same semantic information. For convolution neural network, different depth corresponds to the semantic features of different levels: shallow network layers learn more detail of hight resolution features, deeper layers learn more semantic features from relatively low resolution. Therefore, we introduce the trick of feature pyramid network (FPN) proposed by Lin et al [8]. Exploiting these effective links, each layer we want to predict is a blend of different resolution, different intensity of semantic feature. Illustrated in Fig. 2, we add the FPN into our network.

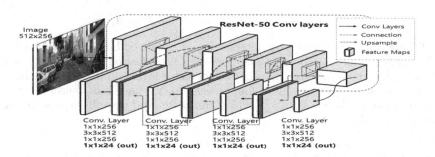

Fig. 2. Improved end-to-end network for 2D object detection, we add FPN

Detector Layer. We use end-to-end neural network to ensure high accuracy when time is limited. Inspired by YOLO method from Joseph Redmon et al. [13], we improve our network in which problem of positioning and classification is solved by regression. After the image has been trained on the pre-training network (ResNet-50 [7]), multiple anchor boxes [14] are presented in each grid of each convolution feature graph at different scales. Each anchor predicts the position of the bounding box size information, classification and the confidence score. These scores reflect the fitting degree of the prediction with the ground trues. The confidence function here can be defined as: $C = pr(object) \times IOU_{pre}^{truth}$. Where $pr(object)$ represents whether there is an object in the predicted box. When the object exists, it equal to 1, and IOU is the intersection of predicted box and ground truth. Each boxes contains five estimates, including the object center point (x, y), width, height (w, h) and confidence value C. To increase the stability of x and y, and we use track of Anchor from Faster-RCNN [14]:

$$\hat{t}_x = \frac{(\hat{x} - x_a)}{w_a}, \hat{t}_y = \frac{(\hat{y} - y_a)}{h_a}; \hat{t}_w = \log(\frac{\hat{w}}{w_a}), \hat{t}_h = \log(\frac{\hat{h}}{h_a}) \qquad (1)$$

$$t_x^* = \frac{(x^* - x_a)}{w_a}, t_y^* = \frac{(y^* - y_a)}{h_a}; t_w^* = \log(\frac{w^*}{w_a}), t_h^* = \log(\frac{h^*}{h_a}) \qquad (2)$$

Where $\{\hat{x}, \hat{y}, \hat{w}, \hat{h}\}$ denote respectively the central coordinates, width and height of the predicted box. Parameters $\{x_a, y_a, w_a, h_a\}$ are the location box of Anchor box, and parameters $\{x^*, y^*, w^*, h^*\}$ are the ground truth. In short, what the network do is to regress ground truth from anchor box. Then we removed the full link layer of the network in the end of the ResNet-50, then added four convolutional layers convolution layers into each scale, and use anchor box from multi-scale to estimate the bounding box. For detailéd network structure, please browse Fig. 2.

Loss Function for Training. Our loss module was inspired by YOLO [13] and improved with the latest research. For training, we set up 4 different scales, and 3 different ratio anchors at every scale. We define a loss C_s at each output scale s, forming the total loss as the sum $LOSS = \sum(L_s)$. Our loss module computes L_s as a combination of tree main terms,

$$L_S = \lambda_1 Conf_s + \lambda_2 Class_s + \lambda_3 Coord_s \tag{3}$$

Where $conf_s$ encourages the intersection of predicted box and ground truth to be predicted more accurate. $Class_s$ enforces classification and $Coord_s$ prefers the predicted the locations. Note that the detector layer will predict k predicted boxes at each cell, and we have four scales. So, we have four tensors in very output layers s, like $w_s \times h_s \times [k \times (5 + classes)]$. And we will discuss these in more detail below.

$$Conf_s = \lambda_{noobj} \sum_i^{n_s^2} \sum_j^{anchor} (1 - \alpha_{ij})(C_{ij} - C_{ij}^*)^2 + \lambda_{obj} \sum_i^{n_s^2} \sum_j^{anchor} \alpha_{ij}(C_{ij} - C_{ij}^*)^2 \tag{4}$$

$$Coord_s = \sum_i^{n_s^2} \sum_j^{anchor} (\hat{t}_x - t_x^*)^2 + (\hat{t}_y - t_y^*)^2 + (\hat{t}_w - t_w^*)^2 + (\hat{t}_h - t_h^*)^2 \tag{5}$$

$$Class_s = \sum_i^{n_s^2} \sum_j^{anchor} (p_{ij} - \hat{p}_{ij}) \tag{6}$$

Where α denotes if object appears in the anchor j from cell i. Note that we give λ_{obj} more higher weight than λ_{noobj}, because we don't think the features of the non-interest area are effective enough. And about $Coord_s$ we have introduced in last section.

2.2   Improved Depth-Network

In the previous section, we have focused on our improved real-time 2-dimensional object detection model. We have been able to predict two-dimensional information from it. And in this section we will focus on the method that output a depth map from a single image. The basis of the idea relay on binocular stereo matching. Based on the principle of polar geometry, we can easily deduce the formula for depth assuming that there are two left-right images taken at the same time:

$$z = \frac{Bf}{x_1 - x_2} \tag{7}$$

Where B is the distance between the left-right cameras, called baseline. f is the focal length, in general, we assume that the left-right cameras have the same focal length. x_1, x_2 respectively denote the points on the image planes projected from the same point from 3-dimensions space. Usually we call $x_1 - x_2$ as the disparity. Hence, when given disparity, we can calculate the depth information from formula (7). Only given single figure, a lot of previous researches often use a supervised learning to calculate the depth information. But in daily life, depth information acquisition is difficult. Therefore, we adopt a strategy that is an unsupervised method. It switch the problem of estimating depth to the problem of reconstructing images. In simple terms, the depth network method is used to estimate the disparity between the left image and right image. Subsequently, we optimize this prediction by learning.

Specifically, in training time, we are given two calibrated color images (I_l, I_r) that are sampled at the same time. We do not directly estimate depth, rather than using a full convolutional network estimate the left and right disparity (d_r, d_l). Images (I_l, I_r) and the disparities (d_r, d_l) are known, we have ability to reconstructed image $(\hat{I}_l, \hat{I}_r)$. Consequently we will get ideal disparities when $\hat{I}$ is infinitely closed to I.

We adopt the full convolution network, which comes from the network proposed by Clement Godard [6]. It consists of two main parts–encoders and decoders. We made our modifications to this network in order to improve our accuracy. Specifically we switch to a variant based ResNet as the encoder for this network. Similar to the scale pyramid in the previous section, our network also sets four different scales of output so that it can resolve higher resolution details, as shown in Fig. 3.

After completing deep inference operation, pixels on original I can be mixed up to form a new pixel with the help of disparities. Denote I_l as the input left image, we choose to directly warp the left image based on estimated disparity into a corresponding right image. In the same way, the right image can also generate the predicted left image. We compared the reconstructed images with ground truth to make sure our disparity predicted is accurate enough. To supervise the reconstruction quality, we do not propose any special loss function. We find that a simple L1 loss supervising on the reconstructed appearance is sufficient for the task of view reconstructed, where N is the number of pixels:

$$Loss_s = \frac{1}{N}(|\hat{I}_r(i,j) - I_r(i,j)| + |\hat{I}_l - I_l(i,j)|) \tag{8}$$

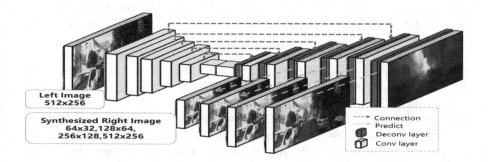

Fig. 3. Improved full convolutional network for depth

2.3   Windowed Point Cloud Separation

We can quickly get rough 3-dimensional information of the detected object through the above two networks, but there is redundant depth information in the box region. It is necessary to remove outlier points to accurately find the position of the object. We propose a windowed point cloud segmentation to deal with this problem. In each small window we can rapidly outline objects wanted. Comparing to segmentation in whole points, it costs less time because of the reduce of redundant regions. In our windowed strategy, we sort these windows according to the average depth. That prevents occlusion phenomenon effectively, on the premise that we remove the points closed to us. The segmentation information the image provide is only gray-scale or RGB vector, while the 3d point cloud can provide more information. Therefore, the advantage of point cloud in segmentation is unmatched. There is no need to use some recent image segmentation algorithms that need a mass of supervised data (such as FCN [10]). We just adopt point cloud segmentation based on curvature, RGB and other information to solve the problem. In this paper, we define the properties of each point cloud as (Fig. 4):

$$\{x, y, z, r, g, b, cur, \boldsymbol{n}\} \tag{9}$$

Where $\{x, y, z\}$ denote the coordinate information of a point in the 3D space, while $\{r, g, b\}$ represent colors. And the cur and $\boldsymbol{n}$ are for the curvature and normal vector. The normal vector and curvature are the typical feature that describe the geometric properties of points on the surface. In strict sense, isolated points have no normal vector and curvature. Here we take advantage of K-Nearest Neighbor method to fit a surface from which we can compute approximate normal vector and curvature. We employ the least squares nonlinear fitting surface, and the following formula is deduced:

$$\begin{bmatrix} \sum(x_i - \bar{x})^2 & \sum(x_i - \bar{x})(y_i - \bar{y}) & \sum(x_i - \bar{x})(z_i - \bar{z}) \\ \sum(x_i - \bar{x})(y_i - \bar{y}) & \sum(y_i - \bar{y})^2 & \sum(y_i - \bar{y})(z_i - \bar{z}) \\ \sum(x_i - \bar{x})(z_i - \bar{z}) & \sum(z_i - \bar{z})(y_i - \bar{y}) & \sum(z_i - \bar{z})^2 \end{bmatrix} \boldsymbol{n} = \lambda_{min} \boldsymbol{n} \tag{10}$$

Where $\{\bar{x}, \bar{y}, \bar{z}\}$ denoted as center of gravity. In order to minimize the loss function of the least square, we need to calculate the minimum eigenvalue of the matrix, and the eigenvector λ correspond to the normal vector. Simultaneously the residual of plane fitting can be think as an approximation of curvature: $cur = (\lambda/k)^{1/2}$.

In this paper, we are inspired from region growing segmentation algorithm [12] that is very effective and fast. And color information is added to the point cloud structure information. Every neighbor is tested for the angle between its normal and normal of the current seed point. If the angle is less than threshold then current point will be added to the current region. After that every neighbor is tested for the curvature value. If the curvature is less than threshold value then this point is added to the seeds. And if the color difference between the current seed point and the neighborhood point is less than the color difference threshold, it will be also added to the seeds. Finally, current seed is removed from the seeds.

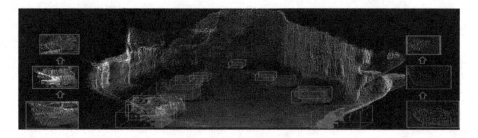

Fig. 4. Our windowed point cloud segmentation. We sort these windowed according to depth to counter occlusion phenomenon.

3 Implementation Details

The networks which is implemented in TensorFlow and Keras. And We performed our experiments on the KITTI [4].

For improved 2D box object detection, we take advantage of the parameters of the ResNet-50 on the ImageNet [3] as our pre-train network and takes on the order of 60 hours to train our detector network on a dataset of the KITTI with double 1080Ti GPUs. Notably, when it runs there are 4 prediction layers of different scales with the application of FPN. In particular, we predict 3 boxes at each cell of different scales. So the tensor is $w_s \times h_s \times [3 \times (5+3)]$. According to ResNet-50, $(w_s, h_s) = R/8, R/16, R/64$, where R denoted raw images. And in our experiment, we resize images as 512×256. So the obvious thing is that we have a mass of predictive boxes (8160). During optimization, we set the weight of the different loss components. Since we care more about the object we interested, we set $\lambda_{obj} = 0.7, \lambda_{noobj} = 0.3$ here, and $\lambda_1 = 0.6, \lambda_2 = 0.2, \lambda_3 = 0.2$. And throughout training we use a batch size of 64, a momentum of 0.9 and a decay of 0.0005.

For depth network, the KITTI dataset has total of 7481 pairs of training left-right images. Inference is fast and takes less than 34ms, for a 512×256 image on double 1080ti GPUs platform. During optimization, the possible output disparities are limited between 0 and d_{max} using a scaled sigmoid non-linearity. In our experiment, we set $d_{max} = 0.5$ at a given output scale. As a result of our multi-scale output, the typical disparity of neighboring pixels will differ by a factor of two between each scale (as we are upsampling the output by a factor of two).

For point cloud segmentation, we test on KITTI. The object of KITTI mainly include some categories of automobile and automobile and pedestrians. And we want to make sure both goals of grouping smooth areas and avoiding over-segmentation. Winded point cloud segmentation affect the result, so we focus on: point cloud segmentation may affect the performance of 3D detection. About the parameters of the region growing segmentation algorithm, we compare different thresholds, and got different results. After our repeated tests, we got a set of ideal thresholds for cars. When we set smooth threshold as 0.06π, curvature threshold

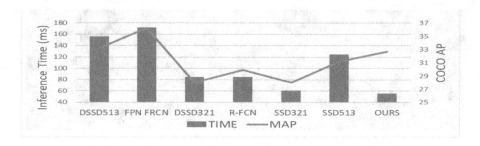

Fig. 5. Comparison of the Average Precision (AP) on MS COCO dataset

as 3.4 and RGB threshold as 30, we can quickly segment the target cloud in a small area. And for other objects, we also got different segment threshold in the same way.

4 Result

We evaluate our approach on the challenging KITTI detection that consist of 7481 training images and 7518 test images. And our detection contains three object classes: car, pedestrian, cyclist. And there are 3 regimes: Easy, Moderate and Hard. In our training process, we split training images into a training set (5984 images) and a validation (1497 images). In particular, for 2d object detector we also evaluate our network on MS COCO dataset [9]. In order to test the accuracy of our algorithm, we bound the segmented point cloud into 3Dbox. We evaluate the whole pipeline of our detection model on two tasks of KITTI: 2D object detection and 3D object detection. Following the standard KITTI setup, we use the Average Precision (AP2D) metric for 2D object detection task, and for joint 3D object detection we use Average Localization Precision (ALP) metric proposed by [15].

Table 1. Comparison of the Average Precision (AP) on official KITTI dataset for car and pedestrian.

Method	Type	Time	Car			Pedestrian		
			Easy	Moderate	Hard	Easy	Moderate	Hard
3DOP [2]	Stereo	4 s	90.09	88.34	**78.79**	82.36	67.46	**64.71**
SubCNN [16]	Mono	2 s	90.47	**88.86**	77.60	**83.17**	**71.34**	66.36
Mono3D [1]	Mono	4.2 s	90.27	87.86	78.09	77.30	66.66	63.44
Ours	Mono	**0.32 s**	**90.91**	88.01	77.02	80.33	72.34	65.32

Table 2. Comparison of the ALP on official KITTI dataset for car.

Car			ALP(1m)			ALP(2m)		
Method	Type	Time	Easy	Moderate	Hard	Easy	Moderate	Hard
3DOP [2]	Stereo	4 s	**81.97**	**68.15**	**59.85**	**91.46**	**81.63**	**72.93**
3DVP [15]	Mono	40 s	45.61	34.28	27.72	65.73	54.60	45.62
Mono3D [1]	Mono	4.2 s	48.31	38.98	34.25	74.77	60.91	54.24
Ours	Mono	**0.32 s**	49.78	40.63	37.32	77.56	62.32	55.74

4.1 Performance of 2D Object Detection

For our 2D object detection we evaluate its performance on both MS COCO and KITTI (Fig. 6).

We test separate 2D object detection inference on MS COCO dataset. As shown in Fig. 5, our approach outperforms many algorithms in terms of accuracy, and the speed control is clearly far ahead. We not only obtain 32.7%mAP on MS COCO, but the calculation time of each picture is only 56 ms.

We test our approach on KTIIT for a task: 2D object detection. We choose our model based on the validation set, and submit our results to the benchmark. For the detection network, we use the test RGB images as the input of our model. As shown in Table 1, our approach significantly maintain a high level. At the same time ours spend a lot less time than all of they do. Our method is several tens of times faster than most of previous methods and capable of applications with real time constraint. After our improvement, our algorithm is precise and fast.

Fig. 6. The result of our method, the first group is our 2D object detection from single view; the second group is the result of depth network; the third group is the point cloud result through the windowed point cloud segmentation.

4.2   Performance of 3D Object Detection

Our KITTI 3D metric is Average Localization Precision (ALP) metric. A test of 3D detection is ideal when its distance is smaller than a distance threshold from the ground truth. As shown in Table 2, it presents results on the a val set for a threshold distance of 1 m and 2 m. We got good grades in the test, compared with other methods. Our framework clearly outperforms other monocular approaches [1,15] for the 3D localization task (about %9 compared to 3DVP [15]). Moreover, in the case of acceptable accuracy, our framework leads to tens times speed up over these methods (about 125 times compared to 3DVP [15]), which heralds it work in real time.

5   Conclusions and Future Work

The problem of object detection is particularly important in the application of robots that need to make decisions or interact with objects in the real world, including auto-driving. To solve this kind of problem, in this work, we show how to fast identify object, and recover the 3D point cloud of object in 3-dimensional space simultaneously from a single view. We combine two improved network models–object detection and depth prediction network–to recognize object and estimate depth. And then, by adopting point cloud segmentation strategy, we can locate accurately the object 3-dimensions point cloud. About this problem, we have a long perspective. One future work is to explore the benefits of augmenting the RGB image input in new CNN with separate depth channel. Another one is optimizing our point cloud segmentation classifier by deep learning method.

Acknowledgements. This work is supported by NSFC under Grant 61860206007 and 61571313, by National Key Research and Development Program under Grant 2016YFB0800600 and 2016YFB0801100, by funding from Sichuan Province under Grant 18GJHZ0138, and by joint funding from Sichuan University and Lu-Zhou city under 2016CDLZ-G02-SCU.

References

1. Chen, X., Kundu, K., Zhang, Z., Ma, H., Fidler, S., Urtasun, R.: Monocular 3d object detection for autonomous driving. In: Proceedings of the IEEE Conference on Computer Vision and Pattern Recognition, pp. 2147–2156 (2016)
2. Chen, X., Kundu, K., Zhu, Y., Berneshawi, A.G., Ma, H., Fidler, S., Urtasun, R.: 3d object proposals for accurate object class detection. Lecture Notes in Business Information Processing, vol. 122, pp. 34–45 (2015)
3. Deng, J., Dong, W., Socher, R., Li, L.J., Li, K., Li, F.F.: Imagenet: a large-scale hierarchical image database. In: IEEE Conference on Computer Vision and Pattern Recognition, CVPR 2009, pp. 248–255 (2009)
4. Geiger, A., Lenz, P., Urtasun, R.: Are we ready for autonomous driving? the kitti vision benchmark suite. In: 2012 IEEE Conference on Computer Vision and Pattern Recognition (CVPR), pp. 3354–3361. IEEE (2012)

5. Girshick, R., Donahue, J., Darrell, T., Malik, J.: Rich feature hierarchies for accurate object detection and semantic segmentation. In: Proceedings of the IEEE Conference on Computer Vision and Pattern Recognition, pp. 580–587 (2014)
6. Godard, C., Mac Aodha, O., Brostow, G.J.: Unsupervised monocular depth estimation with left-right consistency. In: CVPR, vol. 2, p. 7 (2017)
7. He, K., Zhang, X., Ren, S., Sun, J.: Deep residual learning for image recognition. In: Proceedings of the IEEE Conference on Computer Vision and Pattern Recognition, pp. 770–778 (2016)
8. Lin, T.Y., Dollár, P., Girshick, R.B., He, K., Hariharan, B., Belongie, S.J.: Feature pyramid networks for object detection. In: CVPR, vol. 1, p. 4 (2017)
9. Lin, T.-Y., et al.: Microsoft COCO: common objects in context. In: Fleet, D., Pajdla, T., Schiele, B., Tuytelaars, T. (eds.) ECCV 2014. LNCS, vol. 8693, pp. 740–755. Springer, Cham (2014). https://doi.org/10.1007/978-3-319-10602-1_48
10. Long, J., Shelhamer, E., Darrell, T.: Fully convolutional networks for semantic segmentation. In: Proceedings of the IEEE Conference on Computer Vision and Pattern Recognition, pp. 3431–3440 (2015)
11. Mousavian, A., Anguelov, D., Flynn, J., Košecká, J.: 3d bounding box estimation using deep learning and geometry. In: 2017 IEEE Conference on Computer Vision and Pattern Recognition (CVPR), pp. 5632–5640. IEEE (2017)
12. Rabbani, T., Van Den Heuvel, F., Vosselmann, G.: Segmentation of point clouds using smoothness constraint. Int. Arch. Photogramm. Remote. Sens. Spat. Inf. Sci. **36**(5), 248–253 (2006)
13. Redmon, J., Divvala, S., Girshick, R., Farhadi, A.: You only look once: unified, real-time object detection. In: Computer Vision and Pattern Recognition, pp. 779–788 (2016)
14. Ren, S., He, K., Girshick, R., Sun, J.: Faster R-CNN: towards real-time object detection with region proposal networks. In: Advances in Neural Information Processing Systems, pp. 91–99 (2015)
15. Xiang, Y., Choi, W., Lin, Y., Savarese, S.: Data-driven 3d voxel patterns for object category recognition. In: Proceedings of the IEEE Conference on Computer Vision and Pattern Recognition, pp. 1903–1911 (2015)
16. Xiang, Y., Choi, W., Lin, Y., Savarese, S.: Subcategory-aware convolutional neural networks for object proposals and detection. In: 2017 IEEE Winter Conference on Applications of Computer Vision (WACV), pp. 924–933. IEEE (2017)

SalNet: Edge Constraint Based End-to-End Model for Salient Object Detection

Le Han[1,2], Xuelong Li[1], and Yongsheng Dong[1(✉)]

[1] Center for OPTical IMagery Analysis and Learning (OPTIMAL),
Xi'an Institute of Optics and Precision Mechanics, Chinese Academy of Sciences,
Xi'an 710119, Shaanxi, People's Republic of China
hanle2016@opt.cn, xuelong_li@opt.ac.cn, dongyongsheng98@163.com
[2] University of Chinese Academy of Sciences, 19A Yuquanlu, Beijing 100049,
People's Republic of China

Abstract. Salient object detection is a fundamental task in computer vision and pattern recognition. And it has been investigated by many researchers in many fields for a long time. Numerous salient object detection models based on deep learning have been designed in recent years. However, the saliency maps extracted by most of the existing models are blurry or have irregular edges. To alleviate these problems, we propose a novel approach named SalNet to detect the salient objects accurately in this paper. The architecture of the SalNet is an U-Net which can combine the features of the shallow and deep layers. Moreover, a new objective function based on the image convolution is further proposed to refine the edges of saliency maps by using a constraint on the L1 distance between edge information of the ground-truth and the saliency maps. Finally, we evaluate our proposed SalNet on benchmark datasets and compare it with the state-of-the-art algorithms. Experimental results demonstrate that the SalNet is effective and outperforms several representative methods in salient object detection task.

Keywords: Salient object detection · U-Net · Auto-encoder
Image convolution

1 Introduction

Human can automatically pay attention to the *region of interest* (ROI) and selectively ignore the uninterested region when they face a scene. The salient objects are just the contents of the ROI. For instance, when we are looking at a picture with a horse grazing on the hillside, we may concentrate on the horse because it is the visual salient object in this image. The task of salient object detection is to teach computers to identify and extract the salient objects of the input images as humans do. Visual saliency has been explored by numbers of

© Springer Nature Switzerland AG 2018
J.-H. Lai et al. (Eds.): PRCV 2018, LNCS 11259, pp. 186–198, 2018.
https://doi.org/10.1007/978-3-030-03341-5_16

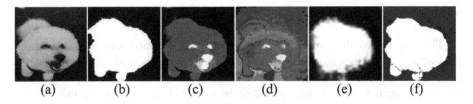

Fig. 1. Comparison of different kinds of models. (a) is the input image and the Ground-truth is (b). The saliency maps output by the background prior based model, global contrast based model and the convolution neural network based model are (c), (d) and (e), respectively. (f) is the output of the SalNet, which accurately extracted the salient objects and the edge of the object is very clear.

scholars from multiple disciplines such as neuroscience [10], cognitive psychology [7] and computer vision [4]. As a fundamental problem in computer visual, saliency detection has been successfully applied to many areas including object tracking and recognition, semantic recognition, video retrieval and scene classification [28]. Therefore, it has attracted the interest of many scholars. Numerous salient object detection models have been proposed, including the conventional models [11,17] and deep learning based models [15,22,28].

The conventional saliency detection models mainly focus on the heuristic priors or the contrast information [18]. Some previous methods utilize various visual informative knowledge as heuristic priors, i.e., the background prior, compactness prior and objectness prior. Background prior based models [6] assume that the area near the boundary of image is probably the background. It is easy to see that they usually have low accuracy if the salient objects are close to the edge of image. In compactness prior based models [27], the salient object region is considered as a connected area with perceptually homogeneous elements. However, the disadvantage of this kind of models is that they cannot detect the images with multiple salient objects very well. The objectness prior based models [27] tend to focus on the regions that are likely to contain salient objects. They are usually empirical and rely on hand-designed formulations. Due to the high-level semantic features are not considered, the objects of the saliency maps output by these prior based models are usually uneven like a heat map. The Fig. 1(c) is the output of the heuristic prior based model, in which the brightness of the different parts of the object is not the same.

The contrast based algorithms aim at investigating the difference between the image pixels or regions and the context [13], and they can be divided into the global and local context based models. Global context based models usually output a saliency map with relatively complete internal information but incomplete details. Besides, it is difficult for them to detect the salient objects with large sizes. On the contrary, local context based models can capture the detailed structures but often lose internal information. The saliency maps output by the contrast based models are usually fuzzy and the edges of the objects are not clear as presented in Fig. 1(d). The reason is that they process the images pixel by pixel or region by region, so the relationship of adjacent pixels or regions is not considered.

The conventional saliency detection models mentioned above just leverage the low-level visual features, such as the color, contrast and various heuristic priors. The high-level information which is about the semantic knowledge has not been taken into account. So these models can hardly distinguish salient objects from the images with complex background and can not output a precise saliency map with clear edges of the objects [26].

To mine the high-level semantic information, deep learning is widely used in salient object detection task in recent years. And they delivered superior performance because the convolutional neural network can hierarchically capture the features of images. The auto-encoder is one of the best architectures of the saliency detection [18]. However, the information loss is serious when the input flows pass through the network. The reason is that the features of shallow layers and deep layers cannot be effectively combined due to the existence of a bottleneck between encoder and decoder. As a result, the saliency maps extracted by the models based on convolution neural network often have fuzzy objects which is illustrated in Fig. 1(e).

In order to alleviate these problems, we should make full use of high-level semantic information and low-level visual information. In this paper, we propose a new method named SalNet for salient object detection. The architecture of the proposed model is the U-Net which can combine multi-level features and avoid information loss [20]. Besides, in order to enrich the edge information extracted by network, we add a convolution-based edge constraint to loss function. The experimental results are presented in Fig. 1 to verify the conclusion discussed above. It can be found that our SalNet can effectively alleviate the uneven of saliency maps and blurring of objects edges, which are usually generated by existing models.

The main contributions of our work are as follows:

- We propose a new loss function to refine the objects details of saliency maps. In order to fully exploit edge information, we add a convolution based edge constraint term to loss function.
- We employ the architecture of U-Net to detect the salient objects of images accurately. Such an architecture can reduce the loss of low-level visual information, which is necessary because the saliency detection task requires the objects of saliency map and input image to be consistent on the visual information, such as shape and edge.
- The proposed SalNet is tested on four benchmark datasets (ECSSD, HKU-IS, SED1 and SED2). And the experimental results show that our saliency detection model outperforms the state-of-the-art methods on benchmark datasets.

The rest of this paper is organized as follows. In Sect. 2, some previous works are briefly introduced. Section 3 presents our model for salient object detection. To validate the proposed method, the experimental results are shown in Sect. 4. At last, Sect. 5 makes a brief conclusion for this paper.

2   Related Work

In recent years, deep learning achieved superior performance in numerous fields in computer vision, including semantic segmentation, image classification, object recognition and so on. *Convolutional Neural Network* (CNN) can fully mine the deep semantic features of images. Therefore, it is widely used in salient object detection tasks.

Zhang *et.al.* proposed a model based on the CNN and the *Maximum a Posteriori* (MAP) principle [25], which has no constraint to the number of objects in image and outputs the bounding boxes of the objects. Wang *et.al.* dealt with the saliency detection with a recurrent architecture combined with prior knowledge [22]. However, the models mentioned above only output the bounding boxes of the objects or rely on certain prior knowledge.

In order to output the saliency maps and not rely on various prior information, Liu *et al.* proposed an end-to-end salient object detection model [18]. They first utilized a convolution neural network to learn a global feature representation, and then hierarchically refined the details of saliency maps with a network named HRCNN. Zhao *et al.* utilized two convolutional neural networks to extract global context and local context information respectively, and then combined these information with a fully-connected layer to predict the saliency map of input image [28]. The *Fully Convolutional Networks* (FCN) [19], which is proposed by Long *et al.* for semantic segmentation, is widely used in the salient object detection tasks and performs well. Zhang *et al.* proposed a deep fully convolutional network based model named UCF [26], which increases the robustness and accuracy of saliency detection by learning deep uncertain convolutional features. The architecture of UCF consists of encoder and decoder. And the auto-encoder-based models are currently the best [29].

The reason why these models work well is that the convolution neural networks can capture relevant information from the convolution layers features. However, the disadvantage of these models is that their saliency maps are relatively blurred, since these salient object detection models don't aggregate the multi-level convolutional feature maps. Besides, there is a bottleneck between encoder and decoder which leads to information loss. Therefore, we adapt the U-Net as the architecture of proposed method due to the fact that it can decrease information loss by adding skip connections between corresponding layers of encoder and decoder. Experiments indicate that the SalNet performs very well in salient object detection task.

3   Proposed Method

In this section, we describe the proposed method named **SalNet**. We first present the model architecture, followed by proposed loss function. The details of the training procedure and inference are given in the last subsection.

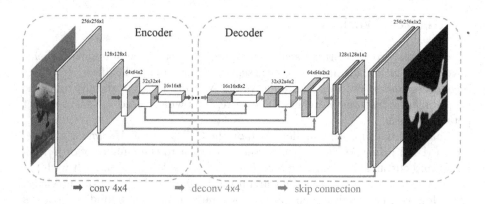

Fig. 2. The architecture we employed in the SalNet.

3.1 The Network Architecture

Many salient object detection models [22,26] use auto-encoder architecture [1,8]. The encoder is composed by a group of downsampling layers, and the size of images decreases progressively during downsampling. On the contrary, the decoder gradually restores the output of layers to input size. The disadvantage of encoder-decoder network is that the information loss is serious when image flows pass through the network. The reason is that there is a bottleneck between the encoder and decoder [9].

We leverage an U-net [20] which is an improvement of encoder-decoder network as the architecture of SalNet. The U-net adds skip connections between corresponding layers of encoder and decoder. Such a structure can reduce low-level visual information loss when image flows through the network [24], which is necessary because the salient object detection problem requires input and saliency maps to be consistent on the shape and edge of objects.

The architecture of the SalNet is illustrated in Fig. 2. The encoder is composed of 8 convolution layers of which the kernel size is 4×4 and stride is 2. The output size of encoder is $1 \times 1 \times 8$. The decoder is composed of 8 deconvolution layers with the kernel size is 4×4. In encoder, the white box of each layer is downsampled from the output of previous layer. And it is upsampled from the output of previous layer in decoder. The blue boxes of decoder are the copied feature maps of the corresponding layers in encoder.

3.2 Loss Function

In order to enrich the detail features of the salient objects extracted by network, we propose a new loss function which can be formulated as

$$Loss = \lambda_1 \mathcal{L}_{L_1}(x,y) + \lambda_2 \mathcal{L}_C(x,y) + \lambda_3 \mathcal{L}_{Conv}(x,y), \tag{1}$$

where the λ_1, λ_2 and λ_3 are the weights of L1 loss, cross entropy term and convolution loss term respectively. The x is the saliency map output by network, and y is ground-truth.

The $\mathcal{L}_{L_1}(x, y)$ is the L1 loss which is presented in Eq. 2. The L1 distance is wildly used to train neural networks. However, the network will produce blurry output if it only rely on L1 loss. So we added additional constraints to capture the high-frequency information.

$$\mathcal{L}_{L_1}(x, y) = \|y - x\|_1. \tag{2}$$

The second term is the cross entropy loss, and the definition of it is

$$\mathcal{L}_C(x, y) = -\frac{1}{M \times N} \sum_{i=1}^{M} \sum_{j=1}^{N} [y(i,j) \times p(i,j) + (1 - y(i,j))ln(1 - p(i,j))], \tag{3}$$

where M and N are the length and width of image respectively, and the $p(i,j)$ is defined as follows:

$$p(i,j) = sigmoid[x(i,j)] = \frac{1}{1 + e^{-x(i,j)}}. \tag{4}$$

It performs a sigmoid calculation on the output saliency map and then calculates its cross entropy with ground-truth. It has optimized the calculation method of cross entropy so that the result will not overflow.

The last term is the convolution loss term, which can be formulated as

$$\mathcal{L}_{Conv}(x, y) = \|Conv(x) - Conv(y)\|_1. \tag{5}$$

As illustrated in Fig. 3, the value in one diagonal of the kernel is 1 and -1 in the other, and the value of the rest, including the center point, of the kernel are 0. We tested many different sizes of the convolution kernel, and some of the results are shown in Table 1. When the size is 21×21, the test results of the trained model are the best. So we set the convolution kernel size to 21×21. Such convolution kernel with a large size can fuse the object edge with information of its neighborhood, rather than just extracting the boundary of the objects as the kernel with a small size do.

3.3   Training Procedure and Inference

The optimization algorithms we used in this paper are the mini-batch *Stochastic Gradient Descent* (SGD) and the Adam solver [12], which can calculate different adaptive learning rates for different parameters. And the outputs of our SalNet can be seen from the Fig. 4.

During the inference phase, we run the network in the same way as the training time. Besides, at test phase, we apply dropout and batch normalization which uses the statistic information of the test batch. And the batch size we used in the experiments is 4.

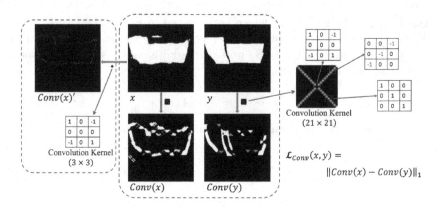

Fig. 3. The graphical diagram of the convolution kernel and comparison of results of the convolution kernels with different size. x and y represent the output of model and ground-truth, respectively. The $Conv(\cdot)$ is convolution with a 21×21 kernel, and the kernel size of $Conv(x)'$ is 3×3. The convolution operation only extracts objects edges because of too small kernel size of the convolution. Thus the relative information of objects edges and nearby regions is ignored.

4 Experiments

In this section, we describe our experimental setting and quantitative results which validate the effectiveness of our model for salient object detection.

4.1 Datasets

To show the effectiveness of the proposed method, we test it on several widely used salient object benchmark datasets, including ECSSD [23], HKU-IS [28], SED1 and SED2 [2]. ECSSD contains 1,000 semantically meaningful images with complex structure. HKU-IS has 4,447 high quality images. Many images in this dataset contain multiple salient objects, and the salient objects in many images touch the image bounding. The SED is composed of two subsets named SED1 and SED2, and both of them contain 100 images. Each image in SED1 contains one salient object, while there are two in each image in SED2.

4.2 Evaluation Metrics

In order to measure the performance of the different algorithms for salient object detection, we used three objective metrics in this paper, including the *Precision-Recall* (PR) curves, F-measure and *Mean Absolute Error* (MAE) [3].

The PR curve is based on the overlapping area between the ground-truth and estimated saliency map. We can divide the binary mask M, which is binarized by saliency map S with different thresholds, into *True Positive* (TP), *False Positive* (FP), *True Negative* (TN) and *False Negative* (FN), according

Fig. 4. Examples of our SalNet output results: the images in the first row are the inputs, the saliency masks in the second are the outputs of our method, and these in the last are the ground-truth saliency masks. It is not hard to see that the edges of the objects extracted by our model are very clear. The first column of images show that the proposed model can accurately extract the salient objects even if their colors are close to the background. The images in the second and third column indicate that the model can preserve the details and subtle structures of the object very well, and the last two columns indicate that our model can precisely detect the multiple salient objects.

to whether the $M(x, y)$ is equal to $G(x, y)$. And the precision and recall can be calculated by

$$Precision = \frac{TP}{TP + FP}, \quad Recall = \frac{TP}{TP + FP}. \tag{6}$$

The F-measure is a weighted harmonic mean of average precision and average recall with a non-negative weight β and can be calculated by

$$F_\beta = \frac{(1 + \beta^2) \times Precision \times Recall}{\beta^2 \times Precision + Recall}. \tag{7}$$

As suggested by existing works [3,5,18], β^2 is set to 0.3 because the precision is more important than recall. And we set the adaptive threshold T to be twice of the mean saliency value of.

The defect of the overlap-based evaluation measures is that they don't consider the true negative saliency assignments [3], so they usually give a higher score to the models which can classify the saliency areas correctly. In order to evaluate the models comprehensively, we calculate the *Mean Absolute Error* (MAE) which assess the saliency detection accuracy. The MAE can be calculated by

$$MAE = \frac{1}{W \times H} \sum_{x=1}^{W} \sum_{y=1}^{H} |S(x, y) - G(x, y)|, \tag{8}$$

in which G is the ground-truth.

Table 1. The comparison of the F-Measure and MAE results of different salient object detection models on four benchmark datasets. The models named SalNet-Kernel55 and SalNet-Kernel5151 are our models with the kernel size of convolution loss equal 5×5 and 51×51, respectively. The values in red, blue and green are the best three results of each term, respectively. The results of the proposed SalNet are almost always the best on these datasets.

	ECSSD		HKU-IS		SED1		SED2	
	F-Measure	MAE	F-Measure	MAE	F-Measure	MAE	F-Measure	MAE
DS	0.8255	0.1216	0.7851	0.0780	0.8445	0.0931	0.7541	0.1233
LEGS	0.7853	0.1180	0.7228	0.1193	0.8542	0.1034	0.7358	0.1236
UCF	0.8517	0.0689	0.8232	0.0620	0.8647	0.0631	0.8102	0.0680
ELD	0.8102	0.0796	0.7694	0.0741	0.8715	0.0670	0.7591	0.1028
DRFI	0.7331	0.1642	0.7218	0.1445	0.8068	0.1480	0.7341	0.1334
DSR	0.6621	0.1784	0.6772	0.1422	0.7909	0.1579	0.7116	0.1406
SalNet-Kernel55	0.8076	0.1013	0.8502	0.0647	0.8582	0.0827	0.8589	0.0747
SalNet-Kernel5151	0.8459	0.0819	0.8741	0.0530	0.8902	0.0665	0.8739	0.0718
SalNet	0.8468	0.0650	0.8660	0.0546	0.8918	0.0658	0.8892	0.0632

4.3 Performance Comparison with State-of-the-Art

We compare the proposed SalNet with the state-of-the-art algorithms including UCF [26], ELD [14], DS [16], LEGS [21], DRFI [11], DSR [17]. The UCF, ELD, DS and LEGS are the deep learning based algorithms, and the DRFI and DSR are conventional algorithms. The model of us is trained with 2,964 images selected randomly from the HKU-IS dataset. For fair comparison, the parameter settings of the models is the recommended by the authors, and we use some results shown in the original papers of the corresponding algorithm or the benchmark evaluation.

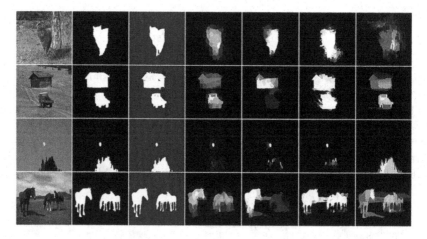

Fig. 5. Comparison with State-of-the-art models. (a) Input images; (b) Ground truth; (c) Our SalNet; (d) DS; (e) LEGS; (f) ELD; (g) DRFI.

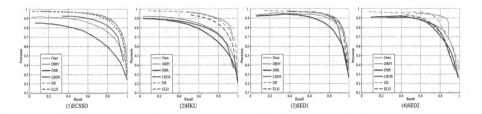

Fig. 6. The PR curves of our SalNet and the state-of-the-arts on 4 benchmark datasets

Figure 5 presents a visual comparison of the state-of-the-art models and the SalNet. As we can see from it that our saliency detection model can detect and localize the salient objects accurately. It preserves the object details which are ignored by other models. The edges of the objects detected by the SalNet is very clear and the saliency mask has a very uniform brightness, which is useful in the applications of it.

The F-measure and MAE of the proposed method and the other models are presented in Table 1, and the PR curves are illustrated in Fig. 6. We can see from them that the proposed SalNet is superior to other state-of-the-art models in all evaluation metrics across the benchmark datasets. The comparison results indicate that the SalNet can provide more accurate saliency maps with clear objects edges. In addition, we can learn from the last three rows of Table 1 that the results are not optimal when the kernel size of convolution loss term is too large or too small.

4.4 Ablation Studies

In order to verify the contributions of different components in our loss function, we evaluate three variants of the loss function and the results are illustrated in Fig. 7(b)–(d). The architecture and parameters setting of the comparison methods and the SalNet are the same. It not hard to see from (b) that the edges of the objects are quite blurred without the convolution loss.

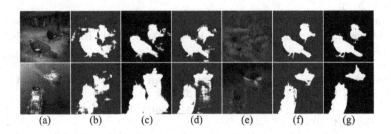

Fig. 7. The results of ablation studies. (a) Input images; (b) The output of the model with a loss function: $\mathcal{L}_{L_1}(x,y) + \mathcal{L}_C(x,y)$; (c) $\mathcal{L}_{L_1}(x,y) + \mathcal{L}_{Conv}(x,y)$; (d) $\mathcal{L}_C(x,y) + \mathcal{L}_{Conv}(x,y)$; (e) The output of the encoder-decoder model created by severing the skip connections of SalNet; (f) The output of the SalNet; (g) Ground-truth.

In order to verify whether the skip connections, which allow the low-level information combined with the features of deep layers, are useful in the SalNet, we train an encoder-decoder model which is created by deleting the skip connections of SalNet. The parameter setting and objective function are the same as the proposed method. The test results are presented in Fig. 7(e), which indicate that the skip connections can improve the detection performance of the model.

5   Conclusion

In this paper, we propose a novel end-to-end salient object detection method based on the U-Net, which can reduce the information loss by combining the features of different layers. In order to fully capture features related with the details of objects, we add a convolution based edge constraint term to the loss function. Extensive experiments demonstrate that the proposed SalNet outperforms the other state-of-the-art methods on four benchmark datasets.

Acknowledgements. This work was supported in part by the National Key Research and Development Program of China under Grant 2018YFB1107400, in part by the National Natural Science Foundation of China under Grants 61871470, 61761130079 and U1604153, and in part by the Program for Science and Technology Innovation Talents in Universities of Henan Province under Grant 19HASTIT026.

References

1. Badrinarayanan, V., Kendall, A., Cipolla, R.: Segnet: A deep convolutional encoder-decoder architecture for image segmentation. IEEE Trans. Pattern Anal. Mach. Intell. **39**(12), 2481–2495 (2017)
2. Borji, A.: What is a salient object? a dataset and a baseline model for salient object detection. IEEE Trans. Image Process. **24**(2), 742–756 (2015)
3. Borji, A., Cheng, M.M., Jiang, H., Li, J.: Salient object detection: a benchmark. IEEE Trans. Image Process. **24**(12), 5706–5722 (2015)
4. Borji, A., Sihite, D.N., Itti, L.: Quantitative analysis of human-model agreement in visual saliency modeling: a comparative study. IEEE Trans. Image Process. **22**(1), 55–69 (2013)
5. Cheng, M.M., Mitra, N.J., Huang, X., Torr, P.H., Hu, S.M.: Global contrast based salient region detection. IEEE Trans. Pattern Anal. Mach. Intell. **37**(3), 569–582 (2015)
6. Han, J., Zhang, D., Hu, X., Guo, L., Ren, J., Wu, F.: Background prior-based salient object detection via deep reconstruction residual. IEEE Trans. Circuits Syst. Video Technol. **25**(8), 1309–1321 (2015)
7. Hayhoe, M., Ballard, D.: Eye movements in natural behavior. Trends Cogn. Sci. **9**(4), 188–194 (2005)
8. Hinton, G.E., Salakhutdinov, R.R.: Reducing the dimensionality of data with neural networks. Science **313**(5786), 504–507 (2006)
9. Isola, P., Zhu, J.Y., Zhou, T., Efros, A.A.: Image-to-image translation with conditional adversarial networks. arXiv preprint (2017)

10. Itti, L., Koch, C.: Computational modelling of visual attention. Nat. Rev. Neurosci. **2**(3), 194 (2001)
11. Jiang, H., Wang, J., Yuan, Z., Wu, Y., Zheng, N., Li, S.: Salient object detection: a discriminative regional feature integration approach. In: Proceedings of the IEEE Conference on Computer Vision and Pattern Recognition, pp. 2083–2090 (2013)
12. Kingma, D., Ba, J.: Adam: a method for stochastic optimization. Computer Science (2014)
13. Klein, D.A., Frintrop, S.: Center-surround divergence of feature statistics for salient object detection. In: Proceedings of the IEEE International Conference on Computer Vision, pp. 2214–2219. IEEE (2011)
14. Lee, G., Tai, Y.W., Kim, J.: Deep saliency with encoded low level distance map and high level features. In: Proceedings of the IEEE Conference on Computer Vision and Pattern Recognition, pp. 660–668 (2016)
15. Li, G., Yu, Y.: Deep contrast learning for salient object detection. In: Proceedings of the IEEE Conference on Computer Vision and Pattern Recognition, pp. 478–487 (2016)
16. Li, X., Zhao, L., Wei, L., Yang, M.H., Wu, F., Zhuang, Y., Ling, H., Wang, J.: Deepsaliency: multi-task deep neural network model for salient object detection. IEEE Trans. Image Process. **25**(8), 3919–3930 (2016)
17. Li, X., Lu, H., Zhang, L., Ruan, X., Yang, M.H.: Saliency detection via dense and sparse reconstruction. In: Proceedings of the IEEE International Conference on Computer Vision, pp. 2976–2983 (2013)
18. Liu, N., Han, J.: Dhsnet: deep hierarchical saliency network for salient object detection. In: Proceedings of the IEEE Conference on Computer Vision and Pattern Recognition, pp. 678–686 (2016)
19. Long, J., Shelhamer, E., Darrell, T.: Fully convolutional networks for semantic segmentation. In: Proceedings of the IEEE Conference on Computer Vision and Pattern Recognition, pp. 3431–3440 (2015)
20. Ronneberger, O., Fischer, P., Brox, T.: U-net: convolutional networks for biomedical image segmentation. In: Proceedings of the International Conference on Medical Image Computing and Computer-Assisted Intervention, pp. 234–241 (2015)
21. Wang, L., Lu, H., Ruan, X., Yang, M.H.: Deep networks for saliency detection via local estimation and global search. In: Proceedings of the IEEE Conference on Computer Vision and Pattern Recognition, pp. 3183–3192 (2015)
22. Wang, L., Wang, L., Lu, H., Zhang, P., Ruan, X.: Saliency detection with recurrent fully convolutional networks. In: Proceedings of the European Conference on Computer Vision, pp. 825–841 (2016)
23. Yan, Q., Xu, L., Shi, J., Jia, J.: Hierarchical saliency detection. In: Proceedings of the IEEE Conference on Computer Vision and Pattern Recognition, pp. 1155–1162 (2013)
24. Yi, Z., Zhang, H., Tan, P., Gong, M.: Dualgan: unsupervised dual learning for image-to-image translation. In: Proceedings of the IEEE Conference on Computer Vision and Pattern Recognition, pp. 2849–2857 (2017)
25. Zhang, J., Sclaroff, S., Lin, Z., Shen, X., Price, B., Mech, R.: Unconstrained salient object detection via proposal subset optimization. In: Proceedings of the IEEE Conference on Computer Vision and Pattern Recognition, pp. 5733–5742 (2016)
26. Zhang, P., Wang, D., Lu, H., Wang, H., Yin, B.: Learning uncertain convolutional features for accurate saliency detection. arXiv preprint arXiv:1708.02031 (2017)
27. Zhang, Q., Lin, J., Li, W., Shi, Y., Cao, G.: Salient object detection via compactness and objectness cues. Vis. Comput. **34**(4), 473–489 (2018)

28. Zhao, R., Ouyang, W., Li, H., Wang, X.: Saliency detection by multi-context deep learning. In: Proceedings of the IEEE Conference on Computer Vision and Pattern Recognition, pp. 1265–1274 (2015)
29. Borji, A., Cheng, M.M., Jiang, H., Li, J.: Salient object detection: A survey, 2(4) (2014). arXiv preprint: arXiv:1411.5878

Gated Feature Pyramid Network for Object Detection

Xuemei Xie[✉], Quan Liao, Lihua Ma, and Xing Jin

School of Artificial Intelligence, Xidian University, Xi'an, China
xmxie@mail.xidian.edu.cn

Abstract. Feature pyramid is a basic component in recognition systems for detecting objects of different scales. In order to construct the feature pyramid, most existing deep learning methods combine features of different levels based on a pyramidal feature hierarchy (e.g. SSD, Faster-RCNN). However, it lacks attention to those informative features. In this paper, we propose a gated feature pyramid network (GFPN) extracting informative features to enhance the representation ability of feature pyramid. GFPN consists of gated lateral modules and a top-down structure. The former automatically learns to focus on informative features of different scales, and the latter is used to combine the refined features. By using GFPN on SSD, our method achieves 80.1 mAP on VOC 2007 with an inference time of 11.9 ms per image, which improves the accuracy of FPN applied to SSD by 0.5% and adds marginal efficiency cost.

Keywords: Object detection · Gated feature pyramid · Informative features · Attention

1 Introduction

Recognizing objects varying from scales and sizes is a fundamental challenge in computer vision. Recent advances in object detection [1, 2] are driven by the success of deep convolutional networks, which naturally integrate rich features with different resolution and semantic information. Different from those which directly use single feature maps (Fig. 1(a)), SSD [11] first exploits the inherent pyramidal feature hierarchy for multi-scale detection (Fig. 1(b)), which facilitates recognition of objects at different scales. However, the low level features in the inherent pyramidal feature hierarchy lack semantic information, which is not good for visual classification.

In order to enhance the semantic of feature maps at all scales, a top-down architecture with lateral connections is developed to combine different-level features to build feature pyramid. FPN [10] first proposes the method to build a feature pyramid based on a basic Faster R-CNN [14] with marginal extra cost, and achieves significant improvements on COCO detection benchmark [23]. RefineDet [20] constructs a feature pyramid based on a pruned SSD [11], and achieves better results than two-stage methods and maintains comparable efficiency of one-stage approaches. However, these constructions of feature pyramid only utilize the existing pyramidal feature hierarches and do not concentrate on the informative features, such as objectiveness features, which is better for prediction.

J.-H. Lai et al. (Eds.): PRCV 2018, LNCS 11259, pp. 199–208, 2018.
https://doi.org/10.1007/978-3-030-03341-5_17

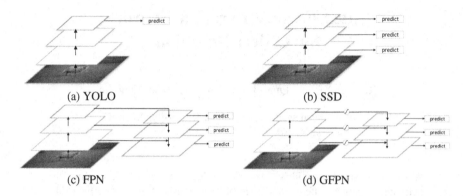

(a) YOLO   (b) SSD

(c) FPN   (d) GFPN

Fig. 1. (a) Recent detector using only single scale features for detection. (b) Detector using feature hierarchy for multi-scale detection. (c) Using a feature pyramid to build high-level semantic feature maps at all scales. (d) Our proposed Gated Feature Pyramid (GFPN) is more accuracy than (c) and of comparable efficiency like (b).

In this paper, we propose a gated feature pyramid network (GFPN) to build the targeted feature pyramid. GFPN consists of gated lateral modules and a top-down structure. The former one automatically learns to focus on informative features of different scales. The lateral one is used to combine the refined features. In order to validate the effectiveness of our method, we use GFPN and FPN on SSD [11] respectively. Without bells and whistles, the former one achieves state-of-the-art result on PASCAL VOC2007 detection benchmark [3], and surpasses the lateral one by 0.5% with marginal extra cost.

2 Related Work

2.1 Object Detection

In general, modern object detection methods based on CNNs can be divided into two groups: two-stage methods and one-stage methods. Two-stage methods, such as R-CNN [5], SPPnet [7], Fast R-CNN [15], Faster R-CNN [14], Mask R-CNN [8], first perform a region proposal generation and then make the prediction on each proposal. R-CNN [6] firstly combines selective search [18] region proposals generation and CNN-based classification. Faster R-CNN [14] replaces the selective search by Region Proposal Network (RPN), making proposal generation become a learnable part. One-stage detectors consider the classification and bounding box regression in a single network, including Over-feat [16], YOLO [13], SSD [11], YOLO9000 [12]. Among them, YOLO [13] uses only single scale features for multi-scale objects detection, and has high efficiency.

SSD [11] firstly predicts objects in multi-scale layers by distributing default boxes with different scales, which improves the accuracy of generic objects with high efficiency. In this paper, we focus on SSD [11] with the consideration of its high efficiency and comparable accuracy of two-stage approaches.

2.2 Feature Pyramid

Combining features from different layers is a basis component in many recent proposed object detectors [4, 9, 10, 17]. FPN [10] first proposes the method to build a feature pyramid based on a basic Faster R-CNN with marginal extra cost, and achieves significant improvements on COCO detection benchmark. TDM [17] proposes top-down modulation to improve performance for hard examples. DSSD [4] first tries to construct the feature pyramid on SSD [11]. In this paper, we propose a gated feature pyramid network to improve the performance of feature pyramid with marginal extra cost.

2.3 Attention Mechanism

Attention mechanism is widely used in object recognition [19, 21, 22]. Residual Attention [19] proposes a soft weight attention to adaptively generate the attention-aware features. SENets [21] introduces a channel attention to existing state-of-the-art classification architectures, and wins first place on ILSVRC dataset. Harmonious attention network [22] proposes the harmonious attention which combines the mentioned two kinds of attention mechanism. In this paper, we introduce a gated connection which is a kind of channel attention.

3 Gated Feature Pyramid Network

We aim to build a gated feature pyramid based on SSD model, which is the state-of-the-art object detector with respect to accuracy-vs-speed trade-off. In this section, first we briefly introduce SSD and the improvement we have made on it. And then we present the gated feature pyramid, which consists of gated lateral modules and the top-down structure.

3.1 Single Shot Multibox Detector

The single-shot multibox detector (SSD) can be divided into two parts: (1) a shared feedforward convolution network, and (2) a set of sub-networks for classification and regression which do not share computation. The former part takes VGG-16 [24] as base network and adds several additional feature layers, which produce a pyramidal feature hierarchy consisting of feature maps at several scales. The lateral one spreads dense predefined anchors on selected feature maps provided by the former part, and then applies two convolutional layers to predict the classification and location of objects respectively. In total, SSD adopts 6 prediction layers to predict different size of objects, for example, conv4_3 for smallest objects, conv11_2 for largest objects. Considering that shallow layers are lack of enough semantic information, SSD [11] forgoes using shallower layers (e.g. conv3_3). Thus it misses the opportunity to use the high resolution maps of the feature hierarchy.

Considering that feature pyramid can introduce semantic information to all scales of the feature hierarchy, we add a new prediction layer on conv3_3 to improve the performance for small objects. To avoid adding too much computational burden, we only use one size of anchors with one kind of aspect ratios, as Table 1 shows.

Table 1. The resolution of selected feature layers in VGG and the corresponding anchor sizes of different aspect ratios.

VGG	conv3_3	conv4_3	conv7	conv8_2	conv9_2	conv10_2	conv11_2
Resolution	75 × 75	38 × 38	19 × 19	10 × 10	5 × 5	3 × 3	1 × 1
Anchor size (min/max)	16	30/60	60/111	111/162	162/213	213/264	264/315
Stride	4	8	16	32	64	128	256
Aspect ratios	{1}	{1/2, 1, 2}	{1/3, 1/2, 1, 2, 3}	{1/3, 1/2, 1, 2, 3}	{1/3, 1/2, 1, 2, 3}	{1/2, 1, 2}	{1/2, 1, 2}

3.2 Gated Lateral Modules

Our goal is to ensure that the feature pyramid network can select the meaningful features at different scales, so it can enhance the useful features which will further improve the representation ability of feature pyramid network. To achieve this, we propose the gated lateral modules. As Fig. 2 shows, it consists of a normal convolutional layer, a channel attention mechanism and an identity mapping, which is inspired by Residual Attention [19] and SENets [21]. In the following, we will give a detailed presentation of these modules.

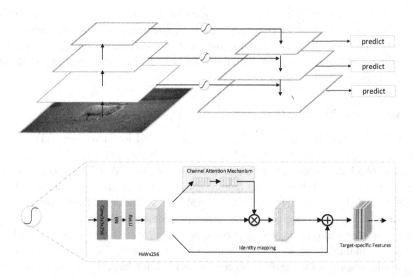

Fig. 2. An overview of our proposed GFPN and a detailed structure of gated lateral modules.

Convolutional Layer. This convolutional layer is designed to reduce the channel dimensions of input feature maps. In this paper, the channel dimensions of each selected feature maps are reduced to 256 by a 3 × 3 convolutional layer, which also play a role in enhancing the representation ability of networks.

Channel Attention Mechanism. The aim of channel attention is to enhance the targeted features. We apply Squeeze-and-Excitation block [21] as our channel attention, which consists of two stages, namely, the *squeeze* stage and the *excitation* stage. The former stage is designed for global information embedding, and the latter one for inter-channel dependency modelling. This channel attention mechanism will enhance the sensitivity of targeted features so that they can be exploited by feature pyramids.

Identity Mapping. We apply an element-wise sum operation to obtain the final outputs, which consists of the weighted features and original features. The motivation of this design is to ensure that the channel attention mechanism will not break the good property of original features, particularly inspired by Residual Attention [19].

As Fig. 3 shows, the mean activations of some feature maps become smaller after the gated lateral modules, which means that useless features are suppressed, and useful features are enhanced.

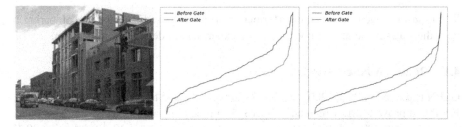

Fig. 3. Visualization of mean activations before and after gated lateral modules. The left column is the input image, the two columns on the right show the mean activations of feature maps of each selected layer. We only show the results of conv3_3 and conv4_3 for better exhibition.

3.3 Top-Down Structure

Each feature combination module is designed to combine the targeted features and the high-level features, which aims to further enhance the representation ability of the feature pyramid. A detailed example of the feature combination module is illustrated in Fig. 4. It consists of three parts: a deconvolution layer, an element-wise sum operation and a 3×3 convolutional layer. The deconvolution layer transforms the dimensions of high-level feature maps from $H \times W \times 256$ to $2H \times 2W \times 256$. Then an element-wise sum operation is applied to obtain the combined features, which are high spatial resolution and semantic strongly. In order to enhance the representation ability of each prediction module, we add a 3×3 convolutional layer, particularly inspired by DSSD [4].

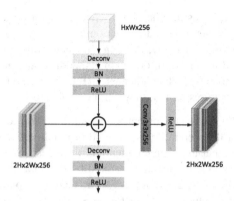

Fig. 4. An example with details of top-down structure.

4   Experiments on Object Detection

In this section, we evaluate the performance of the proposed detector by comparing it with the state-of-the-art methods. And the experimental details are also given.

4.1   Result on Pascal VOC

GFPN is trained on VOC 2007 and 2012 trainval sets, and tested on VOC 2007 test set. For the improved SSD which adds conv3_3 to predict smaller objects, we use a batch size of 16 with 300×300 inputs, and started the learning rate at 10^{-1} for the first 80 K iterations, then decrease it at 120 K iterations and 160 K iterations by a step of 10^{-1}. We take this well-trained SSD model as the pre-trained model for the GFPN. Meanwhile, the gated lateral modules, the top-down structure and the prediction subnetworks are initialized with bias b = 0 and 'Xavier' weight [6]. After that, the initial learning rate is set as 10^{-1} for the first 80 K iterations, and decreases to 10^{-3} at 120 K and 10^{-5} at 160 K.

Table 2 shows the comparisons of GFPN with the state-of-the-art one-stage detectors. It can be seen that GFPN reaches 80.1% for the 300×300 input. GFPN surpasses SSD300 and SSD321 by 2.8% and 3.0%. Compared with those approaches that utilize FPN (e.g. DSSD321, RefineDet), GFPN also achieves relatively higher accuracy. In summary, our proposed detector achieves the state-of-the-art performance.

4.2   Running Time Performance

The running time of GFPN is evaluated with batch size 8 on a machine with NVIDIA Titan Ti, CUDA8.0 and cuDNN v7. Table 3 shows the comparisons of speed with the state-of-the-art one-stage detectors. It is clear that our detector takes 11.9 ms to process an image with input sizes 300×300. The speed of GFPN is slightly lower than that of the fastest SSD300 but still satisfies the requirement of real-time detection. Moreover, our detector can achieve the most excellent accuracy. For practical applications, GFPN achieves the state-of-the-art performance with the best trade-off between accuracy and efficiency.

Table 2. Detection results on PASCAL VOC2007 test set (with IOU = 0.5). RefineDet use input images whose size is 320. Although many two-stage approaches also achieve good performance on VOC2007, we only list the single-stage approaches in consideration of practical application.

Method	Network	mAP	Aero	Bike	Boat	Bottle	Bus	Car	Cat	Chair	Cow
SSD300	VGG	77.3	78.8	85.3	75.7	71.5	49.1	85.7	86.4	87.8	60.6
SSD321	ResNet101	77.1	76.3	84.6	79.3	64.6	47.2	85.4	84.0	88.8	60.1
DSSD321	ResNet101	78.6	81.9	84.9	80.5	68.4	53.9	85.6	86.2	88.9	61.1
RefineDet	VGG	80.0	83.9	**85.4**	**81.4**	**75.5**	**60.2**	86.4	**88.1**	**89.1**	62.7
GFPN	VGG	**80.1**	**86.8**	**85.4**	79.7	74.0	54.0	**87.9**	87.7	88.3	**64.7**
Method	Network	mAP	Table	Dog	Horse	Bike	Person	Plant	Sheep	Sofa	Train
SSD300	VGG	77.3	76.5	84.9	86.7	84.0	79.2	51.3	77.5	78.7	86.7
SSD321	ResNet101	77.1	76.9	**86.7**	87.2	85.4	79.1	50.8	77.2	**82.6**	87.3
DSSD321	ResNet101	78.6	78.7	**86.7**	**88.7**	86.7	79.7	51.7	78.0	80.9	87.2
RefineDet	VGG	80.0	77.0	85.4	87.1	86.7	**82.6**	55.3	**82.7**	78.5	**88.1**
GFPN	VGG	**80.1**	80.3	85.9	88.6	**86.9**	80.0	**56.9**	79.8	80.6	**88.1**

Table 3. The running time of different models.

Method	Base network	mAP	Time(ms/img)	FPS	Batchsize
SSD300	VGG16	77.3	12.7	78.7	1
SSD321	ResNet101	77.1	68.1	14.7	1
GFPN	VGG16	81.4	20.1	49.8	1

4.3 Ablation Study

To demonstrate the effectiveness of different components in GFPN, we design three variants and validate them on PASCAL VOC2007 [3]. As shown in Table 4, the three variants, namely, gated lateral modules, feature pyramid and conv3_3, are added to the single-shot framework respectively. Meanwhile, for a fair comparison, we set the training iteration, batch size and input size as the same. The models are trained on PASCAL VOC 2007 and 2012 trainval sets, and tested on PASCAL VOC 2007 test set.

Table 4. Ablation experiments on GFPN

Method	GFPN				SSD
conv3_3	✓	✓		✓	
feature pyramid	✓	✓	✓		
gated lateral module	✓				
mAP	**80.1**	79.6	79.2	77.6	77.3

How important is low-level features? To evaluate the effectiveness of the conv3_3, we add a new prediction layer on conv3_3, as Table 1 shows. Table 4 of col 4 and col 5·shows the results of our improved SSD and the pure SSD. It is clear that the accuracy

Fig. 5. Qualitative results of GFPN on the PASCAL VOC 2007 test set. VGG16 is used as the backbone network. The training data is PASCAL VOC 2007 and 2012 trainval sets.

increase 0.3% mAP from 77.3% to 77.6%. The result shows that the low-level features do helps promote the performance of detectors. To further validate this conclusion, we conduct experiments based on feature pyramid. As col 1 and col 2 of Table 4 shows, the addition of conv3_3 improves the accuracy of FPN based on pure SSD by 0.4%.

How important are gated lateral modules? To validate the effectiveness of gated lateral modules, we apply the gated lateral modules on each chosen layer of SSD. As shown in col 1 and col 2 of Table 4, we observe a significant improvement of performance with gated lateral connection. The result shows the gated lateral modules play a critical role in enhancing the target-specific features to improve the detection performance.

4.4 Detection Analysis on PASCAL VOC2007

We show some qualitative results on PASCAL VOC2007 test set in Fig. 5. A score threshold of 0.6 is used to display these images. Different colors of the bounding boxes indicate different object categories. From Fig. 5, GFPN achieves an excellent performance on generic object detection. Even for the occlusion, the detection result is satisfactory.

5 Conclusion

In this paper, we propose a gated feature pyramid network (GFPN) for object detection. To address the problem that feature pyramid does not focus on the targeted features, we introduce a gated feature pyramid, which utilizes the idea of attention mechanism to enhance the meaningful features. We apply the GFPN on SSD, and train the combined module on PASCAL VOC 2007 and 2012 datasets. The result demonstrates the effectiveness of our method.

Acknowledgements. This work is supported by Natural Science Foundation (NSF) of China (61836008, 61472301).

References

1. Sean, B., Zitnick, C.L., Kavita, B., Ross, G.: Inside-outside net: detecting objects in context with skip pooling and recurrent neural networks. In: Proceedings of the IEEE Conference on Computer Vision and Pattern Recognition, pp. 2874–2883 (2016)
2. Jifeng, D., Yi, L., Kaiming, H., Jian, S.: R-FCN: object detection via region-based fully convolutional networks. In: Advances in Neural Information Processing Systems, pp. 379–387 (2016)
3. Mark, E., Luc, V.G., Christopher, K.W., John, W., Andrew, Z.: The pascal visual object classes (voc) challenge. Int. J. Comput. Vis. **88**(2), 303–338 (2010)
4. Cheng-Yang, F., Wei, L., Ananth, R., Ambrish, T., Alexander, C.B.: Dssd: Deconvolutional single shot detector. arXiv preprint arXiv:1701.06659 (2017)

5. Ross, G., Jeff, D., Trevor, D., Jitendra, M.: Rich feature hierarchies for accurate object detection and semantic segmentation. In: Proceedings of the IEEE Conference on Computer Vision and Pattern Recognition, pp. 580–587 (2014)
6. Xavier, G., Yoshua, B.: Understanding the difficulty of training deep feedforward neural networks. In: Proceedings of the Thirteenth International Conference on Artificial Intelligence and Statistics, pp. 249–256 (2010)
7. He, K., Zhang, X., Ren, S., Sun, J.: Spatial pyramid pooling in deep convolutional networks for visual recognition. In: Fleet, D., Pajdla, T., Schiele, B., Tuytelaars, T. (eds.) ECCV 2014. LNCS, vol. 8691, pp. 346–361. Springer, Cham (2014). https://doi.org/10.1007/978-3-319-10578-9_23
8. Kaiming, H., Georgia, G., Piotr, D., Ross, G.: Mask R-CNN. In: IEEE International Conference on Computer Vision (ICCV), pp. 2980–2988 (2017)
9. Tao, K., Fuchun, S., Anbang, Y., Huaping, L., Ming, L., Yurong, C.: Ron: reverse connection with objectness prior networks for object detection. In: IEEE Conference on Computer Vision and Pattern Recognition, vol. 1, pp. 2 (2017)
10. Tsung-Yi, L., Piotr, D., Ross, G., Kaiming, H., Bharath, H., Serge, B.: Feature pyramid networks for object detection. In: CVPR, vol. 1, p. 4 (2017)
11. Liu, W., et al.: SSD: single shot MultiBox detector. In: Leibe, B., Matas, J., Sebe, N., Welling, M. (eds.) ECCV 2016. LNCS, vol. 9905, pp. 21–37. Springer, Cham (2016). https://doi.org/10.1007/978-3-319-46448-0_2
12. Joseph, R., Ali, F.: Yolo9000: Better, faster, stronger. In: IEEE
13. Joseph, R., Santosh, D., Ross, G., Ali, F.: You only look once: unified, real-time object detection. In: Proceedings of the IEEE Conference on Computer Vision and Pattern Recognition, pp. 779–788 (2016)
14. Shaoqing, R., Kaiming, H., Ross, G., Jian, S.: Faster R-CNN: towards real-time object detection with region proposal networks. IEEE Trans. Pattern Anal. Mach. Intell. 39(6), 1137–1149 (2017)
15. Ross G.: Fast R-CNN. In: IEEE International Conference on Computer Vision, pp. 1440–1448 (2015)
16. Pierre, S., David, E., Xiang, Z., Micha, M., Rob, F., Yann, L.C.: Overfeat: integrated recognition, localization and detection using convolutional networks. In: International Conference on Learning Representations (2014)
17. Abhina, S., Rahul, S., Jitendra, M., Abhinav, G.: Beyond skip connections: Top-down modulation for object detection. arXiv preprint arXiv:1612.06851 (2016)
18. Uijlings, J.R.R., et al.: Selective search for object recognition. Int. J. Comput. Vis. 104(2), 154–171 (2013)
19. Fei, W., et al.: Residual attention network for image classification. arXiv preprint arXiv: 1704.06904 (2017)
20. Shifeng, Z., Longyin, W., Xiao, B., Zhen, L., Stan, Z.L.: Single-shot refinement neural network for object detection. arXiv preprint arXiv:1711.06897 (2017)
21. Hu, J., Shen, L., Sun, G.: Squeeze-and-Excitation Networks. In: CVPR (2017)
22. Li, W., Zhu, X., Gong, S.: Harmonious attention network for person re-identification. In: CVPR (2018)
23. Lin, T.-Y., et al.: Microsoft COCO: common objects in context. In: Fleet, D., Pajdla, T., Schiele, B., Tuytelaars, T. (eds.) ECCV 2014. LNCS, vol. 8693, pp. 740–755. Springer, Cham (2014). https://doi.org/10.1007/978-3-319-10602-1_48
24. Simonyan, K., Zisserman, A.: Very deep convolutional networks for large-scale image recognition. In: Computer Science. (2014)

Learning Non-local Representation
for Visual Tracking

Peng Zhang[1,2,3] and Zengfu Wang[1,2,3(✉)]

[1] Institute of Intelligent Machines, Chinese Academy of Sciences, Hefei, China
[2] University of Science and Technology of China, Hefei, China
hizhangp@mail.ustc.edu.cn, zfwang@ustc.edu.cn
[3] National Engineering Laboratory for Speech and Language
Information Processing, Hefei, China

Abstract. Discriminative Correlation Filter (DCF) based trackers have tremendously improved the tracking performance. They adopt the first frame of video sequence to initialize the tracker and provide a fast solution due to its formulation in the Fourier domain. Previous work that applies a DCF layer on the top of pretrianed CNN, however, has not taken full advantage of CNN feature maps. In this paper, we propose a tracking architecture to fuse the local and global response map for visual tracking in an accuracy and robust way. The feature map extracted from pretrained CNN is applied to a fully-convolutional DCF layer and a non-local layer for capturing local and global response map. Experiments show that our method achieves state-of-the-art performance on three popular benchmarks: OTB-2013, OTB-2015 and VOT2016.

Keywords: Visual tracking · DCF · Non-local · Feature pyramid

1 Introduction

Visual tracking is one of the fundamental problems in the field of computer vision and has a variety of applications, such as human-computer interactions, smart surveillance systems and autonomous driving. Given the initial state of target object in the first frame of video sequence, visual tracking aims to describe the movement of target object by motion modeling and keeping estimating its trajectory under the hard computational constraints of real-time vision system (e.g., deformation, illumination variations, motion blur and occlusion).

Discriminative Correlation Filters (DCF) is an efficient algorithm which learns to discriminate the target object from surrounding background by solving a ridge regression problem extremely efficiently [4,15]. Recently, DCF based trackers [10,20] have shown great performance improvements on several popular tracking benchmarks [18,31,32] on the part of accuracy, robustness and speed. Compared to other tracking algorithms, DCF owns its performance to a Fourier domain formulation as an cheap element-wise operation and dense response scores over all searching locations. In contrast, sparsely sampling used

J.-H. Lai et al. (Eds.): PRCV 2018, LNCS 11259, pp. 209–220, 2018.
https://doi.org/10.1007/978-3-030-03341-5_18

by other algorithms only generates sparse response scores and may lose the target object in complex environment.

Instead of using multi-dimensional features [12], robust scale estimation [10] or non-linear kernels [15], recent DCF based trackers try to learn DCF directly over a deep convolutional neural network (CNN) [7,11,19] and benefit from the end-to-end training [26]. This has shown that with the discriminate CNN feature map pretrianed on ImageNet dataset offline, DCF gains much improvements on performance. However, in the aforementioned work, these algorithms simply integrate pre-trained deep model with DCF, without considering the limitations of CNN features.

In this paper, we propose a non-local neural network learning scheme for better visual tracking. We first modify a given CNN model into a fully-convolutional network in which we can provide search image with arbitrary size and get more accuracy location. Then we reformulate DCF as a convolutional layer without bias on the top of CNN feature map, which generate local response map of the input image. Meanwhile, CNN feature map is fed into a non-local layer for capturing global response map, which is response for modeling background objects. Similar to DCF, finial response map combined by local response map and global response map generates dense response scores over all searching locations in an input image. For scale estimation, rather than feeding several search patches extracted based on the center location of the target in different scales, we crop feature maps in different scales from original feature map after CNN. This operation helps to efficiently speed our model in one forward propagation. Moreover, fully-convolutional DCF layer and non-local layer are fully differentiable, this allows us to train and update the model through back propagation algorithm (Fig. 1).

Fig. 1. A comparison of our proposed model NNVT with C-COT [11] and CREST [26]. Our tracker outperforms these DCF based trackers and is more robust in scale estimation.

In summary, our contributions are as follows:

- We propose a non-local network architecture for visual tracking by using a combination of fully-convolutional DCF layer and non-local layer, which capture local and global response map for better discriminating target object from background objects.
- We replace image pyramids with feature map pyramids to save more than half the time in scale estimation progress.
- Extensive experiments on three popular tracking benchmarks, OTB-2013 [31], OTB-2015 [32] and VOT-2016 [18], show that our tracker achieves state-of-the-art performance.

2   Related Work

Visual tracking has been widely studied in the literature [25, 33]. In this section we mainly introduce two aspects which are most related to our work.

Correlation Filter: Since the seminal work of Bolme (et al.) [4] employed Correlation Filter for visual tracking, Several algorithms [2, 9, 10, 15] were built upon it and devoted notable efforts to its improvement, such as using multi-dimensional features [12], robust scale estimation [10], reducing boundary effects [13] and non-linear kernels [15]. Recently, CNN based DCF trackers have been introduced [2, 6, 26], they reformulate DCF as one convolutional layer and apply it on the top of pretrained CNN models to obtain response map. Since DCF is interpreted as a differentiable convolutional layer, the loss function can be easily back-propagated through DCF layer to the CNN model.

Non-local Neural Network: Non-local operations [30] is the extension of non-local means which is a classical filtering algorithm that computes a weighted mean of all pixels in an image. It is an efficient and simple approach for capturing long-distance dependences in CNN by enlarging receptive fields. Unlike convolutional operations which processes a local neighborhood in space and needs to stack much operations to capture long-range dependences, non-local operations capture long-range dependencies directly by computing interactions between any two positions, regardless of their positional distance. Thus, we can apply non-local operations for capturing global feature map for modeling the background objects with only a few layers (Fig. 2).

3   Learning Non-local Representation

In this section, we present a convolutional framework for learning the combination of local and global response map. The local response map is captured through a fully-convolutional layer which is formulated as standard DCFs, and global response map obtained by non-local operations is the response at a position as a weighted sum of the features at all positions. Then, we sum the local and global response map for final response map.

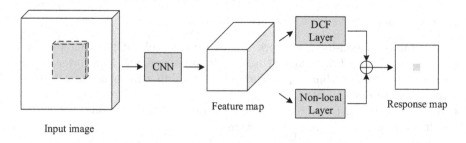

Input image

Feature map   Response map

Fig. 2. Overview of our proposed tracking architecture. We apply one search image into the pretrained CNN for feature extraction, then the feature map is fed into fully-convolutional DCF layer and non-local layer for capturing local and global response map respectively, an accumulative operation is employed for final response map.

3.1   Fully-Convolutional DCF Reformulation

We adopt VGG16 network [24] for base model, and modify it in order to allow the model to be interpreted as a feature extractor for DCF layer.

A *fully-convolutional* neural network is a transformation that it commutes with translation [3]. It can benefit from a much larger input image with more background information, rather than a search image of the target size. To be specific, given the position of target object in the first frame of video sequence, we can obtain an input image centered on the target object and the size is 5 times larger than it, without worrying about decrease of accuracy. For a translation operator L_τ and an input image X, we have $(L_\tau X)[\mu] = X[\mu - \tau]$, a neural network f_ρ with learnable parameters ρ that maps input image X to feature map $f_\rho(X)$ is fully-convolutional with integer stride n if

$$f_\rho(L_{n\tau}X) = L_\tau f_\rho(X) \tag{1}$$

for any translation τ.

On the basis of fully-convolutional neural network, we follow the DCF reformulation in [26] and reformulate it into a fully-convolutional DCF layer. We crop a search patch (denoted as X as well) from the given input image X, which represents the object of interest and typically larger than the target object. DCF layer learns a discriminative classifier with correlation filter $\mathcal{W}$ by minimizing the L2 loss between response map and the corresponding Gaussian function label Y:

$$\mathcal{W}^* = \arg\min_{\mathcal{W}} \|\mathcal{W} \star f_\rho(X) - Y\|^2 + \lambda\|\mathcal{W}\|^2 \tag{2}$$

where λ is the regularization parameter. Equation 2 amounts to predicting the target translation through an exhaustive search of the maximum value in the response map.

We take $\mathcal{W} \star f_\rho(X)$ as the convolution operation on feature map $f_\rho(X)$, which can be achieved through one convolutional layer without bias term. Thus we can reformulate the Eq. 2 in convolution neural network, which learns a convolutional layer by minimizing the following loss function:

$$L(\mathcal{W}) = \|\mathcal{F}_{\mathcal{W}}(X) - Y\|^2 + \lambda r(\mathcal{W}) \tag{3}$$

where $\mathcal{F}_{\mathcal{W}}(X) = \mathcal{W} \star f_\rho(X)$, and $\lambda r(\mathcal{W})$ is the weight decay. We simply use the first frame of video sequence as training image and set the batch N of each iteration 1. We take the L2 norm as $r(\mathcal{W})$ based on DCF function. In order to cover the target object, we set the size k of filter $\mathcal{W}$ equal to the target object after several down-samplings.

In general, target object with large size will provide more representations in feature map and result in more accuracy and robust tracking performance, so we tend to enlarge small size target object to an appropriate size through bilinear interpolation in the search patch. However, as mentioned above, the size k of filter $\mathcal{W}$ must be set equal to the target object, this constraint will highly increase the computation of DCF layer and slow down tracking speed.

Considering above weakness, we introduce large separable convolution layer [27] to act as DCF layer, its structure is illustrated in Fig. 3. A large separable convolution layer is composed of two separate convolution sequences, each convolution sequence is made up of a $k \times 1$ convolution layer followed by a $1 \times k$ convolution layer or a $1 \times k$ convolution layer followed by a $k \times 1$ convolution layer.

The standard DCF layer is parameterized by convolution kernel $\mathcal{W}$ of size $k \times k \times C \times 1$ where C is the channels of feature map, and it has the computational cost of:

$$k \cdot k \cdot C \cdot 1 \cdot H \cdot W \tag{4}$$

where the computational cost depends on the kernel size $k \times k$, channels of feature map C and feature map size $H \times W$.

Considering large separable convolution layer cost:

$$(k \cdot 1 \cdot C \cdot 1 \cdot H \cdot W + k \cdot 1 \cdot 1 \cdot 1 \cdot H \cdot W) \cdot 2 \tag{5}$$

which is the sum of two separate convolution sequences.

By replacing standard DCF layer with two separate convolution sequences, we get a reduction in computation of:

$$\frac{(k \cdot 1 \cdot C \cdot 1 \cdot H \cdot W + k \cdot 1 \cdot 1 \cdot 1 \cdot H \cdot W) \cdot 2}{k \cdot k \cdot C \cdot 1 \cdot H \cdot W}$$
$$= \frac{2(C + 1)}{k \cdot C} \tag{6}$$

In our architecture, we set k to be equal to the size of target object and $C = 64$, the large separable convolution layer uses nearly $2/k$ times less computation than standard DCF layer at only little reduction in performace.

Then, we get the fully-convolutional DCF layer in the form of two separate convolution sequences with L2 loss as the objective function, We name it as fully-convolutional DCF layer.

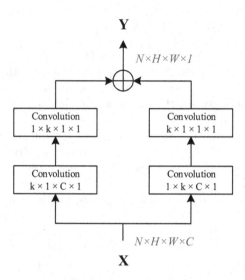

Fig. 3. A large separable convolution layer. It replaces standard $k \times k$ DCF layer with two separate convolution sequences. The computational complexity is reduced by nearly $2/k$ times.

3.2 Non-local Neural Network

DCF layer captures local response map using two separate convolution sequences with fixed kernel size. As a result of convolution operation, DCF layer is only sensitive to the neighborhood of target object, the background objects far away from the center location of target object are not considered sufficiently, thus it is unlikely to be able to agree with the ground truth soft label. Some tracking algorithms have suggested to use more discriminative deep features (e.g. Deep-SRDCF [7] and CCOT [11]) or learn complex deep trackers (e.g. MDNet [21]). Instead of using more complex deep features which may dramaticly increase network computation and result in overfitting, we employ non-local operations as a residual layer for capturing global response map of background objects.

Non-local [30] is a lightweight stack of several convolution layers and softmax layer, we apply a non-local block in our neural network to compute the response at a position as a weighted sum of the feature map of all positions:

$$y_i = \frac{1}{J(x_i)} \sum_{\forall j} g(x_i, x_j) h(x_j) \tag{7}$$

where y is the computed response map, i is the position of the input feature map x whose value is to be computed and j is the index that enumerates all possible positions, g is a pairwise function which computes responses based on relationships between different locations. The unary function h computes a representation of the input feature map as position j. We set $J(x_i) = \sum_{\forall j} g(x_i, x_j)$ to normalize the response (Fig. 4).

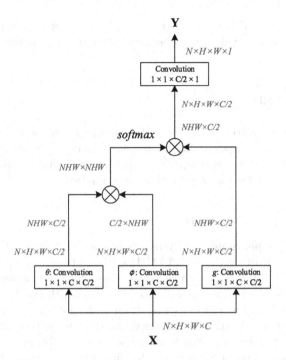

Fig. 4. A spacetime embedded Gaussian non-local layer. The input feature map X is of the shape $N \times H \times W \times C$, Y denotes output response map of the shape $N \times H \times W \times 1$.

Here we apply Embedded Gaussian to compute similarity in an embedding space: $g(x_i, x_j) = e^{\theta(x_i)^T \phi(x_j)}$, $h(x_j) = W_g x_j$ and $\theta(x_i) = W_\theta x_i$, $\phi(x_j) = W_\phi x_j$ are two embeddings. These operations can be achieved through a softmax layer and several convolutional layers without bias term. For arbitrary position i in an input feature map, non-local layer computes the similarity between position i and all positions j to model the global residual response map.

Compared to DCF layer which sums up the weighted feature map in a local neighborhood (e.g., $i - s \le j \le i + s$ with kernel size equal to the object size $2s + 1$), non-local layer can caputer weighted feature all over the feature map, which enhances the influence of background objects over the target object.

3.3 Scale Estimation

Instead of feeding several search images extracted based on the center location of the target object in different scales, we crop feature maps in different scales from original feature map after VGG16 network. These feature maps are then resized into a fixed size before fed into DCF layer and non-local layer to generate final response map. This operation helps to share process of feature extraction and save much computation without degrading performance.

We use a smooth function to update the size s_t of the predicted target object:

$$s_t = \beta s_t^* + (1 - \beta) s_{t-1} \tag{8}$$

where $s = (w, h)$ and s_t^* is the predicted size of the target object in frame t with the maximum response value, β is the weight function to smooth the update of predicted size.

4   Experiments

In this section, we investigate the effect of incorporating of local response map by DCF layer and global response map by non-local layer. We first introduce implementation details. Then we compare our tracker with state-of-the-art trackers on the benchmark datasets for performance evaluation.

4.1   Implementation Details

Our experiment is performed in Python based on Tensorflow [1], and runs at around 5 FPS on a PC with an i7 3.7 GHz CPU and speeded up by a NVIDIA GeForce Titan X GPU. For each new video sequence, we obtain the training image from the first frame whose size is 5 times the width and height of the target object through padding or cropping. Then we feed it into pretrained VGG16 network [24] for feature extraction. After extracting the feature map, we respectively apply DCF layer and non-local layer on it to obtain local and global response map, and sum them together for final response map. The regression target map for computing loss is generated by a two-dimensional Gaussian function with a peak value of 1.0. We calculate the difference between response map and regression target map using L2 loss function and apply the adam optimizer with a learning rate of 5e−8 for back propagation. We stop training until the loss is below the given threshold and update the model when the final response map has a variance above another given threshold with a learning rate of 5e−9.

4.2   Comparison with State-of-the-Art

Here, we extensively consider to evaluate our tracker on three popular tracking benchmarks OTB-2013 [31], OTB-2015 [32] and VOT-2016 [18], comparing with several state-of-the-art trackers.

OTB-2013 Dataset: OTB-2013 benchmark [31] contains 50 fully annotated video sequences with various challenges in object tracking, such as deformation, fast motion and occlusion. We compare our method with most recent state-of-the-art trackers including KCF [15], ECO [6], Staple [2], SRDCF [8], LCT [20], SINT [28], SiamFC [3], SRDCFdecon [9], DeepSRDCF [7], Struck [14], MDNet [21], CF2 [19], C-COT [11], SCT [5], MEEM [34], TCNN [22], HDT [23], STCT [29], MUSTer [17] and CREST [26]. We adopt the one-pass evaluation (OPE) with precision and success plots metrics defined in [31] to evaluate the robustness of trackers. Figure 5 shows the comparison of our tracker with other trackers. The figure legend indicates the average distance precision score and the area-under-curve score at 20 pixels for precision plots and success plots. We can see that our

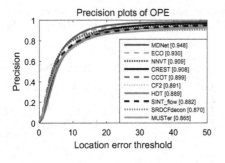
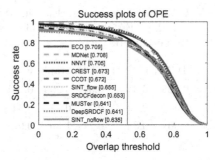

Fig. 5. Precision and success plots on OTB-2013 dataset using one-pass evaluation. The legend shows the average distance precision score and the area-under-curve score at 20 pixels for precision plots and success plots.

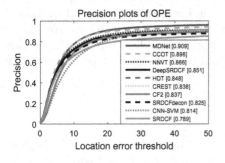
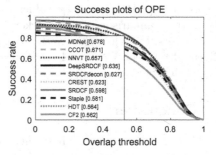

Fig. 6. Precision and success plots on OTB-2015 dataset using one-pass evaluation. The legend indicates the average distance precision score and the area-under-curve score at 20 pixels for precision plots and success plots.

tracker achieves state-of-the-art performance among all the trackers. The higher precision score at low location error threshold (5 10) means that our tracker hardly misses the target even though at a strict threshold. It is worth noticing that, compared with CREST [26] which also uses one convolutional layer to formulate the DCF, our tracker outperforms it in both measures.

OTB-2015 Dataset: OTB-2015 benchmark [32] contains 100 fully annotated video sequences. We also compare our tracker with several trackers, include MDNet [21], C-COT [11], SRDCFdecon [9], HDT [23], Staple [2], SRDCF [8], DeepSRDCF [7], CNN-SVM [16], CF2 [19], LCT [20], DSST [10], MEEM [34], KCF [15] and CREST [26]. We adopt the one-pass evaluation (OPE) with precision and success plots metrics defined in [31] to evaluate the robustness of trackers. Figure 6 shows the comparison of our tracker with other trackers. We can see that our tracker also achieves state-of-the-art performance among all the trackers. Our tracker is slightly underperform the C-COT [11] when compared with OTB-2013 benchmark [31], it means that our tracker is not as robust as C-COT [11] in much challenging conditions.

Table 1. Evaluation of our tracker with the state-of-art trackers in terms of expected average overlap (EAO), accuracy values (Av) and robustness values (Rv) on the VOT-2016 benchmark.

	TCNN	C-COT	ECO	Staple	EBT	MDNet	SiamFC	SSAT	CREST	**NNVT**
EAO	0.325	0.331	0.374	0.295	0.291	0.257	0.277	0.321	0.283	0.323
Av	0.54	0.52	0.54	0.54	0.44	0.53	0.55	0.57	0.51	0.54
Rv	0.96	0.85	0.72	1.35	0.90	1.20	1.38	1.04	1.08	0.88

VOT-2016 Dataset: VOT-2016 benchmark [18] contains 60 challenging videos from a set of more than 300 videos. We compare our model with the top-ranked trackers, including TCNN [22], C-COT [11], ECO [6], Staple [2], EBT [35], MDNet [21], SiamFC [3] SSAT [18] and CREST [26], in terms of expected average overlap (EAO), accuracy values (Av) and robustness values (Rv). Table 1 shows the comparison of our tracker with the state-of-art trackers. Among all the trackers, ECO [6] achieves the best performance. These top five trackers are all based on deep CNN and our tracker achieves the similar performace with other trackers.

5 Conclusion

In this paper, we present a novel network architecture for accuracy and robust visual tracking by fusing the local and global response map. Instead of applying a DCF layer on the top of the pretrianed CNN and merely regressing the local response map, we introduce a convolutional DCF layer for capturing local response map and a non-local layer for global response map, which helps the model to distinguish the target object from the background. Also, we replace image pyramids with feature map pyramids in scale estimation, this operation help to save half the time in one forwarding. Experiments on three popular tracking benchmarks show that our model achieves state-of-the-art performance.

References

1. Abadi, M., et al.: Tensorflow: a system for large-scale machine learning. In: Proceedings of the 12th USENIX Conference on Operating Systems Design and Implementation, vol. 16, pp. 265–283. USENIX Association (2016)
2. Bertinetto, L., Valmadre, J., Golodetz, S., Miksik, O., Torr, P.H.S.: Staple: complementary learners for real-time tracking. In: 2016 IEEE Conference on Computer Vision and Pattern Recognition, pp. 1401–1409. IEEE (2016)
3. Bertinetto, L., Valmadre, J., Henriques, J.F., Vedaldi, A., Torr, P.H.S.: Fully-convolutional siamese networks for object tracking. In: Hua, G., Jégou, H. (eds.) ECCV 2016. LNCS, vol. 9914, pp. 850–865. Springer, Cham (2016). https://doi.org/10.1007/978-3-319-48881-3_56
4. Bolme, D.S., Beveridge, J.R., Draper, B.A., Lui, Y.M.: Visual object tracking using adaptive correlation filters. In: 2010 IEEE Computer Society Conference on Computer Vision and Pattern Recognition, pp. 2544–2550. IEEE (2010)

5. Choi, J., Chang, H.J., Jeong, J., Demiris, Y., Choi, J.Y.: Visual tracking using attention-modulated disintegration and integration. In: 2016 IEEE Conference on Computer Vision and Pattern Recognition, pp. 4321–4330. IEEE (2016)
6. Danelljan, M., Bhat, G., Khan, F.S., Felsberg, M.: Eco: efficient convolution operators for tracking. In: 2017 IEEE Conference on Computer Vision and Pattern Recognition, pp. 21–26. IEEE (2017)
7. Danelljan, M., Häger, G., Khan, F.S., Felsberg, M.: Convolutional features for correlation filter based visual tracking. In: 2015 IEEE International Conference on Computer Vision Workshop, pp. 58–66. IEEE (2015)
8. Danelljan, M., Häger, G., Khan, F.S., Felsberg, M.: Learning spatially regularized correlation filters for visual tracking. In: 2015 IEEE International Conference on Computer Vision, pp. 4310–4318. IEEE (2015)
9. Danelljan, M., Häger, G., Khan, F.S., Felsberg, M.: Adaptive decontamination of the training set: a unified formulation for discriminative visual tracking. In: 2016 IEEE Conference on Computer Vision and Pattern Recognition, pp. 1430–1438. IEEE (2016)
10. Danelljan, M., Häger, G., Shahbaz Khan, F., Felsberg, M.: Accurate scale estimation for robust visual tracking. In: Proceedings of the British Machine Vision Conference. BMVA Press (2014)
11. Danelljan, M., Robinson, A., Shahbaz Khan, F., Felsberg, M.: Beyond correlation filters: learning continuous convolution operators for visual tracking. In: Leibe, B., Matas, J., Sebe, N., Welling, M. (eds.) ECCV 2016. LNCS, vol. 9909, pp. 472–488. Springer, Cham (2016). https://doi.org/10.1007/978-3-319-46454-1_29
12. Galoogahi, H.K., Sim, T., Lucey, S.: Multi-channel correlation filters. In: 2013 IEEE International Conference on Computer Vision, pp. 3072–3079. IEEE (2013)
13. Galoogahi, H.K., Sim, T., Lucey, S.: Correlation filters with limited boundaries. In: 2015 IEEE Conference on Computer Vision and Pattern Recognition, pp. 4630–4638. IEEE (2015)
14. Hare, S., et al.: Struck: structured output tracking with kernels. IEEE Trans. Pattern Anal. Mach. Intell. **38**(10), 2096–2109 (2016)
15. Henriques, J.F., Caseiro, R., Martins, P., Batista, J.: High-speed tracking with kernelized correlation filters. IEEE Trans. Pattern Anal. Mach. Intell. **37**(3), 583–596 (2015)
16. Hong, S., You, T., Kwak, S., Han, B.: Online tracking by learning discriminative saliency map with convolutional neural network. In: Proceedings of the 32nd International Conference on International Conference on Machine Learning, pp. 597–606. JMLR.org (2015)
17. Hong, Z., Chen, Z., Wang, C., Mei, X., Prokhorov, D., Tao, D.: Multi-store tracker (muster): a cognitive psychology inspired approach to object tracking. In: 2015 IEEE Conference on Computer Vision and Pattern Recognition, pp. 749–758. IEEE (2015)
18. Kristan, M.: The visual object tracking VOT2016 challenge results. In: Hua, G., Jégou, H. (eds.) ECCV 2016. LNCS, vol. 9914, pp. 777–823. Springer, Cham (2016). https://doi.org/10.1007/978-3-319-48881-3_54
19. Ma, C., Huang, J.B., Yang, X., Yang, M.H.: Hierarchical convolutional features for visual tracking. In: 2015 IEEE International Conference on Computer Vision, pp. 3074–3082. IEEE (2015)
20. Ma, C., Yang, X., Zhang, C., Yang, M.H.: Long-term correlation tracking. In: 2015 IEEE Conference on Computer Vision and Pattern Recognition, pp. 5388–5396. IEEE (2015)

21. Nam, H., Han, B.: Learning multi-domain convolutional neural networks for visual tracking. In: 2016 IEEE Conference on Computer Vision and Pattern Recognition, pp. 4293–4302. IEEE (2016)
22. Nam, H., Baek, M., Han, B.: Modeling and propagating cnns in a tree structure for visual tracking. arXiv preprint arXiv:1608.07242 (2016)
23. Qi, Y., et al.: Hedged deep tracking. In: 2016 IEEE Conference on Computer Vision and Pattern Recognition, pp. 4303–4311. IEEE (2016)
24. Simonyan, K., Zisserman, A.: Very deep convolutional networks for large-scale image recognition. CoRR (2014)
25. Smeulders, A.W.M., Chu, D.M., Cucchiara, R., Calderara, S., Dehghan, A., Shah, M.: Visual tracking: an experimental survey. IEEE Trans. Pattern Anal. Mach. Intell. **36**(7), 1442–1468 (2014)
26. Song, Y., Ma, C., Gong, L., Zhang, J., Lau, R.W.H., Yang, M.H.: Crest: convolutional residual learning for visual tracking. In: 2017 IEEE International Conference on Computer Vision, pp. 2574–2583. IEEE (2017)
27. Szegedy, C., Vanhoucke, V., Ioffe, S., Shlens, J., Wojna, Z.: Rethinking the inception architecture for computer vision. In: 2016 IEEE Conference on Computer Vision and Pattern Recognition, pp. 2818–2826. IEEE (2016)
28. Tao, R., Gavves, E., Smeulders, A.W.M.: Siamese instance search for tracking. In: 2016 IEEE Conference on Computer Vision and Pattern Recognition, pp. 1420–1429. IEEE (2016)
29. Wang, L., Ouyang, W., Wang, X., Lu, H.: Stct: sequentially training convolutional networks for visual tracking. In: 2016 IEEE Conference on Computer Vision and Pattern Recognition, pp. 1373–1381. IEEE (2016)
30. Wang, X., Girshick, R., Gupta, A., He, K.: Non-local neural networks. arXiv preprint arXiv:1711.07971 (2017)
31. Wu, Y., Lim, J., Yang, M.H.: Online object tracking: a benchmark. In: 2013 IEEE Conference on Computer Vision and Pattern Recognition, pp. 2411–2418. IEEE (2013)
32. Wu, Y., Lim, J., Yang, M.H.: Object tracking benchmark. IEEE Trans. Pattern Anal. Mach. Intell. **37**(9), 1834–1848 (2015)
33. Yilmaz, A., Javed, O., Shah, M.: Object tracking: a survey. ACM Comput. Surv. **38**(4), 13 (2006)
34. Zhang, J., Ma, S., Sclaroff, S.: MEEM: robust tracking via multiple experts using entropy minimization. In: Fleet, D., Pajdla, T., Schiele, B., Tuytelaars, T. (eds.) ECCV 2014. LNCS, vol. 8694, pp. 188–203. Springer, Cham (2014). https://doi.org/10.1007/978-3-319-10599-4_13
35. Zhu, G., Porikli, F., Li, H.: Beyond local search: tracking objects everywhere with instance-specific proposals. In: 2016 IEEE Conference on Computer Vision and Pattern Recognition, pp. 943–951. IEEE (2016)

Discriminative Visual Tracking Using Multi-feature and Adaptive Dictionary Learning

Penggen Zheng[1,2], Jin Zhan[1,2], Huimin Zhao[1,2(✉)], and Jujian Lv[1,2]

[1] School of Computer Science, Guangdong Polytechnic Normal University,
Guangzhou, China
zhaohuimin@gpnu.edu.cn
[2] Guangzhou Key Laboratory of Digital Content Processing and Security
Technologies, Guangzhou, China

Abstract. We propose a novel tracking method using color features and texture features to obtain accurate target appearance model. Each feature dictionary is independent and learned by labeled consistent K-SVD. In the subsequent frames, we exploit the maximum similarity of sparse features by the minimal reconstruction error criterion to locate the best tracking result. When a significant change occurs, we propose an adaptive dictionary learning which update the background template incrementally using the positive and negative samples of the current target. We compared our method with the existing techniques in OTB100 and VOT2017 dataset, and the experimental results show that our proposed method achieved substantially better performance.

Keywords: Visual tracking · Sparse representation · Multiple features
Adaptive updating

1 Introduction

In computer vision field, visual tracking problem is still a challenging task due to its complex scenes, such as target occlusions, target deformation, rotation, scale changes and cluttered background. In recent years, there have been many improved visual tracking methods based on different theoretical frameworks. Most of these methods can be roughly divided into generative models and discriminant models. Generative models [1–4] typically find the most similar candidates or search the highest likelihood with the initial target in the subsequent frames. This kind of tracking methods may easily drift away when the object matching or prediction method is not is accurate enough. Discriminant models [5–9] classify the foreground and background of target by finding the decision boundaries. The performance of discriminant tracking methods depends on the number of training samples and update strategy.

Recently, deep learning based trackers [14, 15] and correlation filters (CF) based trackers [10–13] have attracted considerable attention because of their powerful characterization of depth features and fast tracking performance, respectively. Sparse representation based trackers [3, 4, 6, 7] often model the target appearance with dictionary and locate the target by comparing the reconstruction errors between the target and the samples.

© Springer Nature Switzerland AG 2018
J.-H. Lai et al. (Eds.): PRCV 2018, LNCS 11259, pp. 221–232, 2018.
https://doi.org/10.1007/978-3-030-03341-5_19

Representation model of target appearance is an important issue of tracking method. To address the issues, Ross et al. [2] use an incremental feature space to adapt to the appearance changes. Wang et al. [16] learn a set of feature space to represent the object by partial least squares (PLS) analysis which takes both target and surrounding backgrounds into consideration. Although these methods have strong tracking robustness when target deformation occurs, target appearance with single feature lacks of considering color distribution and gradient information of target, and fixed dictionary with overall appearance ignores the variations cues of target foreground.

Motivated by the success of the L_1 sparse based tracker [3, 22], we propose a new multi-feature based tracking method and introduce an adaptive dictionary learning to model the target appearance. We classify the foreground and background by Label Consistent K-SVD optimization [20], which has discriminative property. Experimental results demonstrate that our method performs better performance than similar methods. The contributions of our method can be summarized as follows:

(1) We propose a novel sparse tracking framework by using multiple features which composed of color and texture characters. Each kind of feature corresponding one dictionary. These independent dictionaries enhance the characterization capabilities of the target appearance model and produce complementary effects that improve tracking stability.

(2) We introduce an additional incremental dictionary updating step which helps effectively handle the target deformation during the tracking process. The background basis in dictionaries will be replaced by new samples when the target posture changes dramatically in the current frame. This adaptive updating is critical to avoid target drifting and suppress the interference of the background information.

(3) Our method shows many attractive properties with different scene videos in OTB100 and VOT2017 datasets, such as robustness to target various, avoiding target drifting, and handling occlusions effectively.

2   Proposed Method

In this section, we will describe the proposed method. Our method extracts color feature and non-color feature from target template and construct independent dictionary to model target appearance. We maintain two sets of samples, T for target and B for background. Then, we use the LC-KSVD [20] method to learn multiple features discriminative dictionaries which have. We also introduce an adaptive dictionary updating method by similar measure to improve the tracking performance. Figure 1 shows the process of the proposed method.

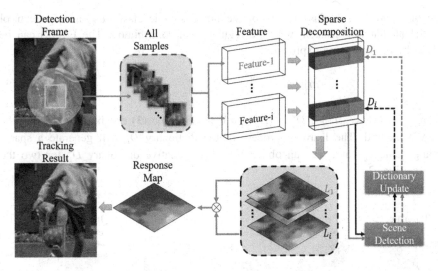

Fig. 1. Proposed method

2.1 Target Appearance Model

In our tracking method, the target y can be represented by sparse expression formula as follow:

$$y \approx Dc = [T, B, I] \begin{bmatrix} z \\ v \\ e \end{bmatrix}, \tag{1}$$

where D is a dictionary composed by samples T, B and diagonal matrix I, c is sparse coefficients including target coefficients z, background coefficients v and noise coefficient e.

With respect to the dictionary D, we extract texture feature and color feature for each sample in the first frame to construct the dictionary, and obtain two feature dictionaries $D_k(i = 1, 2, \ldots)$, where k is a feature tag.

2.2 Discriminative Dictionary Learning

In dictionary learning, we use LC-KSVD [20] method to obtain multiple features discriminative dictionaries D_k. It is expressed as an equation that mixes the reconstruction error and classification error. The solution expression of the discriminative dictionary is as follows:

$$arg\,min_{D_k, c_k^i} \left\| y_i - D_k c_k^i \right\|_2^2 + \alpha \left\| H - A c_k^i \right\|_2^2 + \beta \left\| c_k^i \right\|_1. \tag{2}$$

The first term in Eq. (2) is the reconstruction errors. The second term is the sample class coding error which makes c has stronger ability of discriminating samples category, and H is a class matrix of the initial sample class. α is a range control coefficient that is consistent with the regular term contribution. The Eq. (2) can be solved by the following expression:

$$arg\ min_{D_k^*, c_k^{i*}} \left\| y_i^* - D_k^* c_k^{i*} \right\|_2^2 + \beta \left\| c_k^{i*} \right\|_1 \qquad (3)$$

where $y_i^* = \left(y_i^T, \sqrt{\alpha} H^T \right)^T$, $D_k^* = \left(D_k^T, \sqrt{\alpha} A^T \right)^T$. Formula (3) can be solved using the K-SVD method. The learning process of the dictionary D_k^* will generate a sparse coding value c_k^{i*}, and we can obtain two discriminative dictionary D_k^* for two the features (Fig. 2).

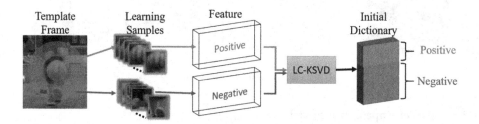

Fig. 2. Discriminative dictionary learning diagram

2.3   Target Matching and Tracking

We exploit a sparse feature matching method [22] which exploits the maximum similarity of sparse features by the minimal reconstruction error criterion. In the current dictionary, we denote the initial target basis vector as d_1 and the target basis vector of previous frame as d_p. In current frame, the j-th sample y_j with the prime coefficient c_k^i and basis vector d_j, where i is the feature label. We define $g_k(j)$ is the distance between d_1 and d_j, and $s_k(j)$ is the distance between d_p and d_j. The objective function of searching result $L_k(j)$ is given as,

$$L_k(j) = \frac{1}{2} g_k(j) + \frac{1}{2} s_k(j) + \eta \ exp\left(\frac{-\left\| y_k^j - D c_k^j \right\|}{2\sigma^2} \right) \qquad (4)$$

where the second term in Eq. (4) indicates the influence of minimal reconstruct error, and η is a regularization parameter. We maximize the product multiplication of $L_k(j)$.

$$\hat{j} = arg\ max \prod_k L_k(j) \qquad (5)$$

where j is the label of the samples. The optimizing result of Eq. (5) ($\hat{j}$-th sample) is the best tracking result.

3 Adaptive Dictionary Update

In the target tracking process, the change of target and background will impact the tracking effect obviously. Many tracking methods update the target appearance model using these change information. However, it is easy to accumulate errors during the update process which will result in tracking drift. It is necessary to reduce error accumulation and over-fitting while maintaining good tracking efficiency.

In the sparse coefficient c_k^i, the noise factor e_k^i has smaller value than the maximum coefficient which reflects the degree of target occlusion and tracking drift to some extent. Our method analyzes the samples noise energy to determine the update time of the dictionary and use an incremental dictionary update method. At frame t, the average noise energy expression for all samples is defined as $\overline{u_k^t} = \sum_{i=1}^{n} u_k^i$, where u_k^i is the noise energy of sample s_i. The expression of the average noise energy set U_k is as follows:

$$U_k = \left\{ \overline{u_k^1}, \overline{u_k^2}, \ldots, \overline{u_k^{t-1}} \right\}. \tag{6}$$

We define the expression of the threshold x_k^α as follows:

$$P\left\{ U_k > x_k^\alpha \right\} = \alpha, \tag{7}$$

where x_k^α reflects the overall level of noise energy during the tracking process. The threshold x_k^α is the upper quintile value of the average noise energy U_k. If the tracked average noise energy $\overline{u_k^t}$ crosses the threshold, it shows that the background information of the current frame begins to change more obviously. At the same time, we also set the minimum update interval tm, the interval between two updates must be more than tm. Setting a minimum updating interval can make update more efficient.

The dictionary is updated when the current frame satisfies the following three conditions simultaneously: (1) The noise energy of the current best sample is less than the average noise energy of all samples. (2) The average noise energy of the samples intersects with the threshold curve which indicates scene change. (3) The interval between two updates must be more than tm.

The incremental dictionary updating and new dictionary learning process is shown in Fig. 3. We resample the positive and negative samples centered on the target position of the current frame and use LC-KSVD to learn the new feature dictionary from the new sample set. Such an update strategy guarantees the reliability of the positive sample features and reduces the accumulation of errors in the update process.

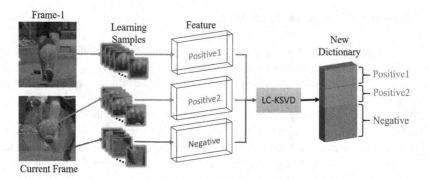

Fig. 3. Dictionary update process.

4   Experimental Results and Comparison

In this section, we validate the proposed tracking method with extensive experiments. Firstly, we perform comparative analysis experiments on different feature combinations and select the multiple features that are optimal for our framework. Secondly, we compare our method with related tracking methods based on intensive sampling and sparse representation. Finally, we conduct performance analysis both quantitatively and qualitatively in various sequences.

4.1   Experimental Setup

We selected 14 color sequences in OTB100 [19] and 8 color sequences in VOT2017 [18] for experiments. These sequences cover a variety of challenging attributes, such as target occlusion, target deformation, lighting changes, target rotation, background interference and so on. In the comparative experiment, we not only selected 9 similar methods (ASLA [1], IVT [2], L1APG [3], CT [5], CXT [6], ORIA [8], OAB [7], TLD [9], Struck [17]), but also selected 7 excellent methods (DCF [10], KCF [10], DSST [11], SRDCF [12], LMCF [13], SiamFC [14], SAMF [21]) for Comprehensive evaluation. We adopt the public code and initial parameters for these methods and carry out a same running environment tracking experiment. We implement the proposed method in MATLAB with matlabR2017a, and the computer environment is: Intel(R)Core(TM) i3-3.7 GHz, RAM-12 GB.

Our method adopts uniform parameter setting. For positive and negative samples, the sampling radii are $r_0 = 4$, $r_1 = 7$ and $r_2 = 15$, from which we can obtain 45 positive samples. The dimensions of all features are controlled between 100 and 200. The method of updating the dictionary is LC-KSVD, updating time interval is $tm = 6$ frames, and noise energy threshold parameter is $\alpha = 0.2$. The number of samples in the tracking process is 500. The experiment evaluation indicators are center location error (CLE), average overlap score (AOS), precision plot and success plot [19]. The center location error (CLE) is the Euclidean distance between the tracking result and the standard target position. The overlap score is a measure of the overlapping range between the tracking result and the standard result tracking box.

4.2   Multiple Features Comparison

In this experiment we mainly discuss the best combination of features in our method framework. We have selected five features that are suitable for our method. They are non-color features: *haar-like* and *hog*, and color features: *rgb*, *lab* and *hsv*. The method in this paper combines non-color features and color features. We use eight color sequences in the VOT2017 for this experiment. And this experiment does not use the dictionary update mechanism.

In Table 1, the average CLE of the *hog* features is slightly better than the *haar-like* feature, but they have great differences in tracking speed. The average tracking efficiency of the method using the *haar-like* feature [22] has reached the real-time level, while the average efficiency of the *hog* feature is only 1.7 f/s.

Table 1. Center location error and frame rate for single feature (non-color) tracking

	HAAR-LIKE	FPS	HOG	FPS
ball1	62.6743	18.9287	107.0594	1.5515
blanket	24.1887	48.6034	56.7963	1.9071
butterfly	234.9816	17.8908	41.4621	1.1416
crossing	32.8666	11.7027	18.5116	1.2541
godfather	75.2504	29.3724	36.9541	2.0616
pedestrian1	107.0762	47.0686	54.6996	2.0101
sheep	11.1645	41.1277	50.6836	1.9869
wiper	27.2947	36.1075	97.9491	1.7385
Average	71.9371	31.3502	58.0144	1.7064

Table 2 shows the experimental results of the *haar-like* features combined with the three color features. We can see that the *rgb* feature does not improve the performance of the method, but the tracking effect is significantly improved in the combination with the *lab* or *hsv*. The *hsv* feature shows better tracking accuracy and tracking efficiency when combined with *haar-like*. When using three feature combinations, there is no effective improvement in tracking performance. Therefore, we adopt a multiple features combination of *haar-like* and *hsv* in our framework.

4.3   Comparison with Similar Methods

In comparison experiments with other methods, we used 14 color sequences (*lemming, mountain, bikedeer, david3, football1, boy, bolt, bolt2, rubik, kitesurf, gym, dragonboy, clifbar, blurowl*) selected in OTB100 [19]. The average CLE and AOS for our method and ten similar methods (ASLA [1], IVT [2], L1APG [3], CT [5], CXT [6], ORIA [8], OAB [7], TLD [9], Struck [17]) are shown in Tables 3 and 4.

From the results in the Tables 3 and 4, we can see that our method is quite outstanding in comparison with other sparse representation methods. In addition, we also add a CF-based method (KCF [10]) to the comparison experiment.

Combined with the tracking results in Fig. 5, it is not difficult to find that the CF-based method has strong tracking robustness in the case of target rotation (In-Plane

Rotation (IPR) and Out-of-Plane Rotation (OPR)) and Background Clutters (BC). On the other hand, the tracking effect of our method on these attributes is quite close to KCF. Our proposed also shows good performance on Scale Variation (SV), fast motion (FM) and motion blur (MB) attributes compared to the similar methods.

Table 2. Center location error and frame rate for multiple features tracking

	RGB and HAAR-LIKE	FPS	LAB and HAAR-LIKE	FPS	HSV and HAAR-LIKE	FPS
ball1	45.3176	9.2322	4.5223	3.3232	5.1713	7.0766
blanket	26.7002	15.0012	14.2856	10.9472	14.0118	9.6928
butterfly	35.9191	6.1486	26.3854	4.5505	34.0104	6.6796
crossing	36.0102	6.8751	34.5094	3.2681	24.7449	6.3169
godfather	11.6728	15.4714	7.8487	11.8826	7.4205	16.4923
pedestrian1	11.8181	15.112	14.1993	12.2403	20.7932	10.7984
sheep	54.2181	14.3322	39.7936	8.5632	10.9163	11.0918
wiper	251.5448	11.6803	28.0519	6.3869	22.4473	9.6831
Average	59.1501	11.7316	21.1995	7.6452	**17.4395**	**9.7289**
	RGB and HAAR-LIKE and HOG	FPS	LAB and HAAR-LIKE and HOG	FPS	HSV and HAAR-LIKE and HOG	FPS
ball1	13.053	1.6034	4.2547	1.2001	3.9515	1.4779
blanket	10.7274	1.6624	10.9618	1.6478	14.4787	1.6329
butterfly	30.7162	1.008	23.143	0.9359	27.8699	1.0045
crossing	35.8374	1.173	37.5716	1.0045	30.007	1.2039
godfather	9.1704	1.8685	10.3247	1.8311	12.0086	1.9767
pedestrian1	12.5084	1.7975	16.6428	1.8142	18.8113	1.8826
sheep	18.0914	1.8116	42.8788	1.6445	32.9777	1.8916
wiper	242.115	1.608	39.3049	1.4539	18.7001	1.5993
Average	46.5274	1.56655	23.13529	1.4415	**19.8506**	**1.583675**

Table 3. The average CLE of similar methods (bold indicates the best two methods)

	OURS	ASLA	IVT	KCF	OAB	STRUCK	L1APG	TLD	CT	ORIA	CXT
BLUROWL	8.86	64.59	167.17	183.43	11.83	67.66	120.61	30.28	164.71	179.43	**6.93**
BOLT2	10.52	284.19	83.13	329.81	135.55	190.37	304.09	304.68	**9.44**	169.35	261.45
CLIFBAR	12.50	49.06	59.20	36.72	37.13	72.59	59.06	20.44	18.87	48.08	31.48
DRAGONBABY	18.90	63.26	92.75	50.39	76.70	89.92	95.66	66.46	70.26	92.72	21.77
GYM	13.22	30.57	27.33	16.26	110.96	122.82	137.89	14.23	28.18	**13.80**	19.82
KITESURF	17.26	**14.97**	59.94	17.26	64.60	38.97	46.17	34.14	93.77	76.37	**7.17**
RUBIK	19.09	15.40	70.01	**9.38**	34.99	45.44	86.53	18.20	112.32	**4.86**	21.35
BOLT	10.08	391.59	376.27	**6.36**	252.04	387.54	390.78	87.99	378.33	83.33	304.05
BOY	4.26	56.32	91.25	**2.87**	**3.33**	3.61	31.13	4.09	40.94	179.32	5.99
FOOTBALL1	4.75	8.04	24.07	5.47	28.81	**4.47**	9.20	52.94	18.99	69.55	4.79
DAVID3	12.03	104.58	52.95	**4.30**	91.07	105.20	85.97	135.75	68.48	182.57	221.80
DEER	9.51	130.43	194.19	21.15	12.64	16.85	25.69	117.70	242.10	215.39	11.17
MOUNTAINBIKE	15.52	**6.52**	7.66	7.66	12.99	12.13	138.40	213.01	118.24	**6.97**	182.19
LEMMING	16.25	186.68	184.13	77.87	25.57	21.06	172.88	16.80	110.48	182.25	42.41

Figure 4 shows the tracking results of several related methods. It is not difficult to find that our method still maintains a good tracking effect when the target appears motion blur and fast motion (e.g., *blurowl*, *deer* and *clifbar* in Fig. 4), and effectively suppresses the influence of similar objects around the target (e.g., *david3*, *deer* and *bolt2* in Fig. 4).

Table 4. The AOS of similar methods (bold indicates the best two methods)

	OURS	ASLA	IVT	KCF	OAB	STRUCK	L1APG	TLD	CT	ORIA	CXT
BLUROWL	**0.743**	0.194	0.055	0.195	**0.768**	0.214	0.253	0.610	0.067	0.069	0.312
BOLT2	**0.598**	0.011	0.015	0.011	0.011	0.010	0.011	0.010	**0.578**	0.011	0.012
CLIFBAR	**0.472**	0.307	0.242	0.260	0.281	0.197	0.266	**0.436**	0.382	0.248	0.396
DRAGONBABY	**0.542**	0.205	0.250	0.313	0.190	0.131	0.214	0.154	0.158	0.138	**0.485**
GYM	**0.466**	0.379	0.087	0.426	0.036	0.081	0.017	**0.443**	0.360	0.431	0.349
KITESURF	0.380	0.317	0.256	**0.475**	0.314	0.186	0.242	0.231	0.152	0.137	**0.590**
RUBIK	0.502	**0.522**	0.160	**0.614**	0.375	0.371	0.120	0.469	0.193	**0.808**	0.268
BOLT	**0.577**	0.011	0.010	**0.679**	0.020	0.019	0.022	0.159	0.014	0.199	0.016
BOY	0.735	0.379	0.260	**0.778**	**0.776**	0.760	0.523	0.621	0.396	0.154	0.563
FOOTBALL1	**0.697**	0.527	0.557	**0.710**	0.356	**0.713**	0.557	0.369	0.286	0.085	0.693
DAVID3	0.657	0.314	0.512	**0.772**	0.286	0.283	0.292	0.276	0.400	0.132	0.122
DEER	**0.665**	0.043	0.033	0.624	**0.690**	0.595	0.548	0.247	0.025	0.034	0.645
MOUNTAINBIKE	0.473	**0.771**	**0.726**	0.712	0.610	0.633	0.361	0.188	0.421	0.662	0.225
LEMMING	**0.628**	0.143	0.126	0.384	0.540	**0.592**	0.134	0.512	0.260	0.042	0.520

4.4 Quantitative Evaluation

We use CLE and overlap score [19] under different thresholds to further evaluate the tracking performance. Figure 4 shows the overall precision plots of OPE and success plots of OPE. In comparison the area under curve (AUC) score with other advanced trackers, our method also shows excellent tracking evaluation results.

Fig. 4. Tracking results of several related methods

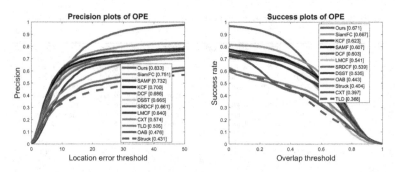

Fig. 5. Comprehensive precision plots (left) and Success plots (right) for different tracking methods

More detailed performance evaluation are showed in Fig. 6. It shows the attribute names and attribute frequency in all sequences. From the comparison of these results we can see that the tracking effect of our method has reached the level of tracking of some advanced methods (e.g. SAMF, SiamFC and SRDCF) in some attributes.

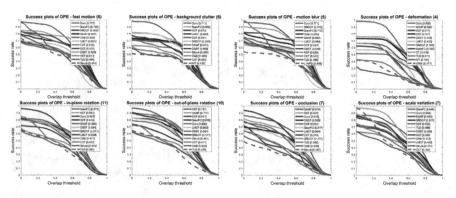

Fig. 6. Attribute based evaluation. Success plots compare our tracker with other 16 trackers on all test videos. Our tracker has outstanding tracking effects in most attributes.

The color features have properties that are insensitive to the deformation of the target. The use of color feature dictionary greatly enhances the tracking effect of our tracking model when the target is blurred. As shown in Fig. 6, our tracker performs the best evaluation result on *motion blur*, *background clutter* and *fast motion* attribute, and the AUC score is over 0.7.

The tracking effect of most methods is easily affected by target scale change. When the target scale changes, the method is difficult to adapt to the internal changes of the target, which is easy to cause misjudgment of the tracking model. Using multiple features can reduce the number of false positives. Our tracking effect is second only to SiamFC on attribute *scale variation*, as shown in Fig. 6.

5 Conclusion

In this paper, we have proposed a novel multi-feature sparse dictionary learning based tracking method. The proposed framework exploits incremental dictionary learning to establish the target appearance model by using noise energy analysis and sample similarity measure. Multiple features combination can complement the representation capabilities of target, and can reduce background noise interference to increase tracking accuracy. The sample similarity measure is used to narrow the search range of the optimal sample to select candidate samples, which can effectively reduce the interference of abnormal samples. An adaptive updating strategy has been proposed by noise energy analysis which comparing the noise energy with the dynamic threshold. Experimental results on OTB100 and VOT2017 dataset show that our proposed method achieved substantially better performance.

Acknowledgments. This research is supported by National Natural Science Foundation of China (61772144, 61672008), Guangdong Provincial Application-oriented Technical Research and Development Special Fund Project (2016B010127006), the Natural Science Foundation of Guangdong Province (2016A030311013), and the Scientific and Technological Projects of Guangdong Province (2017A050501039), Foreign Science and Technology Cooperation Plan Project of Guangzhou Science Technology and Innovation Commission (201807010059), Innovation Team Project (Natural Science) of the Education Department of Guangdong Province (2017KCXTD021), and Characteristic Innovation (Natural Science) Program of the Education Department of Guangdong Province (2016KTSCX077).

References

1. Lu, H., Jia, X., Yang, M.H.: Visual tracking via adaptive structural local sparse appearance model. In: Proceedings of Computer Vision and Pattern Recognition (CVPR), pp. 1822–1829. IEEE (2012)
2. Ross, D.A., Lim, J., Lin, R.S., et al.: Incremental Learning for Robust Visual Tracking. Int. J. Comput. Vis. (IJCV) **77**(1–3), 125–141 (2008)
3. Bao, C., Wu, Y., Ling, H., Ji, H.: Real time robust l1 tracker using accelerated proximal gradient approach. In: Proceedings of Computer Vision and Pattern Recognition (CVPR), pp. 1830–1837 (2012)
4. Liu, Q.: Decontaminate feature for tracking: adaptive tracking via evolutionary feature subset. J. Electron. Imaging **26**(6), 1 (2017)
5. Zhang, K., Zhang, L., Yang, M.-H.: Real-time compressive tracking. In: Fitzgibbon, A., Lazebnik, S., Perona, P., Sato, Y., Schmid, C. (eds.) ECCV 2012, Part III. LNCS, vol. 7574, pp. 864–877. Springer, Heidelberg (2012). https://doi.org/10.1007/978-3-642-33712-3_62
6. Dinh, T.B., Vo, N., Medioni, G.: Context tracker: exploring supporters and distracters in unconstrained environments. In: Proceedings of Computer Vision and Pattern Recognition (CVPR), pp. 1177–1184. IEEE (2011)
7. Grabner, H., Bischof, H.: On-line boosting and vision. In: Proceedings of Computer Vision and Pattern Recognition (CVPR), pp. 260–267 (2006)
8. Ling, H.: Online robust image alignment via iterative convex optimization. In: Proceedings of Computer Vision and Pattern Recognition (CVPR), pp. 1808–1814. IEEE (2012)

9. Kalal, Z., Mikolajczyk, K., Matas, J.: Tracking-learning-detection. IEEE Trans. Pattern Anal. Mach. Intell. **34**(7), 1409–1422 (2012)
10. Henriques, J.F., Rui, C., Martins, P., et al.: High-speed tracking with kernelized correlation filters. IEEE Trans. Pattern Anal. Mach. Intell. **37**(3), 583–596 (2014)
11. Danelljan, M., Häger, G., Khan, F.S., et al.: Accurate scale estimation for robust visual tracking. In: British Machine Vision Conference, pp. 65.1–65.11 (2014)
12. Danelljan, M., Hager, G., Khan, F.S., et al.: Learning spatially regularized correlation filters for visual tracking. In: Proceedings of the International Conference on Computer Vision (ICCV), pp. 4310–4318. IEEE Computer Society (2015)
13. Wang, M., Liu, Y., Huang, Z.: Large margin object tracking with circulant feature maps. In: Proceedings of Computer Vision and Pattern Recognition (CVPR), Honolulu, Hawaii, pp. 4800–4808 (2017)
14. Bertinetto, L., Valmadre, J., Henriques, J.F., Vedaldi, A., Torr, P.H.S.: Fully-convolutional siamese networks for object tracking. In: Hua, G., Jégou, H. (eds.) ECCV 2016, Part II. LNCS, vol. 9914, pp. 850–865. Springer, Cham (2016). https://doi.org/10.1007/978-3-319-48881-3_56
15. Choi, J., Chang, H.J., Yun, S., et al.: Attentional correlation filter network for adaptive visual tracking. In: Proceedings of Computer Vision and Pattern Recognition (CVPR), pp. 4828–4837. IEEE (2017)
16. Wang, Q., Chen, F., Xu, W., Yang, M.-H.: Object tracking via partial least squares analysis. IEEE Trans. Image Process. **21**(10), 4454–4465 (2012)
17. Hare, S., et al.: Struck: structured output tracking with kernels. IEEE Trans. Pattern Anal. Mach. Intell. **38**(10), 2096–2109 (2015)
18. Kristan, M., et al.: The visual object tracking VOT2017 challenge results. In: IEEE International Conference on Computer Vision Workshop, pp. 1949–1972. IEEE Computer Society (2017)
19. Wu, Y., Lim, J., Yang, M.H.: Object tracking benchmark. IEEE Trans. Pattern Anal. Mach. Intell. **37**(9), 1834–1848 (2015)
20. Jiang, Z., Lin, Z., Davis, L.S.: Label consistent K-SVD: learning a discriminative dictionary for recognition. IEEE Trans. Pattern Anal. Mach. Intell. **35**(11), 2651–2664 (2013)
21. Li, Y., Zhu, J.: A scale adaptive kernel correlation filter tracker with feature integration. In: Agapito, L., Bronstein, M.M., Rother, C. (eds.) ECCV 2014, Part II. LNCS, vol. 8926, pp. 254–265. Springer, Cham (2015). https://doi.org/10.1007/978-3-319-16181-5_18
22. Jin, Z., Su, Z., Wu, H., et al.: Robust tracking via discriminative sparse feature selection. Vis. Comput. **31**(5), 575–588 (2015)

Oscillation Detection and Parameter-Adaptive Hedge Algorithm for Real-Time Visual Tracking

Bolin Lv, Xiaolong Zhou$^{(\boxtimes)}$, and Shengyong Chen

College of Computer Science and Technology,
ZheJiang University of Technology, Hangzhou, China
zxl@zjut.edu.cn

Abstract. Although correlation filter-based method performs high efficiency for visual tracking, its tracking precision may be greatly degraded when occlusion occurs. To remedy this, this paper proposes a new spectrum oscillation detection algorithm and an online learning strategy for real-time tracking. Firstly, to facilitate the tracking online learning to adjust weights itself, a weighted parameter-adaptive Hedge algorithm is presented to reduce the parameters of the adjustment. Secondly, since the spectrum of the correlation filter will fluctuate when occlusion occurs, a spectrum oscillation detection algorithm is proposed to detect the frequency spectrum response at target oscillation level. Thirdly, a backtracking algorithm is proposed to predict object position when the spectrum oscillation has been detected. Finally, an update index is introduced to determine whether the current frame is updated to improve tracking accuracy and robustness. Experiments conducted on VOT2016 and OTB-2015 demonstrate the good performance of the proposed tracking method and competitive performance against the state-of-the-art tracking methods.

Keywords: Visual tracking · Spectrum oscillation detection
Correlation filter · Online learning

1 Introduction

Tracking targets in video plays a significant role in many vision-based applications such as intelligent video surveillance, autonomous robots, visual navigation etc. Currently, although there is extensive literature on visual tracking and many advanced tracking methods have been proposed, it is still a challenging task to track target in real time especially when the target suffers from occlusion. Although many deep learning methods [1,2] could handle with occlusion problem to a certain extent, it is uneasy to deploy in real-world application due to the large computational burden.

Correlation filter (CF) based tracking methods have been proven a high efficient way to track target in real-time. In recent years, many improvements have

J.-H. Lai et al. (Eds.): PRCV 2018, LNCS 11259, pp. 233–244, 2018.
https://doi.org/10.1007/978-3-030-03341-5_20

Fig. 1. Tracking results comparison of our method with other state-of-the-art track-ers. **Our Staple ECO ECO-HC CSR-DCF VITAL SiameseFC SCT SRDCF DSST CREST --BACF   CFnet-conv1 --CFnet-conv2 --CFnet-conv5 --ACFN   ADNet-fast** (Color figure online)

been investigated, such as using multidimensional features [3], max-margin clas-sifiers [4], nonlinear kernel methods [5], scale estimation [6], multi-target [7], designing complex learning frameworks [8], and focusing on solving boundary effects [9,10], to achieve high accuracy and robustness. However, there is few literature coping well with occlusion scenes. Since classifiers tend to learn a dis-criminative boundary between positive and negative samples, the majority of the existing CF-based methods emphasize on the most discriminative samples. However, as the target appearance varies frame-by-frame in the whole video sequence, the most discriminative samples in the current frame may not persist over a long temporal span. Appearance changes caused by occlusion or out-of-plane rotation would easily result in model-drift, as current training samples may differ much from the previous ones. To alleviate this problem, existing trackers incrementally update the classifier through online sample collections. However, the occured noisy updates will bring the trackers drift problem. Therefore, it is crucial to develop a tracker that can track target with high accuracy when occlusion occurs and simultaneously achieve real-time performance.

In this paper, we propose an improved CF-based tracking method to han-dle with occlusion problem by investigating a feature weight adaptation algo-rithm and a spectrum oscillation detection algorithm. Figure 1 shows the tracking results of the proposed tracking method and some state-of-the-art methods in occlusion handling. With the improvement, the proposed method can success-fully track the target in occlusion with a speed of 70.8 fps.

1.1   Motivation

Although many factors can affect the performance of CF-based trackers, selection of effective features and model update strategy are the two key factors to be considered in this paper to alleviate model drift and occlusion.

Number and Proportion of Effective Features: Many high-dimensional features will cause the number of model parameters to be exponentially increased, which usually exceeds the dimensions of the input image. For example, C-COT [11] continuously updates about 800,000 parameters during the operation of the algorithm. However, because of the scarcity of tracking samples, the approach is easy to overfit. In addition, high-dimensional calculations require large computational cost.

The Model Update Strategy: Most CF-based trackers use indiscriminately updated strategies for each frame. In contrast, the latest work LMCF [12], uses a multi-peak detection algorithm to determine whether the model is updated. Inspired by this discovery, we believe that many algorithms are indifferently over-updated, such as sudden changes caused by scale changes, deformations, and out-of-plane rotations. This over-update strategy leads to less robustness.

1.2   Contributions

We propose a novel way to solve the above-mentioned problems and the corresponding contributions are sumarrized as follows.

(1) We propose a weight adaptive algorithm that reduces the parameters of the adjustment to a certain extent, which will facilitate the online learning to adaptively adjust weights.
(2) We design a spectrum oscillation detection algorithm that can detect the frequency spectrum response in target oscillation level.
(3) We present a backtracking algorithm to predict object position when spectrum oscillation occurs.
(4) We design a update index to determine whether the current frame is updated.

The comprehensive experiments show that our method can improve the tracking accuracy and robustness, especially when target suffers from occlusion. The tracking precision of our method ranks the 2nd in the VOT2016 dataset, which is higher than the newest ECO [13] and CSR-DCF [14] tracking methods. Moreover, our method can reach real-time requirement. In the OTB-2015 dataset, although our method is slower than those deep learning-based tracking methods, it outperforms the CF-based trackers (ECO,CSR-DCF [14]) especially in occlusion scenes.

2   Baseline Approach: Staple

In this paper, we propose to solve the problem of model drift in occlusion caused by inappropriate update strategies in the most advanced CF-based algorithms as well as the problem of feature weight adaptation. We use the recently developed Staple [15] algorithm as the baseline. The Staple algorithm ranks the fifth overall in the VOT2016 Challenge [16], and it is the only algorithm in the top five algorithms that achieves real-time performance. Unlike other CF-based algorithms using deep features, the Staple only uses two features including color and HOG features. The color features are employed to learn the target with deformation and motion blur, while the HOG features are incorporated to handle with illumination changes.

Here we briefly introduce the Staple algorithm. In frame t, the rectangle p_t that gives the target location in image x_t is chosen from a set S_t to maximize a score:

$$p_t = argmax_{p \in S_t} f(T(x_t, p); \theta_{t-1}) \tag{1}$$

The function T is an image transformation such that $f(T(x, p); \theta)$ assigns a score to the rectangular window p in image x according to the model parameters θ. The model parameters should be chosen to minimize a loss function $L(\theta; X_t)$ that depends on the previous images and the location of the object in those images $X_t = (x_i, p_i)_{i=1}^{t}$:

$$\theta_t = argmin_{\theta \in Q}(L(\theta; X_t) + \lambda R(\theta)) \tag{2}$$

The space of model parameters is denoted as Q. A regularisation term $R(\theta)$ with relative weight λ is used to limit model complexity and prevent over-fitting. The location p_1 of the object in the first frame is given. To achieve real-time performance, the functions f and L must be chosen not only to locate the object reliably and accurately, but also solve some problem effciently.

A origin score function that is a linear combination of template and histogram scores is then formulated.

$$f(x) = \gamma_{tmpl} f_{tmpl}(x) + \gamma_{hist} f_{hist}(x) \tag{3}$$

The template score is a linear function of a K-channel feature image $\phi_x : \tau \rightarrow \Re^K$, obtained from x and defined on a finite grid $\tau \subset \mathbf{Z}^2$:

$$f_{tmpl}(x; h) = \sum_{u \in \tau} h[u]^T \phi_x[u] \tag{4}$$

where the weight vector (or *template*) h is another K-channel image. The histogram score is computed from an M-channel feature image $\psi_x : \mathbf{H} \rightarrow \Re^M$, obtained from x and defined on a (different) finite grid $\mathbf{H} \subset \mathbf{Z}^2$:

$$f_{hist}(x; \beta) = g(\psi_x; \beta) \tag{5}$$

The histogram score is invariant to spatial permutations of its feature image, such that $g(\psi) = g(\prod \psi)$ for any permutation matrix $\prod$. We adopt a liner function of the (vetor-valued) average feature pixel

$$g(\psi; \beta) = \beta^T \left(\frac{1}{|\mathbf{H}|} \sum_{u \in \mathbf{H}} \psi[u] \right) \qquad (6)$$

3   Our Approach

In this paper, we mainly focus on improving the tracking accuracy and efficiency when target suffers from occlusion by proposing a novel algorithm with online adaptive learning and oscillation detection.

Online Adaptive Learning: Valid features selection plays a crucial role in the tracking results. We improve the standard parameter-free Hedge algorithm [17] to a parameter-adaptive algorithm. We revise the HDT [18] algorithm and apply it for real-time tracking.

Oscillation Detection and Backtracking: Through extensive experiments on correlation filtering, we have found that whenever an occluded or similarly interfering object appears, the spectral response graph tends to oscillate. The exsiting algorithms update the model at every frame, which may cause tracker learn something that should not be learned and thus cause the model drift and the tracking fail. To remedy this, we design a new detection algorithm and a target backtracking algorithm triggered with a certain probability.

3.1   Online Adaptive Learning

The standard parameter-free Hedege algorithm [17] is proposed to deal with the decision-theoretic online learning issue. In contrast, we propose to use const confidence weights γ and dynamic confidence weights w. In the every frame, a final result is made based on weighted decison of all trackers. The weights of trackers are then updated to reflect each tracker's decision loss. We predict the target position in the every frame by

$$f(x) = (\gamma_{tmpl} + w_{tmpl}) f_{tmpl}(x) + (\gamma_{hist} + w_{hist}) f_{hist}(x) \qquad (7)$$

Once the ultimate target position is predicted, every tracker will incur a loss. We define a new loss function in the frame t:

$$l_{tmpl}^t = |max(f_{tmpl}^t(x)) - f_{tmpl}^t(x_p)| \qquad (8)$$

$$l_{hist}^t = |max(f_{hist}^t(x)) - f_{hist}^t(x_p)| \qquad (9)$$

where $max()$ operates on a matrix and returns the largest value of the matrix and $f^t(x_p)$ denotes the vlaue at target position. Our algorithm generates a last weight distribution on all trackers by introducing a measure function defined by

$$m^t = \bar{l}^t - l^t \qquad (10)$$

where the weight average loss among all trackers is computed as $\bar{l}^t = \sum_{n=1}^{N} w_n^t l_n^t$.

By optimizing the cumulative measure

$$M^t = \sum_{\tau=1}^{t} m_\tau^t \tag{11}$$

We value the stability of tracker at frame t using

$$s^t = \frac{|l^t - \mu^t|}{\sigma^t} \tag{12}$$

where μ^t is the historic mean of $l^1, l^2, \ldots, l^t$ and σ^t is the standard variance of $l^1, l^2, \ldots, l^t$. A small s^t implies that this tracker tends to be more stable than the one with a larger s^t, and therefore we prefer a larger proportion on its current measure. In contrast, a larger s^t means that this tracker varies greatly. The proposed algorithm's result mainly depends on its historic information. Based on the principle, we define the following adaptive measure

$$M^t = (1 - \eta)M^t + \eta m^t \tag{13}$$

$$\eta = min(\delta, exp(-\rho s^t)) \tag{14}$$

where ρ is a scale factor and δ defines a maximum ratio on current measure to avoid that no historic information is premeditated.

Finally, we update the w by

$$w^{t+1} \propto \frac{M^t}{c} exp \frac{(M^t)^2}{2c} \tag{15}$$

where c is a scale parameter like in [17], which is determined by

$$\frac{1}{N} \sum_{n=1}^{N} exp(\frac{(M^t)^2}{2c}) = e \tag{16}$$

3.2   Oscillation Detection and Backtracking

We propose an oscillation detection algorithm to avoid model drift. As we know, frequency domain response function is a two-dimensional Gaussian function. For the extremum of function we have the following definition:

Definition 1. *If the domain X is a metric space then f is said to have a local (or relative) maximum point at the point x^* if there exists some $\epsilon > 0$ such that $f(x^*) \geq f(x)$ for all x in X within distance ϵ of x^*.*

To extract the position of the extreme value, we designed a mask operation, defined as

$$B = mask(f(x^*)) \tag{17}$$

The formulation indicates the position of the extreme value. Matrix B is a mask matrix consisting of **0** and **1**. Extreme value matrix equals to $f(x).{}^*B$. After getting all the extrema of the response graph, we extract the extremum according to a certain proportion of the maximum value. Then we define an oscillation index to show the level of oscillation in the current spectrum response graph. The index is defined by

$$index = \frac{|max(f(x^\star)) - min(f(x^\star))|^2}{avg(f(x^\star))} \tag{18}$$

where $avg()$ operates on a vector and returns the average value of the vector. If the updated $index$ is greater than the historical average by a certain percentage, we regard the current image has the updated value. Otherwise we will trigger our extra designed backtracking algorithm with a low probability. This algorithm is based on the position of the previous valid frame to estimate the position of the current object. The motion of the object between the consecutive frames can be modeled as uniform linear motion. We use the position predicted by the latest frame and then follow a certain amount of historical frames displacement to calculate the current position of the target:

$$P = P_{last} + \zeta avg(\triangle P) \tag{19}$$

where ζ is a scale parameter to avoid $avg(\triangle P)$ too big.

4 Experiments

In this section, we evaluate the proposed tracking method on two benchmark datasets: OTB-2015 dataset [19] and VOT-2016 [16]. The former is an extension of OTB-2013 [20] consisting of 100 video sequences and the latter includes 60 video sequences complied from a set of more than 300 videos. We compare our method with the baseline (Staple) and the state-of-the-art trackers respectively to show the superior performance on occlusion handling.

4.1 Baseline Comparison

For the VOT-2016 dataset, tracking performance is evaluated both in terms of accuracy (average overlap during successful tracking) and robustness (failure rate). The overall performance is evaluated using Expected Average Overlap (EAO) which accounts for both accuracy and robustness. For the OTB2015 dataset, the overall performance is evaluated using one-pass evaluation (OPE).

Table 1 shows the comparison of our method with the Staple method on the VOT2016 and OTB2015 datasets. The intergration of online adaptive learning, oscillation detection and backtracking into the baseline leads to a performance improvement and a significant speed up. The online adaptive learning improves the perfomance by a relative gain of 3.8% in Precision of OPE. Moreover, by incorporating the proposed model update strategy, our method achieves a Success of OPE with 0.742, leading to a final relative gain of 4.3% compared to the Staple method. In Table 1, for a fair comparison, we report the tracking speed

Table 1. Tracking performance comparison on the VOT2016 and OTB2015 datasets.

Item	Staple	Our
OTB2015 Success of OPE	0.699	0.742
OTB2015 Precision of OPE	0.784	0.82
VOT2016 Accuracy	0.54	0.55
VOT2016 Failures	1.42	1.16
Speed (fps)	56.7389	70.8563

measured on a same database (OTB2015) and a single CPU. The proposed model update strategy improves the speed of the tracker and achieves 70.8 fps that is faster than the baseline method. Moreover, online adaptive learning algorithm makes better the perfomance by a relative gain of 1% in Accuracy of VOT2016, and the model update strategy reduces the Failures (robustness) from 1.42 to 1.16 for VOT2016. Obviously, our method systematically improves both accuracy and efficiency.

4.2   State-of-the-Art Comparison

We also compare our method with the state-of-the-art trackers on two challenging tracking benchmarks.

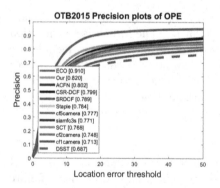

Fig. 2. Precision plot on the OTB2015   **Fig. 3.** Success plots on the OTB2015

Table 2. Tracking speed comparion on OTB2015 dataset

Methods	Our	Staple	SRDCF	DSST	ECO	CFnet	ACFN	CSR-DCF	SCT4
Speed(FPS)	70.8	56.7	3	15.2	2.1	13	15	13	40

For OTB2015 Dataset: We compare our tracker with 9 state-of-the-art methods: ECO [13], ACFN [21], CFnet(conv1,2,5) [2], CSR-DCF [14], SRDCF [9], Staple [15], SiameseFC [22], SCT [23], DSST [24], MCPF [25] and CREST [1].

Figures 2 and 3 show the Precision and Success plots over all the 100 videos in the OTB-2015 datasets. Our method ranks the 2nd both in precision and success plots. In terms of accuracy and success rate, we have absolute advantages in speed, accuracy, and robustness compared to other methods (ACFN [21], CFnet(conv1,2,5) [2], CSR-DCF [14], SRDCF [9], Staple [15], SiameseFC [22], SCT [23] and DSST [24]). Although the ECO [13] achieves a slightly higher score than ours in terms of accuracy and robustness, it requires a large computational cost and cannot achieve real-time performance. In contrast, our method can track target in real-time (as shown in Table 2). Particularly, our method ranks the 2nd and 3rd in Precision and Success plots respectively when tracking the target in occlusion (see Figs. 4 and 5).

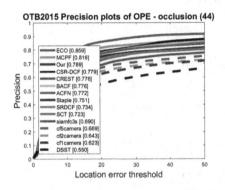

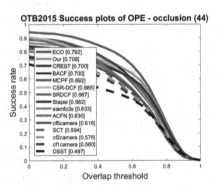

Fig. 4. Precision plot (occlusion)   **Fig. 5.** Success plots (occlusion)

For VOT2016 Dataset: Table 3 shows the comparison of AR ranking (accuracy and robustness) with the top-ranked treackers in the VOT2016 challenge: TCNN [26], Staple [15], CCOT [11], SSAT [27], MLDF [28], DDC [29], ECO [13], ECO-HC [13] and CSR-DCF [14]. Our tracker achieves the 2nd accuracy of 1.70 while maintaining a competitive robustness and the highest speed. Figures 6 and 7 illustrate the occlusion tracking performance and EO curves, which show the superiority of our tracker in tracking target during occlusion period. Different from the first two top trackers CSRDCF and ECO that use deep features to learn occlusion model with a high computational cost, our tracker only uses the color and HOG features with a very fast tracking speed (around 70.8 fps).

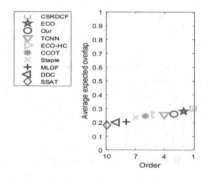
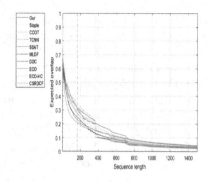

Fig. 6. Expected overlap scores for baseline (occlusion)

Fig. 7. Expected overlap curves for baseline (occlusion)

Table 3. AR ranking

	Baseline		Overall	
	Accuracy	Robustness	Accuracy	Robustness
Our	1.70	3.70	1.70	3.70
Staple	2.13	4.37	2.13	4.37
CCOT	2.33	2.72	2.33	2.72
TCNN	1.93	3.60	1.93	3.60
SSAT	1.67	3.50	1.67	3.50
MLDF	3.77	2.63	3.77	2.63
DDC	2.20	4.17	2.20	4.17
ECO	2.20	2.37	2.20	2.37
ECO-HC	2.23	3.57	2.23	3.57
CSR-DCF	2.87	2.68	2.87	2.68

5   Conclusions

In this paper, we have proposed a novel visual tracking method by introducing a parameter-adaptive Hedge algorithm and an oscillation detection and backtracking algorithm to accurately and robustly track the target especially when the occlusion occurs. We have improved the standard parameter-free Hedge algorithm to a parameter-adaptive version that reduced the parameters of the adjustment, which facilitated the online learning adaptively adjust the weights. We have designed a spectrum oscillation detection algorithm to detect the frequecy spectrum response in target oscillation level. We also have proposed a backtracking algorithm to predict object position when spectrum oscillation occurs and designed a update index to determine the update status. We have conducted experiments on the OTB2015 and VOT2016 datasets and compared the proposed method with the state-of-the-art trackers. Experimental results have demonstrated the good performance of the proposed method both in accuracy and efficiency, especially during the occlusion tracking.

Acknowledgement. This work was supported in part by National Natural Science Foundation of China (61876168, 61403342, 61325019, 61603341), Hubei Key Laboratory of Intelligent Vision Based Monitoring for Hydroelectric Engineering (2017SDSJ03), and Zhejiang Provincial Natural Science Foundation of China (LY18F030020).

References

1. Song, Y., Ma, C., Gong, L., Zhang, J., Lau, R., Yang, M.-H.: CREST: convolutional residual learning for visual tracking. In: ICCV (2017)
2. Valmadre, J., Bertinetto, L., Henriques, J.F., Vedaldi, A., Torr, P.H.S.: End-to-end representation learning for correlation filter based tracking. In: CVPR (2017)
3. Danelljan, M., Shahbaz Khan, F., Felsberg, M., van de Weijer, J.: Adaptive color attributes for real-time visual tracking. In: CVPR (2014)
4. Zuo, W., Wu, X., Lin, L., Zhang, L., Yang, M.-H.: Learning support correlation filters for visual tracking (2016). arXiv:1601.06032
5. Henriques, J.F., Caseiro, R., Martins, P., Batista, J.: High-speed tracking with kernelized correlation filters. TPAMI **37**(3), 583–596 (2015)
6. Danelljan, M., Häger, G., Khan, F.S., Felsberg, M.: Discriminative scale space tracking. TPAMI **39**(8), 1561–1575 (2017)
7. Zhou, X., Li, Y.F., He, B., Bai, T.: GM-PHD-based multi-target visual tracking using entropy distribution and game theory. IEEE Trans. Ind. Inform. **10**(2), 1064–1076 (2014)
8. Galoogahi, H.K., Fagg, A., Lucey, S.: Learning background-aware correlation filters for visual tracking. In: ICCV (2017)
9. Danelljan, M., Häger, G., Shahbaz Khan, F., Felsberg, M.: Learning spatially regularized correlation filters for visual tracking. In: ICCV (2015)
10. Galoogahi, H.K., Sim, T., Lucey, S.: Correlation filters with limited boundaries. In: CVPR (2015)
11. Danelljan, M., Robinson, A., Shahbaz Khan, F., Felsberg, M.: Beyond correlation filters: learning continuous convolution operators for visual tracking. In: Leibe, B., Matas, J., Sebe, N., Welling, M. (eds.) ECCV 2016, Part V. LNCS, vol. 9909, pp. 472–488. Springer, Cham (2016). https://doi.org/10.1007/978-3-319-46454-1_29
12. Wang, M., Liu, Y., Huang, Z.: Large margin object tracking with circulant feature maps. In: CVPR (2017)
13. Danelljan, M., Bhat, G., Khan, F.S., Felsberg, M.: ECO: efficient convolution operators for tracking. In: CVPR (2017)
14. Lukežič, A., Vojíř, T., Čehovin, L., Matas, J., Kristan, M.: Discriminative Correlation filter with channel and spatial reliability. In: CVPR (2017)
15. Bertinetto, L., Valmadre, J., Golodetz, S., Miksik, O., Torr, P.H.S.: Staple: complementary learners for real-time tracking. In: CVPR (2016)
16. Kristan, M., et al.: The visual object tracking VOT2016 challenge results. In: Hua, G., Jégou, H. (eds.) ECCV 2016, Part II. LNCS, vol. 9914, pp. 777–823. Springer, Cham (2016). https://doi.org/10.1007/978-3-319-48881-3_54

17. Chaudhuri, K., Freund, Y., Hsu, D.: A parameter-free hedging algorithm. In: NIPS (2009)
18. Qi, Y., et al.: Hedged deep tracking/hedging deep features for visual tracking. In: CVPR (2016)
19. Wu, Y., Lim, J., Yang, M.-H.: Object tracking benchmark. IEEE Trans. Pattern Anal. Mach. Intell. **37**(9), 1834–1848 (2015)
20. Wu, Y., Lim, J., Yang, M.-H.: Online object tracking: a benchmark. In: CVPR (2013)
21. Choi, J., Chang, H.J., Yun, S., Fischer, T., Demiris, Y., Choi, J.Y.: Attentional correlation filter network for adaptive visual tracking. In: CVPR (2017)
22. Bertinetto, L., Valmadre, J., Henriques, J.F., Vedaldi, A., Torr, P.H.S.: Fully-convolutional siamese networks for object tracking. In: Hua, G., Jégou, H. (eds.) ECCV 2016, Part II. LNCS, vol. 9914, pp. 850–865. Springer, Cham (2016). https://doi.org/10.1007/978-3-319-48881-3_56
23. Choi, J., Chang, H.J., Jeong, J., Demiris, Y., Choi, J.Y.: Visual tracking using attention-modulated disintegration and integration. In: CVPR (2016)
24. Danelljan, M., Häger, G., Khan, F.S., Felsberg, M.: Accurate scale estimation for robust visual tracking. In: BMVC (2014)
25. Zhang, T., Xu, C., Yang, M.-H.: Multi-task correlation particle filter for robust object tracking. In: CVPR (2017)
26. Nam, H., Baek, M., Han, B.: Modeling and propagating CNNs in a tree structure for visual tracking (2016). arXiv preprint: arXiv:1608.07242
27. Qi, Y., Qin, L., Zhang, S., Huang, Q.: Scale-and-state aware tracker. In: ECCV Workshops (2016)
28. Nam, H., Han, B.: Learning multi-domain convolutional neural networks for visual tracking. In: CVPR (2016)
29. Gao, J., Zhang, T., Xu, C., Liu, B.: Discriminative deep correlation tracking. In: ECCV Workshops (2016)

Asymmetrical Reverse Connection and Smooth-NMS for Object Detection

Juan Peng[1]([⊠]), Zhicheng Wang[1], Xuan Lv[2], Gang Wei[1],
Jingjing Fei[1], and Hongwei Zhang[1]

[1] Research Center of CAD, Tongji University, Shanghai,
People's Republic of China
{1631726,zhichengwang,weigang,feijingjing,
1631727}@tongji.edu.cn
[2] Chongqing Land Resources Housing Surveying and Planning Institute,
Chongqing 401121, China
shixuanlv305@126.com

Abstract. In this paper, we propose a new network structure, a more efficient object detection framework. Inspired by the original RON, we also joint the region-based and region-free methodologies of object detection. There is a lifting space in the accuracy of the original RON, so we design the following two structures: (a) design a new reverse connection structure, which can obtain much more information in small object detection; (b) design a new inception structure based on asymmetric convolution to improve the efficiency of object detectors. The conventional of non maximum suppression is replaced by more efficient Smooth-NMS in the object detection phase. With the use of low resolution 320 * 320 input size, the new network structure achieved 75.6% mAP (our method is 1.2% higher than the original RON) and 71.8% mAP on the standard PASCAL VOC 2007 and 2012 datasets respectively. The experimental results show that our method can generate higher detection accuracy.

Keywords: Object detection · Region proposal · Convolutional neural network

1 Introduction

In recent years, with the emergence of a variety of deep networks, the speed and accuracy of the CNN-based object detector has been improved to a certain extent. The mainstream object detectors based on CNN are divided into two categories: the one-stage based detector [2–4] and the two-stage detector [1, 5]. Two-stage detector is divided into two stages: the first stage generates a large number of candidate interest regions, and the second stage is to identify, classify and locate these candidate regions. One-stage detector regards object detector as single shot problem directly, straight from image pixels to bounding box coordinates, and the detector is usually able to achieve high speed. Recently the most popular one-stage networks, such as YOLO [5] and SSD [1], demonstrate promising results and yield faster detectors with accuracy higher about 10%–40% is relative to state-of-the-art two-stage methods. However, the two-stage detector generates a large number of candidate proposal boxes in the first stage,

J.-H. Lai et al. (Eds.): PRCV 2018, LNCS 11259, pp. 245–259, 2018.
https://doi.org/10.1007/978-3-030-03341-5_21

the speed of detection is relatively slow but the rate of accuracy is higher. For example, the two-stage detector consistently achieves top accuracy on the challenging COCO benchmark [6].

Inspired by the two mainstream object detection models mentioned above, we want to ensure that the frame is small and exquisite (reduce the number of parameters), so we try to use a new network [7, 9] model as mentioned below. In the RON framework, we found a reverse connection and the objectness prior [8, 9] are proposed, which are combined successfully. The purpose of reverse connection is to get the default boxes with multi-scales and aspect ratios extracted from the feature map, however only a small proportion of them can be covered to the detected targets. In other words, that is why the running speed of the two-stage detector is slower than that of one-stage. In the process of optimization, Fast R-CNN [10] and Faster R-CNN [4] generally use selective search and region proposal network (RPN) respectively. However, the RPN network will do a lot of repetitive calculations in the detection phase and that will pose a question to us: how to reduce the calculation? RON proposes to use the objectness prior instead of the new proposal region which first calculates the approximate position of the object at multi-scales and takes this position as a reference. At the time of detection, a volume layer behind softmax function calculates the location of each box object, and then matches with the reference before. The performance and accuracy of the method based on the objectness prior are improved from the experimental data.

2   Related Works

Object detection is the process of finding and classifying objects in a picture.

Traditional Methods. The following models are two most popular and widely used models in traditional object detection. The first is the Viola-Jones framework proposed by Viola and Jones [11]. This method is relatively simple and the camera with low processing ability can handle real time facial recognition tasks. It is implemented by using Haar features to generate many simple binary classifiers. These classifiers are evaluated by a multi-scale cascaded sliding window, and the evaluation is completed in advance once the wrong classification results are encountered. Another traditional method is using the direction gradient histogram (HOG) feature and support vector machine to classify. This method still needs a multi-scale sliding window. Although it is better than Viola-Jones, but the speed is much slower.

Deep learning, one field of machine learning, has defeated other traditional models with its excellent performance, especially in computer vision. Over Feat [12], proposed by New York University, is one of the earliest methods using deep learning for object detection. They proposed an algorithm that uses a convolutional neural network (CNN) to deal with multi-scales sliding windows. After that, Ross Girshick and colleagues from University of California published R-CNN [2]. This method has three main steps: using candidate region method to extract objects; using CNN to extract features from each region; using SVM [13] to classify each region. Although R-CNN can achieve good recognition results, it has a lot of problems of training. The main problem is that the training model produces a large number of redundant candidates.

Shortly after R-CNN was published, Ross Girshick released a version of deep learning (Fast R-CNN) which is used widely nowadays. The biggest disadvantage of Fast R-CNN is that this model still relies on Selective Search. Shortly after Fast R-CNN was put forward, Redmon and other authors published a paper named You Only Look Once [5]. YOLO proposed a simple convolutional neural network with both high accuracy and fast speed, and realized real-time object detection for the first time. But YOLO has a bad effect on small objects. Then, Shaoqing Ren published Faster R-CNN [4], the third iteration of R-CNN. In order to make it independent of Selective Search, the Region Proposal Network was added to it, which enabled the model to achieve end-to-end training completely. Soon the researchers proposed SSD and R-FCN [14]. The former uses a multi-scale convolutional feature map on the basis of YOLO to improve both accuracy and speed. The latter is based on the architecture of Faster R-CNN, but only the convolutional network is used.

3   Network Architecture

This section describes the original RON object detection framework and our architecture. We first introduce the improved reverse connection on traditional CNNs in Sect. 3.1. Then in Sect. 3.2, we will explain how to improve the inception structure to produce abundant features on different scales. Next, we present a new method for suppressing overlapping bounding boxes during the detection phase in Sect. 3.3.

This paper is an improvement based on the RON model. We make the improvements as follows (1) The asymmetric convolution kernel of $1 \times 3, 3 \times 1$ is added in the process of reverse connection. (2) Improving the structure of Inception, to replace the original Inception structure with the structure of Inception designed in this paper. (3) Using improved and more efficient NMS instead of NMS to get higher average accuracy in the object detection phase (Fig. 1).

3.1   Improvement of Reverse Connection

As mentioned above, the main role of reverse connection is to make the previous features easier to get more information, so we add $1 \times 3, 3 \times 1$ convolutional kernel based on the original reverse connection model, as is shown in Fig. 2.

Firstly, the result of the next layer (rpn_lrn n + 1) is deconvolved. The convolutional kernel is 2×2 and stride is 2, which is used as the feature map for reverse fusion. Then, the convolutional layers from the 4th to the 6th are respectively operated through a convolutional kernel size of $1 \times 3, 3 \times 1$, a stride of 1, and a pad of 1, and then, convolution kernels 3×3, stride 1, pad 0 convolution operation, and then BN, Scale and Relu will get processed respectively. The results obtained will be a fusion feature map. Finally, we get the final result of rpn_lrn n layer by doing the sum operation of the two feature maps, and get four kinds of inverse fusion features of different sizes. The last layer (rpn_lrn 7 in this paper) is a feature fusion map obtained by convolving a 2×2 convolutional kernel with stride 2, as is shown in Fig. 3.

In contrast to single-level object detection [15], the positioning of multi-scale object detection on an object makes the result more obvious. Further more, reverse connection

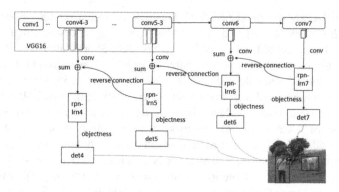

Fig. 1. The entire network structure of our method. The first part of the RON model is based on VGG16, and the three fully connected layers of VGG16 are changed into two convolutional layers, and the last fully connected layer is discarded. Given an input image, resize it. The network firstly generate feature maps. at each detection scale: (a) adds reverse connection; (b) generates objectness prior; (c) detects object on its corresponding CNN scales and locations. Finally, all detection results are fused and selected with smooth non-maximum suppression.

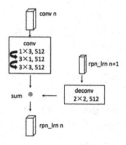

Fig. 2. Improved reverse connection structure model. Add 1×3, 3×1 convolutional kernel to it. Although the detection speed is several milliseconds slow, the details are fully expressed in the process of information transmission, which is conducive to get richer information and identify small objects better.

Fig. 3. Flow chart of the last layer of the reverse fusion feature

can be learned in which case the previous layer can get more semantic information, as reflected in the experimental results in the back.

3.2 Improvement of Inception

Inception structure model [16, 17] first appeared in the Google Net model. This structural model helped Google Net win the category test in the ILSVRC 2014 competition, which thrusted the detection and recognition of objects to a higher level.

The structure uses convolutional kernels of different scales, thus generating different scale of receptive fields, and finally the multi-scale feature fusion map can be obtained by splicing. The purpose of using convolutional kernel of 1×1, 3×3 and 5×5 is convenient alignment. When the step size is set to 1 and the pads are set to 0, 1 and 2 in turn, the feature dimensions obtained after performing the convolution operation will be the same, so that the obtained features can be spliced and fused together. However, the deeper the network, the more abstract the features will be, and the receptive field of each feature is also getting larger. Therefore, the deeper layers of the network, the more convolutional operations with convolutional kernel sizes of 5×5 and 3×3 will be. However, the computational complexity of 5×5 convolutional kernel is also very high, which makes it easy to lead to program collapse in the calculation process, and the processing efficiency will be reduced accordingly. Therefore, by referring to NIN2 (Network In Network [18]), 1×1 convolutional kernel is added to reduce the dimension, thus reducing the convolution parameters and saving operation time. The main purpose of using Inception is to find the approximate optimal local sparse structure. Besides, by using dense matrix for high-performance computing, it is easy to improve the efficiency of the operation.

The original RON adopts the same two consecutive Inception structures, which are the results of rpn_lrn n convolutional kernel 3×3, pad 1, step stride 1 and convolution kernel 1×1, pad 0, step stride 1 convolutional operation (Fig. 4).

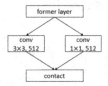

Fig. 4. The RON Inception structure model

In the above content, we use convolutional kernels of the same length and width. Whether we can use the rectangular convolutional kernel with different length and width for information transfer, such as the $n \times 1$ convolutional kernel. To verify this, we have improved the RON Inception structural by adding convolutional kernels of 1×3 and 3×1. The improved structural model can diversify the extracted features. On the other hand, it keeps the structure of RON's Inception. Finally, the splicing makes the expression of the features more detailed, as is shown in Fig. 5.

3.3   Smooth-NMS Algorithm

In the process of object detection, many overlapping bounding boxes will be generated. The Non-maximum suppression [19] algorithm will be used to suppress the boxes with obvious overlapping areas. By sorting the score of the bounding boxes from high to low, the boxes with high score will be retained. This method will improve the average accuracy of the object detection.

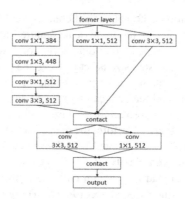

Fig. 5. Improved Inception Structural. adding convolutional kernels of 1×3 and 3×1.

The NMS algorithm filters the bounding box by the user-set threshold. The main problem with the original NMS is that the algorithm resets the score of overlapping boundary boxes within the threshold to 0. If there is a valid object within the overlapping areas, the result will miss a object, which reduces the average accuracy of the algorithm. To solve this problem, we designed a function to smoothly attenuate the score of the bounding box with a large overlapping area instead of resetting it to 0. The core function of our proposed Smooth-NMS algorithm is shown in Eq. 1, which is based on the improvement of the original NMS

$$
s_i = \begin{cases} s_i, & iou(M, b_i < N_t) \\ s_i\left(1 - (iou(M, b_i))^2\right), & iou(M, b_i \geq N_t) \end{cases} \tag{1}
$$

In the above equation, s_i represents the score of the bounding box, $iou(M, b_i)$ represents the overlap threshold calculated during detection, and Nt represents the overlap threshold set by the user. The simple summary is that within a range of overlapping thresholds that are greater than a set value, if a bounding box has a large area of overlap, its score will be lower. If the overlap of the border box is small, then its score will be lower too, but higher than the larger overlapping method. Compared with the original method, our method is the same in time original complexity. Suppose there are N bounding boxes in the picture, then the time complexity is $\theta(N^2)$. The new method does not affect the speed of detection, nor require retraining the model. Experiments show that using the network model designed in this paper for object detection, Smooth-NMS increases the average accuracy by approximately one percentage point over the original NMS on the voc2007 data set. Figure 6 shows the experimental result of the Smooth-NMS algorithm. The left side of the figure is the result of the original NMS, and the right side is Smooth-NMS's result.

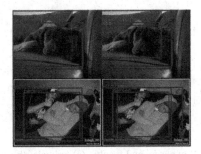

Fig. 6. The experimental results of Smooth-NMS.

4 Experiment

4.1 Experimental Environment

This experiment was performed under the Ubuntu16.04 operating system and used the deep learning framework of the caffe GPU version. We used the NVIDIA GTX1080 GPU to train the model. All experiments are based on VGG16 network. For data sets, we mainly used PASCAL VOC 2007 and PASCAL VOC 2012 for training and testing.

4.2 The Result on PASCAL VOC 2007

We used a learning rate of 10^{-3} for the previous 90k iterations. In the next 90k iterations we reduced the learning rate to 10^{-4}. In the last 40k iterations, the learning rate dropped to 10^{-5}. According to the GPU memory capacity, for a 320×320 image, we set the batch size to 12, the momentum parameter to 0.9, and the weight attenuation to 0.0005. Experimental results show that when the size of the training set image is 320×320, our method is better than other methods such as SSD, RON and Faster R-CNN. As the original RON, we use the precision and recall rate to evaluate the quality of the results.

In this experiment, we classified the 20 categories of PASCAL VOC 2007 test set into three categories to demonstrate the precision-recall experimental results, which are animals, vehicles and furniture. Among them, bird, cat, cow, dog, horse, person and sheep are in the animal category. Bottle, chair, dining table, sofa, TV monitor and potted plant are in the furniture category. Aero plane, bicycle, boat, motor, bike and train are in the vehicles category, as are shown in Fig. 7.

The model is better at detecting animal categories and vehicle categories than furniture categories. Figure 8 shows the detection of animals, vehicles and furniture exhibited by this method in the VOC 2007 test suite. The images show the cumulative scores for Correct Detection (Cor), errors due to poor bounding box location (LOC), Similar categories confused (Sim), Background related (BG) and others cumulative scores (Oth). The red real line indicates that the "strong" standard (0.5 jaccard overlap) recall changes with the increasing of the number of detection. The red dotted line represents the "weak" standard (0.1 jaccard overlap). The testing tools we used are uniformly provided by [20].

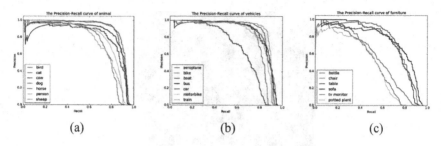

Fig. 7. The precision-recall experimental results, (a) animals, (b) vehicles and (c) furniture

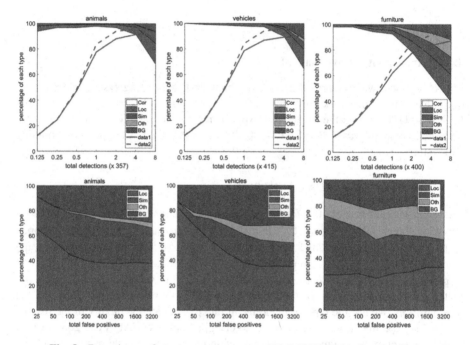

Fig. 8. Detection performance on the test set VOC 2007 (Color figure online)

In order to ensure the fairness of the experimental results, In this model we also used the training set of VOC 2007 and VOC 2012 to train the model, and the test set uses the VOC 2007. Testing and error analysis of the overall experimental results in 20 categories by the diagnosis code [7] shows the proportion of Cor, Loc, Sim, Oth, and BG. Figure 9 shows the test results of Faster R-CNN [14] on VOC07+12 dataset, of which BG accounts for 11.6%, Loc 8.1%, Cor 77.1%, Sim 2% and Oth 1.3%. Figure 10 shows the test results of our method. The proportion of BG is 5%, Loc 8%, Cor 81%, Sim 4% and Oth 2%.

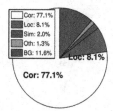

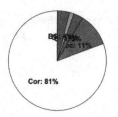

Fig. 9. The test results of Faster R-CNN on VOC07+12 dataset. BG accounts for 11.6%, Loc 8.1%, Cor 77.1%, Sim 2% and Oth 1.3%

Fig. 10. The test results of our method. The proportion of BG is 5%, Loc 8%, Cor 81%, Sim 4% and Oth 2%

It can be seen from the above comparison chart that the method in this paper proves better than Faster R-CNN. We can also use the diagnostic code to test the sensitivity degree of the model to the size of the bounding box, as shown in Fig. 11, which shows that our model is very sensitive to the size of the bounding box. The figure shows the effect of the bounding box area for each category on the test result. It can be seen from the figure that the model in this paper will be better at detecting the large bounding box. But compared with SSD, our detection of small object is also better than SSD. Because our method also considers aspect ratio, this method has better detection effect on objects when they have different aspect ratios. Figure 12 shows the effect of different aspect ratios on detection results. It can be seen from the above figure that the method of this paper is better for the detection of high, medium and wide aspect ratios.

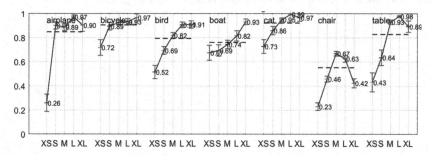

Fig. 11. The influence of the bounding box area on the test results. Where XS is for very small, S for small, M for medium, L for large, and XL for very large.

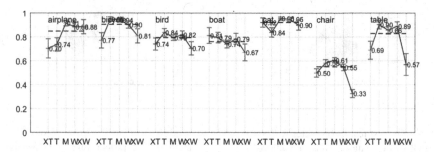

Fig. 12. Effect of aspect ratio on the detection results. XT is for extremely high or very narrow, T for high, M for medium, W for wide, XW for extremely wide.

In this experiment environment, it takes 2 GB memory to test the pictures, and the detection speed is 20FPS. This method promises good applicability in real-time detection. Table 1 shows the test results of VOC 2007 test set.

4.3   The Result on PASCAL VOC 2012

In this paper, we use the evaluation platform of Pascal VOC 2012 competition official website to test this method. The comp4 part of evaluation platform is suitable for the evaluation of the object detection method in this paper. We use VOC 2007 and VOC 2012 training set to train the model. The training models and parameters are the same as those in the last section. The VOC 2012 test set is tested with the same model. The result is shown in Table 2. This method has a good effect compared with the classical methods such as Fast R-CNN, Faster R-CNN, Hyper Net, and SSD. The Table 2 is the comparison between our experimental results and others' experimental results. The size of the experimental data used in this paper is 320 * 320 (Fig. 13).

Table 1. Detection results on the PASCAL VOC 2007 test set

Method	mAP	aero	bike	bird	boat	bottle	bus	car	cat	chair	cow	table	dog	horse	mbike	person	plant	sheep	sofa	train	tv
Fast R-CNN	70.0	77.0	78.1	69.3	59.4	38.3	81.6	78.6	86.7	42.8	78.8	68.9	84.7	82.0	76.6	69.9	31.8	70.1	74.8	80.4	70.4
Faster R-CNN	73.2	76.5	79.0	70.9	65.5	52.1	83.1	**84.7**	86.4	52.0	81.9	65.7	**84.8**	84.6	77.5	76.7	38.8	73.6	73.9	83.0	72.6
SSD	72.1	75.2	79.8	70.5	62.5	41.3	81.1	80.8	86.4	51.5	74.3	**72.3**	83.5	84.6	80.6	74.5	46.0	71.4	73.8	83.0	72.6
RON	74.2	75.7	79.4	**74.8**	66.1	53.2	83.7	83.6	85.8	**55.8**	79.5	69.5	84.5	81.7	**83.1**	76.1	49.2	73.8	75.2	80.3	72.5
Our method	**75.6**	**78.9**	**84.8**	74.0	**66.2**	**53.4**	**84.0**	83.5	**87.0**	55.2	**82.2**	71.7	83.2	**86.3**	81.5	**77.8**	**49.7**	**75.5**	**77.0**	**86.2**	**74.3**

Table 2. Detection results on the PASCAL VOC 2012 test set

Method	mAP	aero	bike	bird	boat	bottle	bus	car	cat	chair	cow	table	dog	horse	mbike	person	plant	sheep	sofa	train	tv
Fast R-CNN	68.4	82.3	78.4	70.8	52.3	38.7	77.8	71.6	**89.3**	44.2	73.0	55.0	**87.5**	80.5	80.8	72.0	35.1	68.3	65.7	80.4	64.2
Faster R-CNN	70.4	84.9	**79.8**	**74.3**	53.9	49.8	77.5	75.9	88.5	45.6	77.1	55.3	86.9	**81.7**	80.9	79.6	40.1	72.6	60.9	81.2	61.5
Hyper Net	71.4	84.2	78.5	73.6	55.6	**53.7**	78.7	**79.8**	87.7	49.6	74.9	52.1	86.0	**81.7**	**83.3**	**81.8**	**48.6**	73.5	59.4	79.9	65.7
SSD	70.3	84.2	76.3	69.6	53.2	40.8	78.5	73.6	88.0	50.5	73.5	**61.7**	85.8	80.6	81.2	77.5	44.3	73.2	66.7	81.1	65.8
RON	71.7	84.1	78.1	71.0	56.8	46.9	**79.0**	74.7	87.5	**52.5**	75.9	60.2	84.8	79.9	82.9	78.6	47.0	75.7	66.9	82.6	68.4
Our method	**71.8**	**85.8**	77.9	70.7	**58.7**	45.8	**79.0**	74.3	89.0	51.5	**77.3**	57.3	86.7	80.8	82.0	79.0	45.4	**75.8**	**67.2**	**82.7**	**68.6**

Fig. 13. The results of our method on PASCAL VOC 2007

5 Conclusion

This paper first introduces the RON-based [9] object detection method, generally introduces the overall flow of the method. Then we introduce the improvement of these modules in reverse connection, objectness prior, Non-Maximum suppression. Finally, we tested the improved model on the PASCAL VOC 2007 and PASCAL VOC 2012. Besides, we analyzed the test results in detail with the help of the tools provided by [7]. In addition, we also analyzed the RON, Faster R-CNN, and Fast RCNN in contrast to the more cutting-edge approaches to CNN and SSD in recent years. We used a pre-trained VGG 16 network and trained on the same dataset. It proved that our method in this paper have more advantages than other methods in recognition accuracy and time performance.

Acknowledgments. The authors would like to express their gratitude to the anonymous reviewers for their valuable comments and suggestions to improve the quality of this paper. This work is supported by the Fundamental Research Funds for the Central Universities and Science and Technology Innovation Project of Shanghai under Grant 16111107602.

References

1. Liu, W., et al.: SSD: single shot MultiBox detector. In: Leibe, B., Matas, J., Sebe, N., Welling, M. (eds.) ECCV 2016, Part I. LNCS, vol. 9905, pp. 21–37. Springer, Cham (2016). https://doi.org/10.1007/978-3-319-46448-0_2
2. Girshick, R., Donahue, J., Darrell, T., et al.: Rich feature hierarchies for accurate object detection and semantic segmentation. In: CVPR, pp. 580–587 (2013)
3. Kong, T., Yao, A., Chen, Y., et al.: HyperNet: towards accurate region proposal generation and joint object detection. In: CVPR, pp. 845–853 (2016)
4. Ren, S., He, K., Girshick, R., et al.: Faster R-CNN: towards real-time object detection with region proposal networks. IEEE Trans. Pattern Anal. Mach. Intell. 39(6), 1137–1149 (2017)
5. Redmon, J., Divvala, S., Girshick, R., et al.: You only look once: unified, real-time object detection. In: IEEE Conference on Computer Vision and Pattern Recognition, CVPR, pp. 779–788. IEEE Computer Society (2016)
6. Lin, T.-Y., et al.: Microsoft COCO: common objects in context. In: Fleet, D., Pajdla, T., Schiele, B., Tuytelaars, T. (eds.) ECCV 2014. LNCS, vol. 8693, pp. 740–755. Springer, Cham (2014). https://doi.org/10.1007/978-3-319-10602-1_48
7. He, K., et al.: Deep residual learning for image recognition. In: Proceedings of the IEEE Conference on Computer Vision and Pattern Recognition (2016)
8. Bell, S., et al.: Inside-outside net: detecting objects in context with skip pooling and recurrent neural networks. In: Proceedings of the IEEE Conference on Computer Vision and Pattern Recognition (2016)
9. Kong, T., et al.: Ron: reverse connection with objectness prior networks for object detection. In: IEEE Conference on Computer Vision and Pattern Recognition (2017)
10. Girshick, R.: Fast R-CNN. Computer Science (2015)
11. Jones, M.J., Viola, P.: Robust real-time object detection. Int. J. Comput. Vis. 57(2), 87 (2001)
12. Sermanet, P., Eigen, D., Zhang, X., et al.: OverFeat: integrated recognition, localization and detection using convolutional networks. Eprint Arxiv (2013)
13. Ukil, A.: Support vector machine. Comput. Sci. 1(4), 1–28 (2002)
14. Dai, J., Li, Y., He, K., et al.: R-FCN: object detection via region-based fully convolutional networks (2016)
15. Kong, T., et al.: Hypernet: towards accurate region proposal generation and joint object detection. In: Proceedings of the IEEE Conference on Computer Vision and Pattern Recognition (2015)
16. Szegedy, C., et al.: Going deeper with convolutions. In: Proceedings of the IEEE Conference on Computer Vision and Pattern Recognition (2016)
17. Szegedy, C., et al.: Rethinking the inception architecture for computer vision. In: Proceedings of the IEEE Conference on Computer Vision and Pattern Recognition (2016)
18. Lin, M., Chen, Q., Yan, S.: Network in network. Computer Science (2013)

19. Hosang, J., Benenson, R., Schiele, B.: A convnet for non-maximum suppression. In: Rosenhahn, B., Andres, B. (eds.) GCPR 2016. LNCS, vol. 9796, pp. 192–204. Springer, Cham (2016). https://doi.org/10.1007/978-3-319-45886-1_16
20. Hoiem, D., Chodpathumwan, Y., Dai, Q.: Diagnosing error in object detectors. In: Fitzgibbon, A., Lazebnik, S., Perona, Petro, Sato, Y., Schmid, C. (eds.) ECCV 2012, Part III. LNCS, vol. 7574, pp. 340–353. Springer, Heidelberg (2012). https://doi.org/10.1007/978-3-642-33712-3_25

External Damage Risk Detection of Transmission Lines Using E-OHEM Enhanced Faster R-CNN

Lei Qu[✉], Kuixiang Liu, Qi He, Jun Tang, and Dong Liang

Key Laboratory of Intelligent Computation and Signal Processing,
Ministry of Education, Anhui University, Hefei, China
qulei@ahu.edu.cn

Abstract. External damage risk detection of transmission lines suffers from complex background information and small-sized objects, thereby leading to numerous false negatives and false positives. Although faster R-CNN with OHEM algorithm can achieve impressive results for the task of external damage risk detection, data imbalance remains an obstacle when applying OHEM. In object detection, one of the major challenges is how to learn an effective model from imbalanced data. To address this issue, we propose a variant of OHEM named Enhance Online Hard Example Mining (E-OHEM) algorithm for external damage risk detection of transmission lines, which can not only effectively learn more hard examples but also avoid data imbalance. Moreover, we fine-tune the learned model by selecting negative examples around false positives at the RPN stage. The fine-tuning model outperforms the original Faster R-CNN model by 0.5% on the mAP value on the PASCAL VOC2007 dataset. The application of E-OHEM algorithm and fine-tuned model render our detector more robust and efficient for the task of external damage risk detection. Meanwhile, our model makes a significant improvement on recognition accuracy.

Keywords: External damage risk detection · E-OHEM
Data imbalance · Fine-tuned model

1 Introduction

Long-distance power transmission mainly uses overhead transmission lines and undertakes huge power transmission. The safe operation of overhead power transmission lines has significant influence on the stability of the power grid. With the unprecedentedly rapid development of urban construction, construction operations are widespread throughout rural areas. Consequently, the potential external damages mainly caused by illegal construction operation of engineering vehicles have been a major threat to the safe and stable operation of transmission lines. As the scale of power grids is surprisingly tremendous, the automatic and accurate transmission lines inspection techniques are in high demand. Recently, many

© Springer Nature Switzerland AG 2018
J.-H. Lai et al. (Eds.): PRCV 2018, LNCS 11259, pp. 260–271, 2018.
https://doi.org/10.1007/978-3-030-03341-5_22

image recognition based algorithms have been proposed [3,16] to deal with this issue. However, these existing techniques still suffers from low accuracy and high costs.

The past few years witnessed the impressive success of of many computer vision tasks by using deep learning techniques. The deep learning based object detection techniques also find its great potential in the automatic inspection of transmission line, including the detection and localization of engineering vehicles. Current object detection algorithm can be roughly divided into two major categories, i.e., one-stage detectors [2,10–12] and two-stage detectors [1,4–6,8,13]. One-stage detectors are applied over a regular, dense sampling of possible object locations. Although one-stage detectors are faster and simpler, they have trailed the accuracy of two-stage detectors thus far. In the two-stage object detectors, the first stage generates a set of candidate object locations and the second stage classifies each candidate location as one of the foreground classes or as the background. Motivated by the fact that the state-of-the-art Faster R-CNN framework of two-stage object detectors can be efficiently trained on large-scale datasets and achieve top accuracy, we adopt Faster R-CNN framework to detect external damage risks of transmission lines. External damage risk detection of transmission lines often suffers from complex background and small-sized objects. Moreover, the detection accuracy is sensitive to the variations of illumination and viewing angle. In practical applications, many false negatives may be produced, which stands a big obstacle for our task.

The main cause of false negatives can be boiled down to data imbalance and fewer hard examples in our task. Although the model of Faster R-CNN is elegant, the challenge of learning from data remains an open problem. In Fast R-CNN and Faster R-CNN, it is difficult to find a balance between foreground and background, even though the foreground-to-background ratio (1:3) is fixed at the second classification stage. And the training procedure is dominated by more easily classified examples of random sampling. Therefore, sampling by a fixed foreground-to-background ratio (1:3) is not an effective strategy to tackle data imbalance. Ross Girshick proposed a hard example mining scheme named Online Hard Example Mining (OHEM) [14] to cope with data imbalance. This algorithm integrates bootstrapping technique [15] with region-based detectors, which can be effortlessly implemented on most of the region-based detectors. However, OHEM algorithm only increases the weight of hard classified examples, whilst ignoring easily classified examples. To address this issue, we propose an variant of OHEM named Enhanced Online Hard Example Mining (E-OHEM) algorithm to overcome the imbalance of hard classified examples and easily classified examples with region-based detectors. On the PASCAL VOC2007 dataset, the mAP of Fast R-CNN with E-OHEM outperforms Fast R-CNN with OHEM by 0.4%. Moreover, it boosts the performance of Faste R-CNN and surpasses that of Faster R-CNN OHEM algorithm by 0.6%.

We detect and locate engineering vehicles based on the Faster R-CNN framework, such as excavators, cement tankers, cement pump trucks, scoops, tower cranes, cranes, bulldozers and engineering cars. Additionally, the E-OHEM algorithm and fine-tuned model are used to achieve the mAP value of 73.2%.

2   Related Work

2.1   The Framework of Transmission Lines External Damage Risk Detection System

As shown in Fig. 1, we use the Faster R-CNN framework as the basic framework for external damage risk detection of transmission lines. At first, we make our datasets and mark the samples of engineering vehicles. Secondly, we input the samples into the RPN network until the network converges. Then, we extract the bounding boxes from the trained binary class detection model by RPN network, and train Fast R-CNN with E-OHEM algorithm until the network converges. Finally, the trained model is used to classify the engineering vehicles.

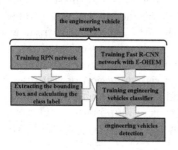

Fig. 1. The framework of transmission lines external damage risk detection

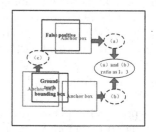

Fig. 2. Selecting negative examples mechanism in RPN stage

2.2   Sampling Heuristics

Balancing Foreground and Background RoIs in Mini-batch Sampling. Using stochastic gradient descent (SGD), Fast R-CNN and Faster R-CNN are trained. Besides, SGD mini-batches are created to share convolution network computation between RoIs. For each mini-batch, N images are first sampled from the dataset, and then B/N ($B = 128$, $N = 2$) RoIs are sampled from each image. Each RoI, which will be labeled as foreground or background according to its intersection over union (IoU), overlaps with a ground-truth bounding box. Figure 3 shows the algorithm structure of Faster R-CNN. To handle the data imbalance, [4] proposed heuristics to fix the foreground-to-background ratio in each mini-batch to 1:3. Consequently, it ensures that 25% of a mini-batch is foreground.

Online Hard Examples Mining. However, most of randomly-selected samples for training are easily classified in mini-batch sampling. OHEM can not only more efficiently learn hard examples but also remove the need for several heuristics and hyperparameters. As shown in Fig. 4, for inputted images, we first compute a convolution feature map using the convolution network.

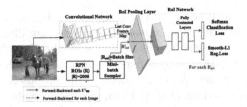

Fig. 3. Architecture of the Faster R-CNN algorithm

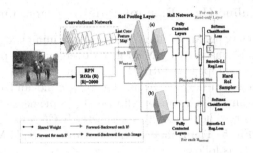

Fig. 4. Architecture of Faster R-CNN using OHEM algorithm

Furthermore, the RoI network uses this feature map and all the input RoIs (R), instead of a sampled mini-batch, to do a forward pass. Besides, we calculate the loss of each example and apply non-maximum suppression (NMS). Hard examples are selected by sorting the input RoIs by loss and taking the B/N ($B = 128$, $N = 2$) examples for which the current network performs worst.

3 Model Design

In this section, we discuss that online hard example mining algorithm focuses on enough hard examples. We will show that our approach results in better training and higher average precision. Firstly, we discuss the design motivation. Then, we present the design and implementation of Enhance Online Hard Example Mining algorithm (E-OHEM). Finally, a method is proposed to fine-tune the Faster R-CNN model.

3.1 Motivation

In Sect. 2.2, we introduce the algorithm of a fixed foreground-to-background ratio (1:3) in mini-batch sampling. The majority of selected examples are easily classified in mini-batch sampling. Besides, the OHEM algorithm is proposed to select more hard examples. Although the OHEM algorithm can achieve high detection accuracy, the problem of data imbalance still exists. The data imbalance indicates that OHEM does not consider the ratio of positive and negative examples and completely ignores the easily classified examples. Additionally, the experiment [9] found that the ratio (1:3) of positive and negative examples is limited and the recognition accuracy is reduced. Thus, the important part of OHEM data imbalance is that the easily classified examples are discarded completely. Moreover, we propose a method to increase the weight of easily classified examples. In fact, most of examples by a fixed foreground-to-background ratio (1:3) in mini-batch sampling are easily classified. In the proposed study, we add the sampled mini-batch based on OHEM to increase the weight of easily classified examples.

3.2 Enhance Online Hard Example Mining Algorithm

We propose an effective enhance online hard example mining algorithm for training Fast R-CNN and Faster R-CNN so as to overcome the problem of ignoring easily classified examples to OHEM algorithm. E-OHEM algorithm is the fusion of mini-batch sampling by balancing foreground and background RoIs and OHEM algorithm, which can be effortlessly implemented on most of the region-based detectors. The architecture of Faster R-CNN using E-OHEM algorithm is shown in Fig. 5. The Enhance Online Hard Example Mining algorithm (E-OHEM) proceeds as follows.

Calculation of forward network in the VGG16 network, the ROI pooling layer uses the con5_3 convolution feature map and all inputted RoIs (about 2000 RoIs) to calculate the forward network through the fully-connected layer. Each RoI calculates the loss value and non-maximum suppression (NMS) works by iteratively selecting the RoI with the highest loss, and then removing all lower-loss RoIs that possess high overlap with the selected region. B/N ($B = 128$, $N = 2$) hard examples are chosen by sorting the RoIs by loss.

RoIs Gradient Updating. Setting foreground and background samples for all inputted RoIs (about 2000 RoIs) by the IoU threshold. B/N ($B = 128$, $N = 2$) easily classified examples (R_{sel}) are chosen by 1:3 ratio of foreground and background samples sampling. Finally, $2 * B/N$ ($B = 128$, $N = 2$) examples ($R_{merge-sel}$) of hard examples and easily classified examples are used for gradient updating and the specific process can be found in Algorithm 1.

3.3 The Fine-Tuning Model Method

In the current study, the fine-tuning model method is proposed to overcome false positives of Faster R-CNN model. As shown in Fig. 2, the specific algorithm proceeds as follows.

Selecting Bounding Boxes. Firstly, we use the trained model to test the training set and set the threshold value of the bounding box as 0.05. Then, we perform non-maximum suppression (NMS) on the bounding box (the threshold value is set as 0.3). Finally, each image selection does not exceed 2000 bounding boxes.

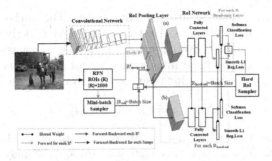

Fig. 5. Architecture of Faster R-CNN using **E-OHEM** algorithm

---

Algorithm 1. Selecting hard examples and easily classified examples by E-OHEM algorithm.

Input:
  The con5_3 convolution feature map and all inputted RoIs (about 2000 RoIs);
Output:
  $2 * B/N$ RoIs of hard examples and easily classified examples;
  1: The forward network calculated by all RoIs of RPN stage extracted and con5_3 feature map;
  2: Calculating loss of each RoI by softmax and bounding-box regression loss;
  3: Non-maximum suppression (NMS) works by the loss;
  4: Selecting the sorted RoIs ($R_{hard-sel}$) with the highest loss;
  5: All ROIs by RPN stage extracted calculate IoU values;
  6: The RoI of IoU $\geq$ 0.5 as foreground and the RoI of IoU $<$ 0.5 as background in the second stage;
  7: RoIs are selected by 1:3 ratio of foreground and background and obtaining B/N RoIs (R_{sel});
  8: $2 * B/N$ RoIs ($R_{merge-sel}$) are obtained by the RoIs ($R_{hard-sel}$) of step 4 and the RoIs (R_{sel}) of step 7;
  9: Gradient updating with $2 * B/N$ RoIs ($R_{merge-sel}$);
  10: **return** $R_{merge-sel}$;

Saving False Positives. We determine whether the bounding box obtained from Sect. 3.3 is false positive by calculating intersection over union (IoU) overlaps with all ground-truth bounding boxes of each image. the bounding box that has an IoU overlap lower than 0.5 is a false positive, and saved in the text.

Training Parameter Settings. According to Faster R-CNN alternate optimization training, the trained model of Faster R-CNN is employed as a pretraining model. Both the RPN and Fast R-CNN stage initial learning rates are set to 0.0001 by dropped an order of magnitude.

Selection Mechanism of Negative Samples in Training. In original RPN stage, Faster R-CNN algorithm selects samples according to the IoU overlap of anchor boxes and ground-truth bounding boxes. The anchor box with IoU overlap lower than 0.3 is taken as negative sample (Neg_{sel}) (box (b) in Fig. 2) and the anchor box with IoU overlap higher than 0.7 is taken as positive sample (box (c) in Fig. 2). In the fine-tuning stage, we propose the negative samples selection mechanism for overcoming false positives. It can be described as follows:

$$Neg = \alpha Neg_{sel} + \beta Neg_{fp} \tag{1}$$

where Neg_{fp} is the anchor box that has an IoU overlap higher than 0.7 with any false positives box. Neg is the total negative samples. As displayed in Fig. 2, We set the different weights of Neg_{sel} and Neg_{fp}. In the experiment, We can get higher recognition accuracy by $\alpha : \beta$ as 3:1.

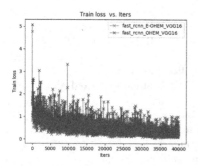

Fig. 6. Comparing training loss for E-OHEM and OHEM in Fast R-CNN

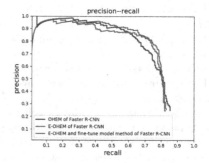

Fig. 7. Precision-Recall curve comparison in testing sets of external damage risk detection

4   Experiments and Results

In this section, we carry out the experiment to evaluate the proposed E-OHEM and compare with OHEM. Furthermore, we evaluate the fine-tuning model experiment and analyze the experiment result of external damage risk detection. We describe the experimental setup in Sect. 4.1, and subsequently demonstrate the efficiency and accuracy of the E-OHEM algorithm by examining the training loss and average precision in Sect. 4.2. In addition, we show the experimental results of the fine-tuning model in PASCAL VOC2007. Finally, we analyze and compare the experiment result of external damage risk detection.

4.1   Experimental Setup

In this paper, we not only use the VGG16 convolutional neural network structure in Caffe [7] framework but also evaluate the performance of the algorithm in PASCAL VOC2007. In the PASCAL VOC2007 experiment, training is conducted on the trainval sets and tested on the test set. All models are trained with stochastic gradient descent (SGD) with an initial learning rate of 0.001. We use gradient accumulation with $N = 2$ forward-backward passes of single image mini-batches and $B = 128$. Moreover, our method does not exploit many popular improvement, such as multi-scale training, multi-scale testing, stronger data augmentation [10], etc. In the Fast R-CNN experiment, the model is trained for 40K iterations. Additionally, the learning rate is dropped in "steps" by a factor of 0.1 every 30K iterations. In the Faster R-CNN experiment, we employ alternate optimization training method. The RPN stage iterates 80K, and the learning rate is dropped in "steps" by a factor of 0.1 every 60K iterations. Fast R-CNN stage iterates 40K and the learning rate is dropped in "steps" by a factor of 0.1 every 30K iterations.

4.2   Experimental Results and Analysis

Training Convergence. In the Fast R-CNN experiment, we compared the training loss for E-OHEM and OHEM algorithms. Figure 6 shows the training loss curve for OHEM and E-OHEM algorithm in Fast R-CNN based on VGG16 network. It can be concluded that the training loss of E-OHEM is smoother and easier to converge than that of OHEM algorithm. Besides, it is verified that the E-OHEM algorithm gets a lower loss value than the OHEM algorithm.

PASCAL VOC2007 Experimental Results Analysis. In the current work, we compare E-OHEM and OHEM algorithms for Fast R-CNN and Faster R-CNN based on VGG16 network in the PASCAL VOC2007. As shown in Table 1, on VOC2007, when the IoU threshold is 0.5, E-OHEM improves the mAP of OHEM from 71.5% to 71.9% in the Fast R-CNN. The Faster R-CNN uses the E-OHEM algorithm to obtain the mAP of 71.3% and it is increased by 0.6% than OHEM algorithm. According to the data, the E-OHEM algorithm effectively solves the problem of data imbalance for OHEM, which not only lays emphasis on misclassified examples but also focuses on easily classified examples.

The Fine-Tuning Model Experiment. In the fine-tuning model stage, we use the trained model as a pre-training model for Faster R-CNN based on VGG16 network. In addition, the initial learning rate is set to 0.0001. As shown in Table 2, on VOC2007, the fine-tuning model method improves the mAP from

Table 1. VOC 2007 test detection average precision (%). All methods use VGG16 and bounding-box regression

Object detection algorithm	Method	IoU	mAp	aero	bike	bird	boat	bottle	bus	car	cat	chair	cow	table	dog	horse	mbike	person	plant	sheep	sofa	train	tv
Fast R-CNN		0.5	67.6	74.7	79.0	66.8	56.2	39.7	76.9	78.7	78.8	48.9	73.3	64.6	76.6	78.0	75.8	72.7	33.7	69.1	68.2	75.5	65.7
	OHEM	0.5	71.5	73.1	79.4	72.4	59.8	48.1	82.6	79.2	83.3	55.4	77.1	70.1	82.1	81.2	75.3	74.8	42.4	68.5	72.8	76.1	76.2
	E-OHEM	0.5	71.9	75.1	81.8	72.4	61.8	46.3	83.4	79.9	84.5	54.1	77.0	72.1	82.2	81.6	78.0	74.9	43.9	68.4	70.6	76.6	74.1
	improv	0.5	0.4	2.0	2.4	0.0	2.0	-1.8	0.8	0.7	1.2	-1.3	-0.1	2.0	0.1	0.4	2.7	0.1	1.5	-0.1	-2.2	0.5	-2.1
Faster R-CNN		0.5	69.9	70.0	80.6	70.1	57.3	49.9	78.2	80.4	82.0	52.2	75.3	67.2	80.3	79.8	75.0	76.3	39.1	68.3	67.3	81.1	67.6
	OHEM	0.5	70.7	70.5	80.6	68.4	56.4	54.7	80.8	80.1	80.7	52.0	75.8	66.8	79.9	83.1	75.7	77.4	39.9	69.9	69.5	78.4	72.9
	E-OHEM	0.5	71.3	69.7	79.8	69.0	60.6	57.7	80.8	80.0	83.5	55.1	75.4	68.0	81.7	82.5	77.1	77.8	39.7	70.0	67.8	76.9	72.0
	improv	0.5	0.6	-0.8	-0.8	0.6	4.2	3.0	0.0	-0.1	2.8	3.1	-0.4	1.2	1.8	-0.6	1.4	0.4	-0.2	0.1	-1.7	-1.5	-0.9

Table 2. VOC2007 test detection average precision (%) of fine-tuning model

Object detection algorithm	Whether to fine-tune the model	mAP
Faster R-CNN	No	69.9
	Yes	**70.5**
	Improv	**0.6**

Table 3. The false positives rate of negative examples detection

	The total number of negative examples (42380)	
Whether to join negative examples training	No	Yes
The number of false positives	2800	124
False positives rate (%)	6.60	**0.29**

Table 4. Faster R-CNN uses different algorithms to compare the detection accuracy of external damage risk detection datasets

Method	Faster R-CNN			
OHEM	✓			
E-OHEM			✓	✓
Fine-tuning model				✓
mAP	71.2	72.3	72.8	**73.2**

69.9% to 70.5% for an IoU threshold of 0.5 in the Faster R-CNN. Interestingly, the fine-tuning model method performs quite well in overcoming false positives of Faster R-CNN model.

4.3 Analysis of the Experiment Result of External Damage Risk Detection

In this study, we convert Faster R-CNN detection into binary class object detection (engineering vehicles and background). The engineering vehicles include eight categories, respectively, excavators, cement tankers, cement pump trucks, scraper trucks, tower cranes, cranes, bulldozers and engineering cars. We make the dataset of 14542 images and it includes data augmentation in external damage risk detection. Data augmentation methods have rotation transformation and examples superposition in this study. We use 7300 images to form the training set and the remaining 7242 images to conduct the test. In the external damage risk detection experiment, the initial learning rate is set to 0.001. The RPN stage iterates 120K, and the learning rate is dropped in "steps" by a factor of 0.1 every 90K iterations. Fast R-CNN stage iterates 60K and the learning rate is dropped in "steps" by a factor of 0.1 every 45K iterations. The evaluation result on the datasets of external damage risk detection is presented in Table 4. Based on VGG16 network, the E-OHEM algorithm and the fine-tuning model method can get the mAP of 73.2% in the Faster R-CNN. As displayed in Fig. 7, external damage risk detection compares the OHEM and E-OHEM algorithm by plotting Precision-Recall curves in testing sets with the Faster R-CNN of VGG16 network.

Practically, the object detection algorithm of deep learning has a common problem. That is to say, there are many false positives. Figure 9 shows the false positives of external damage risk detection. The main reason is that object detection of deep learning selects negative samples around positive samples of each image and learns less negative samples. We adopt two methods to deal with the problem of false positives in the practical application.

- In order to learn more negative samples, as shown in Fig. 8, we make datasets by adding samples of positive and negative examples superposition.
- External damage risk detection is trained by directly adding the negative examples. For the RPN stage, if it is a negative example, we randomly select 256 anchor boxes as negative samples in all anchor boxes. If there are any negative examples in Fast R-CNN stage, each image randomly selects B/N RoIs and the label is set to background.

Through using the above two methods, the false positive of external damage risk detection is significantly reduced to meet the practical need. As shown in Table 3, we test false positives rate (the ratio of the number of false positives and the number of total negative examples) in the 42,380 negative examples.

Fig. 8. Positive and negative examples superposition

Fig. 9. The false positive examples of external damage risk detection

Fig. 10. The results of external damage risk detection

The false positive rate of the image dropped to 0.29%. Figure 10 presents the results of external damage risk detection.

5   Conclusion

In this study, E-OHEM algorithm and fine-tuned model are applied to the Faster R-CNN framework to yield higher detection accuracy in the external damage risk detection of transmission lines.

- Compared with OHEM algorithm, E-OHEM algorithm can be trained more easily and converge faster in the Fast R-CNN and Faster R-CNN framework. Additionally, E-OHEM algorithm makes a remedy for the weakness that OHEM ignores the easily classified examples.
- Under the framework of Faster R-CNN, E-OHEM algorithm not only greatly reduces the number of false negatives but also achieves high recognition accuracy in the external damage risk detection.
- False positives are inevitably produced by the deep learning based object detection algorithms. Thus, the negative example learning is incorporated during the training phase, significantly reducing the number of false positives. Furthermore, we fine-tune the model to achieve higher recognition accuracy to meet the practical application detection requirements.

The major shortage of the proposed algorithm is that it is unable to precisely identify and detect small objects in some remote scenes. We will focus on this problem in our future research.

Acknowledgement. This work was supported by Natural Science Foundation of China (No. 61871411, 61772032), and Scientific Research Foundation for the Returned Overseas Chinese Scholars, State Education Ministry and Technology Foundation for Selected Overseas Chinese Scholar, Ministry of Personnel of China.

References

1. Dai, J., Li, Y., He, K., Sun, J.: R-FCN: object detection via region-based fully convolutional networks (2016)
2. Fu, C.Y., Liu, W., Ranga, A., Tyagi, A., Berg, A.C.: DSSD: deconvolutional single shot detector (2017)
3. Fu, Y., Rong, S.A., Zhao, W.B., Shen, H.: Research on monitoring device for indicating external damage risk of overhead line based on image recognition technology with binocular vision cameras. In: International Conference on Condition Monitoring and Diagnosis, pp. 156–159 (2016)
4. Girshick, R.: Fast R-CNN. Computer Science (2015)
5. Girshick, R., Donahue, J., Darrell, T., Malik, J.: Rich feature hierarchies for accurate object detection and semantic segmentation. In: IEEE Conference on Computer Vision and Pattern Recognition, pp. 580–587 (2014)
6. He, K., Gkioxari, G., Dollár, P., Girshick, R.: Mask R-CNN (2017)

7. Jia, Y., Shelhamer, E., Donahue, J., Karayev, S., Long, J.: Caffe: convolutional architecture for fast feature embedding, pp. 675–678 (2014)
8. Lin, T.Y., Dollar, P., Girshick, R., He, K., Hariharan, B., Belongie, S.: Feature pyramid networks for object detection, pp. 936–944 (2016)
9. Lin, T.Y., Goyal, P., Girshick, R., He, K., Dollar, P.: Focal loss for dense object detection, pp. 2999–3007 (2017)
10. Liu, W., et al.: SSD: single shot MultiBox detector. In: Leibe, B., Matas, J., Sebe, N., Welling, M. (eds.) ECCV 2016, Part I. LNCS, vol. 9905, pp. 21–37. Springer, Cham (2016). https://doi.org/10.1007/978-3-319-46448-0_2
11. Redmon, J., Divvala, S., Girshick, R., Farhadi, A.: You only look once: unified, real-time object detection. In: Computer Vision and Pattern Recognition, pp. 779–788 (2016)
12. Redmon, J., Farhadi, A.: Yolo9000: better, faster, stronger, pp. 6517–6525 (2016)
13. Ren, S., He, K., Girshick, R., Sun, J.: Faster R-CNN: towards real-time object detection with region proposal networks. IEEE Trans. Pattern Anal. Mach. Intell. **39**(6), 1137–1149 (2017)
14. Shrivastava, A., Gupta, A., Girshick, R.: Training region-based object detectors with online hard example mining, pp. 761–769 (2016)
15. Sung, K.K.: Learning and example selection for object and pattern detection. Ph.D. thesis Mit Al Lab (1996)
16. Zhen-Chun, L.E., Liu, W.T., Zhao, W.B.: Embedded monitoring system for high-voltage transmission line based on image recognition. East China Electric Power (2014)

Parallel Search by Reinforcement Learning for Object Detection

Ye Huang, Chaochen Gu$^{(\boxtimes)}$, Kaijie Wu, and Xinping Guan

Key Laboratory of System Control and Information Processing, MOE of China,
Shanghai Jiao Tong University,
Shanghai 200240, China
{lutein,jacygu,kaijiewu,xpguan}@sjtu.edu.cn

Abstract. Object detection algorithms generally search through extensive potential areas without considering spatial correlations. To fully utilize rich information contained in high-level image features, a hierarchical object detection method with parallel search formulated as Markov Decision Process, is presented. Starting from independent initial locations, our model generates adequate region proposals by Reinforcement Learning (RL) method for subsequent refinement of bounding boxes. An attention-based state initialization algorithm combined with a novel reward function for RL training are proposed to facilitate the agent's control over window transformations. Following a coarse-to-fine detection strategy, we adopt adjustable action parameters and perform profound refinement for the generated proposals. Compared with existing detection algorithms, experiments on PASCAL VOC 2007 & 2012 dataset indicate the proposed model achieves encouraging object detection performance with fewer proposals generated.

Keywords: Object detection · Reinforcement learning
Attention mechanism · Neural network

1 Introduction

Existing object detection methods typically adopt a region proposal strategy combined with a classifier to predict the objectness scores of attended areas. Region proposal algorithms always generate excessive windows to capture multiple objects in all scales first (using image segmentation, sliding windows or fixed grids), then utilize image features to reduce the number of potential regions. Low-level features such as color and texture (Selective Search), edge (Edge Boxes [23]), gradient (HoG features used by DPM [5]), high-level features such as Fully Convolutional Network feature maps prove effective in providing adequate positive regions for subsequent classifiers. R-CNN [7] generates about 2,000 windows on raw images through Selective Search method. Fast R-CNN [6] improves the speed by applying traditional image segmentation algorithms on feature maps, decreasing overlapping windows and repetitive computation of features. Faster

© Springer Nature Switzerland AG 2018
J.-H. Lai et al. (Eds.): PRCV 2018, LNCS 11259, pp. 272–283, 2018.
https://doi.org/10.1007/978-3-030-03341-5_23

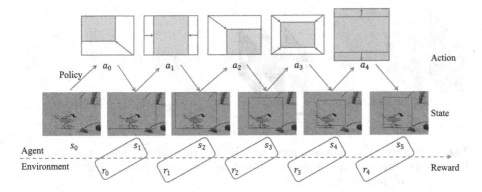

Fig. 1. At each step, the agent chooses one specific action from available predefined transformations based on current state, and gathers the next state deterministically after action taken.

R-CNN [18] and a similar approach, SSD [13] utilize sliding windows with several scales named "anchors" on different layers of feature maps. YOLO [17] segments images into grids of fixed size and detects objects on those grid segments.

Both traditional and deep learning based region proposal methods are capable of generating massive candidate areas. Nevertheless, these predefined sizes, fixed grids or time-consuming sliding windows bring in unnecessary regions that become a burden to consecutive classifiers. The independent generation operation ignores the sequential location correlations contained in extracted areas, which is incompatible with human perception procedure. Humans normally recognize multiple objects across complicated backgrounds quickly and precisely. Research on biological visual attention suggests that the visual system in humans uses attention mechanisms to focus on specific areas of the visual input [3]. Further studies [15] suggest that optimal eye movement strategy integrates the information of the whole visibility map and successively searches for fixation locations. Similar to this attention-based search procedure, the proposed method utilizes an attention map to locate salient areas coarsely, and formulates the following search movement as an agent transforming detection windows according to a RL-optimized policy.

In this paper, an effective object detection pipeline that directs a reinforcement learning agent to explore potential target areas on feature maps from fine designed initial locations, is disclosed. With less candidate regions proposed, this hierarchical detection method combines sequential object bounding box search with attention-based model to detect objects in multiple scales accurately. Under the guidance of an optimal policy learned in RL, the model utilizes a parallel candidate region generation method. This means the entire search procedure starts at differing initial locations and adopts adaptive exploration strategies. Objectiveness scores of all attended regions are then predicted to generate adequate positive proposals, which will be fed into classification and regression layers to be

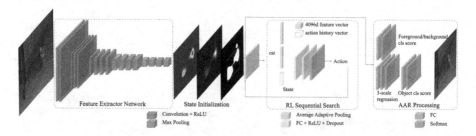

Fig. 2. Architecture of proposed pipeline. Including three main components: attention-based state initialization, parallel search with reinforcement learning and all attended regions (AAR) processing.

better evaluated and refined. The final detection results including the bounding boxes and classes of target objects are given by the refinement network.

Similar works [1,2,10] that use reinforcement learning to optimize detection process all adopt fixed search step size and predefined initial location, resulting in the lack of transformation flexibility. While in our method, an adaptive step size related to current window scales and attention-based initial search position improve the performance of an agent. Also, differing from previous method [10], the proposed reward function reflects the value of an agent's actions in a more reasonable way, driving the agent to make more informed judgements on actions selected. [2] and [1] mask searched regions with settled shapes such as a black cross, which impedes the agent detecting potentially smaller objects contained within masked areas. In contrast, by not limiting the accessibility of an agent but allowing it to exploit all attended regions by feeding them all into subsequent refinement networks.

Our pipeline is explained in detail in Sect. 2. Experiments on PASCAL VOC [4] dataset demonstrate that our method achieves competitive performance compared with similar RL methods. Comparisons with other region generation algorithms demonstrate there are fewer regions involved in the proposed model. A more detailed ablation study and an analysis of experimental results are presented in Sect. 3.

2   Approach

As shown in Fig. 2, the proposed approach includes three main components; (1) attention-based state initialization, (2) parallel search with reinforcement learning, and (3) all attended regions (AAR) processing. The method starts from the global image and local salient areas simultaneously, then performs zoom in/out exploration to locate large scale targets and local exploitation to find small objects. Based on image features and previous search path, the agent of RL balances the exploration of uncovered areas and exploitation among the discriminative regions. Thus the semantic correlation and relevant spatial information contained in feature maps may be fully utilized. All attended regions are then classified into positive or negative samples according to their foreground/background scores, with processed positive regions selected as proposals for subsequent object classification and bounding box regression to refine the results.

2.1 Attention-Based Initialization Strategy

Two individual schemes are implemented to approximate the initial state; a predetermined region and an attention-based location. These two initialization strategies are followed by different action groups described in Sect. 2.2.

In the experiment, this predetermined region in the first stream is designed as the whole image for better analysis of global information. Corresponding transformation groups are mainly composed of large scale zoom in/out actions (Fig. 1). The fixed location is computationally efficient, while it generally takes more steps to reach targets.

In order to reduce the number of steps needed for reaching ideal destination, we adopt Grad-CAM [16] method for the second stream to coarsely extract an attention-based location, which directs the agent to focus on discriminative regions. Based on CAM [22], Grad-CAM works on the explanation and visualization of deep neural networks, producing heat-map that illustrates salient areas of an image. Gradients computed, with respect to feature maps, are then forwarded through Global Average Pooling (GAP) layer to obtain the weights for the heat-map. A binary map processed from the heat-map is then used to compute the minimal circumscribed rectangles as initial locations (Fig. 3). The subsequent action group consists of translations with relatively small step size.

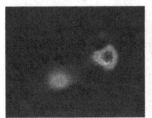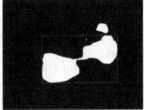

Fig. 3. Preprocessing of attention-based initialization. The image is first fed into a pretrained feature extraction network to obtain the heat-map according to Grad-CAM method. Then the minimal circumscribed rectangles in the binary map of attained heat-map, are computed.

A more effective localization for Grad-CAM state initialization, involves training a feature extraction network from scratch based on VGG [19] model. This is also used to obtain state vectors of RL and feature vectors for later region proposal classification task. More basic models like ResNet [8] and AlexNet [11] are also used in the experiment section to test performance. This extraction network is optimized using a criterion that optimizes a multi-label one-versus-all loss based on Binary Cross Entropy between the target and the output:

$$\mathcal{L}_{cls} = -\sum_i (x[i] * \log(y[i]) + (1 - x[i]) * \log(1 - y[i])) \qquad (1)$$

where $x[i], y[i]$ denote the ith element of the model output and one-hot-encoded target.

2.2   Parallel Search with Reinforcement Learning

The process of starting from an attention-based initial location to generally zoomed-in ROIs could be interpreted as discrete stochastic control task. Figure 1 illustrates a basic RL search path. With decision making involved, the recurrent searching is modelled as MDP optimized by Deep Q-Network [14] (DQN). The search procedure directly exploits feature vectors extracted from feature map to avoid forwarding images repeatedly, (Fig. 2), with the two agents trained to perform parallel search.

In the hierarchical detecting procedure, series of bounding boxes with adjustable scales and aspect ratios are generated, which shares the spirits of Faster R-CNN and SSD. While both of them utilize exhaustive windows fixed to predefined scales, in our method, these scales are flexible and optimized during training, with fewer candidate regions produced and time consumed. The parallel detection procedure is depicted in Fig. 4. **Action, State, Reward** and **Q-learning algorithm** are illustrated in details as follow:

Action: Similar to human perception procedure, applicable bounding box transformation contains two main branches: translation to move the window horizontally or vertically, scaling to change aspect ratio. In addition, a special action that indicates the termination of search is defined to prevent the agent from being trapped in endless detection.

The location of a bounding box is illustrated by the coordinates of its two diagonal vertices $[x_1, y_1, x_2, y_2]$, all the translation moves then could be described as increasing or decreasing corresponding values without changing aspect ratio, and scaling moves are formulated as modifying the width or height individually with centric coordinate fixed to $(\frac{x_2-x_1}{2}, \frac{y_2-y_1}{2})$ and update:

$$w = (x_2 - x_1) * \alpha_w, h = (y_2 - y_1) * \alpha_h \qquad (2)$$

α_w, α_h are related to current width and height, $\alpha_w = \beta * w_c, \alpha_h = \beta * h_c$.

Larger box moves with bigger scale factor could quickly localize objects in uncovered areas, then these potential regions are explored more carefully using smaller scale factors to refine. This zoom-in-out strategy facilitates the search for objects in various scales.

State: The state is designed to cover local feature vector, global feature vector and history of actions gathered from the beginning of the search sequence. Global

Fig. 4. Two searching paths are utilized to focus on both global and discriminative regions. Blue windows are produced by global search with mainly rescaling actions, and red windows start from salient areas. Deeper color represents later steps of the whole search path. The result shows that the jointly search could detect multiple objects with high precision. (Color figure online)

features related to the whole image provide the agent with rich visual content of potential areas that may serve as essential guidance for later exploration. Similarly, local features corresponding to current observed region utilize high-level image features to sufficiently exploit the context and spatial correlation information. State contains all relevant information from history [20], thus history vector is consist of one-hot action vectors that have been taken. As depicted in Fig. 2, feature vectors are directly obtained from an adaptive average pooling layer that follows the last convolutional layer. Before calculating state vector, boxes are mapped back to image coordinate to remove tiny and cross-boundary ones using method proposed by [12].

Reward: Focusing on goal-directed learning, we adopt proportion of intersection area and union area (IoU) to measure the value of actions and design an intuitive reward function that directs the agent to pay more attention to those actions that move current window closer to targets.

Work [1,2,10] both use a binary reward function that gives +1 for actions improving IoU and −1 for those decreasing it. To quantify the value of actions more distinctly, the newly developed reward function is proportional to the improvement of IoU rather than the sign of it. Actions that move current window towards targets closer are given higher rewards corresponding to the amount of change. For translation and scaling actions, the value of reward signal $R(s,a)$ after taking action a under state s can be computed by:

$$R = \begin{cases} k \cdot (\text{IoU}(b',g) - \text{IoU}(b,g)), \text{if IoU } (b',g) > \text{IoU}(b,g) \\ \text{sign}(\text{IoU}(b',g) - \text{IoU}(b,g)), \text{else} \end{cases} \tag{3}$$

where g, b, b' denote the ground truth bounding box, current window, next window after action taken and k represents the scale factor for positive actions.

Terminal action does not transform current window but records its location and restarts new refinement, which is beneficial to limit the sequential search within an adaptive number of steps. Reward for terminal action is:

$$R = \begin{cases} +\eta, \text{if IoU}(b, g) > \text{threshold} \\ -\eta, \text{else} \end{cases} \tag{4}$$

Q-Learning: Q-learning is an off-policy Temporal Difference control algorithm that learns to optimize the long-term cumulative reward by searching for an optimal policy function. Q function is trained to predict the value given current state s and action a. We use a deep neural network to approximate the Q function:

$$Q(s, a) = r + \gamma \max_{a'} Q(s', a') \tag{5}$$

The loss function of Deep Q-network is Mean Squared Error Loss (MSE Loss) of target Q and the output of Q-network. To guarantee the convergence, experience replay buffer and asynchronous update with target network are also adopted in our experiment. Since we use two initialization schemes, there are two corresponding policy models to be trained independently.

2.3 All Attended Regions Processing

The successively explored regions via sequential attention patterns are categorized as positive and negative samples according to their IoU with ground-truth boxes, the assignment criterion is the same with Faster R-CNN. To avoid degeneration of model due to the imbalance between positive and negative samples, we keep all the positive samples and randomly sample negative regions to restrain the ratio to 1:3. In case there are insufficient positive samples, additional windows generated by random combination of current regions are also fed into classification network.

All attended regions in various scales are labelled and then scored. The classification network utilizes Smooth L1 Loss to evaluate the possibility of a region being foreground. To restrain windows with high overlap, we use nonmaximum suppression (NMS) based on the first classification score.

Three regressors are trained for regions with different aspect ratios: $1 : 1$, $1 : a$ and $a : 1(a > 1)$. A multi-task loss function for both object classification and bounding box regression is used at the end of Fig. 2.

3   Experiment

Extensive experiments with different neural networks are performed on PASCAL VOC 2012 dataset which contains about 20k images (train + validation + test) of 20 object categories. The detection results are evaluated using mean

Average Precision (mAP) as this metric reflects both accuracy and generalization of model, which is widely applied in object detection task. As a region proposal method, our model is compared with existing region generation algorithms. Comparative experiments to other RL-based object detection methods are conducted by analyzing the detection results. To validate the effectiveness of our parallel strategy, ablation experiments are performed carefully: we analyze the two branch of initialization and searching policy individually, in addition, the consumption of action steps to convergence is also evaluated.

Experimental Details: The output size of adaptive average pooling layer is 2×2 to obtain 2048d feature vector. We use 5 composite scaling actions for global search and 8 translating actions for saliency search agent. 20 steps of actions are encoded as history vector to be concatenated with two 2048d feature vectors, accounting for the full state. The maximum step length is set to be 36, with 3 additional window scales $h : w, w : w, h : h$ adopted as alternative regions at each step of parallel search path. Threshold for terminal action's reward is set to be 0.6, and we choose $\beta = 5/6, \eta = 5.0, k = 10.0$.

Policy training strategy is $\epsilon - greedy$ with ϵ decreasing from 1.0 to 0.1 linearly during the first 9 epochs, and then fixed to 0.1 in last 41 epochs to ensure that the agent keeps balance between exploration and exploitation. Experience replay buffer has the size of 10,000 and the batch size of 64, discount factor γ for Q function is 0.9. SGD back-propagation method is utilized with momentum value fixed to 0.9 during training.

Threshold of NMS in background/foreground classification is 0.7, then we change it to 0.3 when dealing with the final output. Since in attention-based state initialization, the classification mean Average Precision (mAP) of feature extractor network has reached 83.7, we directly use the parameters of its classifier as pre-trained model for object classification.

Detection Results: mAP results evaluated on PASCAL VOC 2007 dataset are shown in Table 1. Given results by [9], Fast R-CNN models that utilizes BING [12], EdgeBoxes [23], Selective Search [21] as region proposal methods respectively, R-CNN, Faster R-CNN, YOLO and SSD models, as well as other RL-based detection models are presented in the table. We adopt VGG16 with RoI pooling as basic extraction structure. Our model has achieved relatively higher mAP score with much more fewer candidate regions generated compared with other algorithms.

Comparison of the recall rates between other region proposal generation methods is shown in Fig. 5(a). It's worth mentioning that though these approaches are traditional, they are combined with Fast R-CNN structure to evaluate the results. This experiment demonstrates that our model can achieve a similar recall rate as current proposal generation algorithms while we exploit a significantly smaller number of candidate regions. When IoU threshold varies within [0.5,1], the recall of our model performs relatively promising among other methods.

Table 1. Detection mAP of existing methods on VOC07 test set. All methods use VGG16 structure, and are trained on VOC07 except work [10], it's trained on VOC07+12 trainval set and adopts Fast R-CNN(ResNet101) as subsequent network.

Method	Data	mAP (%)	Proposals
Ours(VGG16)	07	69.4	200
FRCNN+Bing [12]	07	49.0	1k
FRCNN+EdgeBoxes [23]	07	60.4	1k
FRCNN+SelectiveSearch [21]	07	59.5	2k
R-CNN [7]	07	54.2	2k
RPN+VGG [18]	07	69.9	300
SSD300 [13]	07+12	68.0	8k
YOLO [17]	07	66.4	49
RL-based [10]	07+12	76.6	Not provided
RL-based [2]	07	46.1	4k

Analysis of Action Steps: As depicted in Fig. 5(b), the saliency search agent normally requires fewer action steps to detect possible regions. In most cases, both agents consume all 36 steps, generating about 100 proposals. Though R-CNN family remains state-of-the-art method, Faster R-CNN produces about 2k proposals generally. We found that the selection of action groups is flexible because it has a negligible effect on the final result. Specifically, appropriate combination of these two basic branches could strengthen the agent's ability of exploration, and composite actions generally reduce the number of requisite steps to locate targets.

Ablation Experiment: To investigate the performance of our parallel strategy, we conduct several ablation experiments including different extraction network shown in Table 2 and individual test of saliency search and global search.

Table 2. Classification score and detection mAP of different basic extraction networks on PASCAL VOC 2012 data set.

Method	Mean accuracy (%)	Val score (%)	Test score (%)	mAP (%)
VGG16+RoI pooling	69.71	75.1	82.1	69.4
ResNet18 [12]+resize	58.20	54.9	45.0	58.6
AlexNet [23]+resize	39.55	44.36	35.80	46.1
VGG16 [21]+resize	65.55	72.50	71.75	65.5

We adopt different basic feature extraction network to evaluate their performance. This basic network is applied to extract feature vectors that can be used

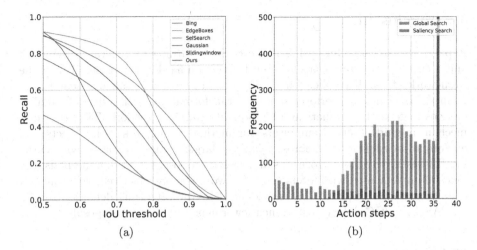

Fig. 5. (a) is the comparison of recall with other region proposal generation methods evaluated on PASCAL VOC 2007 test data. (b) shows the distribution of the number of action steps used in parallel search procedure.

to calculate state and generate grad-cam initial areas, thus we treat it as a typical classification task using multi-label classification loss function and stochastic gradient descent to optimize. Different deep neural networks are trained from scratch under similar training process.

Table 2 shows the classification scores and corresponding detection results evaluated on both validation and test set, with test scores provided by official PASCAL VOC evaluation server. The input image of three basic models are resized to 224 × 224 and augmented with randomly horizontal flip. We further analyze the performance of model VGG16 by alternating image resize to feature map adaptive pooling (RoI pooling). Model that adopts adaptive pooling achieves better classification and detection results than those use image resize, since image resize would lost more information than adaptive pooling.

Table 3 demonstrates the detection results of the two parts of parallel strategy separately. Each search is capable of detecting some objects while the combined parallel search achieves better performance. Given global information at the beginning, global search can locate more objects than saliency search does since the latter focuses on relatively smaller areas.

Table 3. Detection mAP of individual saliency search and global search strategies.

Method	Data	mAP (%)	Average steps
Parallel	07	69.4	31
Saliency search	07	30.9	30
Global search	07	48.2	33

4 Conclusion

A parallel search pipeline using reinforcement learning to generate distinctive and accurate region proposals for object detection has been disclosed. Under the framework of parallel policies including global search and saliency search, the trained RL agents can perform adaptive transformations within limited number of steps to generate adequate and high-quality candidate regions. The attention-mechanism-guided search empowers our method to locate salient objects and explore all possible objects across relatively larger areas. Compared with existing RL-based detection algorithms and region proposal generation methods, the method implemented with a refinement network is more effective in locating and classifying target objects. This is evidenced by the promising detection results on PASCAL VOC dataset with much fewer generated region proposals.

References

1. Bellver, M., Giró-i-Nieto, X., Marqués, F., Torres, J.: Hierarchical object detection with deep reinforcement learning (2016)
2. Caicedo, J.C., Lazebnik, S.: Active object localization with deep reinforcement learning. In: Proceedings of the 2015 IEEE International Conference on Computer Vision (ICCV), pp. 2488–2496. IEEE (2015)
3. Carrasco, M.: Visual attention: the past 25 years. Vis. Res. **51**, 1484–1525 (2011)
4. Everingham, M., Van Gool, L., Williams, C.K.I., Winn, J., Zisserman, A.: The Pascal visual object classes (VOC) challenge. Int. J. Comput. Vis. **88**, 303–338 (2010)
5. Felzenszwalb, P., McAllester, D., Ramanan, D.: A discriminatively trained, multiscale, deformable part model. In: Proceedings of the IEEE International Conference on Computer Vision and Pattern Recognition, CVPR 2008, pp. 1–8. IEEE (2008)
6. Girshick, R.: Fast R-CNN (2015)
7. Girshick, R., Donahue, J., Darrell, T., Malik, J.: Rich feature hierarchies for accurate object detection and semantic segmentation. In: Proceedings of the IEEE Conference on Computer Vision and Pattern Recognition, pp. 580–587 (2014)
8. He, K., Zhang, X., Ren, S., Sun, J.: Deep residual learning for image recognition. In: Proceedings of the IEEE Conference on Computer Vision and Pattern Recognition, pp. 770–778 (2016)
9. Hosang, J., Benenson, R., Dollr, P., Schiele, B.: What makes for effective detection proposals? IEEE Trans. Pattern Anal. Mach. Intell. **38**, 814–830 (2016)
10. Jie, Z., Liang, X., Feng, J., Jin, X., Lu, W., Yan, S.: Tree-structured reinforcement learning for sequential object localization. In: Advances in Neural Information Processing Systems, pp. 127–135 (2016)
11. Krizhevsky, A., Sutskever, I., Hinton, G.E.: Imagenet classification with deep convolutional neural networks. In: Advances in Neural Information Processing Systems, pp. 1097–1105 (2012)
12. Lenc, K., Vedaldi, A.: R-CNN minus R, vol. abs/1506.06981 (2015). http://arxiv.org/abs/1506.06981
13. Liu, W., et al.: SSD: single shot MultiBox detector. In: Leibe, B., Matas, J., Sebe, N., Welling, M. (eds.) ECCV 2016, Part I. LNCS, vol. 9905, pp. 21–37. Springer, Cham (2016). https://doi.org/10.1007/978-3-319-46448-0_2

14. Mnih, V., et al.: Human-level control through deep reinforcement learning. Nature **518**, 529–533 (2015)
15. Najemnik, J., Geisler, W.S.: Optimal eye movement strategies in visual search. Nature **434**, 387–391 (2005)
16. Ramprasaath, R., Abhishek, D., Ramakrishna, V., Michael, C., Devi, P., Dhruv, B.: Grad-CAM: why did you say that? Visual explanations from deep networks via gradient-based localization (2016)
17. Redmon, J., Divvala, S., Girshick, R., Farhadi, A.: You only look once: unified, real-time object detection. In: Proceedings of the IEEE Conference on Computer Vision and Pattern Recognition, pp. 779–788 (2016)
18. Ren, S., He, K., Girshick, R., Sun, J.: Faster R-CNN: towards real-time object detection with region proposal networks. In: Advances in Neural Information Processing Systems, pp. 91–99 (2015)
19. Simonyan, K., Zisserman, A.: Very deep convolutional networks for large-scale image recognition (2014)
20. Sutton, R.S., Barto, A.G.: Reinforcement Learning: An Introduction, vol. 1. MIT Press, Cambridge (1998)
21. Uijlings, J.R., Van De Sande, K.E., Gevers, T., Smeulders, A.W.: Selective search for object recognition. Int. J. Comput. Vis. **104**, 154–171 (2013)
22. Zhou, B., Khosla, A., Lapedriza, A., Oliva, A., Torralba, A.: Learning deep features for discriminative localization. In: Proceedings of the 2016 IEEE Conference on Computer Vision and Pattern Recognition (CVPR), pp. 2921–2929. IEEE (2016)
23. Zitnick, C.L., Dollár, P.: Edge boxes: locating object proposals from edges. In: Fleet, D., Pajdla, T., Schiele, B., Tuytelaars, T. (eds.) ECCV 2014, Part V. LNCS, vol. 8693, pp. 391–405. Springer, Cham (2014). https://doi.org/10.1007/978-3-319-10602-1_26

A Novel Visual Tracking Method Based on Moth-Flame Optimization Algorithm

Huanlong Zhang$^{(\boxtimes)}$, Xiujiao Zhang, Xiaoliang Qian, Yibin Chen, and Fang Wang

College of Electric and Information Engineering,
Zhengzhou University of Light Industry, Zhengzhou, China
zhl_lit@163.com

Abstract. Moth-flame optimization algorithm (MFO) is a new meta-heuristic optimization algorithm that mimics the motion of moths flight around the flames. In this work, a novel MFO-based visual tracking method is proposed by interaction between flames and moths. Firstly, visual tracking is expressed as searching for target in whole search space. Then, the spiral flight of moths is employed to enhance search capabilities. And the mechanism of reducing the number of flames gradually is applied for improving the convergence rate of the proposed algorithm. Finally, an appearance model based HOG feature is established to measure the similarity between the target and the candidate samples. In light of the best confidence value, the tracking target is located. Extensive experiments have demonstrated the effectiveness of proposed tracker.

Keywords: Moth-flame · Visual tracking · Swarm optimal
HOG features

1 Introduction

Visual tracking is one of the fundamental problems in computer vision. It has long been playing a key role in numerous applications like visual surveillance, military reconnaissance, motion recognition, traffic monitoring et al. Although researchers have made significant progress over the past decade, there still exist many challenging problems, such as motion blur, illumination variation, fast motion, et al. To overcome these problems, several algorithms are proposed, they can be classified into two categories, the generative-model-based approaches [1–5] and the discriminative ones [6–12].

In a sense, visual tracking can be reduced to a search task and formulated as an optimization problem. Among them, swarm intelligence algorithm has

This work is supported by National Natural Science Foundation of China (61873246, 61503173, 61501407, 61603347) and Doctor fund project of Zhengzhou University of Light Industry (2016BSJJ002).

J.-H. Lai et al. (Eds.): PRCV 2018, LNCS 11259, pp. 284–294, 2018.
https://doi.org/10.1007/978-3-030-03341-5_24

attracted more and more attention and has been applied to tracking problems successfully. Minami et al. [13] introduced the genetic algorithm into 1-step-GA (Genetic Algorithm) evolution for expressing the deviation of the target in the images. Meanwhile, with the help of the PD-type controller, the fish obtained the better identification and tracking results. Zhang et al. [14] incorporated the temporal continuity information into the PSO (Particle Swarm Optimization) for forming a multilayer importance sampling in the framework of particle filter. In this case, the tracker got better performance especially when the object has an arbitrary motion or undergoes large appearance changes. Chen et al. [15] proposed a Euclid distance based HQPSO (hybrid quantum particle swarm optimization) method, which overcome the problem that the population diversity gets easily lost during the latter period of evolution in PSO for an improved Mean Shift tracker. Hao et al. [16] proposed a particle filtering algorithm based on ACO (ant colony optimization) to enhance the performance of particle filter with small sample set, effectively improved the efficiency of video object tracking system. Nguyen et al. [17] presented a modified BFO (bacterial foraging optimization) algorithm, and designed a visual tracking system based on the bacterial foraging optimization to handle the some challenges. Gao et al. [18] proposed FA-based (firefly algorithm based) tracker which can robustly track an arbitrary target in various challenging conditions. Ljouad et al. [19] proposed a modified version of the CS (Cuckoo Search) algorithm combined with the well-known Kalman Filter, and designed a visual tracking system based on the HKCS (Hybrid Kalman Cuckoo Search) algorithm, the tracker outperforms better than the PSO-based tracker, especially in terms of computation time. In addition, Gao et al. [20, 21] presented bat algorithm and flower pollination algorithm to solve tracking problem.

Recently, Moth-flame optimization algorithm (MFO), a new swarm intelligent optimization algorithm, was proposed by researcher Seyedali Mirjalili [22], which inspired by the spiral convergence toward artificial lights of moths. Since being put forward, MFO algorithm has received more and more attentions because of its good robustness, fast convergence speed and global optimization. In this paper, visual tracking is viewed as the process of searching the best solution using the MFO method in the sequence images. A new visual tracking framework based on MFO is designed to obtain a better tracking performance by high exploration and exploitation. The spiral flight of moths and reduce the number of flames gradually is hired to enhance search capabilities and speed up convergence respectively. To demonstrate the tracking performance of the MFO-based tracker, the comparison of the proposed method and the three representative optimization based trackers was given, which were CS-based tracker, PSO-based tracker and SA-based (Simulated Annealing based) tracker respectively.

2   MFO Algorithm

Inspired by the navigation method of moths in nature called transverse orientation, Seyedali Mirjalili proposes Moth-flame optimization (MFO) algorithm. In this method, a moth flies through a relatively fixed angle to the moon, which is a very effective mechanism for travelling long distances in a straight path. However, when the light source (for example, flame) is close, moths fly spirally around it and finally converge toward it after just a few corrections. This mechanism is called Moth-Flame Optimization (MFO).

The key components in the MFO algorithm are moths and flames, which are considered to be a solution, however, they differ in the way they are handled and updated. The moth is the actual search body that moves in the search space, and the flame is the best solution that the moth has acquired so far.

2.1 Spiral Flight of Moth

In order to simulate the moths behavior of convergence in the mathematical model, a logarithmic spiral is defined in the MFO algorithm:

$$P\left(A_m, B_n\right) = F_m \bullet e^{\lambda t} \bullet \cos\left(2\pi t\right) + B_n \tag{1}$$

where F_m indicates the distance between the $m-th$ moth and the $n-th$ flame. λ is a constant that impacts the shape of the logarithmic spiral. And t is a random number in $[-1,1]$, where -1 and 1 indicate the closest and farthest to the flame, respectively. F_m can be calculated as follows:

$$F_m = |B_n - A_m| \tag{2}$$

where A_m indicates the $m-th$ moth, B_n indicates the $n-th$ flame.

Equation (1) describes the spiral flying path of moths. As may be seen in this equation, the next position of a moth is defined with respect to a flame. The t parameter in the spiral equation determines how much the next position of the moth should be close to the flame. In order to further emphasize exploitation, it is assumed that t is a random number in $[r,1]$. Adaptive convergence constant r linearly decreases from -1 to -2 to accelerate convergence around the flames over the course of iteration.

2.2 The Number of Flames

Another concern here is that the position updating of moths with respect to flame positions in the search space may degrade the exploitation of the best promising solutions. To solve the problem, an adaptive mechanism is employed for the number of flames, as shown in Eq. (3):

$$flame\_no = round\left(N - k * \frac{N-1}{K}\right) \tag{3}$$

where k is the current number of iteration, N is the maximum number of flames, and K is the maximum number of iterations.

In MFO algorithm, the spiral equation is equipped with efficient local exploitation and global exploration capabilities. Global exploration occurs when the next position is outside the space between the moth and flame, local exploitation happens when the next position lies inside the space between the moth and flame. The gradual decrement in number of flames balances the search space for global exploration and local exploitation. It shows superior capabilities of challenging optimization problems with unknown search spaces.

3   MFO Algorithm-Based Tracking System

Suppose there is a ground-truth corresponding to the object (best flame) in the image (state space) being searched and a group of target candidates (moths and flames) are randomly generated in the image (state space). The aim of the MFO-based tracker is to find the best target candidate in all candidates using the MFO algorithm.

In the tracking system, the moths are actual search agents that searching the candidate image patches in the image, whereas flames can save the best positions of image patches that moths have searched so far. Meanwhile, the flames guide the next searching of moths. The best image patches are saved in the flames so they never get lost. Based on this, a MFO-based tracking architecture is designed.

Algorithm 1. MFO-based tracking system

Input: Image sequence
Initialization: Locate the target object T in the first frame manually; Define objective function E; Set initial parameters: The initial number of moths and flames N; Maximum number of iterations K; Logarithmic spiral shape constant b.
Tracking:

1: **for** (i from 2 to the last frame) **do**
2:      Generate the initial positions of moth candidates and flame candidates
3:      **for** ($k = 1 : K$) **do**
4:          Calculating the similarity value of moths candidates and flame candidates
5:          Replace an flame candidate with its corresponding moth candidate it if becomes more similarity
6:          Select the best flame candidate.
7:          Update the number of flames candidates using Eq.(3)
8:          Update the position of moths candidates using Eq.(1)
9:      **end for**
10:     Display the frame indicating the best flame candidate, which is the target.
11: **end for**

In the Algorithm 1, the candidates similarity value is computed as:

$$\rho(X,Y) = \frac{Cov(X,Y)}{\sqrt{D(X)}\sqrt{D(Y)}} \tag{4}$$

where $D(\bullet)$ denotes the variance and $Cov(\bullet)$ denotes covariance. X and Y is the HOG feature of the target and candidate samples respectively. The objective function E is introduced as follows:

$$E = 2 + 2 * \rho(X, Y) \tag{5}$$

The similarity value affects how to update the search of moths and select the positions of flames.

After that, visual tracking is considered an optimization problem and the search space of the optimization problem is the image. The MFO method is used to find the best candidate the image as the tracking output according to the maximizing similarity value.

4   Experiments

The MFO-based tracker that was proposed in this paper should be tested in MATLAB R2014a. The experiments were managed on a PC with Intel Core i5 2.50 GHz and 16GB RAM. To prove the ability of MFO-based tracker in visual tracking, we compared MFO-based tracker with three representative optimization based tracker, including CS-based tracker, PSO-based tracker and SA-based tracker.

In MFO-based tracker, the parameters are set as follows: the number of moths/flames $N = 500$, maximum number of iterations $K = 50$ and the constant of logarithmic spiral shape $b = 2$. To make a fair comparison, the same feature (HOG feature), and each algorithm executed for 25000 objective function evaluations, which is adequate for relative the performances of the trackers. In MFO-based tracker, when the search space is too small or too large, the parameters can be adjusted to prevent overwork or underwork. We keep the parameters constant in this test.

There are 10 challenging sequences in our experiments. The source of the FACE1 is the dataset AVSS2007, and ZXJ is our own. Others are available on the website http://visualtracking.net. Note that we extract the frames 306–310 in BLURFACE sequences, which can represent the problem of frame dropping.

4.1   Qualitative Analysis

As shown in Fig. 1(a), there are the severe motion blur at frame #0150 and #0272, which reduces the discriminative information in feature vectors, it is difficult to predict their locations. At the beginning, all trackers perform well in sequences but SA-based tracker drifts when target objects undergo abrupt motion at frame #0311. In the BLURFACE sequence, the MFO-based tracker and CS-based tracker outperform the other trackers.

As shown in Fig. 1(b), it describes several deer run and jump in a river. The target undergoes large motion and some frames are blurred, for example frame #0036. Meanwhile, there are similar targets at frame #0052 that interfere with

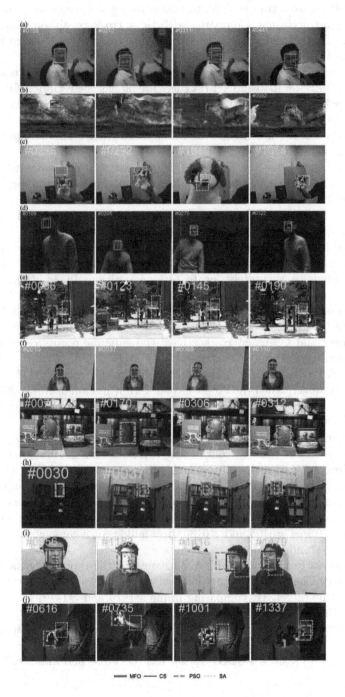

MFO —— CS — — PSO ···· SA

Fig. 1. A visualization of tracking results

tracking. MFO-based tracker generates accurate results even with heavy motion blur and water occlusion. Compared with these trackers, although all trackers keep track of the target object, the tracking accuracy of MFO-based tracker is better than the others.

As shown in Fig. 1(c), in the DOG1 sequence, a toy dog moves towards the camera. At frames #1046 and #1314 there are large scale variation. In addition, at frames #0236 and #0292 the target is rotated. All methods can merely track the target to the end. Only SA-based tracker failure in some frames. The PSO-based tracker has the best merit, the MFO-based tracker and CS-based tracker are the next simultaneously.

As shown in Fig. 1(d), at frame #0109, the target occur scale changes. Furthermore, at frames #0322 and #0275 the target becomes blurry. From Fig. 1(d), we observe that SA-based tracker took the worst to execute. The average execution merit of MFO-based tracker, CS-based tracker, and PSO-based tracker are all comparable.

As shown in Fig. 1(e), in the HUMAN7 sequence, the target undergoes fast motion at frames #0096 and #0123 with camera drastic camera shaking. It is rather tough to accurately locate targets position. In addition, at frame #0190 the brightness of the light changes when target through the shade. The SA-based tracker had lost the target before the frame #0096, MFO-based tracker, CS-based tracker and PSO-based tracker work well. However, MFO-based tracker and CS-based tracker have the superior results compared with PSO-based tracker.

As shown in Fig. 1(f), for ZXJ sequence, before the frame #0037, all tracker work well. However, when the target has an abrupt motion at frame #0069, SA-based tracker off its track to some extent. The MFO-based tracker and CS-based tracker obtain the best performance.

As shown in Fig. 1(g), for FISH sequence, the target occurs slight motion blur because camera shaking continuously. In addition, the illumination of the target at frame #0306 and #0312 is larger than the target at frame #0170. Due to the relative smooth motion, four trackers show good tracking results.

As shown in Fig. 1(h), for MAN sequence, the target experienced a large change in brightness. The tracker of CS fails at frame #0037. Although it catches the target at frame #0105 and #0130, it is failing for a complete video. MFO-based tracker stands out in all trackers.

As shown in Fig. 1(i), for MHYANG sequence, the target deformed and the light changed. Comparing frame #0956 with #1183, we can see the changes in the light of the target. By comparing frame #1416 and #1479, we can see the changes in the appearance of the target.

As shown in Fig. 1(j), for SYLVESTER sequence, as the toy continues to flip, the shape of the target changes dramatically. At the same time, the target has a large change in light. SA-based tracker has the worst performance.

4.2   Quantitative Analysis

Table 1 list image sequences comparison of MFO-based tracker to CS-based tracker, PSO-based tracker and SA-based tracker. The table mainly refers to average overlap rate.

Table 1. Average overlap rate

Sequence	MFO	CS	PSO	SA
BLURFACE	0.71	0.71	0.66	0.49
DEER	0.74	0.73	0.69	0.69
DOG1	0.46	0.46	0.47	0.32
FACE1	0.69	0.69	0.70	0.56
HUMAN7	0.47	0.47	0.46	0.16
ZXJ	0.85	0.85	0.82	0.67
FISH	0.84	0.84	0.82	0.78
MAN	0.83	0.37	0.70	0.67
MHYANG	0.75	0.75	0.60	0.47
SYLVESTER	0.63	0.65	0.63	0.29

Figure 2 shows the average success plot. The y-axis shows ratio of frames, where, amount of overlap is above threshold, to total frames. More the area under the curve then better is the tracker. Figure 3 shows the precision plot of the average precision values of all sequences. Here, also the y-axis shows the ratio of frames, where, distance of predicted and ground truth bounding box is below the threshold, to total frames. In precision plots if the slope is higher, then the tracker is better, this is because more sequences have distance of centers lower than the threshold. It is clearly seen, in Table 1, Figs. 2 and 3 that MFO-based tracker and CS-based tracker performs much better than 2 other trackers. It's worth noting that although the MFO-based tracker has better performance in the DOG1 and HUMAN7 sequences, we can see from the tracking field that the MFO-based tracker does not adapt to the video sequence with the scale change.

4.3   Average Time Costs

In order to analyze the time complexity, the average time costs of the trackers in the tracking process are recorded and the comparative results are shown in Table 2.

It can be seen from Table 2 that the average time cost of the MFO-based tracker is a little more than that of the SA-based tracker, but it is much better than the other three trackers. The time cost of the MFO-based tracker is especially advantageous compared with the CS-based tracker, although their tracking accuracy is often similar.

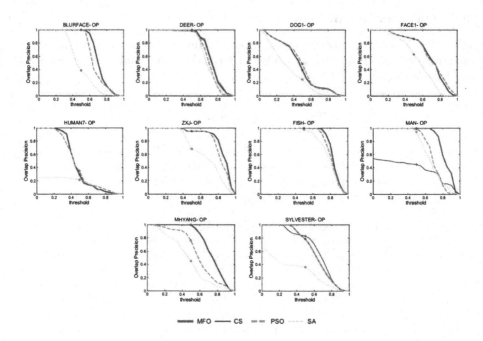

Fig. 2. Precision plots of OPE

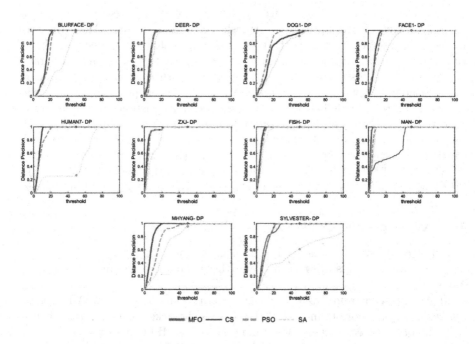

Fig. 3. Success plots of OPE

Table 2. Average time costs of the trackers

Sequence	MFO	CS	PSO	SA
BLURFACE	33.5	34.5	32.1	21.9
DEER	21	40.3	23.3	15.6
DOG1	9.7	12.6	9.9	8.9
FACE1	19.5	24.5	22	15.3
HUMAN7	15.3	20.6	17.4	12.7
ZXJ	12.8	30.1	15.5	10.7
FISH	12.2	15	9.1	9.7
MAN	4.7	14.1	6.7	4.6
MHYANG	9.8	13.2	12.1	8.3
SYLVESTER	8.7	11.7	9.9	7.4

5 Conclusion

In this paper, visual tracking is considered to be a process of searching for target using MFO in sequential images. The moths are the actual exploit body that move in the search space to determine candidate sample set, and the flames are the best solutions that the moth has acquired so far. Meanwhile, an appearance model based on HOG feature is constructed to measure the similarity between the target and candidates. Finally, according to the best fitness value, the tracking states are obtained. To the best of our knowledge, this is the first time that MFO has been adapted for use in a visual tracking system.

A tracker can be evaluated in many ways, and in this article, we mainly analyze MFO-based tracker from the perspective of optimization. The accuracy of the MFO-based tracker compared with three optimization based tracker including the CS, PSO and SA. Experimental results show that the accuracy of MFO-based tracker outperformed the PSO-based tracker and SA-based tracker, and the time cost is much better than CS-based tracker and PSO-based tracker. However, optimization algorithm is used to solve the problem of tracking that is a very time-consuming especially the number of image sequence is large. Future work is expected to combine MFO-based tracking system with the traditional tracking algorithm for high efficiency and high accuracy of target tracking.

References

1. Wang, D., Lu, H., Xiao, Z., Yang, M.: Inverse sparse tracker with a locally weighted distance metric. IEEE Trans. Image Process. **24**(9), 2646–2657 (2015)
2. Meshgi, K., Maeda, S., Oba, S., et al.: An occlusion-aware particle filter tracker to handle complex and persistent occlusions. Comput. Vis. Image Und. **150**, 81–94 (2016)

3. Bibi, A., Zhang, T., Ghanem, B.: 3D part-based sparse tracker with automatic synchronization and registration. In: Proceedings of the IEEE Conference on Computer Vision and Pattern Recognition (CVPR), Las Vegas, pp. 1439–1448 (2016)

4. Zhang, H., Wang, Y., Luo, L., et al.: SIFT flow for abrupt motion tracking via adaptive samples selection with sparse representation. Neurocomputing **249**(2), 253–265 (2017)

5. Zhou, T., Bhaskar, H., Liu, F., et al.: Graph regularized and locality-constrained coding for robust visual tracking. IEEE Trans. Circ. Syst. Video Technol. **27**(10), 2153–2164 (2017)

6. Zhou, T., Liu, F., Bhaskar, H., et al.: Robust visual tracking via online discriminative and low-rank dictionary learning. IEEE Trans. Cybern. **PP**, 1–13 (2017)

7. Zhao, H., Wang, X.: Robust visual tracking via discriminative appearance model based on sparse coding. Multimedia Syst. **23**(1), 75–84 (2017)

8. Sun, C., Li, F., Lu, H., et al.: Visual tracking via joint discriminative appearance learning. IEEE Trans. Circ. Syst. Video Technol. (2016)

9. Liu, F., Zhou, T., Fu, K., et al.: Robust visual tracking via constrained correlation filter coding. Patt. Recog. Lett. **84**, 163–169 (2016)

10. Nam, H., Han B.: Learning multi-domain convolutional neural networks for visual tracking. In: Proceedings of the IEEE Conference on Computer Vision and Pattern Recognition (CVPR), Las Vegas, pp. 4293–4302 (2016)

11. Du, D., Zhang, L., Lu, H., et al.: Discriminative hash tracking with group sparsity. IEEE Trans. Cybern. **46**(8), 1914–1925 (2016)

12. Zhang, H., Zhang, J., Wu, Q., et al.: Extended kernel correlation filter for abrupt motion tracking. KSII Trans. Int. Inf. Syst. **11**(9), 4438–4460 (2017)

13. Minami, M., Agbanhan, J., Asakura, T.: Manipulator visual servoing and tracking of fish using a genetic algorithm. Indus. Robot Int. J. **26**(4), 278–289 (1999)

14. Zhang, X., Hu, W., Maybank, S., et al.: Sequential particle swarm optimization for visual tracking. In: IEEE Conference on Computer Vision and Pattern Recognition, CVPR 2008, pp. 1–8. IEEE (2008)

15. Chen, J., Zhen, Y., Yang, D., et al.: Fast moving object tracking algorithm based on hybrid quantum PSO. WSEAA Trans. Comput. **12**, 375–383 (2013)

16. Hao, Z., Zhang, X., Yu, P., et al.: Video object tracing based on particle filter with ant colony optimization. In: 2010 2nd International Conference on Advanced Computer Control (ICACC), vol. 3, pp. 232–236. IEEE (2010)

17. Nguyen, H., Bhanu, B.: Real-time pedestrian tracking with bacterial foraging optimization. In: 2012 IEEE Ninth International Conference on Advanced Video and Signal-Based Surveillance (AVSS), pp. 37–42. IEEE (2012)

18. Gao, M., He, X., Luo, D., et al.: Object tracking using firefly algorithm. IET Comput. Vis. **7**(4), 227–237 (2013)

19. Ljouad, T., Amine, A., Rziza, M.: A hybrid mobile object tracker based on the modified Cuckoo Search algorithm and the Kalman Filter. Patt. Recogn. **47**, 3597–3613 (2014)

20. Gao, M., Zang, Y., Shen, J., et al.: Visual tracking based on flower pollination algorithm. In: Proceedings of the 35th Chinese Control Conference, Chengdu, pp. 3866–3868 (2016)

21. Gao, M., Shen, J., Yin, L., et al.: A novel visual tracking method using bat algorithm. Neurocomputing **177**, 612–619 (2016)

22. Mirjalili, S.: Moth-flame optimization algorithm: a novel nature-inspired heuristic paradigm. Knowl.-Based Syst. **89**, 228–249 (2015)

Learning Soft-Consistent Correlation Filters for RGB-T Object Tracking

Yulong Wang[1], Chenglong Li[1,2(✉)], and Jin Tang[1]

[1] School of Computer Science and Technology, Anhui University, Hefei, China
wylemail@qq.com, lcl1314@foxmail.com, tj@ahu.edu.cn
[2] Center for Research on Intelligent Perception and Computing,
NLPR, CASIA, Beijing, China

Abstract. To track objects efficiently and effectively in adverse illumination conditions even in dark environment, this paper presents a novel soft-consistent correlation filters (SCCF) using RGB and thermal infrared (RGB-T) data for visual tracking. The proposed SCCF uses soft consistency to take both collaboration and heterogeneity into account for joint learning of the correlation filters of RGB and thermal spectra, while the computational time is reduced significantly by employing the Fast Fourier Transform (FFT). Moreover, a novel weighted fusion mechanism is proposed to compute the final response map in the detection phase. Extensive experiments on the benchmark dataset show that the proposed approach performs favorably against state-of-the-art methods, while runs at 50 frames per second.

Keywords: Visual tracking · RGB and thermal fusion
Correlation filter · Soft-consistent

1 Introduction

Visual tracking is an active research area in the computer vision community, since it is an essential and significant task in various applications, such as visual surveillance, robotics, human-computer interaction, and self-driving systems, to name a few [8,21,22]. Despite of many breakthroughs recently [16,23,29], the visual tracking mainly relies on traditional RGB sensors and tracks target objects in case of cluttered background and low visibility at night and in bad weather, and is thus still regarded as a challenging problem.

The adoption of thermal infrared sensors has provided new opportunities to advance the state-of-the-art trackers by handle the aforementioned challenges [13,15,17–20,26]. However, how to perform efficient and effective fusion of different modalities for boosting tracking performance is an open issue.

In recent years, many methods [13,18–20,26] have been proposed to fuse different spectra for improving tracking performance. Some trackers [13,20,26] focus on the sparse representation in Bayesian filtering framework because of its capability of suppressing noises and errors. Some trackers [13,19] introduce

© Springer Nature Switzerland AG 2018
J.-H. Lai et al. (Eds.): PRCV 2018, LNCS 11259, pp. 295–306, 2018.
https://doi.org/10.1007/978-3-030-03341-5_25

spectral weights to fuse RGB and thermal information. Despite all these significant progress, these methods [13,19] still have some limitations. These methods only consider the collaboration of different source data. However, different spectra are usually heterogeneous (e.g., RGB and thermal), and thus direct fusion that only employs the collaboration might be ineffective. On the other hand, the method [13] based on collaborative sparse representation in Bayesian filtering framework is time-consuming. However, most applications demand real-time tracking.

To deal with these issues, we present a novel multi-spectral approach based on correlation filters [10] to perform efficient object tracking. Specifically, we propose a novel scheme to deploy the inter-spectral information by imposing soft consistency in the correlation filters. Our method take both the collaboration and the heterogeneity of different spectral information into account for more effective fusion. For the collaboration, we observe that the learned filters should select similar circular shifts such that they have similar motion. While for the heterogeneity, we intend to allow filters have sparse different elements to each other. Moreover, we design a novel mechanism to fuse RGB and thermal information for robust visual tracking. We calculate the spectral weights according to the response map in the detection phase, and the final response map is obtained by weighted fusion of each spectral response map.

We validate the effectiveness and efficiency of the proposed method on the benchmark dataset, i.e., GTOT [13], and the results show that our approach achieves big superiority in terms of accuracy and comparable performance in terms of efficiency.

To summarize, the main contributions of this work are three-fold.

- A novel soft-consistent correlation filters for RGB-T object tracking is proposed. In order to take both collaboration and the heterogeneity of RGB and thermal spectra into account, the correlation filters of multi-spectral are learned jointly by imposing soft consistency. And the computational time is reduced significantly by employing the Fast Fourier Transform (FFT).
- A spectral fusion mechanism is designed. The spectral weights are obtained according to the response map in the detection phase, and the final response map is obtained by weighted fusion of different spectra.
- It performs favorably against a number of state-of-the-art trackers with the running speed over 50 frames per second. To facilitate further studies, our source code will be made available to the public.

2   Related Work

We review the related work to us from two research streams, i.e., RGB-T object tracking and Correlation filter tracking.

2.1   RGB-T Object Tracking

RGB-T object tracking has drawn a lot of attentions in the computer vision community with the popularity of thermal infrared sensors [3,13,14,18–20,26].

Cvejic et al. [3] investigate the impact of pixel-level fusion of videos from RGB-T surveillance cameras, and accomplish their tracker by means of a particle filter with the fusion of a color cue and the structural similarity measure. Wu et al. [26] and Liu and Sun [20] directly employ the sparse representation to calculate the likelihood score using reconstruction residues or coefficients in Bayesian filtering framework. They ignore modality reliabilities in fusion, which may limit the tracking performance when facing malfunction or occasional perturbation of individual sources. Li et al. [13] and Li et al. [19] introduce modality weights to handle this problem, and propose sparse representation based algorithms to fuse RGB and thermal information. Different from these methods, we take both collaboration and the heterogeneity of RGB and thermal spectrums into account by imposing soft consistency in the correlation filter tracking framework to perform efficient and effective multispectral tracking.

2.2   Correlation Filter Tracking

Correlation filters have achieved great breakthroughs in visual tracking due to its accuracy and computational efficiency [1,4–7,10,11,29]. Bolme et al. [1] first introduce correlation filters into visual tracking, named MOSSE, and achieve hundreds of frames per second, and high tracking accuracy. Recently, many researchers further improve MOSSE from different aspects. For example, Henriques et al. [10,11] extend MOSSE to non-linear one with kernel trick, and incorporate multiple channel features efficiently by summing all channels in kernel space. To handle scale variations, Danelljan et al. [4] learn correlation filters for translation and scale estimation separately by using a scale pyramid representation. Dong et al. [7] propose a sparse correlation filter for combining the robustness of sparse representation and the efficiency of correlation filter. Zhang et al. [29] integrate multiple parts and multiple features into a unified correlation particle filter framework to perform effective object tracking.

3   Proposed SCCF Tracker

In this section, we first present the technical details of the proposed algorithm and then describe the optimization process of the model.

3.1   SCCF Formulation

For a typical correlation filter, many negative samples are used to improve the discriminability of the track-by-detector scheme. In this work, denote $\mathbf{x}_k$ as the feature vector of $M \times N \times D$ of k-th spectrum, where M, N, and D indicates the width, height, and the number of channels, respectively. We consider all the circular shifts of $\mathbf{x}_k$ along the M and N dimensions as training samples of k-th spectrum. Each shifted sample $\mathbf{x}_{m,n}^k$, $(m, n) \in \{0, 1, ..., M - 1\} \times \{0, 1, ..., N - 1\}$, has a Gaussian function label $y(m, n) = e^{-\frac{(m - M/2)^2 + (n - N/2)^2}{2\sigma^2}}$, where σ is the kernel width. Let $\mathbf{X}_k = [\mathbf{x}_{0,0}, ..., \mathbf{x}_{m,n}, ...\mathbf{x}_{M-1,N-1}]^{\mathrm{T}}$ denote all training samples of the k-th spectrum $(k = 1, ..., K)$. The purpose is to find the optimal correlation filters $\mathbf{w}_k$ for K different spectra,

$$\min_{\mathbf{w}_k} \sum_{k=1}^{K} \frac{1}{2}||\mathbf{X}_k\mathbf{w}_k - \mathbf{y}||_2^2 + \lambda_1||\mathbf{w}_k||_2^2, \tag{1}$$

where λ_1 is a regularization parameter. The objective function (1) can equivalently be expressed in its dual form,

$$\min_{\mathbf{z}_k} \sum_{k=1}^{K} \frac{1}{4\lambda_1}\mathbf{z}_k^{\mathrm{T}}\mathbf{G}_k\mathbf{z}_k + \frac{1}{4}\mathbf{z}_k^{\mathrm{T}}\mathbf{z}_k - \mathbf{z}_k^{\mathrm{T}}\mathbf{y}. \tag{2}$$

Here, the vector $\mathbf{z}_k$ contains $M \times N$ dual optimization variables $\mathbf{z}_{m,n}^k$, and $\mathbf{G}_k = \mathbf{X}_k\mathbf{X}_k^{\mathrm{T}}$. The two solutions are related by $\mathbf{w}_k = \frac{\mathbf{X}_k^{\mathrm{T}}\mathbf{z}_k}{2\lambda_1}$. The discriminative training samples $\mathbf{x}_{m,n}^k$ are selected by the learned $\mathbf{z}_{m,n}^k$ to distinguish the target object from the background. Obviously, the training samples $\mathbf{x}_{m,n}^k$, $(m, n) \in \{0, 1, ..., M - 1\} \times \{0, 1, ..., N - 1\}$ are the all possible circular shifts, which denote the possible locations of the target object.

Most of existing works only consider the collaboration of different source data [13,19]. However, different spectra are usually heterogeneous (e.g., RGB and thermal), and thus direct fusion that only employs the collaboration might be ineffective. Therefore, in this paper, we propose a novel scheme to take both the collaboration and the heterogeneity of different spectral information into account for more effective fusion. For the collaboration, we observe that the learned $\{\mathbf{z}_k\}$ should select similar circular shifts such that they have similar motion. While for the heterogeneity, we intend to allow $\{\mathbf{z}_k\}$ have sparse different elements to each other. Taking the above considerations together, we propose a soft-consistent constraint on $\{\mathbf{z}_k\}$ that makes them consistent while allowing the sparse inconsistency exists, and formulated as a l_1-optimization based sparse learning problem. Finally, we obtain the soft-consistent correlation filter(SCCF) for multi-spectral tracking as

$$\min_{\mathbf{z}_k} \sum_{k=1}^{K} \frac{1}{4\lambda_1}\mathbf{z}_k^{\mathrm{T}}\mathbf{G}_k\mathbf{z}_k + \frac{1}{4}\mathbf{z}_k^{\mathrm{T}}\mathbf{z}_k - \mathbf{z}_k^{\mathrm{T}}\mathbf{y} + \lambda_2 \sum_{k=2}^{K} ||\mathbf{z}_k - \mathbf{z}_{k-1}||_1, \tag{3}$$

where λ_1 and λ_2 are regularization parameters.

3.2 Optimization Algorithm

In this section, we present algorithmic details on how to efficiently solve the optimization problem (3). Two auxiliary variables $\mathbf{P}$ and $\mathbf{q}_k$ are introduced to make Eq. (3) separable:

$$\min_{\mathbf{z}_k, \mathbf{P}, \mathbf{q}_k} \sum_{k=1}^{K} \frac{1}{4\lambda_1}\mathbf{q}_k^{\mathrm{T}}\mathbf{G}_k\mathbf{q}_k + \frac{1}{4}\mathbf{q}_k^{\mathrm{T}}\mathbf{q}_k - \mathbf{q}_k^{\mathrm{T}}\mathbf{y} + \lambda_2||\mathbf{P}||_1 \tag{4}$$

$$s.t. \mathbf{P} = \mathbf{CZ}, \mathbf{z}_k = \mathbf{q}_k,$$

where $\mathbf{Z} = [\mathbf{z}_1; \mathbf{z}_2; ...; \mathbf{z}_K]$, $\mathbf{C}$ is the consistency matrix, which is defined as:

$$\mathbf{C} = \begin{bmatrix} -\mathbf{I}^1 & \mathbf{I}^2 & & \\ & -\mathbf{I}^2 & \mathbf{I}^3 & \\ & & ... & ... \\ & & & -\mathbf{I}^{K-1} & \mathbf{I}^K \end{bmatrix}. \ \mathbf{I} \text{ is the identity matrix.}$$

We use the fast first-order Alternating Direction Method of Multipliers (ADMM) to efficiently solve the optimization problem (4). By introducing augmented Lagrange multipliers to incorporate the equality constraints into the objective function, we obtain a Lagrangian function that can be optimized through a sequence of simple closed form update operations in (5).

$$\min_{\mathbf{z}_k, \mathbf{P}, \mathbf{q}_k} \sum_{k=1}^{K} \frac{1}{4\lambda_1} \mathbf{q}_k^T \mathbf{G}_k \mathbf{q}_k + \frac{1}{4} \mathbf{q}_k^T \mathbf{q}_k - \mathbf{q}_k^T \mathbf{y} + \langle \mathbf{Y}_{2,k}, \mathbf{q}_k - \mathbf{z}_k \rangle + \frac{\mu}{2} ||\mathbf{q}_k - \mathbf{z}_k||_2^2$$

$$+ \lambda_2 ||\mathbf{P}||_1 + \langle \mathbf{Y}_1, \mathbf{P} - \mathbf{C}\mathbf{Z} \rangle + \frac{\mu}{2} ||\mathbf{P} - \mathbf{C}\mathbf{Z}||_F^2$$

$$= \sum_{k=1}^{K} \frac{1}{4\lambda_1} \mathbf{q}_k^T \mathbf{G}_k \mathbf{q}_k + \frac{1}{4} \mathbf{q}_k^T \mathbf{q}_k - \mathbf{q}_k^T \mathbf{y} + \frac{\mu}{2} ||\mathbf{q}_k - \mathbf{z}_k + \frac{\mathbf{Y}_{2,k}}{\mu}||_2^2 - \frac{1}{2\mu} ||\mathbf{Y}_{2,k}||_2^2$$

$$+ \lambda_2 ||\mathbf{P}||_1 + \frac{\mu}{2} ||\mathbf{P} - \mathbf{C}\mathbf{Z} + \frac{\mathbf{Y}_1}{\mu}||_F^2 - \frac{1}{2\mu} ||\mathbf{Y}_1||_F^2$$

$$\tag{5}$$

Here, $\langle \mathbf{A}, \mathbf{B} \rangle = \mathrm{Tr}(\mathbf{A}^T \mathbf{B})$ denotes the matrix inner product. $\mathbf{Y}_1$ and $\mathbf{Y}_{2,k}$ are Lagrangian multipliers. We then alternatively update one variable by minimizing (5) with fixing other variables. Besides the Lagrangian multipliers, there are three variables, including $\mathbf{q}_k$, $\mathbf{Z}$ and $\mathbf{P}$, to solve. The solutions of the subproblems are as follows:

q-subproblem. Given fixed $\mathbf{P}$ and $\mathbf{Z}$, $\mathbf{q}_k$ is updated by solving the optimization problem (6) with the solution (7)

$$\min_{\mathbf{q}_k} \sum_{k=1}^{K} \frac{1}{4\lambda_1} \mathbf{q}_k^T \mathbf{G}_k \mathbf{q}_k + \frac{1}{4} \mathbf{q}_k^T \mathbf{q}_k - \mathbf{q}_k^T \mathbf{y} + \frac{\mu}{2} ||\mathbf{q}_k - \mathbf{z}_k + \frac{\mathbf{Y}_{2,k}}{\mu}||_2^2, \tag{6}$$

$$\mathbf{q}_k = (\frac{1}{2\lambda_1} \mathbf{G}_k + \frac{1}{2}\mathbf{I} + \mu\mathbf{I})^{-1}(\mathbf{y} + \mu\mathbf{z}_k - \mathbf{Y}_{2,k}). \tag{7}$$

Here, $\mathbf{G}_k = \mathbf{X}_k \mathbf{X}_k^T$. $\mathbf{I}$ is an identity matrix. Note that, all circulant matrices are made diagonal by the Discrete Fourier Transform (DFT), regardless of the generating vector. If $\mathbf{X}_k$ is a circulant matrix, it can be expressed with its base sample $\mathbf{x}_k$ as

$$\mathbf{X}_k = F diag(\hat{\mathbf{x}}_k) F^H, \tag{8}$$

where $\hat{\mathbf{x}}_k$ denotes the DFT of the generating vector, $\hat{\mathbf{x}}_k = \mathcal{F}(\mathbf{x}_k)$, and F is a constant matrix that does not depend on $\mathbf{x}_k$. The constant matrix F is known as the DFT matrix. $\mathbf{X}_k^H$ is the Hermitian transpose, i.e., $\mathbf{X}_k^H = (\mathbf{X}_k^*)^T$, and $\mathbf{X}_k^*$ is the complex-conjugate of $\mathbf{X}_k$. For real numbers, $\mathbf{X}_k^H = \mathbf{X}_k^T$. It (Eq. (7)) can

---

Algorithm 1. Optimization Procedure to Eq. (4).

Input: The spectra feature matrix $\mathbf{X}_k(k = 1, 2..., K)$ and Gaussian function label $\mathbf{y}$, the parameters λ_1 and λ_2;
Set $\mathbf{q}_k = \mathbf{Y}_{2,k} = 0, \mathbf{P} = \mathbf{Y}_1 = 0, \mathbf{Z} = 0, \mu_0 = 0.1, \mu_{max} = 10^{10}, \rho = 1.2, \epsilon = 10^{-15}, maxIter = 10$ and $t = 0$.
Output: The filter $\mathbf{z}_k$.
    while not converged **do**
        Update $\mathbf{q}_{k,t+1}$ by Eq. (9);
        Update $\mathbf{P}_{t+1}$ by Eq. (11);
        Update $\mathbf{Z}_{t+1}$ by Eq. (13);
        Update Lagrange multipliers as follows:
            $\mathbf{Y}_{1,t+1} = \mathbf{Y}_{1,t} + \mu_t(\mathbf{P} - \mathbf{CZ})$;
            $\mathbf{Y}_{2,k,t+1} = \mathbf{Y}_{2,k,t} + \mu_t(\mathbf{q}_k - \mathbf{z}_k)$;
        Update μ_{t+1} by $\mu_{t+1} = \min(\mu_{max}, \rho\mu_t)$;
        Update t by $t = t + 1$;
        Check the convergence condition, i.e. the maximum element changes of $\mathbf{q}_k, \mathbf{P}$ and $\mathbf{Z}$ between two consecutive iterations are less than ϵ or the maximum number of iterations reaches maxIter.
    end while

---

be calculated very efficiently in the Fourier domain by considering the circulant structure property of $\mathbf{X}_k$,

$$\mathbf{q}_k = \mathcal{F}^{-1}\left[\frac{2\lambda_1(\hat{\mathbf{y}} + \mu\hat{\mathbf{z}}_k - \hat{\mathbf{Y}}_{2,k})}{\hat{\mathbf{x}}_k^* \odot \hat{\mathbf{x}}_k + \lambda_1 + 2\lambda_1\mu}\right]. \tag{9}$$

Here, $\mathcal{F}^{-1}$ denotes the inverse DFT, while $\odot$ as well as the fraction denote the element-wise product and division, respectively. The $\mathbf{x}_k$ is the base sample of circulant matrix $\mathbf{X}_k$.

P-subproblem. Given fixed $\mathbf{Z}$ and $\mathbf{q}_k$, Eq. (5) can be rewritten as

$$\min_{\mathbf{P}} \lambda_2||\mathbf{P}||_1 + \frac{\mu}{2}||\mathbf{P} - \mathbf{CZ} + \frac{\mathbf{Y}_1}{\mu}||_F^2. \tag{10}$$

According to (Lin et al. 2009), an efficient closed-form solution can be computed by the soft-thresholding (or shrinkage) method:

$$\mathbf{P} = S_{\frac{\lambda_2}{\mu}}(\mathbf{CZ} - \frac{\mathbf{Y}_1}{\mu}), \tag{11}$$

where the definition of $S_\lambda(a)$ is $S_\lambda(a) = \text{sign}(a)\max(0, |a| - \lambda)$.

Z-subproblem. Given fixed $\mathbf{q}_k$ and $\mathbf{P}$, Eq. (5) can be rewritten as

$$\min_{\mathbf{Z}} \frac{\mu}{2}(||\mathbf{P} - \mathbf{CZ} + \frac{\mathbf{Y}_1}{\mu}||_F^2 + ||\mathbf{Q} - \mathbf{Z} + \frac{\mathbf{Y}_2}{\mu}||_F^2). \tag{12}$$

where $\mathbf{Q} = [\mathbf{q}_1; \mathbf{q}_2; ...; \mathbf{q}_K]$. The solution of Eq. (12) is:

$$\mathbf{Z} = (\mu\mathbf{C}^\mathrm{T}\mathbf{C} + \mu\mathbf{I})^{-1}(\mu\mathbf{C}^\mathrm{T}\mathbf{P} + \mathbf{C}^\mathrm{T}\mathbf{Y}_1 + \mu\mathbf{Q} + \mathbf{Y}_2) \tag{13}$$

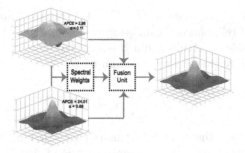

Fig. 1. Pipeline of the proposed spectral fusion mechanism. The spectral weights are obtained according to the response map in the detection phase, and the final response map is obtained by weighted fusion of different spectra response maps.

Since each subproblem of Eq. (4) is convex, we can guarantee that the limit point by our algorithm satisfies the Nash equilibrium conditions [27]. And the main steps of the optimization procedure are summarized in Algorithm 1.

3.3   Tracking

Target Position Estimation. After solving this optimization problem, we obtain the correlation filter $\mathbf{z}_k$ for each type of spectrum. Given an image patch in the next frame, the feature vector on the k-th spectrum is denoted by $\mathbf{s}_k$ and of size $M \times N \times D$. We first transform it to the Fourier domain $\hat{\mathbf{s}}_k = \mathcal{F}(\mathbf{s}_k)$, and then the k-th correlation response map is computed by

$$\mathbf{R}_k = \mathcal{F}^{-1}(\hat{\mathbf{s}}_k \odot \hat{\mathbf{x}}_k^* \odot \hat{\mathbf{z}}_k). \qquad (14)$$

Some existed trackers [13] learn spectral weights in a single unified algorithm. Actually, this may increase the complexity of the proposed model. In this work, we use a novel criterion called average peak-to-correlation energy ($APCE$) measure, as proposed in [25], to calculate the priori influence factor. The definition of $APCE$ is

$$APCE = \frac{|R_{max} - R_{min}|^2}{mean(\sum_{m,n}(R_{m,n} - R_{min})^2)}, \qquad (15)$$

where R_{max}, R_{min} and $R_{m,n}$ denote the maximum, minimum and the m-th row n-th column entry of the response map $\mathbf{R}$, respectively. $APCE$ indicates the degree of fluctuation of the response maps. For sharper peaks and fewer noise, i.e., the target apparently appearing in the detection region, $APCE$ will become larger and the response map will become smooth except for only one sharp peak. Otherwise, $APCE$ will significantly decrease if the response map is multi-peaks. Based on the nature of the $APCE$, we design a new method to calculate the weights of different spectra as follow:

$$\alpha_k = \frac{APCE_k}{\sum_{k=1}^{K} APCE_k}, \qquad (16)$$

where $APCE_k$ denotes the value of $APCE$ of the k-th spectrum. As illustrated in Fig. 1, the weight of reliable spectrum is larger than unreliable spectrum because the $APCE$ of reliable spectrum is much larger than unreliable spectrum. Then the final correlation response map is computed by

$$\mathbf{R} = \sum_{k=1}^{K} \alpha_k \mathbf{R}_k. \tag{17}$$

The target location then can be estimated by searching for the position of maximum value of the correlation response map $\mathbf{R}$ of size $M \times N$.

Model Update. Similar to other CF trackers [10,23,24,29]. To improve our robustness to pose, scale and illumination changes, we adopt an incremental strategy, which only uses new samples $\mathbf{x}_k$ in the current frame to update models as shown in (18), where t is the frame index and η is a learning rate parameter.

$$\begin{aligned}
\mathcal{F}(\mathbf{x}_k^t) &= (1-\eta)\mathcal{F}(\mathbf{x}_k^{t-1}) + \eta\mathcal{F}(\mathbf{x}_k^t), \\
\mathcal{F}(\mathbf{z}_k^t) &= (1-\eta)\mathcal{F}(\mathbf{z}_k^{t-1}) + \eta\mathcal{F}(\mathbf{z}_k^t).
\end{aligned} \tag{18}$$

4   Experiments

In this section, we present extensive experimental evaluations on the proposed soft-consistent correlation filters (SCCF) tracker. We first introduce the experimental setups, and then extensive experiments are conducted to evaluate the SCCF tracker against plenty of state-of-the-art trackers on GTOT benchmark.

4.1   Experimental Setups

Implementation Details. We set the regularization parameters of (3) to $\lambda_1 = 0.038$ and $\lambda_2 = 0.012$, and use a kernel width of 0.1 for generating the Gaussian function labels. Their learning rate η in (18) is set to 0.025. To remove the boundary discontinuities, the extracted feature are weighted by a cosine window. In addition, we utilize an adaptive multi-scale strategy to adapt to the scale variations. We implement our tracker in MATLAB on an Intel I7-6700K 4.00 GHz CPU with 32 GB RAM. Furthermore, all the parameter settings are available in the source code to be released for accessible reproducible research.

Dataset. Our algorithm is evaluated on a large visual tracking benchmark dataset: GTOT [13]. GTOT includes 50 aligned RGB-T video pairs with about 12 K frames in total. They are annotated with ground truth bounding boxes and various visual attributes.

Evaluation Protocol. All trackers are evaluated according to widely used metrics, precision rate (PR) and success rate (SR), as defined in GTOT [13]. PR is the percentage of frames whose output location is within the given threshold distance of ground truth. SR is the ratio of the number of successful frames whose overlap is larger than a threshold. By changing the threshold, the SR plot can be obtained, and we employ the area under curve of SR plot to define the representative SR.

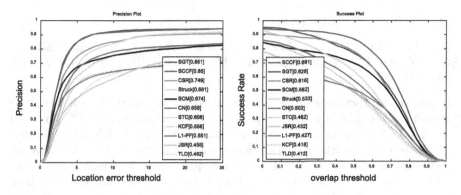

Fig. 2. The evaluation results on public GTOT benchmark. The representative score of PR/SR is presented in the legend.

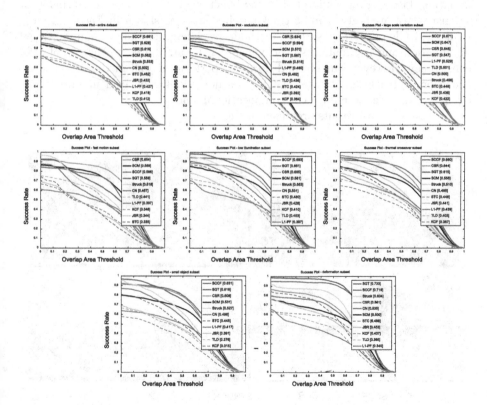

Fig. 3. Attribute-based evaluation on 50 sequences. We also put the overall performance here (the first one) for comparison convenience facing a single challenge and their combination.

4.2   Performance Evaluation

We evaluate our SCCF algorithm with 10 trackers on GTOT, including CSR [13], SGT [19], Struck [9], SCM [30], CN [6], STC [28], KCF [10], L1-PF [26], JSR [20] and TLD [12].

Quantitative Evaluation. As shown in Fig. 2, we report the PR/SR score for each tracker in the figure legend. Among all the trackers, our SCCF method occupies the best one in terms of SR. Compared with CSR, SCCF achieves about 6.5% improvement with SR. Furthermore, compared with SGT, SCCF achieves much better performance with about 5.3% improvement. Although SGT tracker performs the best against the other trackers in PR score, its model is more complex than ours. Moreover, the proposed tracker performs at about 50 FPS (frames per second) which is much faster than SGT (about 5 FPS).

Attribute-Based Evaluation. We further analyze the robustness of the proposed tracker performance in various scenes (e.g., thermal crossover, low illumination, fast motion) annotated in the benchmark. Our tracker performs well against other methods in most tracking challenges as shown in Fig. 3. In particular, SCCF outperforms other methods by a huge margin in handling low illumination and thermal crossover, which can be attributed to the use of soft consistency. However, our method does not perform as well in the presence of occlusion and deformation, as SCCF does not adopt a delayed update strategy [2, 25] in order to reduce the computational load.

More qualitative results are given in Fig. 4.

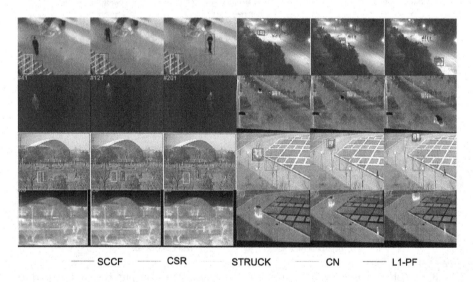

Fig. 4. Sample results of our method against other tracking methods, including L1-PF, CSR, Struck, and CN.

5 Conclusion

In this paper, we propose a novel learning soft-consistent correlation filters for RGB-T object tracking. The proposed tracking algorithm can effectively exploit collaboration and heterogeneity among different spectra to learn their correlation filters jointly. Moreover, we design a novel mechanism to fuse RGB and thermal information for robust visual tracking. Experimental results compared with several state-of-the-art methods on visual tracking benchmark demonstrate the effectiveness and robustness of the proposed algorithm. In the future, we will investigate the performance of multi-channel features (such as HOG) and design a new algorithm based on this work to calculate the correlation filters and spectral weights simultaneously.

Acknowledgment. This work is jointly supported by National Natural Science Foundation of China (61702002, 61472002), China Postdoctoral Science Foundation, Natural Science Foundation of Anhui Province (1808085QF187), Natural Science Foundation of Anhui Higher Education Institution of China (KJ2017A017), and Co-Innovation Center for Information Supply & Assurance Technology, Anhui University.

References

1. Bolme, D.S., Beveridge, J.R., Draper, B.A., Lui, Y.M.: Visual object tracking using adaptive correlation filters. In: CVPR, pp. 2544–2550 (2010)
2. Choi, J., Chang, H.J., Yun, S., Fischer, T., Demiris, Y., Jin, Y.C.: Attentional correlation filter network for adaptive visual tracking. In: IEEE Conference on CVPR, pp. 4828–4837 (2017)
3. Cvejic, N., et al.: The effect of pixel-level fusion on object tracking in multi-sensor surveillance video. In: Proceedings of IEEE Conference on CVPR (2007)
4. Danelljan, M., Häger, G., Khan, F.S.: Accurate scale estimation for robust visual tracking. In: BMVC, pp. 65.1–65.11 (2014)
5. Danelljan, M., Bhat, G., Khan, F.S., Felsberg, M.: ECO: efficient convolution operators for tracking. In: Proceedings of IEEE Conference on CVPR (2017)
6. Danelljan, M., Khan, F.S., Felsberg, M., Weijer, J.V.D.: Adaptive color attributes for real-time visual tracking. In: Proceedings of IEEE Conference on CVPR, pp. 1090–1097 (2014)
7. Dong, Y., Yang, M., Pei, M.: Visual tracking with sparse correlation filters. In: IEEE ICIP, pp. 439–443 (2016)
8. Emami, A., Dadgostar, F., Bigdeli, A., Lovell, B.C.: Role of spatiotemporal oriented energy features for robust visual tracking in video surveillance. In: IEEE Conference on AVSS, pp. 349–354 (2012)
9. Hare, S., Saffari, A., Torr, P.H.S.: Struck: structured output tracking with kernels. In: ICCV, pp. 263–270 (2011)
10. Henriques, J.F., Caseiro, R., Martins, P., Batista, J.: High-speed tracking with kernelized correlation filters. IEEE TPAMI **37**(3), 583–596 (2015)
11. Henriques, J.F., Caseiro, R., Martins, P., Batista, J.: Exploiting the circulant structure of tracking-by-detection with kernels. In: Fitzgibbon, A., Lazebnik, S., Perona, P., Sato, Y., Schmid, C. (eds.) ECCV 2012. LNCS, vol. 7575, pp. 702–715. Springer, Heidelberg (2012). https://doi.org/10.1007/978-3-642-33765-9_50

12. Kalal, Z., Mikolajczyk, K., Matas, J.: Tracking-learning-detection. IEEE TPAMI **34**(7), 1409–1422 (2012)
13. Li, C., Cheng, H., Hu, S., Liu, X., Tang, J., Lin, L.: Learning collaborative sparse representation for grayscale-thermal tracking. IEEE TIP **25**(12), 5743–5756 (2016)
14. Li, C., Hu, S., Gao, S., Tang, J.: Real-Time Grayscale-Thermal Tracking via Laplacian Sparse Representation. Springer, Cham (2016)
15. Li, C., Liang, X., Lu, Y., Zhao, N., Tang, J.: RGB-T object tracking: benchmark and baseline. arXiv:1805.08982 (2018)
16. Li, C., Lin, L., Zuo, W., Tang, J., Yang, M.H.: Visual tracking via dynamic graph learning. IEEE TPAMI (2018). https://doi.org/10.1109/TPAMI.2018.2864965
17. Li, C., Wang, X., Zhang, L., Tang, J., Wu, H., Lin, L.: Weighted low-rank decomposition for robust grayscale-thermal foreground detection. IEEE TCSVT **27**(4), 725–738 (2017)
18. Li, C., Wu, X., Zhao, N., Cao, X., Tang, J.: Fusing two-stream convolutional neural networks for RGB-T object tracking. Neurocomputing **281**, 78–85 (2018)
19. Li, C., Zhao, N., Lu, Y., Zhu, C., Tang, J.: Weighted sparse representation regularized graph learning for RGB-T object tracking. In: Proceedings of ACM MM (2017)
20. Liu, H.P., Sun, F.C.: Fusion tracking in color and infrared images using joint sparse representation. Inf. Sci. **55**(3), 590–599 (2012)
21. Liu, L., Xing, J., Ai, H.: Multi-view vehicle detection and tracking in crossroads. In: ACPR, pp. 608–612 (2011)
22. Liu, L., Xing, J., Ai, H., Xiang, R.: Hand posture recognition using finger geometric feature. In: ICPR, pp. 565–568 (2013)
23. Ma, C., Huang, J.B., Yang, X., Yang, M.H.: Hierarchical convolutional features for visual tracking. In: IEEE ICCV, pp. 3074–3082 (2016)
24. Qi, Y., et al.: Hedged deep tracking. In: CVPR (2016)
25. Wang, M., Liu, Y., Huang, Z.: Large margin object tracking with circulant feature maps. In: CVPR, pp. 4800–4808 (2017)
26. Wu, Y., Blasch, E., Chen, G., Bai, L., Ling, H.: Multiple source data fusion via sparse representation for robust visual tracking. In: ICIF, pp. 1–8 (2011)
27. Xu, Y., Yin, W.: A block coordinate descent method for regularized multiconvex optimization with applications to nonnegative tensor factorization and completion. SIIMS **6**(3), 1758–1789 (2015)
28. Zhang, K., Zhang, L., Liu, Q., Zhang, D., Yang, M.-H.: Fast visual tracking via dense spatio-temporal context learning. In: Fleet, D., Pajdla, T., Schiele, B., Tuytelaars, T. (eds.) ECCV 2014. LNCS, vol. 8693, pp. 127–141. Springer, Cham (2014). https://doi.org/10.1007/978-3-319-10602-1_9
29. Zhang, T., Xu, C., Yang, M.H.: Multi-task correlation particle filter for robust object tracking. In: IEEE Conference on CVPR, pp. 4819–4827 (2017)
30. Zhong, W., Lu, H., Yang, M.H.: Robust object tracking via sparse collaborative appearance model. IEEE TIP **23**(5), 2356 (2014)

Performance Evaluation and Database

A Touching Character Database from Tibetan Historical Documents to Evaluate the Segmentation Algorithm

Quanchao Zhao[1,2(✉)], Long-long Ma[3], and Lijuan Duan[1,4]

[1] Faculty of Information Technology, Beijing University of Technology,
Beijing, China
quanchaozhao@yeah.net, ljduan@bjut.edu.cn
[2] Beijing Key Laboratory of Trusted Computing, Beijing, China
[3] Chinese Information Processing Laboratory, Institute of Software,
Chinese Academy of Sciences, Beijing, China
longlong@iscas.ac.cn
[4] Beijing Key Laboratory on Integration and Analysis
of Large-Scale Stream Data, Beijing, China

Abstract. The benchmarking database plays an essential role in evaluating the performance of the touching character string segmentation algorithm. In this paper, we present a new touching Tibetan character strings database. Firstly, using the previous proposed layout analysis and text-line segmentation algorithms, we segment scanned images of historical Tibetan documents into text-line images. Then, we find candidate touching Tibetan character strings using connected component analysis and screen out the correct touching samples. Finally, we annotate the data manually and establish the touching character database. The database contains 5,844 images of two-touching characters and 1,399 images of more than two-touching characters. It is applicable to evaluate the segmentation algorithms for the touching Tibetan character strings. For each image, the annotated ground truth file includes class labels, candidate segment points, baseline and average stroke width of a Tibetan single character. According to the type of touching, we divide the touching character string into three types: AB, OB and BB. We also count the number of different type of samples and find that 76.27% of the samples belongs to the third type (BB). In the end, we measure the performance of the over-segmentation algorithm on this database for reference.

Keywords: Historical tibetan documents · Touching character
Benchmarking database

1 Introduction

Digitalization of historical documents can protect the literature and improve the reading efficiency. Through an optical character recognition (OCR) system, we can get the content of the literature. A complete OCR system for historical documents includes: image preprocessing, layout analysis, text-line segmentation, character segmentation

© Springer Nature Switzerland AG 2018
J.-H. Lai et al. (Eds.): PRCV 2018, LNCS 11259, pp. 309–321, 2018.
https://doi.org/10.1007/978-3-030-03341-5_26

and character recognition. For the layout analysis of historical Tibetan documents, Zhang et al. [1] extract the texts by connected component analysis (CCs) and corner point detection. For the text-line segmentation, Li et al. [2] propose a baseline-based text-line segmentation algorithm to obtain the text lines of historical Tibetan documents. The research on the segmentation of the touching character string plays an essential role in character segmentation. It is a traditional but not yet fully solved problem, and related researches have started since the 1980s [3]. At present, the segmentation about touching character strings (usually are digital, letters and Chinese characters) has achieved satisfactory results, which has important applications in ZIP code recognition, bank check reading and text recognition. In this field, few scholars pay attention to the touching Tibetan character strings.

Most of the time, researchers use different databases to verify the segmentation algorithm. Finally, the algorithm proposed by researchers can display good performance in their database. It is not accurate to evaluate the performance of different algorithms on different databases. To compare the efficiency and performance of different algorithms and avoid the impact of different databases, some scholars have established the touching character string benchmarking database. Handwritten touching digital database (HWD-TD) [4] and offline Chinese touching character string database (CASIA-HWDB-T) [5] are the representatives. HWD-TD contains several different kinds of touching type and it was generated by connecting 2,000 images of isolated digits extracted from the NIST SD19. However, there is different between factual touching character string and synthesis touching character string. To better evaluate the performance of the segmentation algorithms, Xu et al. [5] extracted touching character string from CASIA-HWDB [6] by CCs. CASIA-HWDB-T includes 56,469 touching character strings, most of which belong to two-touching character type, and the 1,818 are multi-touching character type.

Inspired by the work of Oliveira et al. [4] and Xu et al. [5], we establish a touching Tibetan character strings database (TTCS-DB). THCS-DB contains 5,844 images of two-touching characters and 1,399 images of more than two-touching characters. We have annotated ground truth file for each image, which includes class labels, candidate segment points, baseline and average stroke width of a Tibetan single character. A foreground-based segmentation algorithm has been carried out on our database. In the following chapter, we will introduce our database in detail.

2   Database

To the best of our knowledge, no database about touching historical Tibetan character strings have been built so far. Next, we will introduce the collection and annotation information of the database.

2.1   Data Collection

In native Tibetan syllables, there are thirty consonants and four vowels. The structure of the Tibetan syllable is shown in Fig. 1(a). When segmenting and recognizing Tibetan characters, we usually combine the letters (consonants or vowels) in the vertical direction as a character (in the red rectangle). There is a base consonant (BC) in each syllable. Other consonants, according to their relative position to the base consonant, are called prefix consonant (PC), head consonant (HC), foot consonant (FC), the first suffix consonant (SC1), the second suffix consonant (SC2) respectively. From top to bottom, a Tibetan character may have the top vowel (TV), HC, BC, FC and the bottom vowel (BV). TV and BV can't appear in the same character simultaneously. A typical Tibetan syllable can be made of seven letters at most and only one vowel can be included. Figure 1(b) shows a typical Tibetan syllable which has four Tibetan characters [7]. To get touching Tibetan character strings, we scan the historical Tibetan documents named 'The complete works of Panchen Lama', as shown in Fig. 2. We can see that there are many touching character strings in the scanned image.

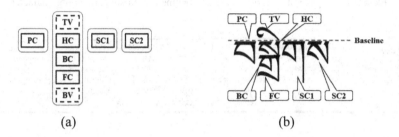

(a)   (b)

Fig. 1. Example of (a) the structure of Tibetan syllable, (b) a typical Tibetan syllable.

Firstly, we use the method proposed by Zhang et al. [1] to obtain the text regions of historical Tibetan documents. Zhang et al. [1] extract text regions of historical Tibetan documents based on CCs and corner point detection. We mark the text regions with a red polygon, as shown in Fig. 3(a). Then we divide the text regions into the text-lines by a text-line segmentation method proposed by Li et al. [2], which is based on baseline detection. The text-line segmentation result is shown in Fig. 3(b). We can see that different text-lines are labeled by different colors.

In touching character strings extraction, we mark the foreground pixel to 0 and the background pixel to 1. We use CCs to extract possible candidate connected components. Due to the cause of the ink diffusion and illumination, we delete the outliers with pixels less than 30 in foreground pixels. At last we collect the candidate connected components.

Considering the overlapping of Tibetan characters, we use the algorithm proposed by [8] to merge the connected components. The four nearest neighbor pixels are used to mark text-line images, and we save the boundary information and pixels of each connected component. We can mark the four end points of the boundary as x^l, x^r, y^t, y^b respectively. We assume that the boundary information of two components are $(x_1^l, x_1^r, y_1^t, y_1^b)$ and $(x_2^l, x_2^r, y_2^t, y_2^b)$, where x_1^l less than x_2^l. According to the formula (1), (2) and (3), we can calculate $ovlp$, $span$ and $dist$. $ovlp$ r represents the length of the overlapping of two components. $span$ represents the total length of the two components. $dist$ represents the distance between the centroids of the two components. The relationship between $ovlp$, $span$ and $dist$ can be shown in Fig. 4.

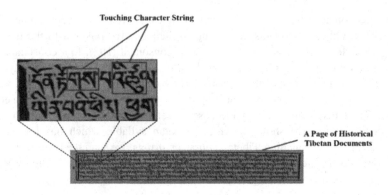

Fig. 2. Example of a page of historical Tibetan documents and some touching character string.

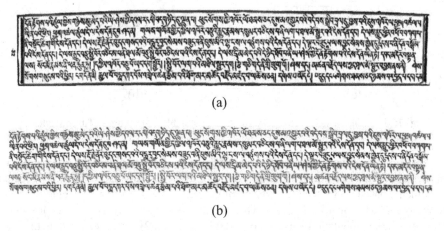

Fig. 3. Example of (a) the text region (in a red rectangle) obtained by method [1], (b) the different text-lines with different labeled colors obtained by method [2]. (Color figure online)

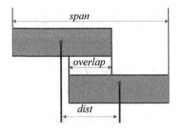

Fig. 4. The relationship between *ovlp*, *span* and *dist*.

$$ovlp = x_1^l - x_2^l \tag{1}$$

$$span = \max\left(x_1^r, x_2^r\right) - x_1^l \tag{2}$$

$$dist = \frac{1}{2}\left|\left(x_2^l + x_2^r\right) - \left(x_1^l + x_1^r\right)\right| \tag{3}$$

nmovlp is used to measure the degree of overlapping, where *w*1 and *w*2 represent the width of two connected components, respectively.

$$nmovlp = \frac{1}{2}\left(\frac{ovlp}{w1} + \frac{ovlp}{w2}\right) - \frac{dist}{span} \tag{4}$$

If *nmovlp* > 0, two connected components can be merged. After the whole text-line images processing is completed, the ratio (L_r) of the length to width of the average character is calculated. If $L_r > 1.3$, it is initially determined to be touching character string. Then, we remove the incorrect samples and obtain the final dataset. Figure 5 shows the touching character strings extracted from the text-line images. In the following, we will introduce the ground truth file's format for each touching character string.

Fig. 5. Some touching character string images extracted from historical Tibetan documents, which contain incorrect samples. The overlapping characters are marked with a red rectangle. The single characters are marked by a blue rectangle and the error characters are marked by a green rectangle. (Color figure online)

2.2 Data Annotation

All the characters and punctuation in Tibetan script are aligned according to the baseline [2], as shown in Fig. 1. This feature is helpful for the segmentation and recognition of Tibetan character. And we divide the touching type into three categories, as shown in Table 1. The three categories are touching points above the baseline (AB), on the baseline (OB) and below the baseline (BB). Through our observation, most of the images in the database belong to the two-touching characters. We partition TTCS-DB into two sub databases according to the number of characters in touching character string: TTCS-DB-T and TTCS-DB-M. Each image in TTCS-DB-T contains two characters and TTCS-DB-M is composed of more than two characters, as depicted in Fig. 6(a) and (b).

Table 1. Touching type of two-touching Tibetan character pair.

Type	Touching Stroke Relation	Examples	Rate (%)
AB			1.37
OB			22.36
BB			76.27

To accurately evaluate the efficiency of the segmentation algorithm, we have annotated the touching character string. The information of the ground truth file includes the baseline (BL), the class labels (CL), the height and width of the touching character string, the average stroke width (SW), and the candidate segmentation points. BL is an important parameter. The top vowels are located above the BL, and other letters are located under the BL. Using BL to divide the touching characters into two parts can improve the accuracy of segmentation. SW and CL are used to evaluate the accuracy of segmentation and recognition of Tibetan character respectively. We save the annotation information in an XML file. Figure 7 depicts an example of an XML file for a touching character string. The tag TextRegion represents a segmentation path. If the touching character string has two touching points, TextRegion will has four coordinate points.

2.3   Data Analysis

We count the number of characters, touching points and Multi-touching (a segmentation path has multiple points) and touching character string, as shown in the Table 2. In our database, single-touching character string is about ten times than multi-touching

(a)

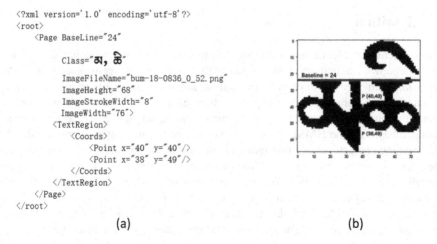

(b)

Fig. 6. Examples of touching character string samples extracted from the database: (a) each image contains two characters from TTCS-DB-T. (b) Each image contains more two characters from TTCS-DB-M.

```
<?xml version='1.0' encoding='utf-8'?>
<root>
    <Page BaseLine="24"

        Class="ཟ, ཆེ"

        ImageFileName="bum-18-0836_0_52.png"
        ImageHeight="68"
        ImageStrokeWidth="8"
        ImageWidth="76">
        <TextRegion>
            <Coords>
                <Point x="40" y="40"/>
                <Point x="38" y="49"/>
            </Coords>
        </TextRegion>
    </Page>
</root>
```

(a)   (b)

Fig. 7. Example of (a) the annotated information, (b) the touching point (indicated by the red arrow), the baseline (in blue line). (Color figure online)

316   Q. Zhao et al.

Table 2. Statistics of TTCS-DB according to the number of characters in touching character string, an overwhelming majority of which is single-touching character string.

Database	#String	#Multi-touching	#Character	#Touch point
TTCS-DB-T	5,844	427	11,688	6,300
TTCS-DB-M	1,399	163	4,350	2,835
Total	7,243	690	16,038	9,135

character string. For TTCS-DB-M, each touching character string has 2.03 touching points and 3.11 characters on average.

In follow-up investigation, we find a common phenomenon. Due to the degradation of historical Tibetan documents, the strokes of character are broken, as shown in the Fig. 8. When we annotate data, we spend a lot of time to identify touching character string. In the character recognition for Tibetan, broken strokes will bring great challenge.

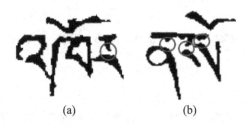

(a)   (b)

Fig. 8. Example of the broken strokes in the touching character string (in the red ring). (Color figure online)

3 Algorithm

The segmentation algorithm for touching character string can be roughly divided into two categories, implicit segmentation algorithm and explicit segmentation algorithm [9]. The main idea of implicit segmentation algorithm is to traverse the touching character string from left to right to get a feature sequence by a narrow sliding window. Then, the character recognition and segmentation result of the whole text-line are obtained based on the HMM of text-line. The explicit segmentation algorithm divides the touching character string into multiple components according the feature points in the image. It can be further divided into two categories, one is weak-segmentation and the other is over-segmentation. The main feature of the weak segmentation algorithm is that only one segmentation path is generated, which is suitable for less touching. The representative algorithm includes vertical projection [10], drip algorithm [11] water reservoir [12] and so on. The over-segmentation algorithm produces multiple segmentation paths. It can be roughly divided into three categories: foreground-based [13, 14], background-based [15], and recognition-based [16].

We have measured the performance of a foreground-based segmentation algorithm on this database for reference, which is based on feature points detection.

The flowchart of our algorithm is shown in Fig. 9. Firstly, the foreground profile and skeleton are detected. Secondly, we detect the feature points and the baseline of touching character string. The feature points are obtained by adding affine transformation to KLT algorithm [17]. According to the baseline of the touching Tibetan character string, we divide it into two parts: upper vowels and consonants. In the end, we will remove all the useless feature points. For the upper vowels part, we use feature points directly to segment upper vowels. Then, we design a support vector machine (SVM) classifier [18] to predict the probability that the image is a vowel. When the probability of each part is acceptable, we keep this feature point, otherwise we delete it. For the consonant part, all the feature points located near the end points in the skeleton are deleted.

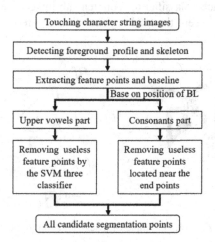

Fig. 9. The flowchart of our segmentation algorithm.

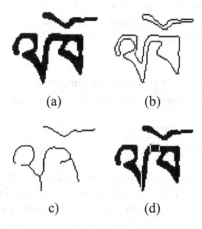

Fig. 10. Example of (a) original touching character string, (b) foreground profile and feature points, (c) foreground skeleton and end points in skeleton, (d) segmentation path.

4 Experiments

We extract the connected components by 8-connected regions for each image, and we delete components where width and height less than SW*2. Figure 10 shows candidate segmentation points and segmentation paths generated by our algorithm. Due to the irregular position of the feature points, we design two methods to construct the segmentation paths. When two feature points are located on either side of the stroke, we connect the two feature points to form a segmentation path. In other cases, we cut the strokes directly based on the feature points to form a segmentation path.

Figure 11 shows an example of an image segmented by our algorithm and its corresponding segmentation graph. Three paths (SP_0, SP_1 and SP_2) and four components (C_0, C_1, C_2 and C_3) be generated in the end. According to Tibetan character characteristics, we assume that a Tibetan character can be composed of three components at most. The touching character string can produce ten sub-images. We need use the candidate character classifier to score ten sub-images and find the largest score path in the graph to represent the final segmentation and recognition results.

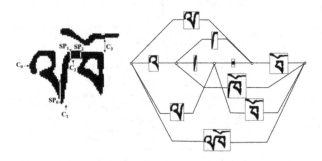

Fig. 11. Example of a segmentation graph.

We evaluate the performance of the algorithm based on the distance (d) between a touching point and a candidate point. When d is less than a threshold d_{th}, we think that the candidate point is a correct segmentation point. In our paper, we set d_{th} equal to 1.4*SW. We also calculate recall rate R and precision rate P [4] to evaluate our algorithm, as following.

$$R = \frac{\#\text{the number of correct separating points}}{\#\text{the number of total truth touching points}} \times 100\% \tag{5}$$

$$P = \frac{\#\text{the number of correct separating points}}{\#\text{the number of total candiate spatating points}} \times 100\% \tag{6}$$

Table 3 reports the performance of the foreground-based segmentation algorithm on the proposed database. In our algorithm, we extract the Tibetan baseline with an accuracy rate of 95%. Since we forcibly split upper vowels and consonants, the actual

Table 3. Performance of the foreground-based segmentation algorithm on the database.

Database	R (%)	P (%)
TTCS-DB-T	87.54	27.56
TTCS-DB-M	80.78	32.98
Average	86.60	30.25

segmentation result is better than the calculated value. Over-segmentation algorithm can achieve better segmentation results, but too many candidate points will bring expensive calculations. Table 4 reports the average number of candidate points generated by our algorithm and the time to process each file in Python program.

Table 4. The number of candidate points generated from one image on average and the time to process each file.

Database	Average number	Time for each file (s)
TTCS-DB-T	3.22	0.0905
TTCS-DB-M	5.21	0.1286
Average	3.60	0.0978

5   Conclusion and Future Works

In this paper, we present a new touching Tibetan character string database. We introduce the methods how to obtain the touching Tibetan character string from historical Tibetan documents and the ground truth file's format for each touching character string in details. The database we have established can be used to evaluate the segmentation algorithm for the touching Tibetan character string. We have implemented a foreground-based segmentation algorithm and analyzed the experimental results on our established database. 86.60% of the samples can be correctly segmented and a touching character string generates 3.6 candidate points on average. In the future, we hope to extend our database further by add touching characters and improve the precision of the algorithm. Meanwhile, we will evaluate other segmentation algorithms on our database for reference. We are also preparing to create a dataset for isolate character recognition in Tibetan historical documents.

Acknowledgment. This work was supported by the Science and Technology Project of Qinghai Province (no. 2016-ZJ-Y04) and the Basic Research Project of Qinghai Province (no. 2016-ZJ-740). The authors would like to thank Qilong Sun, the Department of Computer Science, Qinghai Nationalities University for providing the experimental dataset of historical Tibetan document images.

References

1. Zhang, X., Duan, L., Ma, L., Wu, J.: Text extraction for historical tibetan document images based on connected component analysis and corner point detection. In: Yang, J., Hu, Q., Cheng, M.-M., Wang, L., Liu, Q., Bai, X., Meng, D. (eds.) CCCV 2017. CCIS, vol. 772, pp. 545–555. Springer, Singapore (2017). https://doi.org/10.1007/978-981-10-7302-1_45

2. Li, Y., Ma, L., Duan, L., Wu, J.: A text-line segmentation method for historical tibetan documents based on baseline detection. In: Yang, J., Hu, Q., Cheng, M.-M., Wang, L., Liu, Q., Bai, X., Meng, D. (eds.) CCCV 2017. CCIS, vol. 771, pp. 356–367. Springer, Singapore (2017). https://doi.org/10.1007/978-981-10-7299-4_29

3. Casey, R.G., Lecolinet, E.: Survey of methods and strategies in character segmentation. IEEE Trans. Patt. Anal. Mach. Intell. 18(7), 690–706 (1996)

4. Oliveira, L.S., Britto, A.S., Sabourin, R.: A synthetic database to assess segmentation algorithms. In: 8th International Conference on Document Analysis and Recognition, pp. 207–211. Institute of Electronics and Electrical Engineering Computer Society, 445 Hoes Lane - P.O. Box 1331, Piscataway, NJ, 08855-1331, United States, Seoul, Republic of Korea (2005)

5. Xu, L., Yin, F., Wang, Q.F., et al.: A touching character database from chinese handwriting for assessing segmentation algorithms. In: 13th International Conference on Frontiers in Handwriting Recognition, ICFHR 2012, pp. 89–94. IEEE Computer Society, 10662 Los Vaqueros Circle - P.O. Box 3014, Los Alamitos, CA, 90720-1314, United States, Bari, Italy (2012)

6. Liu, C.L., Yin, F., Wang, D.H., et al.: CASIA online and offline chinese handwriting databases. In: 11th International Conference on Document Analysis and Recognition, ICDAR 2011, pp. 37–41. IEEE Computer Society, 445 Hoes Lane - P.O. Box 1331, Piscataway, NJ, 08855-1331, United States, Beijing, China (2011)

7. Huang, H., Da, F.: General structure based collation of Tibetan syllables. J. Inf. Comput. 6(5), 1693–1703 (2010)

8. Liu, C.L., Koga, M., Fujisawa, H.: Lexicon-driven handwritten character string recognition for Japanese address reading. In: 6th International Conference on Document Analysis and Recognition, ICDAR 2001, pp. 877–881. IEEE Computer Society, Seattle, WA, United States (2001)

9. Rehman, A., Mohamad, D., Sulong, G.: Implicit vs explicit based script segmentation and recognition: a performance comparison on benchmark database. Int. J. Open Probl. Comput. Sci. Math. 3, 352–364 (2009)

10. Chitrakala, S., Mandipati, S., Raj, S.P., et al.: An efficient character segmentation based on VNP algorithm. Res. J. Appl. Sci. Eng. Technol. 4(24), 5438–5442 (2012)

11. Congedo, G., Dimauro, G., Impedovo, S., et al.: Segmentation of numeric strings. In: Proceedings of the Third International Conference on IEEE Computer Society, pp. 1028–1033 (1995)

12. Pal, U., Belaid, A., Choisy, C.: Touching numeral segmentation using water reservoir concept. Patt. Recogn. Lett. 24(1), 261–272 (2003)

13. Jayarathna, U.K.S., Bandara, G.E.M.D.C.: A junction based segmentation algorithm for offline handwritten connected character segmentation. In: CIMCA 2006: International Conference on Computational Intelligence for Modelling, Control and Automation, Jointly with IAWTIC 2006: International Conference on Intelligent Agents Web Technologies and International Commerce, Institute of Electronics and Electrical Engineering Computer Society, 445 Hoes Lane - P.O. Box 1331, Piscataway, NJ, 08855-1331, United States, Sydney, NSW, Australia (2006)

14. Xu, L., Yin, F., Liu, C.L.: Touching character splitting of chinese handwriting using contour analysis and DTW. In: 2010 Chinese Conference on Pattern Recognition, CCPR, pp. 814–818. IEEE Computer Society, 445 Hoes Lane - P.O. Box 1331, Piscataway, NJ, 08855-1331, United States, Chongqing, China (2010)
15. Lu, Z., Chi, Z., Siu, W., et al.: A background-thinning-based approach for separating and recognizing connected handwritten digit strings. Patt. Recogn. **32**(6), 921–933 (1999)
16. Cheung, A., Bennamoun, M., Bergmann, N.W.: An Arabic optical character recognition system using recognition-based segmentation. Patt. Recogn. **34**(2), 215–233 (2001)
17. Tomasi, S.J.: Good features to track. In: Proceedings of the 1994 IEEE Computer Society Conference on Computer Vision and Pattern Recognition, pp. 593–600. Publ by IEEE, Los Alamitos (1994)
18. Chen, J., Takagi, N.: Gray-scale morphology based image segmentation and character extraction using SVM. In: 46th IEEE International Symposium on Multiple-Valued Logic, ISMVL 2016, pp. 177–182. IEEE Computer Society, Sapporo (2016)

Nighttime FIR Pedestrian Detection Benchmark Dataset for ADAS

Zhewei Xu[1], Jiajun Zhuang[2], Qiong Liu[1(✉)], Jingkai Zhou[1], and Shaowu Peng[1]

[1] School of Software Engineering, South China University of Technology,
Guangzhou 510006, China
{se_xuzhewei,201510105876}@mail.scut.edu.cn,
{liuqiong,swpeng}@scut.edu.cn
[2] College of Computational Science, Zhongkai University of Agriculture
and Engineering, Guangzhou 510225, China
zhuangjiajun@zhku.edu.cn

Abstract. Far infrared (FIR) pedestrian detection is an essential module of the advanced driver assistance system (ADAS) at nighttime. Recently, a wave of deep convolutional neural networks (CNN) has taken the visible spectrum pedestrian detection benchmarks top ranks. However, due to the lack of dataset, we could not evaluate the performance of CNN methods on FIR images. In this paper, we introduce a nighttime FIR pedestrian dataset, which is the largest nighttime FIR pedestrian dataset. The dataset contains fine-grained annotated video, recorded from diverse road scenes and we provide detailed statistical analysis. We selected three kinds of advanced pedestrian detection methods as the baseline and evaluated their performance. Benefit from training data volume and diversity, the experimental results show that CNN-based detectors obtained good performance on FIR image. We also propose three suggestions for improving performance, which reduces the average miss rate of the vanilla Faster R-CNN by 12.97% and 9.77% on KAIST and our dataset respectively. The dataset will be public online.

Keywords: FIR pedestrian detection
Convolutional neural networks · Dataset

1 Introduction

Far infrared (FIR) pedestrian detection is an essential module of the advanced driver assistance system (ADAS) [8,12,14,28]. It aims to alert drivers about a possible collision with pedestrians, especially at nighttime scenes where it is hard to ensure enough illumination. Physically, pedestrians are more visible in FIR cameras than in visible spectrum cameras at night.

Recently, a wave of deep convolutional neural networks (CNN) [3,16,22, 23,26] has taken the visible spectrum pedestrian detection benchmarks top ranks. Comparing with visible spectrum, pedestrian detection from FIR imagery present as objects with lower resolution and less texture information is still a

© Springer Nature Switzerland AG 2018
J.-H. Lai et al. (Eds.): PRCV 2018, LNCS 11259, pp. 322–333, 2018.
https://doi.org/10.1007/978-3-030-03341-5_27

challenging problem. However, due to the lack of large nighttime FIR pedestrian detection dataset, we could not evaluate the performance of CNN methods on FIR images. Besides most of the presented FIR pedestrian detectors [18–20] using handcraft features give performance comparing on some small dataset, which often leads to some bias because the handcraft features depend on some prior knowledge from a specific dataset.

Fig. 1. Example images (cropped) and annotations. The solid green, red, yellow boxes denote 'walk_person', 'ride_person' and 'people' respectively. The dashed boxes denote occluded objects.

With this in mind, we proposed a large FIR pedestrian detection dataset to promote relativity study. The main contributions of this paper are: (1) we introduce a nighttime FIR pedestrian dataset, which is the largest nighttime FIR pedestrian dataset with fine-grained annotated video. Figure 1 shows some examples of this dataset. The pedestrians vary widely in appearance, pose and scale. (2) We provide a detailed statistical analysis of the dataset. (3) Benefit from training data volume and diversity, the experiment results show that CNN-based detectors obtained good performance on FIR image. (4) We also propose three modifications for improving CNN-based detector performance, which reduces the average miss rate of the vanilla Faster R-CNN by 12.97% and 9.77% on KAIST and our dataset respectively.

This paper is organized as follows. Section 2 briefs the related work. Section 3 introduces SCUT dataset and carries out corresponding statistical analysis. Section 4 introduces three kinds of advanced pedestrian detection methods and a modified Faster R-CNN fitted for FIR pedestrian detection. In Sect. 5, we report the performance evaluation results by experiments under several different conditions on SCUT dataset. The final is the summary of this work.

2   Related Work

2.1   Pedestrian Detection Datasets

Several early pedestrian datasets in visible spectrum include INRIA [4], ETH [11], TudBrussels [24], and Daimler [10]. But they are superseded by larger and richer datasets such as Caltech [8] and KITTI [12]. Recently, Zhang et al. [28] proposed a new diverse dataset namely CityPersons which make CNN show strong generalization ability as training set.

Table 1. Comparing pedestrian datasets. The horizontal lines divide the datasets based on the image types (e.g. color, thermal, and color-thermal). The first four columns indicate pedestrian number and image number in training and testing dataset (k = 10^3). Properties column summarizes some dataset characteristics.

	Training		Testing		Properties						
	# pedes-trians	# images	# pedes-trians	# images	# total frames	color	thermal	occ. labels	videos	moving cam	publication
Caltech [9]	192k	128k	155k	121k	250k	✓		✓	✓	✓	'09
KITTI [12]	12k	1.6k	-	-	80k	✓		✓	✓	✓	'12
CityPersons [28]	20k	3k	11k	1.6k	5k	✓		✓		✓	'17
KAIST [14]	42k	50k	45k	45k	95k	✓	✓	✓	✓	✓	'15
CVC [13]	4.8k	3.5k	4.3k	1.4k	5k	✓	✓	✓	✓	✓	'16
OSU-T [5]	984	1.9k	-	-	2k		✓		✓		'05
LSI [1]	10.2k	6.2k	5.9k	9.1k	15.2k		✓		✓	✓	'13
TIV [25]	-	-	-	-	63k		✓		✓		'14
SCUT(Our)	175k	108k	177k	103k	211k		✓	✓	✓	✓	'18

There are few of available FIR pedestrian detection datasets. OSU-T [5] is probably the first benchmark dataset. But the images were captured by a static camera mounted on a building in campus. Hence, it lacks diversity and reasonable background clutter and not suitable for on-road pedestrian detection. LSI dataset [1] is captured from a vehicle under different illumination and temperature scenes, but contains only 15K image frames with a low resolution. TIV dataset [25] provides a high-resolution FIR images with rich annotation of person (e.g. walk person, running person and bicyclist) and other scenario participants (e.g. vehicles and motorbikes). It is more appropriate for the task in video monitoring scene. Recently, multispectral (color-thermal) datasets [13,14] are proposed for all day pedestrian detection. But only 30K frames and 37K bounding boxes (BB) recorded from nighttime. Table 1 provides an overview of above datasets.

2.2   Pedestrian Detection Evaluating

For improving on-road FIR pedestrian detection, the early work mainly focuses on various reformative hand-crafted features [14,18–20]. Olemda et al. [19] propose phase congruency feature to resist illumination change, Liu et al. [18] design pyramid entropy weighted HOG to highlight object profile and Qi et al. [20] adopt sparse representation to get rich semantic context. Following the success of integral channel features, Hwang et al. [14] proposed multispectral ACF in which intensity and HOG are used as extend thermal feature channels.

Recently, multifarious convolutional neural network variants achieve top ranks on Caltech benchmark [3,16,22,23]. Most of them are custom architectures derived from Faster R-CNN. Cai et al. [3] propose a multi-scale CNN (MSCNN) with a multiple output layers proposal sub-network, so that receptive fields can match the objects of different scales. Li et al. [16] propose scale-aware CNNs (SA-FastRCNN), capturing features for pedestrians of different image sizes by a scale gate function. Zhang et al. [26] proposed RPN+BF, combining RPN (the first part of Faster RCNN) with a following boosting forest. RPN generates region proposals, confidence scores and features, all of which are used to train a cascaded Boosted Forest classifier (BF). The bootstrapping strategy used in BF largely promotes pedestrian detection accuracy. The result of RPN+BF on Caltech reaches 9.6% log-average miss rate.

Further, Liu et al. [17] proposed a multispectral detector built upon Faster R-CNN and performed 37% miss rate on KAIST. König et al. [15] proposal RPN+BDT classifier for reducing potential false positive detection. As baseline model, it is hopeful to adapt Faster R-CNN for on-road FIR pedestrian detection as well.

3   SCUT FIR Pedestrian Dataset

We introduce SCUT dataset as a benchmark of on-road FIR pedestrian detection for researcher and engineer of this field. The image sequences are collected from several driving scenarios over one month in Guangzhou, China. A fine-grained set of high-quality annotations and corresponding statistics are presented. SCUT dataset is highlighted in data volume, data diversity and a wide range of imaging distance. Besides, the work of this paper has excellent practical significance to boost ADAS or intelligent vehicle in China because Chinese road traffic occupies a large market share and the road environment is more complex than some other countries.

3.1   Data Collection and Annotation

Data Capture. Image sequences in SCUT dataset are captured by a monocular FIR camera mounted on a car (Fig. 2). The spatial resolution of the camera is 384×288 with 13 mm focal length, and the field of view is $28° \times 21°$. The output resolution is resized to 720×576 pixels by an image acquisition card for better observation and annotation. We collect about 11 hours-long image sequences ($\sim 10^6$ frames) at 25 fps by a vehicle driving through diverse traffic scenarios at

Fig. 2. Camera setup

a speed less than 80 km/h. The driver is independent of the authors. The image sequences all include 11 road sections under 4 kinds of scenes, i.e. downtown, suburbs, campus and expressway (Fig. 1).

Ground Truth Annotation. Piotr's Computer Vision Toolbox [6] is adopted to annotate ground truth for pedestrian in a image frame. If a pedestrian or person group is visible, a tight bounding box (BB) is drawn around the object. For occluded pedestrian, a BB involves estimating the location of hidden parts. Among all, we annotated 211,011 frames for a total of 477,907 BBs around 7,659 unique pedestrians. Newly, an annotation protocol [27] is presented by drawing a center line from head to the central point between both feet and then generate a BB with a fixed aspect ratio. Although this procedure ensure the BB is well centered on the subject, it may also lose some parts of the limbs.

SCUT dataset provides a set of fine-grained labels to divide all BBs into six categories by following rules. An individual person when walking, running or standing posture is labeled as 'walk_person'. An individual person when sitting or squatting is labeled as 'squat_person'. An individual person when riding bicycle or motorbike is labeled as 'ride_person'. A person group that are hard to distinguish each other is labeled as 'people'. In addition, an individual person and a person group who is ambiguous or occluded area >2/3 are labeled as 'person?' and 'people?' respectively.

Training and Testing Data. The annotated image sequences randomly divided into training and testing dataset. There are 21 subsets, each video recorded in one of 11 road section. We divide the data randomly in half, S0~S10 as training set, S11~S20 as testing set. The total number of both image frames and BBs in each dataset is similar. Details about the amount of SCUT training/testing dataset can be seen in Table 1.

Table 2. Dataset summary

Label	Frames with anno.	BB	Occluded	Unique	Avg. frames per obj
walk person	92,278	193,765	57815	3,136	61.79
ride person	83,672	157,994	17386	1,824	86.62
squat person	50,483	71,930	18708	1,259	57.13
people	30,267	39,303	15702	1,138	34.54
person?	10,254	12,470	4061	250	49.88
people?	2,330	2,445	508	36	67.92
Summary	148,132	447,907	114180	7,659	62.40

3.2 Dataset Statistics

The statistics on SCUT dataset is discussed here based on Table 2. As a whole, about 70% frames have at least one BB annotation and about 78% BBs contain walk person or ride person, who must be detected in ADAS-oriented applications. A walk person appears 2.47 seconds and a ride person appears 3.46 seconds averagely. We analyze further some sub-theme, i.e. scale and distance, data diversity, pedestrian occlusion and pedestrian position etc. The statistics may be basic supporting when establishing a road FIR pedestrian detection system.

Scale and Distance. Similar to Dollár et al. [9], we group pedestrians by dividing the pixel height of BBs into three scales: near (more than 80 pixels), medium (30~80 pixels) and far (less than 30 pixels). The statistics of histogram distribution in the pixel height of BBs is investigated respectively on walk person

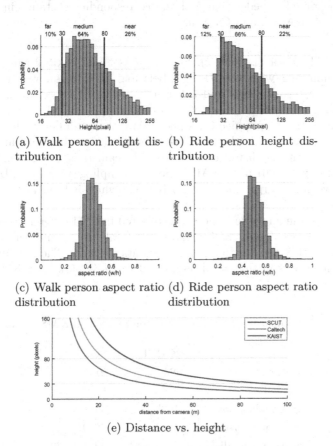

(a) Walk person height distribution

(b) Ride person height distribution

(c) Walk person aspect ratio distribution

(d) Ride person aspect ratio distribution

(e) Distance vs. height

Fig. 3. (a) and (b) Distribution of walk person and ride person pixel heights respectively. (c) and (d) Distribution of walk person and ride person aspect ratio respectively. (e) Pixel height h as a function of distance d.

and ride person, as shown in Fig. 3(a) and (b), which is similar each other. Cut-off for near/far scale is marked respectively. Most observed walk person (~64%) and ride person (~65%) lie in medium scale. At far distance region, the number of pedestrian decreases sharply because it is difficult to identify reliably a small pedestrian. Furthermore, the statistics of BBs aspect ratio histogram is shown in Fig. 3(c) and (d) respectively on walk person and ride person. The log-average aspect ratios of walk person, ride person and the both are 0.43, 0.50 and 0.46 respectively.

Medium and far pedestrian is usually more important than near because it is necessary to have enough reaction time for a driver when alerting him to a possible collision. The focal length in pixels of our FIR camera is 1554 (due to $576/2/f = tan(21°/2)$). Using a pinhole camera model, an object observed pixel height h a pedestrian observed is inversely proportional to the distance d from the camera: $h \approx Hf/d$, where H is a true height of a pedestrian. Assuming $H \approx$ 1.7 m, we gain $d \approx 2641.8/h$ m. Figure 3(e), compare the relationship between the pixel height of a pedestrian and the corresponding distance in meter on SCUT dataset, KAIST, and Caltech.

Diversity. The data diversity on SCUT dataset and KAIST can be seen in Table 3. Comparing with KAIST (4 labels and 103k BBs), we provide fine-grained data category labels and a larger number of BBs (6 labels and 448k BBs), which is the first difference of data diversity.

Following common practice for a pedestrian, the minimum high is 20 pixels and the maximum high is the image resolution [9]. Due to the camera with a longer focal length, the distance range from the camera is 4.6~132 m on SCUT dataset, but only 2.4~61 m on KAIST. So, the sampling space on SCUT dataset is around two times larger than that of KAIST, which is the third difference of data diversity.

In addition, the image sequences are collected from 11 different road sections under four kinds of scenes on SCUT dataset, but only from 3 different road scenes on KAIST, which is the fourth difference of data diversity. The last difference of data diversity works in that total number of frame is 211k on SCUT but only 95k on KAIST.

Table 3. Comparison of data diversity on SCUT and KAIST datasets

	KAIST	SCUT
# frame	95k	211k
# label	4	6
# bounding box	103k	448k
# unique person	1182	7659
# pedestrian distance	2.4 m~61 m	4.6 m~132 m
# road scene	3	4

Pedestrian Occlusion. Since a camera is usually at a horizontal perspective in a traffic scene, a pedestrian may be occluded by another pedestrian or object. We individualize every BB by adding an attribute tag for occlusion. An unoccluded object (person or people) is tagged as 'no occlusion'. An occluded object is tagged as 'occlusion'. Among all, ~25% BBs are marked as 'occlusion'. Also, among all walk persons, the occluded BB accounts for ~30% while occluded BB only accounts for ~11% in ride persons. A walk person could be occluded by trees, parking cars, and another pedestrian when appearing on a sidewalk. The ratio of walk person occluded is larger than the ride person because there are a lot of walk persons on a sidewalk, as shown in Fig. 1.

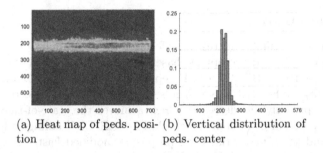

(a) Heat map of peds. posi- (b) Vertical distribution of
tion   peds. center

Fig. 4. (a) Center position heat map of pedestrian (walk person and ride person) BBs, which are log-normalized. (b) Vertical center position histogram of pedestrian BBs.

Pedestrian Center Position. Figure 4(a) shows log-normalized heat map to annotate pedestrian center position. Viewpoint and ground plane geometry constrain a pedestrian appearing only in a narrow band running horizontally across the center of the image. Because the vehicle drives under the right-handed traffic condition, more pedestrians appear on the right side of the image. Corresponding pedestrian vertical (y-coordinate) distribution is shown in Fig. 4(b). The average y-coordinate is 216, and about 97% of the pedestrians are in the range of 166 – 266 y-coordinate.

4   Experiments Results

According to the baseline verified in Sect. 3, we benchmark SCUT dataset. In Sect. 4.1, we evaluate performance under different conditions using SCUT dataset. Next, we report the impact of training data volume in Sect. 4.2.

We employ the evaluation strategy proposed by Dollar et al. [8]. It stated a detected BB (BB_{dt}) and a ground truth BB (BB_{gt}) have an IoU ratio ≥0.5. And each BB_{dt} and BB_{gt} may be matched at most once and the ignored BB_{ig} need not to be matched. In our dataset, six types of BBs are always set to ignore: any BB under 20 pixels high or truncated by image boundaries, containing a 'person?', 'people?', 'people' or 'squat_person'. Detections within these regions will not affect performance.

Table 4. Step by step improvements on KAIST FIR image from vanilla Faster R-CNN to TFRCN, we gain 12.97 MR points total.

Detector aspect	MR	Δ MR
vanilla Faster R-CNN	56.01	-
+ M1 Handling class imbalance	49.20	6.81
+ M2 Adjusting anchors distribution	48.55	0.65
+ M3 Reducing the feature stride	43.04	5.51
TFRCN-ours	43.04	12.97

4.1 Baseline Detectors

To evaluate the training and testing effect for the benchmark, we select three promising pedestrian detectors as baselines, i.e., ACF-based [2], Faster R-CNN [21] and RPN+BF [26]. ACF represents the Integral Channel Feature detector family [7]. Faster R-CNN stands for the CNN-based detector. RPN+BF acts like a typical hybrid detector, which achieves the state-of-the-art performance on pedestrian detection. As vanilla Faster R-CNN failing to handle class imbalance and small pedestrians, we propose a modified Faster R-CNN model to promote performance. We show the step-by-step improvements in Table 4 on the KAIST FIR datasets under the 'reasonable' setting [14]. In total, the MR of TFRCN reduces from 56.01% to 43.04% on KAIST dataset.

4.2 Benchmarking on SCUT Dataset

We sampled images from train subset videos with 2-frame skips (53976 images) for training CNN-based detector and sampled 75-frame skip (1413 images) for training ACF-T+ detector family. The BB_{gt} for training exclude occluded, truncated and small pedestrian (<50 pixels). We plot the miss rate using a per-image evaluation scheme (FPPI) and summarize the performance with a single value by using log-average miss rate (a short for MR) over the range of $[10^{-2}, 10^{0}]$. In all experiments, the image interval of the testing dataset is set to 25 frames. Figure 5 shows the evaluation results for the various subsets of the test set described below.

Reasonable. For this experiment, we use a representative subset of the proposed dataset, named reasonable all. The reasonable all subset (Fig. 5(a)) consists of walk person and ride person which are taller than 50 pixels. This subset is also divided into reasonable walk person and reasonable ride person subsets based on the label. In Fig. 5(a–c), RPN+BF perform best and TFRCN achieves the second rank. We noticed that the CNN-based detectors on ride person subset (Fig. 5(c)) perform better than walk person (Fig. 5(b)). According to Sect. 2.2, we believe this is due to there are more occluded walk persons than ride persons.

Scale. Reasonable subset doesn't cover small pedestrian. As discussed in Sect. 2.2, we have enough high-quality data to group pedestrians by pixel height

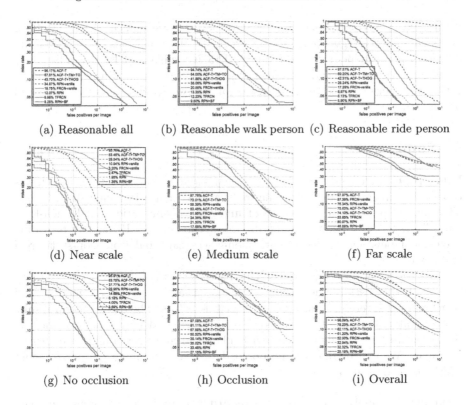

(a) Reasonable all   (b) Reasonable walk person (c) Reasonable ride person

(d) Near scale   (e) Medium scale   (f) Far scale

(g) No occlusion   (h) Occlusion   (i) Overall

Fig. 5. False positive per image (FPPI) versus miss rate in various conditions.

into the near (80 or more pixels), medium (30–80 pixels) and far (30 pixels or less) scales. Results for each scale, on unoccluded pedestrians only, are shown in Fig. 5(d)–(f). In general, as the height of a pedestrian gets smaller, the performance degrades dramatically. FRCN-vanilla and RPN-vanilla are more sensitive to scale. At the far scale, there are more negative samples and smaller convolutional feature size. With our modification, TFRCN achieves 33.54% MR improvement.

Occlusion. The impact of occlusion on detecting pedestrians with a minimum height of 50 pixels is shown in Fig. 5(g)–(h). For this experiment, we build two subsets based on the occlusion tags: no-occlusion, occlusion (0~2/3 of area occluded). Performance drops significantly under occlusion situation in all detectors.

Overall. In this experiment, we examine detectors on entire dataset in Fig. 5(i). It is most similar to the real driving scene. RPN+BF outperforms the remaining methods. With our modification, TFRCN achieves the second rank, with a MR of 32.32%. FRCN-vanilla and ACF-T+ family detector performance are poor, with a MR of over 50%.

Summary. CNN-based detectors achieve better performance. Benefiting from bootstrapping strategy, the RPN+BF excels the other methods. ACF-T+ family detectors perform poorly on all subset. FRCN-vanilla and RPN-vanilla likely suffer from feature size and unfit anchor setting. With our modification, TFRCN gets better performance than RPN, except for two special cases (far scale and occlusion).

5 Summary

In this paper, we introduced a large FIR pedestrian detection dataset, which was collected from several driving scenarios over one month in Guangzhou, China. The dataset provides a large-scale of fine-grained annotations with high-level data diversity. As we know, SCUT dataset is the largest FIR dataset providing occlusion labels and temporal correspondences captured from non-static real traffic scenes.

After the detailed analysis of the basic statistics of SCUT dataset, we evaluated the performance using ACF-based and CNN-based models and benchmarked several promising CNN-based detectors. The experimental results demonstrated that the CNN-based detectors achieved better performance on SCUT dataset, especially provided with a larger training set of high-level diverse examples. We expect that the proposed dataset can promote the development of FIR detection method.

Acknowledgement. This paper are supported by the Science and Technology Planning Project of Guangdong Province (2017A020219008), the Project on the Integration of Industry, Education and Research of Guangdong Province (2017B090901047) and the Science, and the Technology Program of Guangzhou Province (201607010069).

References

1. Pedestrian classification and detection in far infrared images. Integr. Comput. Aided Eng. **20**(4), 347–360 (2013)
2. Fast feature pyramids for object detection. IEEE Trans. Patt. Anal. Mach. Intell. (TPAMI) **36**(8), 1532–1545 (2014)
3. Cai, Z., Fan, Q., Feris, R.S., Vasconcelos, N.: A unified multi-scale deep convolutional neural network for fast object detection. In: Leibe, B., Matas, J., Sebe, N., Welling, M. (eds.) ECCV 2016. LNCS, vol. 9908, pp. 354–370. Springer, Cham (2016). https://doi.org/10.1007/978-3-319-46493-0_22
4. Dalal, N., Triggs, B.: Histograms of oriented gradients for human detection. In: CVPR, pp. 886–893. IEEE Press (2005)
5. Davis, J.W., Keck, M.A.: A two-stage template approach to person detection in thermal imagery. In: IEEE Workshops on Application of Computer Vision, pp. 364–369. IEEE Press (2005)
6. Dollár, P.: http://vision.ucsd.edu/~pdollar/toolbox/doc/index.html
7. Dollár, P., Tu, Z., Perona, P., Belongie, S.: Integral channel features. In: The British Machine Vision Conference (BMVC), pp. 91.1–91.11. BMVA Press (2009)

Nighttime FIR Pedestrian Detection Benchmark Dataset for ADAS   333

8. Dollár, P., Wojek, C., Schiele, B., Perona, P.: Pedestrian detection: an evaluation of the state of the art. IEEE Trans. Patt. Anal. Mach. Intell. (TPAMI) **34**(4), 743–761 (2012)
9. Dollár, P., Wojek, C., Schiele, B., Perona, P.: Pedestrian detection: a benchmark. In: CVPR, pp. 304–311. IEEE Press (2009)
10. Enzweiler, M., Gavrila, D.M.: Monocular pedestrian detection: survey and experiments. IEEE Trans. Patt. Anal. Mach. Intell. (TPAMI) **31**(12), 2179–2195 (2009)
11. Ess, A., Leibe, B., Schindler, K., Van Gool, L.: A mobile vision system for robust multi-person tracking. In: CVPR, pp. 1–8. IEEE Press (2008)
12. Geiger, A., Lenz, P., Urtasun, R.: Are we ready for autonomous driving? the Kitti vision benchmark suite. In: CVPR, pp. 3354–3361. IEEE Press (2012)
13. González, A., et al.: Pedestrian detection at day/night time with visible and FIR cameras: a comparison. Sensors **16**(6), 820 (2016)
14. Hwang, S., Park, J., Kim, N., Choi, Y., Kweon, I.S.: Multispectral pedestrian detection: benchmark dataset and baseline. In: CVPR, pp. 1037–1045. IEEE Press (2015)
15. König, D., Adam, M., Jarvers, C., Layher, G., Neumann, H., Teutsch, M.: Fully convolutional region proposal networks for multispectral person detection. In: CVPR Workshops, pp. 243–250. IEEE Press (2017)
16. Li, J., Liang, X., Shen, S., Xu, T., Feng, J., Yan, S.: Scale-aware fast R-CNN for pedestrian detection. IEEE Trans. Multimedia **20**(4), 985–996 (2018)
17. Liu, J., Zhang, S., Wang, S., Metaxas, D.N.: Multispectral deep neural networks for pedestrian detection. In: The British Machine Vision Conference (BMVC), pp. 1–13. BMVA Press (2016)
18. Liu, Q., Zhuang, J., Ma, J.: Robust and fast pedestrian detection method for far-infrared automotive driving assistance systems. Infrared Phys. Technol. **60**, 288–299 (2013)
19. Olmeda, D., de la Escalera, A., Armingol, J.M.: Contrast invariant features for human detection in far infrared images. In: IEEE Intelligent Vehicles Symposium, pp. 117–122. IEEE Press (2012)
20. Qi, B., John, V., Liu, Z., Mita, S.: Pedestrian detection from thermal images: a sparse representation based approach. Infrared Phys. Technol. **76**, 157–167 (2016)
21. Ren, S., He, K., Girshick, R., Sun, J.: Faster R-CNN: towards real-time object detection with region proposal networks. In: NIPS, pp. 91–99. Curran Associates, Inc. (2015)
22. Tian, Y., Luo, P., Wang, X., Tang, X.: Pedestrian detection aided by deep learning semantic tasks. In: CVPR, pp. 5079–5087. IEEE Press (2015)
23. Tian, Y., Luo, P., Wang, X., Tang, X.: Deep learning strong parts for pedestrian detection. In: ICCV, pp. 1904–1912. IEEE Press (2016)
24. Wojek, C., Walk, S., Schiele, B.: Multi-cue onboard pedestrian detection. In: CVPR, pp. 794–801. IEEE Press (2009)
25. Wu, Z., Fuller, N., Theriault, D., Betke, M.: A thermal infrared video benchmark for visual analysis. In: CVPR, pp. 201–208. IEEE Press (2014)
26. Zhang, L., Lin, L., Liang, X., He, K.: Is faster R-CNN doing well for pedestrian detection? In: Leibe, B., Matas, J., Sebe, N., Welling, M. (eds.) ECCV 2016. LNCS, vol. 9906, pp. 443–457. Springer, Cham (2016). https://doi.org/10.1007/978-3-319-46475-6_28
27. Zhang, S., Benenson, R., Omran, M., Hosang, J., Schiele, B.: How far are we from solving pedestrian detection? In: CVPR, pp. 1259–1267. IEEE Press (2016)
28. Zhang, S., Benenson, R., Schiele, B.: CityPersons: a diverse dataset for pedestrian detection. In: CVPR, pp. 3213–3221. IEEE Press (2017)

How Many Labeled License Plates Are Needed?

Changhao Wu[1], Shugong Xu[1(✉)], Guocong Song[2], and Shunqing Zhang[1]

[1] Shanghai Institute for Advanced Communication and Data Science,
Shanghai University, Shanghai 200444, China
{wuchanghao,shugong,shunqing}@shu.edu.cn
[2] Playground Global, Palo Alto, USA
guocong@playground.global

Abstract. Training a good deep learning model often requires a lot of annotated data. As a large amount of labeled data is typically difficult to collect and even more difficult to annotate, data augmentation and data generation are widely used in the process of training deep neural networks. However, there is no clear common understanding on how much labeled data is needed to get satisfactory performance. In this paper, we try to address such a question using vehicle license plate character recognition as an example application. We apply computer graphic scripts and Generative Adversarial Networks to generate and augment a large number of annotated, synthesized license plate images with realistic colors, fonts, and character composition from a small number of real, manually labeled license plate images. Generated and augmented data are mixed and used as training data for the license plate recognition network modified from DenseNet. The experimental results show that the model trained from the generated mixed training data has good generalization ability, and the proposed approach achieves a new state-of-the-art accuracy on Dataset-1 and AOLP, even with a very limited number of original real license plates. In addition, the accuracy improvement caused by data generation becomes more significant when the number of labeled images is reduced. Data augmentation also plays a more significant role when the number of labeled images is increased.

Keywords: GANs · Data augmentation · License plate recognition

1 Introduction

License plate recognition is one of the most important components of modern intelligent transportation systems. It has attracted the attention of many researchers. However, most existing algorithms [3,13,14,18] can only work normally under certain conditions. For example, some recognition systems require sophisticated hardware to shoot high-quality images, while other systems require the vehicle to slowly pass through a fixed access opening or even stop. Accurately detecting license plates and recognizing characters in an open environment is a

© Springer Nature Switzerland AG 2018
J.-H. Lai et al. (Eds.): PRCV 2018, LNCS 11259, pp. 334–346, 2018.
https://doi.org/10.1007/978-3-030-03341-5_28

challenging task. The main difficulties are different license plate fonts and colors, character distortion caused by the image capture process and non-uniform illumination, and low-quality images caused by occlusion or motion blur.

In this paper, we propose a license plate recognition system, in which we cope with challenge such as, low light, low resolution, motion blur, and other harsh conditions. Figure 1 shows the license plates which can be correctly recognized by our proposed method. From top to bottom are the license plate images affected by the shooting angle, uneven illumination, low resolution, detection error and motion blur.

Fig. 1. The complex license plates images.

In general, supervised learning requires a large amount of labeled data in order to achieve good results. However, real data is not easy to obtain, the acquisition process is slow, and the data needs to be processed and annotated before it can be used for training. To achieve a higher accuracy of the annotation, manual inspection is also required.

However, the acquisition of a large amount of real data and manual annotations is very expensive. Therefore, data generation is very important for the training of license plate recognition network. We believe that the information contained in a small number of real license plates is sufficient to recognize most of the existing license plate images. However, there is no clear common understanding on how much labeled data is needed to get satisfactory performance. In this paper, we try to address such a question in vehicle license plate character recognition.

The main contributions of this paper can be summarized as the following three points:

1. We propose various methods of data generation and data augmentation. As long as we have a few labeled license plate images, a large amount of generated data can be created. We can achieve and even exceed the recognition accuracy and results of systems trained only on real images.
2. We compare the performance of various data generation and data augmentation methods to find that both data generation methods and data augmentation methods can significantly improve license plate recognition accuracy.

Data augmentation plays a larger role in accuracy improvement when there are many labeled license plates but when the number of labelled license plates is small, data generation more significantly increases accuracy.

3. We apply a network that is modified from DenseNet to license plate recognition to reduce network parameters and inference time and improve accuracy.

The rest of paper is arranged as follows. In Sect. 2 we review the related works briefly. In Sect. 3 we describe the details of networks used in our approach. Experimental results are provided in Sect. 4, and conclusions are drawn in Sect. 5.

2   Related Work

The section introduces previous work on license plate recognition and GANs.

2.1   License Plate Recognition

Existing license plate recognition systems are either text segmentation-based [3,6], or non-segmentation-based [13]. Methods that depend on segmentation first preprocess the license plate image and then segment individual characters through image processing. After this, each character is classified by a convolutional neural network. This method is very dependent on the accuracy of text segmentation, and the recognition speed is slower. A recognition method that does not require segmentation is proposed by Li et al. [13]. It is composed of a deep convolutional network and a Long Short-Term Memory (LSTM), where the deep CNN is directly applied for feature extraction, and a bidirectional LSTM network is applied for sequence labeling. DenseNet [9] is a highly efficient convolutional neural network. Because of its low parameter number and fast inference time, DenseNet is widely used. Our method is also a segmentation-free approach based on the framework proposed by [9], where DenseNet is applied for feature extraction.

Data generation is used in license plate recognition to improve the accuracy of recognition. The labeled license plates generated by CycleGAN as a pretraining data set for the recognition network are used in [18], and the model is fine-tuned with the real license plate data set. This data generation method can significantly improve the recognition accuracy. License plate detection and recognition is combined in [14], and it finally improves the recognition speed and recognition accuracy of the system.

2.2   Generative Adversarial Networks

Generative adversarial networks(GANs) [2,15] train a generator and discriminator alternatively. The output of the discriminator acts as a generator's loss function. Zhu et al. [21] propose Cycle-Consistent Adversarial Networks(CycleGAN), which learns the mapping relationship from one domain to another and is mainly used for the style conversion of pictures. Wasserstein GANs(WGAN) [1] are proposed to improve the stability of GAN training. Applying Wasserstein loss to

CycleGAN, creating CycleWGAN, also improves its training stability in [18]. Gradient penalties in WGAN(WGAN-GP) [5] are proposed to solve the WGAN generator weight distribution problem.

2.3   Data Generation for Training

A large number of real labeled images are often difficult to obtain, so the role of data generation is very significant [17]. The synthesized images are used to train scene text detection networks [7] and recognition networks [11]. The generated data is shown to improve the performance of person detection [20], font recognition [19], and semantic segmentation [16]. However, when the difference between the generated data and the real data is very large, the performance is poor when applied to a real scene. Therefore, [18] applies CycleGAN to convert the style of license plate generated by the script into a real license plate, which can greatly reduce the gap between the generated image and the real image. We apply data generation and data augmentation methods at the same time, and use the data generated by different methods directly as the training set for recognition network. Therefore we need very little real data.

3   License Plate Recognition Based on Data Generation and Augmentation

In this section, the pipeline of the proposed method is described. We train the GAN model using synthetic images and real images simultaneously. We then use the generated images to train a model modified from DenseNet.

3.1   CycleGAN

CycleGAN [21] learns to translate an image from a source domain X to a target domain Y in the absence of paired examples. Our goal is to train a mapping relationship G between the script license plate domain X and the real license plate domain Y. CycleGAN contains two mapping functions $G : X \rightarrow Y$ and $Y \rightarrow X$, and associated adversarial discriminators D_Y, D_X.

The techniques proposed in WGAN [1] are applied in CycleGAN, and CycleWGAN is proposed in [18]. WGAN points out why the traditional GAN is difficult to converge and improve during training, which greatly reduces the training difficulty and speeds up the convergence. There are two main improvements: the first one is to remove the log from the loss function, and the second is to perform weight clipping after each iteration to update the weight, and limit the weight to a range (e.g., the limit range is $[-0.1, +0.1]$. Outside weights are trimmed to -0.1 or $+0.1$). CycleWGAN solves the problem of training instability and collapse mode, which makes the result more diverse.

We apply the techniques in WGAN-GP [5] to CycleWGAN and propose the CycleWGAN-GP. WGAN-GP also proposes an improvement plan based on WGAN. WGAN reduces the training difficulty of GAN, but it is still difficult to converge in some conditions, and the generated pictures are worse than DCGAN. WGAN-GP applies gradient penalty, and solves the above problem along with the problems of vanishing gradient and exploding gradient during training. It also converges faster than CycleWGAN and produces higher quality pictures.

We apply a CycleGAN equipped with WGAN and WGAN-GP techniques to train the mapping relationship between the fake license plate and the real license plate. First of all, we apply OpenCV scripts to generate synthetic license plates as a source domain X, and then choose real license plates without labels as a target domain Y. Before the training of CycleWGAN-GP, these license plates are randomly cropped and randomly flipped horizontally or vertically.

3.2 Recognition Network Design

DenseNet is a densely connected convolutional neural network. In this network, there is a direct connection between any two layers. The input of each layer of the network is the union of the output of all previous layers, and the feature map learned by this layer is also directly transmitted to all subsequent layers. DenseNet allows the input of lth Layer to directly affect all subsequent layers. Its output is:

$$x_l = H_l([x_0, x_1, ..., x_{l-1}]) \tag{1}$$

where $H_l(\cdot)$ refers to a composite function of three consecutive operations: batch normalization (BN) [10], followed by a rectified linear unit (ReLU), and a 3×3 convolution (Conv). Additionally, since each layer contains the output information of all previous layers, it only needs a few feature maps, so the number of parameter of DenseNet is greatly reduced compared to other models.

Table 1. Construction of recognition network. The output size represents w × h × c. Note that each "conv" layer shown in the table corresponds the sequence BN-ReLU-Conv

Layers	Output size	Recognition network
Input	$136 \times 36 \times 1$	
Convolution	$68 \times 18 \times 64$	5×5 conv, stride 2
Dense block (1)	$68 \times 18 \times 128$	[3×3 conv] × 8
Transition layer (1)	$68 \times 18 \times 128$	1×1 conv
	$34 \times 9 \times 128$	2×2 average pool, stride 2
Dense block (2)	$34 \times 9 \times 192$	[3×3 conv] × 8
Transition layer (2)	$34 \times 9 \times 128$	1×1 conv
	$17 \times 4 \times 128$	2×2 average pool, stride 2
Dense block (3)	$17 \times 4 \times 192$	[3×3 conv] × 8

Our network structure is shown in Table 1, which is different from the network structure of [9], because the input license plate image is smaller and is a gray scale image of 136×36, so the network only has 3 dense blocks. The transition layers used in our network consist of a batch normalization layer and an 1×1 convolutional layer followed by a 2×2 average pooling layer. A 1×1 convolution can be introduced as bottleneck layer before each 3×3 convolution to reduce the number of input feature-maps. To improve model compactness, we reduce the number of feature-maps from 192 to 128 at transition layers 2.

The last DenseNet layer is followed by a fully-connected layer with 68 neurons for the 68 classes of label, including 31 Chinese characters, 26 letters, 10 digits and "blank". We train the networks with stochastic gradient descent (SGD). The labelling loss is derived using Connectionist Temporal Classification (CTC) [4]. The optimization algorithm Adam [12] is then applied, as it converges quickly and does not require a complicated learning rate schedule. Another advantage of using the modified DenseNet network is that it does not require the Long Short-Term Memory(LSTM) networks. The use of LSTM complicates the solution and increases computational cost.

4 Experiment

In this section, we conduct experiments to verify the effectiveness of the proposed methods. Our network is implemented capitalizing keras. The experiments are trained on a NVIDIA Tesla P40 with 24 GB memory and are tested on a NVIDIA GTX745 GPU with 4 GB memory.

4.1 Dataset

The image in the Dataset-1 [18] are captured from a wide variety of real traffic monitoring scenes under various viewpoints, blurring and illumination. Dataset-1 contains a training set of 203,774 plates and a test set of 9,986 plates. The first character of Chinese license plates is a Chinese character which represents the province. While there are 31 abbreviations for all of the provinces, Dataset-1 contains 30 classes of them.

The second data set is the application-oriented license plate (AOLP) [8] benchmark database, which has 2049 images of Taiwan license plates. This database is categorized into three subsets: access control (AC) with 681 samples, traffic law enforcement (LE) with 757 samples, and road patrol (RP) with 611 samples.

4.2 Implementation Details

Network. The recognition network is shown in Table 1. We implement it with Keras. The images are resized to 136×36 and converted to gray scale and then fed to the recognition network. We change the last layer of fully connected layers to 68 neurons according to the 68 classes of characters-33 Chinese characters, 24 letters, 10 digits and "blank". We train the networks with SGD and learning rate of 0.0001. The labelling loss is derived using CTC. We set the training batch size as 256 and predicting size as 1.

Evaluation Criterion. In this work, we evaluate the model's performance in terms of recognition accuracy and character recognition accuracy, which is similar to Wang et al. [18]. Recognition accuracy is defined as :

$$RA = \frac{Number\ of\ correctly\ recognized\ license\ plates}{Number\ of\ all\ license\ plates} \tag{2}$$

Character recognition accuracy is defined as:

$$CRA = \frac{Number\ of\ correctly\ recognized\ characters}{Number\ of\ all\ characters} \tag{3}$$

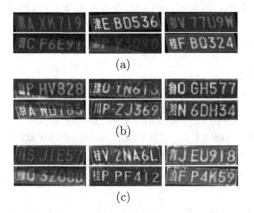

Fig. 2. Three data generation methods (a) Examples of license plates generated by OpenCV scripts. (b) Examples of license plates generated by CycleWGAN. (c) Examples of license plates generated by CycleWGAN-GP.

GAN Training and Testing. Three data generation methods are shown in Fig. 2. To train CycleWGAN, first we use the OpenCV scripts to generate 1000 blue fake license plates as a source domain X, and then select 1000 real blue license plates from Dataset-1 as a target domain Y. We train the CycleWGAN model with these fake license plates and real license plates. The training real plates do not require character labels. All the images are resized to 143×143, cropped to 128×128 and randomly flipped for data augmentation. We use Adam with $L_1 = 0.9$, $L_2 = 0.999$ and learning rate of 0.0001. We stop training after 300,000 steps and save the model. When testing, first we use the OpenCV scripts to generate 40,000 blue fake license plates, and then we apply the last checkpoint to generate 40,000 license plates. The same goes for CycleWGAN-GP. Finally we get 80,000 blue license plates generated by CycleWGAN and CycleWGAN-GP.

Data Augmentation. The six data augmentation methods are proposed in order to increase the training data of the recognition network. The data was augmented through affine transformation, motion blurring, uneven lighting, stretching, erosion and dilation, downsampling and the application of gaussian noise. Examples of these transformations are shown in Fig. 3. A real license plate image randomly passes through the six data augmentation methods, allowing for the creation of much more training data. First, we select a small number of labeled real license plates from Dataset-1, such as 300. And then using data augmentation methods in Fig. 3, we generate 80,000 augmented license plates with these selected real license plates.

Mixed Training Data. Our mixed training data consists of four parts, including 40,000 license plates generated by OpenCV scripts, 40,000 license plates generated by CycleWGAN, 40,000 license plates generated by CycleWGAN-GP, and 80,000 license plates augmented from a small number of labeled real license plates. All 200,000 training images are generated with license plate character labels. The license plates that need manual labeling are only selected from Dataset-1. After converting the training data to gray scale, 400,000 more training images are obtained by flipping pixels in order to simulate gray images of yellow and green license plates. Then, these images are fed to the recognition network modified from DenseNet.

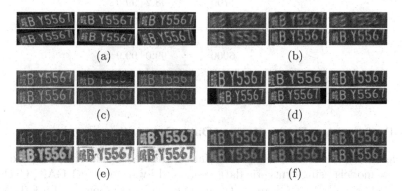

Fig. 3. Six data augmentation methods (a) Affine transformation (b) Motion blur (c) Uneven light (d) Stretching transformation (e) Erosion and dilation (f) Down sampling and gaussian noise.

4.3 Performance Evaluation on Dataset-1

With the above methods, our mixed training data is generated from 300, 700, 3,333, 4,750 and 6,000 real license plates selected from Dataset-1 training set respectively. Our baseline is the [18] using the license plate images generated by the CycleWGAN pre-training recognition network, and then using 9,000, 50,000 and 200,000 real labeled license plate images in a fine-tuning model. From the results in Table 2, it is concluded that when data generation, data augmentation and DenseNet are used, we only need 300 real labeled license plates to achieve the effect of 200,000 real license plates. In the same way, when the number of real license plates reaches 4,750, the final recognition accuracy has reached 99.0%, an increase of 1.4%. When the number of real license plate images exceeds 4,750, license plate recognition accuracy and character recognition accuracy are not improving. We conjecture that 4,750 real images contain enough information to recognize most of the license plates. Thus, by increasing the number of real license plates, the total amount of information after data augmentation will not change, and the recognition accuracy will not increase any further.

Table 2. The accuracy of other methods compared with the proposed method on Dataset-1. Recognition accuracy (%) and character recognition accuracy (%) are listed.

Method	Training data	RA	CRA
Baseline	9000	96.1	98.9
	50000	96.7	99.1
	200000	97.6	99.5
Ours	300	97.5	99.3
	700	98.2	99.5
	3333	98.6	99.8
	4750	99.0	99.9
	6000	99.0	99.9

4.4   Performance Evaluation on Data Generation

In order to evaluate the effect of the data generated by different methods, we train the models using synthetic data generated by script, CycleGAN, CycleW-GAN, and CycleWGAN-GP respectively. The results are shown in Table 3. When we only use the data set generated by script for training, the recognition accuracy on the test set of Dataset-1 is 42.2%. As shown in Fig. 2(a), our synthetic license plates generated by script also contain noise such as low light, low resolution, motion blur. The CycleGAN images achieve a recognition accuracy of 51.2%. Accuracy is not much improved because of the instability and lack of diversity in CycleGAN training. As shown in Fig. 2(b) and (c), the CycleWGAN and CycleWGAN-GP images display more various styles and colors, and part of them can not really distinguish from real images. The CycleWGAN and CycleWGAN-GP images achieve a recognition accuracy of 62.5% and 64.5% respectively. We also compare the impact of data generation and data augmentation on accuracy. When the number of real license plates is 3333, the recognition accuracy of the augmented data on Dataset-1 is 97.9%, far exceeding the recognition accuracy of the generated data.

Table 3. Single data augmentation recognition results with 3333 real images compare with [18]. Recognition accuracy (%), character recognition accuracy (%) are shown. "CRA-C" is the recognition accuracy (%) of the Chinese characters of the first character, and "CRA-NC" is the recognition accuracy (%) of the letters and numbers of the last six characters.

Method	Ours				Baseline			
	RA	CRA	CRA-C	CRA-NC	RA	CRA	CRA-C	CRA-NC
Script	42.2	80.3	43.8	90.8	4.4	30.0	20.0	31.7
CycleGAN	51.2	87.6	51.2	93.1	34.6	82.8	41.3	89.8
CycleWGAN	62.5	92.5	66.8	96.8	61.3	90.6	66.2	94.8
CycleWGAN-gp	64.5	93.7	65.2	98.4	-	-	-	-
Augmentation	97.9	99.1	99.2	99.7	-	-	-	-

Table 4. The effect of the number of plates and data generation on the results. Recognition accuracy (%), character recognition accuracy (%) are shown. RA(A) indicates the recognition accuracy of the data augmentation. CRA(A) indicates the character recognition accuracy of the data augmentation. RA(A+G) indicates the recognition accuracy of the training data composed of data augmentation and data generation. CRA(A+G) indicates the character recognition accuracy of the mixed training data composed of data augmentation and data generation.

Training data	RA(A)	RA(A+G)	CRA(A)	CRA(A+G)
60	47.5	79.3	88.3	94.4
150	83.8	93.8	96.6	98.7
200	92.4	96.7	98.4	98.7
300	96.1	97.5	98.7	99.3
700	97.1	98.2	98.9	99.5
3333	97.9	98.6	99.2	99.8
4750	98.8	99.0	99.8	99.9
6000	98.9	99.0	99.8	99.9

In order to understand how much number of real license plates improves recognition accuracy, we compare data augmentation results from 60 to 6000 real license plates. The result in Table 4 shows that the greater the number of real license plates, the higher the recognition accuracy obtained. Up to 4750, the highest recognition accuracy of the Dataset-1 is 99.0%. Even if the number of real license plates is increased from 4750, the result is no longer improved.

In order to understand the impact of GAN on recognition accuracy, we did some additional comparative experiments. It can also be seen in the Table 4 that training data composed of data augmentation and data generation can get better results than training data composed of only data augmentation. The conclusion is that the recognition accuracy of augmented data can be improved with data generation. In addition, the fewer real license plates, the more recognition accuracy increases contributed from generated data.

4.5   Performance Evaluation on AOLP

For the application-oriented license plate(AOLP) dataset, the experiments are carried out by using license plates from different sub-datasets for training and test. This data set is divided into three sub-datasets: access control (AC), traffic law enforcement (LE), and road patrol (RP). For example, in Table 5, we use the license plates from the LE and RP sub-datasets to train the DenseNet, and test its performance on the AC sub-dataset. Similarly, AC and RP are used for training and LE for test, and so on. Since there is no AOLP license plate font, only the data augmentation methods are used, without script and GAN generated license plates. In Table 5, through data augmentation and DenseNet, our method achieves the highest recognition accuracy on the AOLP dataset.

Table 5. The accuracy of other methods compared with the proposed method on dataset AOLP. Recognition accuracy (%), character recognition accuracy (%) are shown. AOLP is categorized into three subsets: access control (AC) with 681 samples, traffic law enforcement (LE) with 757 samples, and road patrol (RP) with 611 samples

Method	AC(%)		LE(%)		RP(%)	
	RA	CRA	RA	CRA	RA	CRA
Hsu et al. [8]	-	96	-	94	-	95
Li et al. [13]	94.85	-	94.19	-	88.38	-
Li et al. [14]	95.71	-	97.21	-	84.60	-
Ours	**96.61**	**99.08**	**97.80**	**99.65**	**91.00**	**97.22**

5   Conclusion

In this paper, we have investigated how many real labeled license plates are needed to train the license plate recognition system. We have proposed three data generation methods and six data augmentation methods in order to fully obtain all the information in a small number of images. The experimental results show that the proposed method only requires 300 real labeled license plates to achieve the effect achieved by 200,000 real license plates. The result shows that the greater the number of real license plates, the higher the recognition accuracy obtained. Up to 4750, the highest recognition accuracy of the Dataset-1 is 99.0%. Even if the number of real license plates is increased furthermore, the result is no longer improved. Additionally, training data composed of both augmented and generated data can achieve better results than training data composed of only augmented data. Furthermore, the fewer real license plates, the more recognition accuracy increases contributed from generated data.

References

1. Arjovsky, M., Chintala, S., Bottou, L.: Wasserstein gan. arXiv preprint arXiv:1701.07875 (2017)
2. Goodfellow, I.J.: Generative adversarial nets. In: International Conference on Neural Information Processing Systems, pp. 2672–2680 (2014)
3. Gou, C., Wang, K., Yao, Y., Li, Z.: Vehicle license plate recognition based on extremal regions and restricted Boltzmann machines. IEEE Trans. Intell. Transp. Syst. **17**(4), 1096–1107 (2016)
4. Graves, A., Fernández, S., Gomez, F., Schmidhuber, J.: Connectionist temporal classification: labelling unsegmented sequence data with recurrent neural networks. In: Proceedings of the 23rd International Conference on Machine Learning, pp. 369–376. ACM (2006)
5. Gulrajani, I., Ahmed, F., Arjovsky, M., Dumoulin, V., Courville, A.C.: Improved training of wasserstein gans. In: Advances in Neural Information Processing Systems, pp. 5767–5777 (2017)
6. Guo, J.M., Liu, Y.F.: License plate localization and character segmentation with feedback self-learning and hybrid binarization techniques. IEEE Trans. Veh. Technol. **57**(3), 1417–1424 (2008)
7. Gupta, A., Vedaldi, A., Zisserman, A.: Synthetic data for text localisation in natural images. In: Proceedings of the IEEE Conference on Computer Vision and Pattern Recognition, pp. 2315–2324 (2016)
8. Hsu, G.S., Chen, J.C., Chung, Y.Z.: Application-oriented license plate recognition. IEEE Trans. Veh. Technol. **62**(2), 552–561 (2013)
9. Huang, G., Liu, Z., Van Der Maaten, L., Weinberger, K.Q.: Densely connected convolutional networks. In: CVPR, vol. 1, p. 3 (2017)
10. Ioffe, S., Szegedy, C.: Batch normalization: accelerating deep network training by reducing internal covariate shift, pp. 448–456 (2015)
11. Jaderberg, M., Simonyan, K., Vedaldi, A., Zisserman, A.: Synthetic data and artificial neural networks for natural scene text recognition. arXiv preprint arXiv:1406.2227 (2014)
12. Kingma, D.P., Ba, J.: Adam: a method for stochastic optimization. Computer Science (2014)
13. Li, H., Shen, C.: Reading car license plates using deep convolutional neural networks and LSTMs. arXiv preprint arXiv:1601.05610 (2016)
14. Li, H., Wang, P., Shen, C.: Toward end-to-end car license plate detection and recognition with deep neural networks. IEEE Trans. Intell. Transp. Syst. **99**, 1–11 (2018)
15. Radford, A., Metz, L., Chintala, S.: Unsupervised representation learning with deep convolutional generative adversarial networks. arXiv preprint arXiv:1511.06434 (2015)

16. Ros, G., Sellart, L., Materzynska, J., Vazquez, D., Lopez, A.M.: The synthia dataset: a large collection of synthetic images for semantic segmentation of urban scenes. In: Proceedings of the IEEE Conference on Computer Vision and Pattern Recognition, pp. 3234–3243 (2016)
17. Shrivastava, A., Pfister, T., Tuzel, O., Susskind, J., Wang, W., Webb, R.: Learning from simulated and unsupervised images through adversarial training. In: CVPR. vol. 2, p. 5 (2017)
18. Wang, X., Man, Z., You, M., Shen, C.: Adversarial generation of training examples: applications to moving vehicle license plate recognition. arXiv preprint arXiv:1707.03124 (2017)
19. Wang, Z., et al.: Deepfont: identify your font from an image. In: Proceedings of the 23rd ACM International Conference on Multimedia, pp. 451–459. ACM (2015)
20. Yu, J., Farin, D., Krüger, C., Schiele, B.: Improving person detection using synthetic training data. In: 2010 17th IEEE International Conference on Image Processing (ICIP), pp. 3477–3480. IEEE (2010)
21. Zhu, J.Y., Park, T., Isola, P., Efros, A.A.: Unpaired image-to-image translation using cycle-consistent adversarial networks. arXiv preprint (2017)

Evaluation of Lightweight Local Descriptors for Level Ground Navigation with Monocular SLAM

Weiya Chen, Yulin Wan, Shiqi Ou[✉], and Zhidong Xue[✉]

School of Software Engineering, Huazhong University of Science and Technology, Wuhan, China
{weiya_chen,zdxue}@hust.edu.cn, {wanyulin,oushiqi}@isyslab.org

Abstract. Mobile robots play an important role in Ambient Assisted Living (AAL) by supporting or guiding people with reduced mobility to move in an indoor environment. Visual SLAM algorithms have become an important component of such robots by largely reducing the cost of tracking components. These AAL robots represent a typical situation in which robots move on level ground with merely in-plane navigation tasks. In order to find an optimized configuration of monocular SLAM systems in level ground navigation scenarios, we compared different lightweight local descriptors (LDB, BRIEF and ORB) by evaluating their influence on system performance based on the framework of ORB-SLAM. The results indicate that BRIEF outperforms others in metrics like time and trajectory accuracy, while LDB provides best descriptor matching quality. To conclude, BRIEF would be preferred for indoor level ground navigation with a monocular SLAM system, and LDB can be used instead if matching quality is the primary concern.

Keywords: Monocular SLAM · Level ground navigation
Local descriptor · Evaluation

1   Introduction

Simultaneous Localization and Mapping (SLAM) systems have been widely used for autonomous robot exploration both in indoor and outdoor environments. One major application field of SLAM-based mobile robot is Ambient Assisted Living (AAL) [7]: assistive robots are designed to help disabled individuals or people with reduced mobility to move more easily in daily life. In most cases, these robots provide their service on level ground in an indoor environment (from room to room, or inside a building with corridors) in forms of wheelchair [22], smart walker [33] or robot coach [12]. AAL robots often combine inputs from multiple sensors (e.g. LiDAR, sonars and cameras) to achieve more robust localization capability, which leads to complex hardware integration and excessive cost [6].

With the rapid developments of visual SLAM [35], many SLAM systems are able to track and build the map in real-time from purely visual information. This

© Springer Nature Switzerland AG 2018
J.-H. Lai et al. (Eds.): PRCV 2018, LNCS 11259, pp. 347–358, 2018.
https://doi.org/10.1007/978-3-030-03341-5_29

kind of visual SLAM has been an active research topic for more than twenty years with contributions coming from Robotics, Computer Vision and other related fields.

The emergence of visual SLAM systems like ORB-SLAM [25] makes it possible to build mobile AAL robots with low cost hardware, e.g. a single camera run on an embedded system. Visual SLAM can also help to build 3D map of the environment, which will provide more useful information of the surrounding for tasks like obstacle avoidance than traditional 2D maps. Since AAL robots only involve in-plane navigation on level ground of indoor environments, visual SLAM systems like ORB-SLAM can be further optimized by reducing from 6DoF tracking to 3DoF. For example, ORB-SLAM is based on ORB feature [27], which is a fast alternative of SIFT [19] or SURF [2]. ORB is composed of a rotation-invariant descriptor - rotated-BRIEF, which is useful for 6DoF tracking (e.g. hand-held camera), but not necessary for in-plane navigation.

Aiming to build a monocular SLAM system for AAL robots that usually run on embedded systems, we want to further optimize the state-of-the-art visual SLAM framework by finding appropriate lightweight descriptors that improve real-time tracking performance and reduce computational cost for in-plane navigation. So in this paper, based on the framework of ORB-SLAM - a milestone of feature-point based SLAM system, we compared different lightweight local descriptors by evaluating their influence on system performance in level ground navigation scenarios.

2   Related Work

2.1   Monocular SLAM

Visual SLAM can be performed with a single monocular camera, which is the simplest and cheapest sensor setup among all choices. This simplicity allows monocular SLAM to run on embedded systems or smartphones with minimal hardware integration effort, which encourages many years of research on this topic. Monocular SLAM algorithms have evolved from filtering to keyframe-based bundle adjustment (BA) algorithms, with many implementations lying in the middle ground between them. Filtering methods create a model based on the information gained over all past frames with a probability distribution, every frame is processed by the filter to jointly estimate the map feature locations and the camera pose [8]. Unlike filtering methods, keyframe-based approaches [23] estimate the map using global bundle adjustment for only a small number of past frames, which remain relatively efficient even processing large number of features from the keyframes. The work of Strasdat et al. [29] demonstrated that keyframe bundle adjustment outperforms filtering in term of accuracy per unit of computing time by measuring entropy reduction and tracking error.

The most representative keyframe-based system is marked by PTAM [16], which first introduced the idea of splitting camera tracking and mapping into parallel threads. Various systems are proposed in recent years targeting different issues in the front end and back end such as iSAM [14], FrameSLAM [17], etc.

Another type of methods standing out of framework of filtering and keyframe approaches is called direct SLAM, e.g. LSD-SLAM [9]. Direct SLAM method builds large scale semi-dense maps directly upon optimization over image pixel intensities instead of bundle adjustment over features, which offers more potential for related applications.

However, some intrinsic problems of monocular vision systems, e.g. scale drift and failing with pure rotations, still make monocular SLAM difficult to initialize despite simple hardware setup, which lead to the development of stereo and RGB-D vision systems.

2.2 Keypoint Features

Keypoint features are generally salient points (e.g. corners) encoded by information from local image regions that are invariant to viewpoint and lighting condition changes. Many visual SLAM systems use corner detectors in their tracking pipeline, e.g., a machine learning approach called FAST [26] is often used in real-time applications, and its improved version is integrated in other methods like ORB [27]. Besides corner detectors, another popular local descriptor is the Scale Invariant Feature Transform (SIFT) [19], which first achieves scale-invariant keypoint detection using histograms containing main properties of local appearance. However, the high dimension descriptor of SIFT makes it difficult to be used in real-time situations, which leads to different variants such as the Speeded-Up Robust Features (SURF) [2], PCA-SIFT [15] and other types of lightweight local descriptors.

Lightweight local descriptors are mainly designed to be computation-efficient, so the generating and matching of descriptors can run at frame rate. For example, the BRIEF descriptor [5] directly generates bit strings by simple binary tests in a smoothed image patch, and is augmented with rotation invariance by rotated-BRIEF (ORB). Unlike BRIEF, BRISK [18] and its successor FREAK [1] use a circular sampling pattern to compute intensity comparisons between point pairs. Another descriptor named LDB [34] computes a binary string for an image patch using simple intensity and gradient difference tests on pairwise grid cells, which is demonstrated to achieve greater accuracy and faster speed for tracking tasks than state-of-the-art algorithms.

Lots of evaluations and comparisons of keypoint detectors and descriptors have been done to help us choose among enormous options for a given application. Some surveys compare a special group of algorithms like Juan & Gwun's work [13] on SIFT-related methods, while others include more detectors and descriptors to compare with [20,32]. In the field of visual SLAM, there are also many existing work on the performance comparison of interest point detectors and descriptors [3,10,24]. The common conclusion that we can draw from these surveys is that there is a trade-off between accuracy and computation cost. SIFT and related methods offer better matching performance with high computational cost, while lightweight descriptors provide less precise matching at a much higher speed [21].

350 W. Chen et al.

The aforementioned evaluations have covered a wide range of detectors and descriptors, but some recent advances like LDB haven't been compared altogether. Moreover, these studies mostly target at general 6DoF tracking scenarios, cases for 3DoF in-plane level ground navigation haven't been addressed yet.

3 Experiment

In order to find an optimized configuration of monocular SLAM systems in level ground navigation scenarios, we compared different lightweight local descriptors by evaluating their influence on system performance based on the framework of ORB-SLAM. The descriptor used in ORB-SLAM is rotated-BRIEF (or rBRIEF), which is BRIEF enhanced with rotation-invariance. Since we only have yaw rotation in level ground scenarios, BRIEF is already sufficient and we expect more efficient tracking with BRIEF as rotation is not considered. Another lightweight, and claimed to be ultra-fast descriptor that we included in the evaluation is LDB [34]. As mentioned in Sect. 2, LDB is an efficient binary descriptor that has the same length as BRIEF (32 bits), and is much shorter than BRISK and SURF (both have 64 bits). Other popular descriptors exceeding a length of 64 bits are excluded from comparison.

So in this experiment, we choose to compare three lightweight descriptors: BRIEF, ORB (rotated-BRIEF) and LDB (without rotation invariance).

3.1 Dataset

Existing Datasets. We first considered existing public visual SLAM datasets for the evaluation task undertaken. The datasets that satisfy our testing requirements should only involve yaw rotation and in-plane translation (3DoF), which excludes most hand-held sequences such as the TUM RGB-D benchmark [30] and NYU Depth dataset [28]. Moreover, we prefer video recordings of indoor environment as AAL robots are mostly designed for indoor service, which again filters out datasets for large-scale outdoor environments, e.g. KITTI dataset [11] for car driving and the EuRoC dataset [4] for aerial vehicle navigation.

Finally we selected two sequences from the TUM RGB-D dataset (we use only the color images) that are designed for testing and debugging purpose - fr1/xyz and fr2/xyz. These two sequences only contain translation movements within a small movement range, which is not strictly "in-plane", but no rotation is involved. The TUM dataset also provides a tool that implements two methods for calculating the error between the estimated trajectory and the real one, namely Absolute Trajectory Error (ATE) and Relative Pose Error (RPE), both are useful for comparison of tracking performance.

Level Ground Sequences. Since we found little existing datasets for level ground indoor navigation, we decided to make some recordings that satisfy the requirements mentioned above. We mounted a monocular camera on a robotic walker - a standard four-wheel (no motor control) assistive walker combined with different sensors. The user stands behind the walker and walks forward while pushing the walker by holding the handles. A laptop computer running the SLAM algorithm is put on the robotic walker and connected to the camera mounted in front of the walker via a USB cable.

We choose three types of trajectories to be tested, including straight line, zigzag and octagon paths (Fig. 1). These segments have increased complexity and their combination can represent most use case that we encounter for level ground navigation. The length of each segment for these trajectories is chosen arbitrarily according to the room size.

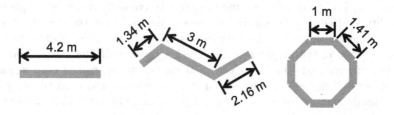

Fig. 1. Trajectories of the level ground video sequences, from left to right: line, zigzag and octagon.

The level ground sequences used in this experiment were captured by a Logitech C525 camera, with the auto-focus function turned off. The intrinsic parameters of the camera are: focal lengths - $f_x = 820.2028$ and $f_y = 819.9700$, the principal point $(u,v) = (255.4357, 222.3254)$, and the radial distortion - $K_1 = 0.0378$ and $K_2 = -0.3324$. The three sequences that we recorded are stored as $640 * 480$ images with a frame rate of 30 fps. The line, zigzag and octagon sequences last respectively 33, 54 and 110 s, and are saved as 803, 1291 and 2647 images.

3.2   Performance Metrics

Time and accuracy are two fundamental aspects that represent the real-time responsiveness and quality of a SLAM system. The performance metrics that we use to evaluate the influence of different descriptors are thus divided into the following groups:

Time: We logged time used for descriptor generation and matching since they directly reflect a descriptor's time efficiency. We also want to see the impact of changing keypoint descriptor on system performance, so we measured the execution time of the whole SLAM process along with the time for different states - initialization, tracking and relocalization. A good SLAM system should spend less time to initialize and relocate, leaving more time for tracking.

Matching Accuracy: Keypoint matching between frames is used to recover the camera's change of pose. We counted the number of matched keypoints as more correct matches generally lead to more accurate recovered pose. When regarding descriptor matching as a classification problem and each keypoint to be an individual class, we can use J3 (Eq. 1) to quantify class separability which is based on within and between class scatter matrix: S_w and S_b (Eq. 2) [31].

$$J_3 = trace\{S_w^{-1}S_m\} \tag{1}$$

$$S_m = S_w + S_b = \sum_{i=1}^{M} p_i s_i + \sum_{i=1}^{M} p_i(\mu_i - \mu_0)(\mu_i - \mu_0)^T \tag{2}$$

where S_m is the global covariance matrix. To compute S_w, p_i and s_i are the probability and covariance matrix of class i. For S_b, μ_i is the average feature vector for class i and μ_0 is the average vector for all classes. Higher J3 value computed from all the binary strings of a descriptor indicates better matching capability. To compute J3, we selected 50 images at the end of each sequence and collected all descriptor binaries for keypoints extracted from the very first image. Finally, only keypoints that have more than 30 binary strings for all three descriptors are included.

Tracking Accuracy: Since we use part of the TUM RGB-D dataset, we can make use of some useful tools provided by the authors. Absolute Trajectory Error (ATE) and Relative Pose Error (RPE) are two methods well-suited for measuring the performance of visual SLAM systems when ground-truth trajectory is available. In this experiment, our level ground recordings don't have ground-truth data that are compatible with TUM tools, so these two methods are only applied to TUM dataset.

4   Results

We performed our tests on a laptop computer with Intel (R) Core (TM) i7-5700HQ CPU @ 2.70 GHz with 8G RAM, running Ubuntu 16.04 LTS. For each video sequence, we run the SLAM system under each testing condition for 10 times to see their averaged performance. Hereafter we name each testing condition by the name of the descriptor in use, i.e. LDB, BRIEF and ORB condition.

4.1   Time

Figure 2 shows the time performance for the whole video sequences under each condition for two descriptor-related tasks: descriptor generation and matching. The results show that, LDB is slightly quicker for keypoint matching, but takes more time to generate the binary code than two other methods, and the result is almost consistent across different video sequences.

In addition to absolute time duration for a task, we also computed the proportion of that task in the total time of the whole SLAM process since the total time differs under each condition. On average, LDB has the highest time rate for descriptor generation (57.9%) and lowest time rate for keypoint matching (5.9%). Regarding ORB, it has the highest matching time cost rate (7.6%), but has similar performance in descriptor generation (52.3%) with BRIEF (51.5%).

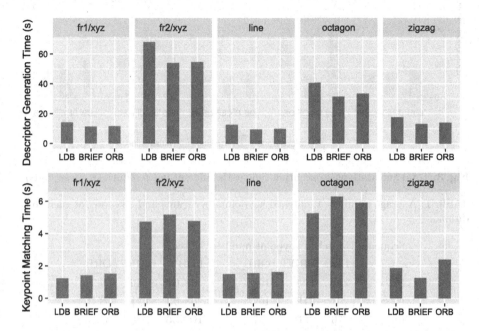

Fig. 2. Descriptor-related time performance for different video sequences (in seconds)

As mentioned in previous section, we collected the execution time for the whole process as well as for each system state. As shown in Fig. 3, all conditions have good performance in fr2/xyz with most time spent on tracking (from 98.8% to 99.3%), while with other sequences all conditions take more time to initialize, among which ORB suffers a steeper increase (up to 12.6%).

Both zigzag and octagon sequences include yaw rotations, relocalization occurred under all conditions on these two sequences. In the zigzag sequence, initialization remains acceptable for LDB and BRIEF (6.9% and 7.4%), whereas ORB increases rapidly (41.3%). LDB spends most time for tracking (85.7%) and least for relocalization (7.4%), BRIEF (52.9%) has similar tracking time as ORB (44.2%), but much more time for relocalization (39.7%). Octagon sequence contains multiple in-place rotations with relatively short transition, as a consequence, all conditions have bad performance. The best condition in this case - BRIEF is able to run tracking for half of the total time (54.8%), while the others have to relocate from time to time.

If we take the sum for all video sequences, ORB condition spends more time for initialization than LDB and BRIEF, while BRIEF condition outperforms others in tracking, relocalization and total time with a slight advantage.

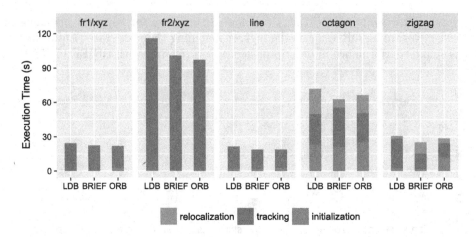

Fig. 3. Total and state-wise execution time with different video sequences (in seconds).

Table 1. Average number of matched keypoints per frame and J3 score for each condition.

Sequence	Matched keypoint number			J3 score		
	LDB	BRIEF	ORB	LDB	BRIEF	ORB
fr1/xyz	261	**295**	198	**98.67**	89.46	56.39
fr2/xyz	201	**219**	169	**88.63**	84.71	58.75
line	276	**280**	237	**102.36**	91.82	57.85
zigzag	225	**244**	204	**84.05**	72.27	61.99
octagon	210	**214**	189	**97.79**	95.02	60.82
mean	235	**250**	199	**94.30**	86.66	59.16
sd	32.4	36.4	25.0	7.64	8.88	2.25

4.2 Matching Accuracy

Table 1 shows the average number of matched keypoints per frame and J3 score for the whole sequences. We can see that for the number of matched keypoints, LDB (mean = 235) has similar performance with BRIEF (mean = 250), while ORB (mean = 199) has much lower number than both of them. Regarding J3 score, from the frames we choose (all three conditions run tracking during this period), we find that LDB has the highest score in all sequences (mean = 94.30), and the mean score of ORB (mean = 59.16) is far lower than the other two.

4.3 Tracking Accuracy

We use ATE and RPE to compute the trajectory error of fr1/xyz and fr2/xyz. As shown in Table 2 and Fig. 4, all conditions have similar performance for ATE (0.3625 ∼ 0.3666) in sequence fr2/xyz, however, BRIEF gets much smaller error than the other two in fr1/xyz with an error of 0.057 m. For RPE, we sum translation and rotation error separately. Same as ATE, the performance for all conditions are close in fr2/xyz, but BRIEF still outperforms the others in fr1/xyz.

Table 2. Measurement of tracking accuracy for each condition (in meter and degree).

Sequence		ATE			RPE-T error			RPE-R error		
		LDB	BRIEF	ORB	LDB	BRIEF	ORB	LDB	BRIEF	ORB
fr1/xyz	mean	0.1039	**0.0570**	0.1009	0.1251	**0.0634**	0.0922	5.2664	**2.5152**	5.7203
	sd	0.0496	0.0500	0.0800	0.0490	0.0539	0.0863	3.7171	3.2312	4.6535
fr2/xyz	mean	0.3666	0.3625	0.3651	0.0637	0.0635	0.0635	2.1105	1.7682	2.0970
	sd	0.0014	0.0042	0.0022	0.0002	0.0007	0.0004	0.7405	0.0461	0.6862

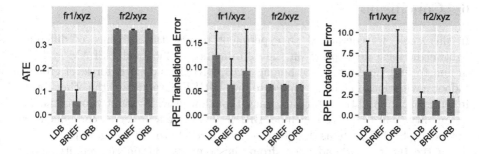

Fig. 4. Measurement of tracking accuracy for each video sequence.

5 Discussion

From the above results, we can see that descriptor generation is still the most time-consuming task for local feature based SLAM system that takes more than half of the total system running time. The use of BRIEF provides faster binary code generation that allows more time for tracking and less total time than with the other two descriptors.

The ORB descriptor is indeed rotated-BRIEF, with additional rotation-invariance ability compared to BRIEF, however, according to our tests, this augmentation largely reduced the number of matched keypoints per frame, which hinders not only the system time efficiency, but also matching ability (as more matched keypoints lead to better tracking result). This reduction is mainly due to the additional angular constraints during keypoint matching. Since rotation invariance is not required in level ground navigation, ORB descriptor is not recommended for this type of application.

Through all the tests with various sequences, we find the performance of different descriptors tends to diverge as the camera motion becomes more complicated (from line to octagon), and remains at the same level with very smooth and slow motion (e.g. in fr2/xyz). Globally, BRIEF retains robust tracking performance in difficult situations, although more sequences should be included to further confirm this observation on trajectory estimation quality.

In fact, when running pilot test for our robotic walker with ORB-SLAM, we found that the system struggled to initialize in indoor environment with many white walls around. The keypoints that the system can extract at runtime are too few to support functional tracking. We had to paste some texture-rich pictures on the walls to facilitate keypoints extraction. On the contrary, if tests were taken in an outdoor environment, the number of keypoints should no longer be a problem. In this case, LDB would be an appropriate choice since it has highest J3 score among our tested descriptors.

6   Conclusion

In this work, we conducted an experiment to test the influence of different lightweight local descriptors on the performance of monocular SLAM system, in aim to find the best choice among LDB, BRIEF and ORB for level ground indoor navigation. The results indicate that BRIEF outperforms the others both in terms of time and trajectory accuracy, though it provides slightly lower matching quality than LDB. To conclude, BRIEF would be a preferred component of monocular SLAM systems designed for indoor level ground navigation.

In the future, with advances from the computer vision community, more lightweight descriptors can be included for comparison and we can also evaluate the impact of keypoint extraction methods. To further improve the usability of SLAM systems for robotic walker as monocular SLAM systems are sometimes delicate to initialize, we can take stereo, RGB-D and even inertial sensors into consideration.

Acknowledgement. This work was funded by the Chinese Universities Scientific Fund (2017KFYXJJ225) and Science and Technology Program of Guangzhou (201803010067).

References

1. Alahi, A., Ortiz, R., Vandergheynst, P.: Freak: fast retina keypoint. In: 2012 IEEE Conference on Computer Vision and Pattern Recognition (CVPR), pp. 510–517. IEEE (2012)
2. Bay, H., Tuytelaars, T., Van Gool, L.: SURF: speeded up robust features. In: Leonardis, A., Bischof, H., Pinz, A. (eds.) ECCV 2006. LNCS, vol. 3951, pp. 404–417. Springer, Heidelberg (2006). https://doi.org/10.1007/11744023_32
3. Bayraktar, E., Boyraz, P.: Analysis of feature detector and descriptor combinations with a localization experiment for various performance metrics. arXiv preprint arXiv:1710.06232 (2017)

4. Burri, M., et al.: The EuRoC micro aerial vehicle datasets. Int. J. Robot. Res. (2016). https://doi.org/10.1177/0278364915620033
5. Calonder, M., Lepetit, V., Strecha, C., Fua, P.: BRIEF: binary robust independent elementary features. In: Daniilidis, K., Maragos, P., Paragios, N. (eds.) ECCV 2010. LNCS, vol. 6314, pp. 778–792. Springer, Heidelberg (2010). https://doi.org/10.1007/978-3-642-15561-1_56
6. Cavanini, L., Benetazzo, F., Freddi, A., Longhi, S., Monteriu, A.: Slam-based autonomous wheelchair navigation system for AAL scenarios. In: 2014 IEEE/ASME 10th International Conference on Mechatronic and Embedded Systems and Applications (MESA), pp. 1–5. IEEE (2014)
7. Costa, R., et al.: Ambient assisted living. In: Corchado, J.M., Tapia, D.I., Bravo, J., et al. (eds.) 3rd Symposium of Ubiquitous Computing and Ambient Intelligence 2008, pp. 86–94. Springer, Heidelberg (2008)
8. Davison, A.J., Reid, I.D., Molton, N.D., Stasse, O.: Monoslam: real-time single camera slam. IEEE Trans. Pattern Anal. Mach. Intell. **29**(6), 1052–1067 (2007)
9. Engel, J., Schöps, T., Cremers, D.: LSD-SLAM: large-scale direct monocular SLAM. In: Fleet, D., Pajdla, T., Schiele, B., Tuytelaars, T. (eds.) ECCV 2014. LNCS, vol. 8690, pp. 834–849. Springer, Cham (2014). https://doi.org/10.1007/978-3-319-10605-2_54
10. Gauglitz, S., Höllerer, T., Turk, M.: Evaluation of interest point detectors and feature descriptors for visual tracking. Int. J. Comput. Vis. **94**(3), 335 (2011)
11. Geiger, A., Lenz, P., Urtasun, R.: Are we ready for autonomous driving? the kitti vision benchmark suite. In: Conference on Computer Vision and Pattern Recognition (CVPR) (2012)
12. Gross, H.M., et al.: Roreas: robot coach for walking and orientation training in clinical post-stroke rehabilitation-prototype implementation and evaluation in field trials. Auton. Robot. **41**(3), 679–698 (2017)
13. Juan, L., Gwun, O.: A comparison of sift, pca-sift and surf. Int. J. Image Process. (IJIP) **3**(4), 143–152 (2009)
14. Kaess, M., Ranganathan, A., Dellaert, F.: iSAM: incremental smoothing and mapping. IEEE Trans. Robot. **24**(6), 1365–1378 (2008)
15. Ke, Y., Sukthankar, R.: PCA-SIFT: a more distinctive representation for local image descriptors. In: Proceedings of the 2004 IEEE Computer Society Conference on Computer Vision and Pattern Recognition, CVPR 2004, vol. 2, p. II. IEEE (2004)
16. Klein, G., Murray, D.: Parallel tracking and mapping for small AR workspaces. In: 6th IEEE and ACM International Symposium on Mixed and Augmented Reality, ISMAR 2007, pp. 225–234. IEEE (2007)
17. Konolige, K., Agrawal, M.: FrameSLAM: from bundle adjustment to real-time visual mapping. IEEE Trans. Robot. **24**(5), 1066–1077 (2008)
18. Leutenegger, S., Chli, M., Siegwart, R.Y.: BRISK: binary robust invariant scalable keypoints. In: 2011 IEEE International Conference on Computer Vision (ICCV), pp. 2548–2555. IEEE (2011)
19. Lowe, D.G.: Distinctive image features from scale-invariant keypoints. Int. J. Comput. Vis. **60**(2), 91–110 (2004)
20. Mikolajczyk, K., Schmid, C.: A performance evaluation of local descriptors. IEEE Trans. Pattern Anal. Mach. Intell. **27**(10), 1615–1630 (2005)
21. Miksik, O., Mikolajczyk, K.: Evaluation of local detectors and descriptors for fast feature matching. In: 2012 21st International Conference on Pattern Recognition (ICPR), pp. 2681–2684. IEEE (2012)

22. Morales, Y., Kallakuri, N., Shinozawa, K., Miyashita, T., Hagita, N.: Human-comfortable navigation for an autonomous robotic wheelchair. In: 2013 IEEE/RSJ International Conference on Intelligent Robots and Systems (IROS), pp. 2737–2743. IEEE (2013)
23. Mouragnon, E., Lhuillier, M., Dhome, M., Dekeyser, F., Sayd, P.: Real time localization and 3d reconstruction. In: 2006 IEEE Computer Society Conference on Computer Vision and Pattern Recognition, vol. 1, pp. 363–370. IEEE (2006)
24. Mozos, Ó.M., Gil, A., Ballesta, M., Reinoso, O.: Interest point detectors for visual SLAM. In: Borrajo, D., Castillo, L., Corchado, J.M. (eds.) CAEPIA 2007. LNCS (LNAI), vol. 4788, pp. 170–179. Springer, Heidelberg (2007). https://doi.org/10.1007/978-3-540-75271-4_18
25. Mur-Artal, R., Montiel, J.M.M., Tardos, J.D.: ORB-SLAM: a versatile and accurate monocular slam system. IEEE Trans. Robot. **31**(5), 1147–1163 (2015)
26. Rosten, E., Drummond, T.: Machine learning for high-speed corner detection. In: Leonardis, A., Bischof, H., Pinz, A. (eds.) ECCV 2006. LNCS, vol. 3951, pp. 430–443. Springer, Heidelberg (2006). https://doi.org/10.1007/11744023_34
27. Rublee, E., Rabaud, V., Konolige, K., Bradski, G.: ORB: an efficient alternative to SIFT or SURF. In: 2011 IEEE International Conference on Computer Vision (ICCV), pp. 2564–2571. IEEE (2011)
28. Silberman, N., Fergus, R.: Indoor scene segmentation using a structured light sensor. In: Proceedings of the International Conference on Computer Vision - Workshop on 3D Representation and Recognition (2011)
29. Strasdat, H., Montiel, J.M., Davison, A.J.: Visual SLAM: why filter? Image Vis. Comput. **30**(2), 65–77 (2012)
30. Sturm, J., Engelhard, N., Endres, F., Burgard, W., Cremers, D.: A benchmark for the evaluation of RGB-D slam systems. In: Proceedings of the International Conference on Intelligent Robot Systems (IROS), October 2012
31. Theodoridis, S., Koutroumbas, K.: Pattern Recognition, 4th edn. Academic Press, Boston (2009)
32. Tuytelaars, T., Mikolajczyk, K., et al.: Local invariant feature detectors: a survey. Found. trends® Comput. Graph. Vis. **3**(3), 177–280 (2008)
33. Wachaja, A., Agarwal, P., Zink, M., Adame, M.R., Möller, K., Burgard, W.: Navigating blind people with a smart walker. In: 2015 IEEE/RSJ International Conference on Intelligent Robots and Systems (IROS), pp. 6014–6019. IEEE (2015)
34. Yang, X., Cheng, K.T.: Local difference binary for ultrafast and distinctive feature description. IEEE Trans. Pattern Anal. Mach. Intell. **36**(1), 188–194 (2014)
35. Yousif, K., Bab-Hadiashar, A., Hoseinnezhad, R.: An overview to visual odometry and visual SLAM: applications to mobile robotics. Intell. Ind. Syst. **1**(4), 289–311 (2015)

Establishing a Large Scale Dataset for Image Emotion Analysis Using Chinese Emotion Ontology

Lifang Wu, Mingchao Qi, Heng Zhang, Meng Jian[✉], Bowen Yang, and Dai Zhang

Faculty of Information Technology, Beijing University of Technology, Beijing, China
lfwu@bjut.edu.cn, {mingcchao_qi,zhangheng}@emails.bjut.edu.cn,
jianmeng648@163.com, yangbowen108@qq.com, davidzhangdai@aliyun.com

Abstract. With the development of visual social network, more and more people like to present themselves using images or videos. Visual emotion analysis is becoming one of hot research topics. According to Jou's idea [1], emotion presentations of the Western and the Eastern are much different due to the culture difference. There are some popular emotion models such as Plutchik's model and so on. And there is not one-to-one correspondence between these emotion models. All of the existing image databases for emotion analysis are built by Plutchik's and Mikels's emotion models. However, most researches on Chinese text emotion analysis used Xu's model [2]. And there are not the corresponding image datasets for emotion analysis with Xu's model. In this paper we establish an image dataset for emotion analysis by collecting images from Flickr using Chinese Emotion Ontology of Xu's model. In addition, we design a dataset refinement (de-noising) strategy to promote the confidence of emotion labels for the images. Finally, we establish the dataset CH-EmoD which includes a sub dataset with single emotion label and a sub dataset with multiple emotion labels. Furthermore, we provide the baselines of emotion classification and multi-label emotion classification by using state-of-the-art emotion/sentiment classifications algorithms Alexnet [3] and PCNN [4]. The experimental results demonstrate that the dataset works well on emotion classification and multi-label emotion classification and the proposed dataset refinement strategy is effective.

Keywords: Emotion models · Chinese emotion ontology
Image dataset for emotion analysis · Dataset refinement (de-noising)
Social network

1 Introduction

With the rapid development of social networks, people tend to express themselves in the form of texts with images or videos on the Internet. Therefore, the

J.-H. Lai et al. (Eds.): PRCV 2018, LNCS 11259, pp. 359–370, 2018.
https://doi.org/10.1007/978-3-030-03341-5_30

Internet has become an important source for opinion mining, affective computing, or emotion analysis. Influenced by development of social network, the text based emotion analysis has made great progress [5–7]. While the visual emotion analysis has lagged behind a lot. In recent years, visual contents become more and more popular on social network, human computer interaction and so on, visual emotion analysis is becoming one of hot research topics [8–10].

Human emotion is a kind of complex feelings. There are more than one kinds of emotion models. The emotion categories in these models are compared in Table 1. The most popular emotion model is Plutchik's Wheel of Emotions [11] in which emotions are organized into eight basic categories: *joy, trust, anticipation, anger, sadness, fear, disgust* and *surprise*, each with three different emotional valences. Mikels *et al.* [12] also divide emotions into eights categories but replace *joy, trust, anticipation, surprise* in Plutchik's model with *amusement, contentment, excitement, awe*. Ekman did a lot of cross-cultural comparative studies all over the world, and found that people with different cultural backgrounds are basically consistent with six emotions, including *happiness, angry, sadness, fear, disgust* and *surprise*. Based on the findings, he proposed Ekman's facial expression system [13], which involves a more universal emotion model with the above six emotions. Ekman's model is much unequal to positive and negative sentiments because only "happiness" is positive, while other five emotions are negative. To address this problem, Xu *et al.* [2] add "like" into Ekman's model to express the positive emotion more exhaustively. These seven kinds of emotions are fundamentally consistent with the traditional Chinese presentation of "seven emotion". Furthermore, Xu *et al.* construct an emotion ontology consisting of Chinese words corresponding to the seven emotions. Most existing researches on Chinese text emotion analysis [14–16] utilized this emotion model and ontology.

Table 1. The popular Emotion models and the emotion categories

Models	Emotion categories							
Plutchik	Joy	Trust	Anticipation	Anger	Sadness	Fear	Disgust	Surprise
Mikels	Amusement	Contentment	Excitement	Anger	Sadness	Fear	Disgust	Awe
Ekman	Happiness	Anger	Sadness	Fear	Disgust	Surprise	-	-
Xu	Happiness	Like	Anger	Sadness	Fear	Disgust	Surprise	-

Image datasets is of great importance for image emotion analysis and some datasets have been available for researches. Lang [17] built a dataset IAPS-Subset based on Mikels's emotion model. And ArtPhoto is composed of photos by professional artists [18]. These two datasets include only hundreds of images, and they are a little small in the era of big data. Based on Plutchik's Wheel of Emotions, Borth et al. [19] build a large scale dataset called SentiBank, in which more than 450,000 images are crawled from Flickr by the Adjective Noun Pairs (ANPs). And the emotion labels are assigned by the ANPs. With the same emotion model, Jou *et al.* [1] set up a large scale multilingual visual sentiment ontology and more than 7.36 million images and their metadata are also released.

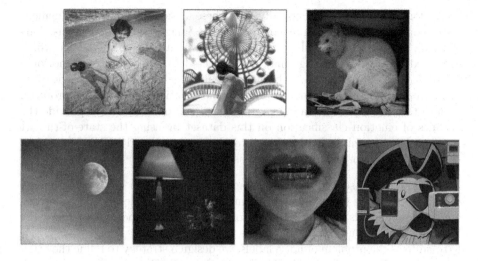

Fig. 1. Example images of seven emotions in CH-EmoD.

This large dataset is mainly created for different cultures, including 12 different languages. You *et al.* [20] query the image search engines (Flickr and Instagram) using Mikels's eight emotion categories as keywords and established a dataset with 23,308 images. These datasets are frequently used in emotion/sentiment classification, and they are built based on Mikels's models. According to Jou's idea [20], emotion presentations of the Western and the Eastern are much different due to the culture difference. Xu's emotion model [2] is popularly utilized in Chinese text emotion analysis. And they proposed a Chinese Emotion Ontology library for emotion analysis. If we could build an image dataset based on Xu's model, it would be helpful for Chinese emotion analysis and emotion matching of Chinese-text and images.

In the era of big data, large scale image data is required. Where could we get a large number of images with emotion labels? There are a lot of images in social network that can be a resource for our dataset. But how could we get the emotion labels for these images? Inspired by SentiBank [19], we also collect the images and the labels from the visual social networks. Flickr is a popular visual social network, It has the characteristics as follows: (1) It is an image social network with lots of images free for public. (2) The images on Flickr have rich metadata such as tags, description texts which can help to attach the image to the corresponding emotional label. (3) A large number of images are shared with Chinese tags and text on Flickr every day.

Motivated by above, we establish an image dataset for emotion analysis by collecting images from Flickr using Chinese emotion ontology of Xu's model. Xu's model is usually used by Chinese, therefore, this dataset is named as CH-EmoD, some example images are shown in Fig. 1. Firstly, the emotion keywords of Chinese emotion ontology is used to crawl images as well as their tags and description text from Flickr. Secondly, with these metadata, a dataset refinement (de-noising) strategy is designed to remove the images with noise labels. Furthermore, we preserve a small set of images with multiple emotion labels, which is resulted from that an image may be connected to more than one emotional keywords. The sub dataset can be used for multi-label emotion classification. Therefore, we not only intend to address the emotion classification problem, but also to carry out multi-label emotion classification. Finally, we provide the baselines of emotion classification on this dataset by using the state-of-the-art sentiment/emotion classification frameworks Alexnet [3] and PCNN [4].

The contributions of this paper are as follows:

- We build a large scale dataset for image emotion analysis by crawling images from Flickr using Chinese emotion ontology of Xu's model [2]. Because Xu's emotion model is usually utilized for Chinese text emotion analysis, the dataset is more suitable for analyzing Chinese emotion.
- To address the problem of noise labels, we design a strategy to refine the original dataset automatically. And the final dataset CH-EmoD could be obtained. The Compared experimental results show that the dataset refinement strategy is effective.
- We practice state-of-the-art sentiment/emotion classification algorithms on CH-EmoD and get the baselines of emotion classification as well as multi-label emotion classification.

2   Establishing the Image Emotion Dataset CH-EmoD

In this section, we build the dataset with Xu's emotion model [2] which defines seven emotions: *happiness, like, anger, sadness, fear, disgust, surprise*. Meanwhile, a dataset refinement (de-noising) tactics is proposed to promote the confidence of emotion labels.

2.1   Crawling Images from Flickr by Emotion Keywords

In the Chinese emotional ontology library [2], there are totally 26,453 emotion keywords, as shown in Table 2. Each keyword is labeled with emotion category, emotion intensity and sentiment polarity. The emotion intensity is divided into five levels of 1, 3, 5, 7, and 9. The bigger the value, the stronger the emotion. From Table 2 we can see that distribution of the number of emotion keywords is imbalance. The number of emotion "surprise" is 228, it is the minimum. And the maximum number of keywords is 10,282 for "disgust". On one hand the imbalance of number of keywords possibly results in the imbalance of images. On the other hand, it is a heavy work to crawl image using all of these keywords. Therefore, we select some of the keywords to represent the corresponding emotions. Based on the number 228, the number of keywords for each emotion category is not more than 300. We first delete the words of network words, idiom and prepositional phrase. Then based on the understanding that keywords with

Table 2. The number of emotion keywords for querying images of each categories

Emotion	Number of keywords	Number of selected keywords
Happiness	1,967	300
Like	10,095	296
Anger	388	223
Sadness	2,314	300
Fear	1,179	296
Disgust	10,282	298
Surprise	228	222
Sum	26,453	1,935

small emotion intensity possibly represent the emotion ineffectively, we select the keywords by the emotion intensity. Finally total 1935 keywords are selected as shown in Table 2. Using these keywords we obtain the raw dataset with 546,472 images whose labels are assigned by the corresponding emotion keywords.

2.2   Dataset Refinement

As is well known, the raw dataset crawled from social network is with noise. It is necessary to refine the raw dataset. By observing the raw dataset, there are some problems as follows:

Problem 1: The emotion presented in some images is different from the labels assigned by the corresponding emotion keywords. In Fig. 2(a), the image is

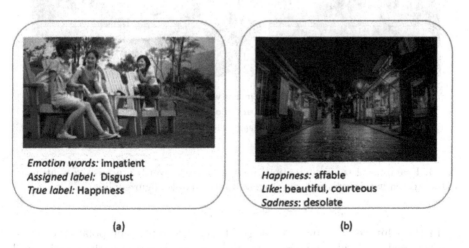

Fig. 2. Example images with problems in the raw dataset ((a)Example image with noise label; (b) Example image with keywords of different emotion categories).

crawled by the keyword of "impatient" and it is assigned as emotion "disgust". But it is clear that this image presents the emotion "happiness" which is much different from the assigned label.

Problem 2: Some images are crawled by different keywords. In Fig. 2(b), the image is crawled by "affable", "beautiful", "courteous" and "desolate". Therefore, it is assigned as the emotions of "happiness", "like" and "sadness".

For Problem 1, we should find the images with such problem and remove them from the raw dataset. Wu *et al.* [21] found such images by the sentiment polarity confliction of ANP and Tags in SentiBank [19]. Inspired by Wu's idea, we try to refine the raw dataset by the sentiment polarity confliction of different text contents. In the raw dataset, most images involves emotion keywords, the tags and description texts. We look key words, the tags and the description text as three parties. If there is emotion confliction among these three parties for an image, we think the emotion label is confident, the image will be removed from the dataset. Otherwise, three parties give the sentiment polarity consistent or without confliction. And the label from the keywords is high confident. In Fig. 3, image in Fig. 2(a) is labeled as "disgust", it presents a negative sentiment. However the sentiment polarities of tags and description text both are positive. There is sentiment polarity confliction between the emotion keywords, description text and tags for this image, and this image should be removed from the raw dataset.

Emotion words: lilac flowers
Description text: harm, protect, disease
Tags: diseases and insect pests

Emotion words: impatient
Description text: happy
Tags: happy, comfortable life

Fig. 3. Examples of some contentious images. The red words are positive sentiment, and the green words represent negative sentiment. (Color figure online)

In the Chinese emotional ontology library, the sentiment polarity of emotion keywords is divided into neutral, positive, negative and both (positive and negative). For the convenience of statistics, we mark positive as 1, negative as -1, neutral and both as 0. We first use TextRank [22] algorithm to extract the keywords of description text. The sentiment of every text keyword is obtained from the Chinese emotional ontology library. If a keyword is not included in the library, its polarity is labeled as 0. Eventually, the sum of the polarity of the text keywords is the sentiment polarity of description texts. Secondly, the polarity of image tags is also determined by the same principle. Finally, an image preserved in or removed from the dataset is determined according to the sentiment polarity of emotion keywords, description text and tags. The detailed judgment rules are shown in Table 3. For example, if the sentiment polarity of the keyword is 1, and the sentiment polarity of description text and tags are 1 or 0, it means that there is not sentiment polarity contradiction, the image will be preserved. Otherwise, it will be removed.

Table 3. The rule of de-noising strategy.

Sentiment of keywords	Sentiment pairs of (Description text, Tags)	Result
1	(1,1)(1,0)(0,1)(0,0)	Preserved
	(−1,1)(1,−1)(−1,−1)(0,−1)(−1,0)	Removed
0	(0,0)(0,1)(1,0) (0,−1)(−1,0)(1,1) (−1,−1)	Preserved
	(1,−1)(−1,1)	Removed
−1	(−1,−1)(−1,0)(0,−1)(0,0)	Preserved
	(−1,1)(1,−1)(1,1)(0,1)(1,0)	Removed

After the above step, 120,429 images have been removed and the size of dataset become 426,043. To address Problem 2, we collect the images with multiple emotion labels and form a multiple label dataset. It includes total 29,022 images, each image includes almost 6 keywords on average. For an image, the number of keywords with the corresponding emotion is counted. And the number of keywords of each emotion category is divided by the total number of keywords so that we can obtain the probability of the corresponding emotion categories. As shown in Fig. 4.

[0.45, 0.35, 0.0, 0.15, 0.05, 0.0, 0.0]   [0.0, 0.0, 0.0, 0.25, 0.375, 0.125, 0.25]   [0.33, 0.67, 0.0, 0.0, 0.0, 0.0, 0.0]

Fig. 4. Example multi-label images. Each element of the seven dimensional vector represents *happiness, like, anger, sadness, fear, disgust, surprise*, sequentially.

Finally, the dataset CH-EmoD is composed of two parts: single label dataset and multi label dataset. In multi label dataset, the label of an image is presented as the probability distribution. Table 4 shows the number of images in each emotion category in dataset CH-EmoD. For multi-label dataset, we only give the total number of images.

Table 4. The distribution of every category

Dataset	Happiness	Like	Anger	Sadness	Fear	Disgust	Surprise	Sum
Raw dataset	128,496	120,799	42,017	76,344	63,358	64,691	50,767	546,472
Refined dataset (single-label)	74,509	68,961	14,184	37,859	31,945	24,774	23,455	275,687
Refined dataset (multi-label)	-	-	-	-	-	-	-	29,022

3   Image Emotion Analysis Using Convolutional Neural Network

In recent years, convolutional neural network has achieved great success in many image processing tasks, for example, Hand written numeral recognition, Image classification etc. At the same time, there also exist effective results by fine-tuning the AlexNet model pre-trained from ImageNet model [3]. In our work, the same tactics is conducted to fine-tune the Alexnet. We keep the same network structure as ImageNet reference network [23]. For the task of emotion, we only change the output of last fully connected layer from 1000 to 7. Additionally, we use the sigmoid cross entropy loss function instead of the softmax loss function for multi label classification. The other layers are exactly the same as ImageNet reference network which includes five convolutional layers and three fully connected layers.

Especially, because the label of multi-label data is probability distribution, we first processed it into binary labels based on formula as follows:

$$label_i = \begin{cases} 0 & prob_i < C_{th} \\ 1 & prob_i \geq C_{th} \end{cases} \quad i = 1, 2, ..., 7 \tag{1}$$

where $label_i$ represents each emotion category, $prob_i$ is the probability of every emotion class in one image, and C_{th} is threshold ranging from 0 to 1. It is determined by experiments. At the end, the label of each image is a vector with seven binary values.

4   Experimental Results

Considering the diversity of data structures, we test our dataset from two different aspects: emotion classification, multi-label emotion classification.

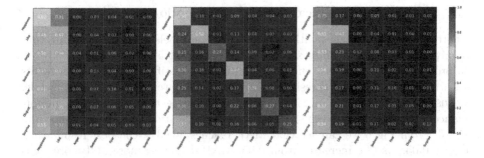

Fig. 5. Confusion matrix for the three models on the testing data.

4.1 Emotion Classification

There are totally 275,687 images with single labels in our dataset CH-EmoD. And we randomly select 2,000 images as testing set, 1,000 images as validating set and the rest of them as training data. We fine-tune the pre-trained AlexNet [3] using the training data. Then the trained mode is tested using the testing data. In order to evaluate the effect of the dataset refinement, we fine-tune the same model using the raw dataset. We also practice the PCNN framework [4] on the dataset CH-EmoD. For these algorithms, the same testing set is utilized. The experimental results are shown in Table 5. The accuracy of the Alexnet on the refined dataset is 46.32%, which is higher by 14.37% than that of the same model on the raw dataset. The results show that the data refinement strategy is effective. The accuracy of PCNN is better than Alexnet on raw dataset while worse than Alexnet on CH-EmoD.

Table 5. Emotion multi-classification accuracy on different models.

Model	Correct samples	Accuracy
Alexnet on raw data	639/2,000	31.95%
Alexnet on CH-EmoD	926/2,000	46.32%
PCNN on CH-EmoD	734/2,000	36.74%

We further compare the confusion matrix of these three models from their prediction results, as shown in Fig. 5. In general, the false positive rates of "happiness" and "like" is high on the three models, especially on the model of raw data. It is consistent with the fact that these two categories have the largest number of images in the dataset. Meanwhile, the true positive rates on model of refined data are the best in all emotion categories except "happiness" that is 0.75 on PCNN. These results demonstrate again that the proposed dataset refinement (de-noising) strategy works well.

4.2   Multi-label Classification of Image Emotion

There exist 29,022 images with multiple emotion labels. These images are randomly separated into training set (80%), validating set(5%) and testing set(15%). In order to obtain the best effect for multi-label classification, the experiments with different values of threshold C_{th} (in Sect. 3) are conducted. Meanwhile, we use Mean Average Precision (MAP) to evaluate the classification performance which is generally used in multi-label classification problems, as shown in Fig. 6. From Fig. 6 we can see that MAP reaches 36.63%, the best result when $C_{th} = 0.05$. As C_{th} increases from 0.05, MAP decreases more and more. It is reasonable because the labels of images become more and more sparse as C_{th} increases.

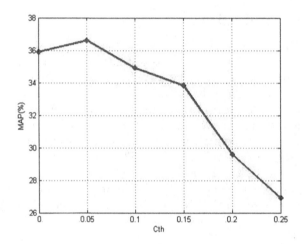

Fig. 6. The effect of multi-label emotion classification with different C_{th}.

5   Conclusion

In this work, we address the challenging task of visual emotion classification since the sentiment analysis is difficult to present human emotions adequately. Due to the difference of Chinese and Western cultures, we use Chinese Emotion Ontology published by Dalian University of Technology to estabilsh an image dataset for emotion analysis. In addition, we design a refinement (de-nosing) strategy to promote the confidence of labels of each image. Furthermore, we obtain the dataset with multi emotion labels. Finally we provide the baselines of emotion classification and multi label emotion classification by using state-of-the-art emotion/sentiment classifications algorithms Alexnet and PCNN. The provided emotion dataset is the first emotion dataset involving seven emotion categories with Xu's emotion model, which is popular in Chinese text emotion analysis. Therefore, the provided dataset is possibly useful for analyzing Chinese emotions from the images they uploaded or generated. The baselines could provide reference for the following researches. In future, we will continue to improve the credibility of the image labels and transform weakly labeled dataset into strongly labeled dataset. Furthermore, we will pay more attention on multi-label emotion classification.

Acknowledgements. This research was supported by National Natural Science Foundation of China (NO. 61702022), China Postdoctoral Science Foundation funded project (NO. 2018T110019), Beijing excellent young talent cultivation project (NO. 2017000020124G075) and Beijing Municipal Education Commission Science and Technology Innovation Project (NO. KZ201610005012).

References

1. Jou, B., Chen, T., Pappas, N., Topkara, M., Topkara, M., Chang, SF.: Visual affect around the world: a large-scale multilingual visual sentiment ontology. In: ACM International Conference on Multimedia, pp. 159–168 (2015)
2. Xu, L., Lin, H., Pan, Y., Ren, H., Chen, J.: Constructing the affective lexicon ontology. J. China Soc. Sci. Tech. Inf. **27**, 180–185 (2008)
3. Krizhevsky, A., Sutskever, I., Hinton, G.E.: ImageNet classification with deep convolutional neural networks. In: International Conference on Neural Information Processing Systems, pp. 1097–1105 (2012)
4. You, Q., Luo, J., Jin, H., Yang, J.: Robust image sentiment analysis using progressively trained and domain transferred deep networks. In: Twenty-Ninth AAAI Conference on Artificial Intelligence, pp. 381–388 (2015)
5. Patodkar, V.N., Sheikh, I.R.: Twitter as a corpus for sentiment analysis and opinion mining. In: International Conference on Language Resources and Evaluation, pp. 17–23 (2010)
6. Bao, S., et al.: Mining Social Emotions from Affective Text. IEEE Trans. Knowl. Data Eng. **24**, 1658–1670 (2012)
7. Wang, D., Li, F.: Sentiment analysis of Chinese microblogs based on layered features. In: Loo, C.K., Yap, K.S., Wong, K.W., Teoh, A., Huang, K. (eds.) ICONIP 2014. LNCS, vol. 8835, pp. 361–368. Springer, Cham (2014). https://doi.org/10.1007/978-3-319-12640-1_44
8. Zhao, S., et al.: Predicting personalized emotion perceptions of social images. In: ACM on Multimedia Conference, pp. 1385–1394 (2016)
9. Yang, J., She, D., Sun, M.: Joint image emotion classification and distribution learning via deep convolutional neural network. In: Twenty-Sixth International Joint Conference on Artificial Intelligence, pp. 3266–3272 (2017)
10. Yang, J., She, D., Sun, M., Cheng, M., Rosin, P., Wang, L.: Visual sentiment prediction based on automatic discovery of affective regions. IEEE Trans. Multimed. **20**, 2513–2525 (2018)
11. Camras, L., Plutchik, R.: Emotion: a psychoevolutionary synthesis. Am. J. Psychol. **93**, 751 (1980)
12. Mikels, J.A., Fredrickson, B.L., Larkin, G.R., Lindberg, C.M., Maglio, S.J., Reuter-Lorenz, P.A.: Emotional category data on images from the international affective picture system. Behav. Res. Methods **37**, 626–630 (2005)
13. Ekman, P.: Facial expression and emotion. Am. Psychol. **48**, 384–92 (1993)

14. Wang, M., Liu, M., Feng, S., Wang, D., Zhang, Y.: A novel calibrated label ranking based method for multiple emotions detection in Chinese microblogs. In: Zong, C., Nie, J.Y., Zhao, D., Feng, Y. (eds.) Natural Language Processing and Chinese Computing. CCIS, vol. 496, pp. 238–250. Springer, Heidelberg (2014). https://doi.org/10.1007/978-3-662-45924-9_22

15. Li, C., Wu, H., Jin, Q.: Emotion classification of Chinese microblog text via fusion of BoW and vector feature representations. In: Zong, C., Nie, J.Y., Zhao, D., Feng, Y. (eds.) Natural Language Processing and Chinese Computing. CCIS, vol. 496, pp. 217–228. Springer, Heidelberg (2014). https://doi.org/10.1007/978-3-662-45924-9_20

16. He, F., He, Y., Liu, N., Liu, J., Peng, M.: A microblog short text oriented multi-class feature extraction method of fine-grained sentiment analysis. Acta Sci. Nat. Univ. Pekin. **50**, 48–54 (2014)

17. Lang, P.J: International affective picture system (IAPS): technical manual and affective ratings. In: Center for Research in Psychophysiology University of Florida (1999)

18. Machajdik, J., Hanbury, A.: Affective image classification using features inspired by psychology and art theory. In: ACM International Conference on Multimedia, pp. 83–92 (2010)

19. Borth, D., Rong, J., Chen, T., Breuel, T., Chang, S.F.: Large-scale visual sentiment ontology and detectors using adjective noun pairs. In: ACM MM (2013)

20. You, Q., Luo, J., Jin, H., Yang, J.: Building a large scale dataset for image emotion recognition: the fine print and the benchmark. In: Thirtieth AAAI Conference on Artificial Intelligence, pp. 308–314 (2016)

21. Wu, L., Liu, S., Jian, M., Luo, J., Zhang X., Qi, M.: Reducing noisy labels in weakly labeled data for visual sentiment analysis. In: IEEE International Conference on Image Processing, pp. 1322–1326 (2018)

22. Mihalcea, R.: TextRank: bringing order into texts. In: Conference on Empirical Methods in Natural Language Processing, pp. 404–411 (2004)

23. Jia, Y., Shelhamer, E., Donahue, J., Karayev, S., Long, J.: Caffe: convolutional architecture for fast feature embedding (2014)

Remote Sensing

Attention-Based Convolutional Networks for Ship Detection in High-Resolution Remote Sensing Images

Xiaofeng Ma, Wenyuan Li, and Zhenwei Shi[(✉)]

Image Processing Center, School of Astronautics, Beihang University, Beijing, China
{max15,liwenyuan,shizhenwei}@buaa.edu.cn

Abstract. Environmental information, like sea-land distribution, plays an important role in detecting ships from remote sensing images. However, the huge scale difference between environments and ship targets makes current CNN-based detection models hard to learn large-scale geographical information and focus on small targets at the same time. We propose an attention-based method by adding a Fully Convolutional Networks (FCN) to a detection networks as an attention branch to extract environmental features. Within a detection phase, the target detection branch is guided by the attention branch so as to focus on the potential target locations while in a training phase, the losses of other locations are simply ignored. We test our method on a public available remote sensing target detection dataset: LEVIR. By taking the classical Single Shot MultiBox Detector (SSD) as baseline, our method improves its detection accuracy in ship detection task while with an acceptable computational overhead.

Keywords: Ship detection · High-resolution remote sensing image
Attention model · Feature fusion · Convolutional Neural Networks

1 Introduction

With the development of imaging technology in remote sensing field, research work about image content interpretation like ship detection is of great importance for both military and civil applications. Researchers have spent a lot of time in developing detection methods and achieved many brilliant results in last few years. Before CNN-based methods, most detection systems are limited because they could only collect low level features and need a lot of time to locate targets. The most popular way to calculate features of candidate targets is block-wise methods, such as HOG [1] and SIFT [2]. Moreover, there are mainly two kinds of method to locate targets. One kind is morphological methods based on threshold processing. This method is simple but performs poorly in images with complex background. The other kind is sliding window methods. This way is time-consuming but works better than the former. Even so, this location method is still rough and inefficient.

© Springer Nature Switzerland AG 2018
J.-H. Lai et al. (Eds.): PRCV 2018, LNCS 11259, pp. 373–383, 2018.
https://doi.org/10.1007/978-3-030-03341-5_31

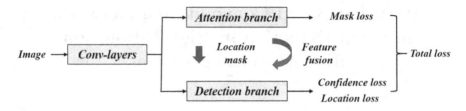

Fig. 1. An overview of our attention-based networks. We add an FCN to a detection networks as an attention branch. The attention branch produces a prediction mask for the locations of ship targets. Mask-loss will be calculated during training and FCN features will be fused into the detection feature maps.

Researchers in vision community developed CNN ways in order to extract more efficient features. The mostly adopted frameworks are R-CNN [3], fast R-CNN [4], faster R-CNN [5] which are two-staged and YOLO [6], SSD [7] which are one-staged. Besides, FCN [8], a special kind of CNN, is popularly used in image segmentation. It can get pixel-wise information and label images pixel by pixel [9].

There are many challenges to apply these models to ship target detection of remote sensing images. Ship targets in remote sensing images, compared with targets in vision images, are highly communicative with the environment. Environmental information, like sea-land distribution and ship wake, plays an important role in detecting ship targets. However, the huge scale difference between environments and ship targets makes current CNN-based detection models hard to learn large-scale geographical information and focus on small targets at the same time. This is a common problem in detecting targets from remote sensing images.

Lei etc. in [10] propose a method to make the detection system focus on the sea-area by extracting a sea-land mask before detecting ships. But this work is unsupervised and is separate from the detection backbone which means that it has little effect in improving the CNN-based model. Inspired by the attention model [11] used in neural network community, we construct our networks which is trained end-to-end to solve the problem mentioned above. Attention models generate attention maps besides feature maps to reveal regions where the following network parts should focus on. Zou etc. in [12] propose a network based on SVD which is more friendly in extracting features of ship targets in spaceborne optical images.

In this paper, we propose an attention-based method to extract environmental features and obtain the potential locations of ship targets which is implemented by adding an FCN to a detection networks shown in Fig. 1. Within a detection phase, the detection branch is guided by the attention branch so as to focus on the potential target locations while in a training phase, the losses of other locations are simply ignored. Besides, we also use a feature fusion strategy where features from the two branches are crossly fused to further improve the detection performance on small targets.

The main contributions of our work are as follows,

(1) By adding an attention branch to a classical network, the networks can focus on the area where ship targets exist with high probability. The detection branch is able to extract cleaner and more accurate features which is of great importance for targets detection in remote sensing images.

(2) By using a feature fusion strategy where features from the two branches are crossly fused, the network can integrate environmental information into detection feature maps. The detection branch achieves improvements in detection performance on detecting small targets.

2 Related Work

CNN is widely used in image related tasks and performs much better than typical methods. Current CNN-based object detection methods are widely used in vision community. Faster R-CNN [4] introduces a region proposal networks (RPN) to get proposal regions. Then features for each region are extracted from feature maps using roipooling. YOLO [6] frames object detection as a regression problem to spatially separated bounding boxes and associated class probabilities. Features are extracted based on the boxes from feature maps. SSD [7] discretizes the output space of bounding boxes into a set of default boxes over different aspect ratios and scales per feature map location. It extracts different features for different default boxes at the same location from different feature layers. Due to the extremely effective performance of CNN-based features, hand-crafted features gradually fade out from recent detection systems.

Considering the scale difference between ship targets and remote sensing images and the scale variation of ship themselves [13], researchers proposed many specialized methods to improve the CNN-based detection models performance in detecting ships from remote sensing images. Lin etc. in [9] utilize an FCN to tackle the problem of inshore ship detection and design a ship detection framework that possesses a more simplified procedure and a more robust performance. And in [14], they propose another FCN to accomplish the tasks of sea-land segmentation and ship detection simultaneously. Liu, etc. in [15], mainly focus on the rotation information of the ship targets. They propose a Rotation Region-of-Interest (RRoI) method to project arbitrary-oriented proposals to a feature map. This framework performs better than axis-aligned pooling frameworks due to the large aspect ratio of targets. The framework is also adopted in text detection field and achieves competitive results [16,17]. Besides, new research works beyond detection begin to be studied like in [18], they try to generate humanlike language descriptions for remote sensing images. Chen, etc. in [19], proposed a method based on CNN to detect airports which is very significant.

Attention mechanism used in artificial neural networks simulates the attention model of the human brain so as to make network systems focus on the extraction of key information. Attention mechanism is extensively used in Natural Language Processing (NLP) and models [20] using this mechanism have achieved the best results on many difficult sequence prediction problems (such as text translation). These approaches train the networks to generate both feature maps that encode the information of the input, and the attention maps that reveal regions of the feature maps where the following parts of the network should focus on. Similarly, we propose a method by using an FCN to guide the detection branch to focus on locations where ship targets exist with high probability during detecting. Losses of other locations are simply ignored during training. The attention branch can also integrate environmental information from high level into target features.

3   Method

3.1   Overview of Our Method

We take SSD as our detection branch. As shown in Fig. 1, we add an FCN branch to a detection networks to apply attention mechanism in the detection system. The attention branch is used to extract environmental features and obtain potential locations of targets.

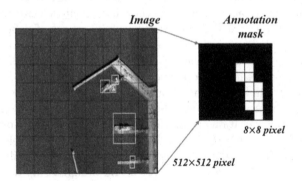

Fig. 2. Annotation mask for the attention branch. Left: ground truth of the input image, yellow bounding boxes denote the locations of each target ship and black grids denote the area of each pixel in the annotation mask. Right: annotation mask for the attention branch which is of the same shape with prediction mask of the attention branch. (Color figure online)

During training, we use heterogeneous annotations in the networks. Figure 2 denotes an annotation mask for the attention branch. Multitasking losses will be calculated to optimize parameters in the networks by adding the location mask loss to SSD losses. The losses of no-ship locations are simply ignored according to the predicted location mask. Moreover, by operating deconvolution, the high-level information about the environment will be fused with features in detection branch. A better feature extracting model will be gained after training. During detection, the attention branch will guide the detection branch to focus on the potential target locations and provide environment information for the detection feature maps which will improve performance of the detection networks in remote sensing images.

3.2   Network Architecture

This section describes the design details of our Attention-based Networks. Important structural parameters are shown in Fig. 3. In detection branch, we take SSD as the base model. Layers in this branch decrease in size progressively so as to make predictions at multiple scales. At attention branch, we add an FCN at the end of Conv5_4 in detection branch. Then we apply softmax layer to produce prediction of the location mask. The annotation mask will be given when calculating mask loss in the train phase. Moreover, the features of reverse layers will be added to the detection layers to fuse large-scale environment information to single-scale feature maps. Through these improvements, the detection system is able to focus on the target-hot zone and obtain higher-quality feature maps.

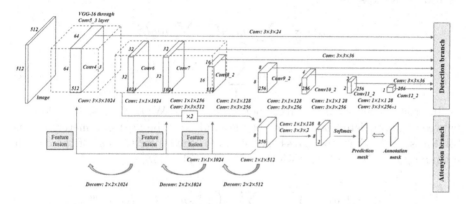

Fig. 3. Network architecture of our Attention-based Networks based on SSD. We achieve an attention-based networks with SSD as our base detection network. Attention branch uses the same structure as marked in the red dotted cube. (Color figure online)

We adopted deconvolution as our up-sampling method in the attention branch. Deconvolution is defined as transpose convolution. The operation of deconvolution can be described as that during backward convolution with stride f, the size of the input gradient map is f times that of the output-map. Thus, up-sampling with factor f can be seen as convolution with a fractional stride of $1/f$, accomplished by transpose convolution. The advantages of deconvolution include high efficiency and learnable convolution kernels.

3.3   Training Objective

The detection branch takes an image X as its input, and outputs a normalized score vector $L(X;\theta)$ for each default box. The objective of the detection branch is to minimize error between ground-truths and estimated class labels, and is formally written as

$$\min_{\theta} \sum_i e_{cls}(y_i, L(X; \theta))$$ (1)

where $y_i \in \{0, 1\}$ denotes the ground-truth of the ith example and $e_{cls}(y_i, L(X; \theta))$ denotes the classification loss of $L(X; \theta)$ with respect to y_i.

The attention branch obtains a prediction mask $M(g_i; \theta)$ by applying softmax function after the last layer. z_i denotes the binary ground-truth location mask of the targets shown in Fig. 2. The objective of the attention branch can be formulated as per-pixel regression, which minimizes

$$\min_{\theta} \sum_i e_{mask}(z_i, M(g_i; \theta))$$ (2)

We use the following formulas to calculate the confidence loss ($conf$) and the location mask loss ($mask$)

$$L_{conf} = -\sum_{i \in pos} y_i log L - \sum_{i \in neg} log L^0$$ (3)

$$L_{mask} = -\sum_i ||M - z_i||^2$$ (4)

In order to get accurate target bounding boxes. We add Smooth L1 loss [5] between the predicted box (l) and the ground truth box (g) parameters to the total loss, with which to regress the offsets for the center ($cx; cy$) of the default bounding box (d) and for its width (w) and height (h).

$$L_{loc}(x, l, g) = \sum_{i \in pos}^{N} \sum_{m \in \{cx, cy, w, h\}} x_{ij}^k smooth_{L1}(l_i^m - \hat{g}_j^m)$$ (5)

$$\hat{g}_j^{cx} = (g_j^{cx} - d_i^{cx})/d_i^w, \; \hat{g}_j^{cy} = (g_j^{cy} - d_i^{cy})/d_i^h$$ (6)

$$\hat{g}_j^w = log(g_j^w/d_i^w), \; \hat{g}_j^h = log(g_j^h/d_i^h)$$ (7)

The overall objective loss function is a weighted sum of the localization loss (loc), a weighted sum of the mask loss and the confidence loss

$$L_{total} = \frac{1}{N}(L_{conf} + \alpha L_{loc}) + \beta L_{mask}$$ (8)

where N is the number of matched default boxes. If $N = 0$, we set the loss to 0.

4   Experiments

4.1   Dataset and Evaluation Metrics

We train and test our method on dataset LEVIR introduced by [21]. LEVIR consists of a large number of high resolution Google Earth images with over $22k$ images of 800×600 pixels and $0.2\,\mathrm{m} - 1.0\,\mathrm{m}$/pixel's resolution. There is a total of $11k$ independent bounding boxes including $4,724$ airplanes, $3,025$ ships and $3,279$ oil-pots. The average number of targets per image is 0.5. We just detect ship targets in the images. Table 1 shows the analysis of the ship targets in LEVIR based on scale.

Table 1. Analysis of ship targets in LEVIR based on scale.

Scale (*pixel*)	Scale1 (<100)	Scale2 (100–200)	Scale3 (200–300)	Scale4 (>300)	Total -
Number	1659	870	375	121	3025

We select the target-involved images from LEVIR as our dataset. The train dataset consists of 2844 images with 2325 ship targets and the test dataset consists of 947 images with 700 targets. We evaluate the detecting performance of our networks using average precision (AP) with different preset recalls and detecting speed using the number of frames that the network processes per second (FPS).

4.2   Training Details

We build our attention-based networks using the framework of tensorflow. Training parameters are listed in Table 2. We train base networks SSD with the same parameters. Both networks have been trained about 8 h. Pre-trained VGG model is used in both networks.

Table 2. Preset training parameters.

Parameter	Value
Learning rate	10^{-3}
Batch size	10
Momentum	0.9
Weight decay	5×10^{-4}
α	1.0
β	0.25

4.3   Results and Analysis

Table 3 presents the detected results of the base networks SSD (512 × 512) and our attention-based networks. We set the value of IoU to be 0.5 which means that the predicted bounding box whose IoU overlap is higher than 0.5 with the groundtruth box is confirmed as a correct detection. Our proposed networks achieve ~3% improvement on detection AP on testing dataset. Both networks gain a ~27 FPS speed during processing images.

Our proposed networks achieves almost the same precision as SSD but a much better recall. This indicates that the detection branch gets optimized under the guide of attention branch and is able to focus on the potential target locations. By deploying the mechanism of attention, the networks overcomes the problem of the huge scale difference between environments and ship targets to some degrees. It is able to gain environment information and target information at the same time.

Table 3. Detecting results of SSD and Attention-based Networks (IoU = 0.5).

Results	SSD	Our networks
AP (%) on training dataset	78.58	**84.17**
AP (%) on testing dataset	71.47	**74.44**
Prec (%) on testing dataset	**95.93**	95.76
Rec (%) on testing dataset	71.98	**75.03**
AP (%) of scale_1 targets	57.11	**61.58**
AP (%) of scale_2 targets	75.11	**79.29**
AP (%) of scale_3 targetst	69.83	**75.94**
AP (%) of scale_4 targets	69.23	69.23
FPS	**27.05**	26.72

According to the detection results of different-scale ship targets, both networks perform well in detecting large-scale ship targets. But in detecting small-scale ship targets, our attention-based networks performs much better. This indicates that the feature fusion strategy where features from the two branches are crossly fused really improve the detection performance on small targets. This also verifies that environmental information is of great importance in detecting ship targets.

In addition, we use the losses respectively to constrain the ship targets confidence, locations and environment mask. This is useful in improving the networks properties for training. Our whole networks is trained in an end-to-end mode which is helpful in obtaining a better model.

We list some result images on testing dataset using Attention-based Networks in Fig. 4. It demonstrates that our networks performs well in detecting small ships. As shown, ships with tail wakes and ships inshore are well detected.

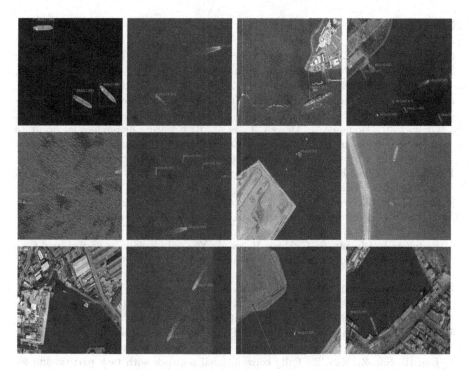

Fig. 4. Detection results on testing dataset using Attention-based Networks.
Our attention branch improves the performance of detection branch based on SSD in
detecting ship targets in remote sensing images. Especially, small-scale targets are well
detected.

5   Conclusion

In this paper, we propose an Attention-based Networks to detect ship targets in
high-resolution remote sensing images. By taking SSD as our baseline detection
model, the proposed method achieves 3% AP improvement on testing data while
with almost the same detecting speed. Our networks overcomes the problem of
huge scale difference between environments and ship targets to some degrees
which is of great importance for ship detection of remote sensing images. The
attention mechanism in our networks can be easily applied to other detecting
CNN-based models for targets detection of remote sensing images. Our networks
currently cannot detect ships in instance level when ships are connected together.
For future work, we aim to modify our networks to detect ships with various
complicated backgrounds in instance level and to apply our method to detect
other kinds of targets in remote sensing images.

Acknowledgments. The work was supported by the National Key $R\&D$ Program of
China under the Grant $2017YFC1405600$ and the National Natural Science Foundation
of China under the Grant 61671037.

References

1. Dalal, N., Triggs, B.: Histograms of oriented gradients for human detection. In: IEEE Computer Society Conference on Computer Vision & Pattern Recognition, pp. 886–893. IEEE Computer Society (2005)
2. Lowe, D.G.: Distinctive image features from scale-invariant keypoints. Int. J. Comput. Vis. **60**(2), 91–110 (2004)
3. Girshick, R., Donahue, J., Darrell, T., et al.: Rich feature hierarchies for accurate object detection and semantic segmentation. In: IEEE Conference on Computer Vision and Pattern Recognition, pp. 580–587. IEEE Computer Society (2014)
4. Girshick, R.: Fast R-CNN. In: IEEE International Conference on Computer Vision, pp. 1440–1448. IEEE (2015)
5. Ren, S., He, K., Girshick, R., et al.: Faster R-CNN: towards real-time object detection with region proposal networks. In: International Conference on Neural Information Processing Systems, pp. 91–99. MIT Press (2015)
6. Redmon, J., Divvala, S., Girshick, R., et al.: You only look once: unified, real-time object detection. In: Computer Vision and Pattern Recognition, pp. 779–788. IEEE (2016)
7. Liu, W., et al.: SSD: single shot multibox detector. In: Leibe, B., Matas, J., Sebe, N., Welling, M. (eds.) ECCV 2016. LNCS, vol. 9905, pp. 21–37. Springer, Cham (2016). https://doi.org/10.1007/978-3-319-46448-0_2
8. Long, J., Shelhamer, E., Darrell, T.: Fully convolutional networks for semantic segmentation. IEEE Trans. Pattern Anal. Mach. Intell. **39**(4), 640–651 (2017)
9. Lin, H., Shi, Z., Zou, Z.: Fully convolutional network with task partitioning for inshore ship detection in optical remote sensing images. IEEE Geosci. & Remote. Sens. Lett. **14**(10), 1–5 (2017)
10. Lei, S., Shi, Z., Zou, Z.: Super-resolution for remote sensing images via local-global combined network. IEEE Geosci. Remote. Sens. Lett. **14**(8), 1–5 (2017)
11. Ba, J., Mnih, V., Kavukcuoglu, K.: Multiple object recognition with visual attention, arXiv preprint arXiv:1412.7755 (2014)
12. Zou, Z., Shi, Z.: Ship detection in spaceborne optical image with SVD networks. IEEE Trans. Geosci. Remote. Sens. **54**(10), 5832–5845 (2016)
13. Ding, H., Luo, Q., Zou, Z., Guo, C., Shi, Z.: Object detection with proposals in high-resolution optical remote sensing images. In: Yin, H., et al. (eds.) IDEAL 2017. LNCS, vol. 10585, pp. 242–250. Springer, Cham (2017). https://doi.org/10.1007/978-3-319-68935-7_27
14. Lin, H., Shi, Z., Zou, Z.: Maritime semantic labeling of optical remote sensing images with multi-scale fully convolutional network. Remote. Sens. **9**(5), 480 (2017)
15. Liu, Z., Wang, H., Weng, L., et al.: Ship rotated bounding box space for ship extraction from high-resolution optical satellite images with complex backgrounds. IEEE Geosci. Remote. Sens. Lett. **13**(8), 1074–1078 (2017)
16. Jiang, Y., Zhu, X., Wang, X., et al.: R2CNN: rotational region CNN for orientation robust scene text detection (2017)
17. Ma, J., Shao, W., Ye, H., et al.: Arbitrary-oriented scene text detection via rotation proposals. IEEE Trans. Multimed. **PP**(99), 1 (2017)
18. Shi, Z., Zou, Z.: Can a machine generate humanlike language descriptions for a remote sensing image? IEEE Trans. Geosci. Remote. Sens. **55**(6), 3623–3634 (2017)
19. Chen, F., Ren, R., Van de Voorde, T., Xu, W., Zhou, G., Zhou, Y.: Fast automatic airport detection in remote sensing images using convolutional neural networks. Remote Sens. **10**(3), 443 (2018)

20. Schlemper, J., Oktay, O., Chen, L., et al.: Attention-gated networks for improving ultra-sound scan plane detection (2018)
21. Zou, Z., Shi, Z.: Random access memories: a new paradigm for target detection in high resolution aerial remote sensing images. IEEE Trans. Image Process. **27**, 1100–1111 (2018)

An Improved Camouflage Target Detection Using Hyperspectral Image Based on Block-Diagonal and Low-Rank Representation

Fei Li[1,2], Xiuwei Zhang[1,2(✉)], Lei Zhang[1,2], Yanning Zhang[1,2]
Dongmei Jiang[1,2], and Genping Zhao[3]

[1] School of Computing Science, Northwestern Polytechnical University,
Xi'an 710071, Shaanxi, China
xwzhang@nwpu.edu.cn
[2] Shaanxi Provincial Key Laboratory of Speech and Image Information Processing,
Xi'an 710071, Shaanxi, China
[3] School of Computers, Guangdong University and Technology,
Guangzhou 510006, China

Abstract. Accurate camouflage target distinction is often resorted to hyperspectral spectral imaging technique as for the rich spectral information contained in hyperspectral images. In this paper, a novel block-diagonal representation based camouflage target detection method is proposed for hyperspectral imagery. To better represent the multi-mode cluster background, an hyperspectral image is first clustered into different background clusters according to their spectral features. Then, an orthogonal background dictionary is learned for each cluster via a principle component analysis (PCA) learning scheme. The background and camouflage target often show different structures when projected onto those dictionaries. The former exhibits block-diagonal structure while the latter shows sparse structure. Inspired by this fact, we cast the block-diagonal structure into a low-rank representation model. With proper optimization of such model, the sparse camouflage targets can be accurately separated from the block-diagonal background. Experimental results on the real-world camouflage target datasets demonstrate that the proposed method outperforms the state-in-art hyperspectral camouflage target detection methods.

Keywords: Hyperspectral image · Camouflage target detection
Block-diagonal structure · Sparse representation · Dictionary learning

X. Zhang—Supported by the National Natural Science Foundation of China (No. 61231016, No. 61303123, No. 61273265, No. 61701123), the Fundamental Research Funds for the Central Universities (No. 3102015JSJ0008).

J.-H. Lai et al. (Eds.): PRCV 2018, LNCS 11259, pp. 384–395, 2018.
https://doi.org/10.1007/978-3-030-03341-5_32

1   Introduction

Camouflage target plays an important role in modern warfare. Therefore, various strategic and tactical targets rely on the camouflage or covert technology to avoid being discovered. How to quickly and accurately detect and identify camouflage targets has become an important research topic for the military target detection. To conceal target or reduce its detectability, camouflaged and stealth materials are widely used to reduce the differences of scattering and radiation intensity between target and background in optical bands. With the rapid development of spectral imaging technology, an hyperspectral image (HSI) [16] contains not only the two-dimensional geometric spatial information of the target, but also the one-dimensional spectral information of the target. Since, most of the camouflage targets are designed to hide mainly at certain bands, which makes it hard to realize all-wave stealth [11], hyperspectral imaging technology [13] shows great potential for the camouflage target detection by utilizing the abundant spectral information.

To give a better reconnaissance result of camouflage target, researchers investigated the hyperspectral camouflage target detection methods on early days [3,5,6], such as, HUA *et al.* [5] employed the constrained energy minimization (CEM) hyperspectral target detection method to extract the camouflage targets, YANG *et al.* [11] utilized the spectral angle distance and mathematical morphology to detect the camouflage target in hyperspectral image. The common strategies of these methods is to use the prior spectrum information of the camouflage target to complete the detection task, but it is not practical in real applications. The reason is that the prior spectral information of camouflage target is hardly available as it is often effected by some uncertain environmental factors, such as the absorption and scattering of the atmosphere, change of illumination, spectral response of sensor, etc. Additionally, the military secrets also interferes with the acquisition of spectra information of camouflage targets. In this case, it is appropriate to exploit the unsupervised hyperspectral camouflage target detection method.

With the ideas discussed above, this paper proposes a novel camouflage target detection method via hyperspectral image. Since there is no prior spectral information for the camouflage target, we first cluster the HSI into different background clusters according to their spectral features in order to describe the background accurately. Then, a spectral-based background dictionary is learned for each cluster through the principle component analysis (PCA) learning method. Based on the representation theory, the background can exhibit block-diagonal structure while camouflage target has sparse property when the HSI is represented onto those background sub-dictionaries. Following this investigation, the block-diagonal-based low-rank and sparse representation model has been built. When solving this model, the HSI can be decomposed into the background part and sparsity part. Since the camouflage target has a sparse property, we can extract it from the sparsity part.

The rest of this paper is organized as follows. In Sect. 2, we give a detailed description of the proposed model, the spectral-based background dictionary construction method and the optimization procedure for the proposed model. The experiments and results analyses are provided in Sect. 3, and Sect. 4 concludes the paper.

2   The Proposed Method

2.1   Background Block-Diagonal Structure for the Hyperspectral Image

It is important to describe the background accurately without prior spectral information of camouflage target. However, due to the cluttered imaging scene, an HSI often contains different categories of materials. And the corresponding background is inhomogeneous but multi-mode. Therefore, to guarantee the camouflage target detection accuracy, it is crucial to consider the multi-mode structure in background modeling. A promising way for the multi-mode structure capturing is to apply the clustering method. As it specializes in collecting similar pixels into a homogeneous cluster and dispersing different pixels into various clusters. In such way, the multi-mode structure is represented with different clusters. In this study, we propose to incorporate the clustering method and dictionary learning scheme to depict the multi-mode structure of background in the representation based detection framework. Through clustering the background, we obtain several homogeneous clusters and different clusters exhibit obvious discrepancy. When being represented on the concatenation of all dictionaries learned from each cluster, the representation matrix of the HSI exhibits obvious block-diagonal structure.

To clarify this point, we first decompose the input HSI X into a background part as well as camouflage target part, which can be formulated as:

$$X = B_{bg} + C, \tag{1}$$

where B_{bg} is the background part and C is the camouflage target part. As discussed above, the background can be represented by a reasonable dictionary while the camouflage target C not. Thus, we can represent $B_{bg} = DZ$ and reformulated Eq. (1) as:

$$X = DZ + C, \tag{2}$$

where $D = [D_1, D_2, \cdots, D_k]$ contains k background sub-dictionaries which is learned from each cluster independently, D_i corresponds to i-th sub-dictionaries, Z is the background representation matrix of the HSI. Suppose the HSI X can be divided into k cluster, it is easy to permute the columns in X according to the cluster result as $X = [X_1, X_2, \cdots, X_k]$, X_i represent i-th cluster and each column in X_i denotes the spectra of a specific pixel. According to [8,12] when D_i and X_i are exactly sampled from independent subspaces, Eq. (2) can reveal the subspace membership among the samples. Therefore, with clustering and permuting the original HSI, the background representation matrix Z will exhibit a block-diagonal structure which means that the background also has this structure characteristics.

2.2 Block-Diagonal Structure Based Low-Rank and Sparse Representation Model

Based on above discussion, the proposed Block-Diagonal Structure Based Low-Rank and Sparse Representation (BDSLRSR) is implemented by integrating the multi-mode structure background and sparse camouflage as follows:

$$\min_{Z,C} \quad \text{rank}(Z) + \lambda \|C\|_{2,1},$$
$$\text{s.t} \quad X = DZ + C, \tag{3}$$

where rank$(\cdot)$ denotes the rank function, parameter $\lambda > 0$ is used to balance the effects of the two parts, and $\|\cdot\|_{2,1}$ is the $\ell_{2,1}$ norm defined as the sum of ℓ_2 norm of the column of a matrix. $X = [x_{11}, \ldots, x_{1n_1}, \ldots, x_{k1}, \ldots, x_{kn_k}] \in \mathbb{R}^{b \times n}$ is a sorted 2-D HSI matrix according to the cluster processing (suppose that there are k clusters for the HSI, $x_{ij}(i = 1, \ldots, k; j = 1, \ldots, n)$ is j-th pixel of the i-th cluster, $n_1 + \cdots + n_k = n$ is the total number of samples, b is the number of hyperspectral bands), DZ denotes the background part, D is the background dictionary learned by each cluster, Z denotes the background block-diagonal representation coefficients, and C denotes the remaining part corresponding to the camouflage target. The reason for the sparsity of camouflage target in Eq. (3) is that the dictionary D stands for background characteristics only and can not be utilized to represent camouflage target reasonably. Moreover, there are very low amounts of camouflage target in the data X compared with the background pixels, thus the camouflage target may have sparsity property rather than low-rank property [14]. Consequently, it is reasonable to add the sparse constraint into camouflage target as shown in Eq. (3).

After getting the sparsity matrix C, the role of i-th pixel can be determined as follows:

$$r(x_i) = \|[C]_{:,i}\|_2 = \sqrt{\sum_j ([C]_{j,i})^2} \gtrless \delta, \tag{4}$$

where $\|[C]_{:,i}\|_2$ denotes the ℓ_2 norm of the i-th column of C, δ is the segmentation threshold, and if $r(x_i) > \delta$, x_i is determined as the camouflage target; otherwise, x_i is labeled as the background.

The main advantages in our model are as follows:

1. We adopt the cluster method to describe background which can exploit background information and characteristics more accurately. This kind of detailed feature has not been considered in the former low-rank-based methods which regarded the background as a whole.
2. The block-diagonal structure is utilized to represent the multi-mode structure information of background based on the cluster result and it is more robust than the low-rank structure. Because, low-rank structure depends on the feature consistency of pixels, and a slight variation may cause the background to be full-rank. While the block-diagonal structure depends on the feature dissimilarity of pixels, which is more robust to feature variation.

3. We employ dictionary leaning method to obtain background dictionary which can extract background feature efficiently. The later section will give a detailed explanation.

2.3 Spectral Feature Based Dictionary Learning

Generally, the background dictionary has a great impact on the representation-based hyperspectral unsupervised target detection methods [7,15]. To construct a robust background dictionary, we utilize the k-means [1] method to divide the hyperspectral data into k clusters and each cluster can represent one background material roughly. By this way, the multi-mode characteristics of background can be well exhibited through selecting a reasonable k (k *should be larger than the true number of ground material clusters in order to make sure that the k cluster represent all the ground materials*).

Through clustering background, the camouflage target will be assigned to one of cluster. Then, we adopt the PCA technique for dictionary learning. It has been shown that the significant components in PCA deliver the major information of the data. In a given cluster, the major information comes from the background pixels. Thus, we remove the less significant components after PCA to eliminate the negative effect of anomalies on the learned dictionary. Finally, we obtain the background dictionary D after using the PCA learning algorithm for each cluster.

The advantages of spectral feature based dictionary learning technique are as follows:

1. By using the cluster way to represent background, both the diversity and multi-mode structure information of background can be well described explicitly. Moreover, the low-rank property of background is enhanced, which is helpful to increase the separability of camouflage targets and background.
2. The PCA learning scheme enables us to learn clean background dictionary by neglecting those less significant principle component.

The entire flow of the proposed method can be shown in Fig. 1. It can be seen clearly that the proposed method mainly contains two modules, dictionary learning and block-diagonal structure based low-rank and sparse representation. Given an HSI, we first divide it into different clusters by utilizing the k-means method. Then, a robust background dictionary D can be learned through PCA method for each cluster. With the background dictionary D and re-ordered HSI X corresponding the dictionary D, the block-diagonal structure based low-rank and sparse representation model in Eq. (3) can be built. Through solving this model, we can get the sparse matrix C containing the camouflage target. As a result, the targets are extracted from this sparse matrix by Eq. (4).

2.4 Optimization Procedure

This section will show the detailed procedure of how to solve the BDSLRSR model. The model in Eq. (3) is non-convex and NP-hard. An effective way to mitigate this problem is to relax Eq. (3) into the following convex problem:

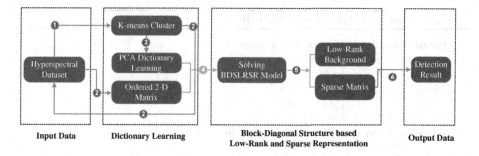

Fig. 1. Framework of the proposed method.

$$\min_{Z,C} \quad \|Z\|_* + \lambda\|C\|_{2,1},$$
$$\text{s.t} \quad X = DZ + C. \tag{5}$$

where the nuclear norm $\|\cdot\|_*$ is utilized to replace the original rank regularization. It has been shown that the solution of Eq. (3) is equal to that of Eq. (5) when some mild conditions hold [8].

In our study, we employ the standard alternative direction method of multipliers (ADMM) to solve the problem in Eq. (5). Specifically, we first reformulate Eq. (5) as follows

$$\min_{Z,E,J} \quad \|J\|_* + \lambda\|C\|_{2,1},$$
$$\text{s.t} \quad X = DZ + C, Z = J. \tag{6}$$

Then, we can obtain the following Lagrangian function:

$$L = \|J\|_* + \lambda\|C\|_{2,1} + \text{tr}(Y_1^T(X - DZ - C))$$
$$+ \text{tr}(Y_2^T(Z - J)) + \frac{\mu}{2}(\|X - DZ - C\|_F^2 \tag{7}$$
$$+ \|Z - J\|_F^2)$$

where Y_1 and Y_2 are Lagrange multipliers and $\mu > 0$ is the penalty coefficient. Similar as [8], given the Lagrangian function the detailed steps for solving Eq. (7) can be summarized into Algorithm 1. The detailed derivation for each step can be found in [8].

3   Experiments and Discussion

3.1   Comparison Methods and Evaluation Index

To give a well and objective evaluation for the proposed method, we employ 4 state-of-the-art hyperspectral unsupervised target detection methods for comparison. They are RX (RX) [9], Sparse Representation-based (SR) Unsupervised Target Detector, Cluster-Based Detector (CBAD) [2] and Low-Rank and Sparse

---

Algorithm 1. ADMM for BDSLRSR

Input: Sorted 2-D Hyperspectral image $\boldsymbol{X}$,
        Sorted cluster-based background dictionary $\boldsymbol{D}$.

Initialize: $\boldsymbol{Z} = \boldsymbol{J} = \boldsymbol{C} = 0$,
        $\boldsymbol{Y_1} = \boldsymbol{Y_2} = 0$, $\lambda = 0.002$
        $\mu = 10^{-6}$, $\mu_{\max} = 10^6$,
        $\rho = 1.1$, $\varepsilon = 10^{-8}$.

while *Stopping criteria is not satisfied* **do**

    1. Fix the others and update $\boldsymbol{J}$ by
       $\boldsymbol{J} = \arg\min \frac{1}{\mu}\|\boldsymbol{J}\|_* + \frac{1}{2}\|\boldsymbol{J} - (\boldsymbol{Z} + \boldsymbol{Y_2}/\mu)\|_F^2;$

    2. Fix the others and update $\boldsymbol{Z}$ by
       $\boldsymbol{Z} = (\boldsymbol{I} + \boldsymbol{D}^T\boldsymbol{D})^{-1}(\boldsymbol{D}^T(\boldsymbol{X} - \boldsymbol{C})$
         $+\boldsymbol{J} + (\boldsymbol{D}^T\boldsymbol{Y_1} - \boldsymbol{Y_2})/\mu);$

    3. Fix the others and update $\boldsymbol{C}$ by
       $\boldsymbol{C} = \arg\min \frac{\lambda}{\mu}\|\boldsymbol{C}\|_{2,1}$
         $+\frac{1}{2}\|\boldsymbol{C} - (\boldsymbol{X} - \boldsymbol{D}\boldsymbol{Z} + \boldsymbol{Y_1})/\mu\|_F^2;$

    4. Update the multipliers:
       $\boldsymbol{Y_1} = \boldsymbol{Y_1} + \mu(\boldsymbol{X} - \boldsymbol{D}\boldsymbol{Z} - \boldsymbol{C});$
       $\boldsymbol{Y_2} = \boldsymbol{Y_2} + \mu(\boldsymbol{Z} - \boldsymbol{J});$

    5. Update the parameter μ:
       $\mu = \min(\rho\mu, \mu_{\max});$

    6. Check the convergence conditions:
       $\|\boldsymbol{X} - \boldsymbol{D}\boldsymbol{Z} - \boldsymbol{C}\|_\infty < \varepsilon$ and $\|\boldsymbol{Z} - \boldsymbol{J}\|_\infty < \varepsilon.$

Output: Sparsity matrix $\boldsymbol{C}$.

Representation (LRASR) based Detection Method [10]. The proposed method is named Block-Diagonal Structure Based Low-Rank and Sparse Representation (BDSLRSR) method. The results are evaluated using receiver operating characteristic (ROC) curves and the area under such curves (AUC) [4].

3.2 Hyperspectral Datasets

In this study, we employed our Hyperspectral Imager shown in Fig. 2(a) bought from Zolix company[1] in Beijing to collect the hyperspectral datasets. The specific parameters of this imager are shown in Table 1. Three kinds of camouflage nets shown in Fig. 2(b)–(d) are utilized as the camouflage targets by placing them in the same color surroundings.

    The first dataset was collected on the fourth floor of the School of Computer Science, Northwestern Polytechnical University. The camouflage target were woodland camouflage net (left) and desert camouflage net (right). There are 174×411 pixels in the whole data with 160 spectral bands as shown in Fig. 3(a). The ground truth of the target is shown in Fig. 3(b). The parameters

---

[1] http://www.zolix.com.cn/index.html.

Table 1. Parameters of hyperspectral imager

Spectral range	Spectral resolution	Detection element	Number of pixels	Frame rate	Interface
400–1000 nm	2–3 nm	Cooled CCD	1392 × 1040	11–62 fps	USB

(a)   (b)   (c)   (d)

Fig. 2. Data acquisition equipments. (a) Hyperspectral Imager, (b) Woodland camouflage net, (c) Desert camouflage net, (d) Digital camouflage net.

(a)   (b)

Fig. 3. First dataset. (a) Pseudo-RGB of the scene, (b) Ground truth of the camouflage targets.

on this dataset are as follows: the number of clusters is 8 and the number of first principle components is 20.

The second dataset was collected at the BaiLu Tableland, Xian, Shaanxi Province. The camouflage targets in the data were woodland camouflage net (left) and digital camouflage net (right). The image size is 174 × 682 pixels with 160 spectral bands as shown in Fig. 4(a). The ground truth of the target is shown in Fig. 4(b). The parameters on this dataset are as follows: the number of clusters is 8 and the number of first principle components is 20.

The third data was also collected at the BaiLu Tableland, Xian. By using a woodland camouflage net, the roadside car was covered as a camouflage target. Its size is 87×181 pixels with 160 spectral bands as shown in Fig. 5(a). Figure 5(b) is the ground truth of the target. The parameters on this dataset are as follows: the number of clusters is 8 and the number of first principle components is 20.

(a)   (b)

Fig. 4. Second dataset. (a) Pseudo-RGB of the scene, (b) Ground truth of the camouflage targets.

(a)   (b)

Fig. 5. Third dataset. (a) Pseudo-RGB of the scene, (b) Ground truth of the camouflage targets.

3.3   Result Analysis

All the two-dimensional plots of detection results for these three datasets are shown in Figs. 6, 7 and 8. For giving a good visualization, we adopt the colormap image to show these results. Background pixels are represented by the blue pixels. The groundtruth location of the targets are shown in Figs. 3(b), 4(b) and 5(b). Compared with other methods, the proposed method has achieved better results both in background representation and background suppression. Although a small amount of man-made objects, such as buildings in Fig. 8, tele-

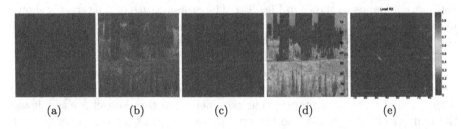

(a)   (b)   (c)   (d)   (e)

Fig. 6. Two-dimensional plots of the detection results obtained by different methods for the first dataset. (a) RX, (b) SR, (c) CBAD, (d) LRASR, (e) BDSLRSR. (Color figure online)

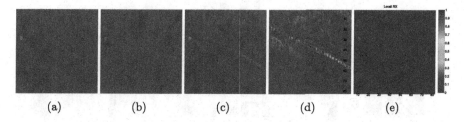

Fig. 7. Two-dimensional plots of the detection results obtained by different methods for the second dataset. (a) RX, (b) SR, (c) CBAD, (d) LRASR, (e) BDSLRSR. (Color figure online)

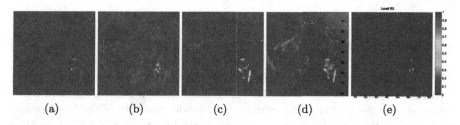

Fig. 8. Two-dimensional plots of the detection results obtained by different methods for the third dataset. (a) RX, (b) SR, (c) CBAD, (d) LRASR, (e) BDSLRSR. (Color figure online)

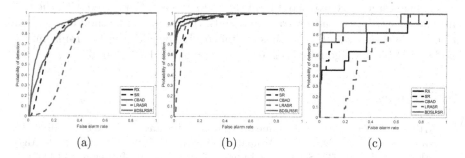

Fig. 9. Detection accuracy evaluation for the first dataset. (a) ROC curves. (b) AUC values.

graph poles in Fig. 7, etc., can be easily judged as a target of interest when the target is detected using spectral information, the proposed method can effectively suppress such objects and reduce interference by considering the overall block-diagonal structure information of the background. Finally, the background and the camouflage targets are effectively separated by solving a block-diagonal structure based low-rank and sparse representation model. Further more, the ROC curves and AUC values in Figs. 9 and 10 show that the proposed method achieved better detection results.

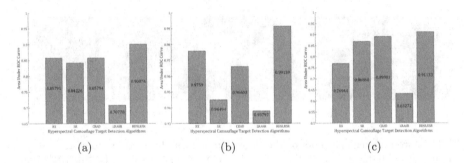

Fig. 10. Detection accuracy evaluation for the second dataset. (a) ROC curves. (b) AUC values.

4 Conclusion

With the hyperspectral image, this paper describes a new camouflage target detection method. To represent the background more accurate, spectral-based cluster strategy is employed to exhibit multi-mode structure of the background. Then, the dictionary of each cluster is obtained by utilizing the PCA method and the whole background dictionary consists of the learned sub-dictionary of each cluster. Next, we cast the block-diagonal structure and background dictionary into a low-rank and sparse representation model. After solving this model, camouflage targets are extracted from the sparsity part. Compared with the traditional cluster-based and low-rank methods, this proposed method can achieve a better detection result, since it simultaneously consider the low-rank, multimodal, and block diagonal structure properties of the background.

References

1. Arthur, D., Vassilvitskii, S.: k-means++: the advantages of careful seeding. In: Proceedings of the Eighteenth Annual ACM-SIAM Symposium on Discrete Algorithms, pp. 1027–1035. Society for Industrial and Applied Mathematics (2007)
2. Carlotto, M.J.: A cluster-based approach for detecting man-made objects and changes in imagery. IEEE Trans. Geosci. Remote Sensing **43**(2), 374–387 (2005)
3. Chen, Y., Chen, X., Zhou, J., Ji, Y., Shen, W.: Camouflage target detection via hyperspectral imaging plus information divergence measurement. In: International Conference on Optoelectronics and Microelectronics Technology and Application, p. 102440F (2017)
4. Fawcett, T.: An introduction to ROC analysis. Pattern Recognit. Lett. **27**(8), 861–874 (2006)
5. Hua, W., Guo, T., Liu, X.: Camouflage target reconnaissance based on hyperspectral imaging technology. In: International Conference on Optical Instruments and Technology: Optoelectronic Imaging and Processing Technology (2015)
6. Kim, S., Shim, M.S.: Cooperative spectral and spatial feature fusion for camouflaged target detection. In: SPIE Defense + Security, p. 94721M (2015)

7. Li, F., Zhang, Y., Zhang, L., Zhang, X., Jiang, D.: Hyperspectral anomaly detection using background learning and structured sparse representation. In: 2016 IEEE International Geoscience and Remote Sensing Symposium, IGARSS 2016, Beijing, China, 10–15 July 2016, pp. 1618–1621 (2016). https://doi.org/10.1109/IGARSS.2016.7729413, https://doi.org/10.1109/IGARSS.2016.7729413
8. Liu, G., Lin, Z., Yan, S., Sun, J., Yu, Y., Ma, Y.: Robust recovery of subspace structures by low-rank representation. IEEE Trans. Pattern Anal. Mach. Intell. **35**(1), 171–184 (2013). https://doi.org/10.1109/TPAMI.2012.88
9. Reed, I.S., Yu, X.: Adaptive multiple-band CFAR detection of an optical pattern with unknown spectral distribution. IEEE Trans. Acoust. Speech Signal Process. **38**(10), 1760–1770 (1990)
10. Xu, Y., Wu, Z., Li, J., Plaza, A., Wei, Z.: Anomaly detection in hyperspectral images based on low-rank and sparse representation. IEEE Trans. Geosci. Remote Sens. **54**(4), 1990–2000 (2016)
11. Yang, J., Hua, W., Ma, Z., Zhang, Y.: Detection of camouflaged targets using hyperspectral imaging technology. In: International Symposium on Photoelectronic Detection and Imaging 2013: Imaging Spectrometer Technologies and Applications, vol. 8910, p. 891006. International Society for Optics and Photonics (2013)
12. Zhang, L., et al.: Adaptive importance learning for improving lightweight image super-resolution network. arXiv preprint arXiv:1806.01576 (2018)
13. Zhang, L., Wei, W., Bai, C., Gao, Y., Zhang, Y.: Exploiting clustering manifold structure for hyperspectral imagery super-resolution. IEEE Trans. Image Process. **27**, 5969 (2018)
14. Zhang, L., Wei, W., Shi, Q., Shen, C., van den Hengel, A., Zhang, Y.: Beyond low rank: a data-adaptive tensor completion method. arXiv preprint arXiv:1708.01008 (2017)
15. Zhang, L., Wei, W., Zhang, Y., Shen, C., Den Hengel, A.V., Shi, Q.: Dictionary learning for promoting structured sparsity in hyperspectral compressive sensing. IEEE Trans. Geosci. Remote Sens. **54**(12), 7223–7235 (2016)
16. Zhang, L., Wei, W., Zhang, Y., Shen, C., van den Hengel, A., Shi, Q.: Cluster sparsity field: an internal hyperspectral imagery prior for reconstruction. Int. J. Comput. Vis. **126**, 1–25 (2018)

Hyperspectral Band Selection
with Convolutional Neural Network

Rui Cai[1,2], Yuan Yuan[1], and Xiaoqiang Lu[1(✉)]

[1] Center for OPTical IMagery Analysis and Learning (OPTIMAL), Xi'an Institute
of Optics and Precision Mechanics, Chinese Academy of Sciences, Xi'an 710119,
Shaanxi, People's Republic of China
crwsr124@163.com, {yuany,luxiaoqiang}@opt.ac.cn
[2] University of Chinese Academy of Sciences, 19A Yuquanlu, Beijing 100049,
People's Republic of China

Abstract. Band selection is a kind of dimension reduction method,
which tries to remove redundant bands and choose several pivotal bands
to represent the entire hyperspectral image (HSI). Supervised band selection algorithms tend to perform well because of the introduction of
prior information. However, The traditional methods are based on the
entire image, without taking into account the differences in ground categories, and cannot figure out which band is discriminative for a specific category. In this paper, a supervised method is proposed based on
the ground category with convolutional neural network (CNN). Firstly,
we propose a structure called contribution map which can record discriminative feature location. Secondly, the contribution map is added
to CNN to generate a new model called contribution map based CNN
(CM-CNN). Thirdly, we apply CM-CNN for HSI classification with the
whole bands. Then, we can get the contribution map which records discriminative bands location for each category. Finally, the contribution
map guides us to select discriminative bands. We found that CM-CNN
model can obtain a satisfactory classification result while preserving the
position information of important bands. To verify the superiority of
the proposed method, experiments are conducted on HSI classification.
The results demonstrated the reliability of the proposed method in HSI
classification.

Keywords: Hyperspectral image classification
Convolutional neural network · Feature extraction · Band selection

1 Introduction

Hyperspectral image contains hundreds of bands which range from the visible
to the near infrared wavelength [8]. In other words, each pixel in the image
captures hundreds of narrow spectral bands from the same area on the Earth.
Hyperspectral remote sensing plays an important role in national economy and

© Springer Nature Switzerland AG 2018
J.-H. Lai et al. (Eds.): PRCV 2018, LNCS 11259, pp. 396–408, 2018.
https://doi.org/10.1007/978-3-030-03341-5_33

national defense, and has been widely used in the field of classification, target detection, agricultural monitoring and mineral mapping [13].

There are many problems in the actual use of hyperspectral data. The most important one is that the band redundancy is too great [4]. A hyperspectral image often contains hundreds of bands, and the rich spectral information can enhance the ability to distinguish objects. However, for specific tasks, such as classifying the types of crops, it may not be necessary to analyze the objects with all the bands. In the contrast, the bands irrelevant to the target object may weaken the classification accuracy [20]. Compared with the high dimensionality of bands, the ground truth of HSI are often very limited under the condition that labeling samples is very time-consuming and expensive [2]. As a well-known conclusion, the generalization ability of the classifier is weakened if the dimensionality of features is too high in the case of limited training samples [4,8]. Therefore, it is necessary to carry out dimension reduction method for hyperspectral data.

Dimension reduction methods are mostly divided into two categories: feature extraction and band selection. The feature extraction based dimension reduction methods consider that hyperspectral data is projected to a lower dimensional space so as to get an abstract representation of the data [16,21]. The research direction includes principal component analysis [18], wavelet transformation [10], independent component analysis [6] and linear discriminant analysis [9]. Although these methods can get relatively satisfactory results, they also have some serious problems. First, these method have a high time complexity [2]. Second, the extracted features may lose the physical meaning for interpretation [19].

Band selection based dimension reduction methods aim to select discriminative bands for a specific task. The ultimate selected bands should be able to represent the whole hyperspectral data with little loss of effectiveness [17]. It is obvious that band selection has advantages of preserving original physical information compared with feature extraction methods. Therefore, we try to figure out a band selection method for hyperspectral task such as HSI classification.

Band selection methods can be divided into unsupervised and supervised according to whether there are training samples [17]. Numerous researches have focused on the unsupervised band selection methods. This is a very versatile method that comprehensively considers the distribution of all ground category in the image and retains an optimal subset distribution of original features [3]. However, it is not very effective for a specific task such as vegetation classification. Not all the band selected are used to distinguish vegetation category. Supervised band selection algorithms often performs better because of the introduction of prior information. However, there are still some problems for supervised method. The traditional methods are based on the entire image, without taking into account the differences in ground categories, and cannot figure out which band is discriminative for a specific category. Another disadvantage is that it is not possible to select the band flexibly according to the type of ground taking into account different task. Moreover, the traditional supervised method is not intuitive and interpretable. It cannot explain the specific role of a band.

To alleviate problems mentioned above, we proposed a convolutional neural network that generates contribution map (CM-CNN) in this paper. Due to excellent feature extraction capabilities, convolutional neural networks are widely used in hyperspectral image classification. Recent research on CNN shows the ability to localize discriminative image regions in the field of natural image processing [23]. We apply this idea to hyperspectral images classification and try to locate the position of discriminative bands through simple spectral classification. In this paper the structure of CNN has been changed sightly, and we proposed a contribution map by replacing the fully-connected layer with pooling features in order to record the location of discriminative band while classifying at the same time. The main contributions of this paper are as follows: (1) We apply neural network interpretability methods to hyperspectral task for the first time and have achieved remarkable results. (2) The proposed model is able to locate discriminative bands for a specific category and show the contribution of all the bands. (3) The proposed model can be transfered to other hyperspectral tasks such as anomaly detection.

2   Related Work

Band selection is considered to be an efficient dimension reduction method for HSI. The purpose of this method is to obtain a subset to represent the most discriminative information of HSI. Band selection is able to reduce the amount of data and speed up processing at the same time. Supervised methods and unsupervised methods are the most commonly used approaches [17]. The difference is that supervised methods need training samples with ground truth, while unsupervised methods do not require training and learning.

This paper mainly discusses supervised methods for the reason that they have better performance under conditions of prior knowledge. Existing supervised methods are mostly based on classification. Lots of supervised algorithms are proposed including local spatial information based [22], the hypergraph model based [1], the support vector machine (SVM) based [14], the non homogeneous hidden Markov chain based [7] and the sparse independence criterion based methods [5]. However, there are still some problems for the supervised methods above. The result of selected bands depends on the accuracy and even distribution of the labels. Another shortcoming is that the traditional supervised methods are not intuitive and interpretable. It can not figure out which band is discriminative for a specific type of ground category.

With the development of machine learning and computer vision, methods based on deep learning have become the mainstream of computer science [15, 24]. Therefore, applying deep learning methods to hyperspectral images is an inevitable direction. Recently, convolutional neural networks have been widely applied in the field of HSI [8]. The CNN model is a special type of feedforward neural network which is able to automatically learn high-level semantic features from the samples [11]. A 3D CNN model is proposed for HSI classification in [4]. Spectral-spatial based CNN model also gets a satisfying result [13]. CNN can

even be applied to hyperspectral image reconstruction [12]. It is also effective for
band selection [19]. As far as we know, deep learning methods for band selection
are quite limited. Since the neural network is a black box, the interpretability
of this method needs to be improved. Some works find that CNN can locate the
features that activate the classification result to some extent [23]. The advantage
of the deep learning methods is that it can extract more abstract high-level
semantic features that are thought to reflect intrinsic meaning of the input [4,11].
So, we try to exact location information of input bands with CNN.

3   Proposed Framework

We propose a CNN model that can select bands specifically for each category
while classifying. First, we introduce the specific process of 1D CNN classification
using spectral information. Then, we put forward the contribution map which
tends to retain location information of the bands in classification. Finally, we
introduce how to select bands based on the contribution map.

3.1   Spectral Based Classification

The ultimate goal of hyperspectral image classification is to assign a unique
category to each pixel in an image which contains hundreds of bands. In this
paper, we adopt the typical 1D CNN model for classification that only uses the
spectral information.

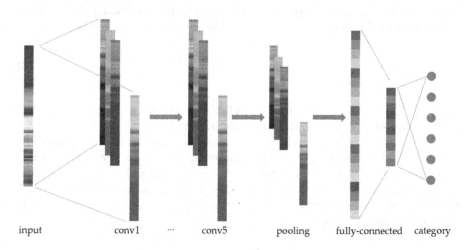

input   conv1   ···   conv5   pooling   fully-connected category

Fig. 1. A typical 1D CNN model for spectral based classification.

Since each pixel is a one-dimensional vector containing hundreds of bands, we
propose a 1D CNN model. The network structure is shown in the Fig. 1. The 1D
CNN consists of 5 convolution layers, 2 pooling layers and 1 fully-connected layer.

Then the last layer of convolution is reshaped to an one-dimensional vector. The feature vector goes through a fully-connected layer lately to reduce dimensions. Finally, we use the softmax function to compute the probability of each category for the pixel.

The main units of 1D CNN include convolution layer, pooling layer and nonlinear function. The formula for the convolution operation is

$$x_j^k = g(\sum_{i=1}^{N} w_{ij}^k x_i^{k-1} + b_j^k), \tag{1}$$

where x_i^{k-1} refers to the i-th feature map in $(k-1)$-th layer. x_j^k refers to the j-th feature map in current k-th layer, and N refers to the number of input channels. w_{ij}^k and b_j^k are trainable parameters in convolution operation.

The output value of convolution layer is subjected to a non-linear operation through the activation function. Typical activation functions include sigmoid, rectified linear unit (ReLU) and tanh. ReLU is adopted in our model for it's excellent performance in training. ReLU works as follows:

$$g(x) = ReLU(x) = \begin{cases} 0 & \text{if } x \leq 0, \\ x & \text{if } x > 0. \end{cases} \tag{2}$$

Max and average pooling are most widely used downsampling method. Max pooling is thought to be robust to rotation and slight translation. Due to the fact that the spectral dimension of hyperspectral images does not have geometric distortion. Pooling layer adopts the average pooling in our model. To a certain extent, it can reduce the impact of noise. The method of average pooling is

$$x_k = \text{average}(x_{k-1}) = \frac{1}{n}\sum_{i=1}^{n} x_i^{k-1}, \tag{3}$$

where x_i^{k-1} refers to the output of convolution layer, and n refers to the size of pooling window. x_i^k refers to the output of pooling layer.

The result of CNN depends on the weight parameters of the network. So it is very vital to find proper weights. In our model, parameters are randomly initialized and trained by a back-propagation algorithm which is the core training algorithm for all sorts of neural networks [23]. Our model adopts mini-batch update strategy, which is efficient for large data set processing. The cost is computed on a mini-batch of inputs

$$c = -\frac{1}{m}\sum_{i=1}^{m} [y_i \log(y_i^{label}) + (1 - y_i) \log(1 - y_i^{label})], \tag{4}$$

where m is the size of mini-batch which means the number of samples per optimization in training. c refers to the total error of cost function for a mini-batch. y_i is the output of network for each sample. y_i^{label} refers to label of each sample.

Since this is a multi-classification problem, we adopt one-hot encoding for the label.

To maximize accuracy, learning rate decay method is added to our training process. With the increase in the number of training epoch, the learning rate slowly declines. It is shown as follows:

$$lr = lrmin + (lrmax - lrmin) * \exp(-\frac{i}{P}), \qquad (5)$$

where $lrmax$ is the initial learning rate of the network. $lrmin$ is the final learning rate of the network. i represents the current training epoch which means once complete training of all training data. P is a constant used to control the rate of decline on learning rate.

3.2   Contribution Map

In this section, we describe the procedure of generating contribution map by changing the last convolution layer in CNN. A contribution map indicates the discriminative spectral regions which are used by the CNN to determine the category. Figure 2 shows the procedure of generating these maps for a particular category.

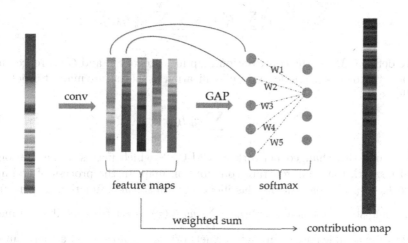

Fig. 2. CM-CNN uses the global average pooling of feature maps for training directly. Right after the training step, the contribution map can be obtained by weighted summation of feature maps.

The proposed method takes into account the ability of CNN to localize the discriminative image regions in the field of natural image processing [23]. We apply this idea to hyperspectral images classification and try to locate discriminative bands which play an important role in the classification results. Before the final output layer, our model performs global average pooling on the feature maps of the last convolution layer. Then we use the pooled vector to sort through a softmax function. In this way, the weight of each feature map which represents the contribution of the feature to the final classification can be obtained. Finally, we compute a weighted sum of the feature maps in the last convolution layer to get our contribution map.

The specific operation is as follows. First, we assume that the values of the elements in the k-th channel(feature map) in the last convolution layer are expressed as $f_k(x)$. x refers to the spacial position at the feature map. Then, global average pooling is performed on the k-th channel. Let $F_k = \sum_{i=1}^{n} f_k(x)$, and $S_c = \sum_{j=1}^{k} w_k^c F_k$. Therefore, for a given category c, w_k^c is the weight corresponding to category c for channel k. Virtually, w_k^c reflects the importance of F_k for category c. In the end, the output of softmax is calculated by

$$p_c = \frac{\exp(S_c)}{\sum_c \exp(S_c)}. \tag{6}$$

A little trick is adopted. We replace F_k in $S_c = \sum_{j=1}^{k} w_k^c F_k$ with $\sum_{i=1}^{n} f_k(x)$. Then S_c can be described as follows:

$$S_c = \sum_{j=1}^{k} w_k^c \sum_{i=1}^{n} f_k(x) = \sum_{i=1}^{n} \sum_{j=1}^{k} w_k^c f_k(x). \tag{7}$$

We define CM_c as the contribution map for category c, and CM_c represents the contribution of each node to the classification in the feature map. It is defined as follows:

$$CM_c = \sum_{j=1}^{k} w_k^c f_k(x). \tag{8}$$

We name this changed network as CM-CNN which means a convolutional neural network that can generate contribution map. In the process of training we use F_k to participate in the classification with softmax function. Right after the training step, we calculate $CM_c = \sum_{j=1}^{k} w_k^c f_k(x)$ to get the contribution map. Every time a sample passes through the network we are able to get a contribution map.

3.3   Band Selection

Once the training of our CM-CNN is completed, each training sample through the network can get a contribution map correspondingly. We assume that it roughly reflects the contribution of each band to the final classification result. Our purpose is to prove that this assumption is credible. Figure 3 shows the contribution map.

Fig. 3. An example contribution map in Indian Pines which belongs to category Wheat. Bands in highlight areas contribute a lot to classification.

For a particular category, we average the contribution map of all the training samples to get the final contribution map of that category. The number of bands selected for each category is determined based on the number of bands we need to select in a total. Two algorithms are proposed taking into account the efficiency and accuracy of band selection. The first method is to ignore the non-uniform distribution of samples. Assuming that the number of all the bands is N, the number of category is l, and M bands need to be selected. For each category, we choose the top M/l bands according to the element value in the contribution map which is ranked beforehand. Consider that the hyperspectral bands are highly correlated. If the former band selected and the latter band selected are adjacent bands, we abandon the latter band and select the next band sequentially until the number of bands meets the requirements. The second method takes into account the uneven distribution of the samples. Especially for the classification task, we recommend the second band selection method. The number of bands selected for a category with a large number of samples should be appropriately reduced so as to leaving more bands to those difficult to classify. Assume that the number of samples in different categories is H_c, and a maximum and minimum normalization $f(x)$ is applied to all categories of $\log(H_c)$. $f(H_c)$ is as follows:

$$f(H_c) = \frac{\log(H_c) - \min(\log(H_c))}{\max(\log(H_c)) - \min(\log(H_c))}, \tag{9}$$

and then the number of bands to be selected for each category is determined based on

$$N_c = \frac{1 - f(H_c)}{\sum\limits_{c=1}^{l} f(H_c)} * N. \tag{10}$$

The method of selecting a fixed number of bands on the contribution map is the same as the first method. For each category, we choose the top N_c bands according to the element value in the contribution map. If the former band selected and the latter band selected are adjacent bands, we abandon the latter band and select the next band sequentially until the number of bands meets the requirements.

4   Experiment

4.1   Visualization

The interpretability of neural network model has always been an important topic in natural image processing. Visualization can helps us to get some intuitive knowledge and improve the understanding of the model. So we try to visualize the contribution map to show whether the location distribution of features is regular. Figure 4 shows the contribution maps of a few samples which are randomly selected in the first category (Alfalfa) of Indian Pines' training data. As we can see, for the same category of samples, the activation region of the contribution map is almost the same. Then, we summarize all the contribution maps for each category in the Indian Pines as shown in Fig. 5. It can be seen that different categories correspond to different activation region.

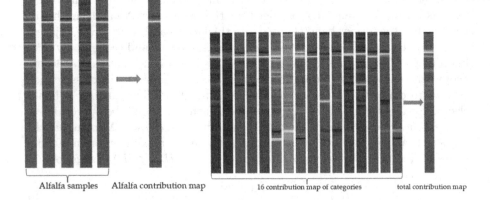

Alfalfa samples   Alfalfa contribution map   16 contribution map of categories   total contribution map

Fig. 4. The contribution map of Alfalfa which is a category in Indian Pines.

Fig. 5. The contribution map of all the 16 categories of Indian Pines. Bands in highlight areas contribute a lot to classification.

4.2   Indian Pines

Indian Pines data set was obtained by the Airborne Visible/Infrared Imaging Spectrometer (AVIRIS). The image size is 145×145 pixels with 220 spectral bands in the range of 0.4–2.5 μm. The final bands adopted is reduced to 200 by abandoning water absorption bands. There are total 16 categories in Indian Pines data set.

For Indian Pines, Table 1 shows the architecture of the CM-CNN used for the experiment. In the figure, Ci means the i-th convolution layer. There are a total of 10,249 labeled samples in the Indian Pines, of which 7,168 are for training and 3,081 for testing. The training epoch is set to 300. With the increase in the number of training epoch, the learning rate slowly declines. The initial learning rate is set to 0.003 and the final learning rate decade to 0.0001. We have found that average pooling always performs better than max pooling, and smaller kernel size can significantly increase training speed but with lower accuracy. So, we choose 4 as the kernel size for both speed and accuracy. In order to preserve location information, stride is mostly set to 1 to keep output size the same as original input. Once the training of CM-CNN is over, we can get the contribution map to make reasonable band selection according to the method in Sect. 3.2.

Table 1. Architecture of the CM-CNN on Indian Pines.

Layers	Input	C1	pooling1	C2	C3	C4	C5	pooling2	CM	Output
Feature maps		8		16	32	64	128			
Kernel size	200 × 1	4 × 1	2 × 1	4 × 1	4 × 1	4 × 1	4 × 1	2 × 1	128 × 1	16 × 1
Stride		1	1	1	1	1	1	2		

We compared two supervised and two unsupervised band selection method with our CM-CNN. As is shown in Fig. 6, CM-CNN outperform all these methods when the number of selected bands is larger than 35. The selected bands are classified by a SVM classifier with RBF kernel to verify the validity of them. Wrapper based SVM (SVMwrapper) method and minimal Redundancy Maximal Relevance (mRMR) method are supervised methods [20]. CEM-BCM and ordinary-clustering-based band selection (OCBBS) are unsupervised methods [17]. When the number of selected bands is small, the performance of our method is not very ideal. We figure that it is because the location information of contribution map is not precise enough. Band correlation makes adjacent bands easily selected at the same time. However, experiment proves that CM-CNN is able to extract location information and has the best performance when the number of selected bands is larger than 35.

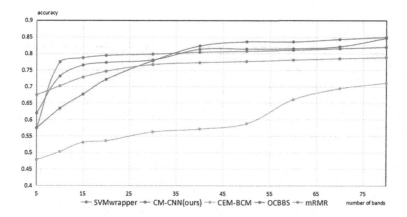

Fig. 6. Classification result of Indian Pines.

4.3   Pavia University

Pavia University data set was obtained by Reflective Optics Spectrographic Imaging System (ROSIS-03) airborne instrument. The image size is 640 × 340 pixels with 115 spectral bands in the range of 0.43–0.86 μm. The number of bands adopted is reduced to 103 by removing noise bands. The spatial resolution is 1.3 m per pixel. There are total 9 categories in Pavia University data set.

For Pavia University, Table 2 shows the architecture of the CM-CNN used for the experiment. Same as Indian Pines, C_i means the i-th convolution layer. There are a total of 42,776 labeled samples in the Indian Pines, of which 29,943 are for training and 12,833 for testing. The training epoch is set to 400. The initial learning rate is set to 0.008 and he final learning rate decade to 0.0005. The following process is the same as Indian Pines.

Table 2. Architecture of the CM-CNN on Pavia University.

Layers	Input	C1	pooling1	C2	C3	C4	C5	pooling2	CM	Output
feature maps		6		12	24	48	96			
kernel size	103 × 1	8 × 1	2 × 1	8 × 1	8 × 1	8 × 1	4 × 1	2 × 1	96 × 1	9 × 1
stride		1	1	1	1	1	1	2		

We compared two supervised and one unsupervised band selection method with our CM-CNN. As is shown in Fig. 7. The selected bands are classified by a SVM classifier with RBF kernel to verify the validity of them. SVMCV is a kind of wrapper based supervised method and minimal redundancy maximal relevance (mRMR) method are also supervised [20]. CEM-BCM is an unsupervised method has been widely compared. CM-CNN performs as good as the two supervised method. Results proved the effectiveness of our method to locate discriminative bands.

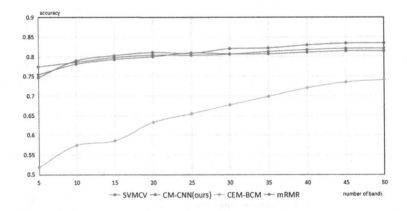

Fig. 7. Classification result of Pavia University.

5   Conclusion

In this paper, a CNN-based supervised band selection model (CM-CNN) is proposed. The main task is to choose the most discriminative bands so as to effectively represent the original image cube. The bands selected by our method prove to perform well on HSI classification. The contribution map we get proves to be sensitive to discriminative bands. Approach in this paper is instructive for many hyperspectral tasks.

References

1. Bai, X., Guo, Z., Wang, Y., Zhang, Z., Zhou, J.: Semisupervised hyperspectral band selection via spectral-spatial hypergraph model. IEEE J. Sel. Top. Appl. Earth Obs. Remote Sens. **8**(6), 2774–2783 (2015)
2. Cao, X., Xiong, T., Jiao, L.: Supervised band selection using local spatial information for hyperspectral image. IEEE Geosci. Remote Sens. Lett. **13**(3), 329–333 (2016)
3. Chang, C.I., Wang, S.: Constrained band selection for hyperspectral imagery. IEEE Trans. Geosci. Remote Sens. **44**(6), 1575–1585 (2006)
4. Chen, Y., Jiang, H., Li, C., Jia, X., Ghamisi, P.: Deep feature extraction and classification of hyperspectral images based on convolutional neural networks. IEEE Trans. Geosci. Remote Sens. **54**(10), 6232–6251 (2016)
5. Damodaran, B.B., Courty, N., Lefévre, S.: Sparse Hilbert Schmidt independence criterion and surrogate-kernel-based feature selection for hyperspectral image classification. IEEE Trans. Geosci. Remote Sens. **55**(4), 2385–2398 (2017)
6. Falco, N., Bruzzone, L., Benediktsson, J.A.: An ICA based approach to hyperspectral image feature reduction. In: Geoscience and Remote Sensing Symposium, pp. 3470–3473 (2014)
7. Feng, S., Itoh, Y., Parente, M., Duarte, M.F.: Hyperspectral band selection from statistical wavelet models. IEEE Trans. Geosci. Remote Sens. **55**(4), 2111–2123 (2017)
8. Ghamisi, P., Plaza, J., Chen, Y., Li, J., Plaza, A.J.: Advanced spectral classifiers for hyperspectral images: a review. IEEE Geosci. Remote Sens. Mag. **5**(1), 8–32 (2017)
9. Imani, M., Ghassemian, H.: Boundary based discriminant analysis for feature extraction in classification of hyperspectral images. In: International Symposium on Telecommunications, pp. 424–429 (2015)
10. Kavitha, K., Nivedha, P., Arivazhagan, S., Palniladevi, P.: Wavelet transform based land cover classification of hyperspectral images. In: International Conference on Communication and Network Technologies, pp. 109–112 (2014)
11. Krizhevsky, A., Sutskever, I., Hinton, G.E.: Imagenet classification with deep convolutional neural networks. In: International Conference on Neural Information Processing Systems, pp. 1097–1105 (2012)
12. Li, Y., Xie, W., Li, H.: Hyperspectral image reconstruction by deep convolutional neural network for classification. Pattern Recognit. **63**, 371–383 (2016)
13. Luo, Y., Zou, J., Yao, C., Li, T., Bai, G.: HSI-CNN: a novel convolution neural network for hyperspectral image (2018)
14. Patra, S., Modi, P., Bruzzone, L.: Hyperspectral band selection based on rough set. IEEE Trans. Geosci. Remote Sens. **53**(10), 5495–5503 (2015)

15. Saeedan, F., Weber, N., Goesele, M., Roth, S.: Detail-preserving pooling in deep networks (2018)
16. Wang, Q., Yuan, Y., Yan, P., Li, X.: Saliency detection by multiple-instance learning. IEEE Trans. Cybern. **43**(2), 660–672 (2013)
17. Yuan, Y., Lin, J., Wang, Q.: Dual-clustering-based hyperspectral band selection by contextual analysis. IEEE Trans. Geosci. Remote Sens. **54**(3), 1431–1445 (2016)
18. Zabalza, J., et al.: Novel two-dimensional singular spectrum analysis for effective feature extraction and data classification in hyperspectral imaging. IEEE Trans. Geosci. Remote. Sens. **53**(8), 4418–4433 (2015)
19. Zhan, Y., Hu, D., Xing, H., Yu, X.: Hyperspectral band selection based on deep convolutional neural network and distance density. IEEE Geosci. Remote Sens. Lett. **14**(12), 2365–2369 (2017)
20. Zhang, H., Huang, B., Yu, L.: Kernel function in SVM-RFE based hyperspectral data band selection. Remote Sens. Technol. Appl. **28**(5), 747–752 (2013)
21. Zhang, Q., Zhang, L., Yang, Y., Tian, Y., Weng, L.: Local patch discriminative metric learning for hyperspectral image feature extraction. IEEE Geosci. Remote Sens. Lett. **11**(3), 612–616 (2013)
22. Zheng, X., Lu, X.: Discovering diverse subset for unsupervised hyperspectral band selection. IEEE Press (2017)
23. Zhou, B., Khosla, A., Lapedriza, A., Oliva, A., Torralba, A.: Learning deep features for discriminative localization. In: Computer Vision and Pattern Recognition, pp. 2921–2929 (2016)
24. Zhou, Z., Shin, J., Zhang, L., Gurudu, S., Gotway, M., Liang, J.: Fine-tuning convolutional neural networks for biomedical image analysis: actively and incrementally. In: Computer Vision and Pattern Recognition, pp. 4761–4772 (2017)

Integrating Convolutional Neural Network and Gated Recurrent Unit for Hyperspectral Image Spectral-Spatial Classification

Feng Zhou, Renlong Hang, Qingshan Liu$^{(\boxtimes)}$, and Xiaotong Yuan

Jiangsu Key Laboratory of Big Data Analysis Technology, School of Information and Control, Nanjing University of Information Science and Technology, Nanjing 210044, China
qsliu@nuist.edu.cn

Abstract. In this paper, we propose a novel deep learning framework for hyperspectral image (HSI) spectral-spatial classification. This framework mainly consists of two components: convolutional neural network (CNN) and gated recurrent unit (GRU). CNN is used to automatically extract the high-level spatial features of each band, which are then fed into a fusion network based on GRUs. This fusion network combines feature-level fusion and decision-level fusion together in an end-to-end manner, thus sufficiently fusing the complementary information from different spectral bands. To demonstrate the effectiveness of the proposed method, we compare it with several state-of-the-art deep learning methods on two real HSIs. Experimental results show that the proposed method can achieve better performance than comparison methods.

Keywords: Hyperspectral image classification
Convolutional neural network · Gated recurrent unit
Spectral-spatial fusion

1 Introduction

Hyperspectral image (HSI) can capture both spatial and spectral information of the specific object on the land surface. Such abundant information in HSI can be applied in a variety of fields, such as resource management, military, and urban development. HSI classification which aims at assigning a specific class to each pixel in the scene is a crucial step for the aforementioned applications.

HSI is usually composed of several hundreds of spectral bands spanning from the visible spectrum to infrared spectrum. A substantial number of spectral bands in the HSI reflect different spectral characteristics of the object in the same location. Traditional spectral feature based classifiers include K nearest

---

F. Zhou—Currently working toward the Master degree in the School of Information and Control, Nanjing University of Information Science and Technology.

© Springer Nature Switzerland AG 2018
J.-H. Lai et al. (Eds.): PRCV 2018, LNCS 11259, pp. 409–420, 2018.
https://doi.org/10.1007/978-3-030-03341-5_34

neighbors (KNN), logistic regression and so on. Due to the high dimensionality of spectral information, most of these methods inevitably suffer from this phenomenon (i.e., curse of dimensionality). To reduce the Hughes phenomenon, support vector machines (SVMs) have been explored for improving the classification performance. SVM-based classifiers often perform better than other supervised classifiers when training samples are limited owing to their low sensitivity to the data with high dimensionality and small sample size.

With the development of hyperspectral sensors, the spatial resolution of HSI is becoming higher and higher. For example, the Airborne Visible/Infrared Imaging Spectrometer (AVIRIS) sensor is able to cover hundreds of spectral bands with a spatial resolution of 3.7 m. To further improve the classification performance, many methods consider incorporating the rich spatial information into spectral information [12,14]. For example, markov random field (MRF) model the joint prior probabilities of each pixel by incorporating its spatial neighbors into the Bayesian classifier as a regularizer [9]. Morphological profile and its extensions are widely used to extract spectral-spatial feature of HSI [1]. Multiple kernel learning designed to improve SVM classifier is a powerful technology to handle heterogeneous fusion of both spectral and spatial features [7].

Recently, deep learning has made promising achievements in spectral-spatial feature extraction for HSI classification [2,13,17]. Compared with traditional classification methods, deep learning models can extract the invariant and discriminant features in a hierarchical manner. Chen *et al.* proposed a deep learning classification framework composed of multilayer stacked autoencoders (SAE) to extract the spectral-spatial feature [3]. Another deep learning network, deep belief network (DBN) was also proposed for HSI classification [4]. Although these two networks can effectively extract deep features for classification, they have to transform the input into a 1-D vector, resulting in the loss of spatial information. Therefore, Yue *et al.* proposed principal component analysis (PCA) based 2-D convolutional neural network (CNN) [15]. Due to the use of PCA on HSI, 2-D CNN may lose the spectral information. To simultaneously learn the spectral and spatial features, 3-D CNN [2] was proposed to take the original hyperspectral image cube as an input. However, CNN cannot model the dependencies between non-adjacent spectral bands due to its local connection property. To address this issue, long short term memory (LSTM) based classification methods were proposed to learn the dependencies between non-adjacent spectral bands. For examples, spectral-spatial LSTMs (SSLSTMs) [17] utilized LSTM to extract spectral and spatial features, respectively; Bidirectional-convolutional LSTM (Bi-CLSTM) [13] incorporate convolution operator into LSTM to extract spectral and spatial features simultaneously. However, these two methods still exist some issues. On the one hand, as a kind of fully-connected neural networks, spatial LSTM of SSLSTMs is inferior to CNN in extracting spatial feature. Although Bi-CLSTM introduces the convolution operator into LSTM, it has only one convolutional layer which may be not enough to extract high-level spatial feature for classification. On the other hand, in the classification phase, Bi-CLSTM directly concatenate all spatial features in each band into a high-dimensional vector, which increases the computational complexity of the network; SSLSTMs only use the last output of LSTM to classify the hyperspectral pixel, leading to the loss of spectral information.

To address the aforementioned issues, we propose a novel deep learning framework to integrate the superiority of CNN and gated recurrent unit (GRU) [5] in this paper. Similar to [15], CNN is used to extract the spatial features of each spectral band, while GRU is used to construct a fusion network to fuse the spatial features from different spectral bands. Different from LSTM, GRU can effectively alleviate the gradient vanishing problem while modeling long term dependency. Similar to LSTM, GRU can also model the dependencies between different spectral bands, which can be considered as a feature-level fusion process. In the classification stage, each band outputs a classification result and a weighted summation method is used to fuse the results from different bands, which can be considered as a decision-level fusion process. All the fusion weights are learned from data itself in an end-to-end manner.

The remainder of this paper is organized as follows. Section 2 gives the detail of the proposed classification framework. Experiments conducted on real HSIs are shown in Sect. 3. Section 4 concludes this paper.

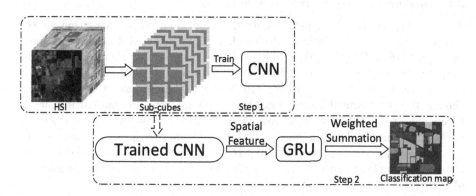

Fig. 1. The flowchart of the proposed spectral-spatial classification framework.

2   The Proposed Classification Framework

To begin with, the original hyperspectral image can be defined as a 3-D matrix $\mathcal{X} \in \mathbf{R}^{M \times N \times K}$, where $M \times N$ is the spatial size and K is the number of spectral bands. To take both spectral and spatial information into consideration, we use the small sub-cube $x \in \mathbf{R}^{S \times S \times K}$ centered at a specific pixel to represent it. Lets assume that we have N training samples $X = [x_1, x_2, \ldots, x_N]$, where each sample is a sub-cube. The goal of the classification framework is to assign these samples to the corresponding classes, $Y = [y_1, y_2, \ldots, y_N]$. The flowchart of the proposed method is shown in Fig. 1. Firstly, we train a CNN for HSI classification which aims at learning spatial feature from HSIs, and then mapping raw training samples into the embedding subspace $Z = [z_1, z_2, \ldots, z_N]$ by the trained CNN. After that, extracted spatial features are fed into GRU to model the dependencies between spectral bands and further fuse spectral information on both feature level and decision level. Finally, we use the weighted summation of all outputs of GRU as the final classification result. In the following subsections, we will introduce the whole process in detail.

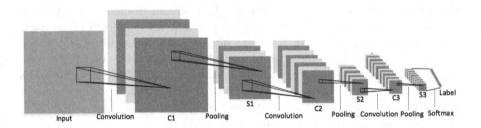

Fig. 2. The structure of CNN.

2.1 Spatial Feature Extraction Network

A CNN [11], is a class of neural networks that excelled at extracting spatial feature from the image. Different from other fully-connected deep learning models (e.g., SAE, DBN, LSTM), CNN takes the original 2-D image as an input, retaining the spatial structure of the image. To capture the spatial information of HSI, we design the CNN illustrated in Fig. 2. The proposed CNN contains three parts: three convolution layers, three pooling layers, and one softmax layer. Meanwhile, to address the small sample problem, we transform the raw sample into K new samples by splitting the HSI sub-cube across spectral channels, i.e., $x_n = [x_{n1}, x_{n2}, \ldots, x_{nK}]$ where $x_{nl} \in \mathbf{R}^{S \times S \times 1}$. The newly generated samples share the same label with the raw sample. Followings are detailed introductions of each component of the CNN.

Convolution Layer: Convolution layer is the most important part in the CNN. By stacking multiple convolution layers, CNN can derive the high-level semantic feature of the input image. Let f_j be the j-th output feature map, x_i be the i-th input feature map. The f_j can be formulated as $f_j = \sum_{i=1}^{C} \sigma(x_i * w_j + b_j)$ where C is the number of input channels, '$*$' represents discrete convolution operation, 'σ' refers to nonlinear function, and w_j and b_j represent the weight and bias of the j-th convolution kernel respectively.

Pooling Layer: The pooling layer mainly reduces the amount of parameters and the computation of the network by reducing the spatial size of the feature map. Specifically, for a $q \times q$ window, the max pooling operation can be formulated as $f = \max\limits_{1 \leqslant i \leqslant q, 1 \leqslant j \leqslant q} x_{ij}$ where x_{ij} is the pixel value corresponding to the position (i, j).

Softmax Layer: The softmax layer takes a hidden vector as the input and obtain the classification result. The probability that the pixel belongs to i-th class can be formulated as $P(Class = i) = \frac{e^{w_i x_i}}{\sum_{j=1}^{L} e^{w_j x_j}}$ where x_i and x_j represent i-th and j-th value of the input respectively, and analogously, w_i and w_j represent the weights corresponding to i-th and j-th class respectively. L is the number of classes.

We train the proposed CNN by optimizing the cross entropy function with Adam algorithm [10]. After that, the trained CNN is used to extract spatial feature of each pixel. Specifically, for a given pixel $x_n \in \mathbf{R}^{S \times S \times K}$, it is firstly split into a sequence across spectral channels i.e., $x_n = [x_{n1}, x_{n2}, \ldots, x_{nK}]$ where $x_{nl} \in \mathbf{R}^{S \times S \times 1}$ denotes the l-th band value and K is the number of spectral bands. Then, each band is fed into the trained CNN successively to obtain the spatial feature $z_n \in \mathbf{R}^{d_z \times K}$ where d_z represents the output dimension of the last pooling layer. Similarly, we apply the trained CNN to all training samples $X = [x_1, x_2, \ldots, x_N]$ and get spatial features $Z = \{z_1, z_2, \ldots, z_N | z_n \in \mathbf{R}^{d_z \times K}\}$.

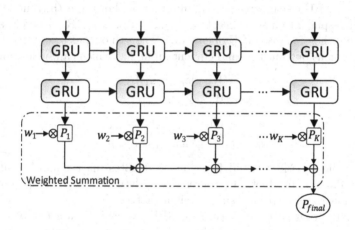

Fig. 3. The proposed fusion network based on GRUs.

2.2 The Fusion Network

In order to efficiently process the high-dimension spectral information, some LSTM-based methods [13,17] (e.g., SSLSTMs, Bi-CLSTM) explore the representation of hyperspectral pixels in a sequential manner instead of treating hyperspectral pixels as vectors. However, there still exist some issues. Bi-CLSTM concatenates spatial features from all spectral bands directly, producing high-dimension feature space. Although SSLSTMs prevent it from producing high-dimension feature space via a decision-level fusion, it only uses the last output of LSTM to classify the hyperspectral pixel, resulting in the loss of spectral information. To address these issues, we propose a fusion network based on GRUs. As shown in Fig. 3, the network contains two GRU-based recurrent layers and a weighted summation layer. GRU, which only contains 'reset' and 'update' gates, is a simplified version of LSTM [8]. It has shown promising results in many sequence-based tasks with long-term dependencies [16]. Besides, compared with LSTM, GRU can effectively reduce the amount of parameters and alleviate the gradient vanishing problem when modeling long term dependency [6]. Therefore, we use GRU rather than LSTM to build a classification network to model long term dependencies between spectral bands. Furthermore, we combine feature-level fusion and decision-level fusion in the proposed fusion network to sufficiently fuse the complementary information from different spectral bands. For feature-level fusion, we fuse spatial features derived from different spectral bands by means of the GRU's recurrent connection instead of concatenating them directly. For decision-level fusion, we regard each output of GRU as one classification result and fuse them with a weighted summation method, avoiding losing spectral information. The detailed computational procedure of fusion network can be summarized as follows.

We feed the spatial features $Z = \{z_1, z_2, \ldots, z_N | z_n \in \mathbf{R}^{d_z \times K}\}$ derived from Sect. 2.1 into GRU to capture spectral information. For the n-th training sample z_n, it is first split into a sequence $\{z_{n1}, z_{n2}, \ldots, z_{nK} | z_{ni} \in \mathbf{R}^{d_z}\}$ across spectral channels and then fed into GRU one by one. The i-th output h_i of GRU is calculated by previous output h_{i-1} and current input z_{ni}, which can be formulated as

$$
\begin{aligned}
u_i &= \sigma(W_u \cdot [z_{ni}, h_{i-1}]) \\
r_i &= \sigma(W_r \cdot [z_{ni}, h_{i-1}]) \\
\tilde{h}_i &= \tanh(W \cdot [z_{ni}, r_i * h_{i-1}]) \\
h_i &= (1 - u_i) * h_{i-1} + u_i * \tilde{h}_i
\end{aligned}
\tag{1}
$$

where σ is the logistic sigmoid function, '$\cdot$' denotes matrix multiplication, '$*$' denotes Hadamard product, W_u represents update gate matrix, W_r represents reset gate matrix, and W is a single weight matrix.

After extracting spectral feature by GRU, we can get a series of predicted values $[P_1, P_2, \ldots, P_K]$. To make full use of these values, we make weighted summation on them. The final classification result P_{final} can be obtained by

$$
P_{final} = \sum_{i=1}^{K} w_i P_i
\tag{2}
$$

where w_i represents the weight of P_i and K is the number of spectral bands.

The weights in Eq. (2) and parameters of GRU can be adaptively determined by optimizing the following loss function with Adam algorithm: $Loss = -\sum Y \log \sum_{i=1}^{K} w_i P_i$ where Y is the real label.

3   Experimental Results

3.1   Datasets and Experiment Setup

We test the proposed deep learning classification framework on two real HSIs, which are widely used to evaluate classification algorithms.

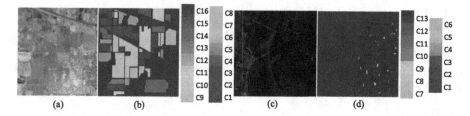

Fig. 4. False-color composite images and ground-truth maps of (a)-(b) IP, (c)-(d) KSC.

Indian Pines (IP): The first dataset was acquired by the AVIRIS sensor over the Indian Pine test site in northwestern Indiana, USA, on June 12, 1992 with 145×145 pixels. It contains 200 spectral bands with the wave-length range from $0.4 - 2.5 \, \mu m$ and the spatial resolution is 20 m. The false-color composite image and the ground-truth map are shown in Fig. 4(a)–(b). The available number of samples is 10249 ranging from 20 to 2455 in each class.

Kennedy Space Center (KSC): The second dataset was acquired by the AVIRIS sensor over Kennedy Space Center, Florida, on 23 March 1996. It contains 176 spectral bands. The spatial resolution is 18 m with 512×614 pixels. For classification purposes, 13 classes representing the various land-cover types that occur in this environment are defined. Figure 4(c)–(d) demonstrate a false-color composite image and the ground truth map.

In order to reduce the effect of random selection, all the algorithms are repeated five times and the average results are reported. Besides, to evaluate the performance of different models for HSI classification, we use the following evaluation indicators: overall accuracy (OA), average accuracy (AA), per-class accuracy, and Kappa coefficient κ. OA defines the ratio between the number of correctly classified pixels to the total number of pixels in the test set, AA refers to the average of accuracies in all classes, and κ is the percentage of agreement corrected by the number of agreements that would be expected purely by chance.

To validate the effectiveness of the proposed classification framework, it is compared with several state-of-the-art deep learning methods, including 2-D CNN, 3-D CNN, SSLSTMs, CNN+LSTM and Bi-CLSTM. Specifically, for 2-D CNN and 3-D CNN, we take the same configuration as described in [2]. For SSLSTMs, we utilize the same configuration listed in [17]. For CNN+LSTM, we apply CNN to extract spatial features from each band and then employ LSTM to fuse them. The configuration of CNN is the same as that in [2], and the number of hidden nodes in LSTM is 128. For Bi-CLSTM, we use the same network structure and the parameters described in [13]. Additionally, for IP and KSC datasets, we select 10% pixels from each class as the training set, and the remaining pixels as the test set.

3.2   Parameter Selection

There are three important influence factors in the proposed method, including the configuration of CNN, the spatial size of input sub-cubes, and the number of hidden nodes in GRU. Firstly, we empirically choose the network parameters listed in Table 1.

Table 1. Architecture of the CNN designed for IP and KSC datasets.

HSIs	IP		KSC	
Layer	Convolution	Max-pooling	Convolution	Max-pooling
1	$7 \times 7 \times 32$	2×2	$5 \times 5 \times 32$	2×2
2	$7 \times 7 \times 64$	2×2	$5 \times 5 \times 64$	2×2
3	$7 \times 7 \times 128$	2×2	$5 \times 5 \times 128$	2×2

Secondly, we fix the number of hidden nodes in GRU and select the optimal spatial size of input sub-cubes from a given set $\{19 \times 19, 23 \times 23, 27 \times 27, 31 \times 31, 35 \times 35\}$. Table 2 shows OAs of the proposed method on two HSIs. It can be observed that as the spatial size of input sub-cubes increases, OA will firstly increase and then decrease on both IP and KSC. Therefore, the optimal spatial size is chosen as 31×31 for IP and KSC datasets.

Table 2. OAs (%) of different spatial size of the HSI sub-cube.

Spatial size	19×19	23×23	27×27	31×31	35×35
IP	87.68	92.91	96.88	98.56	96.63
KSC	94.65	94.50	97.74	99.25	98.29

Finally, we fix the spatial size of input sub-cubes and search for the optimal number of hidden nodes for GRU from five candidate values $\{64, 128, 256, 512, 1024\}$. Note that, the number of hidden nodes of second layer in GRU is determined by the number of class of each data. Thus, we only need to choose the number of hidden nodes in the first layer. Table 3 demonstrates the effects of different numbers of hidden nodes on OA of IP and KSC datasets. From this table, we can observe that the proposed method achieves the highest OA when the number of hidden nodes is set to 128.

3.3   Performance Comparison

The classification maps of the IP dataset obtained by six methods are shown in Fig. 5. Besides, the corresponding accuracy indexes, and the number of training

Table 3. OAs (%) of different number of hidden nodes in the GRU-based classification network.

Number	64	128	256	512	1024
IP	98.30	98.56	98.05	97.32	97.18
KSC	98.87	99.25	98.27	98.00	96.63

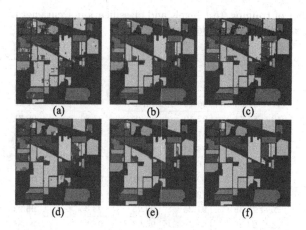

(a)   (b)   (c)

(d)   (e)   (f)

Fig. 5. Classification maps on the IP dataset. (a) 2-D CNN. (b) 3-D CNN. (c) SSLSTMs. (d) CNN+LSTM. (e) Bi-CLSTM. (f) Ours.

and test samples are presented in Table 4. From these results, we can observe that 2-D CNN achieves the lowest OA among six methods. This is because it only uses the first principal component of all spectral bands, leading to the loss of spectral information. Compared with 2-D CNN, CNN+LSTM improves the classification performance because LSTM can extract the spectral feature from all spectral bands. However, the spectral feature extraction and spatial feature extraction processes are independent, making the trained parameters in CNN+LSTM may be not the optimal ones. Therefore, SSLSTMs which attempts to integrate two well-trained LSTMs designed for spectral and spatial features extraction respectively by decision-level fusion, outperforming CNN+LSTM and 2-D CNN. Nevertheless, LSTM is inferior to CNN in spatial feature extraction. 3-D CNN and Bi-CLSTM can address this issue by using convolution operator to extract spatial feature, and achieve the higher OA, AA, and than SSLSTMs. For 3-D CNN, the sub-cube with specific number of spectral bands is taken as an input of the network, ignoring the relationships between non-adjacent spectral bands. Different from 3-D CNN, Bi-CLSTM can model the correlations across all the spectral bands via recurrent connections. Therefore, compared to 3-D CNN, Bi-CLSTM improves OA from 95.30% to 96.78%. However, Bi-CLSTM concatenates all spatial features in each band into a high-dimensional vector, which increases the computational complexity of the network. Besides, Bi-CLSTM cannot sufficiently extract high-level semantic feature of the HSI only with one convolution layer. The proposed classification framework combines feature-level fusion and decision-level fusion to incorporate spatial information into spectral information. Furthermore, a 3-layer CNN is used to extract spatial feature in our proposed method. Owing to these, our method can improve OA from 96.78% to 98.67% compared with Bi-CLSTM.

Table 4. Number of training/test pixels and classification accuracies (in percentages) performed by six methods on IP dataset.

Class	Training	Test	2-D CNN	3-D CNN	SSLSTMs	CNN+LSTM	Bi-CLSTM	Ours
1	5	41	71.22	92.68	88.78	91.06	93.66	89.03
2	143	1285	90.10	95.41	93.76	94.26	96.84	99.11
3	83	747	91.03	96.16	92.42	95.29	97.22	99.82
4	24	213	85.73	92.49	86.38	93.80	96.71	99.06
5	48	435	83.36	87.89	89.79	84.78	92.28	97.70
6	73	657	91.99	95.23	97.41	90.87	99.39	99.85
7	3	25	85.60	86.67	84.80	84.00	92.00	96.00
8	48	430	97.35	99.84	99.91	99.07	99.91	99.53
9	2	18	54.45	72.22	74.44	55.56	76.67	69.45
10	97	875	75.38	91.24	95.95	93.35	95.93	99.73
11	246	2209	94.36	97.59	96.93	98.82	96.31	99.67
12	59	534	78.73	93.01	89.18	89.78	93.33	98.75
13	21	184	95.68	96.56	98.48	95.65	95.76	100.00
14	127	1138	96.80	98.83	98.08	95.36	99.49	99.62
15	39	347	96.54	90.01	92.85	95.53	98.67	97.41
16	9	84	81.90	86.51	87.86	87.62	87.38	98.02
OA	–	–	90.14	95.30	95.00	94.15	96.78	98.67
AA	–	–	85.66	92.02	91.69	90.30	94.47	96.42
κ	–	–	88.73	94.65	94.29	93.50	96.33	98.48

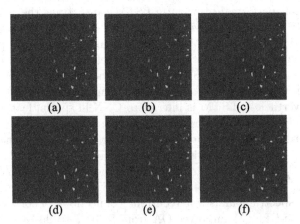

Fig. 6. Classification maps on the KSC dataset. (a) 2-D CNN. (b) 3-D CNN. (c) SSLSTMs. (d) CNN+LSTM. (e) Bi-CLSTM. (f) Ours.

For KSC dataset, we can draw the similar conclusions from Table 5 and Fig. 6. 3-D CNN, SSLSTMs, and Bi-CLSTM achieve better performance than 2-D CNN and CNN+LSTM. Specifically, OA, AA and κ obtained by SSLSTMs and Bi-CLSTM are higher than 3-D CNN, and Bi-CLSTM obtains better performance than 3-D CNN. Similar to IP dataset, the proposed method achieves the highest OA, AA and κ than other methods.

Table 5. Number of training/test pixels and classification accuracies (in percentages) performed by six methods on KSC dataset.

Class	Training	Test	2-D CNN	3-D CNN	SSLSTMs	CNN+LSTM	Bi-CLSTM	Ours
1	76	685	94.86	96.06	99.56	96.00	98.87	99.67
2	24	219	77.53	98.48	90.41	89.04	93.61	97.37
3	26	230	84.52	95.79	100.00	92.96	99.35	99.89
4	25	227	77.71	90.89	99.56	87.31	94.71	99.78
5	16	145	80.97	80.92	93.79	90.48	97.24	99.66
6	23	206	72.62	97.25	95.15	93.30	94.54	100.00
7	11	94	93.19	96.45	100.00	99.36	99.74	99.74
8	43	388	93.87	96.65	88.40	92.11	97.23	99.74
9	52	468	95.85	98.22	99.57	99.44	97.81	99.47
10	40	364	96.81	98.72	100.00	95.71	99.66	99.86
11	42	377	94.27	99.73	99.47	99.84	98.94	100.00
12	50	453	97.35	97.86	98.90	98.28	99.28	99.95
13	93	834	100.00	100.00	99.88	100.00	100.00	99.91
OA	–	–	92.55	97.14	97.89	96.12	98.29	99.69
AA	–	–	89.20	95.92	97.28	94.91	97.77	99.62
κ	–	–	91.69	96.82	97.65	95.68	98.10	99.66

4   Conclusion

In this paper, we propose a hyperspectral image (HSI) classification method based on convolutional neural network (CNN) and gated recurrent unit (GRU). First, we use CNN to extract spatial feature of each band. Then, GRU is utilized to fuse each band's spatial feature. The proposed method is compared with several state-of-the-art deep learning methods on two HSIs. Experimental results demonstrate that sufficiently fusing spectral information and spatial information can improve classification performance. We also evaluated the influences of different parameters in the network, including the spatial size of input sub-cubes and the number of hidden nodes.

Acknowledgements. This work was supported in part by the National Natural Science Foundation of China under Grant Numbers: 61532009 and, in part, by the Foundation of Jiangsu Province, China, under Grant 18KJB520032.

References

1. Benediktsson, J.A., Palmason, J.A., Sveinsson, J.R.: Classification of hyperspectral data from urban areas based on extended morphological profiles. IEEE Trans. Geosci. Remote Sens. **43**(3), 480–491 (2005)
2. Chen, Y., Jiang, H., Li, C., Jia, X., Ghamisi, P.: Deep feature extraction and classification of hyperspectral images based on convolutional neural networks. IEEE Trans. Geosci. Remote Sens. **54**(10), 6232–6251 (2016)
3. Chen, Y., Lin, Z., Zhao, X., Wang, G., Gu, Y.: Deep learning-based classification of hyperspectral data. IEEE J. Sel. Top. Appl. Earth Obs. Remote Sens. **7**(6), 2094–2107 (2014)
4. Chen, Y., Zhao, X., Jia, X.: Spectral-spatial classification of hyperspectral data based on deep belief network. IEEE J. Sel. Top. Appl. Earth Obs. Remote Sens. **8**(6), 2381–2392 (2015)
5. Cho, K., et al.: Learning phrase representations using RNN encoder-decoder for statistical machine translation. arXiv preprint arXiv:1406.1078 (2014)
6. Chung, J., Gulcehre, C., Cho, K., Bengio, Y.: Empirical evaluation of gated recurrent neural networks on sequence modeling. arXiv preprint arXiv:1412.3555 (2014)
7. Gu, Y., Chanussot, J., Jia, X., Benediktsson, J.A.: Multiple kernel learning for hyperspectral image classification: a review. IEEE Trans. Geosci. Remote Sens. **55**(11), 6547–6565 (2017)
8. Hochreiter, S., Schmidhuber, J.: Long short-term memory. Neural Comput. **9**(8), 1735–1780 (1997)
9. Jackson, Q., Landgrebe, D.A.: Adaptive Bayesian contextual classification based on markov random fields. IEEE Trans. Geosci. Remote Sens. **40**(11), 2454–2463 (2002)
10. Kingma, D.P., Ba, J.: Adam: a method for stochastic optimization. arXiv preprint arXiv:1412.6980 (2014)
11. LeCun, Y., Haffner, P., Bottou, L., Bengio, Y.: Object recognition with gradient-based learning. Shape, Contour and Grouping in Computer Vision. LNCS, vol. 1681, pp. 319–345. Springer, Heidelberg (1999). https://doi.org/10.1007/3-540-46805-6_19
12. Liu, J., Wu, Z., Wei, Z., Xiao, L., Sun, L.: Spatial-spectral kernel sparse representation for hyperspectral image classification. IEEE J. Sel. Top. Appl. Earth Obs. Remote. Sens. **6**(6), 2462–2471 (2013)
13. Liu, Q., Zhou, F., Hang, R., Yuan, X.: Bidirectional-convolutional lstm based spectral-spatial feature learning for hyperspectral image classification. Remote Sens. **9**(12), 1330 (2017)
14. Sun, L., Wu, Z., Liu, J., Xiao, L., Wei, Z.: Supervised spectral-spatial hyperspectral image classification with weighted markov random fields. IEEE Trans. Geosci. Remote Sens. **53**(3), 1490–1503 (2015)
15. Yue, J., Zhao, W., Mao, S., Liu, H.: Spectral-spatial classification of hyperspectral images using deep convolutional neural networks. Remote Sens. Lett. **6**(6), 468–477 (2015)
16. Zhao, R., Wang, D., Yan, R., Mao, K., Shen, F., Wang, J.: Machine health monitoring using local feature-based gated recurrent unit networks. IEEE Trans. Ind. Electron. **65**(2), 1539–1548 (2018)
17. Zhou, F., Hang, R., Liu, Q., Yuan, X.: Hyperspectral image classification using spectral-spatial LSTMs. In: Yang, J., et al. (eds.) CCCV 2017. CCIS, vol. 771, pp. 577–588. Springer, Singapore (2017). https://doi.org/10.1007/978-981-10-7299-4_48

Disparity-Based Robust Unstructured Terrain Segmentation

Pengbo Zhang, Xinzhu Ma, Zhihui Wang, Haojie Li[✉], and Zhongxuan Luo

Dalian University of Technology, No. 321, Tuqiang Street, Dalian, Liaoning, China
{bobo96,maxinzhu}@mail.dlut.edu.cn, {zhwang,hjli,zxluo}@dlut.edu.cn

Abstract. Autonomous robot navigation in unstructured outdoor environment is still a challenging problem, and the terrain segmentation is one of the key tasks in robot navigation. Previous methods work well on common terrains like urban roads, but tend to fail in wild conditions due to different illumination, weather and road variations. In this paper, we propose a novel two branches terrain segmentation network based on disparity map and ground plane fitting, introducing geometric characteristics into the network. The terrain segmentation main branch uses convolutional feature layers with multiple sampling rates filters, which effectively considers local and global context information and smooths the holey information in the disparity map. The enhancement branch exploits plane geometry property of the ground plane deviation map calculated from the disparity map, which adaptively generates reference feature maps for improving the robustness of identifying traversable areas under conditions of unseen terrains. Experimental results demonstrate excellent performance of the proposed method on terrain segmentation both qualitatively and quantitatively.

Keywords: Terrain segmentation · Disparity-based
Plane geometry property · Convolutional neural network

1 Introduction

Autonomous robot navigation in unstructured outdoor environment is still an open and challenging problem. The terrain segmentation is one of the core tasks in robot navigation, which is key to the robot to identify traversable areas and avoid obstacles. Unlike the urban roads with clear marking lines, terrain in unstructured outdoor environment is complicated, featured by various combinations of ground types and obstacles. As illustrated in Fig. 1(a), illumination condition causes shadows and oversaturation, in addition, obstacles (trees, haystacks) have high visual similarities to a dirt road surface with foliage. These bring great challenges to terrain segmentation.

In human biological vision system, stereo disparity plays an important role in scene perception, and it can be adopted by machine vision systems in autonomous robot navigation. Thus lots of road segmentation algorithms [11,17,21,24] have been developed based on stereo disparity information.

© Springer Nature Switzerland AG 2018
J.-H. Lai et al. (Eds.): PRCV 2018, LNCS 11259, pp. 421–431, 2018.
https://doi.org/10.1007/978-3-030-03341-5_35

For example, Zhu et al. [24] propose a traversable region detection algorithm in indoor and urban environment by introducing UV-disparity. However, inaccurate estimations in the process of feature extraction and stereo matching tend to bring holey and noisy disparity maps (see Fig. 1(b)). Therefore, it is important to connect global and local information for smoothing holes and noises when applying disparity maps.

(a)   (b)   (c)   (d)

Fig. 1. The process of terrain segmentation: Given an unstructured natural scene (a), stereo disparity map (b) is provided by strongly calibrated Point Grey Research Stereo Rigs. A ground plane model is fitted and subtracted out, obtaining a ground plane deviation map (c). The proposed two branches network is applied to arrive at the final terrain segmentation result (d).

With the rapid development of deep learning technology, fully convolutional networks [13] are driving advances in semantic segmentation. Many excellent research efforts [1,2,6,12,14,23] have improved the accuracy on exposed standard datasets, such as PASCAL VOC [5], Cityscapes [4] and KITTI Road [7]. They work well on common and regular terrains like urban roads or highways, but may lead to failures in unstructured natural scene with changing illumination, weather, and road conditions etc. (see Table 1 Segnet [1] and Baseline-RGB). This is because the network trained on a particular kind of dataset is not flexible enough to adapt different and unseen road conditions. Shashank et al. [20] combine deep convolutional neural network (CNN) with color lines model based prior in a conditional random field framework to adapt to varying illumination conditions, but it fails when the color of the road is close to the surrounding environment. In the practical application of robot navigation, the scene will change over time. For these reasons, it is necessary to study an adaptive and robust terrain segmentation algorithm.

DARPA LAGR program [8] have inspired researches [15,17,18,21] to focus on unstructured terrain segmentation. Procopio et al. [17] obtain stereo labels by ground plane fitting. They compute the difference between predicted ground plane disparity and observed disparity from the stereo readings. Thresholds are used directly to determine whether pixels in the image belong to ground. As shown in the Fig. 1(c), there are some noises and discontinuities in the ground plane deviation map, so the results obtained by threshold segmentation are not applicable. We are inspired by the ground plane fitting techniques [3,17] and proposed a novel method to improve terrain segmentation accuracy.

In this paper, we proposed a disparity-based robust unstructured terrain segmentation network. We first do the calculation of ground plane fitting and deviation, then we choose to use the disparity map and the ground plane deviation map as network inputs instead of the color image. They have stable distributions on different datasets and imply certain plane geometry property, which can help to identify traversable areas and avoid obstacles in the situation where the appearances of the roads have changed greatly. In addition, the segmentation module with multiple sampling rates filters is a powerful visual model that extracts hierarchies of features and incorporates local and global context, which can smooth the holey information in the disparity map. Moreover, the enhancement module adaptively generates reference feature maps for improving the robustness of terrain segmentation results.

The process of terrain segmentation is shown in Fig. 1. For a given unstructured natural scene, stereo disparity map is provided by strongly calibrated Point Grey Research Stereo Rigs. A ground plane model is fitted and subtracted out for obtaining the ground plane deviation map. The trained two branches network is applied to terrain scenes with varying appearances and demonstrates excellent terrain segmentation performance.

2   Proposed Methodology

This section is divided into two major parts. We first give the theory of ground plane fitting and the calculation of ground plane deviation, and then we describe the design methodology of the proposed network.

2.1   Ground Plane Fitting and Deviation Calculation

Stereo vision refers to the inferring of 3D structure from two images taken from different viewpoints. In this research, Stereo disparity and depth data are provided by strongly calibrated Point Grey Research Stereo Rigs. There are many different algorithms to estimate disparity map, but in this paper we don't focus on how to estimate it, but on how to apply the stereo disparity with noise and holes effectively.

Disparity plays an important role of depth and geometric cue in machine vision systems in autonomous robot navigation. Assuming a calibrated stereo camera system with baseline length L and focal length f, and the X, Y, Z axes of the camera coordinate system are aligned with image axes x, y and camera optical axis separately, then the relationship between disparity δ and depth d can be expressed as:

$$\delta = \frac{L \cdot f}{d} \tag{1}$$

The plane P in a camera coordinate system can be expressed as:

$$P : AX + BY + CZ + D = 0 \tag{2}$$

where A, B, C, D are plane parameters. According to the principle of perspective projection and similarity transformation, we can compute an initial estimation of the plane in disparity space that corresponds to a world plane relative to the camera:

$$\delta = \alpha u + \beta v + \gamma \qquad (3)$$

where u, v are pixel coordinates in the image coordinate system and α, β, γ are plane parameters.

Therefore, given a disparity map, the corresponding ground plane can be fitted to image points that have been stereo matched without knowing the intrinsic camera parameters. Then we obtain the ground plane deviation map I_{dev} by calculating the difference between fitted disparity δ_f of ground plane and given disparity δ_g:

$$I_{dev} = \delta_g - \delta_f \qquad (4)$$

We conduct a statistically analysis and comparison using natural data taken from the outdoor environment. For color images, it is important to note that they have some similarities in texture and color when the scene remains the same, but they are going to be significantly different when the scene changes. However, the distributions of disparity maps and ground plane deviation maps in changing conditions are more stable and similar. Consequently, we choose to use the disparity map and the ground plane deviation map as network inputs instead of the color image, introducing their plane geometry property into the network.

2.2 Network Architecture

The proposed network architecture consists of two sub-networks: a terrain segmentation main network and a stability and adaptability enhancement module as shown in Fig. 2. The two modules complement each other and show excellent terrain segmentation results.

Segmentation Module. The terrain segmentation main network is designed based on the Deeplab model [2] by taking a disparity map as input. In our setting, 1×1 convolutional layers are used as dimension reduction modules to remove computational bottlenecks. This design allows for increasing the stability and adaptability enhancement module without significant performance penalty. What's more, we use the multi-sampling rates dilated filters (represented by DConv in Fig. 2), which can be explained by the following formula:

$$H(x,y) = \sum_{i,j} F(x + i \cdot r, y + j \cdot r) W(i,j) \qquad (5)$$

where F are convolution features, W are the filter weights, r is the sampling rate, and H are the output features. Four dilated convolutions with different sampling rates (2, 4, 6, 8) are applied in parallel as a pyramid structure, which effectively consider local and global context information for smoothing the holey and noisy information in the disparity map and ground plane deviation map.

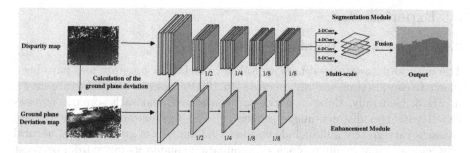

Fig. 2. The proposed novel terrain segmentation network with enhancement module. The disparity map and the ground plane deviation map are used as network inputs to introduce their stable distribution and geometric characteristics into the network. The segmentation module with multiple sampling rates filters extracts hierarchies of features and incorporates local and global context, which can smooth the holey information in the disparity map. Moreover, the enhancement module adaptively generates reference feature maps for improving the robustness of terrain segmentation results.

Enhancement Module. The enhancement module operates on the ground plane deviation map, which is obtained by calculating the difference between the fitted disparity of ground plane and the given disparity. As an auxiliary input, the ground plane deviation map can improve the adaptability and robustness of terrain segmentation with changing illumination, weather, and road conditions etc. Because the ground plane deviation map has stable distributions on different datasets and implies certain plane geometry property.

The proposed enhancement module is clearly different from the threshold discrimination method used in [21]. They feed the noisy and discontinuous ground reference maps obtained by threshold directly into the network decoder, resulting in poor segmentation (See the third line of Fig. 5). However, we respectively use one 3×3 convolutional layer with half dimensions of each corresponding scale layer (1, 1/2, 1/4, 1/8) in the segmentation main network to adaptively generate reference feature maps. Afterwards, the reference feature maps are concatenated to the corresponding layers of the segmentation module, improving the robustness of terrain segmentation results.

In our design, overlapping pooling [10] ($kernel\ size = 3, stride = 2$) is used to shrink the size of the feature maps while retaining representative features. During the pooling process, the holey information will gradually decrease or even disappear. Besides, training models with overlapping pooling is slightly more difficult to overfit. Overall, the stability and adaptability enhancement module is similar to a residual learning module which enables fast and stable training.

3   Experiments

3.1   Datasets and Training Details

The natural data sets used here are taken from LAGR program and have been shown to contain time-varying concepts [15,16]. Representative images are shown in Fig. 3. Generally, three scenarios are considered, and each scenario is associated with two distinct image sequences. The terrains appearing in the six datasets vary greatly and include various combinations of ground types, natural obstacles and man-made obstacles. Illumination conditions range from overcast with good color definition to very sunny, causing shadows and saturation. Each pixel is labeled as one of the three classes: ground plane, obstacle, or unknown.

In this research, Stereo disparity and depth data are provided by strongly calibrated Point Grey Research Stereo Rigs. Our implementation is based on the public platform Caffe [9]. We employ the modified version of the 16-layer DeepLab from [2] for the segmentation model. It is initialized by the VGG-16 [19] pretrained on the ImageNet. We use the 'poly' learning rate policy. The base learning rate is set to 0.001 and the power is set to 0.9. The number of the iterations is set to 10000 and there is no data augmentation strategy using in our experiments. In addition, the unknown labels are regarded as obstacles to provide a fair comparison with existing methods.

The proposed two branches terrain segmentation network can run in real time. The average speed is about 14 frames per second with one NVIDIA Titan X graphic card. The method still has room for speed improvement by optimizing the network structure or upgrading the hardware equipments.

DS1A   DS2A   DS3A

DS1B   DS2B   DS3B

Fig. 3. Representative images from each of the datasets

3.2 Results and Discussion

The performance metric used in this evaluation is the root mean square error (RMSE), where lower scores are better.

$$RMSE = \sqrt{\frac{1}{N}\sum_{i=1}^{N}(p_i - l_i)^2} \tag{6}$$

where $p_1, p_2, \ldots, p_N$ are the predictions on $[0,1]$ for a set of N test points and $l_1, l_2, \ldots, l_N$ are the corresponding class labels in $\{0,1\}$. Used in this manner, RMSE measures the error between the predicted terrain class p_i as output of our network, which is probabilistic, and the actual class label l_i determined by a human, which is discrete.

The terrain segmentation main network operates on color images, disparity images and ground plane deviation images respectively, recorded as baseline-RGB, baseline-Disparity and baseline-Deviation. We can observe that the proposed terrain segmentation method is more stable (by analyzing Table 1 horizontally) and accurate (by analyzing Table 1 vertically) than our baselines. It's because we calculate the ground plane deviation from the disparity, whose stable distributions on different datasets and certain plane geometry property can help to identify safe areas in the situation where the appearance of the scene changes greatly. Experiments show that using the disparity map and the ground plane deviation map as network inputs instead of the color image is effective. Contrastively, when we use a combination of RGB and deviation, the root mean square error is increased by 0.3%.

Table 1. Comparison of terrain segmentation results. We use the terrain segmentation main network (only segmentation module) with the multiple sampling rates filters operates on different inputs as our baselines.

Method	DS1A	DS1B	DS2A	DS2B	DS3A	DS3B	Overall
Baseline-RGB	0.069	0.210	0.195	0.232	0.376	0.504	0.265
Baseline-Disparity	0.144	0.278	0.269	0.271	0.318	0.303	0.264
Baseline-Deviation	0.083	0.186	0.203	0.209	0.206	0.219	0.184
Proposed method	**0.066**	**0.171**	**0.183**	**0.191**	**0.190**	**0.191**	**0.166**

Table 2 shows the comparison of terrain segmentation results. Different from the training strategy using all six datasets proposed by Wei et al. [21] and others, we just choose the first dataset DS1A for training and evaluate the performance over all six datasets. It is important to note that DS1A is a small-scale training set and differs significantly from the testing sets which have diverse natural and road conditions. Procopio et al. [18] use sample balance methods and train the model on the near field data of the image, which does not suffer from the scene change problem. Their method performs well on DS3 (0.104, 0.139), but is not suitable for other datasets, especially on DS2B (0.676). We achieve a precision of 0.066 in a situation where the scene remains the same. Overall, the proposed two branches terrain segmentation network based on disparity map and ground plane fitting is more stable and accurate than others by introducing geometric characteristics into the network and generating reference feature maps adaptively.

Besides, we use the multiple sampling rates filters to incorporate larger context and smooth the holey information, offering a 1–2% decrease in RMSE (see Tabel 3 for details).

Table 2. Comparison of terrain segmentation results. Different from the training strategy using all six datasets proposed by others, we just choose the first dataset DS1A for training and evaluate the performance over all six datasets.

Method	DS1A	DS1B	DS2A	DS2B	DS3A	DS3B	Overall
Segnet [1]	0.582	0.465	0.612	0.477	0.422	0.596	0.526
UV Disparity [24]	0.592	0.559	0.521	0.532	0.487	0.501	0.532
Zhang [22]	0.449	0.504	0.467	0.516	0.438	0.430	0.467
Wei [21]	0.402	0.283	0.329	0.404	0.231	0.229	0.313
Procopio [18]	0.486	0.272	0.393	0.676	**0.104**	**0.139**	0.345
Proposed method	**0.066**	**0.171**	**0.183**	**0.191**	0.190	0.191	**0.166**

Table 3. Comparison results of multiple filters

Multiple filters	DS1B	DS2B	DS3B
No	0.195	0.209	0.205
Yes	**0.171**	**0.191**	**0.191**

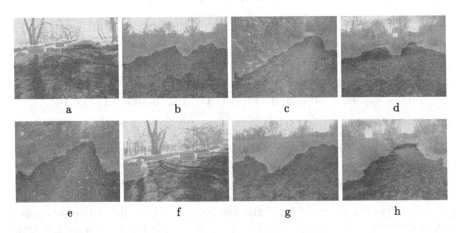

a   b   c   d

e   f   g   h

Fig. 4. Overlapping maps (Green denotes the traversable areas.) of the result images with raw images (Color figure online)

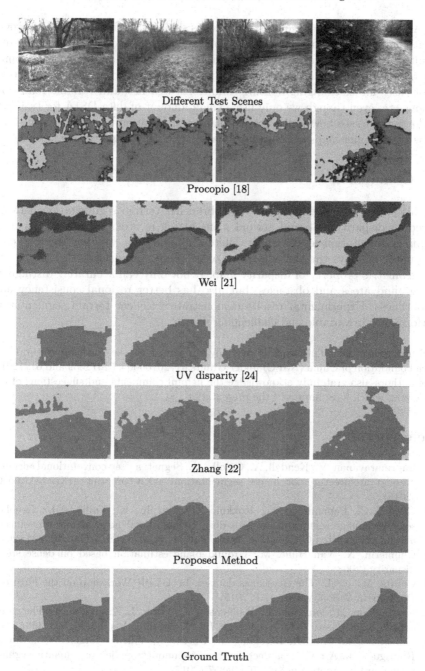

Fig. 5. Comparison of terrain segmentation results. The test images come from different data sets (from left to right, they come from DS1B, DS2A, DS2B, DS3A). Green and gray denote the traversable areas and obstacles respectively. The penultimate row shows our results which demonstrate excellent unstructured terrain segmentation performance. (Color figure online)

As shown in Fig. 5, the qualitative results showing significant visual improvement compared with other methods. For test data from different datasets, our results are closest to the ground truth, and have better smoothness and continuity than others. We can observe that our method performed better than others in most cases under changing lighting conditions, weather, and variable road conditions etc. even though we only use a small amount of data DS1A for training. To be easier to see how well a ground plane segmentation has been achieved, we show overlapping maps of the result images with raw images in Fig. 4.

4   Conclusion

In this paper, we propose a novel two branches terrain segmentation network based on disparity map and ground plane fitting in order to produce accurate terrain segmentation results under different illumination, weather and road conditions. It employs the characteristics of deep convolution neural network and the geometric property of disparity map. It not only can accurately distinguish the ground areas and obstacles, but also has better regional consistency and smoothness. Experimental results demonstrate excellent terrain segmentation performance in variable and challenging scenes.

Acknowledgment. This work is partially supported by the National Natural Science Foundation of China (NSFC) under Grants 61720106005, 61472059 and 61772018. The authors also gratefully acknowledge the helpful comments and suggestions of the reviewers, which have improved the presentation.

References

1. Badrinarayanan, V., Kendall, A., Cipolla, R.: Segnet: a deep convolutional encoder-decoder architecture for image segmentation. arXiv preprint arXiv:1511.00561 (2015)
2. Chen, L.C., Papandreou, G., Kokkinos, I., Murphy, K., Yuille, A.L.: Deeplab: semantic image segmentation with deep convolutional nets, atrous convolution, and fully connected CRFs. IEEE Trans. Pattern Anal. Mach. Intell. **40**, 834 (2017)
3. Chumerin, N., Van Hulle, M.: Ground plane estimation based on dense stereo disparity (2008)
4. Cordts, M., et al.: The cityscapes dataset. In: CVPR Workshop on the Future of Datasets in Vision, vol. 1, p. 3 (2015)
5. Everingham, M., Van Gool, L., Williams, C.K., Winn, J., Zisserman, A.: The pascal visual object classes (VOC) challenge. Int. J. Comput. Vis. **88**(2), 303–338 (2010)
6. Garcia-Garcia, A., Orts-Escolano, S., Oprea, S., Villena-Martinez, V., Garcia-Rodriguez, J.: A review on deep learning techniques applied to semantic segmentation. arXiv preprint arXiv:1704.06857 (2017)
7. Geiger, A., Lenz, P., Stiller, C., Urtasun, R.: Vision meets robotics: the kitti dataset. Int. J. Robot. Res. **32**(11), 1231–1237 (2013)
8. Jackel, L.D., Krotkov, E., Perschbacher, M., Pippine, J., Sullivan, C.: The DARPA LAGR program: goals, challenges, methodology, and phase I results. J. Field Robot. **23**(11–12), 945–973 (2006)

9. Jia, Y., et al.: Caffe: convolutional architecture for fast feature embedding. In: Proceedings of the 22nd ACM International Conference on Multimedia, pp. 675–678. ACM (2014)
10. Krizhevsky, A., Sutskever, I., Hinton, G.E.: Imagenet classification with deep convolutional neural networks. In: Advances in Neural Information Processing Systems, pp. 1097–1105 (2012)
11. Li, F., Brady, J., Reid, I., Hu, H.: Parallel image processing for object tracking using disparity information. In: Second Asian Conference on Computer Vision ACCV 1995, pp. 762–766 (1995)
12. Lin, G., Milan, A., Shen, C., Reid, I.: Refinenet: multi-path refinement networks for high-resolution semantic segmentation. In: IEEE Conference on Computer Vision and Pattern Recognition (CVPR) (2017)
13. Long, J., Shelhamer, E., Darrell, T.: Fully convolutional networks for semantic segmentation. In: Proceedings of the IEEE Conference on Computer Vision and Pattern Recognition, pp. 3431–3440 (2015)
14. Noh, H., Hong, S., Han, B.: Learning deconvolution network for semantic segmentation. In: Proceedings of the IEEE International Conference on Computer Vision, pp. 1520–1528 (2015)
15. Procopio, M.J.: An experimental analysis of classifier ensembles for learning drifting concepts over time in autonomous outdoor robot navigation (2007)
16. Procopio, M.J.: Hand-labeled DARPA LAGR datasets (2007)
17. Procopio, M.J., Mulligan, J., Grudic, G.: Learning terrain segmentation with classifier ensembles for autonomous robot navigation in unstructured environments. J. Field Robot. $26(2)$, 145–175 (2009)
18. Procopio, M.J., Mulligan, J., Grudic, G.: Coping with imbalanced training data for improved terrain prediction in autonomous outdoor robot navigation. In: 2010 IEEE International Conference on Robotics and Automation (ICRA), pp. 518–525. IEEE (2010)
19. Simonyan, K., Zisserman, A.: Very deep convolutional networks for large-scale image recognition. arXiv preprint arXiv:1409.1556 (2014)
20. Yadav, S., Patra, S., Arora, C., Banerjee, S.: Deep CNN with color lines model for unmarked road segmentation. In: IEEE International Conference on Image Processing (ICIP 2017), Beijing (2017)
21. Zhang, W., Chen, Q., Zhang, W., He, X.: Long-range terrain perception using convolutional neural networks. Neurocomputing 275, 781–787 (2018)
22. Zhang, W., Zhang, W., Li, Z., Gu, J.: Visual features for long-range terrain perception. Robot 3, 015 (2015)
23. Zhao, H., Shi, J., Qi, X., Wang, X., Jia, J.: Pyramid scene parsing network. arXiv preprint arXiv:1612.01105 (2016)
24. Zhu, X., Lu, H., Yang, X., Li, Y., Zhang, H.: Stereo vision based traversable region detection for mobile robots using UV-disparity. In: 2013 32nd Chinese Control Conference (CCC), pp. 5785–5790. IEEE (2013)

Author Index

An, Wei   53

Cai, Rui   396
Chen, Kangping   162
Chen, Shengyong   233
Chen, Weiya   347
Chen, Yibin   284

Deng, Qingxu   65
Ding, Wenrui   115
Dong, Yongsheng   186
Duan, Lijuan   309

Fei, Jingjing   245

Gao, Jinyan   53
Ge, Daohui   103
Gu, Chaochen   272
Guan, Xinping   272
Guo, Yulan   53

Ha, Zechen   115
Han, Le   186
Hang, Renlong   409
He, Dongcheng   78
He, Qi   260
He, Weixiong   27
Hong, Weijie   174
Hu, Jian   138
Huang, Linlin   138
Huang, Shihua   65
Huang, Yaping   150
Huang, Ye   272

Jian, Meng   359
Jiang, Dongmei   384
Jin, Xing   199

Lai, Jianhuang   3, 27, 40
Li, Chenglong   295
Li, Fei   384
Li, Haojie   421

Li, Kui   16
Li, Wenyuan   373
Li, Xuelong   186
Li, Zhixin   78
Liang, Dong   260
Liao, Quan   199
Lin, Zaiping   53
Liu, Bo   16
Liu, Chunlei   115
Liu, Eryun   162
Liu, Kuixiang   260
Liu, Qingshan   409
Liu, Qiong   322
Liu, Yiguang   174
Lu, Ruizhi   3
Lu, Xiaoqiang   396
Luo, Zhongxuan   421
Lv, Bolin   233
Lv, Jujian   221
Lv, Xuan   245

Ma, Lihua   199
Ma, Long-long   309
Ma, Qiulin   150
Ma, Xiaofeng   373
Ma, Xinzhu   421
Miao, Qiguang   103

Ou, Shiqi   347

Peng, Juan   245
Peng, Shaowu   322

Qi, Mingchao   359
Qi, Yutao   103
Qian, Xiaoliang   284
Qu, Lei   260

Shi, Xuelei   174
Shi, Zhenwei   373
Song, Guocong   334
Song, Jianfeng   103

Tang, Jin 295
Tang, Jun 260

Wan, Yulin 347
Wang, Chongxiao 103
Wang, Fang 284
Wang, Hongyuan 126
Wang, Lu 65
Wang, Nan 150
Wang, Tingting 16
Wang, Ying 174
Wang, Yulong 295
Wang, Zengfu 209
Wang, Zhicheng 245
Wang, Zhihui 421
Wang, Zhiwen 78
Wei, Gang 245
Wu, Changhao 334
Wu, Kaijie 272
Wu, Lifang 359

Xie, Xiaohua 3, 40
Xie, Xiaomin 16
Xie, Xuemei 199
Xu, Shugong 334
Xu, Zhewei 322
Xue, Zhidong 347

Yan, Hai 90
Yang, Bowen 359
Yang, Enze 138
Yang, Jinyu 115
Yang, Peiyu 65
Yang, Wei 126

Yuan, Xiaotong 409
Yuan, Yuan 396

Zhan, Jin 221
Zhang, Canlong 78
Zhang, Dai 359
Zhang, Heng 359
Zhang, Hongwei 245
Zhang, Huanlong 284
Zhang, Ji 126
Zhang, Lei 384
Zhang, Lin 16
Zhang, Peng 209
Zhang, Pengbo 421
Zhang, Quan 40
Zhang, Shunqing 334
Zhang, Xiujiao 284
Zhang, Xiuwei 384
Zhang, Yanning 384
Zhang, Zhongbao 126
Zhao, Genping 384
Zhao, Huimin 221
Zhao, Quanchao 309
Zhao, Wenqing 90
Zheng, Huicheng 27
Zheng, Penggen 221
Zheng, Yunan 174
Zhou, Feng 409
Zhou, Jingkai 322
Zhou, Xiaolong 233
Zhu, Junyong 40
Zhuang, Jiajun 322
Zou, Qi 150

Printed in the United States
By Bookmasters